The Bloody Chasm

A Descriptive Analysis of the First Reconstruction Period in U.S. American Literature: 1865-1885

By

Rev. Dr. Finley C. Campbell, Chair Emeritus

The Unitarian Universalist Multiracial Unity Action Council

DORRANCE
PUBLISHING CO
EST. 1920
PITTSBURGH, PENNSYLVANIA 15238

Dorrance Publishing Co
585 Alpha Drive
Suite 103
Pittsburgh, PA 15238
Visit our website at www.dorrancebookstore.com

ISBN: 979-8-88925-430-0
eISBN: 979-8-88925-930-5

Dr. Campbell was in the final stages of editing *The Bloody Chasm* when he died in August 2023. Although obvious errors have been corrected, the book is being printed as he left it rather than being edited further without his input.

- Roberta Lammers-Campbell, Ph.D.

The Bloody Chasm

A Descriptive Analysis of the First Reconstruction Period in U.S. American Literature: 1865-1885

CONTENTS

ACKNOWLEGMENTS

Bobbi Lammers Campbell, who encouraged me financially, existentially, and spiritually to finish the prepublication draft.

Barbara Ennis of Dorrance Publishing, who guided me into the mysteries of self-publication, emphasizing both patience and urgency.

Tim Arehart, a member of my church, First Unitarian Church of Chicago, who served as my copy editor, especially in developing a reasonable authors index and in straightening out the footnote sequence.

Fern Lister—I hope I have remembered her name correctly!—the skilled and efficient secretary of the English Department back in 1969 who did the official typescript version of the dissertation.

Elaine North, who did the official Microsoft Word version.

Ethel Werfel, my Morehouse College humanities professor (1952-1955), who introduced me, unknowingly, to neo-Aristotelianism, in her emphasis on elements, genres, etc., as fundamental to appreciating and understanding the arts.

Dr. Thomas D. Jarrett, a brilliant lecturer and my master's thesis advisor, who presided over my first foray into sociopolitical fiction by supporting my efforts to do my master's thesis on the *USA* trilogy by John Dos Passos. His guidance helped me graduate from Clark Atlanta University, known as AU back in the 50s, with highest honors. Most important, his letter of recommendation in support of my application to his old alma mater, The University of Chicago's Department of English, allowed me to get a full first-year Woodrow Wilson Fellowship (1958-1959). His advice to me was that, if I got in, not to do a Negro dissertation. I partially fulfilled that advice. By the way, he was related to Valerie Jarrett, and eventually he became the president of the old Atlanta University.

The U of C Fellowship, my second financial aid package, this time from the UC Department of English itself, which allowed me to finish my second year of on-campus residence (1959-1960).

United Negro College Fund Fellowships, two full-year fellowships that allowed me to spend fruitful time doing my extensive research, as reflected in the bibliography.

Dr. Benjamin E. Mays, the famous president of Morehouse College, who arranged for me to have two years off to take advantage of these UNCF fellowships, with pay.

Liliane Jacot Des-Combes Campbell, my first wife, who created a domestic environment that allowed me to do full-time teaching and work tediously on researching and writing and rewriting the dissertation, and who accompanied me on my two-year research activities at U of C, 1964 and 1966.

Paulette Leonie Campbell, my baby daughter, to whom I would feed breakfast while working on my notecards at 6:30 A.M. and who would sometimes sit in my lap while I wrote out stuff in longhand to be typed eventually.

Dr. Walter Fertig, the chair of the Department of English at Wabash College, who arranged for me to have time off (1968-1969) to work on the monster, with pay.

Prof. Eric Foner, Department of History, Columbia University, one of the outstanding history professors who encouraged me to publish my research (2022) and who gave excellent advice about finding out if someone had already produced such a work as mine. (So far, the answer is none, although a recent historical analysis of the Reconstruction has come out called *The Third Reconstruction*, which erroneously portrays the Reconstruction periods as black power narratives.)

Rev. Wesley Hromatko, comrade in the struggle, a member of the Religious Professionals Task Force of the Unitarian Universalist Multiracial Unity Action Council. He gave me information for the Appendix on Unitarian and Universalist participation in the Reconstruction Period, especially their supporting the Tuskegee Institute. Tuskegee was one of the few Afro-U.S. American schools to survive reconciliation in Alabama. Comrade Hromatko also gave me the names of such idealistic Unitarian and Universalist Carpetbaggers as Louisa Shaw who served in Florida, a Ms. Bottume in a place called Ladies Island, and Caroline F. Putnam, who served in Viriginia.

My U of C dissertation team, one Negro and two white, multiracial unity in its interracial mode: Dr. John Hope Franklin, Negro (as he identified himself back then), a specialist in Negro history, later the John Matthews

Manly Distinguished Service Professor Emeritus in History; Dr. James E. Miller, a U.S. American literature specialist and later The Helen A. Regenstein Professor Emeritus of English; and finally, the chair of my committee, Dr. Robert E. Streeter, also a specialist in 19th-century U.S. American literature, and the Dean of the Humanities Division.

Most importantly, the world's rank and file: the workers (Marie Cobbs), students (Tom Jones), and professionals (Pastor and Pastoress Rev. Stephen C. "Dynamo" and Pauline J. Campbell), symbolized in Reconstruction literature and history by ordinary men and women of all colors who gave their lives in that tragic struggle, which remains an important historical steppingstone toward the Beloved Community. I now add to this group an anonymous white sistah, a salesperson working for Clark Atlanta University Alumni Office, with whom I momentarily bonded during a phone call. She promised to buy my book once it appeared in a Little Rock, Arkansas, bookstore.

It is to this international rank and file of all colors that I ultimately dedicate this book in all its literary, ideological, and theological complexity.

The Unity of the Light- and Dark-Skinned People of the World

PROLOGUE
WHAT TOOK YOU SO LONG?

This book, based on a dissertation, was approved back in December 1969 by three of the top scholars at the University of Chicago at that time: my main advisor in the Department of English, Dr. Robert E. Streeter (also Dean of the Humanities Division); Dr. James E. Miller, also in the department; and most importantly, Dr. John Hope Franklin from the Department of History, one of the leading scholars in the Revisionist approach to the nature of the First Reconstruction Period and a vital contributor to my research.

Thanks to their recommendation, I had received an offer from the University of Chicago Press to transform my dissertation into a book. We agreed there was a book within the dissertation, but it needed to be made more visible through deep editing and extensive rewriting. The University Press was prepared to extend the resources necessary to make this happen, and it was the hope of my three advisors—who had spent so much time and energy since 1960, when I started on the dissertation, in helping me finish it—that such a book would not only be my child but theirs as well.

But that December was a momentous month in my life. On the night of December 4, I had been involved in a violent confrontation with alleged Cointelpro agents—neo-racist members of Ron Karenga's U.S. organization, aka United Slaves—who had come down from Chicago to disrupt a Black Student Union/John Brown Society Conference I had organized (under the leadership of Captain Donald Campbell (no relation) of the Indiana Chapter of the Black Panther Party) at St. Joseph College in Rensselaer, Indiana. We successfully fought off those jackanapes. However, on our way back to Indy, we noticed police cars all along the key streets of Rensselaer. Donald remarked something was up, and then we heard over our car radio that Comrades Fred Hampton and Mark Clark had been killed in a "shootout" with Chicago law enforcement agents.

This took place just days before my graduation ceremony, when I received my Ph.D. with highest honors. While in Chicago, I went with others to the site where Fred and Mark had been brutally assassinated, seeing with my own eyes the bullet holes and blood-soaked mattresses. I read in the newspapers that a progressive member of the Teamsters Union and his family, the Jablonskis, also had been assassinated—husband, wife, children—by a hit squad hired by a fascist leader of the union. Also much on my mind at the time was the ongoing, raging war in Vietnam.

In this fiery context, I felt God had given me a choice: Either spend two or three years working on reconstructing my dissertation into a book, or heed his voice and plunge headlong into the maelstrom of activism opposing the cruel forces of inequality that seemed to be sweeping the world. I made the choice to go back to Wabash College in Crawfordsville, Indiana, where I was teaching, to become the "white" organizer of the Indiana Peace and Freedom Party. Its task would be to reach out to the white community, the so-called silent majority in Indiana, in order to get them to see that neither the Viet Cong and their North Vietnamese comrades nor the Black Panther Party were their enemies. Most of all, my goal was to win my fellow Hoosiers to the struggle of radically reconstructing our state, to get them to see that, symbolically speaking, the forces that had murdered Comrades Mark Clark and Fred Hampton were the same forces that had slaughtered the Jablonskis and were napalming villages in North and South Vietnam. The same power structure was exploiting the workers, students, and professionals in Indiana itself.

By 1972 my political and academical work in Indiana had come to an end with modest success. I then went back into academia more or less full time as Acting Chair and Assistant Professor in the Department of Afro-U.S. American Studies at the University of Wisconsin–Madison (1972–1977). The dissertation still remained in typescript form in a steamer trunk down in the basement of my new home in Middleton, Wisconsin. I focused my energies on organizing the department, which was in shambles, and taking part in founding a new organization called the National Academic Committee Against Racism (CAR) in 1973.

So from 1972 to 1976, I spent my energies building up the Department of Afro-U.S. American Studies using a multiracial approach, focused on interfacing the department with the rest of the university, especially on recruiting white students. I developed new courses and deepened existing ones. My most important decision was bringing on board a competent white historian, a brother named Willliam Van De Burgh with a newly minted Ph.D. from the University of Michigan. This decision angered the black nationalist caucus who wanted an uncredentialed black activist scholar for the post.

I was eventually asked to step down from the acting chair position in 1975, mainly, I assert, because of my outspoken public support of a special educational program for lower-class students, predominantly black, called the Five-Year Program. This program showed that with enough time, support, and encouragement, motivated lower-class kids—white and non-white—could graduate from our prestigious university. However, UW elites—black and non-black—successfully called for its dismantlement. Their rationale allegedly was that having these kinds of students at such a prestigious university compromised our academic excellence. But by this time I had put the department on solid ground; my one regret was a lack of full-time tenured teaching faculty.

Still determined to fight for racial justice, I put my non-classroom energies into the Committee Against Racism (CAR). At that time CAR was battling theories of racial inferiority derived from the fallacious assertions of one Dr. Arthur Jensen, who declared that IQ tests were a true measure of human intelligence and that intelligence itself was genetic in origin. CAR also opposed the concept of cultural determinism, which argued that culture determined individuals' ability to take part in U.S. American society and that those born in a "culture of poverty" could never really get out, no matter how much federal aid was made available to them. Both ideologies had a particular impact upon lower-class black people; interestingly they excluded from their analyses middle- and upper-class Afro-U.S. Americans, members of the black bourgeoisie. It was a new strain of racism—neo-racism, as I came to call it—with a decided class content that distinguished it from older forms.

As the Midwest Chair of CAR, I was helping to organize forums, conferences, and struggles against what we identified as academic racism. This led me to a major encounter with Dr. James Crow, one of the chief defenders of the academic racist, Dr. Arthur Jensen. Dr. Crow was a prominent population geneticist at UW Madison, and we had a major debate over the statewide UW Madison radio network that was covered in the Madison newspapers. I charged him with supporting racism indirectly by defending Jensen's model of genetic IQ as a legitimate thesis worth exploring. My arguments prevailed largely because Dr. Crow—a supposed expert on population genetics—could not give a genetic definition of a black person, instead falling back on an outdated melanin theory of blackness, that "everyone could see what a black person was." But my victory had a cost; as a lifetime NAACP member and a prestigious visiting professor at Morehouse College (my old alma mater and an HBCU), Dr. Crow had major support among the black senior faculty, the arbiters of my department's tenure procedures.

My 1977 bid for tenure became a struggle with complicated issues. The tenure committee made it clear to me that while my service to the university and my teaching evaluations were superb, it was not enough for a professor in an undergraduate department to get tenure; in other words, publish or perish. I went down to the steamer trunk where I had stored a section of my dissertation, which had been trimmed from the final version; I had it typed up, titled it *White Bourbons/Black Jacobins: The Reconstruction Period in U.S. American Non-fictional Literature 1865-1885*, and submitted it to UW Press. To my surprise, it was accepted.

Our department was an undergraduate department, lacking the resources of a traditional graduate department; demanding a tenure candidate to publish or perish was an unfair standard of tenurability. Nor was publication sufficient: One of my top professors, Dr. David Britt, published a book before he came to Wisconsin but was still denied tenure because, in my opinion, he was considered a Campbellian. No one on my tenure committee was from the Department of English, much less from my specialty in U.S. American literature. The chair of my tenure committee was not even a specialist in Afro-U.S. American Studies, but a black astronomer.

Consequently, I took the position at the hearing that I was a victim of neo-racism. When asked if I had any recent evidence of my publication record, I refused to submit my letter of acceptance from UW Press to protest how the tenure committee was using neo-racist criteria in violation of our departmental mission, which was *teach well* or perish.

On the basis of that refusal, I was eventually terminated for not living up to the high standards of UW scholarship—although according to one GW, a spy from the administration who had infiltrated my classes, I was actually denied tenure because I was a Marxist-Socialist. Nevertheless, my struggle led to tenure based on academic work as teachers in an undergraduate department for all the rest of the department…including the sellouts.

In 1977 I was invited to head up the Chicago Chapter of the International Committee Against Racism (InCAR), which I accepted in August. Once more I put the idea of publishing my dissertation on the backburner, choosing instead to continue the struggle against racism more directly. I also turned down a full-time appointment as a tenure track assistant professor at Rutgers University in order to become a member of the proletarianized professoriate, the thousands of part-time and non-tenured instructors employed in a variety of colleges and universities, like Chicago State University, Columbia College, the University of Illinois Chicago Campus, Malcolm X Community College (1977-1987). This eventually led in 1987 to a position as a full-time instructor at a technical school-turned-university, DeVry University—the Chicago campus—in a non-tenure track position, with a heavy teaching load. In this position, I could be terminated/fired at any time for any reason—but unlike at UW Madison, student evaluations were key to maintaining employment. I thrived in that environment, but it left no time for preparing a dissertation for publication.

What time outside my teaching duties I did have, I spent on a myriad of racial justice activities, from leading an InCAR union group to taking part in anti-Nazi activities in Marquette Park. This important project—aiding in that community's final desegregation, which was begun in 1966 by Rev. Martin Luther King, Jr.—included physical confrontations with the Chicago National Socialist Party.

My dissertation languished in that steamer trunk, but I found time for slimmer scholarly writing, focusing on the creation of handouts, "quikbooks," and pamphlets customized for classroom activities. An old colleague of mine, Prof. Irving Thalberg of the Department of Philosophy at the University of Illinois Chicago Campus, identified these forms of publication as written scholarship as valid as those works published by the academic press.

When my formal academic career came to an end in 2006, having reached the highest level in a non-tenure track position, that of senior professor, still more delays kept me from publishing my dissertation. I became an unpaid organizer building a multiracial movement in the Unitarian Universalist Association of Congregations. This racial justice activism culminated in the founding of the Unitarian Universalist Multiracial Unity Action *Caucus*—later *Council*—in 2008. I served first as chair and then as vice chair until December 2022, again as an unpaid organizer and administrator. While I created a variety of essays, booklets, leaflets, "quikbooks," and articles for our journal *The MAC Arrow*, transforming my dissertation into a book became an impossible dream.

But God spoke again. Stricken by a variety of ailments and old age (I am now 88 in February 2023), I consulted my psychic, who advised me that my physical situation could be a chance at a new direction in life. Unable to act out my principles in deeds anymore, it is time to share them in written form. Now is the time to produce scriptures, to produce creeds.

With that advice ringing in my ears like a terrifying truth, I decided to retire from full-scale racial justice activism, but not from the social humanist vision that had sustained that activism. Now I had the God-given opportunity to at last return to what I had always wanted to be: a writer. I want to write new forms of didactic literature, both fiction and nonfiction, dramatizing in symbolic action the power of social humanism—specifically, Marxist-Leninist historical theism, within the framework of a new religious vision, grounded in a hundred thousand years of human evolution. This vision, or more precisely theology, we activists in the Unitarian Universalist Multiracial Unity Action Council call Multiracial Unitarian Universalism.

I am able to do this now, thanks to the power of self-publishing—as recommended by Professor Miller so many years ago!—through the Dorrance Publishing Company, if my health will allow.

Whether you, dear reader, enjoy, endure, or reject this book, *Consumatus Est*—it is now finished, and my three wonderful dissertation advisors, all dead, can now rest in peace.

"Literature is the technology of the human heart—whether defined as the soul, the mind, or …consciousness," (Rev. Dr. Finley C. Campbell, senior professor emeritus, DeVry University-Chicago).

ADDENDUM
AN IMAGINARY CONVERSATION

Professor James E. Miller Goes Over My Pre-Publication Version of *The Bloody Chasm*

"Come on in," he said.

I stood outside his office, nervous about what he had to say because I was anxious to get this thang to Dorrance Publishing as soon as possible.

"Have a seat. I want to go over with you some notes I made about your edited version of the dissertation since clearly you have made some emendations since we approved the original document back in 1969."

"Yes, I confess I certainly have, based on my political and literary development since then."

"So I noticed," he said. "Well, let's get to it. I see you have your footnote sequence in continuous order. That is not an MLA or U of Chicago footnote system."

"Yes, I know. But my original typist, Ms. North, did it that way for efficiency's sake, so I decided to keep it as she did. They seem to work well since they are coordinated with the footnote pages."

"Hmm. What about your use of capitalization? Her decision or yours? How do you decide when you are using a word like 'officer' as a common noun and when using it as a proper noun, the 'Union Officer'?"

"I had some difficulty myself with consistency. My rule of thumb was that when a sociopolitical character is treated as an aesthetic archetype, it is capitalized, like The Radical; when used generally as an adjective it is not, like radical rule. Same thing with Redeemer, Carpetbagger, Yankee School Marm.

I also treat as proper nouns specialized terms reflecting my symbological bias; e.g., the Cult, the Taboo Conjunction, the Cult of Racio-sexuality."

"What about the word 'abolitionist'? Same thing? Seems inconsistent."

"Well, abolitionism is generally a common noun, so in the book 'abolitionist' is capitalized only when used as follows: The Abolitionist Movement, or when I am referring to the abolitionist as a literary symbol, e.g., the Abolitionist."

Dr. Miller continued. "Okay, that's the minor stuff, here is a major issue. What literary critical system are you using? You seem to be all over the map. When dealing with the University of Chicago School of literary criticism—what we called neo-Aristotelianism—you have a strong emphasis on Aristotle's concepts of plot, character, and genre. An example of this is in your discussion of the different kinds of Reconstruction fiction. On top of that, I see traces of Walter Blair, Norman MacLean, and Barbara Foley in your critical system for examining traditional literary elements like character, plot, and setting.

"Then, when you want to deal with irony and the use of figurative imagery, you drift over into the jargon of the old New Criticism crowd—of John Crowe Ransom, Robert Penn Warren, and Kenneth Burke, among others—all those references about symbolic action, for example. I find it surprising that you like those guys considering that they were defenders of what you call Bourbonism (in literary form, of course), what they called the Southern Agrarian Tradition.

"Then there is the psychoanalytical stuff—Jung and Freud. Jung, with your emphasis on the use of archetypes in the literature, and all this Freudian b-s about the Oedipus complex, racio-sexuality, and the Cult of Violence, as mediated through your use of Leslie Fiedler's esoteric approach about the antagonistic contradiction in U.S. American literature between adult sexuality and death.

"And from time to time, I get hints of Marxism-Leninism as an implicit bias. So, where are you coming from in terms of literary criticism?"

"Well," I responded, "Dr. Miller, you raise some important points. I would say in the editing of this book, I have worked toward a more liberal humanist approach, downplaying my personal commitment to Marxist-Leninist Historical Theism, which emerged from my philosophy of social humanism. In terms of literary theory, I admit to being eclectic, though I prefer the term synergistic, with an emphasis on neo-didacticism, with a very limited, selective use of post-modern literary theories, mainly existentialism. I agree that my focus on the aesthetic use of setting, narrative, character, language, and thematic structure grows from my interest in hermeneutics as influenced by the neo-Aristo's like Elder Olsen, one of my favorite U of C professors back then.

"But I also consider John Crowe Ransom's approach of using literary criticism 'to define and enjoy the aesthetic or characteristic values of literature,' right on the mark. And his co-partner, Kenneth Burke, influenced me greatly, especially his concept of literature as a form of symbolic action and his theory of rhetoric as the 'use of words by human agents to form attitudes or to induce actions in other human agents, … using words to move people or encourage action.' So yes, the New Criticism plus Neo-Aristotelianism plus various forms of sociopsychological theorizing were major influences on my description of the power of Reconstruction literature as an example of neo-didacticism."

"Ah, yes," Dr. Miller mused out loud, "your emphasis on looking for layers of linguistic meaning in all those quotations you so liberally sprinkled throughout your book. That shows your interest in hermeneutics, the branch of knowledge that deals with interpretation, especially of the Bible or literary texts. And clearly this is your main literary tool in examining Reconstruction literature, which holds together your eclectic approach to literary criticism. But let me warn you: This approach means that your readers will have to deal with U.S. American literature experts long dead—old Dead White Males—and considered outmoded by contemporary systems of criticism."

"I accept the warning."

"Okay, let us move on to another major problem. I wonder if you will not need a rhetorical glossary about the different ways you use specialized terms.

"One example would be the term 'Irrepressible Conflict.' I think you have clearly explained the historical meaning and your particular definition of it. But what is your rule of thumb in identifying ex-slaves? You seem to mix up Freedmen/Freedman. How do you handle the gender question? And then you also use the terms 'Negro,' 'Afro-U.S. American,' 'African'—are these just synonyms or do they reflect some special points of view?"

"I use the term 'Freedmen' to refer to ex-slaves, both male and female. I use 'Freedman' to refer to males as recipients of the rights of the 15th Amendment. I worked to be sure that this distinction is used consistently in the text."

"Good idea. What about the other terms?"

"I use the term 'Negro' as a synonym for black folks, slave and free, as used by John Hope Franklin. Same thing with 'Afro-U.S. American.' I usually use the word 'African' to describe the ex-slaves prior to their existence as citizens. But in general, these terms are synonyms."

"Seems reasonable. What about the term 'Slavocracy'? Referring to the rule of the slaves or the rule of the slave masters?"

"The latter."

"The Slavery Syndrome. Seems self-explanatory in the context of the book. What about the terms you use for the Southern ruling class? You use 'Slavocrat,' 'Cavalier,' 'Bourbon.' You use the term 'Bourbon' as your key term. Why?"

"Historically, the term is derived from the House of Bourbon, which ruled France and Navarre in the 16th century to the 18th century, when temporarily the dynasty came to an end with the French Revolution and the Napoleonic Era. It was temporarily restored with the defeat of Napoleon by the Grand Coalition, led by England. In my book 'Bourbon' refers to the ideological descendants of that dynasty, the Southern aristocracy, which embodied much of the Bourbons' authoritarian, feudalistic outlook in their sociocultural lifestyles and in their opposition to egalitarianism. It was once said of the Bourbons that they could neither forget their past glories nor learn from their mistakes. And that the only way they got back into power was through the military defeat of the French imperial army, itself a descendant of the French Revolution. So the term 'connotatively' means 'those members of the ex-Confederate elites who would not forget their lost glories nor learn to adapt to their present defeat at the hands of the Union army and Reconstruction revolutionaries and who would eventually need an outside power to restore them to power'" (Campbell).

"Fascinating. Well, let's examine some of your other sociological jargon. You use the terms 'socio-psychic,' 'cultural-psychological,' and 'psychocultural' a lot. Are they synonyms or specialized concepts?"

"Well, I suppose it has to do with the context, but I believe (as do many Marxists—and bourgeois social psychologists) that our complex mental states originate in social institutions and in the rules governing those institutions. So 'socio-' as a morpheme underlines that fact. Like the term socio-psychic. 'Cultural-psychological' indicates that the rules governing those social institutions, what we call culture, precede the evolution of our individual psychology. But to underscore that our minds can achieve a certain autonomy within this process, that is to say, the full introjection of cultural attitudes at the unconscious level of our neurophysiology, I use the term 'psychocultural' and sometimes the term 'psychological.'"

"So," Dr. Miller responded wryly, "you subscribe to the view that the origins of our psychological states are ultimately found in the environment, more of a Pavlovian view of the evolution of the psyche than a psychiatric view, but incorporating Freudian manifestations."

"Yes, sir. That's right. Sort of an aspect of my Marxist-Leninist Historical Theism."

"This is not a major part of the book, right?"

"Correct, sir. Just my personal belief that God works through history as defined by the Marxist-Leninist vision, moving from Primitive Communism, through slavetalism (my word for slave-plebian-based societies), through feudalism, reaching the time of capitalism, and today the highest form of that capitalism, imperialism, all leading through reform, reconstruction, or revolution to Scientific Communism, aka the Kingdom of God."

"Interesting formulation. Well, back to my list. America vs. U.S. America. What's the distinction?"

"Geopolitically speaking, 'America' can only refer to the entire region lying between the Arctic and the Antarctic, thus I use the term 'U.S. America' to indicate that region lying between Canada and Mexico with geographical connections to the Caribbean in the East and Alaska and Hawaii to the West."

He reached for his empty pipe and said, "One way to deal with America First chauvinism. We are doing quite well on my list. Just two more items. Your work seems rather repetitious, especially in the treatment of the Conflict and the key characters in that Conflict. Isn't that a major flaw in your book?"

"I respectfully disagree. The neo-didactic function of this book is threefold: to supplement the work of the Revisionist historians past and present; to bring to the attention of the literate reader the complex, hidden history of this literature as a major part of the Reconstruction Period; and most of all, through the critical analysis used in this book, to celebrate imaginative works that dealt with the Irrepressible Conflict and the characters representing opposing sides of that conflict. Yes, at the level of appearance, this book does reflect the dangers of theme and repetition. But at the level of essence, I see this approach as a form of theme and variation."

Dr. Miller took a suck from his empty pipe. "I would suppose this theme and variation technique would explain your repetitive use of causational analysis. For example, there can only be one essential cause behind specific effects, yet you have in each section several 'essential' causes for the Conflict. And just when we think we have got to the ultimate cause, you introduce another one, supposedly deeper than the last. In the summation section of the book, just when we think we have gotten to the basic cause of the Conflict, you come up with another layer, like a co-eccentric circle. So, which is it? Political economy, social institutions, culture, psychocultural conditioning, or psychological factors?"

"Yes, I admit that this could be a problem. Perhaps in my efforts to approach the causes of the defeat of Reconstruction from a dialectical point of view, I keep shifting the nature of the essential cause because I found so many varieties of important causes generating the Conflict. So, at the risk of being a reductionist, I will assert that political economic factors emerge as the ultimate cause of causes of the Irrepressible Conflict."

"Sounds Marxist enough. One last thing from the point of view of literary criticism: How do you define this neo-didacticism?"

"'Neo,' meaning 'new, a new way'; 'didacticism' meaning 'a philosophy that emphasizes instructional and informative qualities in literature, art, and design' (*Wikipedia*). So, I am trying to develop a new way of uncovering, discovering, the instructional nature of literature, in this case Reconstruction fiction, trying to locate the lessons they can teach us today beyond their immediate purposes. I assert that built into the aesthetic nature of a literary work are aspects of meaning going beyond the writer's conscious (or unconscious) intentions, what have been called the interpretational hypothesis. This is especially important in dealing with sociopolitical literature, the organic interaction between the appearance (the texture) and the essence (the thematic structure) of a literary text, what Professor Barbara Foley calls 'depth.'"

"Oh, one last question. Who exactly is this book for? Who is your intended audience? And what current political issues are you confronting?"

"That is a good question, Dr. Miller. I guess you could say that this book is for Anglo-English majors, those with some knowledge of the First Reconstruction and U.S. American history in general, those who have completed general education courses, those who have intellectual curiosity who will look at this book as a challenge. That's my intended readership. The current political issue I am confronting are those forms of whiteness studies that seek to decenter the leading role white Radicals played during the First Reconstruction, trying to argue it was a form of black power or black liberation. In the person of the Carpetbagger, I re-center that leadership role."

PREFACE

There are two divergent tendencies that have influenced the thematic development of U.S. American literature. One emphasizes psychological and moral states; the other stresses the sociological, those political, social, and cultural conditions that form the human environment.

In post-bellum 19th-century U.S. American fiction, sociological literature—particularly that dealing with the social and political conditions arising immediately in the wake of the Civil War—became an important part of the literary scene, though perhaps not in a qualitative sense. It was during this period that there appeared a cluster of works that, because of their thematic use of Reconstruction history, may be called generically Reconstruction literature, and that for the same reason constitutes an interesting and yet neglected example of sociological fiction and nonfiction in U.S. American literature. While one might question the importance of these works as accurate historical documents and debate their literary value, they are certainly early examples in bulk of sociological writing as it appeared during the period 1865 to 1885. On the one hand, they were a direct part of the local color movement which, with its emphasis on and presentation of regional cultures, was a specific manifestation of the sociological tendency. On the other hand, they are an organic part of that line of essays and novels, stretching from William Byrd through William Faulkner, which features Southern life and culture as the thematic core.

Thus, a possible forerunner of the local color movement in particular and as an example of the sociological in U.S. American literature generally, Reconstruction literature, especially the fiction, deserves description and analysis. But there is another reason for this study more important than these.

This literature not only mirrored the factual events of one of the most extraordinary periods in U.S. American history, it also recreated in literary form the symbolic potential of these events: the dramatic expression of U.S. American democratic idealism in a political form that was both corrupted and yet ironically fulfilled by an irrepressible conflict between North and South. This was the symbolic action at the center of Reconstruction history. Since this history has yet to be fully treated by the great U.S. American writers, it is to the minor Reconstruction authors that we must turn for the evocation of this symbolic action within a specifically aesthetic framework. This is the essential importance of Reconstruction literature; this is the primary reason why it deserves critical investigation.

The cultural symbolism of the Reconstruction period forms the general context of our study. The specific aim is more limited: a description of Reconstruction literature as a 19th-century literary genre and as an exponent of the themes and symbols of the period. Such a description foregoes a critical analysis *per se* since this literature was inferior in itself (although it contains an embryonic literary power, which is frequently actualized) and more so when compared to the works of the more important U.S. American writers of the same period. Instead, this study examines these texts as self-contained writings, as social and political documents, and as carriers of Reconstruction symbolism. The results of this examination will be twofold: an account of this literature as a minor genre in popular U.S. American writing and a study of the Reconstruction as an historical event in 19th-century U.S. American literature (with the accent on the sociological aspects of the period appearing in the fictional image). The key to such analysis and to our study is the Reconstruction canon of Albion Tourgée.

Briefly, Tourgée, an ex-Union soldier and political Carpetbagger, embodied in his novels and short stories the successes and failures of the Reconstruction and in doing so left a distinct example of the power, potentiality, and limitation of Reconstruction literature. It is his literary writings that form the nucleus of this book: *Toinette* (1874), *A Fool's Errand* (1879), *Bricks Without Straw* (1881), *A Royal Gentleman and Zouri's Christmas* (1881), and *John Eax and Mamelon* (1882).

This book is divided into three major sections. The first is an introductory section, which offers a theoretical discussion of North-South sectionalism as the key vision operating through Reconstruction history and its literature.

The second is a presentation of Reconstruction history (featuring Reconstruction nonfiction) as a manifestation of this sectional rivalry. More than a list of dates, events, and names, this section categorizes these elements into the major symbols and themes of the period (Bourbon, Carpetbagger, Freedman, Scalawag); the Interracial Symbiosis between black and white; and the Irrepressible Conflict between Southerner and Northerner—all defined within the success and the failure of the United States' only political experiment with a multiracial, democratic republic in the 19th century.

The third section, central to this book, studies the nature of the literary genre and social documents through the symbolism of the Reconstruction as event and as literature. Chapters III, IV, and V describe, for example, selective examples of Reconstruction writing as the embodiment of the literary trends and the major historical themes and symbols of the period, with the Tourgée canon as the foremost example. In Chapter III, those writings are examined as 19th-century art and as sociological literature. Chapter IV concerns itself with particular examples of Reconstruction fiction. Chapter V culminates the study with a treatment of the key themes in Reconstruction literature as they appear in the fiction of Albion Tourgée.

This study limits itself to works published by Northern writers within the period 1865–1885. This period covers the major historical action of the period, going beyond the official end of Reconstruction (1877) to its symbolic end, 1885, when a nominee from the "Party of Treason" had finally been elected President of the Union mainly because of votes from the Solid South, briefly ending Republican rule. In a symbolic sense this election exorcised from the nation the political animus engendered against the South by the War of Rebellion and by the postwar period. It was in this period (1877-1885) that Reconstruction novels, for example, appeared in quantity; there is a dearth of Reconstruction works immediately after 1885. Dr. John Hope Franklin points out that the period itself was relegated to limbo even by the historians. Although there was a brief resurgence after 1885, climaxing with the Dixon trilogy, Reconstruction literature appeared only sporadically thereafter. In sum, the primary interest of this book is the era in relationship to the works that describe it, a relationship clearer in the literature that appeared during what I have defined in this study the Reconstruction period.

Northern writers are emphasized for three reasons. First, there is the propaganda problem. The literature available to this research reveals that the Northerners are more often closer to the historical facts than their Southern counterparts. The best example of this is De Forest's relative factuality in *The Bloody Chasm* and Sidney Andrews' objectivity in *The South Since the War.*

Second, the Northern writers have a more complex emotional reaction to their subject. In this conception the Northern artists approach the former Confederacy as an alien and somewhat exotic culture, whose people have become their brothers and sisters by the Union victory but who have remained their enemies because of their defeat and humiliation. Our Northern writers exult in this defeat as the inevitable punishment of the Confederates' political heresy, but they also feel pity for the ruin of their slavocratic pride.

In the beginning, the Carpetbaggers, Freedmen, and Scalawags are the moral instruments to purge the South of its dangerous sectionalism. But later the Northern writer sympathizes with the South as the victim of their tragicomic rule. Hence whether the Northern writers became completely pro-Southern (Constance Fenimore Woolson and James S. Pike), remained essentially hostile (Albion Tourgée and Albert Morgan), or were neutral reconciliationists (Charles King and Stephen Powers), their ambivalent relation to the Reconstruction is ultimately more complicated and more ironic than the relationship of the typical Southern writer. Finally, the central themes in Reconstruction literature, particularly in the novels, are most clearly expressed by writers of the North and have their clearest expression for the purposes of this study between 1865 and 1885. This emphasis on Northern works, however, will not totally exclude the Southern writer.

Within such boundaries and using the methods, aims, and assumptions set forth in this preface, this research should have value for students of this historical era and its literature. Furthermore, this study should offer general insights into the nature and meaning of sociological fiction within the broad context of U.S. American literature. This book, so long delayed, should cast needed light on the complex, tragic, and sometimes prophetic events that form the Reconstruction experience and that have haunted the political development of the U.S. American South for generations.[1]

CHAPTER I
INTRODUCTION: THE BLOODY CHASM

"The pastoral rebellion of the earth against machines, against the Age of Steam. . . ."[2]

"I look upon it then, Sir, as a war of sentiment and opinion by one form of society against another form of society."[3]

A cursory reading of the works featured in this book evokes a disconcerting sense of thematic discreteness, a feeling that each work is a separate entity only superficially connected to the others in that all describe Southern Reconstruction. A thorough, chronological reading, however, reveals a master theme lurking within the Victorian prose, the local color descriptions, and the social and political commentary. More than the historical events themselves, this theme binds the history to the literature and the works of fiction and nonfiction to each other.

The theme can be written as a rather commonplace thesis: Between the North and South there arose an irrepressible conflict. Among historians "the Irrepressible Conflict" usually refers either to the slavery debate or the War of Rebellion (now called the Civil War). But this conflict is more profound than these traditional associations; it antedates these issues, existing throughout the development of the U.S. American republic in the 19th century. The compromises preceding the Civil War, the war itself, and Reconstruction following that war were all in a sense dramatic signs of the struggle, rather than the struggle itself. The Irrepressible Conflict was one that sprang up between two differing forms of society occupying the same geopolitical area and possessing antithetical interpretations of the essence of the U.S. American experience. This duality caused the historical conflict between the North and the South, and made the "slave-owning Southern states and the rapidly industrializing North . . . two different nations; . . . two contending power units—each of which was trying to expand at the other's expense . . . [as if they were] two European countries."[4] In the light of how these works emphasize this sectional distinctiveness, the African Presence in the South can be seen as merely the most sensational sign of North-South antagonism.[5]

Both fiction and nonfiction invariably portray the sectional rivalry between North and South, and the North's victory over its rival, as permeating the texture of both the U.S. American experience in general and the Reconstruction experience in particular. The conflict between the North's and South's polarized interpretations of this conflict emerges in the answers to a handful of questions: Was the best mythic apparatus for a cultural ideal the pastoral or industrial vision? Was the best model for U.S. American society derived from rational or "anti-rational modes" of social behavior, modes related to the Rights of Man or the Privileges of Power, respectively? Was the Republic a federal or "con-federal" union? In other countries, some of these polarities occurred within a single society, as a struggle between classes. It was an accident of U.S. American geography that these contrasting values divided so neatly into a sectional conflict between two broad aggregates of states, regardless of class structure or class interest within each aggregate.[6]

The first conflict, industrialism versus agrarianism, will seem familiar to the partisans of Jungian mythology. It can be seen as an archetypal encounter, rooted in the collective unconsciousness where animus and anima reside—between the North and the South represented by the antimony, "The Locomotive and the Garden." The belief that a country as young as the United States had in the 1800s already acquired myths or archetypes might seem dubious. Yet there is an archetypal quality to the sharp, contrasting juxtaposition of cultures that split America apart. It is this quality that carries over into Reconstruction literature, represented by rhetorical descriptions of industrial and natural phenomena.

"The opposing forces [in U.S. American society] are agriculture and technology."[7] In his analysis of this symbolism in *The Machine in the Garden*, Leo

Marx provides the appropriate scholarly apparatus for an explanation of this dimension of the Irrepressible Conflict. For him, the two symbols of this opposition, derived from an older agriculture-pastoral tradition and a newer industrial one, are the Garden and the Locomotive. The struggle for supremacy between the ancient pastoral vision of the *summum bonum* and the newer industrial dreams of the same good generated the basic conflict in U.S. American society.[8]

> The archetype of the Northern industrial triumph is the Locomotive: Associated with fire, smoke, speed, iron, and noise, [it is] the leading symbol of the new industrial power. It appears in the woods, suddenly shattering the harmony of the green hollow, like a presentiment of history bearing down on the U.S. American asylum.[9]

This is a precise, poetic image of the way industrialization of the North took place during the fantastic era, 1840-1877. Only the Locomotive could symbolize a society that would emphasize mechanic skills over agrarian ones, the inventive man over the yeoman-farmer and the gentleman-planter.[10] Only the Locomotive could become the synecdoche for Northern power:

> "And this is the North of which I have heard all my life!" [Horace Dunwoddie] said. . . . He had never seen a locomotive so large—he felt stronger himself at the sight of it. In comparison with the narrow-gauge and dingy cars of the past, how sumptuous the train seemed, and it was so much longer too. The speed, also, after he had got aboard, was greater than he had ever known before, but how could he go slower, since a world so wide had to be crossed![11]

By 1860, the North's burgeoning industrialism was seen as a dangerous force that would corrupt the Republic's moral and social vitality as it had done in 18th-century England. The imagery of crowded, dirty cities; blighted landscapes; and exploited women and children toiling endlessly in grimy, darkened mills filled anti-Northern polemics.[12] Southern ideologists took the position that the cruel exploitation of the laborer, the indifference to his health and living conditions, and the joylessness of his work made slavery by contrast a more humane economic system.

Yet there was another image of industrialism, an image of poetry and romance found in pro-industrial writing:

> And all about flew the white chips from the lathes, and the . . . sawdust gathered in piles everywhere. It was all so neat and clean and airy, and yet so strong and relentless in its ceaseless rush and so wonderful in its transforming power! It was as if the gnomes and fairies had banded together in the broad daylight to disport themselves with the white hearts of our Carolina "shag barks."[13]

In Reconstruction literature, especially in those works that support the Reconstruction cause, it is the political symbolism of the Machine that is paramount. The Locomotive, and what seemed a worldwide revolutionary drive by the poor and propertyless to obtain democratic rights, appeared to be conjoined phenomena. Pistons and governor wheels came to symbolize an unprecedented release of human energy in science, politics, and everyday life: ". . . equality, freedom, and happiness [were] felt to rest on technology." Most important, there was a metaphysical implication in all this. Pro-industrial ideologists felt that "an obscure kinship [existed] between . . . the spirit of the Republic, the machine power, and the progressive forces of history."[14]

Thus, the Locomotive literally and figuratively became the inexorable force of the future. When it entered the Northern Garden, the rural republic was doomed. With the North's adoption of the industrial *mythos* in the forties, the one place that still preserved the pastoral traditions from mechanistic encroachment lay south of the line. By November 1860, the South exemplified many of the attributes of the pastoral myth.

In Reconstruction literature, the South *is* the Garden, "the uncontaminated Eden" on the North U.S. American continent, the last refuge of the pastoral "against time and progress."[15] All the assumptions of pastoral idealism undergirded the Southerners' belief in the superiority of a slave economy and a cavalier society over the Yankee's mercantile culture. The Cotton States' prejudices against native manufactories paralleled the pastoral philosophers' antipathy against native industrialism. Jefferson's advocacy of "dependence on European manufactures" found implementation in the close economic relationship between the Black Belt and the English textile mills, in the postwar South's dependence on Northern industry. In this context the Locomotive becomes in the planter's eyes a "reality alien to the pastoral dreams,"[16] a potential corruption of the Southern landscape: "I had rather see [the plantation] a shrubless waste as it is now. I had a thousand times rather see the bay with its clear sky than blackened by the smoke from [Yankee] factories.'"[17]

The South, then, is the Garden in Reconstruction literature in that, on the simplest level, it fulfills the anti-industrialist bias of the pastoral society. On a more complex level, the South is the Garden because of certain positive and negative traits related to this U.S. American variation on the pastoral theme.

The positive traits relate to "a cluster of metaphors expressing fecundity, growth, increase, and blissful labor in the earth. . . ."[18] The Garden also signified "a virtual cocoon of freedom from anxiety, guilt, and conflict—a shrine of the pleasure principle"; a life "relaxed, quiet, sweet."[19] That the great prewar plantations realized these psychic virtues was a constant theme in the fiction and nonfiction of slavery apologists. Reconstruction literature presented these virtues persisting after the war, despite revolutionary upheaval, in the descriptions of peaceful plantations, fertile cotton fields, and the blissful labor of an African working class:

> For miles along the bank of the river the horizon was blue and misty with the columns of smoke from the trash-gangs on the plantations. Here and there . . . ox-teams . . . hauling willow-poles; [the] negroes . . . at work on every plantation—the plows near the road, . . . [the] trash-gang . . . toward the swamp . . . [The houses appear only at] rare intervals. . . . [The] unvarying double row of quarters, with the little mud-floored porch . . . , and the swarms of little picaninnies tumbling about in the sunshine. . . . Coveys of quails . . . started up with a whirr. . . . [From] the fields came faintly the shout of some plower to his team. [There were no other sounds] none—the country seemed almost as silent as . . . wilderness.[20]

Among those Reconstruction writers who favor the Southern cause, these physical attributes carry the concomitant socio-psychic virtues of freedom from anxiety, guilt, and conflict, virtues organic to that harmonious social interaction between races and classes celebrated by apologists for slavery.

As the Garden, then, the South was a place of pleasure and joy, a self-contained, genteel world in which anxiety about material things, guilt about slavery, conflicts between black and white, between poor-white and quality folk, were nonexistent—at least in the romantic view of the South.[21]

> [If] you wish once again to find the lost gate of Eden . . . if you wish to see in this rude, practical America of ours an "earthly paradise," where life is good, because Nature has invested it with everything that is delicious and fairest; if you wish to see plantations at the height of culture—lawns as fragrant, as clean-shaven, as nobly shaded by graceful trees as any sovereign's—seek the Teche country. It is the pearl of Louisiana; it is the gem of the South.[22]

(That this was written by a Reconstruction writer indicates the persistence of this image in this postwar literature.)

But there were negative aspects to the Garden *mythos*. These aspects became incarnate in what can be called the "Wilderness ambiguity," aspects seen in this study as major attributes of the Southern *pastorale*. Unlike the Arcadia of the traditional myth in which benign forces ruled, the U.S. American Garden had to share territory with a vast wilderness in whose dark forest and expansive wastes daemonic forces, usually in the earlier days of U.S. American society, Indigenous people, lurked. Such also was the condition of the pre-Confederate states. Physiographically, the South of 1860 was still relatively uncultivated compared to the North. Great tracts of a plantation might be nothing but canebrakes and pine forests. Beyond the plantations lay dismal swamps along the Atlantic Coast, gorges and cliffs in the Southern mountains, bayous and everglades near the Gulf. The gothic description of the Southern wilderness recurs persistently in such Reconstruction nonfiction as King's *The Great South* and Powers' *Afoot and Alone*, and this quality of wilderness is presented as the unique feature of the Southern landscape:

> Long naked grapevines swing down from the vast cypresses through which the wind swoops with an inexpressibly ghostly hollow moan. [All] the ground is strewn with the wrecks and rubble of the freshets. And then these snaky bayous, wriggling in the yellow muck, arched over with gloomy gray cypresses and funereal moss.
>
> ....
>
> It was rapidly growing dark; the long moss overhead began to sway with a mysterious and ghostly motion, pre-saging a storm; and the hoarse and eldritch screams of the owls were echoing with a most dismal reverberation among the cypresses.[23]

Socially, the Wilderness is the existential condition and the explanation for the persistence of frontier savagery in the 19th-century South. On the one hand, such savagery refers to the primitive conditions of countryside, rural habitations, and landscape. On the other hand, "savagery" is related to violence and cruelty, a meaning fulfilled in the barbaric aspects of Southern life: the murderings and floggings, bushwhacking and bowie-knife brawls, random mob cruelty and deliberate vigilantism—the Southern forms of that freedom from law that was the social condition of the Wilderness-Frontier.

This freedom also carried over into that anarchic individualism, which became the exasperating emblem of the Southern aristocrats' temperament. It could be seen in the intensely held doctrine of personal independence and personal responsibility, which made the great planters laws unto themselves, especially during the Klan uprisings, and which established independence and honor as the twin virtues of Dixie. Such individualism underlaid the political anarchy that doomed both the Confederacy and the Reconstruction governments.

Thus, in the Wilderness-Garden ambiguity, one locates a further example that identifies the South as the Garden.

Finally, the South exemplifies that submission to the power of nature, which may be described as the essence of the Garden archetype. The interconnection of humans with the cyclical variety of the Southern climate gave the agrarian society its pantheistic tone: Planting, breeding, and harvesting were the clocks by which Southern life was timed. If New Orleans accepted the seasonal occurrences of yellow fever, it was because they were a part of that Priapean nature that made the South the image of fecundity in Reconstruction literature.

> Spring in the South is "glorious summer"; . . . the vines are wrapping themselves with new life up the stems of the sassafras and thorn trees, while the winter-reft and winter-soiled edges of the forest, splashed in color as with the clayey mud of the ditches, become more bright every day; the brilliant light green of the willows touching the landscape with the hues of Eden. . . . This, . . . amidst the deep silence of these parts, without heat or glare of sun. . . .[24]

On the mythic level, then, the North emerges as the Locomotive, the South as its pastoral counterpart. And at this level, the struggle between them can be seen as a clash between "the ideal of agrarian innocence and the mastering impulse of industrial and technological experience."[25] By November 1860, this complex antagonism contracted to more simplistic terms—a struggle between freedom and slavery. By 1861, this conflict, which had simply been a cultural-psychological image of the economic differences between the two sections, became transformed into the harsh reality of a civil war, a war that demanded (symbolically speaking) allegiance to either the Locomotive or the Garden. On April 9, 1865, those allied to the Machine entered the Southern Garden, where they remain to this day.[26]

The rivalry of opposing economic archetypes is, therefore, the first level of the sectional conflict between North and South. The second level is the sociocultural clash between Yankee and Cavalier as rival societies.[27]

The nature of Yankee society by 1860 can be summed up by certain accurate clichés.[28] It was a society in which, for most classes, democratic-egalitarian ideals usually predominated. As a result, there was a great deal of social mobility from one class to another. While a definite class structure did exist, it did not include the kind of impediments against upward advancement that typified an aristocracy. The enterprising individual in commercial and industrial activities could start as low as a janitor and end up owning a company. Such a theme appears in Tourgée's *Figs and Thistles* (1879), in which Markham Churton rises from common-laborer to congressman because of hard work, enterprise, and the exploitation of his opportunities. In such Horatio Alger fantasies was "acted out" the Yankee's belief that freedom of opportunity was the key virtue, symbolizing the egalitarianism and social mobility of their society. This was the dynamic of the rational mode at work as a cultural imperative.

Freedom of opportunity was the essential characteristic of the political and social progressivism of which the North boasted. The celebration of this virtue as the major difference between Yankee and Cavalier recurs constantly in the fiction and nonfiction sympathetic to the Reconstruction. Freedom of opportunity was the answer to the problem of the Freedman: Give him a white man's chance, the chance to move out of his previous condition to a better one, argue Reid and Tourgée, and he will become a free man. And the progress of ex-slaves under Reconstruction from field hand to South Carolina lawmaker represented the fullest flowering of Northern ideals south of the line.

Democratic egalitarianism, social mobility, and freedom of opportunity were sustained in Northern society by a major social institution that rarely existed southward, and that was the public school. For Tourgée and the other pro-Radical Reconstruction writers, this institution bulwarked Northern progressive ideas against the forces of secession and rebellion. Furthermore, Tourgée in *Bricks Without Straw* regards its transplanting to the South as the only way to transform the Southern aristocracy into a democracy. It is precisely because public education is identified with Yankee ways that it is celebrated in pro-Reconstruction works and castigated in the literature of the opposition. That the Yankee Schoolmarm is always featured in the former works as the idealistic heroine testifies to the importance of public schools in the Yankee's imagination as the epitome of rationalism.

If the North could be said to have had a mystique defining her rationalistic virtues other than faith in individual initiative and industrialism, it is Puritanism:

> . . . the Puritan way of thought, harsh and ascetic and intolerant, promising salvation for the few but damnation for the many, became a major intellectual force in U.S. American life. It introduced a discordant element into a society with a heritage of tolerance, moderation, and experimentalism.[29]

Most modern U.S. Americans accept this unflattering (if not biased) Southern view of Puritanism, but it is only partially correct. Puritanism also gave moral and intellectual vigor to the Yankee society. It was the reluctant mother of liberal theology, e.g., Unitarianism and Universalism, and the moral foundation of New England transcendentalism; it was the unifying superego of the diverse groups that made up the North. Its harshness bred discipline; its asceticism found positive expression in the self-sacrificing quality of the Northern soldier during the war and in the commitment of idealistic Carpetbaggers to teaching and working with Freedmen in a hostile South after the war. And most of all, some of the evils the Puritan ethic was intolerant of were the kind no society could tolerate and survive as a humane social order. One such evil was slavery, and the Puritan response was abolitionism as an ideology and as a cultural imperative, a fact to be discussed in more detail in Chapter V. These then were the elements creating what I am calling the rational mode.

In contrast, Southern critics saw Puritanism as the foundation of a society permeated with Uriah Heaps (a symbol of an intolerant hypocrisy) and with a morality masking such antisocial values as selfishness and acquisitiveness. It was the sanction for a society whose institutions were directly or indirectly based on predatory greed.[30] That Simon Legree was a Yankee demonstrates that these negative criticisms were not limited solely to Southerners.

It was a conventional romantic gambit in the 19th century to picture the North as vital and energetic, the South as static and lethargic. The quality of Cavalier culture in this view seemed almost surrealistic, as if time had slowed down and all activity had been reduced to slow motion. Such a dramatic juxtaposition conveniently overlooked the immense amount of energy released in the Southern landscape: steamboats being loaded and unloaded, cotton and tobacco fields being tilled, levees and roads being built and repaired, workdays beginning at sunup and ending at sunset—if then. But the romantic observer would have been blinded to this dynamic black side of Southern life. Instead, the languorous manner of plantation belles, the good-humored conviviality of lazy slaves, and the long summer evenings of cigar-and-whiskey talk would have dominated the pages of his/her report, the epitome of the anti-rationalist mode.

This view coincided with the self-conceptions of Cavalier propagandists. They conceived of a Cavalier culture in which labor was divorced from the aristocratic existence. The planters denigrated the expenditure of energy as being ungentlemanly and properly the work of slaves. In a sense they preferred the image of stasis and lethargy, but for "stasis" they substituted "stability" and for lethargy, "that indefinable quality of a society at ease with itself and the world, a society solely for the supremacy of the planter class,"[31] the cultural triumph of a distinctly anti-rational mode.

Such supremacy emerged from the importance of "place" within class boundaries. This made it difficult to climb from one class to another. Slave and poor whites were fixed in their place, though sometimes a freed slave or a talented "cracker" might mount upward in a limited way. Tourgée in *Bricks Without Straw* describes an enterprising merchant who becomes wealthy enough to marry into a degenerating aristocratic family. But in the main, class rigidity hampered social movement, and this led to the social stability, which was the pride of the Old South and which ensured the supremacy of elite families.

Such stability also derived from the Southerner's strong sense of tradition. He looked backwards to the glorious days of the revolutionary period, the colonial period, the semi-mythical days of the Stuarts and their ill-fated cavaliers,[32] and the completely legendary days of the golden feudal world celebrated in the novels of Sir Walter Scott.[33] The importance of tradition became expressed in a confused form of modern feudalism, found primarily in the Southern romance, which was based on a mythological vision of the Southern past mixed with a novelist's depiction of English feudalism. The chief expression of this mythology was the Cult of Chivalry, a cult in which barbarity and civilization coalesced. If the mystique of the North was Puritanism, at the South it became courtly traditions. These traditions shaped the cultural aspirations and heroic postures of the Southern knighthood: the *code duello*, the *noblesse oblige* toward the slaves, the importance of martial virtues, the intense individualism of the planter-barons, the various rites of leisure, and the exaggerated respect for women. These were the values explicit in the South's medieval conceptions of itself.[34] And in these conceptions, the aristocratic Southern woman dominates.

In the Southern romance and in the sentimental vision of the Cavalier in Reconstruction literature, the master of the Southern knight is his mistress, the Belle. Despite the reality of her legal, social, and political helplessness, she wielded certain powers, powers present in the Southron's idealization of her moral and erotic influence over his life. Such powers formed the keystone in the arch of sexual relationships in the planters' domain—at least in fiction.

In this context, respect, honor, and the ritual of gallantry were real phenomena and, in many instances, acted as a buffer between the Belle and the rigors of her position in a slave society. Moreover, this cult of the Southron woman created an interesting patriarchal-matriarchal tension on the plantations. On the one hand, the plantation was a patriarchy, devolving around the masculine principle of the Cavalier. But if he were, in turn, submissive to his lady—mother or wife, aunt or sister—then the plantation was under quasi-matriarchal control. Such control can be seen in Baker's *Colonel Dunwoddie, Millionaire*; Bonner's *The Valcours*; Morgan's *Yazoo*; and Tourgée's *Bricks Without Straw* and "John Eax." The treatment of the Southern matriarch in these works is freighted with Oedipal overtones that, in light of the Freudian revolution of modern times, are quite explicit, as the following excerpts should demonstrate.

In the first two excerpts, the matriarchal dynamic is defined in purely Oedipal terms, in the symbol of the Belle-Mere:

> [Horace Dunwoddie] was not so tired at night that he could not bear his mother upstairs as well as down again in his arms every morning. She seemed to yield herself up to him more completely each time; and she parted from him so reluctantly . . . , and welcomed him so gladly when he came back at night, that he got into the habit of running into the house at unexpected hours during the day, if it was but to say a word and go again.
>
> [One night, they have a sacramental encounter after Horace returns from a trip.]
>
> '. . . darling mother, it is time for me to take you up-stairs. Not a night while I was gone but I thought of it and wanted to do it.' . . . He laid her upon her bed, . . . and knelt by her side as she lay, and emptied a pile of gold coin upon the bed-cover, while his father fastened up the house below. . . .
>
> [She accepts his gift of gold coins and then makes a request.]
>
> 'You have always been my own boy, . . . but there is another gift I want more, Horace. Will you give me that?'
>
> The young man had never before heard such accents of eagerness from his mother.
>
> 'Why, mother! . . . *you* ask me such a question? I am all I am and have and can be, am already yours. You know it.'
>
> 'That is all I want,' she said; 'I want you to give me yourself! Mind, you belong to me. You cannot . . . give yourself away . . . without my consent! Remember, Horace, it is a promise—a sacrament! And now, dear, keep my gold for me to-night! Kiss me once more.'[35]

The second excerpt is even more explicit. The scene is between Garry Valcour and his young mother:

> [Garry said,] 'You remind me of a Christmas candle . . . rising slim and long from . . . curls of tissue paper. . . . Now keep perfectly still.' He lifted her as if she were a child and . . . placed her carefully . . . , on a lounge. Then he caught her little foot in his hand. 'I knew it,' he cried: '. . . Ah, traitress. Did you not promise me to wear no more such slippers [i.e., with a Louis Quinze heel]?' . . . She took it off, displaying a diminutive foot, in a silk stocking ornamented with three

darns, on which Garry gazed admiringly. [He then jokingly berates her for the] shocking morality [associated with wearing] 'heels as high as new lead-pencils. . . .'[36]

In light of these overtones, it becomes clear that the Cult of the Aristocratic-Slavocratic Woman in the cavalier society is a conscious acknowledgment of a matriarchal energy operating within the patriarchal structure of plantation life.

In Tourgée's sociopolitical tales, the Oedipal byplay between the Cavalier-son and the Belle-Mere is used by Jocasta to control the political or social radicalism of her son. In *Bricks Without Straw*, Madame Le Moyne uses her influence to force her son to give up his Carpetbagger sweetheart:

> He knelt by her side and pressed his lips to hers.
>
> 'Oh, my son, my son!' said the weeping woman, as she pushed back the hair above his forehead and looked into his eyes; 'only give your mother time— . . . It will not be for long, but we must be alone—all alone—as we were before all these things came about.'[37]

However, Jocasta's power is not always complete, at least in pro-Reconstruction works. In "John Eax," a Southern male revolts against the matriarchal energy. The cause of the revolt, in this case, is Charles De Jeunette's desire to marry beneath his station against his mother's wishes:

> She . . . was gazing at me with a wild yearning look, her arms outstretched towards me in mute entreaty. I sprang towards her and caught her in my arms. Her head fell upon by breast, and a torrent . . . of grief . . . burst from her. After a time she . . . directed me to go. As I turned . . . , she caught me again.
>
> 'Once more, one more embrace," she said, as she kissed me again and again. "O Charles! Remember that your poor mother begs . . . you to grant her this one last request. . . . Remember her life is in your answer.'
>
> [His answer was that he would marry the girl.] 'Then go!' she cried. 'Go! You are no longer my son!' She gave a slight cough, and a red stream burst over her thin lips.[38]

What, then, do these examples indicate about Cavalier culture as symbolic of the anti-rationalist mode? We have two basic hints here. First, that the deference and worship directed toward slavocratic women in the prewar South's plantation society are clearly related to "matriolatry" and probably accounts for some of the sexual fantasies related to the male slave and the Belle. Second, that much of the conservatism and traditionalism organic to the planter society can be traced indirectly to the sociopsychological relationship between the Cavalier and the Belle-Mere.

The above discussion represents the psychological aspects of the Cult of the Belle: historically, the specific social acts of the matriarch were more important. In some instances she helped to run the plantation and to care for sick slaves; in most instances, she helped to civilize the patriarch.[39] In a few cases she took the reins of rule away from an inept or vice-ridden master. And during the war in conjunction with a favorite slave, she ran the plantation, often with some success.[40] In these and other ways, the Cult of the Belle balanced the vision of the heroic, all-powerful patriarch and helped to soften the harsh brutalities of a slave-owning class.

The immediate result of the Cult of Chivalry (and its effect upon the Southron and his lady) was to reinforce the traditionalistic emphasis so apparent in the depiction of the prewar South:

> The new ideas which [Garrick] had caught from Ross and her friends were true. . . but they were raw and unaired to him. There was an indescribable sense of content and actuality as he [listened] to Aunt Laura's stories as to old, well-known songs, in settling down into the narrow, warmed, familiar limits of thought and belief.[41]

"The warmed, familiar limits," in turn, structured the values of this society, unified the cavalier culture under the planter and his family (at least on the surface), and constituted the sanction for an aristocratic social system. More important, the Cult of Chivalry, as the mystique of the South, created "the notion that Southerners [were] a separate and homogeneous breed."[42]

This homogeneity as an adjunct to Southern traditionalism was a superficial one, especially as it relates to the anti-slavery movement. First of all, there were anti-slavery slave owners whose conscience, political ideals, and personal values developed attitudes broader than Cavalier dogmas. In a sense, they were abolitionists forced by cultural conformity to remain slaveholders. Reconstruction works like *A Royal Gentleman*, *Yazoo*, and *After the War* allude to the anguish of conscience about and hatred of an institution that some Southrons were compelled by a cultural conformity to support. Andrews and Trowbridge report the curious sense of relief that many slaveowners felt when they were compelled to give up the institution they would have died to preserve. Thus, among the planter class, the homogeneity, the commitment to the warm, familiar ways, was not complete.

Then there was another group, spread throughout the South, who rejected both slavery and the cultural-psychological apparatus built around slavery to create a Dixie-centered nationalism. They were of the "out" classes of white Southerners who struggled, often futilely, with the Cavaliers for economic and political position in a slave-based society.[43] These men formed the Unionist party in the secessionist South. In wavering states, they worked with the Army to save Missouri, Kentucky, and Maryland for the North; in the rebel states, they formed pro-Union enclaves in anticipation of the Federal victory. Most of all, they gave Andrew Johnson to the cause. After the war it would be they who would flourish in triumph over their Cavalier rivals during Reconstruction, supplying, for a while, the ranks of the Radicals with native Southerners, a few of whom were heroic, progressive men. In *A Fool's Errand* John Walters is presented as the embodiment of these characteristics.

But in the myth of the Cavalier and in the nature of his closed society, this and other kinds of heterogeneity are suppressed. The vision of Cavalier supremacy is one of unity, of stability and conformity shaped around tradition and custom. These become the attributes that created the golden world of the prewar South—golden primarily for the elite. It was these same attributes, especially the traditionalism that produced them, that were to cocoon the South against the progressive trends of the 1800s and hamper the efforts to modernize it during Reconstruction.

The Yankee writers of Reconstruction literature are primarily of two minds about the anti-rational mode in Cavalier culture. On the one hand, some were quite sympathetic to certain positive qualities they found beneath the romantic mythology and the evils of slavery. In this view the South was a place of close human relationships. Because it was a settled society, its pleasures tended to be social even between equals and unequals. Its stability was a restful contrast to the social turmoil developing in the North. Besides, it was a culture based on a fixed idea of human relations and human nature, an idea enshrined in the political religion of State's Rights. Such views must have had a certain attractiveness to Northern Conservatives, especially those who envied the Cavaliers as the true U.S. American patricians, seeing them as slave-holding Catos and Solons who were the country's natural leaders.[44] Edward King, Stephen Powers, John W. De Forest, and Robert Somers reflect in their descriptions of Southern society the reappearance of this romantic admiration in Northern literature after the war. It can especially be seen in Somers' nostalgic picture of the planter nobility in the Valley of the Tennessee, a picture that clearly parallels the images given by the romancers of the 1830s and 1840s.

> So the planters put their wives on pads behind the saddle, met at each other's houses, lived a merry and hospitable life; and the Valley of the Tennessee was soon occupied from end to end by lords and ladies of the land—men capable in business, and dames bringing both grace and wisdom from afar—who spread civility and plenty round them by degrees, and gave a tone to society that was spoken of from New York to New Orleans, and the impress of which, after all the havoc of war and revolution, still remains.[45]

In such a vision, the cruelty and exploitation and the anti-rational nature of slavery-capitalism and its bloody destruction through civil war disappear in a haze of nostalgia.

Finally, the persistence of the North's fascination with the South can be seen in Tourgée's prediction in the 1880s of a future greatness for Southern literature, a greatness that would encompass a Faulkner and an Ellison:

> A foreigner studying our current literature . . . would undoubtedly conclude that the South was the seat of intellectual empire in America, and the African the chief romantic element of our population. . . . To the woefulness of the conquered . . . is added the pathos of a myriad of deposed sovereigns. Around them will cluster the halo of romantic glory, and the epoch of their overthrow will live again in American literature. . . . We cannot foretell the form [Southern literature] will bear. . . . It may be sorrowful, exultant, . . . or perhaps terrible, but will certainly be great. . . . Because of the exceeding woefulness of a not too recent past, therefore, and the abiding horror of unavoidable

> conditions which are . . . the present, we may confidently look for the children of soldiers and of slaves to advance American literature to the very front rank. . . ."[46]

From the opposite point of view, the anti-Southern writers of Reconstruction saw the prewar culture as filled with flaws that passed into the Reconstruction experience and generated the turmoil characteristic of that experience. In their eyes, the Cult of Chivalry, which the pro-Southern writers admired, grew out of cultural-psychological and social needs to mask the squalor and the agony created by the influence of the slave-labor capitalist system on Southern society. For example, the persistence of violence in Southern society evolved from the callous sensibilities created by a combination of slavery and frontier brutality. For the anti-Southern writer, such violence contradicted the Cavalier's genteel pretensions and produced an insidious corruption of his *code duello*. The prewar South became the Anglo-Saxon society, which tolerated a Cult of Violence—dueling, feuds, the law of Judge Lynch, knife brawls, rail riding, and tarring[47]—fused with the Cult of Chivalry.[48] It is possible to locate the pervasiveness of the Cult of Violence throughout the slave states as a cultural-psychological, social, and political force in the sadistic impulses of individual Southerners and ultimately in the wilderness crudity of the 19th-century South in general. But for the anti-cavalier writer, it was the permissiveness of violence in a slave society that was the essential source of the ease with which many a Southerner, before and during Reconstruction, turned to whip and gun and rope.

Indeed, for the pro-radical writers, slavery is the corrupt center in the golden circle of Dixie feudalism. This is the fact that Harriet Beecher Stowe explored so well and that was only vaguely or romantically presented in pro-Southron writing. It is slavery and the racism developed to defend it which, in this study, generates the major defects of Southern society—defects that would destroy that society and also the Reconstruction governments raised to supplant it.

As an economic system, slavery was paradoxically the source of the cotton baron's wealth and of his financial dependency. For some critics of slavery, including within the South itself, as an economic structure, the peculiar institution was more liability than asset. Indeed, they insist that by 1860, chattelism had become more and more inefficient as an agricultural technique.

It had already wasted vast tracts of land, and staple crop production was diminishing, except on very large plantations.[49] Moreover, the cash returns from cotton were becoming negligible for the average planter. His investment often led to a spiraling circle of debt. A planter might end up using all his finances, Mary Chestnut bitterly states, "to support a horde of idle dirty Africans. . . ."[50] Yet so important was slavery as a symbol in the planter's romantic, anti-rational conception of his commonweal that he sacrificed his wealth, his best blood, to protect it—as if it were still a dynamic economic force.

Several features made slavery more than simply an economic system, related organically to its cultural-psychological flaws before Reconstruction. First was the racism defining the slave as subhuman. This, aside from certain melodramatic aspects (e.g., the incredibly hard labor of plantation life, the overcrowded living conditions, the general poverty of the slave, and the punishments), created extraordinary limitations on the slave and the slaveowner. For example, because of its dependence of racial definitions, U.S. American chattelism embodied a feature that made it more inhumane than other forms: the almost impossible legal difficulties after 1830 of either granting a slave freedom or of the slave gaining freedom. Because U.S. American slavery became, by 1860, an integral part of racist doctrines, it lacked the redeeming features of, say, Roman or even Turkish slavery, wherein a slave could gain freedom through meritorious service or could advance to a superior rank though still a slave. Tourgée discusses the rigid inflexibility of this kind of slavery at length in *A Royal Gentleman* and *Hot Plowshares*.

Another feature of the peculiar institution was the paradox of "Interracial Symbiosis," which for the anti-cavalier writer was the most significant form of an anti-rational tendency in Southern society before and during Reconstruction. Briefly defined, this term refers to the socially ambiguous relationship between master and slave and indicates that, despite the planter's assertions to the contrary, he was as dependent on his slaves as they were on him. The image of the masterful planter taking care of helpless, childlike slaves whom he does not really need is another myth of the romancers. In addition, the term suggests a vast complex of sociopsychological interaction between the two races that both denied and paradoxically reinforced the racism of slavery.

For example, though the Southerner believed that blackness was the sign of a curse, he felt:

> No physical repulsion from color. . . . White children were suckled by black mammies, and played promiscuously with the picaninnies. In a stagecoach or railroad car, as a squeamish abolitionist observed, a lady makes no objection to ride next to a fat Negro woman . . . ; providing always that her fellow travelers understand she is her property.[51]

This symbiotic intercourse caused the subtle Africanization of Southern life. When the Southron complains that radical rule has Africanized the South, he is already a century too late with his accusation. Slavery had in several ways accomplished that fact. In the first place, the South's exotic nature evolved from the presence of this alien minority (often a majority) within its boundaries, and the myths of the South intertwine the African and the Saxon in a Gordian knot. In the second place, the average Deep South plantation had much of a tribal nature about it. The master ruled with the capricious power of a chief, with royal prerogatives translated into the domestic life of the plantation. He might have had one or more concubines, a number one wife, usually white, and a brood of natural and legal children, often indistinguishable from each other. His priestly duty as moralist combined with his medical duties as witchdoctor. His cruelty to the inferior members of the tribe simply represented the authority of the chief. The way to his favor and hence to a form of tribal status lay, for the women, through his bed. Perhaps it was status and seduction as well as rape that helped to create the Afro-Saxon.

The most melodramatic and anti-rational variation on the Symbiosis was miscegenation or, more correctly, what I call racio-sexuality. I use this term in direct opposition to interracial sexuality, which was and is based on consensual sexual relationship between two persons legally defined as racially different. In contrast, racio-sexuality (or racist-based sexual behavior) can be described as follows: Sexuality between white and black during slavery took on a unique form because of the legal dehumanization and inferiority of the slave or, to be more specific, the female slave. If technically the slave was a wench and not a woman, then there was really no onus attached to a liaison with her. Hence, sexuality was not only permitted between the Saxon male and the African female (this being the only socially acceptable form) but often encouraged. The sexual possession of the slave grew out of the legal distinction between the master and his property; sexual possession was also a sign of property possession defined by racial lines. The liaison with the slave was both a racial as well as sexual act, all bound up in the legal and political doctrines related to slavery.

The social necessity of racio-sexuality was admitted frankly by the planters. It kept their young men from being driven "back on white ladies" and prevented the establishment of Northern "white slavery" in the South. Moreover, it kept the Lady at a level of purity above the Gal.[52] The sons of the aristocrats could enter into manhood via the rites of sexual initiation in the slave quarters or on Rampart Street. The romantic irony is that often what began as lust ended in love. This is the theme of *A Royal Gentleman*.[53]

The pressures of such eroticism on the Cavalier's family structure must have been extraordinary. On the one hand, the Lady was the adored wife and mother, the epitome of U.S. American womanhood; on the other hand, proofs abounded under her nose that she had a rival. The master's mulatto children were, in some cases, given the run of the plantation, while his wife and daughter were assumed to be so innocent that they would not understand the obvious. The conflict between the reputed purity of the Eves and the "open sensuality and slatternly, provocative manner" of their Lilith rivals must have created an interesting domestic situation on the plantation.[54] Master, Lady, and Gal formed the Southern version of the menage à trois: the Gal, possibly ". . . as light-skinned as [the Cavalier's] wives and daughters and sisters . . ."; the Lady, asexual and ethereal, "conveniently converted into disembodied . . . idealizations";[55] and, of course, the Cavalier, the master of the revels.

Although the geometric symbol is a triangle, there lurks in the master's imagination a rectangle, created by another figure who rivals the Cavalier for his Lady, at least in the master's frenzied dreams. It was the black man as a dark alter ego, as a phallic rival to the sexual dominance of the master, what Eldridge Cleaver calls the Super masculine Menial. In this context, a new myth is discernible. The plantation is an erotic Eden in which sexuality is both innocent and guilty. Adam is dual—black and white—in rivalry for Eve and Lilith, who are different (by race) and the same (by sex). And so that the white Adam can possess both Lilith and Eve without a phallic rival, he finds it necessary to create a repressive vision of his black alter ego as the Dark Rapist, cunning, cruel, and inexorably committed to the desecration of Eve. Furthermore, any guilt that White Adam may feel can be relieved by the occasional sacrifice of this alter ego.

There are instances of the taboo form of such sexual conjunctions between white women and black men in Reconstruction literature. Reid refers to liaisons between poor white women and their slave lovers, with unpredictable results for their children: "'One of these children . . . narrowly [escaped] drowning at the hands of his maternal uncles. . . . Another was once sold into slavery by his mother, for a 'flitch of bacon.'"[56] Powers and De Forest also depict examples of similarly rare instances of such forbidden conjunctions that took place during the Reconstruction. De Forest describes "two white women [who] were pointed at . . . as having children of mixed blood," and refers to the fact that a "rosy-cheek girl of nineteen had taken a mulatto husband of fifty. . . ." De Forest also states that once a "full-blooded black walked twenty miles to ask me if he could have a white wife, assuring me that there was a girl down in his" 'settlement' who was 'a teasin' every day about it."[57] Finally, Rebecca Harding Davis makes her chief Reconstruction novel, in part, a chronicle of the passionate agony of an unconsummated love affair between an ex-slave and an anti-Negro white woman.

In general, racio-sexuality relates to the erotic encounter between the Cavalier and the Gal. The general effect of such relationships on a society ostensibly imprisoned by Victorian and Protestant repressions is given a quasi-sociological analysis by Albert Morgan and a romantic treatment by Tourgée in *Toinette* and *A Royal Gentleman*. The blurring and splitting of libidinal energies between the Lady and the Gal, however, is more properly the subject for an psychoanalyst than for two Northern writers inhibited by Puritanism. They overlook the more subtle aspects of the problem by concentrating only on concubinage, rape, and bastardy. They do not describe the ineffectuality of the Protestant ethic in a society in which incest could be possible—with the correct partners, although Whitelaw Reid does refer to the persistent rumor that Jefferson Davis' mistress was the mulatto daughter of his brother Joseph.[58]

In an amazing way racio-sexuality allowed for a marvelous compromise with the Southern form of Evangelical Protestantism. The master could express his unsubdued dark passions with the tacit sanction of his church, provided that it was done discreetly. Geoffrey Hunter, the antagonist of *A Royal Gentleman*, has no religious problems so long as Toinette is simply his wench. In this way, the Southron solved a problem that defeated the more pragmatic Yankee: how to permit sexual drives to coexist with spiritual needs. One comic effect of this compromise was that the master could be both the model of virile accomplishments and a paragon of Baptist morality without being a hypocrite—at least in his own eyes. He is, says Mary Chestnut,

> A magnate who runs a hideous black harem with its consequences under the same roof with his lovely white wife, and his . . . daughters. [Yet he] poses as the model of all human virtues. . . . [He] scolds [at his wife and daughters] as if he never did a wrong in his life. Fancy such a man finding his daughter reading *Don Juan*. 'You with that immoral book!' And he orders her out of sight. You see, Mrs. Stowe did not hit the sorest spot. She makes Legree a bachelor."[59]

Perhaps the best example with which to conclude this mosaic of paradoxes related to racio-sexuality and to bring into sharpest focus the peculiar institution south of the line is the image that haunts all Reconstruction writers, an image that both fascinates them and, one suspects, threatens their own sense of racial purity. It is the racially ambiguous image of the mulatto or Afro-Saxon, the most dramatic sign of the fluid relationship between master and slave and of the anti-rational absurdity of U.S. American racism:

> Nowhere else in the world could that scene [a freedman fair] have been witnessed. There were elegantly dressed ladies, beautiful beside which that of the North is waxwork; with great, swimming, lustrous eyes, half-veiled behind long, pendent lashes, and arched with coal-black eyebrows; complexions no darker than those of the Spanish senioritas one admires in Havana, but transparent as that of the most beautiful Northern blonde, with the rich blood coming and going, under the olive skin, with every varying emotion; luxuriant flowing tresses, graceful figures, accomplished manners—perfect Georgian or Circassian beauties. Yet every one of these were 'only a nigger.'[60]

In this context, the image emerges of the South as a world in which swarthy Cavaliers (labelled white) can buy and sell blond, blue-eyed slaves (labelled colored): "I've seen many a black Samson sold," so states a Freedman, "standing between those posts; and many a woman too, as white as you or I."[61]

The psychological results of this Symbiosis, the knotted intricacy of what began as economics and ended up as existential complexity, have yet to be studied. For example, how much of an Oedipus could survive a Jocasta with two faces—one white and one black, but often with only dark breasts?[62] What nightmare arose in the collective unconsciousness of the Black Belt planters when they looked about their home and fields, in their bed and at their bedside, and saw the Blackness of Darkness?[63] Is it possible that the trauma of the Reconstruction period recorded in its literature grew, in part, from such psychic entanglements, from the attraction-repulsion ambivalence that the Cavalier had for his property? This was the height of the anti-rational element in Cavalier culture.

A motif that might well reflect such an ambivalence is the Cavalier's violence against his slave, the second aspect of the Interracial Symbiosis. This was represented by the specific presence of a pattern of cruel behavior throughout slavocratic culture directed toward the Negro as Negro. This impulse toward racial violence, almost genocidal in nature, grew from the unlimited power that the master wielded over a race treated as both helpless and subhuman. Invariably, racial violence found expression in a mixture of capricious acts of cruelty, ranging from the casual box on the ear of a mischievous picaninny, the flogging to death of runaways, to putting slaves into "hogsheads, with nails driven in all round," and rolling "the poor things down hill."[64]

It is, therefore, around slavery that all the flaws of the Cavalier's society cluster in anti-Southern Reconstruction works: the sadistic impulses of the Cult of Violence, the psycho-sexual and socio-psychic dislocations and complications of the Interracial Symbiosis, the emotionalism over State's Rights, the intolerance of heterodoxy, the obstinate commitment to the secessionist position—in a word, the wide range of activities and attitudes which, by 1860, made the slave society, the Slavocracy, odious to the pro-abolitionist writer as the anti-rational society. Yet it was slavery that somehow invested this society with its idealistic conception of itself.

In this view, slave-labor capitalism with its virtues and vices emerges not only as an economic institution but also as the force that formed the cultural and psychological base of the Cavalier's kingdom. In a sense, as corroborated by Kenneth Stampp's *The Peculiar Institution* and Eugene Genovese's *The Political Economy of Slavery*, slave labor capitalism for the planter class *was* the South and, consequently, remained the essential reason for the conflict between Yankee and Cavalier.

Whether or not the war between Cavalier and Yankee was inevitable in 1860 is debatable; that Yankee and Cavalier were engaged in a cultural conflict of increasing virulence is axiomatic. By 1860 the political conflicts between the two intensified and were intensified by the cultural rivalry. For the ultimate result of the Cavalier's cultural values—social stability, slavery, the Cult of Chivalry—was the formation of a section of the United States that was so distinctive from its Yankee antithesis that it conceived of itself as another country. Secondly, a poetic machinery proved conclusively that a nation of knights could not coexist peaceably with a nation of money grubbers.[65] Thus, the South closed in upon itself—becoming fearful to the point of paranoia about the abolitionist North—as cultural myths became more important than sociopolitical and socioeconomic realities—the Cavaliers became mobilized behind the leaders of unreason. All these factors would make the military encounter with the Yankees inevitable. On April 9, 1865, cultural myths and political realities finally met. The Cavaliers received the first in a series of severe defeats that would eventually lead to the extinction of their class as a slavocratic hegemony at the hands of the despised Yankee plebeians.[66]

This conflict, which has been traced from the archetypal encounter between the Locomotive and the Garden, through the cultural antagonisms of Yankee and Cavalier, designated as a conflict between rational and anti-rational modes of behavior, found its most important crystallization in sociopolitical terms, in those historical struggles that climaxed in the Civil War and, most important for this study, in the First Reconstruction. This sociopolitical struggle over the nature of the Republic divides into two periods. The first, the prewar struggle, will end this chapter. The second, the Reconstruction struggle, will be the subject of the following chapter. It is the conflict between Unionist and Secessionist that defines the final phase of the sectional antagonism:

> The curse of sectionalism had antedated the quarrel over slavery. Almost from the nation's birth North and South had differed in cultural attitudes, in political theory, and in economic bases.
>
> [But by the nineteenth century] the sectional lines, in respect to slavery, the nature of the Union, and the place of the Negro in the American society, soon appeared.

> The divergent cultures had hardened, and for a half century an ever more divided nation sought without success to find an accommodation. Almost every milestone was ominous, and over each hung the shadow of slavery. The Missouri Compromise . . . the Nullification Controversy . . . the Anti-Abolitionist Laws . . . the Mexican War . . . the Compromise of 1850 . . . the Fugitive Slave Act . . . the Kansas-Nebraska Act . . . the Dred Scott Decision.[67]

By December 1860, with the election campaign ended, it may have struck thousands of Midwesterners and New Englanders, like some terrible illumination into the interactions of chance and necessity, that the series of appeasements that the North had made to solve the Irrepressible Conflict had always been only temporary accommodations. The South had been no more content with the Dred Scott decision than it was with the compromises of '87, '20, and '50.[68] Now, with Lincoln's election, there was no possible position that the North could take (aside from nullifying the election returns) that would make that devilish abolitionist acceptable to the South's frenzied imagination. For the Cavaliers, there was only one solution to this long-postponed national defeat: to secede from the Union and to close in upon themselves as a separate nation in the fullest meaning of those words.

Behind these complex historical events lay a profound ideological conflict, revolving around the nature of the U.S. American Republic. It was a battle between those, North and South, who believed in a centralized Hamiltonian-Federalist government, and those believing in a kind of Jeffersonian-Confederalist government.[69] Economic creeds interrelated with these beliefs: the dogma of protectionist tariffs and native manufactories versus the dogma of low tariffs and European imports. The Hamiltonians wanted a government that would give land to railroads and homesteaders and general subsidies to new industries. This strong relationship between industry and government, and the centralizing tendencies of such a government, were repugnant to the Jeffersonians, who emphasized agrarianism on the one hand and limited centralization on the other. By 1860, all these ideological positions had collapsed into the antithesis, Unionism versus Secessionism.

In Washington, December 1860, "[Men] with blue cockades of the secessionists brushed jubilantly past those who wore the colors of the union." By the spring of 1861, the South had abandoned their former capital to the Yankees in favor of Richmond and Montgomery. The Washington of Southern dominance "had vanished forever with the pleasant, provincial society, the grinning slaves and the broad-brimmed hats of the planter-politicians." Some of the planter-politicians "journeyed South in proud expectation of the empire of King Cotton; . . . some in scorn for the Yankee traders and crude Westerners who would supplant them; some in sorrow for lost friendship and old ambitions. A regime had ended in Washington."[70] Thus, what had begun as romantic myth ended in political action. According to one school of thought, Confederate staff officers, afraid that "Davis would clasp hands with Seward, and [that] the chance of war would slip away forever," ordered the attack on Fort Sumter later that spring.[71]

By April 13, 1861, the Union had become divided. What had begun as generalized tendencies and quaint cultural differences resulted in two separate countries. The Garden lay South; the Machine, North. The Yankee—a generic term encompassing the new immigrants from Ireland and Germany, the Old and New West (outside of Southern influence) and diverse Northern interests—had their nation; the Cavaliers—Deep South and Border States, southeastern and southwestern sovereignties—had theirs. Each now had a chance to apply its version of the spirit of '76 to its own national boundaries. By April 13, 1865, however, the conflict was ending in the North's favor. By April 13, 1868, Reconstruction would ensure that the victory of the Machine over the Garden, the Yankee over the Cavalier, the new bourgeois democratic republic over the old, would not be dissipated by a sentimental peace. The First Reconstruction would emerge as the ironic end to the South's quest for certainty that her separated world would have permanent existence; it would become the political and economic complement to Appomattox. By April 13, 1878, the South had more or less capitulated, for a season, on all the major issues—except the African Question. But by then, this was ceasing to be a national issue. The South was free to return to those myths and policies that would not endanger the new Union in military and insurrectionary adventures. The Conflict was, for all practical purposes, finished as a problem to be settled by war or forced political control. The nation's destiny was, for good or evil, in the hands of the Yankee under the aegis of the Locomotive. This is the fact and the myth celebrated in both anti-Reconstruction and pro-Reconstruction literature.[72]

Myth, semi-myth, and fact are found in the fiction and nonfiction of Reconstruction, which will be discussed in this study, and the unifying theme that links them together in a chain of conceptual unity is the Irrepressible Conflict in all its variations and its final resolution. These works have their ultimate importance not as historical documents (though some of them can rightfully claim this distinction), nor as distorted or faithful images of historical truths (though such distortions and fidelity will be infrequently pointed out); rather, it is their portrayal of the values and visions of the two societies and the results of their fatal antagonism to the Southern and U.S. American community that emerges as the defining characteristics of their importance as U.S. American literature. It is in terms of the antitheses set forth in this chapter that the social and political themes of the Reconstruction and its literature derive from their frame of reference.

CHAPTER II
THE FOOL'S ERRAND

> But, then, there has never been an objective book about the Reconstruction Period. It demands friends or enemies.[73]

> The Reconstruction era has properly been called the bloody battleground of American historians. For the issues of post-Civil War history have proved even subtler than those of the war itself.[74]

The presentation of the Reconstruction period in U.S. American historiography divides into two schools. To the right is the Dunningite School, named after William M. Dunning, one of the most influential scholars on Reconstruction history. Its view of the documentary facts and its interpretation of some of the ambiguous issues involved have dominated the depiction of this period in history textbooks for generations. The essence of the position is this:

> The victorious North behaved with far more economic ruthlessness than the victors of Versailles, and it imposed in the name of the 'Reconstruction' the rule of emancipated slaves, local renegades, . . . and imported adventurers.[75]

In the Dunningite version, Reconstruction became an aberrant event in U.S. American history, a perverse corruption of U.S. American political idealism in no way related, except by contrast, either to the nobility and grandeur of the evolution of the Republic, or the heroic war fought to protect that evolution.[76]

In opposition to this view stands the approach of the so-called Revisionist School. As the adjective implies, historians who embrace this position, e.g. C. Vann Woodward, Kenneth Stampp, John Hope Franklin, and Prof. Eric Foner, seek to revise the conclusion of the Dunningites by examining the period "objectively," taking, as it were, "the passion and rancor out of history" and trying to use more scholarly terms than "ruthlessness," "renegades," and "adventurers," to describe the period.[77] Revisionists see the Reconstruction as a mixture of good and evil. They place emphasis on examining the period as a historical phenomenon, seeing it within a national context of historical change. For example, if there were bloc-voting among the Freedmen, it existed also among the New York immigrants; if Republicans corrupted New Orleans, Tammany Democrats led the way in New York City. Further, the Reconstruction Revisionists seek to unearth the valuable and lasting accomplishments of radical rule, emphasizing the idealism codified in Reconstruction constitutions as representative of the best U.S. American political tradition.[78] They insist that Reconstruction was not an aberration but an event necessary to the establishment of modern U.S. America and hence an integral part of the evolution of the Republic.[79] They also demonstrate with extensive evidence that the South was no innocent, helpless victim upon which "Black Rule" was forced by a vengeful North, that to a great extent the South brought on itself many of the revolutionary upheavals by refusing to accept the spirit of Emancipation. Finally, they question the thesis that the Republican left was as radical as it has been presented.[80] It is on the Revisionist view that this study is based.

The functions of this chapter are, first, to see Reconstruction history as social and political events (with their roots in the prewar period), and second to present these events as the "data" that form the thematic structure of Reconstruction fiction, the Irrepressible Conflict as the dynamis. While this chapter's structure is close to being chronological and historical, it is essentially descriptive and thematic, concerned less with dates and political personalities than in the way social conditions in the reconstructing South resulted from onstage and offstage political acts. The aim is to present those basic historical periods forming the Reconstruction experience in the fiction. The context combines the observations and concrete descriptions recorded in the Reconstruction literary nonfiction of the period: Sidney Andrews' *The South since the War* (1866), Whitelaw Reid's *After the War* (1866), John T.

Trowbridge's *The Desolated States* (1868), J. W. De Forest's *A Union Officer in the Reconstruction* (a series of magazine articles 1866-1867 compiled into book form in 1948), Robert Somers' *The Southern States* (1871), Stephen Power's *Afoot and Alone* (1872), James Pike's *The Prostrate State* (1873), Edward King's *The Great South* (1875), "Studies in the South" (1883), and Albert Morgan's *Yazoo* (1884).[81] These works show how the nonfiction provides the historical and sociopolitical background to the themes, incidents, and characters appearing in the short stories and novels.

Reconstruction history consists of four phases. The first phase, restoration (1863-1868), was the period in which Southerners—Unionists and pardoned Confederates both—were in control of their own reconstruction within certain limits. However, it was more than this. Restoration was an attempt to end the varied wars between the states.

Civil strife had spilt the best blood of North and South for four years. Yet as one examines the political workings of the Reconstruction, it becomes clear that this bloodshed solved only one problem specifically: No state could secede from the Union.[82] The surrender of the Confederate armies still left ambiguous the nature and extent of Emancipation, the social and political status of the African, and the possibility of future rebellion. Nor had the war decided the fate of the political South (as distinct from the military South) as a powerful, momentarily subdued rival to the North's aims.[83] And, while militarily the national government seemed the supreme arbiter of states' rights south of the line, the political aspects of this ideological question were still undecided. Ostensibly, it would be the major aim of restoration to settle all of these questions and problems, because the Irrepressible Conflict was contained, not eliminated.

An overall view of the first phase reveals the following landmarks: Johnson issued the June Proclamation of 1865, which began the organization of so-called Johnson governments, staffed mainly by the ex-Confederates. These governments, while not recognized by the Congress, enjoyed a certain vitality and relative independence within their several states from the summer of 1865 to the spring of 1867. However, because of the election of ex-Confederates to major offices, because of anti-Unionist and anti-Freedman activity, the South, through Congressional action, was divided into five military districts and the restoration governments were put under military control, preparatory to

Congressional re-organization.[84] Restoration, then, failed as a policy of Reconstruction.[85]

The second phase, reconstitution (1867-1872), has come to stand for the entire Reconstruction period, represented by the shibboleth "Black Rule." In a real sense, reconstitution began while restoration was ending. During the spring of '67, the Southern wing of the Republican Party was organized, while in the North Congress passed the various Reconstruction Acts. During the period before the 1868 national elections, Southern Republicans created new constitutions and reorganized the old restoration governments in light of Congressional demands. After the election of 1868, a literal reconstitution of the South seemed realized. The Confederate opposition was either numb, cowed, or cooperative. For two years, 1869 and 1870, the Day of Jubilee seemed at hand. The 14th and 15th Amendments had been passed. Negro colleges had been established in Tennessee and Georgia supported, in part, by Unitarians and Universalists. Public schools were a fact of life. New constitutions of a relatively progressive nature operated throughout the South. Despite anti-radical delay in Georgia and Texas, the new states were, one by one, readmitted to the Union. Republicans—black and white, Northern émigré and native Southerner, cooperating ex-Confederate and anti-Negro Unionist, held together in a loose but viable fusion coalition—seemed almost in unchallenged control throughout the Garden[86] with, for the most part, the goodwill of the North and the active support of the Federal government. It seemed that Thad Stevens' dream of a loyal South, solidly backing the Northern Republicans and supporting the rights of Freedmen, had been realized.[87] Thus, 1868 to 1872 formed a brief golden age—before the scandals and the terrorism that would accompany the reconstitutionists' fall from grace.

The third phase, redemption (1871-1877), is the period during which the Bourbon, through political strategy, violence, and fraud, overthrew Republican governments, and Reconstruction returned to the hands of ex-Confederates and their Conservative allies. In the legend, hooded white-robed Southrons and their sons sweep out of the night to wreak righteous violence upon corrupt whites and corrupted blacks. This was one part. The other part involved the political maneuvering of Bourbons and their Northern allies disenchanted with Reconstruction and indignant over the misgovernment of the Grant wing of the party. By 1876, violence and political maneuver returned all of the southern

States except Louisiana, Florida, and South Carolina to Bourbon hands. Then in the confusion, fraud, and violence growing out of the 1876 election, Southern leaders met at Wormley House in Washington, D.C., with Republican leaders who needed the help of the Redeemers to "win" the election. The Republican presidential candidate, Rutherford B. Hayes, agreed to remove Federal troops from the final three Reconstructed states if elected, and Southern Congressional leaders agreed not to contest the results of a special Electoral Commission which, by one vote, made Hayes the president. This Wormley House conference was an event more symbolic than functional, since much of the negotiation had taken place before the meeting, but it stands in history and legend as the place where the Bourbon regained his South.[88]

The final phase is reconciliation. In this study, reconciliation refers to the period 1877-1885, in which the problems within the South, related to a remnant Republican Party and the "Negro", still existed alongside attempts to reach an intersectional accommodation. But it is more than a chronological time as applied to the Southern context; it is also a social, political, and psychological "time" in which the residual problems of the high Reconstruction persist, informing the process of hostile reconciliation *within* the South with unresolved tensions, as distinguished from the apparent solution of Reconstruction problems *between* the North and South. In this view, though Reconstruction as history ends with its so-called Wormley House Compromise, Reconstruction as social and political experience ends when the Democrats with Southern votes elect Grover Cleveland, the first Democratic president since the war, signaling the end of the political nature of the Conflict.

All phases share a common theme: the revolutionary attempt to transform the South from a slave-labor culture to a free labor one, from a "mono-racial" political structure to a multiracial one. It was this revolutionary assay that generated the literature of the Reconstruction, forming its thematic structure and shaping its aesthetic interest, especially as related to plot and character.

Throughout all phases there were four major characters: the Scalawag, the Freedman, the Bourbon, and the Carpetbagger.[89] Because the Scalawag appears always in a tertiary role, it is only necessary here to sketch this figure in this book. In Reconstruction fiction, the Scalawag is a minor character. In the Dunningite legend, he is a key figure, with the reputation of being a traitor to his own way of life and a collaborator with his country's enemies. In reality, he represented a broad range of characters. Some were Southern Unionists who had remained steadfast to the Republic's cause through persecution during Secession and during the restoration violence. Southern Negrophobes, slaveowners, abolitionists, and Christian egalitarians formed their ranks. Some were former Confederates ranging from anti-planter yeoman farmers and poor whites to ex-generals, e.g. James L. Alcorn (Republican governor of Mississippi) and James Longstreet (commander of the New Orleans Negro Metropolitans). In the main, they were men who wanted to break the power of the Bourbon, not so much for the Reconstruction or Negro cause as for their own vision of a New South. Therefore, they seized upon the improvisational machinery of radical rule as a chance to experiment with public schools, general enfranchisement, social welfare, taxation, prison reform, and the like. Finally, while radical politics forced them to work with the black citizens, a significant minority were hostile to the Freedmen as persons and as a political power. With these varied figures were, of course, corrupt opportunists and scoundrels, like Governor Moses of South Carolina.

As interesting as the Scalawags are as dramatic figures, they remain essentially minor characters in Reconstruction literature. Reconstruction history in its literary treatment rests upon the shoulders of Bourbon, Freedman, and Carpetbaggers. In this context, the four periods have two facets. The first relates to those factors that defined the new relationship between the ex-slave and the ex-master during "The Tragic Era." These factors are the dramatic sign of revolutionary changes in the status of the slave and master. From restoration through reconciliation, this transformation remains in this literature as the obvious symbol of the Reconstruction experience. The second facet, the more crucial for this study, is less obviously dramatic but more significant: It is the struggle between the Carpetbagger and the Bourbon as representatives of sectional types, defined as and shaped into symbols by the Irrepressible Conflict. Whatever the conflict or relation is between black and white Southerner, it takes on its reality from the pressures generated in the Garden by the intrusion of the Yankee-as-Radical. This second facet will appear in the discussion of the thematic nature of Reconstruction fiction in the following chapters. The first facet will form the substance of the discussion of Reconstruction history in these chapters: ". . . and frankly announced their purpose to insist on the destruction of the existing state governments in the South and on reorganization through negro [*sic*] suffrage."[90] In this light let us now examine the restoration phase.

The Bourbon appears after Appomattox as the inheritor of chaos. Railroads are in ruins, bridges and telegraph lines are down, crops have been despoiled. Ruins shape the context of this new existence and remind him of what he has lost:

> A city of ruins, of desolation, of vacant houses, of widowed women, of rotting wharves, of deserted warehouses, of weed-wild gardens, of miles of grass grown streets, of acres of pitiful and voiceful barrenness,—that is Charleston, wherein Rebellion loftily reared its head five years ago, on whose beautiful promenade the fairest of cultured women gathered with passionate hearts to applaud the assault of ten thousand upon the little garrison of Fort Sumter.[91]

Related to the physical ruin is the social dislocation. Lawlessness and anarchy, always latent in the Southern Garden, were widespread. Guerrillas and bushwhackers, half bandits and half soldiers, continued a desultory struggle directed more toward their own people than toward the Federals.[92] Joined with criminal Freedmen, they broke the tense equilibrium between the Wilderness and the Garden, filling the Southern pastoral with the danger and reality of rape, robbery, and murder.[93]

More poignant to the returning Bourbon was the sight of his fellow aristocrats, his family and friends, fallen into squalor, incompetence, and despair: a belle-matriarch, the former owner of 655 acres, now in her seventies, reduced to:

> . . . carrying her bag, like a poor white, to beg corn of the miller. . . . Her bed was a mattress spread on the floor [and she] had to do her own cooking. . . . I have seen her trudging slowly up a long hill, at the foot of which was a spring, reeling under the weight of a pail of water [;][94]

A fine gentleman forced to open a beer saloon, a great dame forced to take in boarders, an heiress to broad estates reduced to working as a menial for eight dollars a month.[95] It was a social catastrophe marked by untuned pianos, ragged sofas, curtainless windows, broken china, stockingless legs, displaced persons:

> Seated around that fire on their trunks, in the cold night air and half-blinded by the smoke, were ladies who, before the

> war, had been among the wealthiest and haughtiest in the South. Some of them were going to Texas to hide their poverty.[96]

Finally, there was the economic ruin, not only in terms of lost capital and wrecked plantations but the wreck of an economy that had defined and sustained the Cavalier's world view. What a change greeted the planters returning from the war! The assumption of forced labor, which had undergirded slave-labor capitalism, seemed irrevocably destroyed. In order to get the Freedman to work, the Bourbon was forced to bargain with him:

> The negro was king. Men fawned upon him; carried pockets full of tobacco to bestow upon him; carefully explained to him the varied delights of their respective plantations. Women came too—with coach and coachman—drove into the camp, went out among the negroes, and with sweet smiles and honeyed words sought to persuade them that such and such plantations would be the very home they were looking for. Sambo listened, took the tobacco, drank the whisky, grinned ample return for every smile, and—cogitated.[97]

Thus, military defeat revealed to the homecoming Confederate his dependence on cheap, skilled field hands and the concomitant helplessness without them. The thousands of ex-slaves moving through the Garden indicated the dismal fact of a loss almost equal to that of the Confederate dead. An economic system had fallen and with it, so it seemed, a civilization.[98] Property that had been both a form of capital and a source of labor had been washed away by a rush of blood and ink. For the Cavalier's class, it must have seemed as if the universe had turned upside down to have seen such sights.

Yet there was the possibility of renovation and rebuilding in the midst of these ruins. If the Bourbon could cast off the world view destroyed by the Yankees, he could restore the South. Much of the ruined land was still in ex-Confederate hands; Johnson's plan for restoration called for a charitable program of pardoning; the Bourbon would be allowed to help bring his defeated states back into the Union. Though there was widespread damage, homes, bridges, and railroad tracks could be repaired.[99] Finally, his best tool for renovation was, of course, his former slaves, and they were all around him, willing in many instances to establish a new relationship with ole Massa. The physical and social damage to the Bourbon's Garden, therefore, while severe, was not death-dealing.

What was more severe was the psychological ruin. For the Cavalier to have been defeated by his inferiors, to have his streets patrolled by his bondsmen, to have been reduced to poverty and debt, to see the agonizing inversion in defeat and occupation of his former pride and glory, were traumas that the ruins of the physical and social landscape were barely sufficient reflections. The socio-psychic shock of defeat and Emancipation were the real desolation—more than the ruin of cities and plantation. In this light, the wreck around the ex-Confederates contained, to cite De Forest, that "sense of degradation which must accompany" a fall from pride, a "degradation of dirt and nakedness and slatternly uncomeliness . . . , a degradation which seemed to place them beside the Negro."[100] This was the severest shock.

The Bourbon, however, soon gets his bearing in the midst of chaos. The Union, which has defeated him, now refuses to persecute or prosecute him, so long as he begs for pardon. Very well then; he will use the restoration moment to create out of the shattered Garden a semblance of the old way. He takes over the restoration process, and through the Johnsonian instruments—pardoning, recognition, support—he implements two specific goals in the political and economic arenas. Politically, he replaces provisional Unionists with his old Confederate leadership:

> The Vice-President of the Confederacy, four Confederate generals, five Confederate colonels, six Confederate cabinet officers, and fifty-eight Confederate congressmen were elected to the thirty-ninth Congress. . . . At the state level former Confederate military and civilian officers dominated the governments. {In} both houses of the Louisiana legislature former Confederate officers wore their uniforms.[101]

Economically, he replaces slavery with the Black Codes. Supposedly modelled after the apprenticeship laws of the North, the Bourbon created in reality a rigid form of peonage which, for all practical purposes, put the ex-bondsmen back in slavery without any of the benefits of slavery: "The freedmen must be respectful and polite or pay a fine; no one can come on the plantation without permission; all must be quiet and not have too many dogs; no one can leave the plantation without leave."[102] More viciously, the Codes made Emancipation a kind of cruel joke, violating both the spirit and much of the letter of the Thirteenth Amendment, passed in December 1865:

> Having been without the means to purchase a slave [the outclasses], now that the slaves had become freedmen who could neither own or lease lands, by taking advantage of their lighter complexions and of the "lien laws" framed by their leaders, they could hypothecate the crops they *intended* to plant for the supplies requisite to feed and clothe the labor required to make the crop, *hire* freedmen and *compel* them to do the work required from January to Christmas, during the hours from dawn of day to darkness of night, of the entire period, refuse to pay or divide, and then walk over to the auction block and buy them in for another year as 'runaways.'[103]

These two accomplishments, these political and the economic moves, recreate in the ruins of the Garden the symbolic power of the former Cavalier and enable him to snatch from military defeat a kind of victory:

> [After Appomattox, the Southrons] expected nothing; were prepared for the worst; would have been thankful for anything. . . . the whole body politic was as wax. It needed but a firm hand to apply the seal. . . . But if the plastic moment was suffered to pass——!
>
> ....
>
> [With the Johnson plan,] the reaction . . . set in. Men now began to talk of their rights, and to argue constitutional points; as if traitors had rights, or treason was entitled to constitutional protection. [The Southrons] had discovered that, having laid down their arms, they were no longer Rebels . . . as the thief who is forced to abandon his booty is no longer a thief, and may laugh at penitentiaries.[104]

The Bourbon's plans were thwarted by Congressional Reconstruction, and in 1868 they suffered a political and economic overthrow worse than that experienced that terrible spring of 1865. All that they had sought to prevent with their arrogant disregard for Northern sensibilities came upon them in a final wrenching of their pride and hopes:

> . . . Grant was president. . . . '[The] freedman, free negro, or mulatto' sat on the jury, . . . the auction block for 'runaways' had been destroyed, . . . 'our nigros' could testify in court 'against a white man,' . . . [Radicals] not only had the right but were enjoying it, to buy and carry arms, . . . [Freedmen] were already buying land, [the] rape of a negro girl by a white man was a rape, . . . the white man's 'black sweetheart' began to 'kick against the pricks,' now . . . all these things were no longer *in futuro* but *in esse*, and now . . . all present danger that 'our nigros' were 'about to rise' with intent to 'kill all the white men, women, and children, from the cradle up,' had passed into the limbo of the forgotten ku kluxes. . . .[105]

This final ruin causes varied reactions. For some, reconstitution collapsed their hopes and dreams into an "enforced poverty . . . even bitterer now than it was [after the war], for they are compelled to see, day by day, the poor State, . . . plundered anew and embarrassed further by the action of the ignorant and vicious legislatures."[106] There were those Bourbons who participated as a bitter minority in the new governments, but as members of a futile, passive opposition party—at least in the Dunningite view:

> The frosts of sixty and seventy winters whiten the heads of some of them. There they sit, grim and silent. They say little and do little as the days go by. . . . They hold their places reluctantly. They feel themselves to be in some sort martyrs, bound socially to suffer in behalf of that still great element in the State whose prostrate fortunes are becoming the sport of an unpitying Fate. Grouped in a corner of the . . . chamber, they stolidly survey the noisy riot that goes on in the great black Left and Centre, . . . [dealing with] the fortunes of a once proud and haughty State. In this crucial trial of his pride, his manhood, his prejudices, his spirit, it must be said of the Southern Bourbon . . . that he comports himself with a dignity that [commands] admiration. He feels that the iron hand of Destiny is upon him. He is gloomy, disconsolate, hopeless. . . . [The Bourbons] accept their position with a stoicism that promises no reward here. . . . They are the type of a conquered race. They staked all and lost all. . . . They endure, and wait for the night.[107]

Thus, the first reaction is stoic and bitter endurance. The second reaction is hidden by these melodramatic visions of the Suffering Southron. It is one of biding time, of waiting for the moment to bring to bear on the new governments a remaining nexus of forces based on the real economic, social, and political power that many Bourbons still maintained in their respective communities. It would be these men who would form the White Leagues and Rifle Clubs making up the core of a Southern liberation front.[108] This power can be seen in the happier images of the Bourbon during the reconstitution phase.

These images show that Reconstruction was not necessarily detrimental to the enterprising planter who adapted to the new order. They also reflect the latent power that still persisted in the Southern aristocracy:

> From July until September the season is at its height. The trains bring hundreds of passengers every evening; . . . The lawns are dotting with sprightly parties. . . . The "hotel" . . . is provided with long and solid verandas. . . . From the cottages on Alabama, Louisiana. . . . Virginia, [and] Georgia . . . rows . . . , the belles come slipping across the green sward to dinner, attired in full evening dress. . . . Ex-Generals of the Confederate army—Beauregard, Johnson, the Lees—chat amicably with United States Senators from the North and West. . . .[109]

There is even a picture of a similar amicable meeting between Radical Yankee planters and Bourbons in a rather moving image of a utopian moment set in the midst of the Garden when the antagonists reached a human accord before the calcinating fires of the fast-approaching redemption moment:

> After supper, . . . we were seated on the ample gallery, surrounding the low-story-and-a-half hotel on three sides, enjoying our cigars just as the moon [,] lifting herself above the grove of China trees which surround the courthouse, deepened by contrast the mystic shadows that hung like a pall over the dense forest of cypress and gum which covered the lowlands between us and the . . . River. The notes of the mocking bird reached our ears from the valley below. The soft and gentle air was odorous with the fragrance of sweet flowers. Our journey with horses had been long, our supper excellent and our cigars luxurious. One after another the neighbors and townspeople dropped in—for the Yankees had come—took seats upon the porch . . . or, lay down upon the warm earth; all chatting about their goods, their crops, their

> horses . . . , or politics. Nearly all were smoking like ourselves. . . . Below us lay their homes and firesides.[110]

The Bourbon had suffered two defeats in his combat with the North. He would not make that mistake again. He understood that whatever action he took against the New Order must not antagonize the all-powerful North. He would have to conduct his counter-revolution in such a way that it would not bring down the Federal thunderbolts. Therefore, he set for himself the same goal as reform-minded Democrats and Republicans in the North and South: an end to corrupt rule. He took for his rallying cry the demand of Anti-Radicals in both sections and in both parties: a return to reform government as a way to right his loss of power:

> [South Carolina] lies prostrate in the dust, ruled over by this strange conglomerate, gathered from the ranks of its own servile population. . . . It is the spectacle of a society suddenly turned bottom-side up. The wealth, the intelligence, the culture, the wisdom of the State, have broken through the crust of that social volcano on which they were contentedly reposing, and have sunk out of sight, consumed by the subterranean fires they had with such temerity raved and defied.[111]

In addition, the Bourbon had at the service of his cause those Northerners with a traditional aversion to the Blackness of Darkness. In their struggle to redeem the South, the Bourbons—Whigs, Democrats, apostate Scalawags, all anti-radical Southerners of substance—would cast the imagery of their cause in terms of both a political and racial act of purification, which would purge the South of a corruption engendered by Radicalism and Africanism:

> Looking at . . . the invincible qualities that mark the Anglo-Saxon race, we cannot admit that she is going to . . . relapse into barbarism. . . . The State must burst its bonds. The energy of the American race, the nature of things, the demands of modern civilization . . . , all seem to warrant the conclusion that a change must come. . . . While the laws of the universe remain, these claims must in the end successfully assert themselves. . . . And it is about time for the Federal Administration to take this reflection to heart.[112]

And if the Administration does not, the Bourbon has other forces at his command:

> . . . no depressing circumstances of the present are going to destroy . . . the natural development that comes of race and of blood. Opportunity alone is wanting; and that, we know, is always found by the bold and aspiring. [113]

And so with a clarion call emphasizing race and reform politics, the Bourbon launched his wars of sectional liberation—the redemption phase, with the support of Northern sympathizers (including former Radicals and abolitionists), the wars of redemption, which eventually brought down the Reconstruction governments one by one in acts of blood and political maneuver.

This time, because Bourbon's political, economic, and racial policies do not threaten the security of his Northern counterparts, the counter-revolution succeeds. In the half-fact and half-myth of the reconciliation experience, the Redeemer supplants Freedman and Carpetbagger as the representative of the New Union in the South. He becomes a man "we expect to find in the highest places in the republican party." He is cooperative and loyal to the best interest of the Union, and can be counted on to support mutually beneficial economic progress against hostile Democrats, North and South.[114] In the reconciliation period, the Bourbon becomes the best friend of the Negro, and all the innovations brought to aid the ex-slave by radical rule—education, political rights, even freedom—become seen by some former abolitionists as false turns in the evolution of the Republic:

> I think the experience of the past has made it plain that few things are more dangerous for the mass of men . . . than eloquent, vague talk about a more perfect organization of society, social reform, and the development of a higher civilization. It always attracts the unpractical . . . who have sublime aspirations, but no . . . firm grasp upon realities. It would be far better for a man to be a slave of an intelligent master, who would hold him to some useful work, and flog him for idleness, than to be the dupe of sentimental schemes for the reconstruction of society.[115]

Throughout the four phases of Reconstruction, the Bourbon exhibits two complementary sets of traits. On the one hand, he is the anarchic, anti-rational figure of the Wilderness ethic: audacious, vehement, reckless, passionate, sentimental, vain, full of "whim whams, absurdities, culture, ignorance, courtliness, barbarism."[116] On the other hand, he is the incarnation of all the virtues of the Garden. In comparison with the Yankee, he is:

> more simple, . . . more provincial, more antique, more picturesque; [having] fewer of the virtues of modern society, . . . [more] of the primitive, the natural virtues; . . . careless of wealth, art, learning, and the other delicacies of an urban civilization; they care more for individual character and reputation of honor.[117]

It is this contradictory, powerful figure, then, who emerges triumphant from the Reconstruction experience. It is he who survives the ruins of the war, the failure of his restoration plans and, most of all, the attempt of the Carpetbagger and his comrades to reconstitute his Garden. As a force of history and as a sectional symbol, the Bourbon embodies those characteristics that made the South the archetypal antithesis of the North. In this light, his triumph during redemption was a triumph of Southern ideals over Northern ones. In such a victory the defeated Carpetbagger could only hope that the Bourbons' victory would not be a long-lasting one.

> The fresh tide of Northern enterprise will soon sweep rudely enough against these broken remnants of the *ancien regime*, and wash them under. The "old families" seem . . . exhausted of force and energy. They had enough originally to gain position; they had not enough left to retain it; and it waits the grasping hand of the coming parvenues. "New men" will soon be the order of the day, in Mobile and in many another center of Southern aristocracy.[118]

Here, Whitelaw Reid was speaking in 1866, but it cogently reflected the hopes of the defeated Carpetbaggers in 1876.

• • •

> . . . Here was presented, in its most extreme form, the actualization of the theory of racial equality. [The freedmen] were abandoned by the best men of the South

> and deceived by the worst; their innocence exposed them to temptation and their ignorance betrayed them into the hands of . . . spoilsmen who exploited them for . . . sordid ends.[119]

At the other end of the Garden is the Bourbon's alter ego, the Freedman. He is the former slave to the aristocrats and the new ally of the Yankees. Indeed, he operates in Reconstruction fiction as the symbolic stand-in for the Carpetbagger, and his relationship to the Bourbon is the symbolic expression of the ultimate meaning of Reconstruction history. It is the Freedman and the transformation of this relationship with the Bourbon that forms the social context of Reconstruction fiction as a reflection of the Irrepressible Conflict.

The Freedman during all phases of the First Reconstruction represented to the North more than just the moral justification of the war, and more than just an outward sign of a supposed final solution to the Irrepressible Conflict. He was that element in Southern society that formed the basis for its peculiarity; he was the symbol of that dual heritage—the Anglo-Saxon and African—operating in the New World. He was the *cause célèbre* that gave rise to the Congressional reorganization of the South.

The Congressional Radicals, led by Stevens and Sumner, recognized that Johnson's restoration policies perpetuated an institutional structure, slave-labor capitalism, which had already led to a bloody rebellion, and sought through congressional reorganization to destroy this structure once and for all. What they did not foresee was that slavery as a mythic and cultural apparatus would remain, generating those tensions in Reconstruction society that would eventually destroy their partially planned, partially improvised politico-legal edifice. Slavery has been, ironically, the only extensive, successful experiment with multiracial coexistence in 19th-century America—North, Central, South, Caribbean. Moreover, since slavery and its racist ideologies also defined the archetypal experience of the African in America, its effect would not cease with the U.S. Americanization of the Freedman. For many the experience of slavery left physical and psychological scars that political acts could not change. Some were willing to adapt to the new order, but they were too old. Their physiques were irrevocably branded with the marks of the past:

> A withered little fellow, cramped and dislocated with rheumatism, his legs twisted in a style not suitable for

> traveling. He got himself about with the aid of two sticks, his wrinkled, old face grimacing with the effort, and perhaps with pain. When I heard two sticks and a shuffle on the brick pavement . . . , I knew that the next sound would be the deep, harsh bass of Kangaboonga, trumpeting, "He, he, good morning, Sar."[120]

And there were those Voluntary Slaves, whose scars were within, a mixture of unconditional desire and conditioned reflex. They longed for the days of slavery, and in the hands of the anti-radical writer they would become the model black citizens.[121]

Thus, the social development of the Freedman is dramatized in the arena of the slave labor experience and indirectly within the larger sectional conflict, which this experience had caused. This persistence of the memory and the reality of slavery into Reconstruction is called in this study "the Slavery Syndrome." And it is the conflict between the reality of the Syndrome and the reality of the ex-slave's expectations about freedom that gives to the period and its literature the tragic poignancy of thwarted idealism and shattered hopes.

The thesis of the Dunningites that the Freedmen came out of slavery as a homogeneous group is one of the persistent legends of the period. What the nonfictionists (and Revisionist historians) reveal is the complex nature of the Freedmen, the existence of sub-classes within this single group. Indeed, even uneducated ex-slaves made distinctions between "up-down" and "low-down niggers":

> "We likes you fus-rate, Missah, and we's be glad to stay wid you, but dese niggers is all de time a quarrelin' an' a fightin' wid us; dey aint like folks at all; day's mean, low-down niggers. We's nebber been used to 'sociate wid such; we wasn' raised to it, an' we can't stand it no longer!"[122]

The nonfictionists who report on the restoration are aware of three levels among the new citizens: a minority of "old issue" free men, the most important group living in Louisiana; the so-called "house-servant" group, which might also include artisans and craftsmen; and the "fieldhand" group. But there was much more social variety than this, resulting from the ex-slaves' previous conditions of servitude. Sea-Island Freedmen tended to be "vastly inferior in natural intelligence and ability" to Freedmen from the upper and middle parts of South Carolina;[123] those who lived on large, settled plantations were superior to those on small frontier farms.[124] There were differences between those freed before Emancipation and those freed afterward, between ex-veterans and non-combatants. Most of all, the restorationist nonfictionists show that this class of new citizens contained the two levels common to all social hierarchies within class societies: the ambitious and intelligent versus the indolent and the stupid. When Reid describes an "old issue," Uncle Sandie, who had bought himself out of slavery for $3200 and who came into the restoration a wealthy planter, [125] he is describing a member of that elite among the ex-slaves who not only accounted for their social variety but who would also form the core of the "black" wing of a Southern Republican Party. It would be the members of this elite who would appear as heroes and villains in Reconstruction fiction.

In a more normal situation, the Freedmen as a sub-class would have entered the principle society. The North based its hopes for the reconstruction of the South on the theory that insofar as ambition and talent were involved, there would be social flexibility through which well-bred whites and well-bred blacks would form an interlocking middle class, Victorian in morality and Unionist in politics. It was this ideal that the brief reactionary policies of restoration and the more extensive policies of redemption sought to control by fixing the ex-slaves into a single homogenous class—"Negro"—not citizen and often only barely not slave. The falsity of this position was especially plain to the nonfictionists in the Southron's handling of the mulatto or, more precisely, the Afro-Saxon question.

The division between the upper- and lower-class Freedmen, these writers tentatively assert, existed along "racial lines." The Afro-Saxon came out of Egypt with more of Pharaoh's treasures than his darker brother, and in a real sense these treasures helped to define class status. De Forest points out that the octoroons in the Greenville district tended to be more intelligent and ambitious, tracing these qualities to "blood" and to the favored treatment and encouragement they received from "the family to which they belonged"[126] and to which they were often related. Morgan describes several Negroes as being nearly white or mixed: "Those of the lightest complexion were quite well dressed. Some also were wretchedly clad."[127] Thus, in Reconstruction history and nonfiction, the Afro-Saxon tended to be identified as an elite class among the Freedmen and was counted in the U.S. Census as a separate race during this period.

In Reconstruction fiction, the Afro-Saxon Freedmen also served to identify the historical reality of the racial interpenetration of black and white at the South and the agony resulting from such penetration on white and black as a result of racism. Moreover, the Afro-Saxons emerge in Reconstruction art as a physical symbol, a concrete embodiment, of the cultural and social fusion of white and black realities expected to be attained by all free men of color. Physically, a black Freedman remained black, but in his cultural, political, and social aspirations he was expected by the Radicals to fuse into a U.S. American mixture both African and Saxon attributes, with the greater emphasis on the Saxon. Yet in this same context, the Afro-Saxon suffers the pain of being a white Negro because of the obstacles that U.S. American racism in the New World puts in the way of such fusion, despite the census identification. This pain is a key theme in the mulatto literature of the period and is found as a thematic convention in Negro fiction related directly and indirectly to the Reconstruction experience:

> Then she thrust back her sleeve and noted the texture of the soft white skin— . . . blue veins . . . transparent whiteness . . . nails pink and pearly . . . the mass of hair . . . soft, silken texture . . . the rich brown tinge. . . . Was it possible? . . . It was [her father] who had left as her sole heritage . . . the horror of a tainted blood! How she loathed herself as she thought of it. She tore open her robe and gazed upon her palpitating bosom. She wished [to tear out] the heart that throbbed beneath it. She would willingly pour out her very life if the one drop that corrupted its red tide—the one drop of darker, baser blood—might only flow forth and leave her dead body undefiled. . . . Even the fair white breast seemed foul and loathsome as the tettered leper's skin.[128]

This theme, the Whiteness of Blackness, appears in *Waiting for the Verdict*, *What Answer?* and *Toinette–A Royal Gentleman*. It also appears in Tourgée's non-Reconstruction works, *Hot Plowshares* and *Pactolus Prime*. In these pro-radical works, the mulatto signals the power of white blood in the Freedman to make him strive for the highest level, no matter how mixed with the "baser" fluid. In anti-radical novels, the mixture signals a moral corruption and dangerous racial ambiguity pushing the unhappy owner toward vice and evil.[129] In the end, the result of the general intercourse between the races in the Garden remains for the nonfictionists in their chronicling of the historical events one of the more exotic attributes of the newly freed slaves:

> There were Negro men who in the North would be considered none other than intelligent and polished ornaments of the Anglo-Saxon race. Mingled with these were others of darker hues, ranging down to mulattoes, and even darker still, and among them were several Negro officers. . . . A group of beautiful ladies, apparently white, was suddenly invaded by a quaint old chocolate-colored dame, with high bandana wound about her head. . . . She was the grandmother of two of the young ladies![130]

That white-skinned people could be black reflected those feelings, in the depths of Cavalier (and Yankee) culture, which made even the most tenuous form of African blood the incarnation of the Blackness of Darkness. This was to have a long-range effect on the ex-slaves' role in Reconstruction and beyond. For when the restoration governments fused all this intraracial and class heterogeneity, Afro-French aristocrats in New Orleans and Gullah fieldhands on the Sea-Islands, into a single socio-legal category—"nigger,"[131] based not on physical features or social accomplishment and potential but on parentage and previous condition of servitude, they gave the Northern Radicals a clear demonstration of the bad faith and the basic immorality of the Johnsonian governments as instruments of Reconstruction.

Moreover, as a result of this fusion, the new citizenry was supplied, in many instances, with an articulate and often effective elite during the struggle: Beverly, Revels, Cardozo, Bruce, and Douglass rallied against Bourbon anti-rationality in a common cause and gave to the Carpetbagger a bloc of loyal voters. Reid's description of a black Unionist meeting stands as an image for both the unity and diversity of the Freedman class, a diversity reflecting the complexity of the larger society into which they were denied an entrance by the restoration governments. The meeting consisted of:

> a group . . . the blackest faces, with the flattest noses and the wooliest heads, I ever saw—the mouths now and then broadening into a grin or breaking out into that low, oily,

> chuckling gobble of a laugh which no white man can ever imitate. . . . Some, black and stalwart, were dressed like quiet farm laborers. . . . Others, lighter in color and slighter in build, were dressed in broadcloth, with flashy scarfs and gaudy pins. . . . On the other side of the church was a motley, but brilliant army of bright-colored turbans, . . . and tawdry bandanas, and hats of all . . . shapes. . . . Some . . . wore [fancy] gloves, all were gaudily dressed and a few, barring the questionable complexion, had the air and bearing of ladies.[132]

The essential question in Reconstruction history relates to bringing this class into the U.S. American order. Indeed, the transformation of former Africans into Victorian citizens was, for Anti- and Pro-Radical alike, the first item of business: for the former in order to make him a more efficient laborer, for the latter to make him a more human person. In the nonfiction this process is seen to occur simultaneously on two levels. On the first, there is that melodramatic transformation celebrated or condemned in Reconstruction legend: the elevation of a relatively few ex-slaves to the high ranks of politics, law, and education. On the lower, more prosaic level, there were those gradual and specific changes resulting from Emancipation and the subsequent attempt to assimilate nearly four million non-whites into the new Union. When this attempt is viewed against the backdrop of those socio-legal restrictions devised during the days of the Slavocracy to place the African outside of the human race, then it becomes quite clear that even the most trivial activities of Americanization—getting married, obtaining legal possession of property and children, moving freely around the countryside, earning money and spending it even on brass jewelry, checkered pants, and candied fruits—carry the symbolic weight of the entire experience.

During restoration a significant indication of this new change was discernible. Many Freedmen (always inclusive of women as well, except where noted) survived the agonizing realities of 1865 and 1866 without losing their desire for freedom, despite the passing of the Jubilee excitement and the temptation to return to the familiar anguish of slavery. During this period, such survival was no mean accomplishment. First of all, the Grand Army of the Republic, which had sheltered thousands, was being dismantled; then the Freedman's Bureau had only a limited staff; Northern charity was not yet extensive; and many Southrons refused to aid their ex-slaves: "No loyal household in the North was disturbed . . . when each swarthy corpse went down at midnight, with a cold gurgle into the Mississippi; or was carried out from the putrid camp to be flung like offal to a common infamy."[133] For many who did not die, the first days of restoration were a time of cholera and smallpox, of hunger and desperate idleness, of abandoned Negro quarters "silent as the grave" through which abandoned black children crept "stealthily among the wrecks of the cabins, . . . shivering in the dank blasts of winter."[134] It was, in a word, an agonizing moment: "Thousands died of neglect and starvation. . . . [Some] died in despair and unrest occasioned by their change of condition. [Some became] wanderers . . . blindly starting toward some dimly-defined goal." During this period, between military rescue and the Black Codes, they were in a tragic limbo, sustained only by the Union's promise: "they could only hope and wait."[135]

During this time, the Southrons' ideal of *noblesse oblige* toward his adopted children was given its severest tests, and in the legend and history of Reconstruction there are factual instances of the selfless charity of former slaveowners. But in pro-radical nonfiction, there is an additional picture: that combination of vengefulness and malicious resentment with which ex-masters watched the decimation of many of their ex-slaves.[136] Fortunately, Northern and Southern charity and the ex-slaves' own inventiveness, adaptive skills, and their persistent faith in the transcendental efficacy of freedom enabled them not only to survive but to also earn the citizenship, which was both a gift and a right.

The Carpetbagger proceeded from the simple fact that the Negro was no longer a slave to the more complex legal step that, therefore, citizenship was an essential right. Around these fundamentals white Radicals structured the program for realizing the potential of the new citizens. But relative to the Victorian life, which the Carpetbagger saw as the *summum bonum* to which the new U.S. Americans had to evolve, many ex-slaves were bricks without straw. The Freedman's poverty was widespread:

> At a little distance . . . stood a row of rudest cabins. . . . Entering one, I found a block serving as a chair for a middle-aged negress, who sat on it before the big fire, holding a sick baby. . . . An old bedstead, nailed together by pieces of rough boards and covered with tattered quilt, stood in one corner. In the opposite was a rough table, on which were fragments of a half-eaten, heavy, sodden 'corn-pone.' In the fireplace

> stood a skillet covered by a broken lid, and on an old box were piled some broken dishes. I have enumerated absolutely everything gathered here to make comfortable the happy home of an American freeman.[137]

His language was hardly U.S. American:

> "'Charles, why didn't you come to school earlier?' 'A-couldn't come soon today, sir: de boss he sheer out clo' dis morning.' 'What did he say to you?' 'Me, sir? I ain't git; de boss he de baddest buckra ebber a-see. De morest part ob de mens dey git heaps o' clo'—more'n nuff; n' I ain't nuffin.' 'Where's your brother?' 'Sh'im dar? wid both he han' in he pocket. . . .' 'Where's Polly?' 'Polly de-de.'"[138]

His ignorance reflected the intellectual degradation fostered by slavery:

> "What do you think of Andie Johnson?" . . .
> "Who him?"
> "He's President. . . . Do you know what that is?"
> "Who him?"[139]

His sexual misdemeanors had become institutionalized:

> . . . in the churches, the schools, and . . . social gatherings . . . the colored concubines of white men had been able to maintain their supremacy. These ranked according to the rank of their . . . 'sweethearts.'
>
> While 'Liz' was the concubine of a wealthy planter she stood at the head of colored 'ciety,' when she became the concubine of a merchant . . . she stepped down one point, and when she had dropped down another peg . . . she took her place in the ranks of that 'social Set' and thus she continued to descend in the social scale until she became the wife of a 'po' no 'count nigger.'[140]

His religion in some instances was a Dionysian form of a degenerate Evangelical Protestantism:

> Men and women foam at the mouth, wander about the fields and forests half distracted, a spasm of spiritual insanity having

> taken possession of them. In such moments . . . they sometimes descend to orgies; whiskey and licentiousness do their work, and the whole meeting will be transformed into an assembly of blackamoor maenads and satyrs.[141]

The element accounting for all this among the new citizens was their extreme poverty.[142] This factor remains constant. Its poisonous influence would have negative effects on the Afro-American's eventual assimilation into Southern and U.S. American society. The Carpetbagger's chief mistake during Reconstruction was giving the Freedman political rights without eliminating the abject impoverishment, which made him dependent on white Northerner and Southerner and in which too many black Radicals continued to remain during reconstitution. Three forces kept them in the lower depths of economic dependency: the planter's economic need for cheap labor or even non-paid labor; the planter's stubbornly held and violently defended, deeply held conviction that the freed slave would not work, could not work, without coercion; and ironically, the inadequacy of the Carpetbagger's economic program.

The white Republican's failure to provide economic tools for their allies—land distribution, crop subsidy, loans, guidance and training in agriculture and husbandry (along with ballot, book, and federal power)—became the chief obstacle to the democratization of the South. That some of the new U.S. Americans achieved a relative degree of prosperity testified to the correctness of the Carpetbagger's belief in the potentialities of the new citizens, but at the same time underscored the timidity of his economic program. From his failure to lay the groundwork for a self-sustaining black yeomanry can be traced the South's (and the nation's) racial trouble during and after Reconstruction.

The essential historical problem involved in the socializing process was that "the vices of the Negro [were] the vices of the slave."[143] And insofar as the Freedmen were kept in a condition akin to or modeled on the poverty and the resulting dehumanization of slave-labor capitalism, those vices persisted in a class regarded as the political backbone of the new order:

> [Some Negroes in Alabama] are absolutely dependent upon the charity of the white folks. Their lives are grossly immoral, and the women have . . . little conception of the true dignity of womanhood. One sees men and women, like Italian and Spanish beggars, slouching all day from sun to shade . . .

> living on garbage and the results of begging. . .—a prey to any disease that comes along, and festering in ignorance. Some of them have been trying agriculture, and have given it up in disgust, because they do not understand farming, and there is no one to teach them. They have flocked into towns hoping that something will turn up.[144]

For such new citizens, their political Americanization proved a cruel hoax. Instead of an efficient wage system, some were given patronage; instead of training in the arts of agriculture and husbandry, a few were elected to public office; instead of land, most were given the vote: "'gib us our own lan' and we take care of ourselves; but wid out land, de ole massas can hire us or starve us, as dey please.'"[145] For the landless, impoverished Freedmen, their only place in the new order was between slavery and political rights, their only hope a slow, tedious evolution toward full citizenship over several generations.

Yet despite these obstacles and failures, the Radicals during their brief reign did fulfill some of the Jubilee dreams by codifying Emancipation into law and laying the constitutional bases for assimilation. This was the easiest part of the historical process of Americanization—the 13th, 14th, and 15th Amendments to the Constitution, finding immediate and startling success among the sociocultural elite in the Freedman ranks. And at the same time, there were varied successes for the majority of the ex-slaves.

The first task was the creation of a monogamous institution out of a loosely structured polygamous pattern. For example, Whitelaw Reid describes how by rule of thumb the Bureau disentangled the organic, if artificial and capricious, sexual relations of slavery. In case of conflict, it was necessary to establish uxorial prerogatives between the first wife and the latest one. The Bureau's rule was that the wife with the most children got the man.[146] Sometimes where there was a case of two husbands, it took more than following the rules to arrive at an equitable conclusion. John W. De Forest plays the Solomon with some skill in finding a solution to the problem of one Caesar, his wife, her older second husband, and "their" children. According to South Carolina law, the first husband, Caesar, was supposed to get the wife; according to Bureau orders, "such persons as were living in lawful wedlock at the date of emancipation were husband and wife, to the exclusion of all other claimants." De Forest cuts through the red tape and gives Caesar his wife. But Caesar also wants the children. "'I mean *his* chil'n—the ole woman's chil'n and *his*. She says she won't go ef she can't hev all her chil'n.'" However, the old man wants someone to care for him and also demands his offspring. De Forest, godlike, gives Caesar the children too but advises him to adopt the second husband as well. "The result was that the wife clove to the younger husband, while the elder remained in the family as a sort of poor relation."[147]

Through such improvising and invention, through individual choice, a family pattern was either created, or the existing one legalized. Out of such beginnings, a middle-class family structure was to eventually evolve for many Freedmen.

The creation of the Freedman's family was the first major success of Americanization. The second was education. In the Abolitionist-Radical dream of reconstitution, the schoolhouse became an outpost of Northern civilization in the defeated South. Along with the barrack, the Union League, and the Bureau, public and private schools became a repository of freedom and light, taking its importance from the contrast between the public school and the enslavement school. Morgan points out that the education of the slave was geared only to teach the "human machine" how to "make a bed and—lie in it, or under it, according to the whim . . . of the owner . . . ," how "to wield a hoe, or an ax, hold a plow or drive it, scrape cotton and pick it, wash potatoes and boil them, cut a steak and fry it. . . ."[148]

Because most Slavocratic states forbade the education of the slave, book-learning became for Carpetbagger and Freedman alike an initiation into a forbidden mystery. For the black and white idealists, learning was the critical difference between the African slave and the Afro-American citizen, especially during restoration when such a task was highlighted by the immediacy of the slave past. Then, the Sunday and improvised public schools seemed the fulfillment of the Union's moral struggle, the key to the Freeman's sociopolitical power, and the guide to the transformation of the South:

> Ranged upon the seat . . . sat row after row of closely-crowded, smiling, black-faced, but bright-eyed, Sunday school scholars. . . . On the higher benches . . . were a few young ladies, tastefully attired in white. At that distance, one had difficulty in seeing that their faces were not of the pure Anglo-Saxon tinge; but neat and pretty as they looked, they were only niggers, and nigger Sunday school teachers at that.[149]

It was, of course, a difficult task:

> One of the . . . girls, a remarkably handsome octoroon with Grecian features and chestnut hair, attended recitations in the morning and worked at her trade of dressmaking in the afternoon. There were some grown men who came in the evening to wrestle, rather hopelessly than otherwise, with the depravities of our English spelling. One of them, a gray-headed person in circular spectacles, [was] bent on qualifying himself for the ministry.[150]

But despite such difficulty, the establishment of black colleges and public schools here and there throughout the South by the radical governments was, for the Tourgées and the Morgans, another triumph for the Americanization process in solving the intellectual side of the Irrepressible Conflict.

The most important success of this process was the transformation of the slave-laborer into free-laborer. This change is a recurring theme in the nonfiction, expressed in the varied descriptions of the general wellbeing of those who had become self-sufficient citizens:

> On either side were stone pavements, crowded with Negroes; colored children gamboled on the [flagstones]; colored mammas smoked pipes in the doorways of shops, where colored fathers sold apples, beer, whiskey; colored damsels, with baskets of clean linen in their stout arms, joked with colored boatmen from the canal; colored draymen cursed and pounded their mules; and colored laborers on the streets enveloped one in a cloud of suffocating dust as he (sic) hastened by.[151]

It was, therefore, as "free laborers" and not as political officers that the Freedmen's new citizenship became a reality. Manual labor continued to be their lot, as in slavery, especially since they were the economic sinews of the reconstructing South:

> About [the] boats, . . . the Negroes swarm in crowds. . . . They are clad in garments which hang in rags from their tawney or coal black limbs. Their huge naked chests [resemble] the works of Praxiteles. . . . [Whenever] there is a

> lull in the work they sink down on the cotton bales, clinging to them like lizards to a sunny wall, and croon to themselves, or crack rough and good-natured jokes with one another. [And then the ships come in, swinging] with grace and precision [into their berths] and the instant the cables are made fast and the gangways swung down, the "roustabouts" are on board, . . . wheeling the bales to the spaces allotted to them on the wharves.[152]

It was precisely in the area of "free" labor that the full nature of the dramatic reversal in Southern society, occasioned by Appomattox, was expressed.

There were two forms of free labor economics in the South. For those planters looking for a compromise between slavery and the Yankee methods, there was the option of the sharecropping or tenant-farming system. It was a forced marriage between free labor and the socioeconomic paraphernalia of slavery, looking backward in its agricultural inefficiency, its waste of human resources, and its general pattern of brutal exploitation. More often, for example, instead of receiving wages, the laborer was paid, if he were lucky, with rations; instead of developing some minimal form of independence, the dependency of slavery was reinforced:

> [The Freedmen waited] with a motley collection of tin-buckets, bread-bowls, troughs, old candle-boxes, little boxes [to receive] "de 'lowance." One of the Negroes chopped up the rounds of mess pork, and weighted out four pounds to each.
>
> . . . the meat [was] measured [out] by [the] proprietor . . . Then a Negro took a tin cup, and baring his brawny arm to the elbow, dipped down into the molasses barrel, bringing up cup, hand and wrist clammy with the black, vicous [*sic*] fluid, which was soon daubed over clothes, barrels, and faces. . . .
>
> [There appeared] a wrinkled, white-wooled old auntie, blear-eyed, trembling, and thin-voices. 'Please, massa, can't you git me a little piece ob meat?' and she laughed . . . 'Why, auntie, I thought you were so old and didn't eat anyhow?' 'Bress ye, sah, I eats lots, an' wen de cotton come, sah, I picks some for ye. Aint strong 'nuff to pick much, sah, but I picks little for ye, close to de house.'

> 'Massa' handed her a piece of meat, and filled her outstretched apron with flour; and the old woman stepped back into the crowd, her face fairly aglow. [Then] one of the girls said, as she took her flour, 'I wants meat dis time; had flour las'. 'You g'long!' exclaimed the old woman . . . 'if you can't take what white folks gibs you, go widout.'[153]

In contrast, the fully developed free-labor system involved the payment of good wages and looked toward the time when the Freedmen would buy their own meat and cornmeal. For the idealistic Carpetbagger, it is the one great Northern innovation at the South—even greater, one feels, than general suffrage. The receipt of money for work done marked for even the least intelligent of the ex-slaves the revolutionary difference between freedom and bondage. During restoration, this difference appeared with startling clarity against the background of the immediate slave past. One of the dramatic moments in Reid's *After the War* is a description of ex-Africans receiving their first wages. Reid gives the incident almost incantatory heightening, making it both an actual and archetypal event in which the South's defeat by the North symbolizes the Machine's entrance into the Garden:

> Finally a table was placed in the door of one of the rooms. The pay-roll, store-book, and some piles of green backs and fractional currency were spread out upon it, a couple of candles furnished all the light. A hundred eager eyes watched the proceeding from the doors of the quarters. At last the bell was tapped by one of the drivers. In a moment or two, the gallery was covered by the 'whole stock of the plantation,' . . . men, women and children. They stood at respectful distance in a circle around the table, and with wide-eyed curiosity awaited developments. . . . Then he read over the long pay-roll, told each one how many days he or she had worked. . . . 'Dat's so.' occasionally interrupted one in a reflective manner. 'I did miss five days, I'd done forgot all 'bout it till you tole me.'
>
> . . . Then he began the payments. Looking out from the lighted doorway into the darkness, one could see the fringe of black faces lining the gallery, their eyes shining as the light from the candles struck upon them. Beyond was blackness and a confused murmur of many whispers; within, the circle advanced one and another to the table to receive the currency rapidly counted out. The lessee . . . counted the money note by note, folded it up, and handed it over. The

> Negro looked with a puzzled air, took the money as if it were fragile glass, and must be handled very carefully or it would be broken. . . .[154]

That money as well as law was necessary in defining liberty in a capitalistic democracy was a fact that would have to be rediscovered a hundred years later, symbolized by various Poor People's Campaigns.

Thus, during the brief experiment, enterprising Freedmen in particular, and the race in general, successfully participated in the economic system. Where there was land, wages, and fair employment or where they acted as vigorous partners with ex-masters and ex-Yankees in the economic revival of the South—all without the need of codes, penalties, and terrorism. Beyond the walls of school and legislature, the nonfictionists note a successful process of Americanization that could have reconstructed Dixie much more completely than even Radicals or Redeemers could have conceived. Reid's emotional, dramatic picture of land-clearing on a Louisiana plantation serves as a metaphor for the dynamics of this process—the free-labor system as a tool in the unionization of the former Confederacy:

> The overseer kept the three gangs near each other, the hoes ahead, pushing hard behind them the log-rollers, and shouting constantly to the log-rollers to keep out of their way. The air was filled with a dense smoke from the burning briars and logs. Moving about among the fires, raking together the trash, chopping the briars, now seizing a brand from a burning heap, and . . . firing half-a-dozen new ones, then hurrying forward to catch up with the gang, singing, teasing the log-rollers to "cotch us if you kin," were the short-skirted, black-faced damsels, twenty or thirty who composed the trash-gang. Before the little heaps were half burnt the log-rollers were among them. A stout, black fellow, whiskey bottle in hand, gave directions. . . . [Half] the gang were women, each armed . . . with a formidable handspike. They were . . . proud of their distinction, and wanted it understood that 'dey wasn't none ob you' triflin' hoe han's; dey was log rollers, dey was.' Selecting the log hardest to be moved . . . the driver shouted, 'Now, heah, hurry up dat log dere, and put it on dis sid heah!' A dozen hand-spikes were thrust under the log! Sometimes the spikes were thrust under and the log was lifted bodily, the foreman shouting, 'Man again man dere! Gal agin gal! All togedder wid you, if you 'spec any water out o' dis bottle!'

> `Sometimes, before these heaps were fired, the plows were upon them, every plowman urging his mules almost into a trot, and the driver occasionally shouting, 'Git out o' de way, there, you lazy log roller, or we plow right over ye.' The land was a loose loam, turning up like an ash-heap; and both Negroes and mules seemed to thrive on the hard work.
>
> The overseer rarely left the field. With one leg lazily thrown across the pummel of this saddle, he lounged in his seat, occasionally addressing a mild suggestion to one of the men. . . . All treated him with the utmost respect. I am satisfied that no Northern laborers, of the degree of intelligence, ever worked more faithfully, more cheerfully, or with better results.[155]

Considering the unyielding hostility of the Southrons, the haphazard moral enthusiasm of the Carpetbagger, the rawness of the material, and the brevity of the experiment, it is a wonder that any Americanization took place at all. Yet throughout the reconstructing South, examples of success were, as already shown, everywhere demonstrable: "There were several of this class of colored planters who kept open house, so to speak, and many a 'high-toned, honorable gentlemen,' belated on his journey, was glad to partake of their hospitality."[156] Yet the sensational image of the Freedman's Americanization would not be these relatively mundane social and economic successes but the vision of black political power. It was the sight of Freedmen voting *en masse* in Columbia and New Orleans, of efficient, diligent representatives in Washington, of the scores of legislators in the Southern state houses that filled the idealistic Radicals with pride and enraged the Pro-Bourbons:

> The Speaker is black, the Clerk is black, the door-keepers are black, the little pages are black, the chairman of the Ways and Means is black, and the chaplain is coal-black. At some . . . desks sit colored men. . . whose costume, visages, attitudes and expression, befit the forecastle of a buccaneer.[157]

This picture—the Blackness of Darkness—would remain the essential vision of liberated slaves' accomplishments—and of their non-enslaved black brothers and sisters—in Reconstruction history for generations to come.

Thus, in the main, it is the failures of the Carpetbagger in Americanizing the Freedmen, not his accomplishments, that dominate the anti-radical history and legend of the First Reconstruction. The Freedman's social rehabilitation is seen as a failure, his economic progress is denied, his political errors and vices are magnified into the sole meaning of his political citizenship. Yet even if these exaggerations were true, the Radicals' failures would be more akin to Browning's dictum concerning the necessity of a heaven, than to malice of will or naiveté of intention. When Albert Morgan, one of the archetypal Carpetbaggers in Reconstruction literature and history, insists that his task was to guide his black comrades, especially the women, "to the promised land, where a pure heart, and an enlightened mind possibly might so light up a dark covering that it would be merely a question of tastes which, the light or the dark skin, was most beautiful [,]"[158] he located the essential idealism undergirding the Americanization of the Freedmen. In such insistence can be seen the celebration of an achievement so triumphant that it cancels out all those "facts" of political corruption and misrule that fill the works of anti-Radical literature and history. More subtly, such idealism cancels out the basically incorrect image of the Freedman as being totally dependent on the paternalistic charity of the ex-master, the one person capable of handling the Negro. A Bourbon, looking at a village of Freedmen in 1874, casts this image into the myth that would become the original pattern defining the Afro-American role in Reconstruction in the mind of reactionaries in the South and eventually in the mind of their counterparts in the North:

> "Thar's what they call free niggers. Thar's a change from a few years ago, sir. Them poor things thar are just idlin' away their time, I reckon; and you notice, they're mightily ragged and destitute lookin'. Thar's a d—d nigger a-ridin' a mule, as comfortable like as ye please. Not much like the old times when they were all working quiet-like in the fields. Sundays yo'd seen'em in their clean white clothes and at night, when the plantation bell rung, agoin' peaceful as lambs to quarters. Now it's all frolic. I reckon they'll starve. What kin they do alone, sir?"[159]

And the irony was that his last question could also have been asked of the Bourbon, in terms of his relationship with his symbiotic partner in the context of the Garden, which they both defined and sustained.

• • •

> "Stand aside, uncle," said the planter firmly, but very politely, "we wish to cross at once, and there is not room for us all."
>
> "Yas, sah' yas, Colonel . . . I's willin' to wait on you gemmen, 'cause you is gemmen' but ef yer was no count folks, I'd go for yer. Ride in Colonel."[160]

The Freedman and the Bourbon appear in Reconstruction history and literature within a complex of political, social, and aesthetic values, embodying in their organic relationship with each other the socio-historical context derived from slavery called in this study the Interracial Symbiosis.[161] This, along with Americanization, forms the proscenium in which the drama between Carpetbagger and Bourbon takes place. And it would be the Carpetbaggers' incomplete comprehension of this fact (more than their folly or malice) that would lead them to the catastrophes of redemption. Therefore, since the Symbiosis is the quintessence of the Slavery Syndrome and, as such, frames the ideological structure of Reconstruction fiction, it is appropriate that this discussion of Reconstruction history concludes with a descriptive hypothesis of this social phenomenon.

In the Reconstruction myth, the Bourbon's relationship with the new citizens is not one of mutual need, nor of the inability of both to live alone, but of some kind of paradoxical independence in which the ex-master is unrelated, except as a leader, to the masses toiling in the fields. Such a distortion fulfills both a political and an aesthetic purpose in Dunnningite history. Politically, it shows the Radicals' error in ignoring the power of the planters; aesthetically, it demonstrates the romantic grandeur of a tragic hero who is not only a master but inherently masterful:

> Negroes were toiling in the mud at some of the landings, building ineffectual dams, around which the current of the great river . . . remorselessly ran. The white men, splashing along the overflowed roads on horseback, looked grimly courageous, and give their orders in a cool, collected manner.[162]

In the Reconstruction reality, mutual dependence and co-equal political interaction was the basis of their relationship (though it was equality unrecognized by the master). This was true economically, and it was true in the social and psychological realm as well.

The Bourbon's reaction to this reality, especially political equality, was one of intense hostility. The slave-as-Freedman, his very freedom, was seen as the essential disturbing force in the traditional Symbiosis. In this context, the Bourbon sees the Freedman as worse than the slave simply because he is free. Freedom is not a Negro's natural state, since he will not work without coercion. As a result, the freed slaves will do harm to themselves and will endanger the white community, since they must use illegal means to sustain themselves. The Freedmen must be, consequently, made absolutely subservient to the supervision of the superior race. Once this occurs, they are to be cared for and guided, for in the Bourbon's system of racism they are at best a special sociopolitical entity; at worst, a subhuman species.[163] The identification of the total meaning of Southern culture with this view of the African may be seen as the ultimate cause of the irrepressibility of the conflict between Carpetbagger and Bourbon.

The planters' design for a postwar Symbiosis based exclusively on the denial of important human rights for their Americanized cousins and children and based solely on racial definitions must have disturbed the consciences of the sensitive and the just. Therefore, the Bourbon's racism served to blind him to the symbiotic rationale of Southern society and to protect his mind and cultural ideals from the guilt and self-hatred involved in that denial. This is clearly seen in the ambivalent interpenetration of the two extremes of the Symbiosis—cruelty and eroticism—as a kind of permanent emotional complex in Dixie. In Reconstruction nonfiction the ambivalence can be seen from the Freedman's point of view as a simple love-fear "confusion." From the Southron's point of view, it is a complex coupling of love and lust with hate and disgust, a fusing of paternalism and *noblesse oblige* with sadism and contempt, polarized toward racial violence and the Cult of Racio-sexuality.

The violence that the ex-masters launched against the ex-slaves during all phases of the First Reconstruction is the most paradoxical sign of the Symbiosis. That the violence was never designed to exterminate the Negro but to keep him "in his place" signals a perverse awareness among the Bourbons of their need for black power to support and sustain their world. One might argue that the murders, beatings, insults recorded in

Reconstruction literature and history were never genocidal. Certainly, this is De Forest's view of the violence:

> [The] Southerner was not hostile toward the Negro as a Negro, but only as a possible office-holder, . . . as a political and social equal. He might cuff him, as he would his dog, into what he calls 'his place'; but he was not vindictive toward him for being free, and he was willing to give him a chance in life.[164]

And as a Bureau agent, De Forest followed his own analysis. When a Freedman complained that a white man had ridden into his house on a mule, smashed the furniture, and threatened to murder his brother, De Forest dismissed the incident as no "more than a rough frolic."[165] It is quite clear that the uncontrolled impulse to anti-Negro violence typical of genocide was muted by the Southrons' need for cheap labor and by the paternalistic nature of the plantation system.[166]

But, if the Bourbon's racist-based terrorism was not genocidal, it certainly was near it in those parts of the South where the Freedman took up his rights as political citizen or where he was liable for criminal prosecution. There was a racial motive behind the extreme severity of punishment levied against the Freedman for petty crimes in those states under conservative control, while whites guilty of killing Negroes were often acquitted.[167] One suspects also that even when Freedmen were killed for capital crimes, race as well as ostensible lawlessness was involved:

> Rape and similar crimes, of which in all the States, negroes are occasionally guilty, are invariably punished with death; and the rape, justly considered a capital offence by all nations, is almost always avenged at the hands of Judge Lynch.[168]

And wherever the planters' need for labor or their paternalism had been washed away by the war and reconstitution, the impulse found pathological expression even in the best of the Southerners, exacerbated as they were by defeat, humiliation, and Americanization: "G—d d—n your black heart, you dirty Yankee nigger, I'd just like to cut your throat from ear to ear for your infernal impudence."[169] Such threats were all too often acted out in murders, which were both a technique of social control and a ritualization of a pathological violence: Freedmen were killed for forgetting to remove their hats or for disputing a planter's command;[170] a young girl was beaten brutally and her brother killed for trying to protect her;[171] a white woman murdered a black woman when the latter protested the flogging of her child. In each case, for the Carpetbagger, these outrages carried racist overtones: ""Nigger life's cheap now; nobody likes 'em enough to have any affair of the sort investigated; and when a white man feels aggrieved at anything a nigger's done, he just shoots him and puts an end to it."[172] Violence against the Freedmen during Reconstruction becomes an articulation of the view in Southern racism that the Negro was an animal controlled only through the threat of annihilation:

> ". . . the whole damned nigro tribe. Give them an inch and they'll take an ell. They can be governed only by fear. You'll not be able to do anything with them unless you start right. They are by nature a lazy . . . treacherous people. I wouldn't trust one of them. This fellow, Bristol, is tainted, like all the rest, with those damned notions about freedom, which you damned Yankees—"[173]

A curious form of the impulse to racial violence was the Bourbon's fear of a black insurrection. On the first level, this fear and the insistence on its impending realization represented the projection into the passivity of the Freedmen of the Southron's own murderous fantasies of racial annihilation. On the second level, the Southrons were possessed of a nightmare in which they, not the ex-slaves, were the victims. Such a nightmare, from a Freudian perspective, masked the unconscious desire of the Victimizer to be punished by the Victim. This complex of fear and desire perhaps lay behind the cry "The nigros are rising!" The Bourbons were rarely incredulous about this fantasy; the Radicals rarely sympathetic. Reid finds that whenever Freedmen neglected to touch their hats, when they held meetings, sang freedom songs, played warlike games, refused to be beaten, the Southerners cried "insurrection."[174] Morgan correctly notes the political case of the nightmare as a pretext for "the hightoned gentleman of the county" to vindicate the "superiority of the Caucasian race over the negroes. . . ."[175] And it would be this same gambit that would be used to justify the redemption of Mississippi and South Carolina during that phase.[176]

The mass murders and whippings during the initial and final stages of Reconstruction, especially those used to put down so-called impending insurrections, revealed the prevalence and intensity of the impulse to racial violence in Southern culture. Anti-radical terrorists—the idealistic, the sadistic, and the racially psychopathic, with the "consent of all other classes of whites"[177]—launched the White Insurrection, first in the pre-reconstitution phase of the '60s and then during redemption in the '70s, with a violence that fused into one terrible agony of fire and blood the political, the homicidal, and the genocidal. In the following statement, Reid is referring to the earlier stages of Reconstruction; he could well have been referring to redemption and beyond: "the negroes are worked as hard as ever . . . and they have no more protection from the cruelty of the whites than ever."[178]

In polar opposition to this Cult of Violence in the Symbiosis was the Cult of Racio-sexuality, defined primarily as intercourse between the Bourbon and the Freedwoman. As sketched in Chapter I, it differs from normal sexuality only in its fact that the partners' race defines the nature of the act. Implicit in their copulation is the entire structure of Southern racism which, through social and legal taboos, defines one of the partners as subhuman. It is, further, a conjunction in which the complex ambiguities of Southern culture found expression in a paradoxical framework of sexual taboos and their conscious violation. This theme appears in some of the major Reconstruction writings of the period—*A Royal Gentleman*, *'Toinette*, and *Mose Evans*—in greater or lesser degree. Further, black-white sexuality during the Reconstruction period can symbolize the impact the Radical cause had on the personal relationship between the races North and South. Finally, in terms of Reconstruction in the South, the impact of the Radical cause on the Cult stands for the idealistic meaning of the Americanization of the Freedman and, at the same time, reveals one of the psychological drives underlying much of the violence of the Bourbon's political response to reconstitution.

The fullest discussion of the historical relationship between the Cult of erotic racism and the course of Reconstruction history is found in Albert Morgan's *Yazoo*. And, in terms of the points stressed above, it is not inappropriate to give in detail one Carpetbagger's reflections on this controversial aspect of the Symbiosis. Morgan's analysis concerns three parts: the moral, the social, and the political.

For Morgan, the moral corruption inherent in the entire mechanism of the Cult is its most poisonous feature. Its basic tenet, the permissibility of non-marital sex, is by nature a contradiction of those Victorian standards of modesty and chastity governing the rest of the nation. The Cult makes of each planter a potential Lovelace (the male victimizer) and of every Freedwoman his inevitable Clarissa (the victim), a reference to the 18th-century novel *Clarissa*. Under the restoration laws, for example, the Southron was not ordinarily convicted of such crimes as seduction, bastardy, and adultery or of such capital offenses as rape and sodomy, since his partners were not legally recognized as human. Moreover, the Bourbon as Lovelace had additional legal powers. In Mississippi, through a device called the one-fourth rule, he could decide the race of his white Negroes, i.e., any slave with only one-fourth Negro blood. Such manipulation of the God-ordained color line, states Morgan, enabled the Bourbon, under the restoration codes, to "compel acquiescence" of reluctant, attractive Afro-Saxons "when glamour and bribes failed." And a cursory analysis of the crisis of identity afflicting the Afro-Saxon heroines in Reconstruction fiction reveals just how godlike such power was. In rare instances, the one-fourth rule permitted a sincere Bourbon to marry his white Negro. Sophie Watters, an ex-slave, is permitted by her lover's aristocratic family to become white so that her love-smitten Cavalier can marry her.[179]

But such a Bourbon was a rare person. In the main, the libidinous Southron insisted on his *droit de seigneur*, with the legal acquiescence of the restoration laws:

> . . . to enter a negro's house without knocking . . . , and when evil nature prompted, to suggest an intrigue with wife, mother, sister or daughter. The old rule permitted a white man to pinch or put an arm around a colored woman while shopping, or when she was on the street, to . . . make remarks to or about her . . . or . . . openly invite an intrigue, and when resented by the lady, press it by some coarse speech or action.[180]

With the ascension of the Radicals to power, the entire legal edifice supporting the sexual immorality of the Bourbon was dismantled, but old habits died hard. Morgan recognizes that for women with intellectual capacity and beauty, concubinage offered much more rapid social advancement than the public school, hard work, and thrift. And the Bourbon cajoled and pressured such women with his seductive influence. If many black women were his willing victims, he still, in Morgan's eyes, remained the sinner, generating the pressures that violated the standards of purity, not only between the two races, but more so within the subordinated one:[181]

> Susie Poindexter was but one of the number who began with such bright prospects, only to fall away. Some met ruin in their own home. The Sabbath-school and the day school were the only places where they could stand without besmearing themselves with pitch. If perchance it was not within the dwelling of their parents, it was likely to be in that of their mistress or employers, and almost always upon the streets, or in the fields where, during a large part of the year, they were required to work. At all times liable to the grossest vulgarities and obscenities from white youth and men, and from black, too. The wonder is that many more were not defiled than there were. The fact is, the aspiring young colored girl, black or light complexioned, has always had to be contented with such a multitude of obstacles that those who have conquered them are entitled to wear a crown in this world.[182]

Morgan recounts a comic version of this theme. In the eyes of certain Freedwomen, he has acquired the same rights as the ex-masters, especially as one of Lincoln's Cavaliers. He innocently notices that some Negro ladies are loitering around the plantation, ranging in complexion "from pure Caucasian to brown skins."

> One day when two of those women were sitting thus together, one of them boldly exclaimed:
>
> "Colonel, it 'pears to me yo' are a long time taking a hint!'
>
> Her speech was in every whit as good English as that of the average white lady there, and her manners equally refined and subdued. She was a very comely person, too. . . . To me they were all freed people. All poor, all needy—needing land, . . . clothes, . . . meat, no more than the dignity of self-respect, which everywhere . . . has been the chief want of slaves. . . . To be sure I had been through the war and had seen much of the world for a young man. The truth is; however, such a thing as was about to present itself had never before entered my thoughts. Therefore, I plainly asked her what she meant.

[She replied:]

'Any one might know yo' are a Yankee . . . Colonel, is yo' married?'

'No and don't wish to be.'

. . .

'Doan yo' all fin' heap lonesome up y'here by our own self?'

'Not at all lonesome—too busy.'

'My, yo' Yankees neber will hab no fun, t'wel yo' own dis yar whole blessed worl'! Yo' alwus so mighty busy an' peart.'

'I like to work,' I rejoined.

'Wuck! . . . Yo' doan wuck, I knows. Look at his han's Liz . . . An see his face! No mo' sunburnt than mine is, he! he! he! Ain't he han'some!'

This was too much. I was not accustomed to that kind of fire, and couldn't face it. So turning to my desk with some embarrassment, I resumed my work.

'He! Laws! See um blush!' ejaculated the 'dark' one through her merry laughter.

[Later Morgan is invited into a cabin for a talking to by one of the grannies, the wife of the plantation preacher. She warns him about] 'dose ar town gals. . . . Dar is jes ez good gals an' better tu, I"pect, y"ere on de plantation, honey.'

I was beginning to get my eyes open by this time, and impatiently started to leave her.

She begged me to stop a minute, and went on to explain that 'I must not think myself too good for de colored gals; 'fo' God, the best gen'lemens in de Azoo County neber think deyselves too good! An day ha' wives too. Mighty quar, bein' yo' is sich a likely gen'leman—an' not one dem gals cept'n dey is in lub wid ye, too; white no mor'n de black. . . ! I'z hearn um talk, an' I knows! he! . . . [You're] boun' ter hab one y'here . . . ; I knows that, honey.' Then she bluntly asked me how I liked her "gal" Rose?

Now Rose [who] was her daughter, was only fourteen, and though a pure African, was one of the most perfect natural

> beauties I had ever seen. I had not then, nor have I since, seen such exquisite arms and hands.

The reader is then informed that Rose has been making sly attempts to arouse his interest and that her mother wishes to encourage a liaison. Morgan is dumbfounded and berates the old lady, who apologized for hurting his feelings, explaining that she still "don't understand Yankee ways yit." Then Morgan turns to the reader and asks, "Well! What kind of a country is this, anyway?"[183]

In sum, the Mississippi Radicals' sociopolitical reforms, in Morgan's eyes, give to the Freedwoman legal rights to counterbalance the demoralizing power of the Southron.[184] But, for him, the intransigent presence of racio-sexuality remained a serious obstacle to the moral regeneration of the South:

> It was an evil that no constitution or form of government, however rigidly enforced, could cure. More virulent now than formerly, it was a pustule in the heart of the social order, which could not be reached by the courts. . . . And should any of those upon the 'inferior' side of the old rule dare to do so it would have been an . . . indication of another 'rising' of the negroes. . . .
>
> The evil . . . could be extirpated , if at all, in no other way than by example as well as by precept—by rearing a generation of colored women who could neither be purchased by the blandishments of a system which made household-pets of concubines and prostitutes, nor bulldozed into the subjection to the libidinous demands of dissolute 'masters, mistresses,[185] or employers,' and by rearing a generation of colored men whose manhood would as quickly resent all overtures for the possession, for such evil practices, of their mothers, wives, sisters, and sweethearts, as would the manhood of the 'best white. . . .'[186]

With such a call to arms, Morgan advocates both a moral and social revolution. And his awareness in the 1880s of the social dimension of something as "unmentionable" as sexual relations again exemplifies the surprising perceptions that make his work the best of the nonfiction. For him the sociology of the Cult resides in the caste symbolism inherent in Reconstruction society. Racio-sexuality evolves organically from the aristocrat's postulation of the social non-humanity and hence moral invisibility of the subordinate class.[187] Radical legislation sought to redress the social balance by Americanizing the inferior class, and then protecting that transformation by law. The Freedman was, thus, given weapons to protect his ladies against the coercions and even the blandishments of his rival. He could, if he were bold enough, command respect for his wife, mother, daughter ". . . on the streets, in the stores, and at their homes . . ." since under Radical rule both the Belle and the Gal were equally protected from molestation and "indecent proposals and actions" by statute.[188] Indeed, even black mistresses obtained specific rights under the new rule, since they too had become persons. Such rights instigated a veritable social revolt of the Yazoo concubines:

> So long as the concubines could remain at the head of the Mississippi social order on the 'inferior side of the line' they appeared tolerably content and took advantage of the new constitution [only to protect] their rights. Now that the concubine's position as a social leader . . . was not only in danger, but several of them in Yazoo had been 'turned out of church' because they were 'living in adultery' . . . many . . . began to [seek to marry their] 'white sweethearts.' Finding there was [no legal prohibition] they not only kicked against the pricks, they actually began to wear armor against them. Of course this could never be made by the whites a pretext for another 'nigro rising,' never! It would endanger their standing in the 'civilized world.'
>
> One began the erection of an elegant new residence just south of our home . . . for his concubine . . . ; another satisfied his with promises; some surrendered all 'claims' on theirs, while the great mass 'bided their time.' These last were harassed nigh unto death by the 'insolence' of their concubines, who, . . . became stronger supporters than ever of Republican principles and of that 'miscegenationist, Mawgin'; while the great mass of the colored men . . . were now permitted . . . to call their firesides their own, and to erect within their homes a sacred family altar without imminent peril of . . . pollution from the unholy touch of 'superior, white men.'[189]

Morgan objects to the Cult of Racio-sexuality not so much because of his Puritanism, but because of the social exploitation involved in an act that under normal circumstances was merely sexual sin. Non-marital "miscegenation" involved the very racist nature of Southern society as an act between:

> '*two races*,' one of which had always maintained its 'superiority' by force, and had perpetuated a 'separation' of the two in all those affairs of life which tend to develop the moral nature of man, and perpetuated their contact in all those affairs of life which tend to develop man's lower nature.[190]

Morgan's interest in the Cult leads him to the thorniest social (and political) issue of the First Reconstruction—interracial marriage. In the eyes of many Anti-Radicals, corruption, Republicanism, and interracial marriage were synonymous concepts. The Carpetbagger's social innovations were overshadowed by this issue, and Morgan asserts cogently that this issue was used to discredit the entire political rehabilitation of the Confederacy. At the height of their power, the Mississippi Radicals accepted all the implications of making the black Southerners free men and women. If full Americanization led to intermarriage, such result was neither intended—nor hindered. When slavery was introduced, argues Morgan, the question of marriage was not raised. "When . . . the [Reconstruction] Amendments to the Constitution . . . were ratified, was the question whether a white should be forced to marry a black allowed to have weight against the . . . justice of those acts?"[191] Morgan attacks anti-radical critics head on:

> 'Would you have me marry my daughter to a negro?' What a silly question. . . . No! I would not have you do any such thing. [I prefer] that you marry your daughter to a negro than that you [should have her be his mistress.] How dare I talk that way? . . . How dare you consent, as you have been doing for two centuries, that while your daughter may not marry a 'nigger,' nor yet be the mistress of one, your son may make my daughter his concubine, though he shall not marry her.[192]

And as if to demonstrate the entire irrelevance of the anti-radical position, Morgan marries an Afro-European, Carrie Highgate. If he cannot marry her in Ohio, he can marry her in Mississippi. "I have never denied nor been ashamed [that] my wife and children have . . . negro blood." His grief is that most U.S. Americans ". . . can see no difference between miscegenation . . . at the South, and amalgamation through honorable marriage, or seeing the distinction, nevertheless prefer and honor the miscegenationist above the amalgamationist." And then he concludes rather poignantly, "Wife and I have been married fourteen years; we have six children. During all the dreary years that have passed since the enemy . . took possession of my new field, . . . this woman and these children have been my refuge." At the time when the new field was still his, Morgan's marriage made him the Carpetbagger *compleat*. Further, it stood in his eyes as a moral vindication of every egalitarian ideal implicit in the U.S. American social experiment. Finally, his marriage became for him a demonstration that bourgeois democratic idealism firmly applied through political action could transform even such a land as 19th-century Mississippi: "The leaven of liberty is working here, even here upon this old stubble-ground of African slavery and hot-bed of miscegenation."[193]

The leaven did not take. The political dangers growing out of the social questions became more and more powerful. Redemptionists were preparing to undo the Radical Revolution with an unlikely alliance of economic depression, scandal, racism, and sex. Morgan's discussion of the Cult of Racio-sexuality as a major element in the cause of the Bourbon's political revolution is another demonstration of the radical thinking that continually startles the reader of his memoirs. His entire discussion of the moral and social dimensions of racio-sexuality has implied the political. His most explicit analysis is his treatment of *Your Sister Sallie*, a polemic booklet that was used as a part of the perverse ideological justification of the White Terror launched against the Mississippi Radicals in 1875. Morgan shows how the pamphlet exploits the racial and sexual fears and guilts of the Mississippi Southrons in a call for the extirpation of the Radical Party as an adjunct to destroying the Cult of Racio-sexuality. Ironically, the pamphlet embodies the same criticism of the Bourbon as is found in Morgan's beliefs. Both see the Cult as the overriding cause of the South's troubles, though from opposing political perspectives; both accuse the Southron as the guilty party in the relationship; both call for the destruction of the Cult as a prerequisite for the moral purification of the South. The difference is that Morgan seeks to protect the black woman and his anonymous opponent, the white.

In *Your Sister Sallie*, Appomattox and the black tyranny are God's punishment on the South for those illicit unions that occurred during slavery. The redemption of the Bourbons and their land will only occur when they abandon Lilith/the Gal forever and overthrow the governments, allowing the legalization of these unions. Radical policy, further, will eventually force "the marriage of their sister—their own deah sister Sallie to a buck negro." Only the destruction of the Carpetbagger can save the Sallies from the "terrible doom impending over them by the presence of the negroes."[194] Thus, a political maneuver for power became intricately involved with a crusade to save the purity of the Belle.

Psychiatrists interested in Southern pathology establish sexuality as a basic element. "One of the unconscious drives underlying racial violence and antagonism . . . is fear of the sexuality of the Negro male," related to the myth of his "woman-enslaving jungle magic." Conversely, continues Dr. Louis West, University of Oklahoma psychiatrist, in a May 4, 1965, article of the *Chicago Daily News*, the Negro "tends to fear the white man as a competitor for the colored woman 'with much greater basis in historical reality.'"[195] If this is a correct evaluation, then it suggests the validity of Morgan's observations that during Reconstruction history this sexual Cult corrupted the South's sociopolitical fabric:

> I firmly believe [that] concubinage . . . at the South has already so corrupted [the Southrons'] bodies, so dwarfed their intellects, and so dulled the moral perceptions of the people that it is [a] matter of very grave doubt with me whether the social body has not already become so infected with this form of miscegenation as to exclude all hope of its ability to expel the virus without prompt and skillful aid from without. [This corruption results from] that policy which perpetuates *by force* the subjection of every individual . . . of the weaker race, to the will of the stronger; a policy which creates such a temptation to prey upon the weaker, male and female, as the stronger is unable to resist.[196]

For Morgan this fusion of racism and eroticism in all its complex sociopolitical phases grows from the Southron's relationship with Lilith as the symbol of his superior power, and conversely from his fear of a parallel relationship between Black Adams and White Eves as the symbol of his guilt. For Morgan, in a kind of final vision of the Cult, such complicated emotional needs were important factors lying at the heart of the White Insurrection: "I foresaw that it would shortly become the mainspring—hidden, of course, under a 'nigro rising' as its mask—of future hostility to the workings of the new rule."[197] And it would be this racio-sexuality in all the complexity that would act as the ideological mainspring of those violent tensions that kept the South unsettled during Reconstruction history and that fill out the plots of Reconstruction fiction with images of whippings, burnings, and killings.

Violence and eroticism then, at the level of appearance, form the center of the Interracial Symbiosis between Bourbon and Freedman. These energies become in Reconstruction literature the understood referents in those coloristic descriptions of Cavaliers and happy ex-slaves, of frivolous beauty and heroic gentility, of cotton-fields and moss-festooned cemeteries:

> The sun struggles . . . to penetrate the Gothic arches overhead. . . . Everywhere the arches are . . . draped . . . with the deathly festoons of the Spanish moss, slowly stealing the sap and vigor—fit funeral work—from these giant oaks, and fattening on their decay. [It is sometimes] lit with . . . an accidental ray from above, [and] points its warning, silvery with light, toward the graves beneath your feet; while still it clings, in the embrace of death, . . . to . . . oaks . . . and preaches and practices destruction together. Noble and lusty oaks are these, glorious in spreading boughs, and lofty arches, and fluttering foliage, but dying in the soft embrace of the parasite that clings and droops, and makes yet more picturesque and beautiful in decay—dying, even as Georgia was dying in the embrace of another parasite.[198]

Similarly, over the myth of the one-race South, over the economic and social interdependence, was thrown a Spanish moss of sexual ambiguity and sadistic cruelty, qualities that related the Southrons intimately by ties of blood and bloodshed to a people they could only see as partially human. This emotional ambiguity of attitude, action, and feeling had been more or less contained by the elaborate rituals of slavery. The removal of rituals protecting the patricians from their psyche for nearly a hundred years focused these emotions: Lilith and Eve, Sambo and Sir Knight suddenly made equal. It was too much, in terms of a Jungian vision.

When the Southrons were in charge of Reconstruction, they reinstituted as much of the old order as possible; when the Radicals took over, the planters responded with the most murderous terrorism since the war. In this hypothesis, it was sociopsychological motivation, political aims, and socioeconomic need that explain both the unseemly and self-defeating haste with which the ex-Confederates brought out the Codes and the implacable hatred with which they turned against the Radicals.

As one reads the mass of Reconstruction history and its literature, it becomes apparent that the real agony took place not only in the objective world of voting and Klan raids (though these were the realities) but in a subjective world formed from the interlocking Slavocratic psyches of ex-masters and ex-slaves and the traditions that held their interracial memories and desires. Standing outside this network of what could be designated a "collective unconsciousness" and what has been called the Symbiosis, the Carpetbagger from beyond the Mason-Dixon Line could only superficially understand his allies and his foes, could scarcely understand with what rage and with what lusts demons came out of the night to overwhelm them all—at least in terms of a symbolic action perspective.

• • •

"To the White South they were and remained the unforgettable years of the locust."[199]

Underlying Reconstruction history from both the Dunningite and Revisionist position, underlying the depiction of this history in Reconstruction nonfiction, is, of course, the Irrepressible Conflict. The struggle between North and South simply shifts from the national arena to a sectional one. The North in 1865 and 1867 was not content to destroy the South as an intra-national power; it aimed to assure Appomattox by recreating a dangerous rival in its own image. The essential method was the reconstitution of Southern sociopolitical economic order by giving political power to an alliance of Carpetbaggers, Freedmen, and Scalawags. This alliance would act as the check-and-balance to the remnant power of the ex-Confederates. Yet despite the ravages of war, their brief disenfranchisement, and their disunity, the Bourbons remained a social force to be reckoned with, especially in relationship with the Freedmen. If the Carpetbaggers had been as shrewd, diabolical, and united as their mythical image, the Bourbons would have perhaps remained enthralled. But as cowed as they were, the Southrons had a visceral issue around which even the most moderate would rally: the issue of social and political equality with the black man. And it was precisely in the social sphere—the area the Radicals hoped to change through political action—that the ex-masters remained an unyielding obstacle against which Northern law beat in vain. The symbol of this obstacle was the Slavery Syndrome.

In the midst of the new order—machines, wage systems, individual liberty, efficiency—the presence of that deeper energy, that sociopsychological force originating from the attitudes and emotions conditioned by slavery-capitalism, remained. In a real sense (as Morgan and Servosse discovered), the pressures of the Slavery Syndrome were merely overshadowed by Federal power:

> When slavery was "destroyed," the act no more wiped out [the color line] than it changed the opinions of the slaveowners upon the origin of slavery. The divinity which had hedged about that institution also shielded the lines of caste which had been drawn in defense of it.[200]

Wherever Federal power was weak, wherever it withdrew, or was forced to withdraw, the surrogates of slavery reappeared. In those areas far from the political center of the new order (during reconstitution), the atmosphere of the Garden and not the Machine dominated. It was this atmosphere, this quality of life, that became the real enemy of the Radicals' attempt to fully reconstruct the South and the real victor of the terrorist wars of redemption. And just as actual slavery was only the operative metaphor of the conflict between North and South, so would be its various surrogates—conflict-leasing, peonage, sharecropping, tenant-farming, and their various social and political modifications subsumed under the term "segregation," *de jure* or *de facto*. The Slavery Syndrome emerges in this discussion of Reconstruction history and Reconstruction nonfiction as the chief synecdoche for the conflict between the U.S. American dream and the U.S. American reality.

However, this was within the South; between the North and South the political solutions fashioned by Congressional Reconstruction were more successful. The North wanted three things from the war and the radical governments: the protection of the Union as a powerful political entity, the sustenance of its economic programs, and the expansion of its sociocultural ideals. The North still supported these aims in 1877, but the idealism directed toward the Slave and Freedman earlier was no longer directed toward the Negro but toward improving the moral quality of the new industrialism.[201] Insofar as the South cooperated in these endeavors, it could do what it liked with the North's former allies. The Bourbon Restorers made the mistake of threatening the North's idealism and its socioeconomic and political policies at a time when the horrors of a war fought to defend those aims still haunted the Yankee's imagination. The Bourbon Redeemers were wiser. They had finally realized the significance of 1865. Prior to 1877, Southern reformers, racists, and Conservatives had already established a working relationship with their Northern counterparts through the Democratic Party and the Liberal Republicans.[202] So that when they sat down at Wormley's, they formed a special interest community clustered around the need for the South to participate in the new industrialism.[203] Thus, when outraged Northern Democrats threatened to fight for the presidency in 1876, it was the Bourbons who calmed them down. They had traveled that route in 1861 and did not plan to repeat past mistakes.[204]

This is perhaps the final irony of Reconstruction history. In 1861, when Lincoln won by a majority of 57 electoral votes, the South seceded and fought a war over the symbolic meaning of his majority; in 1877, when Hayes won by only one Congressional Electoral Commission vote, the Southrons quietly assented to this fraud in the spirit of reconciliation. The sociopolitical conflict between the North and South as a national issue was finally over. What would be conveniently forgotten during reconciliation and afterwards was the necessity of Radical Reconstruction in accomplishing that victory.[205]

In the end, the corruption of the Carpetbagger was superior to the honesty of the Bourbon. In the midst of the former's errors and evils could be seen the genius of U.S. American "democracy"; in the midst of the latter's virtue could be seen the daemon of U.S. American slavery.[206] The corruption the Dunningites point at with such indignation was, after all, only economic and political and was susceptible to reform; the corruption the Redeemers would support would be sociopsychological, poisoning not only the relations between black and white Southerners, but distorting the vision of their mutual dependence for generations to come. Such corruption yields only slowly and agonizingly to reform, but eventually it does, though needing the Second Reconstruction (1954-1968).

The final vision of the First Reconstruction as history in this study comes from one of the participants, Thomas E. Miller, before the purge of the black Republicans from the South Carolina capitol in 1895:

> . . . starting as infants in legislation in 1869, many wise measures were not thought of, many injudicious acts were passed. But in the administration of affairs for the next four years, having learning by experience the result of bad acts, we immediately passed reformatory laws touching every department of state, county, municipal and town government. These enactments are today upon the statute books.[207]

CHAPTER III
BRICKS AND STRAW

> . . . the leading characteristics of the American romance novel, as it may be called—[are that it is] . . . freer, more daring, more brilliant fiction that contrasts with the solid moral inclusiveness and massive, equability of the English novel.[208]

> He had learned that the spirit . . . of the North cannot be imposed upon the South in an instant; that if the two divergent civilizations are ever to meet, and harmonize with each other, it must be when the circumstance are more propitious than the present, or when some great convulsion has swerved the currents, that they meet in one overwhelming flood.[209]

This book's first chapter presented the prewar antagonisms between North and South—symbolized as the Locomotive versus the Garden, the Cavalier versus the Yankee, and Unionism versus Secessionism—as cultural context for Reconstruction literature. The second chapter presented the "Tragic Era" in nonfiction as an evolution of these prewar antagonisms. These chapters confer a historical framework for the Irrepressible Conflict as it was understood during the First Reconstruction period. This same conflict is central to this chapter's discussion of Reconstruction fiction as U.S. American literature.

Before delving into character, plot, and setting, it is necessary to discuss the literary frame of reference in which this fiction belongs, both in its general and in its specific configurations—but since the primary aim of this study is an examination of the thematic structure of the fiction, this discussion will not be too extensive.

In general, Reconstruction fiction evolves from the impact of the Civil War on U.S. American literature. The war split the 19th-century U.S. American literary tradition into two phases. The prewar phase, romanticism and its corollary, sentimentalism, may be said to have ended symbolically with Appomattox. The postwar phase—realism and its corollary, the local color movement—may be said to have begun symbolically with the Reconstruction Acts. In 1861, Longfellow's *The Song of Hiawatha*, Emerson's *The Conduct of Life*, and Hawthorne's *The Marble Faun* appeared, representing romanticism in its poetic, philosophic, and novelistic moods. In the period comprising the major phase of Reconstruction (1867-1872), realism was emerging as the dominant mode, typified by Harte's "The Luck of Roaring Camp," Twain's *Roughing It*, and James' "The Passionate Pilgrim." In reality the influence of romanticism persisted, despite the cultural schism created by the war, throughout the emergence of realism and its triumph. The effect of this coexistence was to create a period in which "Victorian acceptance and compromises . . . lingered on" at a time when "a new age . . . was struggling to find its voice."[210]

Thus, the period from 1865 to 1885 is clearly not only a sociopolitical transition, but also the bridge between the romantic and realist era in U.S. American literature. The inherent ambivalence of literary modes characteristic of such a transitional period is found in Reconstruction writings as a Janus-like presence looking back to the fifties and forward to the eighties and nineties. In the best examples of this literature, one finds a hesitant oscillation between idealized and objective presentation of character, action, and scene. Such an oscillation reflects that duality of romantic and realistic modes in Reconstruction fiction that finds a more familiar presentation in the early fiction of Twain, Harte, and James.

But what is of more interest here is that Reconstruction fiction so often reflects a realistic-naturalist mode. Its descriptions of the ruined Confederacy, the downfall of aristocrats, the Klan outrages, and the rule of the Radicals are frequently presented as vivid actualities and not as prettified stereotypes. Its local color depictions have that sentimental precision typical of the U.S. American regionalists. Its examination of the exploitation of the Freedmen, the deterministic effects of the slavery environment, and the inexorable power of the "color caste" system on individual development reflect obliquely the "increasing consciousness of the influence of environment on character and fate."[211] Tourgée's conclusion that the Slavery Syndrome has fatefully conditioned the Southron's hostile response to radical rule is somewhat similar to that naturalistic doctrine that external social and cultural forces deprive man of "that necessary exercise of individual responsibility which had been common to democratic idealism and Christian ethics."[212] Finally, Reconstruction fiction in some of its details (if not in the conception) deals, like much of realist-naturalist fiction, with the ugly facts of the U.S. American Republic during the rise of the new Union: "political corruption, economic injustice, religious unrest, sexual irregularities," and those more general themes of "greed and doubt and hate and cruelty and violence. . . ."[213]

This is especially significant when Reconstruction fiction is placed against the "Godey code" with its demands for purity in language and plot, traditional morality in sentiment and conception, and the avoidance in print of coarse language, evil actions, or immoral references or descriptions.[214] Thus, although Reconstruction fiction oscillates between the romantic and realistic modes, it is as a precursor of the latter mode that it has its essential literary interest in this study.

Romanticism and realism, then, are the two poles of the transition period that form the general literary context framing the thematic structure of Reconstruction fiction. Within this context, it is possible to locate more specific genres in U.S. American literature that also share in the transition aesthetic and that are closely related to the general nature of Reconstruction fiction. These genres are Southern fiction and Negro fiction, types embracing tales of prewar plantation life, the Civil War, and the postwar South. Such a differentiation must be made in order to understand the literary characteristics of Reconstruction fiction and in order to distinguish it from genres that share its *personae* and that appeared at the same time. For example, Tourgée calls his novella "John Eax" a Reconstruction tale when it is clearly Southern fiction. Consequently, it is necessary to show that while his *A Royal Gentleman*, for instance, is such a Reconstruction tale in a certain way, his "John Eax" is not.

The basic forms of Southern fiction are the romance, the local color narrative, and the Civil War tale. The term "Southern romance" refers to a work of fiction in which there is a sentimental description of Southern mores and a sympathetic idealization of the Bourbon and his Belle, contrasted humorously (in most cases) with comic-pathetic pictures of their ex-slaves in the joys of voluntary servitude. Yet while Reconstruction literature is allied to the Southern romance in the use of locale and Southern character types, the difference is quite clear. Reconstruction fiction is sociopolitical in mode and aim while the Southern romance is primarily an apolitical cultural fantasy.[215] At its best, the Southern romance incarnates the mystique of the South, that sentimentality related to the Lost Cause and Lost Slavery nostalgia that would pervade the eighties. At its worst, it is merely a Godey mutation in which the South is only a vague setting for innocuous domestic crises.

Reconstruction fiction does share some of these thematic and narrative trappings. But the basic difference remains: Southern fiction does not deal with the political conflicts of the Second Revolution. Some examples of the Dixie romance are De Forest's *Kate Beaumont* (1871); E. Van Loon's *The Shadow of Hampton Mead* (1878), dedicated to the redemptionist Wade Hampton; and Mary E. Nealy's "Legends of Virginia" (1877-1878).

The second form of Southern fiction is the local color tale. Such works contain passages that parallel the description of Dixie fauna, flora, physiography, and regional types found in Reconstruction fiction. This can be seen in Rebecca Davis' anti-romantic depiction of a degraded Bourbon in "A Night in the Mountains" (1877), in the local color description of an ugly, squalid Southern community in the anonymous "My Village in the South" (1879), and in a similar description in Sherwood Bonner's "In Aunt Mely's Cabin" (1878). The best example of such local color realism is in Edward Spencer's "Low-Down" (1872). The exoticness of a North Carolina fishing village is gradually changed into a portrait of flies, stench, and heat—of houses filled with "the sour odor of shells of oysters, clams, and crabs, and fish refuse . . ."; of the village tavern "squatting by the roadway" while flies swarm inside amid the odors of "rum, sugar, and tobacco-juice." And dominating all, "the unwrinkled, molten surface of the glaring, staring sound."[216]

Reconstruction fiction does, of course, employ such coloristic technique, as in the following un-picturesque description of a vague Virginia countryside during restoration: It was a scene of:

> dull monotonous desolation. . . . The hill-tops were smirched by frost; the untilled fields were covered with a sparse, weedy

> growth; there was a swampy slope crowded with soldiers' graves and rotting headboards; . . . and over all there were stillness and stagnation. A slow, unhindered decay appeared to be thwarting . . . nature. Corruption was at work, . . . that foul life which corruption develops.
>
> . . . there came into my mind a morbid notion, an idea of moral wrong bred like maggots in the dissolution of an evil; . . .[217]

More significantly, Tourgée manipulates the coloristic value of the North Carolina locale in order to take advantage of the interest in the state that seemed to erupt in the journals during redemption and reconciliation.[218] His works are distantly akin to such Southern fiction as Woolson's "Up in the Blue Ridge" (1878), Davis' "The Yares of Black Mountain" (1875), Christian Reid's "The Land of the Sky" (1875), and Jones' "In the Highlands of North Carolina" (1883). But, unlike local color fictionists, Tourgée subordinates his interest in Southern regionalia to his social and political analyses. It is a deliberate political rationale that, again, differentiates Reconstruction fiction from this form of Southern literature.

There is, however, a body of Southern fiction that does carry explicit political meaning, the postwar tales of the Civil War set in the South and, in most cases, involving the impulse toward reconciliation. W. W. Sikes, in his "Absalom Mather," espouses what can be guardedly called a left-of-center view of reconciliation. His tale focuses on a Copperhead Yankee, Absalom, who goes South to escape New Englandism. His hatred for the North leads him to become a leading, fire-eating secessionist:

> "Let . . . Lincoln become President and . . . Yankees will march over the border, . . . set the negroes free, an amalgamate the fair daughters of the South with buck-niggers . . . before your very eyes! Southerners, are you ready to submit to your fate like cowards?"

After Appomattox, he undergoes a striking conversion: "'Don't talk those old lies to me. . . . Lies! . . . See what they have brought us to!'" His penitence is complete when, at the climax of the story, he kneels in tears and kisses the old flag. The symbol here reflects what most Radicals saw as the meaning of reconciliation: the South's complete loyalty to the new order. However, the political symbolism is blurred by the New England origins of the hero.

De Forest may be said to adopt a right-of-center view in "Rum Creeters is Women." This short story is the more conventional version of the reconciliation theme involving the Yankee Lover and his Secessionist Belle. But the difficulty of such a reconciliation appears when the Belle, despite her real love for the Yankee, betrays him to Confederate raiders. The officer survives the betrayal with only a wound, and in an extraordinary act of forgiveness, he marries her. This reunion is so contrived as to be a merely mechanical use of the reconciliation device. (De Forest is to use it again with more extravagance in the Reconstruction novel *The Bloody Chasm*.)

In these two tales, one notes the theme of reconciliation as the key political doctrine. Sikes' tale insists that, in effect, the South must forego forever through penitence and remorse the vision of the Confederacy. De Forest's tale states, in effect, that the defeated South must be accepted as it is—a somewhat irrational, emotional geopolitical area, better brought back into the Union by patience and forgiveness than by reconstitution. However, despite the political symbolism, works like these are not Reconstruction fiction: The theme they articulate deals primarily with the conflict between North and South and not with the Reconstruction aspect of that conflict.

Of course, Southern fiction does reflect through interpolation and inference some of the currents of postwar politics. Like its nonfictional models, Southern fiction helped to foster the partial reunion between the sections. Indeed, it is possible to see the Bourbon victory of 1877 as resulting, however indirectly, from the influence of Southern fiction. In a sense, the popularity of Southern romance, colorist tale, and Civil War narrative during redemption and reconciliation evidenced the re-acceptance of the South as a revived political power. Cryptographically, these works state that if the North would acquiesce in the planters' hegemony over the South, it would no longer need to fear the Bourbon class. In the hands of the Pro-Radicals, Reconstruction fiction would be a futile attempt to warn the indifferent Yankees of the dangers of this revived power.

Similar to and related to Southern fiction in the use of locale and character types is Negro fiction, that body of literature featuring the Negro as its narrative and thematic center and appearing contemporaneously with Reconstruction works. Both often share a common locale and common local color elements; and certain of the Reconstruction novels use the ex-African as a central figure, e.g., *Bricks Without Straw* and *Other Fools and Their Doings*. During the First Reconstruction viewed as a Second U.S. American Revolution, Negro fiction had a double reality. It was a derivative of prewar models, yet at the same time it mirrored obliquely the political stances of that revolution. Works that portray the Freedman sympathetically are descendants of *Uncle Tom's Cabin* and appear in various forms. For example, the slave tales, like Stowe's novel, are postwar, abolitionist narratives attacking the "joys-of-servitude" thesis that continued to pervade Southern fiction. Good examples are Lizzie M. Champney's "Vina's Ole Man" and Sarah Winter Kellogg's "Little Lizay" (1877). At the same time, they offer emotional supports for pro-Negro efforts during (and after) Reconstruction. (The description of the cruelties of slavery in the opening chapters of *Bricks Without Straw* parallels such postwar "abolitionist" tales.) The Civil War tales of the Negro continue this sympathetic depiction. Helen Pierson's "Chips" (1865) and "Queen's Good Work" (1866) chronicle the agonies and joys of military emancipation. Tales about the period immediately following the war center on the problems of general emancipation. All these postwar works—slave tales, war stories, after-the-war sketches—when used to support Negro emancipation, continue the attack on slavery embodied in Stowe's novel and, as such, mirror indirectly the pro-radical position.

There were other homesteads in the prewar period, e.g., *Aunt Phillis' Cabin* and *Uncle Robin and His Cabin in Virginia*, which symbolized the other vision of slavery: that it was a beneficial institution for master and slave alike. This vision is embodied in an ambivalent image of the slave. The African as black child must be guided and loved; the slave as black savage must be restrained and subordinated.[219] These ideas recur frequently in those post-slavery writers who implicitly adopt an anti-radical stance in their Negro fiction. The clearest exponents of the "Uncle Robin" thesis are Jennie Woodville's tales: "Mammy" (1875), "The Death Rain" (1879), and "Uncle Pompey's Christmas" (1878). She celebrates the joys of voluntary servitude and laments the plight of those unfortunate Freedmen who ". . . warn't nuvvur nothin' but a free nigger, an' didn't hav no ole mas' to pattern by." In this light, Woodville's slave and Freedman narratives glorify the joys of slavery and reflect the views of anti-radical writers.

In all cases—whether the writer is sympathetic to the Freedman or not—the evolution of Negro fiction during this period from its prewar models is clear. The persistence of earlier conventions can be seen in Reconstruction fiction. The slave as the "noble child of nature" finds reincarnation in the noble freeman, e.g., Uncle Jerry in *A Fool's Errand*; the "faithful retainer of chivalry" can be seen in the Voluntary Slave, e.g., Anderson Parker in *Colonel Dunwoddie, Millionaire*; and the "comic darkey" continues in the happy-go-lucky ex-slave—Cousin Berry in *Bricks Without Straw*.[220] But while Negro fiction shares themes, characters, and local color elements with Reconstruction fiction, they lack the essential relationship. As with Southern fiction, tales of the Negro are apolitical in their mode, theme, and conception, though there are implications in their texture that allow for political interpretation. This is the key distinction between Reconstruction stories about the Negro ex-slave and fiction about the African.

• • •

Reconstruction authors,
in helping to restore national harmony,
offered superficial description of the post-bellum period;
for they were obviously propagandists for peace,
and their works were not artistically compelling.[221]

Reconstruction fiction is neither Southern fiction nor Negro fiction, though all three forms share common characteristics, and though Reconstruction fiction may be considered a kind of Southern or Negro fiction, Reconstruction novels and short stories are *per se* a self-contained genre, belonging to that large body of sociopolitical literature that appeared during the transition. Therefore, in this study, the texts under discussion are defined in terms of their direct or indirect thematic treatment of the explicit *social* and *political* conflicts of the period and not simply by their aesthetic or thematic use of the South or its unique citizenry. Or, to put it another way, while these novels and short stories are Southern in locale, they are intended to be sociopolitical *exempla* of the four phases defining the period.

Before these simple criteria can be expanded into a full-scale definition, it is necessary to isolate the three forms of Reconstruction fiction from a variety of works, ranging from novels that clearly examine political issues to magazine sketches that carry only their tenuous or symbolic outlines: semi-

Reconstruction fiction, the Reconstruction fable, and sociopolitical fiction. It is sociopolitical fiction that defines the major works in this study.

The semi-Reconstruction work does make use of the period in a clearly explicit manner, but the political elements are so unfocused and vague as to be only tenuously present. The emphasis is on the sociocultural and the economic rather than the sociopolitical conflict between North and South. The antagonists are often the Belle and her Yankee suitor. She must long for but eventually reject her slave-holding past, and then she must accept the non-political aspects of the new era. Sometimes these works are adventure-romances but more often they are love stories in which the theme of reconciliation is the dominant motif.

Examples that research reveals are Sergeant Epes' "Strategy at the Fireside" (1865); Maria Louisa Pool's "Pharaoh's Horses" (1866); Fanny Purdy Palmer's "A Woman" (1866), a pathetic-sentimental treatment of a Freedwoman's problem with two husbands, a problem solved more comically in *A Union Officer*; Rebecca Harding Davis' "Two Women" (1870); William J. Flagg's "A Good Investment" (1872); Davis' "The Rose of Carolina" (1874); Crayon Porte's "Home" (1879); Davis' "The Colonel's Venture" (1879); and three major works of this species in a "conversionist" vein: Jacqueline Thornton's *Di Cary* (1879), De Forest's *The Bloody Chasm* (1881), and M. Sheffey Peters' magazine novel, "The Barren Ridge of Ridgeway" (1882).

An examination of a few of these works in detail should illustrate Reconstruction fiction in its tenuous form. In Rebecca Harding Davis' "Two Women," the Reconstruction elements, revolving around the Belle's social collapse and her ineffectual reaction to the new era, are subordinated to the theme of domestic crisis. Mrs. McIntyre, the pathetic survivor of a once proud family, is an Anti-Radical but in feminine terms only. For her the essential evil is that Reconstruction is destroying the womanliness of the Southern lady and hence is leading inexorably to "Isms, . . . spirit-rapping's, Indiana divorces, and infidelity."[222] However, the work is more concerned with a realistic contrast between "the two women" than with sociopolitical affairs.

Miss Alice McIntyre is the Godey blonde: insipid, childish, and seemingly asexual, seemingly because in Davis' hands her sexuality is merely transposed, not lacking—as demonstrated in this scene with her little playmate: "Presently, as though she had found what she sought, she stooped and . . . kissed [little

Tom] on the lips. When she lifted her head her pretty face and throat were died crimson." She is juxtaposed with Charlotte Vane, the Belle as full-ripened brunette, the unmarried, un-childed woman whose unladylike aggressiveness has a touch of the slattern and whose driving force results from what seems to be sexual frustration. Because Charlotte has lived beyond the fatuous life of the McIntyres (she was a Confederate spy and survived defeat with some wealth), she is more at home in the Radical South. Indeed, her great ambition is to inspire a man to political greatness, since she cannot live "as a man" herself. In sum, Davis reveals through Charlotte Vane a muted picture of the sexual intensity hidden behind the mask of Southern gentility: "He had an odd, . . . fancy that she silently had [gone out of her body] and belonged to the warm-tinted autumnal dusk, full of drowsy harvest smells, darkness, and passion."[223]

To calm such powers, she drinks laudanum like an addict and dreams of an act of passion or sacrifice that will redeem her. When her chance comes, she is left ridiculous and bereft. Disguised as a man, she has attempted to prove her worthiness to act as an equal partner with the fastidious Cavalier hero of the story by helping him tend his sick workers during an epidemic:

> He stopped in the chicken-yard outside, among the coops. It was still daylight, bald, ugly daylight. . . . [There] she stood in her man's coat and trousers, a felt hat on her head, [with] a black feather . . . broken and sagged down behind. She knew that her face was smutted with soot from the boat.[224]

Charlotte Vane is an unusual portrait of the Belle-as-neurotic in 19th-century fiction, the man-woman, admired but mostly pitied for her self-willed destructive frustrations. It is this theme, rather than sociopolitical problems, that pervades the narrative.

William J. Flagg's serialized novel, *A Good Investment,* has as its general aim the presentation of the "conversion" theme *à la* Miss Ravenel, and this, more than the political upheavals, informs the work's texture. In the beginning Bella, the heroine, is a Yankee-phobe who later (and typically) falls in love with an ex-Union officer. Standing between the two lovers is her Southern pride symbolized by the Voluntary Slave, Uncle Hector: "My young missis mustn't marry no Yankee ablishun officer. Think ob de 'spectability ob our family."[225] Bella's feelings are equally severe—and conventional:

> "Peace. . . . There can never be peace between us and them, except the peace of death. . . . Will . . . the men of the South consent to remain under subjugation, not to the cowardly Yankees, but the more cowardly negroes, whom they have raised up to insult and degrade us more effectually than they could do it themselves? No! Southerners will not submit."[226]

Her brother responds in a manner similar to Absalom Mather:

> "Such talk . . . may be pleasant . . . as a parlor amusement. Southern women have been very fond of it, but Southern men—those who survived—have had enough of it."[227]

There are other allusions to the political innovations in the New South:

> Negro Congressmen we have, and Senators too; and if we will, we can choose a President of bronze. . . . But nowhere, not in Congress-halls or Senate-chamber, . . . will the African race appear to so good advantage as a Negro boat's crew, lustily pulling, keeping stroke to songs of their own humor. . . .[228]

But, true to form, the political remains oblique to the main interest of the story: Bella's conversion and her eventual marriage to a Yankee.

Jacqueline M. Thornton's *Di Cary* might be called a Southern romance, in its delineation of Southern peculiarities and in its emphasis on the conflict between Yankee and Cavalier modes of society. However, the Reconstruction is tenuously present. In *Di Cary*, as in most semi-Reconstruction fiction, one witnesses the sectional conflict not so much as a sociopolitical encounter as an economic and cultural one between Northern enterprise and Southern richness of life, between Yankee plebeians and patrician Southerners, the victorious obsequious Unionist and the defeated proud Secessionist—all defined against a background of prewar myths. (This is especially so since Thornton sets her story in restoration Virginia.)

Once again the Cavalier paraphernalia of the forties and fifties—the aristocratic genealogies, the princely portraits, the silver relics—are trundled out in order to make a poignant contrast to defeat and degradation, all haloed by a heavy-handed, partially counterfeit nostalgia. But something irrevocable has modified these illusions of feudal power: Slavery has been destroyed by war and Reconstruction. In the antebellum period, this aristocratic mythology was a part of the cultural justification of slavery as a socioeconomic institution. But since it has been destroyed, Thornton seeks to recreate a myth of aristocratic chivalry without recourse to the force that generated, sustained, and corrupted the myth. She seeks to purify the Southron of the pollution of chattelism by denying its economic function. Within the Reconstruction framework, Thornton considers slavery as the sublime act of charity of a glittering nobility:

> "I hold in trust two hundred souls born on my sod. My grandfather watched and provided for them, my father religiously did the same, and to my wife and me they are a part of our large and helpless family."[229]

The reader is then informed that "before the war" Di's father cared for these hundred-odd Negroes totally since "they made nothing but corn, and not enough to feed themselves. He had the additional expense of meat and clothing."[230]

The major purpose of the romance of Southern culture during the final phase of Reconstruction is to define the formula of reconciliation between the two sections, for only insofar as the Yankee is converted to the Bourbons' mythic vision is reunion possible. But the conversion is twofold. The Cavalier represented by Di Cary, a Virginia Belle, must accept the efficiency and success of Northern economics; the Yankee must accept what may be called Bourbonism. His conversion is more significant because it is not motivated by defeat and upheaval, but by a voluntary acquiescence to the dreams of the Southern way of life. Among the negrophobic Carpetbaggers, this conversion had startling but no longer unexpected dimensions: "Ye ought to have had [*sic*] freed them a hundred years ago, and killed off the black devils."[231]

This is only slightly less extreme than the initiation which Hugh Hunsdon, Di's "carpetbag" lover, undergoes. By the time the novel closes, Hunsdon has not only saved the heavily mortgaged plantation, but he has become its Cavalier. Yet his transformation lacks even the minimal tension of Underhill's in *The Bloody Chasm*. He is more English than Northern. (Worse, he is of noble descent and is related genealogically to the Carys.) He is more in awe of the ex-Confederates than enraged by their rebellion. (Indeed, he was not even in the country during the war.) And he is more prejudiced against the Freedman than the Belle is. He is not only pro-Bourbon, he is pre-Bourbon in his attitude, vision, ideology, and conversion.

The tenuous Reconstruction elements eventually disappear into a suffocating atmosphere of nostalgia. The Cary plantation becomes a Reconstruction version of *Swallow-Barn*, a novel about antebellum life on an Edenic Virginia plantation—with its quaint customs, charming ladies and chivalrous heritage—in its postwar decrepitude and revival. The sociopolitical conflict between Unionist and Secessionist is reduced to the domestic antagonism between virtuous Southern ladies and worldly Northern women whose moral corruption is signaled by acts of malice and wan faces and eyes burning "with a wild, feverish light"; the causes of the irrepressible hatred are reduced to "ignorance of each other"; finally, the solution to the conflict becomes the transformation of Yankees into Southerners.

Thematically, it is the conversion motif more than a simple reconciliation that becomes the archetypal gesture bridging the bloody chasm. Aesthetically, this motif is the thread tying this Godey-ridden romance into a loosely structured whole. In the final analysis, *Di Cary* emerges as an example of the semi-Reconstruction novel superimposed on the Southern romance.

De Forest's *The Bloody Chasm* is only slightly better. After a strong Reconstruction beginning, it degenerates into the sentimental romance—a far cry from De Forest's more clearly defined Reconstruction nonfiction. The novel involves two characters: Harry Underhill, Union veteran, and Virginia Beaufort, fire-eater, daughter of the overthrown Secessionist oligarchy, and Underhill's cousin (by the marriage of his uncle to a Southern Belle before the war). The plot revolves around the attempt of Uncle Mather to unite this Benedict and Beatrice through the promise of a fortune, a fortune they can receive only if they marry. At first Virginia imperiously rejects this arrangement, but fatigue with her postwar poverty—with dry cornbread and baskets of dirty laundry—forces her to accept this conjugal form of a political reconciliation, provided that after the wedding Underhill agrees never to see her again.

By the time the last scenes are reached, Underhill, by undergoing Hunsdon's conversion, is rendered acceptable. To win back his wife, he disguises himself as a Confederate veteran and writes poetry in praise of the CSA. The ruse works and, as the Confederate colonel, he wins her heart. He then reveals himself as her hated husband, but she is so moved by his willingness to accept the Lost Cause that she also gives him her hand. Through Underhill's conversion, the chasm is bridged.

A parallel image of this allegory of reunion is found in the character of Uncle Mather. Mr. Mather is Dr. Ravenel in his 1881 mutation—wealthy, philanthropic, puritan—and no longer sure of the efficacy of freedom of the Negro, though he is still an arch-Unionist. According to the demands of the allegory, he must be converted from exultation in the South's defeat to pity for its sufferings. De Forest's technique of transformation is simple. In the beginning Mather-Ravenel is seen rejoicing over the ruins of Charleston, but then he is exposed to the suffering of specific ex-rebels. The initial feeling of exultation fades; instead, Mather feels:

> Like one who is unexpectedly and painfully forced into pity—whom it . . . dazzled by a sudden glare of misery. . . . It is doubtful whether Mather was quite conscious that he took the ex-Confederate General by the hand.[232]

This gesture mirrors the reconciliationist motto: the clasping of hands across the bloody chasm. Thus, "Ravenel's" spirit of triumph is converted to compassion and charity. By the time Chapter XX is reached, the meaning of reconciliation is clear in the allegorical figures forming the final tableau: The Freedmen characters are in subservient dependence on the Bourbon, and because the Carpetbagger has become a Cavalier the Bourbon accepts his persistent offer of reunion. The spirit of Mather is triumphant.

This work, like all semi-Reconstruction works, does have a generalized sociopolitical matrix. The opening chapters describe images of the first days of restoration: the crushed Confederates, the ruins of Charleston, the allusions to Sherman's pacification, the poverty and helpless struggle of the Belle. Moreover, there can be discerned in the conflict between Underhill and Virginia, the Carpetbagger-Bourbon tension masked, because of the demands of the 1880s, by the old Yankee-Cavalier pattern. Finally, the resolution of this tension in a conjugal embrace is the tiresome fantasy of reconciliation, which in literary terms reflects the slogans of the pro-Bourbon wings of both parties. But, in the main, this story is clearly a sentimental allegory of conversion in which the Reconstruction typically disappears, to be uncovered only through symbolic explication:

> At last she put her mouth softly up to his cheek and kissed him.
>
> "You belong to me . . ." he whispered.
>
> "Yes," she whispered back, kissing his lips and clinging there, as Southern in her love as she had been in her hate.[233]

The final example is M. Sheffey Peters' serialized work, "The Barren Ridge of Ridgeway" (1882), the clearest illustration of what is meant by the expression "semi-Reconstruction fiction." The plot occurs in the right place (Virginia) and during the right period (reconstitution). And it deals clearly with the right themes—the failure of the Old Southrons to adjust to "the Trauma"; the folly of useless, stubborn pride; the contrast between a past of patrician glory and a despairing present. It is around these semi-political themes that the narrative development is woven.

The plot is quite simple. A Belle rejects the useless life of a defeated aristocracy and adapts herself successfully to the new order with the help of her "Yankee" lover and her cooperative ex-slaves. Eventually she becomes an independent, skilled manager of her father's plantation.[234] Moreover, in the two climactic moments of the story—the establishment of a steam sawmill at Ridgeway and the discovery of a vein of valuable iron ore in the Barren Ridge,[235] one can discern the parable of the Locomotive's entrance to a particular garden, as it were, a picture of the "new economics" breaking into the lethargic failure of Southern agrarianism.

This economic transformation is the thematic center of the work. The Southrons, in all their baronial, pre-Sumter splendor, are described by the hero as a "band of lotos-eaters" whom necessity, i.e., the war and Reconstruction, had to shatter so that the land could be profitably redeemed. This necessity becomes for the heroine (who undergoes the conventional conversion) the power needed for "the ultimate development and prosperity of our people and country." Therefore, the work stands primarily as a contrast between the old Ridgeway whose deed goes back to the "King's Patent" and the new Ridgeway of steam sawmills, between the land being plowed for tobacco and the Barren Ridgeway being mined for iron.

The work is also a laborious love-story between "two . . . over-proud souls," paired up along the archetypal axis. Bernard Yorke is the Belle who, under the circumstances of the New South, becomes an economic Radical. Like Di Cary and Virginia Beaufort, she learns that sweet are the uses of adversity. However, she is not left at the subsistence level of the yeoman. Out of the North comes the economic Carpetbagger bearing the cornucopia of capital improvement. He must rescue her from the labor that has purified her for new splendor. Such a character is the hero, Wooten.

He is not immediately recognizable as the Reconstruction protagonist, as he is disguised for the sake of political neutrality as an Englishman (related distantly to the Yorke family). This mask is, of course, a fuller development of the convention that the Belle must always marry an upper-class Yankee. But it is a thin disguise; he is a capitalist-entrepreneur and cattle-speculator; he is an inventor, chemist, and mineralogist. He is then, despite his English accent and aristocratic ancestry, the economic Carpetbagger, the incarnation of the virtues of the Machine.

In terms of narration and characterization, this novel treats the less melodramatic, non-political aspects of Reconstruction: the theme of the industrial potential of the South and the possibility of triumphant recovery through hard work, the rejection of the patrician past, and the acceptance of Northern economics. And while "Ridgeway" avoids the reconciliation cliché as a component of this thematic design, it does continue the conversion motif, limited in this cause solely to the Belle, as the unifying element in this parable of the Locomotive in the Southern Garden.

These five works, as examples of the ten dealing indirectly with the political dimensions of Reconstruction, share basic characteristics. They are concerned with Reconstruction only as a general setting and not with those fierce sociopolitical controversies that formed the period. The authors choose themes that have been drained by the passage of time of the partisan animosities motivating the central Reconstruction novels. The first of these neutralized themes is the intercultural tension between representatives of the sections, usually ending in an erotic union. The second theme is the problem of the Bourbon's socioeconomic rehabilitation. This problem is always solved by "the magic carpetbag": those wills or mineral discoveries that elevate poverty-stricken Southrons to sudden wealth, as in "A Good Investment," *Di Cary*, "The Barren Ridge of Ridgeway," "Mamelon," and *Colonel Dunwoddie*,

Millionaire, just to mention a few. Because these themes—cultural (and sexual) competition and socioeconomic problems—are structured tenuously along Reconstruction lines, they lack the clear ideological design prevalent in the core sociopolitical novels. Instead, the concern is with the juxtaposition of economic Carpetbaggers against destitute Bourbons, of Southern gentility against Northern enterprise. The concern is more with the grounds of reconciliation between the sections—the acceptance by Yankee and Cavalier of aspects of each other's cultures—than their political differences. These, then, are the thematic characteristics of semi-Reconstruction fiction.

The second form is the Reconstruction parable or fable. The fable is a work of fiction written during the Reconstruction dealing with the key social and political themes of this period, the African Question and the Irrepressible Conflict, but with the narrative set historically prior to 1866 and placed geographically in both the North and the South. In other words, the contemporary problems are transferred back into time for a kind of retroactive treatment. Cable's *The Grandissimes* (1880) comes immediately to mind. It is for some critics one of the more famous examples of the Reconstruction fable. But, in the context of this study, it lacks a clear articulation of the African Question or the specific sociopolitical issues involved in the Irrepressible Conflict. The emphasis is more on Southern locale than on the anxieties of the Second U.S. American Revolution (a new birth of freedom), more on the Civil War than its postwar effects. Clearer forms of the fable can be seen in *Miss Ravenel's Conversion*, *Waiting for the Verdict*, *What Answer?* and *A Royal Gentleman*.

De Forest's *Miss Ravenel's Conversion from Secession to Loyalty* (1867), probably the best-known example, is a partial fable; most of it is a Civil War tale. In the Civil War section, the fate of Lily Ravenel and her two union officers dominates; in the fable part, the interest is in her father, Dr. Ravenel—doctor, chemist, inventor, and South Carolina Unionist-abolitionist. It is through the mouth of this pre-Reconstruction Scalawag that De Forest presents his theories on the African Question: "He would make himself analytically acquainted, not only with [Southern] soil, but with the possibilities of the negro soul.[236]

As an analysis of such possibilities, Ravenel works from the realities of slavery as he has seen it and not from those naïve myths of slavery espoused by abolitionist-idealists like Colburne (Lily's Yankee lover). The Colburnes, used to dealing with the slave workers on the abstract plane of *Uncle Tom's Cabin*, approach them with little understanding of their actual plight nor with much patience for their peculiar conditions. The Colburnes are resentful that "the mere gift of freedom has not exalted and purified the negro character notwithstanding, uncounted centuries of barbarism or of oppression."[237] Colburne finds the Afro-American reality—especially the seeming helplessness and the lack of initiative—offensive to his Victorian mores:

> Wendell Phillips says that 'the negro is the only man in America who can afford to fold his arms and quietly await his future.' That is just what the critter is doing, and just what puts me out of patience with him. [And then he makes a correct prophecy.] We shall cease to be negrophilists; we shall kick him out of doors and get in somebody who is not satisfied with . . . waiting for the future.[238]

In contrast to this, Ravenel can look at the totality of the ex-slave and still see his future potential, recognizing that for the mass of former Africans two hundred years would not be undone simply by proclamations of freedom or appeals to self-reliance:

> We must not grumble if [God] chooses to use up a hundred years in civilizing him. . . . What right has . . . Colburne to demand roses of land . . . sown . . . with nothing but thistles? We ought to be thankful if it merely lies barren for a while.[239]

In this statement is found De Forest's essential criticism of Reconstruction: It tried to Americanize the African before the one hundred years were up.

Ravenel's fullest analysis of the Negro soul—its failure, its promises, and the effects of slavery on its development—is found in the fable section of the novel—Chapters XII, XVII, XVIII, and XIX (pp. 217 ff.), especially in those scenes set on the "Ravenel plantation." De Forest's first point is the familiar one of environmentalists: The vices of the ex-slaves derive directly from the vices of slavery and not from the inherent nature of the Freedman. (DeForest would later reverse himself in "The Colored Member.") Because of their bestializing environment, the ex-slaves:

> were liars and hypocrites and thieves. All constituted society lied to them by calling them men and treating them as beasts; it played the hypocrite . . . by preaching to them Christianity, and never . . . practicing it; it played the thief by taking all the earnings of their labor. . . .[240]

Only after an evolution far beyond this state would emancipation lead to Americanization.

During this evolutionary period, De Forest continues, it will be the moral obligation of the emancipators to extend to the Freedman extensive non-political aid in the ethical and economic spheres:

> The conscience of the nation . . . will not be cleared when we have merely freed the negroes. We must civilize them. And we must begin . . . by teaching them the great. . . duty of . . . life—that of working for his [*sic*] own subsistence.[241]

For Ravenel, this is a task only for the idealist: "It is your duty and mine to work patiently, courteously and faithfully to undo the horrid results of a century of selfishness." The antidote to such selfishness is the fullest implementation of free labor economics. Unlike the typical Northern Radical, Ravenel implicitly rejects sociopolitical rights as a solution. In place of the transcendental celebration of the vote, he substitutes his celebration of the Northern socioeconomic system. From wage-payment will flow the inevitable transformation of ex-slaves into ". . . intelligent, industrious, and virtuous laborers"[242] and their realization thereby of the "ideas of justice . . . , honesty, [and] mercy. . . ."[243] When the army of occupation of Louisiana turns over to Ravenel an abandoned plantation and a squadron of contraband (Freedmen), he has a chance to implement his theories.[244]

At first the Freedmen fail. Laziness, bad working habits, and stupidity prove stubborn forces. But Ravenel knows his material and gradually he shapes them into an efficient labor force. But it is more than this. The plantation (like Tokeba in *Yazoo*, Warrington in *A Fool's Errand*, and Red Wing in *Bricks Without Straw*) becomes a reconditioning camp where a new ethic and a new sociocultural order are developed among the Freedmen by a combination of voluntary labor and public education. What Ravenel wants is not only labor efficiency, but the removal from the Freedmen of the "stigma of social contempt" given him by slavery.[245]

But such an undertaking was doomed to failure. The Ravenel-Radicals assumed that the hostility to the Negro was caused solely by his behavior. For the average U.S. American racist the hostility was caused by his blood. In antithesis to Ravenel's workers were the Afro-French aristocrats of New Orleans, proof of the abolitionists' dream of the fruits of liberty. Yet despite their obvious accomplishments, the Negrophobes despised them as much as the plantation field hand—and perhaps even more because of their mixed blood.[246] Therefore, even as Ravenel successfully carried out his experiment in transforming the Negro soul, forces were gathering to render his efforts futile. In terms of the narrative, the plantation is destroyed, like Tokeba, Red Wing, Warrington, and Beaconsville, by Confederate irregulars sweeping Klan-like out of the night. Allegorically, Ravenel's plantation is destroyed, like them, by that persistent racism that shaped many Yankees and Cavaliers alike.[247]

As for the other theme in the Reconstruction fable, the Irrepressible Conflict, the entire work is woven around it, but only in a general way:

> The victory of the North was the triumph of laboring men living by their own industry, over non-laboring men who wanted to live by the industry of others. . . . Slavery meant . . . an idle nobility. Liberty has established an industrious democracy.[248]

Nevertheless, De Forest's novel is primarily Civil War fiction; only in certain chapters is the fable structure fully expressed. A much better example of this structure is Rebecca Harding Davis' *Waiting for the Verdict*. This work first appeared in the journal *Galaxy* in the same year as the publication of *Miss Ravenel's Conversion* (1868).[249] As a fable, *Waiting for the Verdict* demonstrates the pattern from first to last. In contrast to the formal duality of De Forest's novel, Davis' novel centers on the Irrepressible Conflict and the African Question totally. The narrative, one of those multiple Dickensian plots (covering the period 1847-1865), offers two basic constellations: the Ross-Garrick and the Margaret-Broderip stories. The unifying narrative element is the erotic union of these characters across chasms of section and race. Within this complexity reside the two major themes of the fable.

The first constellation graphically expounds the ramifications of the sectional conflict, but in a manner quite intricate for Reconstruction fiction.

Ross Burley, Northerner, and Randolph Garrick, Southerner, seem the stereotypical couple of reconciliation literature. But closer examination of Davis' handling of the convention reveals astonishing innovations. To begin with, Ross Burley is no abolitionist sprung full blown from the womb. She first appears in the novel as a twelve-year-old negrophobe: "Ross laughed tauntingly, glad that she was white, and stronger than this yellow monster of a boy; . . . she never hated anything so much before; never." But her eventual transformation into an abolitionist identifies her clearly as the North. More interesting is the fact that she is a rare creature in Godeyana: the virtuous, idealistic girl-woman who is also a bastard (the daughter of a Southron) and who has passed her younger life with her grandfather in poverty and, compared to her fastidious Cavalier lover, degradation: It was a life of the fish-market, with a "low, dirty-blue roof overhead, [and with] the brick pillars pasted with bills"; a world of "tiresome, muddy" streets; of untidy women: "Scheffer haggling . . . over a bone of meat on one side, and Kit Vance, slimy and red-faced, diving into her filthy mackerel hogshead, on the other."[250]

Davis superbly shapes both Ross' natural and moral environment into clear symbols of the absolute difference between herself and Randolph Garrick. First, there is the ugly decrepitude of Northern physiography, hinting vaguely of the oppressiveness of an industrial landscape:

> A November day, twenty years ago. A chilly, pale, weak-breathed, deadening day everywhere; up where the sun glimmered feebly along through a cold, watery sky; yonder, where the sea yawned to the horizon like lead: up the bay where the water moodily lapped the beach, while pink gentians and saffron weeds mildewed and rotted in the salt hay of the marshes.[251]

Then, there is the moral landscape of the Northern plebeian class:

> I was a market-girl until I was nine years old. . . I had a stall in the public street. Whatever there is to see and hear there, which should be kept from children, I saw and heard. [I] belonged by birth to the class which you place on a par with your slaves. . . .[252]

The physical and the moral landscape combine to render up in an unsentimental manner the complex psychological nature of Ross Burley as a symbol of the North, a complexity of which she herself is all too well aware: "I understand why the nuns found it necessary to use the lash on their own bare flesh sometimes."[253] Yet despite such feelings and within such landscapes, Ross survives honorably.

In comparison, her lover, Randolph Garrick, is the typical Bourbon of pro-radical fiction, standing obviously for the South. And although he does not serve in the CSA, being a Kentucky planter who opts for a kind of physical neutrality, his pro-slavery sympathies leave little doubt that he symbolizes the South. Like the Southron, Geoffrey Hunter, in *A Royal Gentleman*, he is no cliché of aristocratic idealism: He blurs repeatedly back and forth between patrician honor and patrician treachery, a fact exemplified in his dealing with Ross and with an old family slave, Hugh (the father of Broderip, by the way). Garrick's act of honor is his willingness to fulfill his father's promise to free the old slave. But Hugh knows that Ross Burley (now Garrick's wife) is, through complicated plot developments, the unknowing owner of the Garrick plantation. When Garrick discovers this, he sells the old slave (under the guise of freeing him) to certain death as a laborer in the Confederate Army in order to prevent any chance of disclosure:

> Garrick, slowly rising his head, saw the old man's face as it passed him, peering eagerly from the dark car, and heard his weak quaver as it called out something about "how far to Mars' Streblin's," and then died away in the distance.
>
> Then he adjusted his hat, and passing his hand over his parched face, wiped a fleck of foam from his mouth. He had saved the honor of the Randolphs,—by being dishonorable to a slave—he could go back to Rosslyn. At that his eyes turned from the retreating train, and from the stars beginning to shine in the dark blue overhead, and were glued to the ground, where he thrust his boot to and fro among the straw and filth of the platform. He had no will to do otherwise.[254]

Randolph Garrick's complex nature is further revealed in his relationship with his wife. When Ross and Garrick marry, there is no sentimental transformation in Garrick's patrician attitudes through the pure love of the

Yankee Maid. For example, Ross confesses to her new husband the nature of her life; Garrick's reaction is decidedly unusual for the typical hero of the reconciliation fantasy:

> Garrick . . . was silent, looking at her, yet it seemed to him as if horrible, shameful oaths, one after the other, were rushing through his discreet, clean lips, in his dismay and passion. . . . [At first, he assures her that his love can endure her degradation, but he is nevertheless appalled.] It did not seem fitting to him that James Strebling's illegitimate daughter should look with critical eyes at his dead mother's face.[255]

Later, his reaction becomes even more unorthodox: ". . . the shame which Strebling had given to his base-born child he could forgive; but the tenderness—never!"[256]

In light of the characterization of Randolph Garrick and Ross Burley, as symbols of South and North, their wedding night brings together pure and tainted blood, noble man and commoner, slaveowner and abolitionist, Conservative and Radical, Cavalier and Yankee in a clash of "character and creed."[257] Randolph and Ross, then, reflect in their stormy marriage (to be calmed only by the Surrender at Appomattox) the theme of the Irrepressible Conflict.

Davis' treatment of this theme is detailed and corresponds ideologically to Morgan's and Tourgée analyses. She too sees slavery as the essential cause and symbol of the internecine warfare between sections:

> There's thousands of young men gone into this war to give Nathan here, and his kin, the chance of bein' men, and not property, wuth the vally of a horse. "Ef you knew, Nathan," said Joe, with the patronage which black blood always brought to his manner, yet speaking directly to a hungry something [in] the man's eyes . . . , "ef you and your kin knew the price that's bein' paid for your chance, in the best blood of the country, you'd use it when it came."[258]

And in her description of "the best blood of the country" sweeping through Louisville, Davis images the inexorable moral and physical force of the Union's military might purging the nation of rebellion and slavery, and giving to Nathan (Broderip's brother, by the way) his place in the U.S. American sun:

> . . . regiments of muscular lumbermen from Maine: Massachusetts' lawyers and doctors, . . . men from the shores of the great lakes, and from the prairies, with brawny bodies and clear, sensible eyes, swept in endless procession down the streets. . . . It was [Randolph's] first glimpse into the great seething whirlpool. . . . He began to be dully conscious of a mighty current sweeping by, which sucked in all the forces of the air and of life. . . .[259]

Moreover, this is the revolutionary power lying at the center of the Radicals' plan of Reconstruction as the handmaiden of their deeper moral purpose: the purification of the South (and thereby the nation) of the crimes of slavery that poisoned the promise of the New World:

> To leave the slave neither citizenship, family, women's virtue, mind, to shut out God from him, as far as in them lay! I think this country is filled with ghosts of murders done! I hope God may teach the North how to lay them.[260]

Slavery, the war, and the various phases of the First Reconstruction have each, at one time or another, been identified as the Irrepressible Conflict *per se*. But in this study, they are merely tokens of the deeper ideological division existing in the North and South over the significance of 1776. Was this significance defined by Jefferson the Southerner in his dream of white male equality or by Hamilton the Northerner in his dream of equality created for all men by an economic elite?

> There is a fable that all men are born free and equal in this country. . . . It only needs for you and me to prove the baseness of this falsehood. . . . I have heard of equality and brotherhood all my life but there is not a face I meet on the streets which does not bear terrible marks on the difference made in the nature of man by money and rank and the want of them. Sometimes my caste has the advantage, sometimes yours: but the gulf is always there.[261]

The Irrepressible Conflict, therefore, becomes the inexorable hostility generated between democratic and aristocratic idealism, growing in large measure out of two differing attitudes about the hypocrisy, unreality, or possibility of this vision of human equality. Davis' verdict is that the egalitarian proposition encoded in the Declaration of Independence is possible, and such possibility defines the tension pervading the Burley-Garrick narrative.

In the Broderip-Margaret Conrad narrative, Davis turns extensive attention to the other topic of the Reconstruction parable: The African Question. Her treatment is very unconventional in keeping with her unconventional talents. In the main, this analysis centers on the African-as-slave and the African-as-Freedman, represented by the two brothers: the black Negro Nathan and the white Negro Broderip. In one family there appears the nonfictionists' implicit contrast between the two forms of the Negro soul.

In her treatment of slavery, i.e., the Nathan theme, Davis' work shifts into the narrative and thematic dynamics of Negro fiction. But because of a clear political cast, these qualities are subordinated to the novel's Reconstruction thrust. The melodramatic realities typical of the slave narrative—the escapes to the North, the exile down-river, the anguish and triumph of freedom—are used to define explicitly the Freedman's conditions in 1867.

For Davis the chief damage of slavery is more psychological than physical:

> Look at his face; there is unused brain-power there which God never gave to you or me. Look at the hunger, the vacuity, the animal passion, which has taken its place. Why, the man was born with ambition, and most likely, the blood of the best of their Southern families in his veins, and to satisfy it, he has had for work a stable . . . , and for his highest pleasure an extra dish of something to eat . . . ; he is . . . homeless, with neither a name nor a country to call his own. . . . It is late in the day to bring him, and the gray-haired thousands like him, their chance.[262]

The adjunct to the corruption making this degradation both possible and desirable is the white racists' obsessional concern with the "Darkness of Blackness." Davis explores Northern and Southern racism in its two faces. First, it is a sociopolitical ideology against the Negro as slave:

> Why, sir, emancipate them and where can you stop? We will be asked to jostle at the polls with negroes, bring them to our tables, marry them our daughters! Besides . . . the two races differ—differ vitally. If you attempt to put them on the same

> plane, it will end in the destruction of the weaker. There is not an Irish hodman . . . who does not know the negro is his inferior, and will not join to put him down if he tries to compete with him in free labor. It is the old story of the earthen and iron pitcher.[263]

Secondly, racism is a socioculturally inspired revulsion against the slave as Negro:

> The dirty yellow skin of the mulatto made her sick, she was sure; it was the same as if a toad or snake had stood upright, to see his grimaces and monkey tricks of delight at being kindly spoken to. She wished he was dead, . . . and was sure that, if she had been a boy, she would have thrown the yellow, grinning thing into the water.[264]

Even some abolitionists, especially those whose commitment grew more from an Emersonian idealism than from hatred of the brutal realities of slavery, are trapped by a more subtle mutation of these feelings:

> He acknowledged argumentatively the wrong done to the slave, and his right to redress; but in fact, the very scars of the negro, the hurt done to his brain by this slavery, his lazy good-humor, his lustfulness, his blind faith in "de Lord," jarred against him at every point, chafed him with an unreasonable disgust and choler, the more that he could not shake off the consciousness of debt owed to this unwelcome man and brother. With all other Northerners outside of the Radical party, he looked to deportation. It was the old story. Prospero could not easily rid himself of his black Caliban, whose crown of manhood he had stolen for him.[265]

Against such an ideology and such emotions, the Freedman in the North is as helpless as the slave. In the North, there were thousands of "old issue" Freedmen struggling

> to rise, a respectable, industrious, God-fearing class as any in the North, yet tramped under foot by the law, and society finding in the mere color of their skin a disgrace which white criminals and harlots held beneath their shame.[266]

And in the South, there were millions of slaves who were in an even more degrading condition. Both groups were trapped by their blood in Davis' powerful polemic.

There did exist for both Northern and Southern blacks a reality hidden, in many instances, by the Euro-Americans' matrix of racial animosity—the fact that the black U.S. American was the keystone of whatever power accrued not only to the South but to the North because of the peculiar institution:

> I want you, if you're took back into slavery, to learn it by heart. It'll keep you from bein' a lazy nigger as it has me. The money that's bought them plantations and furnished them houses was made out of our sweat an' blood. We bought them; we paid for them. There's them among our people as say if ever they're free they'll claim on-third the crops as pay; an' it would be but fair. If yer father an' me, an' them like us, hed been paid for our labor, we'd not have been the offscouring of the nation to-day, with scars on our backs in place of the wages that's bin our due.[267]

These facts, rather than mere union charity, undergird Nathan's right to legal and constitutional protection against the Negrophobes. And since the Union is ultimately responsible for the racist contingency governing the African's existence as slave and free man, the Union must make amends to him not as an act of pity but as the payment of an economic and moral debt:

> if I were Nathan, or one of his race, I would say the price ought to be paid. I would enter into no abasement of gratitude. What if the best blood of the country does flow to give him his chance? It is late in the day. My God! Look at him.[268]

The only hope for Nathan in Davis' vision is that the Radical and his comrades will move the mass of U.S. Americans across the racial chasm to an awareness of a national Interracial Symbiosis, or at least to an awareness of the necessity of racial toleration:

> . . . Markle, you've not said once by your looks dat you was white and I was black.

> Bah! What's the skin? That prejudice will vanish like the one our Salem grandfathers had against old women. The world moves—it moves![269]

But it would move slowly against the complex emotional strata lying within the intellectual justifications the slave-labor system had created: white supremacist racism as theory and praxes. It is these strata lying above the bedrock of economic demands that Davis analyzes with almost contemporary frankness in her study of Nathan's brother, John Broderip.

The Broderip-Margaret Conrad plot is also Negro fiction used as a Reconstruction fable. The Nathan motif represents Negro fiction in its "slave narrative" form, the Broderip tale in its "tragic mulatto" structure. Broderip's evolution from mulatto pet to white doctor to black Union officer is, in essence, the tradition of the Afro-Saxon narrative. But the socio-psychic tensions engendered by Broderip's racial ambiguity, typical to those stories,[270] are used to elucidate a Reconstruction point of view about the problems of the Freedman in 1867—the interracial, the intraracial, and the personal tensions to which Northern and Southern racism subjected the black aliens: "Whether he loathed or respected the black skin, the mysterious sympathy of race . . . made it more familiar than any other; the whole bond of childhood and its associations brought it close."[271] Moreover, Broderip's feelings are further compounded by his passion for "Eve" and made more poignant by her love for him.

Davis handles the Taboo Conjunction quite subtly. The use of such a rare theme in 19th-century U.S. American literature indicates her unorthodox approach to this subject matter. On the thematic level, this interracial affair becomes an image of a radical solution to the problems of the multiracial Union. On the aesthetic level, Davis uses this theme to play off one of her Charlotte Vane types against an unconventional relationship that will redeem or destroy her.

Margaret's involvement with Broderip creates touching complexities. First of all, she is psychologically an intricate person, that fully developed, passionate, frustrated woman whose emotional intensity hints of depraved feelings, feelings more akin to masculinity than femininity—at least in the Victorian context: "She is not like a woman to me, but a dangerous, lawless man in an iron mask. . . . I could not tell what terrible cry [her lips] would utter if they opened." As such a person she possesses that sensual ambiguity that must have been so repellent and yet so fascinating to the Victorian-minded: "She wore her body unconscious and neglectful of it as a half-used garment, yet never was its beauty so dominant or perilous. . . ." Along with such complex physical and emotional characteristics is Margaret Conrad's moral and psychological ambiguity. She believes in male-female equality but she needs to be dominated. She detests the slaves as Negroes yet favors their liberation. She is semi-atheistic, realistic, and curiously detached from shocking experiences.[272] Like Floyd Reese in a later Reconstruction work, Margaret is conscious of possessing an unexplored sociopsychological force, a "great unmalleable power within her, unused and decaying."[273] Indeed, she is extraordinarily aware of what would later be called the id:

> If I had been a man, and that side of my nature which has been kept hidden had been brought into temptation . . . there is no crime which I could not have committed. None! [I could have expressed] whatever foul possibilities lay there. . . .[274]

It becomes increasingly clear in Davis' analysis that much of Margaret's psychological and moral complexity originates in the problems of feminine sexuality within the restrictive confines of Victorian mores.

Thus, Margaret Conrad emerges in this novel as a kind of 19th-century anti-heroine. She is in complete contrast to those innocuous, asexual Southern belles and Yankee maidens who flit through Reconstruction fiction as acceptable heroines. Consequently, she may be described in sexist terms as the Yankee-Maid as bitch who, through an unendurable, unconsummated passion, evolves into a Madonna figure.

The person to be responsible for this passion and this transformation will be Dr. Broderip. He alone can release Margaret's soul from the stifling sullenness of her painful emotional, physical, and moral complications. But he too has complexity. This results, aesthetically, from the amalgam of literary stereotypes forming his personality: He is both the tragic mulatto and the dark hero. As one of those Byronic bad men beloved by Victorian authoresses and audiences (Rochester, Heathcliff, and St. Elmo come immediately to mind), Broderip encompasses a fascinating diversity of contradictions. Physically, he is an androgynous mixture of femininity and obvious sexual appeal.[275] Morally, he is a cynic, a rumored participant in bachelor orgies, and a connoisseur of the vices of 19th-century masculinity (which Davis describes with surprising precision).[276] He is clearly that urbane but corrupt hero who was so offensive to the Puritan. Yet at the same time, his passion for Margaret makes him capable of humanitarian acts and ethical and physical courage. Because Broderip is also the tragic mulatto, his moral redemption carries an additional thematic energy. Like St. Elmo, Broderip places his talents at the service of a noble action. He deliberately gives up his white mask, forms at his own expense a Negro regiment, and leads it into battle in the Virginia campaign. He is captured and is sent to Andersonville. He is later freed by Sherman troops and leads his regiment in the capture of Richmond. But at the moment of triumph, he is mortally wounded. In this way, he helps to save the old Union and reinforces the Freedman's right to citizenship in the new: "I think this sacrifice for his own people [will] bring out the man in him more'n . . . a wife . . . would have done."[277]

As the tragic mulatto, Broderip incarnates other values, since his racial ambiguity in its intimate and public facets is irrevocably entangled with the overriding social question of the First Reconstruction: the African presence in the Union and the color prejudice arrayed against his presence North and South. Once more there is a return to this repetitive theme—but now in terms of the specific ideologies espoused by Bourbon and Carpetbagger. The fundamental division between them revolves around the nature of the prejudice against Broderip. For the Bourbon and his allies, it grows inevitably from the natural antagonism between a higher race and the genetic depravity of the lower: "The defects are inherent in his blood which will keep him down. He is indolent, treacherous and sensual." As super-Freedman, Broderip is the man of wealth, education, and medical renown; the respected friend of prejudiced Northerners; the Negro as Caucasian; the paragon which the ex-Africans are to emulate. But his "blood" makes such accomplishments irrelevant.[278] In this view, the Bourbons posit the correct solution to the problem of racial aliens in the postwar Union: continued subordination (without slavery, of course) as a permanent condition, especially since the model for such subordination already existed in the North in 1867:

> "John Broderip is the son of a negro; there is not one of his hospitals or patients to-day would open their doors to him .

. . ; there is not a club . . . or restaurant from which he would not be rejected like a felon; the academies of science . . . , where he was a director, would admit him only if he came as the servant of a white child. . . . If he married there would be no citizenship for him, no honor for his wife, no educator for his children. They are the one class which the law and the white man are privileged to trample under foot."[279]

But it is precisely to attack the doctrines of "genetic disability" and subordination that Davis' Reconstruction fable appeared in 1867, featuring a Freedman as a central character. Concurrently, it is because these doctrines encouraged such cruel sanctions against the freed slaves that the radical idealists rallied to their defense. The Radicals posed a counter-thesis to the doctrine of subordination: the idea of a continual progressive evolution of the ex-slave to full development in the new multiracial Union. For if, as Broderip demonstrates, the African in all his mutations is capable of Americanization, and if the antagonism against him is merely the result of fear, hatred and, most of all, ideology, then the solution is clear: constitutional amendments guaranteeing Americanization and legal protection against an irrational phobia.

Broderip's personal conflicts and reactions to this racial hostility give these abstract ideological positions their human urgency. Because of racism, Broderip is torn between becoming white with all its joys or accepting his blackness with all its social and psychic costs:

> To leave this dainty refinement . . . ; to give up Margaret, in order to become a leader among the filthy black swarms of Bedford street, or of the fouler hordes of Southern field hands? . . .Nathan could comprehend the nausea. . . .[280]

In accepting the nausea of this absurd condition, Broderip finds his task: to join in a common cause with all men of "color" and their white comrades against the oppressive, race-based caste-system.

But this system demands its price, the destruction of the love affair that had sustained Margaret and transformed Broderip. Davis' handling of the rejection scene is powerfully sentimental and yet tinged with a subtle realism and serves as a symbol of the system against which the Radicals marshaled their forces:

> To-night, the night when he meant to woo her from the secret depths of her soul the evidence of her love for him, when he meant to touch her lips at last to his, to feel her heart beating against his own, weak and famished, which had never known the love of woman, the desire to be true to her, to strike down the damnable lie in which he moved, became maddening.
>
> [Later that evening, Broderip and Margaret come together.] His hand was on her arm; how white it was—white. His was another color! A few hours back and this woman was a part of himself; he was going to build a barrier between them which not even death could destroy.
>
> ....
>
> She held out her hands, looking up at him. He took them; they slept in his with an utter quiet and trust; he stooped; his hot breath touched her forehead.

But the anti-black racism of this caste system intervenes with brutal disruptiveness. Broderip confesses his race, and Margaret's reaction is painfully realistic. She would rather drain out every drop of her blood than eradicate the color bar:

> "I have no pity. The negro blood—" The white, powerful limbs began to shiver and tremble, as she put out one hand blindly, and caught the wall. "The negro blood is—is abhorrent to me . . . .' and then she slowly dragged herself from the room. . . .[281]

Thus, whatever foul possibilities Margaret is capable of do not include marrying a Negro, no matter how white. Then Davis introduces her most surprising complexity: Margaret's "keen physical disgust . . . to the black skin" keeps her out of Broderip's arms, but her love for him keeps her faithful to him: "I may never see Margaret Conrad's face again, . . . But she will never . . . marry another man. I think there is somewhere a world where my color will not keep me from her."[282] Ironically, it is not his white skin but his African ancestry that is the problem. A 19th century version of *West Side Story*.

In this way, the Broderip-Margaret plot demonstrates as a Reconstruction symbol the persistence of color prejudice as the most adamant force against which radical policy struggled and demonstrates further the persistence of this prejudice even in the face of gratitude, need, and love. However, the novel ends on that note of transracial consummation beyond the grave denied by Hawkeye-Cooper to Uncas and Cora in *The Last of the Mohicans*. Margaret, in an elegiac mood of reconciliation, sits in the failing twilight, communing with her dead love, purged of the hostility that separated them in life: "Someday my friend will come to me; and with all his whims, with all his moods, as he left me. There is no such word as dead, to me." Now at peace with her various selves and curiously fulfilled, Margaret Conrad has decided to answer the call for idealistic Carpetbaggers with which the work ends. She has denied Broderip; she will not deny his race. Her father, a non-political Radical, sums up this transformation: "Well, the black blood is not abhorrent to her now. If she had been less bitter once—"[283] Thus, Davis suggests a controversial solution to U.S. American racism: the use of interracial sexuality to bridge the "blood" chasm.

Waiting for the Verdict, appearing as it did in 1868, prior to the election, opened up all the ramifications of the Darkness of Blackness lying athwart the U.S. American polity:

> Dar's power in Tom's head, Missus, and Dar's bad passions in his blood, and ef dar's no work given to de one, de oder has its work ready. He must be a man or a beast, an' dat soon. . . . Dar's four millions of his people like him; waitin' for de whites to say which dey shall be—men or beasts. Waitin' for the verdict, madam.[284]

In ideology and narrative thrust, the development of the Broderip-Margaret plot placed Davis on the side of the Radicals. In the final chapter of *Waiting for the Verdict*, the two major questions of the Reconstruction fable—the Irrepressible Conflict and the African Question—find an ultimate solution in symbols of erotic union. Garrick has become a pro-Unionist and an abolitionist; Margaret has picked up the torch from Ross and will become a future Freedman-teacher. Consequently, the two major narratives terminate with both an intersectional and an interracial reconciliation.[285]

Other examples of the fable are *What Answer?* (1868), *'Toinette* (1874), and *A Royal Gentleman* (1881). These works share a common heroine (the Mulatto Lilith) and a similar ideological interest in the Question and Conflict. As usual the sociopolitical issues are placed geographically and historically in a non-Reconstruction context (though each work ends with the restoration phase). As with Davis' novel, the plots of these three works follow the Broderip figure in his feminine guise through the racio-social problems, especially interracial passion, which act as similes for the problems of the freed slave in 1868.

Anna E. Dickinson's *What Answer?* appearing the same year as the book form of *Waiting for the Verdict*, examines the African Question in the period 1861 to 1865 as manifested primarily in the North and primarily in one family, the Ercildoune clan. The chief character is Franscesca [*sic*] Ercildoune, the daughter of an Afro-Saxon planter and an English noblewoman.[286] Like Broderip, she is the super-mulatto of pro-radical fiction: intelligent, courageous, pious, beautiful, the accomplished member of the highest rank of "old issue" society in Philadelphia.[287] Typically, she falls in love with an Anglo-Saxon, William Surrey, the scion of white society in the same city. Untypically, he accepts her Negro blood, marries her and, according to the convention, is ostracized by friends and family. From their erotic conciliation across the blood chasm comes the impetus of the plot and the development of the sociopolitical meanings of the Question in 1868.

The initial problem is the common one: What is the symbolism of the white-skinned black man within the context of "this devilish U.S. American prejudice,—wholly U.S. American, for it is found nowhere else in the world . . ."—which permeates the new Union? Dickinson poses a radical answer, even for the radical left: Franscesca is a kind of Caucasian, having no community with the slaves who are, by contrast, "ragged, dirty, . . . shabby, . . . bareheaded, [with] great clumsy feet, stupid and heavy-looking heads; slouching walk, stooping shoulders. . . .":

> "Here's Miss Ercildoune . . . one-eight negro, seven-eights [*sic*] Anglo-Saxon. You make that little bit of negro master of all the lot of Anglo-Saxon. [Any of them with] any mixture at all, and that knows anything, and keeps a clean face,—and ain't a rebel, nor yet a Copperhead—I call him . . . one of us."[288]

Certainly, during the brief moment before restoration, many Negroes had this dream. But the "devilish U.S. American prejudice" made such simplification impossible. Franscesca, like Broderip, is a kind of Negro united by race to the most barbaric ex-slave. Worse, her Saxon mask makes her even more dangerous, representing the Blackness of Whiteness and, thereby, incarnating that terrible fear of unknowing conjugality with the African. In our time of racial desegregation, it is hard to understand the thrilling horror of the "drop of savage blood" that obsessed the 19th-century racists and that impelled them to insult and persecution: "Quadroon, mulatto, negro, it is all one. I have no desire to split hairs of definition. You could not be more obnoxious were you black as Erebus."[289] Thus, the Afro-Saxon is both white and black. In this ambivalence there are present again, as in De Forest and Davis, the two poles of the "Negro soul" in their intra-racial antithesis.

What emerges in pro-radical fiction as a more comprehensive symbol is that the Afro-Saxon represents the potential development and actual accomplishment of all talented, intelligent Freedmen within the new Union. Franscesca becomes, consequently, the model possibility intrinsic to the radical plan of Americanization. And since such possibility is already manifest in her varied accomplishments, then any political ideology based on inferiority and place becomes an unreal, contradictory doctrine:

> If he stays in the position to which the Anglo-Saxon assigns him, he is a *worthless* nigger; if he protests against it, he is an *insolent* nigger; if he rises above it, he is a nigger not to be tolerated at all. . . .[290]

The second point grows out of the first and has that shock of recognition that characterizes Reconstruction fiction. A major part of the racial obsession of many Victorians evolves from their ambiguous sexual attitude toward the African as creature and person, generated by both Victorian anti-sensualism and the fascination with and revulsion against the Negro as an erotic partner. The fear of "mis"-cegenation and yet the continued commission of it become the tangled web in which the myth of black *mana* grows. The Southrons (and their Northern counterparts), says a minor character, speak so much about amalgamation, and yet they ". . . and their friends . . . made a race of half-breeds all over the country." It is not "the living together that troubles squeamish stomachs; it's the marrying." Thus, when a Northern Democratic newspaper uncovers Francesca's marriage, the paper uses the marriage as a political issue to discredit the anti-slavery struggle: "MISCEGENATION.

DISGRACEFUL FREAK IN HIGH LIFE. FRUIT OF AN ABOLITION WAR."[291] It is within this web of sexual and racial hostility that the anti-Republicans make their attacks on Americanization. In *What Answer?* this position is cast back during the war, but the reader in 1868 well understood its contemporaneity. This is the anti-rationalism afflicting from the South becoming national.

Dickinson's final and essential point is that the Question and the Conflict are the same. The Negro is the cause and their condition the meaning of the antagonism between and within the sections. Two major incidents illustrate this fusion. The first is the attack on Fort Wagner by Negro soldiers. In the rhetoric and in the allegoric juxtaposition of black knights and perfidious rebels, one can clearly discern the emphasis on the war as primarily a force of Emancipation.[292] The second incident is the Draft Riot of July1863, bloody protests against Lincoln's plan of national conscription. The Copperhead uprising is not only a projection of the conflict between the North and South, but because of the racist ferocity of the Democratic mobs, it is a genocidal attack on the Union's staunchest supporters.[293] It becomes, in a word, a Northern version of the White Insurrection, an insurrection in which the dominating image is the murder of black Unionists on the streets of New York:

> The child fell while thousands of heavy, brutal feet trod over it till the hard stones were red with its blood, and the little prostrate form, yet warm, lost every likeness of humanity, and lay there a sickening mass of mangled flesh and bones; some men [were] assaulted, clubbed, overborne . . . or tied to some convenient tree or lamp-post to be hacked and hewn, or flayed and roasted, yet living, where they hung. . . .[294]

And, of course, Franscesca and Surrey are also killed—in front of the home of Surrey's parents. The riot, then, becomes the murderous articulation of Northern race hatred in its genteel and vulgar forms, and in terms of radical ideology in 1868, racial violence is the necessary outcome of keeping the postwar Freedmen in a sociopolitical and socio-psychic limbo between citizenship and slavery.[295]

This pathetic-sentimental tale ends with the answer to the question of Freedman rights not yet assured. The camera, as it were, focuses on Robert Ercildoune, almost the last survivor of a family destroyed by pogroms, a veteran of Fort Wagner, a gentleman and philanthropist. He is standing in front of a polling station, waiting to vote:

> Robert stood leaning upon his cane; a support which he would need for life; one empty sleeve pinned across his breast, over a deep and yet unhealed wound. The . . . sun shone down upon his . . . face, upon the . . . flag that waved in triumph above him. . . .[296]

But he is refused admittance by a band of Irish (translated Democratic) ruffians. 1861 or 1865, the Negro was still not a citizen.[297]

In 1868, the Radicals were waiting for a confirmation of their solution to the Question and the Conflict: The war is not over, says Russell, Robert Ercildoune's white pro-radical friend: "How and when will it be closed?"

> 'That is for the loyal people of America to decide. . . .'
>
> . . . Among the living is a vast army: black and white, shattered, and maimed, and blind: and these say, 'Here we stand . . . that the body politic might be perfect! blind forever, that . . . liberty might shine abroad, . . . for all people.' . . .
>
> And the dead speak too. From their crowded graves come voices of . . . persistent pathos, . . . 'Finish the work that has fallen from our nerveless hands. Let no weight of tyranny, nor taint of oppression, nor stain of wrong, cumber the soil, nor darken the land we died to save.' [298]

The specific political purposes of this work in the context of the Reconstruction are clear. According to Miss Lee (Smith) in her unpublished dissertation, *What Answer?* was a polemic for Grantist and leftist Republicans during the 1868 campaign. (Indeed, its title was used as one of their rallying cries.)[299] Its sympathetic treatment of the ex-African reminded the reader of the debt owed to the Freedman North and South. Its description of the Draft Riot reminded the Unionists with which side of the Conflict the Northern Democracy sympathized. The Irish proletariat—the Tammany power to which the New York Democrats owed most of their strength—is pictured as a Copperhead fifth column striking at the Union's vitals. The reader is further reminded that during the height of the atrocities, Governor Seymour, the

Democratic candidate for President in 1868, refused to call up the National Guard. The implicit contrast to General Grant is clear.

In this light, *What Answer?* as a fable has two functions: to support Carpetbagger policies in their broad sociopolitical applications to the Freedman's plight and, more precisely, to discredit the Democrats' bid for power in 1868. It is that political campaign that forms the particular rationale for Dickinson's fable.

The Afro-Saxon maiden as Reconstruction symbol continues in Tourgée's *Toinette* (1874) and *A Royal Gentleman* (1881), the final fables in novelistic form.[300] These works are basically two versions of the same story—the interracial passion between Geoffrey Hunter, a young Southron, and Toinette, his mulatto slave-mistress. Within Tourgée's pro-radical ideology, the problems engendered by this passion correspond allegorically to the antagonisms the Question generated between Bourbon and Carpetbagger. This can be clearly seen in the two conclusions he wrote to the story.[301]

A review of the common events immediately leading up to these differing endings is illustrative. On the eve of the Civil War, Geoffrey arrives in Oberlin, Ohio, with his pregnant Toinette. He frees her, settles her in a maternity home, and goes off to the war.[302] Toward the war's end, Toinette goes to work as a white volunteer nurse at a prison hospital in hopes of a chance meeting with Geoffrey. The quality of her love is evidenced by the horrors she is forced to witness in hopes of finding her master:

> Blood, flowing or clotted, was everywhere. Dirty, powder-blackened faces were smeared with it. Unkempt, tangled heads of hair were still more closely matted with the crimson ooze.
>
> ....
>
> The matted locks must be cleaned and smoothed, the clammy brow bathed, the grimy face washed, the fevered tongue cooled, the wound dressed, the bleeding stanched, death in its most horrible forms faced. . . . The canvas tent-wall alone separated the receiving from the operating ward. The half-whispered words of hurried consultation, the grating of the saw, the keen shudder-bringing rush of the sharp knife, deftly wielded, the groan, the curse, the gasp, and amid all, the sickening, fearful drip, drip, of the everflowing blood. . . . . The surgeons, red-handed, perhaps

> with red drops upon the face and clothing, passed to and fro. One whose face had been literally bathed in the jet from a severed artery, stopped to examine the wound of a new arrival, whose only anxiety on earth seemed to be to pick the clotted blood from his clammy hands and from under his long nails. When the horrible pictures separated, Toinette washed the stiffening hands and pallid brow. . . . [303]

Sure enough, Toinette is rewarded. Geoffrey is blinded in battle, captured by the Federals, and taken to Toinette's hospital. She nurses him through the pain of his incurable blindness, but when he discovers she is masquerading as a white woman he denounces her to her Confederate patients as a "nigger gal."

After this point, significant differences between the two novels appear. At the end of *Toinette*, Geoffrey surrenders to the love that, despite his denunciation, continues to sustain him in his blindness. Reunited with Toinette and his son, Geoffrey, filled with remorse, gratitude, responsibility, and love, accepts them gladly in marriage. *A Royal Gentleman*, on the other hand, Geoffrey is cured of his blindness by an improbable combination of Toinette, Lincoln, and a famous surgeon. When he meets Toinette again, he is overwhelmed by the memory of their passion, a memory symbolized by reveries over a kiss secretly given him by the still disguised Toinette in the hospital:

> He had heard her . . . come into the tent. . . . Then she . . . kissed his lips—a trembling, fervent, dewy kiss, freighted with hope and love. . . . What lips! . . . How they spoke in that silent pressure! . . . in its trembling, tender eagerness! He had never felt but one kiss like it, and that was Toinette's. . . . The girl had exquisite lips. A Sybarite could not have helped kissing them, if she *was* a nigger. He remembered thinking she was only a pretty pet; yet, somehow, he trembled when he gave her that first kiss. . . . He remembered, too, how her kisses ripened from simple childish jests, to tender, clinging endearments. [Her lips were] nearly matchless—full, tender, mobile, and exquisitely cut and penciled. He remembered now that last kiss she had given him, when he left her a free woman, waiting for maternity in her new Northern home. She hung around his neck, and her lips had the same clinging tenderness, only it was a burden of beseeching which they bore.[304]

Now, during the restoration period, Geoffrey asks Toinette to be his concubine once more. However, she recognizes that while slavery had made their racio-sexual affair "as the unconscious indelicacies of rollicking childhood[,]"[305] Reconstruction now makes its continuance a deliberate vice.[306] She pleads for marriage—for the sake of their son and their own honor. But because of those conscious and unconscious influences of slavery that shape his psychology and his culture, such an act of "honor" is intolerable to a "seeing" Geoffrey; he *cannot* legalize the natural relationship between himself, his "nigger gal," and his "darky brat"; cannot make the transition from racio-sexuality to interracial sexuality, despite his passionate need to do so. He denounces Toinette's plea as a Reconstruction plot, and they separate forever.

In terms of the Question and the Conflict, Tourgée's contrasting conclusions take on allegoric meaning: The blinded Geoffrey of the earlier version is the helpless Bourbon, compelled by defeat and radical power to accept on the level of equality his black *alter ego*. Toinette represents those Freedmen who are or have become "white," i.e., Americanized. She further represents the Carpetbaggers' belief that as the Freedman's legal transformation became a sociocultural one, he would be less odious to the Bourbons as a co-sharer of the sociopolitical development in the New South. But *Toinette* was written before the total dissolution of pro-Carpetbagger power in the Union. By the publication of the second version, Radical Reconstruction had not only been defeated in the South but discredited by Conservatives in the North. The Bourbon was no longer helpless ("blinded"); he had emerged as the triumphant redeemer. He would accept his black *alter ego* (Toinette) only in terms of the subordination (concubinage) that governed their pre-restoration relationship. Thus, the "seeing" Geoffrey contains a dual symbolism: His rejection of Toinette represents the triumph of Bourbonism in 1877; it also represents, in this view, the persistence of the evils in Southern culture (with the support of liberal Republicans) that defeat and Reconstruction did not overcome. What *A Royal Gentleman* is ultimately about, then, is the Slavery Syndrome.

The influence of the Southern past, what has been called the Slavery Syndrome, is presented in Tourgée's two stories as the central theme linking the Question and the Conflict into an ideological unit:

> I saw, or thought I saw [wrote Tourgée in *A Royal Gentleman*], that the conscious evils of slavery—the cruel lash, the impossible task, and whatever of opportunity for malice the system gave rise to—had been, if not magnified, at least disproportionately dwelt upon by the anti-slavery writer of the north. At the same time, . . . the unconscious evils of the system . . . had been allowed to drop out of sight. . . . I noticed, too, that these unconscious evils were the very ones which had left their marks upon character, and that everyone who had been submitted to their influence was more or less scarred by them—especially the master race; and that these influences were a part of slavery which could not be abolished.[307]

I would argue that, at least not without sustained effort by a united Federal government.

Consequently, the roots of the conflict between the Carpetbagger and the Bourbon in *A Royal Gentleman* reside in the syndrome of unconscious evils forming Geoffrey's vision of Toinette's transformation. For him (as a Bourbon), Toinette's white skin and white aspirations and behavior are irrelevant. Like all other Freedmen of whatever degree of Americanization, she is fixed by a racial doom to remain a "nigro wench." Neither erotic passion nor Reconstruction politics can change this, precisely because the cultural-psychological machinery of slavery had not changed:

> [While] slavery in name had been abolished, it was actually as much alive as ever, because the results of the Civil War had not changed, but rather strengthened, the belief of the Southerners in their superiority to the people of the North, and in their rights to dominate the negro, if not physically, at least socially and politically. In other words, the War had merely lopped off a few branches for the tree of slavery, but had left its roots and trunk untouched.[308]

A syndrome of ancient symptoms—racism, racio-sexuality, and a concomitant impulse to racial violence—becomes, in a symbolic sense, the force that shatters this intense, generous love affair. Upon such shoals would founder those radical governments built on the possibility of bridging the chasm between a Toinette and a Geoffrey Hunter merely by amendments to the U.S. Constitution.[309]

It is evident thus far that, in all cases, the Reconstruction fables side sympathetically with the Negro. Their essential message is that while Emancipation will make life difficult for the ex-slave, such difficulty need not be fatal—provided that the Freedman is given social, economic, and political help. Two fables that take an opposing view are G. C. Eggleston's "My Friend Phil" (1875) and Joel C. Harris' "Free Joe and the Rest of the World" (1884).

In each of these short stories, the plot, set in slavery, shows through the chief characters the pain of liberation—the isolation from the life of the plantation, the sense of vulnerability in a hostile South and, worst of all, the lack of a master and his sustaining paternal concern: "[Free Joe] realized the fact that though he was free, he was more helpless than any slave. Having no owner, everyman was his master."[310] As a result of freedom, both characters die. On the surface, these stories join with the Bourbons in their assertion that since slavery was necessary to the life of the African in America, it followed, therefore, that only in volunteer servitude could the Negro survive in the post-Emancipation South. Both tales are pro-Bourbon fables attacking not only Americanization but Emancipation as well. This is the total meaning of Eggleston's sketch and part of the meaning of Harris' tale, meanings that would eventually cancel out the heroic-pathetic images in Davis, Dickinson, and Tourgée.

But a closer look at Harris' work reveals some complexity. Free Joe dies not so much because he has been freed, but because he has been cut away by freedom from the intimate ties that had been formed in slavery. Moreover, Free Joe (and possibly Phil) is not so much a victim of freedom as a victim of the antagonism against Freedmen in the harsh, anti-abolitionist South. Unintentionally, Harris' pro-Bourbon parable is an indictment against the subtle inhumanity of a system in which freedom for a slave must lead to death.

These two anti-radical fables, "My Friend Phil" and "Free Joe and the Rest of the World," along with *Miss Ravenel's Conversion*, *Waiting for the Verdict*, *What Answer?*, and *Toinette–A Royal Gentleman*, form the basis for the definition of the Reconstruction fable operating in this discussion. These seven fables have, to sum up, the following characteristics: The plot is placed in the North and/or South prior to reconstitution. The themes are based on the sociopolitical issues of this Second U.S. American Revolution but placed backwards in time. Superficially, the "fabulists" avoid controversy by placing the problem in another period. But the rhetoric, the subject matter, and incident in Davis, Dickinson, De Forest, and Tourgée are clearly used to initiate controversy. They exploit the shift to the immediate past in order to identify the issues of the Radical South organically with those issues (i.e., abolitionism and chattelism, Union and Secession) which, for pro-Southerners and pro-Northerners, had acquired the holiness of a crusade. For the Pro-Radicals, the turbulence of reconstitution was the direct heir of the idealistic agitation against slavery and secession. Consequently, they sought to tap that vast reserve of emotion and commitment that they hoped was still active in the thousands of survivors of the moral and military crusades against slavery. The pro-radical fables, with their emphasis on the problems, potentials, and accomplishments of the African, are therefore placed in the past, not to avoid controversy but to sanctify it. By using the African Question as the symbol of the Irrepressible Conflict in terms of the two dramatic metaphors—the peculiar institution and the war—these parables create a literary (and thematic) energy missing from works that treat the Conflict as merely a problem soluble by marriage and economic innovation.

To reiterate: The spectrum of works making the fiction of the First Reconstruction in its general definition divides into three bands: the semi-Reconstruction narrative, the fable, and the sociopolitical tale. Of these three, it is the last band that has been operating implicitly as a general norm against which Reconstruction fiction has been distinguished from Southern and Negro narratives and through which the three forms of this fiction have been identified and described. Moreover, the sociopolitical will determine the specific meaning of the major Reconstruction fiction in the rest of this study. The first step, then, is a detailed analysis of sociopolitical fiction as the literary form to which the central works more correctly belong. A second related step, in the following chapters, involves the presentation of a descriptive survey of these works as both a demonstration of this concept and as a summary of the chief works in this study.

What do I mean by sociopolitical literature? Reconstruction fiction as sociopolitical literature combines both cultural sociology and political comment. The social aspects appear in the scenes, incidents, and characters that are exponents of both the class structure of Southern society and the interrelationships operating within that structure. More specifically, the social facts of Reconstruction culture—the life and manners of Freedmen, poor whites, "new rich" businessmen, Carpetbagger politicians, and Southern aristocrats—become the data through which the reader confronts the familiar (or exotic) folkways and traditions creating the peculiar patterns of behavior in Southern society. The political aspect appears in three guises. First, there is the case in which the subject matter deals specifically with the maneuvers and character of Reconstruction politicians as *dramatis personae* and as symbols. Second, the political aspect appears in the use of Reconstruction fiction as a podium for pro-Bourbon and pro-Carpetbagger propaganda and ideological commentary on the historical problems of the period. In its third guise, this fiction is concerned with political ideology as a general theory of public conduct and public action related to the specific social issues. This is the most generalized form of sociopolitical fiction.[311]

However, the defining attribute of Reconstruction fiction is the treatment of the social and the political not as separate dimensions but as interrelated forces. Such interrelationship finds a clear articulation in the major literary and thematic elements of the novels and short stories. Ideally, the plot must center on incidents that "act out" the political ideology of the author within a specific Reconstruction context; the characterization must share a like symbolism, combining "impersonated characters with fiction, and [adding] to the result some significant political [and] social moral." The setting must express in no uncertain terms the historical data of the First Reconstruction as it was evolving and not as some past event. Finally, these literary elements must combine to give in these narratives a didactic thrust, involving "a strong moral emphasis" and an "ever developing spirit of reform."[312]

Indeed, in keeping with the thematic bias of this study, the didactic thrust is much more important as an index to the basic characteristic of this form than the literary elements. It is the effect of political decisions on social traditions and the operation of these decisions as both the cause and the results of social change that form the thematic structure of sociopolitical fiction. In the Reconstruction-as-event, this structure is clear: A Northern proclamation in 1863 leads to social transformation in the South in 1865, created by passage of the Thirteenth Amendment; these changes result in the "Black Codes" of 1866 which, in turn, provoke the ratification of the 14th and 15th constitutional amendments of 1868 and 1870. Out of such social and political causation evolve the conflicts between Carpetbagger and Bourbon in the seventies. In other words, the meaning of the Reconstruction-as-event, ". . . a people defeated, a race enfranchised, and a society overthrown,"[313] is a social *and* political reality. It is this interplay between cultural and legislative forces that shapes the thematic design typical of the Reconstruction-as-literature. This thematic design relates Reconstruction literature to those tales of instruction and persuasion typical of U.S. American literature since its inception, tales that seek "to agitate, and to carry out investigation and reform of various kinds."[314]

To sum up: In terms of our three bands, Reconstruction fiction has been defined in its general and specific dimensions: as tenuous or semi-political fiction, it uses Dixie in its postwar setting as the frame for the reconciliation romance and the depiction of sectional contrast; as fable, it is quasi-historical fiction, presenting the problems of the Second Revolution behind a mask of retrospection; as sociopolitical fiction, it combines cultural sociology, history, and political comment to express a position—pro, con, or neutral—on the definitive events of the Carpetbagger-Bourbon conflict, e.g., the Ku Klux violence against an ex-slave, the problems of a Northern schoolmarm in a small Southern town, the degradation of a proud Southern family, the rise and fall of a brave Carpetbagger. These sociopolitical conflicts, central to Southern Reconstruction during the twenty years following the Civil War, are the dominant symbols in literary form of the works that the following chapters present as illustrative texts.

CHAPTER IV
THE YEARS OF WRECK

> Scarcely any age or nation presents so rich a field of romantic incident as the conflict of these forces viewed at first by the glare of battle and afterward by the fitful gleam of the embers of revolution.[315]

> As the fruit of a remarkable minuteness of observation and tenderness of feeling . . . [these novels] have a high value, especially when regarded in the light of the *voicelessness* of the conquered and reconstructed South. [The Reconstruction novelists strike] the reader as having a compassionate sense of this pathetic dumbness—having perceived that no social revolution of equal magnitude had ever reflected itself so little in literature, remained so unrecorded, so unpainted, so unsung.[316]

The general purpose of this chapter is to give an account of the key form, the sociopolitical genre, of Reconstruction fiction in terms of the aesthetic framework described in Chapter III and in terms of the thematic context described in the first two chapters. Reconstruction fiction takes an interest in the revolutionary shift in the traditional social relationship between the African and the Saxon in the Southern Garden. Growing out of and yet generating this social revolution are the political dynamics of the Reconstruction: the political conflict between the Carpetbagger and the Bourbon who, in their half-satiric names, mask those deep cultural and political divisions between the North and South subsumed under the image of the Irrepressible Conflict. This political struggle and its bloody resolution during redemption underlie the social revolution depicted in Reconstruction fiction. Consequently, this descriptive analysis is neither a source study nor an evaluation of historical accuracy, nor a biographical-critical analysis of the authors who produced this fiction. Rather, the aim is to lay before the student of U.S. American literature during the Reconstruction period in general, but from a specific point of view, the nature, meaning, and importance of these works in the American literary tradition.

The classification of Reconstruction fiction in this sociopolitical analysis is divided into three groups: anti-radical, neutral, and pro-radical fiction. The neutral writers occupy the middle ground between the extremes, resisting the temptation to espouse the ideological position of the Anti-Radicals or the Pro-Radicals. However, most of the Reconstruction writers treated in this chapter do choose sides. Such partisanship invariably distorts historical "facts," and the kinds of distortions used form a discernible pattern signaling the author's ideological allegiance:

> [The Pro-Radical] ignores the misdemeanors of Negroes: [the Anti-Radicals] exaggerate their crimes. [The former] censures the Southern gentleman as a white supremacist who is unwilling to provide the Negro . . . equality; [the latter depicts] the gentleman as a man defending a civilization [against venal] carpetbaggers. In [pro-radical] works, the Republican is the humanitarian . . . ; in the fiction of [the pro-Bourbon], he is indifferent to the best interests of the South—the good work attempted by any Republicans is almost totally ignored.[317]

These historical distortions are not absolute lies. They are imagistic analogues to that polarization of passion, attitudes, and ideology intrinsic to the Conflict. As emotionally charged images the emphasis on melodramatic simplicity, the omission of the opponent's virtues, and the misuse of generalizations give to the inferior art of Reconstruction its dramatic antitheses. Further, these images give to the reader the feeling that Reconstruction narratives are not merely ideological polemics, but hallucinatory visions as well. As in the distortions of a vision, a kind of truth is projected. The partisanship espoused by pro-Bourbon and pro-Carpetbagger fiction afford the reader flaring glimpses into the depths of the emotions permeating the clash of cultures and races "at" the U.S. American South.

In considering the Anti-Radicals, let us begin with Herman Melville. In this context, Melville is a literary curiosity. He alone among the great prewar giants left a literary record of his interest in the initial stages of Reconstruction: an anti-radical essay and some pro-Southern poetry. This handful of works illustrates the influence of the historical event on the minor art of a major artist, while foreshadowing just how small the impact of that event would be on the art of the great postwar giants.

Melville's "Supplement" to *Battle-Pieces and Aspects of the War* (1866) deals with the Civil War and Reconstruction as interrelated events within the restoration context and articulates a clear pro-Johnson point of view. Whether Melville speaks retrospectively about the war ("The Released Rebel Prisoner" and "A Grave Near Petersburg"), or contemporaneously about the congressional debates in 1866, he is a champion of reconciliation through a lenient peace.

In the Reconstruction essay, Melville attacks the Radicals' plan of reconstitution along two lines of reasoning. For him, the problem of reunion exists as a choice between two mutually exclusive alternatives: reconciliation with the white Southerner or Americanization of the black Negro. Melville advocates reconciliation at the expense of Negro rights by arguing that the Emancipation Proclamation, the initial step toward Americanization in the radicals' view, was not enacted by the collective will of the U.S. American people; it was, as has been argued by the Conservatives since 1865, merely an act of military expediency and hence of dubious constitutional legality in peacetime (even though the U.S. Supreme Court had indirectly established its legality in March of 1863). Melville implies that additional attempts to make the ex-slave a citizen would create a similar legal dubiety. But his main objection to Americanization is to the penalties it would entail for the ex-rebels:

> In our natural solicitude to confirm the benefit of liberty to the blacks, let us forebear from measures of dubious constitutional rightfulness toward our white countrymen—measures of a nature to provoke, among other of the last evils, exterminating hatred of race toward race.[318]

Melville's Johnsonian view of restoration finds clear expression in "Lee in the Capitol," a polemic poem recounting General Lee's appearance before the

Congressional Committee on Reconstruction to 1866.[319] Speaking through the hero of the Virginia uprising, Melville calls for a reconstruction that will, in a sense, implement the mood of Lincoln's final inaugural: "Push not your triumph; do not urge/Submissiveness beyond the verge." Such a magnanimous gesture becomes a practical one, since the South is willing to return to the Union, though with pride intact: "You ask if she recants: she yields./ Nay, and would more, would blend anew."[320]

If, on the other hand, the more rigorous policy of the Radical Republicans is adopted, then the bitterness and passion of secession, war, and defeat will continue to plague the new Union:

> Intestine rancor would you bide
> Nursing eleven sliding daggers in your side?
>
> Shall the North go Sylla's way?
> Proscribe? prolong the evil day?
>
> Confirm the curse? Infix the hate?
> In Union's name forever alienate?[321]

Melville's essay and poem are quite pedestrian as art, but they have a more important value. They record his aesthetic response to the Reconstruction-as-event and as such are a rare glimpse of the effect of this event on the conscience and sensibility of a great U.S. American writer.

The discussion of Melville is merely an interesting prologue; this descriptive analysis begins in earnest with John W. De Forest's "The Colored Member" (1872). De Forest's narrative is a satiric attack on Carpetbag rule in South Carolina, the place in anti-radical mythos of the utter gracelessness, opportunism, and corruption of Southern Radicalism.[322]

On the first level, this semi-picaresque tale revolves around Pompey Howard, a Freedman legislator, and his adventures among the Radicals. One follows him through the labyrinth of South Carolina misrule to high repute among his fellow Republicans as a pliable fool. But all ends in disaster. When he demands more than five dollars for his vote on a fraudulent bill, he is summarily disqualified from office. He returns to his village, Alligatorsville, sadder but wiser in the ways of Carpetbag politics.

On a second level, this narrative is an allegory of Republican corruption. The corrupter is a Carpetbagger, Jack Hunt, and Pompey his ignorant dupe.

De Forest shows Hunt as the representative Yankee Radical: arrogant, opportunistic, malignant, a "slimy and impudent scoundrel" with a wheedling voice, "fat and warm to sickishness, like machine grease." His interest in the Freedmen springs solely from political expediency and the need to exploit their votes for political and financial power. His relationship with Pompey has all the integrity of a grafting, "jolly policeman in communing with a pickpocket." Moreover, while he corrupts his Pompeys through a variety of legislative frauds, the graft goes primarily in his direction, as his pawns receive only crumbs.[323] Thus, while the story is ostensibly about the colored member, it is more clearly an assault on the white Carpetbagger. The climax of this satiric attack is the radicals' ball at the Governor's mansion:

> It's a free lunch for all, white, and colored, and semi-colored, and demi-semi-colored; and all you've got to do is just what you want to do; eat, drink, smoke, and be sweet on the ladies. The Governor pays and the secret service fund pays the Governor, and everybody that votes is welcome to all he can use.[324]

The ball becomes a compendium of all the sociopolitical offensiveness attributed to Carpetbagger misrule in anti-radical polemic: the back parlor wheeling-and-dealing, the selling of votes over champagne, the gullibility of Freedmen who surrender the Fifteenth Amendment for a mess of pottage, the utter crudity and vulgarity of plebeian legislators. De Forest exploits this last element with gusto and seems to hint at a contrast between this rabble and the patrician charm and grace of the offstage Bourbons. A Scalawag spills food and drink on the floor; a black Radical stretches "at full-length along a sofa, with his boots on the silk damask"[325]; legislators fight over cream-dessert and chicken. In a word, such swinishness becomes for De Forest the synecdoche for radical power at the South:

> Honorable gentleman ladled up jellies and raked in cakes . . . as if they were spading rice-swamp mud. . . . Saucers of floating-island struggled to and fro in the air, their contents slopping over heads and coat-collars and coat tails and into sleeves. . . . One white dignitary had just filled a plate with luxuries for his wife when a dusky hand . . . removed it from his wondering sight. . . . Pompey . . . smashed two plates and a goblet in the process of devouring a peck of goodies and drinking. . . champagne.[326]

Worst of all is the ostensible social intimacy between the races. De Forest here used a typical anti-radical gambit. If he cannot shock the Northern reader with his descriptions of political misdeeds and official vulgarity, he will play upon their racio-sexual fears, relating political corruption intimately with the threat of "miscegenation." He describes Negro ladies flirting with white gentlemen and white ladies entertaining black gentlemen.[327] The white wife of the white Speaker of the House is shown turning her charms on Pompey to secure votes for her husband's reelection to that position: "So for half-a-minute, Pompey Howard promenaded among the stars with the white kid gloves of a goddess of fashion just touching the sleeve of his slop-shop coat." However, this interracial gathering is only apparently egalitarian. De Forest depicts drunken Negroes being dumped by the Governor's butlers "at a distance, as if they were so many loads of garbage."[328]

In this scene, then, De Forrest used this Reconstruction ball as the operating metaphor for the Radical's corrupting activity at the South: the railroad speculation, the watered stock, the graft, the interracial licentiousness, the hypocrisy of Negro enfranchisements, the utter gracelessness of Carpetbag rule.

If De Forest had been content merely to present what were, despite the exaggerations, the facts of much a Governor Moses' brief reign, his work would have been a distorted but powerful attack on Carpetbaggery. But his attack goes beyond such limits: He includes in his diatribe a vicious stream of racist rhetoric, which is quite surprising coming from a former Union officer.

The doctrine of the inherent inferiority of the Negro, that key theme in all anti-radical fiction, forms the ideological center of De Forest's attack on the Freedman and, by analogy, the Carpetbagger. De Forest's major point is the familiar assertion of the pro-slavery apologists: the genetic non-humanity of the Negro. He presents the Freedman's African physique—the flat forehead, the thick lips, the wooly hair, the big nose—as signs not of a different race of men but of a different kind of creature. And he underscores this view with his continual use of bestial imagery to describe the ex-slave, especially those stock caricatures related to the primate. (It is no comic accident that Pompey Howard's village is called Alligatorsville.) Through direct description and metaphoric indirection, the Freedmen emerges in De Forest's rhetoric as the "living creature," the animated technology of pro-slavery anthropology.[329]

He then parallels these physical defects with the Freedman's cultural ones: "Pompey Howard was descended from men . . . who had for two hundred years been slaves; he was further descended from men . . . who, for thousands of years had been slaves, savages, idolators, and cannibals on their own native soils." Even the gift of language was new to them. Thus, the U.S. American Freedman had inherited all the cultural-psychological vices of his barbarous forebears: "subjugation, servility, poltroonery, helplessness and ridiculousness."[330]

It is these genetic disabilities that form the basis of three implicit objections to the ex-slave as a sociopolitical person: The Negroes contributed nothing to the saving of the Union, yet were given political power; the ex-slaves were totally inexperienced in the rudiments of social behavior, yet were given equality with the elite of Southern Saxondom; finally, they were uncivilized and could not be made civilized, yet were gratuitously made citizens. And while De Forest does not explicitly propound these anti-radical doctrines, they are nevertheless relevant derivatives from his ideas.

Such distortions represent a surprising contrast to the attitude articulated by Dr. Ravenel. However, there are several possible explanations for this change. De Forest, like most of the pro-Bourbon Northern writers, had mixed feelings toward Reconstruction. While he accepted the necessity of preventing future rebellions, he did not accept Radical Reconstruction as the best method. In *A Union Officer*, there can be seen rather clearly his objection to the elevation of uncivilized Negroes to citizenship at the expense of moderates among the ex-Confederate patrician class. Further, his personal relationship with South Carolina patricians before the war and during (and after) his Bureau days were quite cordial. Moreover, the operation of black politics between 1869-1872 in Louisiana and South Carolina (at least under Governor Moses' reign) must have appalled De Forest's conservative nature. Finally, De Forest had by 1872, symbolically speaking, gone over to the political position of the Colbournes and the Knoxes, the future masters of the Republican Party. He had become the spokesman for their disenchantment with the process of Americanization as practiced by the Jack Hunts and the Pompey Howards; he thus codifies in fictional form the various fantasies about the Negro (and his white comrade), which this disenchantment had engendered. Five years later these fantasies would help to justify the abandonment of the Southern Radicals by key leaders of the Republican Party.[331]

By 1872, the tenuous anti-Radicalism of De Forest's Freedman Bureau days had become, in terms of this short story, a savage antipathy. And, for the sake of this antipathy, he abandoned the honest realism of his earlier Reconstruction literature for the distortions of a crude burlesque.[332]

The second work, William Baker's serialized novel, *Mose Evans* (1874), while anti-radical in tone and implications, makes none of the explicit attacks on the Carpetbaggers found in De Forest. Being a Southerner, Baker could little afford to offend the *Atlantic* or its readership in 1874 with the kind of diatribes found in Northern pro-Bourbon prose. However, his biases are clear: He is against slavery since it has been outlawed, but not for Americanization; he counsels endurance of Reconstruction as a fact of life, but articulates the bitterness against it; he is, finally, not so much anti-Carpetbagger as pro-Bourbon. This can be seen in his treatment of General Throop and his family, South Carolina nobles in exile in Mississippi. They are presented as the incarnation of Southern aristocratic *élan*, a force expressed in their defeat not in the objective symbols of power but "in certain inflections of voice, the heritage in the blood for generations," an *élan* whose roots lie in the Golden Age of Southern nobility: the post-revolutionary epoch of Washington, Jefferson, Patrick Henry, and the first Lee. Despite defeat, such a class remains heroic and still superior to the best of Northern society. For though the Bourbon is "behind the times . . . absurd in his exasperation at the new era, intensely prejudiced," he is nevertheless the proud remnant of the Republic's aristocracy of '76, an eagle among carrion-eating predators (to use Baker's terms). It is as a picture of the agonizing pressures of the new era on such a class that the Throop narrative acts as a secondary plot.[333]

The central plot deals with the love affair between Mose Evans, a young backwoods Mississippi planter, and Agnes Throop. The Reconstruction elements framing this plot are somewhat muted, though not quite as fully as in semi-Reconstruction fiction. The Freedman as a character is present, but as a political force he is primarily offstage. He appears in three forms: the recalcitrant fieldhand, the wanton concubine, and that cliché of anti-radical fiction, the Voluntary Slave, who conceives of the Abolitionist-Radical as "the vilest and most venomous of mankind" and who remains chattel out of religious conviction.[334] The Carpetbagger appears in the novelette primarily as the economic entrepreneur. His primary function is to admire the Bourbon and to buy out his old plantation (thereby giving him enough money to recreate his aristocratic splendor in the midst of a Mississippi wilderness). Through his power as the carrier of the "magic carpetbag," he transforms the heroine.

In the beginning Agnes Throop is to be the sacrifice that General Throop and his wife will lay on the altar of the Lost Cause. It is symbolized by a dead son, for whose sake she is called upon to make up for "the whole world they had forever lost . . . ." Agnes fulfills this role as a grieving, nostalgia-ridden fire-eater. However, when the Throops waste away under the pressures of the New Era, the Carpetbagger intervenes. Through a variety of complications, he converts her into a healthy-minded, Northernized woman who eventually becomes Moses' wife, thereby making up for the Throops' lost world. Besides fulfilling these various functions, the Carpetbagger narrates the story.

It is clear from this description that the political issues of the epoch are not emphasized; what Baker is primarily interested in is the social dimension. The work depicts the pathetic anguish of defeated, unreconstructed rebels; their futile memories of prewar power; and their paralysis of morale in the new era, a paralysis that Baker describes as ". . . the inertia of two hundred years of position and power!" In contrast to their spiritual lassitude are the vigor and enterprise of a new aristocracy, represented by Evans, which has developed under the Second Revolution. Thus, Baker acknowledges the positive effects of the Reconstruction; nevertheless, he hopes that the innovations of radical rule (as well as the radicalism itself) will pass away in the course of time. Till then, stoic endurance is the best mode for the old Bourbon, as action and enterprise are the best for the young.[335]

The setting of the story is the most interesting feature of Baker's concern with class and class-types under Reconstruction. In a sense the key scenes are merely a series of anecdotes dealing with the lives of the inhabitants of Browntown, a settlement of partially civilized types in the wilds of Mississippi and the place of exile for the chief Bourbon family in the tale. It is here that Mose meets his well-beloved. Browntown's isolation from the seats of radical power protects it from the full weight of Carpetbag rule. Except for the presence of Freedmen, the village is almost a replica of antebellum life. Here is presented a variety of Southern-frontier incidents—shootings, poor-white church services, a sacrilegious communion, and blatant racio-sexuality.

Baker handles this last topic only as a brief allusion, but in the context of Interracial Symbiosis it has more symbolic weight. On the one hand, the Bourbon "instinctively invested his white women with certain chivalric attributes of sister, daughter, wife, mother. . . ."[336] On the other hand, he invested his black women with earthier attributes that often made them powers in the Southern households:

> The flaunting concubines of the [landlord's] seraglio, black, yellow, ash-colored, were in and out of the room . . . with that peculiar impudence of manners which we would think a woman would shrink . . . from showing toward a wife . . . ! [The concubines] sent scorn and defiance to [the wife's] ears . . . in their shrill songs for the washtub . . . — songs offensively religious.[337]

The result in the physical health of the supposed mistress of the household was "pallor and emaciation [,] but I dare not say a syllable here as to the effect upon a Southern wife or a Negro concubine. . . ."[338] Since "Mose Evans" is a redundant celebration of Bourbon magnificence, the inclusion of the Liliths seems a contradictory gesture. However, Baker avoids this problem by making the Cult of Racio-sexuality a part of the frontier vices of Browntown and not a part of the more patrician world of the Throops.

In the main, the Browntown setting is a frame for Southern portraiture. Here is found a variety of exotic character-types. There is old New Hampshire, an antebellum economic Carpetbagger. There is also Archer, a St. Elmo figure, committed from childhood to a life of exhausting sensuality through the influence of Negro lasciviousness. Baker is rather blunt in describing this influence: "Sparks which should have slept in the soul for ten years longer, blown by the lips of our Negroes into consuming fires—poor, miserable, utterly helpless child!"[339] He later becomes a pious minister through the influence of Agnes Throop. Another character is Squire Robinson, the Bourbon as crude yeoman. And, of course, Mose Evans, the Bourbon in a state of natural virtues.

Baker describes these coloristic elements within a context of both the direct and indirect influence of Reconstruction. Therefore, on the archetypal level, Browntown becomes the incarnation of the South in its profane, anarchic state, unchanging and resistant to the power of the invisible but all-powerful Carpetbaggers. In the end, as in the semi-Reconstruction novel, these sociopolitical elements, clustering around descriptions of local color phenomena and the influence of reconstitution on Carolina aristocrats, disappear as the work becomes more and more sentimental.

Radical defeat in 1877 removed all obstacles to a full-scale attack on the Carpetbagger and his sociopolitical creations. In the chronological sequence of this analysis, a Northern writer leads the way and is followed by a Southerner, William Baker, who continues the criticisms set forth tentatively in "Mose Evans" and, more explicitly, in "Little Miss Mouse and Her Marvelous Scholar" (1878) and in *Colonel Dunwoddie, Millionaire* (1878). That "Little Miss Mouse" could have appeared in a formerly pro-radical organ like *Harper's New Monthly Magazine* reveals the changes wrought in the Republican establishment by the events of '76 and '77.

Baker's short story typically attacks the Carpetbaggers through their most important creation, the Freedmen. The ideology of the work is not precisely stated but it seems to have the following familiar outline. The essential force underlying radical power in the South was the ex-slaves. The essential doctrine governing the Carpetbaggers' alliance with their inferiors was not only their opportunism, but also their mistaken belief in the possibility that the ex-slave could be made into a full, co-equal partner through education and political rights. Against these assumptions, Baker poses the anti-radical thesis of genetic disability, assaulting head-on the belief in the educability of the Freedman. To give his refutation a more ironic edge, Baker develops his story as if it were a pro-radical tale.

Baker's heroine seems to be a Yankee schoolmarm teaching Freedmen in an antagonistic South Carolina community.[340] The narrative describes Miss Mouse's struggle to survive the passive hostility of her neighbors, on the one hand, and the attempts, on the other, of a Yankee-phobe—Tom Terrell—to dispossess her of her school.

Baker spells out rather sympathetically Miss Mouse's isolation from those social amenities and acts of neighborliness that sustained the Victorian woman in the small U.S. American communities. To invite her to dinner would be like "asking a negro to the table! Horror! Who knows but the visitor actually ate with negroes?" To be kind to her would be like offering comfort to Yankee invaders. When, in a moment of unendurable helplessness, Mouse goes to a neighbor, Mrs. Dunwoddie (the wife of the millionaire), for aid, she is refused, despite Mrs. Dunwoddie's sympathetic recognition of her plight: as "if [Miss Mouse] were fathoms deep under the sea, the atmosphere of [Mrs. Dunwoddie's] region stifled her. . . ."[341] Thus, Miss Mouse, like Mollie Ainslie in a later work, must bear alone the full antagonism of a community that hates her as a nigger-lover, a Carpetbagger, and a Northerner.

Baker also depicts with apparent compassion her brave struggle to transform her pupils into the radical ideal, appropriating the tropes that the pro-radical nonfictionists used to describe the Freedman school. One is shown first the difficulties of educating black rascals "who would lie and steal, [and] little yellow girls who would laugh and not learn,"[342] and then the triumph found in the attainment of just one dedicated student. This is Marcellus, Mouse's marvelous scholar, whom she sees as a future Numa of his people. Marcellus clearly stands for all the virtues of Freedman education espoused in pro-radical fiction and nonfiction: the enthusiasm, the facility, the diligence, and the progress.

Baker does an excellent job of masking his Anti-Radicalism in Tourgéan prose. But at the climax of the story, he unleashes a series of surprises via the conversion technique that reveal his true colors. Typically, Yankee and Southern unite: in this case, Terrell and Miss Mouse. Terrell even confesses that his antagonism against her was solely because of her birthplace and not because of her nigger school-teaching. But surprisingly, it is discovered that Miss Mouse is not a New Englander but a Southern Belle reduced by the circumstances of defeat and Reconstruction to a choice of begging or teaching Freedmen. Moreover, one learns that her devotion to her Negroes is not as noble as it had seemed. She had all along regarded them as a superior kind of vermin, to use Baker's term, with which she whiled away her "prison-hours" (though she did believe she could help an exceptional student like Marcellus). Finally, the motivation for her valiant struggle against the sentiments of the community lay solely in her Southern pride and stubbornness and not in any idealistic commitment.[343]

But most important of the central theme of the story, the theme of genetic disability, is the evolution in Marcellus:

> But Marcellus was a failure . . . Alas! Miss Mouse was not the only instructor [of Negroes] doomed to sad disappointment. . . . After a certain point he degenerated from mental arithmetic in a manner frightful to see. . . . Marcellus could no more help it than if he had been drifting down toward Niagara. Nature must have laughed in doing it, but it was nature. . . . In the end the smart boy utterly disappeared, swallowed up in a phenomenal way in the big and stupid field hand.[344]

Thus perished Mouse's Numa. If this happens to the best, what of the average? Education, like political rights and citizenship, Baker is saying, is a useless force against the granite bedrock of inherent inferiority. "Little Miss Mouse and Her Marvelous Scholar" would be but one of the myriad works of fiction in the post-1877 era denouncing the Americanization amendments under the guise of a spurious, racist, genetic anthropology.

Such attacks on the Freedmen augmented during the reconciliation phase, reflecting their change of status in some Northern eyes. In a cultural sense, they were the sacrificial scapegoat for the failures of Republican Reconstruction; they were the scapegoat necessary to bless the reconciliation between Southern and Northern Conservatives. This is a possible explanation for the crude sketches of irremediable savagery in S. A. Shields' work, "Sambo: A Man and Brother" (1878).

In this hypothesis, the function of these rather third-rate sketches (recounted by one "Cap'n S," a De Forest-type, ex-Bureau officer) is to discredit the Negro as a political ally by discrediting him as a person, thereby justifying to wavering Northerners the necessity of his abandonment by the Republican party. To do this, Shields seeks to counter the moral-emotional vision of the Freedman as the North's special responsibility. In terms of this study, the literary origins of the vision lie in the fiction, reports, and journalistic essays of sympathetic Northern observers during restoration. It was they who emphasized the North's responsibility to the Freedman, who depicted the Freedman as the pro-Republican loyalist in the defeated Confederacy and who warned the Northern Republicans that because of this loyalty (and their race, regardless of color) the ex-slaves were in danger of being re-enslaved—unless the Union intervened. From this complex vision, to put it in a simplified way, came part of the idealistic thrust that sustained and motivated reconstitution policy *vis-à-vis* the Negro in the late sixties. Shields seeks to destroy this vision by returning to the restoration period and restructuring the images generated then. In 1866, to simplify again, the Freedman was the representative of a New Southern Unionism; in 1878, Shields describes him during the same period as the representative of a savage primitivism.

To disabuse his fellow Northerners of the sentimental illusion that the Freedman was human and, therefore, could change his condition if given Northern help, "Cap'n S," aka Cap, demonstrates that the Reids and Andrews were in error in their assessment of Negro character, primarily because they were only passing through: ". . . the romance and sentiment of negroism dissolves" when one has lived "amongst them for a time." Cap implies in the shaping of his sketches and the movement of his ideas that those who *did* know the ex-African at first hand (the Southron and the realistic Yankee) could have foreseen the crudities of black rule in the seventies evolving inevitably from the savagery of black primitives in the sixties. Moreover, where Reid and Andrews recount cases of cruelty and violence during and after slavery, Cap indicates that these were rare exceptions. Where Reid describes enterprising ex-slaves supporting both themselves and old Marse, or old retainers being evicted by vengeful masters, Cap shows the Freedmen to be improvident thieves whom ex-masters do not have the heart to turn out. In a word, he espouses that other vision of the restoration phase: the Freedman's shiftless dependence on the Bureau, the breakdown in the discipline created by slavery, the varied social failures, the anguish and suffering of freedom. In place of the piety, courage, and family affection depicted in restoration nonfiction, Cap shows a phantasmagoria of ridiculous bestiality. When a white employer tells a Freedwoman to get rid of her children if she wants to work for him, she literally complies: "I jes' waited till day was asleep, and 'cut their throats. Dey nebber screeched."[345]

The work, then, is obviously another variant on the theme of genetic disability. Yet for a Ravenel, even such a work can be seen, in reality, as a depiction of *environmental disability*, an unintentional description of the extent to which the ex-slaves' vices resulted from the sociopsychological corruption of slave-labor capitalism. This fact becomes even clearer when "S" admits, almost as an afterthought, that his observations are based only on Negroes from the interior plantations,[346] which in Revisionist lore were as conducive to the development of the higher instincts as a fascist labor camp. Revisionists would further argue that many of Cap's criticisms evolve from an absurd sentimentalism. Like Colbourne in *Ravenel* and Knox in *Verdict*, he, too, is disillusioned that the mere gift of emancipation has not automatically created black Anglo-Saxons.

Shields' minor story, then, is contradictory and distorted; nevertheless, it is in itself an accurate reflection in miniature of a political economic process developing in the North to discredit the Carpetbaggers, testifying to the resurgence of a type of moral isolationism *vis-à-vis* supporting any more

Federal intervention in Dixie. Shields' tale is, like all pro-Bourbon Northern fiction after 1876, an apology to the Southrons for the intervention on behalf of the Negro.[347] And that the First Reconstruction was enacted solely for the Negro would be one of the enduring historical distortions of the period.

A more significant example of anti-radical fiction is *Colonel Dunwoddie, Millionaire* (1878). The work deals with that other distortion: the reiterated assertion that reconstitution was instigated solely for the benefit of Carpetbaggery.[348] Baker's novel (published anonymously) deals with the theme of carpetbag knavery within a mosaic of images typical of the sociopolitical form: political rallies; violent denunciation of Bourbons and Radicals; political terrorism that includes barn and church burnings, vigilantism, and brutal floggings; and recurring specific allusions to the political misdemeanors in an unspecified locale in the South (it seems to be South Carolina).

The unifying image in all this is the corrupting Carpetbagger. The novel develops this image along three lines of narration. There is first the story of a Bourbon family, the Dunwoddies and their personal defeats and sudden rise to fortune during Reconstruction through the power of the magic carpetbag. In this line of action, Baker sets forth his fullest analysis of the Bourbon in the new era. He depicts the scenes of the Bourbon's desolation, not only as physical ruins, but as a psychological shattering:

> It is not merely that people who were accustomed to wealth have lost everything, but that with everything else, . . . they have lost ... their faculty of hoping. The strain upon them during the war; the sudden shock with which it ended; the breaking-up of the whole system of *labor*, the death or maiming of the men—a thousand things made it impossible for them to go to work all at once.[349]

However, the most maddening aspect of the Reconstruction is the painful circumstances of the Belle, the metaphor for the agony of the Southern planter-class:

> She had been born to social pre-eminence, to great wealth, to be petted at home and admired abroad, to be waited upon by multitudes of people who seemed to be, in all social senses, at least, as much her slaves as those who worked in her father's fields.[350]

Now, Southern ladies are left open to all contingency in a "howling wilderness of free negroes and insolent poor whites, their income exposed and uncertain . . . ," unfitted "by their training, as well as by the climate, for work, even if they knew what to do."[351] Alice Dunwoddie, the Colonel's saintly wife, becomes the chief symbol of this psychological agony:

> Then, being all alone, she leaned her head weeping upon the edge of the table at which she sat until her tears had ceased to flow. It was the darkest hour of her life. Her tired heart was beating in her as if against the future, and as if that future was a darkness so dark as to be felt. She never forgot the past; to her it was but a little less vivid than the present. As to the future, it was to her as a stone wall; the utmost she could do was to lie prostrate at its base, she was so tired, tried.[352]

Then Baker presents the power and resiliency of this class as it battles against adversity, sustained only by its aristocratic *élan*:

> I often think of the followers of the Stuarts, and there was something sturdy in their detestation of their Hanover conquerors at the time for generations afterwards. [Then Colonel Dunwoddie compares the Stuarts to the Southern Bourbons.] We were shamefully wronged before, during, and worse, than all, since the war. Others may plunge into the petty bitterness of the moment, but . . . I won't![353]

While the older Southrons survive mainly as stoic heroes, their progeny are profoundly affected for the better by the New Era. Emmeline Anderson, one of the heroines, is transformed into a wiser, more developed, stronger person. Horace Dunwoddie, her lover, is the new Southron, coming of age under Reconstruction, saturated with the ethics and principles of his parents, Alice and the Colonel, and prepared to possess the new time as the future of the South.[354] Therefore, whether old or new, the Bourbon becomes in Baker's hands, despite the defeats of 1865 and 1868, the ultimate victor in the Reconstruction struggle, both sectionally and nationally:

> We influenced the country, notwithstanding the heat, up to the war. If it had not been for a mere handful of weak and

> wicked men, North and South, . . . we would have done so still, and had no war. We were overpowered by your numbers then, less than we were by the weakness of a few of our own leaders. Our day is coming again.[355]

The force allowing the Dunwoddies to have their own "day" is the magic carpetbag, created by complicated plot coincidences by the economic Carpetbagger. The patricians become millionaires, now able to make up with financial power what is lacking in political power (although the new millions also bring sorrow and painful complications). It is with the new wealth that Colonel Dunwoddie comes to the fore as the archetypal Bourbon. He uses his new power in futile attempts to alleviate the sufferings of his fellow aristocrats and to mediate in the battles between the pro-Bourbon and pro-Carpetbagger terrorists. All the while, however, he remains relatively aloof from the political warfare: "I hated politics before the war, and I abhor them [*sic*] tenfold since. I cannot . . . go with one party, and I cannot go to the extremes of the other."[356] Nevertheless, he defends anti-radical terrorists and condemns the radical tyranny which, for him, generates the violence.

Dunwoddie's political philosophy of Reconstruction, presented in two speeches, is a rather surprising call for a "New South" attitude (surprising, that is, considering Baker's peculiar antipathies). Dunwoddie assumes a sectional and racial interdependency: If South Carolina is in trouble, Pennsylvania will suffer:

> . . . if the meanest negro, Yellow Jessamine say, is wronged, or left to his ignorance and wickedness, which is the same thing, every man in the county, the state, the South, the country, is more or less injured thereby.[357]

And while defending the Cavalier vision of the old Union, including the beneficence of slavery, Dunwoddie nevertheless attacks the irreconcilables' absurd attempt "to live in a dead past . . . !"[358] However, he saves his most savage diatribes for the Reconstruction politicians on both sides, though with emphasis on Carpetbagger villainy:

> In every place . . . there are dangerous classes—wretches who are the scum and refuse, the offal and excrement, of society, the ruffianism and disgrace of humanity. Do not we have

> them also? We have our Hiddikel Queasy. . . . They are not natives to our soil. Locusts they are, which come from the hand of offended Heaven to devour, during their brief moment, and then depart. Very soon will they fly before the vengeance of the people they have plundered; but shall *we* escape who sin and remain? Because a man is born here; because he adds to the infernal fires of alcohol the fury of an insane patriotism, shall he escape?[359]

Dunwoddie climaxes his key speech with an impassioned plea for reconciliation, but on Southern terms:

> And shall this our glorious South be forever given over to lag in the rear of the land . . . the helpless victim of the unjust rule of the North and the apathy or passion of its own children as well? . . . Only give us time, and we will prove to you what we are! . . . there is a war here . . . upon ignorance and passion . . . and lawlessness. . . . *War* upon these by all true men of the South, and God—God—![360]

Dunwoddie's speech ends with a stroke and eventual death. Thus, in a sense, the Colonel as Bourbon hero is a martyr to that New South to be born, in his eyes once the Radical tyranny is overthrown.

But despite Dunwoddie's espousal of a New South rhetoric, his roots, and hence his adaptation to the new era, is generated by an ethics and a cultural reality originating in the Old South. The ethics evolves from the chivalric rules of the Cavalier code:

> . . . but always be southern. . . . Don't make money your chief object. Never lie, cheat, or steal, when you are in Congress. Never be mean. Be energetic, but be honorable. Never let your honor be suspected, as when . . . any indebtedness is concerned. Treat women with all deference, but detest strong-minded females. Be a gentleman, Horace—a gentleman.[361]

These rules evolve from the historical myths and facts of the Southron's lifestyle:

> When I was in the North . . . people . . . ridiculed [my father's class]. And yet, does not that class embrace Washington, as well

> as John Randolph . . . ? Was it not the highest flower of the time? An order in fact, of nobility—and of nobility in the truest sense of the word? People laugh at the defects [of the Southron] . . . when every paper they read is filled with the rascality of men in politics and business. . . . I prefer the old ideas of gentlemen, if it is perishing from the earth, to the new.[362]

And, of course, both Cavalier ethics and cultural nobility were created by slavery: "What an influence it has on these people—the very tradition of having owned slaves—it's in the blood." Because of such influences, the wealth that corrupts the Carpetbaggers in the story merely frees the poetic, intelligent powers of the Southern.[363]

Therefore, in Baker's hands, the Bourbon emerges as the superior character. His aristocratic vision becomes the mainstay against radical progress and revolutionary change. And, acting as the very essence of the conservative temperament, such a vision becomes transformed from reactionary negativism into ethical and cultural pressure on sociopolitical excess.

The Dunwoddie narrative ends sadly and happily. The Colonel and his wife die, Horace and Emmeline marry and, with his younger sisters and brothers (save one), they go away to Europe.

The second narrative line deals with the fortunes and misfortunes of the black Bourbon, Anderson Parker, and his conflict with the Radicals, especially one Yellow Jessamine. The third line features the Carpetbagger Middleton, and his schemes to capture the Dunwoddie fortune. The unifying element between these three lines is the corrupting influence of the Yankee ex-patriate.

The vilification of the Carpetbagger follows the ideological stance first appearing in terms of this descriptive analysis in "The Colored Member" and continuing beyond Reconstruction in *Red Rock*, *Gabriel Tolliver*, and *The Klansman*. But what is particularly interesting in Baker's work is his timing. The virulence of his attacks disregards Republican sensibility at a time when the spirit of reconciliation was strong in the land. He insults men who, despite the defeat of 1877, still retained some influence in the national party as representatives of its Southern wing. Moreover, he denounces them not only as corrupt politicians, but also as Northerners. This latter point distinguishes Baker clearly from the other reconciliationist-minded anti-radical writers.

The Yankees are represented by three stereotypes. First, there is Clara Middleton, the Northern female as "Carpetbaggage"; trivial, artificial, and sensual, she is the showy, strong-minded, decadent mature woman contrasted to the chaste Southern Maiden.[364]

Second, there is Hiddikel Queasy, the physical, moral, and political archetype of Carpetbagger caricatures. With such a name, Queasy cannot help but be a knave. Indeed, his name and character are "acted out" in a grotesque physique combining in one person poor-white scum and Yankee devil as a metaphor for the ugliness of radical rule:

> He was a stoop-shouldered, thin-visaged, lank, lean specimen of the Yankee, when, North as well as South, the name is used as curse, his outer man corresponding closely to the typical Brother Jonathan as . . . portrayed in caricatures . . . except . . . he was homelier, meaner, more cowering in appearance. Pitted with small-pox . . . the lower part of his face was disfigured by a scanty beard of reddish hue. . . . [His] eyes were singularly small of a watery blue, and set close together under a low forehead. His complexion was cadaverous, and there was a slimy writhe of . . . thin lips. . . . Underneath the film of his propitiatory demeanor there was a nature evidently as cold as it was stony . . . [He] was the most powerful man in the region. . . . He had been in the employ of the Federal Government immediately after the war; had gone from that, by negro votes, to the legislature. There he had been made Speaker of the House, and was known to be aspiring still higher. He knew every negro in the county; and there was not a secret league among the freedmen which he had not originated; not a document circulating among them which did not come through his hand. . . . [He] plundered as rapidly and as largely as possible, like a man rifling the dead on the night following a battle, knowing that his opportunity was short, and that it was his last for a lifetime.[365]

As the radical leader, Hiddikel leads a lynch-raid against Anderson Parker, works in cahoots with the perfidious Middleton, and is an ally with Yellow Jessamine, the Negro villain in the work. In Hiddikel Queasy, one finds the fullest depiction in anti-radical fiction of the political Carpetbagger as an evil force.

Baker saves his intensest scorn for Clara's brother, the symbol of Northern culture in all its vulgar dimensions. He is "a superior sort of Hiddekel Queasy," made more subtle by urbane vices and sophisticated degradations. Middleton is the typical Yankee in his versatility in all the professions. He has been a teacher, lawyer, solicitor, actor, medium, preacher, Negro minstrel—and murderer. His background contrasts to patrician genealogy: his father, "if he is my father, is a broken-down billiard-saloon keeper[,]" his mother "eloped with a negro minstrel." And his spiritual and mental life contains "a shade of blackness so much beyond that of printer's ink that it cannot well be used in these pages."[366] As the symbol of the North, Middleton reflects the inhuman urbanity and crude materialism of Northern cities:

> The shop windows, the rattle and crush of vehicles along the streets, the lines of granite buildings, the piles of merchandise . . . the throngs of people . . . the slighted streets, the gorgeous theatres, the very policemen with their stars and clubs. . . .[367]

His fancy clothes, energetic bearing, white handkerchief, ostentatious diamond ring, and cologne exude the vulgar power of the Yankee entrepreneur. And in his attempt to convince the Dunwoddie's to invest in his schemes, he becomes in their eyes the articulation of Northern swinishness, to use Baker's term: ". . . your millins [*sic*] keeps turning itself over . . . under your feet like the globe. Not making any noise, without any help from you, while you are eating and sleeping." And the fruits of such processes are trips to Europe, famous paintings, "diamonds, yachts, fast horses, fine houses!"[368] Therefore, through Middleton as the Carpetbagger, Northern vulgarity is juxtaposed against Southern nobility.

This contrast is given further heightening in the competition between Middleton and Horace Dunwoddie, Carpetbagger and Bourbon, respectively, for the hand of Emmeline Anderson (the South). In the scene in which Middleton offers himself as a suitor, Baker gives the contrast satiric heightening:

> [There] was something in the coming of [Horace Dunwoddie] like the rushing of air into a heated room. . . .—it was the advent of nature, and who could oppose that? In spite of himself, Middleton felt as if he were a ragged tramp in the act of stealing something, and here was the owner down upon him in the very deed.[369]

In the beginning, Middleton seems to be that good Yankee relieved of the general curse: the economic Carpetbagger of semi-Reconstruction fiction who comes with the magic bag and reconciliationist goodwill to an impoverished Southern town to transform it into a bustling community—with the suddenness of nitroglycerine (to use Baker's term).[370] But he soon becomes involved in political and economic scheming. For the Baker of *Colonel Dunwoddie, Millionaire*, the Carpetbagger as investor or politician is an opportunist and the natural enemy of the Bourbon's way of life. This is shown more especially in Middleton's relationship with the Freedmen.

Like Queasy, he has an ambivalent relationship to the ex-slaves. On the one hand, he needs their support to gain political help for his economic plans; on the other, he is willing to assent to their subjugation if thereby he can win Bourbon support. For example, a key scene in the work is the lynching of an Afro-Saxon Radical for the murder and what seems to be the rape of two white women.[371] Middleton's *apologi*a for lynching is supposed to reflect the hypocrisy in his political idealism and in his relationship with the ex-slaves and perhaps hint at his own Negrophobia:

> "'Outside the South they think it is horrible,' Middleton remarked at last, 'to lynch even as atrocious a wretch as that mulatto. They want the law to take its course. The law! When lawyers are well paid, and the natural horror has had time to cool, if the worst criminal does not escape conviction, his sentence is almost always for less than his desert. . . . You people are right!'"[372]

Thus, in all three guises—as Yankee Lady, as political power, as economic symbol—the Northerner appears in the novel as the ugly antithesis to Southern ethics and culture.

The Freedman, as the creation of the North, appears both as villain and, interestingly enough, as hero in Baker's novel. In doing this, Baker divides the ex-slaves into two races: the Afro-Saxons (the creatures of the Queasys and the Middletons) and the Africans, the Voluntary Slaves of the anti-radical fantasies. And against the former Baker levels the same hostility used against the Carpetbagger.

Baker's attack on the Afro-Saxon disregards the feelings of many Northerners toward this figure. These feelings resulted from mixed ingredients. In this hypothesis, Negro-U.S. Americans like Douglass, Cardoza, and Revels were links of communication between Saxon and African interests in that racio-political structure that evolved from abolitionism and Reconstruction. They were also the racial link between white and black, their dark blood containing the white power that would, theoretically, facilitate their assimilation into the multiracial union, and through them the assimilation of their darker brothers. In addition, the Afro-Saxon carried that special moral and emotional freight created by the literature of the Tragic Mulatto. When Baker portrays him as vicious and depraved, he is insulting the moral feelings of those Northerners raised on the melodramatic exalting the mixed-blooded Negro. Finally, Baker is attacking the Carpetbagger through what he feels is a special creature of Union misrule.

Because Baker's anti-mulatto assaults are a clear exposition of the racio-political obsession in Bourbonist thought, a full presentation of his vision is necessary. Baker's novel marks the first appearance of the mulatto as villain in Reconstruction fiction, and the rhetorical excesses generating this image reflect his almost pathological antagonism. His target is Yellow Jessamine, who is described as physically repugnant, his slight build and unmasculine appearance giving him a distasteful sexual ambiguity (a fact further intensified by his name). He is the chief of the black Radicals, an active participant in the various phases of Carpetbagger misrule, and a demonstration of the evils attendant to Negro suffrage. Morally, he is treacherous, dishonest, and lecherous:

> Middleton had noticed a number of highly colored and still more highly objectionable pictures on the walls of an inner room. From that, as well as from long observation among the white men, he knew well what sort of character this mulatto was. The snaky thinness of his body, the pallor of his yellow face, an indescribable way in which the man held his eyes half closed, these indicated the lewdness which made Yellow Jessamine . . . a proverb in the place. Middleton was no Puritan, and he had but slight ideas, at last, of the depths of pollution in which, like a maggot in carrion, this man habitually lived; . . .[373]

The mulatto as a racial type then becomes the incarnation of a montage of decadent behavior calculated to shock the Godeyists. Furthermore, this behavior evolves directly according to this theory of Baker's anthropology from the Afro-Saxon's "monstrous syncretism."

To amplify these libels, Baker sets up a series of explicit and implicit contrasts between the mixed Freedman (Yellow Jessamine) and the black (Anderson Parker). Through this structure of differentiation, Baker is able to malign not only the mulatto but his Carpetbagger master as well. His first point is that the two groups are completely different races. This assertion involves a startling adaptation of the genetic disability doctrine:

> ... the black represented the original African—slow, sensible, faithful, capable of any amount of heat and work; the mulatto was quick in body and mind, smart—not sensible—treacherous, incapable in general of anything beyond the work of barber or waiter—the twilight, in a word, between the two races, and destined . . . to perish.[374]

That it is only the Negro with white blood who inherits the disabilities is quite a change from the view that black blood was the corrupting agent. This is the genetic basis for Baker's insistence on an interracial dichotomy among the Freedmen. It is also the assumption that sanctions Baker's political view of the Freedman. This image will also appear in a later, post-Reconstruction anti-radical novel, *The Klansman*, by Thomas Dixon. Dixon takes the Afro-Saxon hero from *Uncle Tom's Cabin*, George Harris, and makes him into the radical villain.

His second point is that the mulatto differs from the other ex-slaves because of his dangerous political attitude. The anthropological contrast between the androgenous, depraved mulatto and the masculine, pious non-mulatto implies antithesis between the politically aggressive Freedman and the faithful Uncle Robin. This antithesis is fully elaborated in this Jessamine-Parker polarity.

Yellow Jessamine is the chief of the pro-Carpetbagger Freedmen, a henchman of Hiddikel Queasy, and an important member of the radical legislature. It is around his leadership that those ex-slaves who have accepted Radicalism rally. Yellow is also the head of the Carpetbaggers' terrorists, which he leads on bulldozing expeditions against pro-Bourbon Freedmen. It is he who instigates the burning of Parker's church and leads the flogging attack that costs Parker his life. Jessamine, then, is the Freedman-Radical complete, the dreaded figure in the Bourbon nightmare of black rule.

The contrast to Parker's docility seems obvious enough; however, there is some subtlety. Interesting enough, Anderson Parker was also a black Radical who had, during the initial stages of reconstitution, accepted wholeheartedly the doctrine of political action as the best way to transform the Freedman's condition. He had advanced rapidly through Carpetbagger circles, a progress climaxed by his being elected Speaker of the House. But gradually he had become disillusioned as growing radical malfeasance destroyed the early ideals of Reconstruction:

> The mean white man, and the ignorant dupes among the negroes; the members openly paid for their votes; the champagne and cigars, and almost everything else, charged as stationery; the lying and perjury; the whole miserable story over again of corruption and gluttonous greed.[375]

His election to the United States Senate, ironically, was the last straw, and he had abandoned the capital, returning to his former station as head-Negro in his massa's plantation.

It is this surrender of power then that gives Parker's political docility complex overtones. Moreover, not only does Parker give up political power, he also gives up any manifestations of power that would be offensive to the Bourbon. His ambition, as it were, is to live up to the ideal of Uncle Robin, whose peace was his place. Consequently, though he takes legal control of the Anderson plantation and makes it a successful concern, he is content to remain behind the scenes as the head Negro, fulfilling his place as the complete darkey.[376] It is these surrenders that make him, in Baker's eyes, morally superior to the ambitious Jessamine. Says Col. Dunwoddie approvingly:

> He has lived among you all his life. . . . No man has been such a help to Judge Anderson's family. He is honest, industrious, respectful in his bearing toward all . . . and hates scallawags [sic], white and black, with all his soul. Gentlemen . . . *be* gentlemen, . . . Remember, whatever else he may be, he is a *Southern* man! I introduce to you the owner of Judge Anderson's plantation, Anderson Parker.[377]

Parker is not content quietly to live out the doctrine of subordination; he must aggressively proselytize it. At a major political rally, he delivers a speech to the Bourbons and Freedmen (previewing the Atlanta Compromise Speech) in which he joins cause with the Bourbons and asserts the doctrine of voluntary subordination as the only route to Freedman progress. This performance reveals a degradation of spirit far more noxious than Jessamine's varied vices: "All dat you white folks hab got . . . is what you or your farders earned. We black people will hab to do de same; we will hab to earn it—*earn* it by hard work!" (This is Parker's version of the myth that somehow black people did not work during slavery.)[378] Parker then literally metamorphosizes into a Voluntary Slave before the approving eyes of the Southrons.

> 'And oh, my marsters,' he continued, using the disused term with great humility and —'oh, my marsters! . . . be patient with us . . . [and you] colored fooks, you stop rushin' away from your work into de towns; stop your laziness an' stealin' and' . . . foolin' away you money. Vote if you want it, but you keep out of bein' voted for till you fitten for it. You *earn* it, an' you'll get it. You think, now . . . you free from de whites, it's all dun and ober. You fool niggers!' this blackest of them all said with the sadness of utter pity, 'a nigger marster is thousand times worse an ebb'ry colored man in de sound ob my voice is under jest dat. You got to break out ob your own ign'rant mis'rable hands 'fore you will stop being' slaves, wus slaves dan ebber! [Then he returns to his former plea;] But oh, marsters, my marsters, . . . be merciful to us colored folks. You are higher than us. Then be dat much more like god. *We* din't make ourselves black. *We* didn't put ourselves here. Was it *us* made ourselves free? Gib us a chance, marsters. Let de law touch un an' nothin' else. Be patient wid us—patient—patient—until we kin learn somethin'. De Yankees are a million ob miles away, an' we are in your hands under God. Onny gib us a chance, marsters—gib us a chance!'[379]

What Parker is advocating, then, is that the ex-slaves abandon Americanization in the more active political forms and the adoption, instead of a kind of indeterminate apprenticeship—voluntary subordination—under their former masters.[380] On the political level, therefore, the chief difference between the black Bourbon and the yellow Radical is the latter's espousal of Americanization in all its dimensions. And when the political aggressiveness is added to his racial traits, the Afro-Saxon emerges in the novel as an utterly distinct figure in the Reconstruction drama.

But Baker must push the differences one step further. He must show not only that the Afro-Saxon differs from the faithful African in terms of color, racial characteristics, and political philosophy, but also that there is a deep innate hostility between the two Negro races that these differences reflect. By presenting the Afro-Saxon as isolated from his black brothers and his white family, Baker amplifies further what he considers to be the freakish nature of the racially mixed as the truly undesirable sociopolitical alien in the South. Hated by black and white, the mulatto is doomed to perish.[381]

The key scene that images this hostility is the lynching of a mulatto Radical by Parkerite Freedmen. Yellow Jessamine and a colleague have seemingly raped and murdered a Belle and her daughter out of the evil propensity of mulatto nature.[382] Anderson Parker and his Africans join with outraged Southrons to avenge this brutal deed, thus forming the first biracial lynching party in U.S. American literature: "We know who is de onny men in de county who could do dat. You be on the spot, but oh, Mars Horace, . . . You all leab dem mulattos to me!"[383] The posse captures Jessamine's partner in crime, ". . . . a lank mulatto with the face of a cat."[384] And, he is also a member of the Republican Party. Parker and his cohorts act as judge, jury, and executioners in one of the most unusual lynchings in Southern literature. But much uglier than the act is the rationale that Parker offers for the deed:

> I hope de day is comin' when dere will be onny two colors in dis land, white and black. People say I is too hard against de yeller people, dat dere is as many good yaller folks as dar is black. Maybe so. I is an ign'rant man myself. De blue is *blue* on de flag, de red is *red*, and de white is *white*. Please God to bring dat day when it will be black and white! And de day is comin' when no man can do what this poor sinner has done. [As Parker prayed for such divine determination, his] hand closed, as if it would crush the yellow flesh to the bone. . . .[385]

Such hatred is identified by Baker as the normative attitude of both black and white Southerners:

> [Leonidas Dunwoddie] was, like many of his shade of color, an excellent, industrious, and deserving man. But people were, like Anderson Parker, . . . prejudiced against mulattos on the principle that, even in buying a cow or a horse, it is safest to rely upon one of some definite and decided color. A mere prejudice, of course.[386]

The ends to which Anderson Parker and Yellow Jessamine come conclude Baker's prejudiced view of the two Negro races. The African dies in the best tradition of the demise of the faithful darkey: mourning Freedmen to the right of the stage; young missy toward the front, weeping copiously; dying uncle, with face illumined by celestial light:

> "Have you nothing to say to me Parker?"
>
> "No Miss Emmeline . . . ; 'cept to ask, please gib my service to Miss Julia. I dun de best I know how."[387]

And, of course, the funeral scene:

> The funeral services took place two days later in Mrs. Anderson's parlors. The Rev. Gen. Atchison, . . . conducted the exercises . . . , all of the leading white men of the region being present. Mrs. Anderson, her daughter by her side, sat at the head of the coffin almost as rigid and still as the black who lay, his calm brow exposed to view, like the fallen statue of an heroic age. The porch and lawn were crowded with colored people.[388]

In contrast, a fate worse than death awaits the treacherous Afro-Saxon Yellow. As the curtain falls, Yellow Jessamine can be seen languishing in prison for Parker's murder and heartsick with apprehension that his complicity in the unmentionable crime will soon be revealed.

Baker's antagonism against the mulattos, then, is rather complete. He sees few redeeming features in the best of them, and the majority of them are depicted as politically, morally and physically inferior to inferiors. And unlike the typical Anti-Radical, who describes the mulattos as Negroes, Baker isolates them from the blacks and whites as a separate race, doomed, he hopes, to some divine act of genocide.

It would be easy to dismiss Baker's vicious distortions as the results of a mere prejudice. But the rhetoric, descriptions, and narrative events related to these distortions suggest more complex motives, which are consciously and unconsciously involved with the Reconstruction trauma and the Carpetbagger. In the following discussion, the socio-psychic and racio-political factors will be described, which account for Baker's somewhat obsessive concern with racial syncretism *per se* as his all-pervading symbol of Carpetbaggerism.

To begin with the broadest generalization, Baker's attack on the "miscegenate" is related to the essential aim of all Bourbon counter-Radical activity: the maintenance of a sociopolitical "stability" similar to that of pre-Emancipation days. Those forces that disturb this stability have to be removed or at least severely curbed. Such a force was the Carpetbagger and, in Baker's fantasy, the Afro-Saxons became the symbols of the Radicals' disturbing energies. Baker's implication is that the racio-cultural instability of Reconstruction would somehow cease if the mulatto were not such a viable part of the Southern social and political landscape.

The social myths of the Southern racial system, as pointed out in Chapters I and II, defined the Interracial Symbiosis in terms of a God-based barrier between superior and inferior races characterized by the phenomenon of "place," of "role," as the one divinely sanctioned social reality in Southern life. The essential characteristics of "place" were first the emphasis on the inferiority of Blackness to Whiteness and second the structured pattern of social subordination that such inferiority made necessary. Place became the norm by which the acceptable behavior of the Negro was judged, and hence place (not caste) can best describe this sociological foundation which, in the myth, gave the pre-Emancipation South its stability and glory. It was this social reality that had to be maintained during the disruptions of the Carpetbagger dictatorship at all cost.

But in the Bakerite obsession, the Afro-Saxon is the glaring contradiction to such social verities. His skin bespeaks an intimacy across God-made barriers not sanctioned by Christian teachings. His very physiognomy introduces the element of ambiguity into a system of placements and roles defined by the physical reality of Blackness and Whiteness. And during the First Reconstruction, the Afro-Saxon was, for the Bakerite, the Freedman who broke out of his traditional place, who acted like a white man—precisely because he was created in part by a white man—or woman. Since patrician blood often ran in his veins, he was envisioned the natural rebel against Southern stability. During the pre-Emancipation period, this blood was the reputed cause of the aggressive spirit of the white-skinned slave. During Reconstruction, according to De Forest in *A Union Officer*, his white blood accounted for the alacrity with which the Cardozos adapted to the new era. Finally, the syncretizing of *both* white and black genes becomes, in the theory of the Afro-Saxon operating in this study, the symbol of the possibility of the Americanization and, hence, the equalization of *all* Freedmen.

Therefore, under Carpetbag rule, the Jessamines seek a forbidden equality with their white parent. Unlike the dependable faithful Parkers, they flaunt their newly given rights: jostling quality folks on the street, demanding respect for their ladies, dressing in the latest fashion, and supporting their neighborhood Freedman teacher. And since they also demonstrate to the African Freedman the possibility of his own political rebellion against role and place, the Afro-Saxon becomes the dangerous example of social equality, in terms of both blood and ambition, for all Negroes:

> The women, as they passed in all their shades of blood and color, from a blackness only less than that of Anderson Parker up to a fairness almost rivaling that of the purest Caucasian race, were alike in being almost superbly dressed . . . silks, shawls, finely worked underskirts, gloves, and expensive parasols [.] . . Leonidas Dunwoddie [the other mulatto leader, was] a . . . perfectly dressed gentleman. . . . All that broadcloth and white Marseilles, snowy linen and yellow kids, gold chain and highly polished boots could do to set off the person was done and overdone. A woman accompanied [Leonidas], and Middleton would have sworn to her . . . as one of the most striking, and . . . the most expensively arrayed, of white women. . . . Small wonder, apart from the hard times, that the whites came to church dressed so plainly. The throngs of colored people poured along the dusty and dull streets like a pageant . . . , leaving more the impression of a circus than a Sunday. . . .[389]

Such a demonstration could only have been intolerable to a Baker.

Therefore, Yellow Jessamine's face becomes the visible sign of the force, unleashed by Carpetbaggery, which threatens the very bases of Southern stability: place, subordination, and inferiority. For Baker, the removal of all ambiguities and contradictions offers the best way to recreate the racio-social order founded on clear, social and political distinctions between Blackness and Whiteness. There is also an additional point: If the ultimate social aim of Carpetbag politics is legalized miscegenation (as it seemed to the Bourbon), Yellow Jessamine's flesh is not only a prophecy but a fulfillment.

The libidinal strain in Reconstruction politics leads inevitably to a discussion of the Cult of Racio-sexuality. In terms of the kind of limited psychoanalytic tropes used in this study, the Cult is the psychological source of much of the Bourbon's violent implacability against Reconstruction. Racio-sexuality gives the mulatto's activism an extra dimension of racist dread and resentment. His skin becomes a reminder of the confusion of racial identity that a racistic eroticism engendered in a world of Blackness and Whiteness, of the breakdown in the spiritual and social distance so carefully cultivated between the races. And during the First Reconstruction Yellow Jasmine's skin foreshadowed the legalization of this breakdown among all Southerners. In addition, his skin stood for the dread power of the Gal in a world dedicated to the racial and sexual purity of the Belle,[390] a purity that figured so persistently and prominently in the vision of Southern polity. In terms of this analysis, the roots of Baker's hostility would seem to lie in the general Southern ambivalence toward race and sexuality. Small wonder, then, that Baker prophesies with such a fierce longing the divine extermination of such creatures.[391] And interestingly enough this same antipathy would be found in the racist philosophy of Marcus Garvey, a hero to many black liberation adherents.

In the overall view of the sociopolitical and cultural-psychological structure of Southern society, the triumph of the Carpetbagger shattered the Bourbon's ancient social, political, and sexual supremacy in the Southern Garden. This, from this limited perspective, was the chief trauma of the Reconstruction event, and in Baker's fantasy the mulatto Freedman becomes the chief symbol of that trauma, reflecting the monstrous proportions that the Freedmen's alliance with the Carpetbaggers assumed in the Bourbon's mind. It is, therefore, this complex of reasons that generates his attacks on the mulatto Freedmen.[392]

In *Colonel Dunwoddie*, Baker castigates the North, its representatives, and one of its wards. Even the theme of reconciliation undergoes a nasty mutation in his hands. It is Alice Dunwoddie, the most neurotic of the Dunwoddie's, who marries Middleton.[393] It becomes clear, then, that Baker's denunciation of the Carpetbagger and his creations is a part of an assault against all things Northern, reflecting a revival of the sectional chauvinism of a Calhoun and a Fitzhugh. In this attack, the North's evils are internal to its very sociopolitical structure, while the evils of the South—the violence and the passion, the ". . . pine-trees and sassafras, swine all snout, negroes all rags, poor whites . . . all lice and laziness" are to the South "as the husk to the corn."[394] Baker's chief Bourbon underscores such chauvinistic celebration of Southern virtues:

> . . . the South was that portion of Christendom fully equal if not superior in any other, which had been, by some fatality, isolated from the rest, and, standing thus at bay, was bound to assert as well as to defend itself against the world. . . . This was gospel denied by none except wicked and prejudiced people.[395]

Colonel Dunwoddie, like the novel itself, goes further: to assert the old Southern view that the South would regain "its ancient supremacy" over the new union once she was redeemed and her internal strife resolved.[396] Such an assertion was, in literary terms, a red flag to those Republicans and old-time Unionists who still feared the power of a revived Dixie. Such an assertion also reflects the chauvinistic celebration of Southern virtues that form the thematic thrust of the work. Small wonder that Baker had to hide behind a mask of anonymity.[397]

Ideologically, Baker's novel is the most distasteful of anti-radical works. (Woodville runs a very close second.) His racist crudities and pro-Southern exaggerations are quite offensive to the Revisionist-minded. However, his work does have some value. It reveals how unreliable the Southern description of the Reconstruction would become. Baker's work expresses the kind of distortions that would pervade both the fiction and the nonfiction written by Southerners and those Northerners who sympathized uncritically with the Bourbon position.[398] Still, there is a raw aesthetic energy in the novel that is directly attributable to its splenetic depiction of the Reconstruction and that gives the work a certain narrative force. In the context of this study, then, *Colonel Dunwoddie, Millionaire*, is the first novel expressing the Dunningite vision of the Carpetbagger-Bourbon conflict to U.S. American literature.

Baker appears for the last time in this descriptive analysis with the short story "Two Couples: A White and Yellow" (1879),[399] in which he continues his attack on Carpetbaggerism by attacking the Afro-Saxon. The hero of the story, Milton M. Berrien, the male member of the yellow couple, is merely Jessamine in his purely political guise. He is the symbol of all the ills of radical rule, ills now generalized outward to include ". . . the whole process of the evolution of the slave into freemen,"[400] and the evolution is, as typical with Baker, rather dismal.

The chief sign of Milton's progress is, of course, his political cooperation with the Carpetbagger:

> He was in the legislature, on the stump, in the newspaper offices, along the streets, reigning in his fine horse beside the cotton fields to have, contemptuous of the helpless overseer, a political talk with the freedmen at work there.[401]

As the result of such activism, Milton, who commences in the story as a sober hardworking slave, is gradually transformed by Reconstruction into an exponent of Radical vices: graft, treachery, dishonor, opportunism, arrogant ambition, lying, and political terrorism. As a slave, pontificates Baker, it was Milton's body that was bought and sold; as a Freedman, it is his soul that is for sale.[402] In the end, Berrien is brought low by the righteous indignation of the redemptionist reaction and, like Jessamine, his evolution ends in the courts of Southern justice, where he is on trial for his political felonies.

Significantly, Baker feels that both Berrien's "evolution" and the general sociopolitical disorders that accompanied it were necessary in order to demonstrate once and for all to the idealistic North (and the Freedmen themselves) the incapacity of the Afro-Americans to become responsible citizens. The lesson has been learned, Baker seems to imply; now the North will leave the Freedman to the guidance and care of his former masters. Moreover, since the Carpetbag governments have been destroyed, he will have to live in Southern society without the artificial support of Federal intervention; he will now have to earn his citizenship through hard work, thrift, discipline, and sacrifice.[403]

Yet Baker seems to doubt that, even with these virtues, the Freedman will ever be a full citizen. The social, cultural, and genetic flaws inherent in his race are too overpowering to afford him civic partnership with the godlike Saxon. He is destined to remain an unassimilable entity in the Southern states. The original mistake giving rise to this problem was, of course, the Emancipation Proclamation. If the Negro had remained a slave or in some form of servitude after the defeat, he would have avoided all the frustration and agony the Reconstruction upheaval brought upon him and the South. He would have avoided the continuing resentment of a dominant group accustomed to seeing him in a certain place. In his total relationship to Southern society, the Freedman was better off as a slave.

Baker's final word is a pessimistic prophecy. Since re-enslavement is no longer possible and assimilation out of the question, the only answer seems to be deportation. And if Milton McPherson Berrien is not deported, and he remains a free person, he and the yellow and black Negroes he represents will continue to plague the social and political structure of the reunited states for generations to come. Baker turns the final solution, as in *Colonel Dunwoddie*, over to Providence: "May God solve and save you! He alone can."[404]

The next two works, "Dogwood Bitters" (1880) and "The Call Meeting" (1881), by one Jennie Woodville, are rather minor works, sketches more than short stories.[405] Like Baker's tales her Reconstruction works are racist fantasies setting forth her attack on the Northerner's belief that the average Freedmen wanted equality. Her works contrast the "placed" Negroes with their "displaced" egalitarian-minded brothers and sisters.

"Dogwood Bitters" opens with an indignant picture of the intolerable presence of displaced Freedmen (or in this case, Freedwomen) in the fabric of Southern life:

> It was these Negro ladies who defiantly took possession of the inner portion of the sidewalk, right or left; who strapped lace veils across their dusky noses and twirled their parasols against ladies' hats; who grazed people's toes with their baby-carriages and entangled ladies' skirts in their wheels. . . .[406]

It is in light of such arrogant equality that Woodville develops her narrative.

The first story involves two incidents that image the crimes the new order permits. In the first incident, an impudent young Freedgirl, Carrie Defridge, accidentally strikes her father's old owner, Mrs. Darring, while playing. In place of an effusive apology, Carrie merely delivers a curt remark. Worse, when Mrs. Darring tries to reprimand her, she talks back to her and refuses to answer to her old slave name, Kyarline. The second incident is less complex. Carrie's mother as an act of courtesy invites the old Missie to attend her daughter's birthday party. Around these two incidents is woven Woodville's ideological disquisition on the meaning of place.

Her narrative voice for this analysis is Addum Lefridge. Old Addum, a Parkerite type, lectures his wife and daughter on the impropriety of seeking any form of social equality with their former owners.[407] For him, the source of his ladies' rebellion against place lies in the vice of ambition unleashed by Carpetbag rule among contented, docile Freedmen: "What would a nigger be ef 'twarn't for ambitions: He wouldn' nuvvur git 'buv' hisse'f, he wouldn' nuvvur be no 'better'n de white foaks—which de sword is done levelled 'em down to him—ef 'twarn't for ambitions!"[408]

Therefore, it is Addum's task to burn this vice out of his wife with stinging mustard plasters ("Does you still want de white lady, my ole mis', to set down wid a passel o' niggers?") and to brutally flog it out of his daughter with dogwood striplings ("A nigger, 'specially a young nigger, will take larnin' on his back dat you nuvvur could ha' got it in his head. De back way is de nachul way for niggers, sho'."). In the end, dogwood bitters and mustard plasters win the day. Carrie and her mother leave the ranks of those obnoxious Freedwomen with whom the sketch opens, having learned that, despite the leveling created by Reconstruction, the ex-master is still supreme over the ex-slave thanks to the power of the Voluntary Slave.[409]

Woodville continues her thesis in "The Call Meeting." Like "Dogwood Bitters," "The Call Meeting" is a racist fantasy on the theme of voluntary servitude, but this time with a female version of Addum Lefridge. For Aunt Milly slavery was and is her golden time, especially as it continues to define her relationship to the Bourbon world and her white family. And as with her male counterpart, Aunt Milly's re-enslavement gives her a superior status over the freed Negroes and allows her to share as a kind of equal the Bourbon's contempt, anger, and resentment toward the Freedmen and their ambition.

Milly arrives at such commitment through the conditioning of slavery and through her rejection by the North. In an only partially explained act, Milly goes North for, one would suppose, the Jubilee. But a few weeks among the negrophobic Yankees disabuse her of the good intentions of abolitionists. She returns to the safety of the old plantation, sadder but wiser.[410] Thus, a part of Milly's fierce loyalty to the Bourbon Massa grows from the hostility of what she thought would be her new masters in Yankeedom.[411] The title of the work indicates the main incident: Milly's trial before her church members ostensibly for stealing; in reality, her more radical neighbors use the call meeting to chastise her for her fierce allegiance to their enemies. But the meeting ends up in her hands as she chastises *them* for their evil, radical ways. The work ends in a triumph for her position.

Lefridge and Milly emerge in the Woodville analysis as the exponents of the two major points of her thesis. The first point is that the Negro is essentially a different species from the Caucasian. As is usually true in anti-radical fiction and nonfiction, the Freedman church service is presented as an all-inclusive symbol of this contention. The service is described as the barbarous expression of an absurd, ignorant, hypocritical people.[412] The uproar and disorder of the call meeting, the overwrought emotionalism, and the illiterate use of religious rite reflect the lack of any redeeming virtues in what was, in Carpetbagger lore, the essential sign of the Freedmen's humanity—their Christian idealism and fervor. If their religion is so superficial, as the author suggests, what of their other virtues?

This is the point of Aunt Milly's rebuttal against her accusers—that beneath the superficial acquisitions of freedom lie the thievery and adultery of the lazy, helpless slave: "I tell you . . . Mas' Jeems, a nigger is a nigger [is] a nigger. You may bile him, an' you may scrape him an' you may white wash him . . . ; de fust rain would wash him back to a nigger;—a dead nigger,—like he really was."[413] It is the Northern belief in the humanness of the slave that is, therefore, the error underlying Emancipation; it is also the error underlying Radical Reconstruction. Thus, on a metaphoric level, Aunt Milly and Uncle Addum strip away that moral idealism and political bravery associated with the Nimbus Desmit prototype (a symbol of the politically active ex-slave) in pro-Carpetbagger literature; they emerge in his place as a new prototype in the Woodville thesis: the authentic Negroes, uncorrupted by the Carpetbaggerism which, indirectly, has poisoned their friends. They are that model of Freedman rectitude, which the Anti-Radicals trundle out with such monotonous frequency, the Voluntary Slaves who, in their dedicated servility, demonstrate that, if left to natural development, the Negro wants no equality with Old Massa. This is the second point in the Woodville position.

Since there has been rather constant reference to the Voluntary Slave, an examination of this figure in detail, especially in terms of his relationship to the Conflict, is instructive. The Voluntary Slave—whether male or female—as already indicated, remains a slave out of the personal conviction that the niche in Southern society assigned to him/her by the master race is the only viable one. His/her successful occupation of this place, in the Woodville tales, becomes his/her refuge of permanence in the violent revolution of the South from restoration through reconstitution to redemption. S/he avoids the traumata afflicting the Jessamines and Berriens, who are involved in the cycle of ambition, success, and failure, which the Carpetbagger permitted—and encouraged.

In addition, as the personal servants of the Massa, these postwar slaves, at least in their own eyes, partake of that power and occupy a position above white trash and uppity blacks. By opting out of the political conflict, the Voluntary Slaves emerge as the black Bourbon counterpart to the black Radical and as the model of Freedman servility in contrast to the self-destructive ambition of Freedman activists. Their voluntary servitude is their real emancipation. As examples of ex-slaves (for these types obviously existed), Milly and Addum unintentionally represent the socio-psychic wounds of the Slavery Syndrome. This can be clearly seen in the vehemence with which they defend their inferior status and in the way they appropriate, for their own survival, ole Massa's contempt toward Negroes in general and toward themselves in particular. In either case, their placement allows them a protective dissociation from their fellows and from *themselves as Negroes*. And, in either case, they must undergo rites of self-abasement, as it were, a type of self-mutilation, in order to prove the depth of their loyalty. Finally, it is not that Lefridge and Milly continue to act as slaves that is most significant; rather, it is their exaltation of their debasement that is the fullest exponent of their loss of humanness. It is this loss that Woodville unknowingly presents in the punishment scene and the call-meeting incident.

Aunty Milly and Uncle Addums, therefore, are the good darkies in the pro-Bourbon allegory of the South as Eden, the Garden in which slaves and masters lived in racial harmony before the Yankee serpents came and destroyed the balance forever with the Apple of Equality. In this light, the Woodville allegories are not only an attack against radical politics *vis-à-vis* the Freedman, they also constitute a denunciation of the roots of those policies: the 1863 Proclamation and the Thirteenth Amendment.[414]

The last anti-Radical work is the anthology *Rodman the Keeper: Southern Sketches* (1886) by Constance Fenimore Woolson. Although published in 1886, the key stories are Reconstruction fiction. Woolson is among the ranks of those Reconstruction writers who had some renown as a writer. (The others are Melville, Davis, and De Forest.) This fact is illustrated by the extensive, favorable criticism she receives in Hubbell's and Quinn's literary histories and, more interestingly, by the admiring critical response *Southern Sketches* elicited from her friend and idol, Henry James. Woolson places in the service of the anti-Carpetbagger cause her very considerable prominence as a 19th-century U.S. American writer.[415]

All the fiction in the collection was written during Reconstruction, but not all of it is about this period. The collection divides between purely local color tales—"The South Devil," "Sister St. Luke," "Aunt Elisabetha, "Felipa," and "Bro"; and Reconstruction stories—"Rodman the Keeper," "Old Gardiston," "In the Cotton Country," and "King David."[416] However, both the apolitical and sociopolitical fiction center attention on the North-South conflict. It is only in the Reconstruction tales that this conflict is spelled out in terms of the Carpetbagger archetype.

The first story in this latter group is "Rodman the Keeper," set in North Carolina in 1869. The tale deals with the activities of John Rodman, a wounded but active ex-Union soldier who works as the custodian of a national cemetery, raised on the grounds of an unnamed but infamous prisoner-of-war camp.[417] In a sense, his preference to live at the South in this rather unusual capacity makes him a kind of idealistic Carpetbagger. He certainly undergoes the same initiation. As is typical in the pro-Carpetbagger tale, Rodman is ostracized by the Southrons' prejudice and resentment against him as a symbol of the Northern victory and the continuing tyranny. And typically, his only initial contact with the community is through the Freedmen, the sole visitors to the cemetery.

The Freedmen attempt to enter into that conventional relationship with Rodman typical of Carpetbaggerism. During a Memorial Day celebration (in which the ex-slaves are the only participants), they ask him to lead the procession they have formed commemorating the death of their liberators. He accepts. By pushing the symbological bias a little, this could hint at the potential political control that Rodman could have had over his wards. The conventional relationship is further established *in embryo* in Rodman's attempt to teach a Freedman reading and writing. As the sole representative of the North and as a friend of the Freedman, Rodman seems the model idealistic Carpetbagger.

But in reality, he is the Copperhead mutation; that is, he is both a Unionist and an anti-abolitionist. His relationship with the ex-slaves remains aloof and perfunctory; his teaching exercise is tainted with pro-Bourbon sentiments: ". . . and an old black freedman allowing himself to be taught the alphabet in order to gain permission to wait on his master—master no longer by law—with all the devotion of this loving old heart."[418] In a word, a Voluntary Slave.

In contrast to this his relationship with the Southron, at least with an ex-

Confederate veteran and an old doctor, is cordial and intimate. Through a series of narrative maneuvers, Rodman becomes involved with a severely wounded rebel-soldier. Rodman eventually brings the wounded man from his old decrepit plantation to the comfortable, well-provisioned quarters in the cemetery. There, with the ghostly approval of the Union dead, Rodman cares for him until he dies. Rodman's loyalties, then, lie ultimately with the Bourbon and not with the new order.

The story is a reconciliation fable, but not in the traditional form. While there is a hint of erotic reunion in a tentative romance between the Confederate's cousin, the Bitter Belle, and his newfound friend, Woolson realistically allows no conjugation across the chasm. She is primarily interested in a more comprehensive vision of reunion. The center of this vision is the myth of the Civil War. In this myth, the North did not fight a loose collection of rebellious states, but a "nation" coexisting with the North in the Union. The South's conception of itself was, for Woolson, an error in judgment, but it was not treason. Therefore, the War of Rebellion metamorphoses in this vision into a civil war between two opposing factions with a degree of right on both sides.[419] Moreover, since the North's victory gave its conception of the Union an ideological hegemony over the new nation, it could well afford a lenient peace. The formula for such a policy is articulated by the dead soldiers in the cemetery: "We do not object to the brave soldier who honestly fought for his cause, even though he fought on the other side. . . ."[420] In terms of anti-radical attitude during the reconciliation period, "Rodman the Keeper" is another fable of reunion that attacks in retrospect the Radicals' plan of Reconstruction.

As a type of Reconstruction fiction, Carpetbaggerism *per se* does not figure in the tale. Yet there is a foreshadowing of what it would mean to the Southern way of life in the conclusion of the story. An "energetic Maine man" has taken over the home of Rodman's Confederate friend, and in tearing it down he is uprooting the greenery "that once screened the piazza." Rodman, in a sentimental gesture, asks for the plants: "'Worth about twenty-five cents, I guess,' said the Maine man, handing them over."[421] Destructiveness and avarice: These would be the salient characteristics of the Carpetbagger in anti-radical legend.

There are some similarities between "Rodman" and the second tale, "Old Gardiston." Both are modified sociopolitical fiction,[422] having as chief characters a Union soldier (this time in reluctant duty in support of reconstitution) and an embittered Belle. Both stories present in greater and lesser degrees the deprivation of the Bourbon during the new era. Both are reconciliation tales: "Rodman" in a general view, "Gardiston" in the conventional romantic view. The prominent difference between the stories is emphasis: In "Rodman" the reconciliation center is the Yankee's life in and relation to the reconstructing South; in "Gardiston" the center is the Bourbon's struggle to survive in that South.

Woolson describes the difficulties of the last of the Gardiston's, the young Belle and her futile old cousin, trying to exist within the social dislocations of the new politics. The chief obstacle is an irrational pride that prevents them from adapting in any particular to reconstitution and that causes the Belle to refuse that kind of Northern magnanimity championed by Rodman. The result of this *hubris* is folly and futility: cold nights, damp food, insufficient clothing, degrading poverty:

> The winter was rainy, with raw east winds from the ocean, and the old house leaked in many places. If they had lived in one or two of the smaller rooms, which were in better condition and warmer than the large apartments, they might have escaped; but no habit was changed, and three times a day the table was spread in the damp dining-room, where the atmosphere was like that of a tomb, and where no fire was ever made. The long evenings were spent in the somber drawing-room by the light of one candle, and the rain beat against the old shutters. . . .[423]

The symbol of this pride and folly is the family mansion, old Gardiston; the symbol of Northern magnanimity is the Union officer, Captain Newell. So long as the mansion stands, there can be no love between Newell and Miss Gardiston. In the climax of the sketch, the mansion burns down. As a result of the fire and the patient love of the officer, the Belle finally accepts his hand and lives happily ever after. In the image of the burning mansion, one finds Woolson's call for the destruction of those Bourbon emotions standing in the way of reconciliation.

The Bourbon-Carpetbagger conflict is muted in this reconciliation romance. Yet there are clear signs of its presence. In contrast to "Rodman," the Carpetbaggers act more as characters, especially in their role as villains. It is a vulgar Yankee merchant who, taking advantage of the helplessness of the

Gardistons, seeks to buy the old mansion in order to destroy it and construct in its place a more financially profitable operation. (The house, suspecting such designs, kills itself with the fire referred to above.) It is the Carpetbagger who brings the dislocations that afflict the Gardistons and their class:

> The unhappy State had fallen into the hands of double-faced, conscienceless whites, who used the newly enfranchised blacks as tools of their evil purposes. These leaders were sometimes emigrant Northerners, sometimes renegade Southerners, but always rascals.[424]

Finally, within Woolson's anti-radical symbology, the Carpetbagger has another role. He stands as the implicit foil for the heroic Union Army.

This contrast is very important in the reconciliationist convention. The Grand Army is a sacred cow. Attacks may be made on idealistic schoolmarms, abolitionists, Northern policies, Freedmen, Emancipation, and anti-secessionism. But in some unverifiable understanding, the Army is never attacked, not even in its Shermanesque manifestation.[425] Indeed, the Army's support of the radical governments is seen as the distasteful duty of brave but obedient soldiers. The reason for this attitude is complex. For the Northern Anti-Radicals, the Grand Army of the Republic is, allegorically, the heroic protector of the westward expansion. It is also the only institution related to the anti-secessionist war that has survived the peace with its moral idealism intact, mainly because of its so-called political neutrality. For the Southern anti-radical writer, the Grand Army is a heroic conqueror who defeated a heroic foe fairly and honorably. On a less lofty level, it could be that the presence throughout the Northern readership and media of so many members of the G.A.R. acted as a control over any rhetorical attacks. At any rate, reconciliation symbolism makes full use of the Army: Whereas the Bourbon and the Carpetbagger are unalterable enemies, the Union soldier (if he is apolitical) and the Confederate veteran are Kiplingesque foes who turn into brave friends. The Union Officer becomes the readymade character to effect reunion with the Bitter Belle. He becomes the representative of those Northern virtues, e.g., bravery, honor, and duty, to which the Bourbon as Belle can respond without surrendering her own principles. The Officer is for anti-radical Northern writers the symbol of Northern excellence contrasted to the opportunism and avarice of the Carpetbagger.

But aside from a limited narrative and thematic role, the Carpetbagger is merely the understood antagonist to the Gardistons; their real antagonist is their Southern irrationality. The sketch then is a tale of the defeated but pride-filled Bourbon forced to come to terms through necessity and love with an order totally alien to her former glory and power. This is the narrative and thematic substance of the sketches.

"In the Cotton Country," Woolson's third Reconstruction tale, also deals with the suffering Southern as Belle, this time in her fatalistic posture. This theme is developed in an episodic narrative built around the character of an anonymous Southern Belle. Her fictional narrative (masked, by the way, as nonfiction) divides into two parts. The first deals with the hardship faced by refined, aristocratic ladies during the war: the lack of necessities and those luxuries that had defined their genteel life. The second part pictures the psychological agony such women underwent during radical rule:

> It may be that my grandchild will prosper under the new regime; people do prosper, they tell me. It seems we were wrong, all wrong; then we must be very right now, for the blacks are our judges, councilors, postmasters, representatives, and law-makers. That is as it should be, isn't it? What! Not so? But how can it be otherwise?[426]

The purpose of these episodes is not hard to locate: They are anti-radical counter-images to the depictions of the suffering Radicals-Carpetbaggers in *A Year of Wreck*, Freedmen in *Other Fools and Their Doings*, and Scalawags in *A Fool's Errand*—which pro-radical writers set before the Northern eyes during reconciliation. These episodes in Woolson's hands are, furthermore, the images that would in future literature and history dominate the meaning of the Reconstruction event.[427]

The final work in Woolson's tetralogy and in this account of anti-radical fiction is "King David," her clearest example of Reconstruction fiction. Here for the first time in her stories, the Carpetbagger appears as a major character and, for the first time, his conflict with the Bourbon forms the thematic center. In this work, Woolson foregoes ideological indirections and launches a direct attack upon the Radical in both his idealistic and opportunistic modes. The former is condemned for his naïve folly, the latter for his knavery. Moreover, she assails the moral ends of Reconstruction: the belief that the Freedman had the right to and the capacity for full citizenship in the new Union. Along all fronts, Woolson's assault seems uncompromising.

The setting of this attack is the Freedman's village in an unspecified Southern community, called allegorically and ironically Jubilee Town. To this village comes David King, the Carpetbagger as idealist and missionary, fresh from the hills of New Hampshire. He is described as a nearsighted, delicate, thin boy who could not fight in the war, but who will answer the call in peacetime for idealistic Carpetbaggers. David's neighbor seems to express Woolson's view of such Reconstruction efforts: "We've paid dear enough to set 'em free, goodness knows, and now they ought to look out for themselves."[428] But driven by the pro-Freedman conviction that through education and example he can win over the ex-slaves to the Yankee ideals of learning, honesty, and hard work, he opens up a Freedman school and rents land for free-labor sharecropping. The result is failure.

Instead of meeting Sojourner Truths and Frederick Douglasses, David runs into the ignorance and vice that gave Whitelaw Reid such a start on the Sea-island. At first undaunted, David launches his attack against such moral and social chaos by following the advice of the Ravenel—teach them to read and write and understand Puritan values—all good flows from such small beginnings:

> So he began at "a, b and c," "you must not steal," "you must not fight," "you must wash your faces," which may be called . . . the first working out of the emancipation problem.[429]

But the novelty wears off for both the teacher and pupils. Instead of the immediate affection and trust typical of the pro-radical myth, there is mistrust, misunderstanding, and disappointment. Woolson describes with felicitous strokes the abrasions between Carpetbagger and Freedman. The learning process becomes a tedious, futile rite: The students learn easily and forget easily. The personal relation is more painful: Although he is working for their moral reconstruction, he cannot stand their physical presence. They, in turn, distrust his Northern puritanism and fastidiousness, and long for Old Marse with his "moral carelessness." Indeed, they sneer at him because he is not a gentleman: "Old Mars Ammerton would nebber wash his dishes ef dey was nebber washed."

Thus, standing outside the Symbiosis, David is only tolerated by the black Southerners and can "only blunder on in his slow Northern way."[430] But his blundering ways lead to disaster. He loses influence over the ex-slaves to the Captain, a Queasy-Jack Hunt type, who takes over David's best student and uses his newly acquired education to stir up the Freedmen to license and riot, thereby provoking threats of Bourbon counterstrikes. David's free-labor experiment ends in weeds and unplowed fields because his sharecroppers, under such demagogic influence, refuse to work. Not only do the more ignorant ex-slaves remain enchained by their defects, but those who do learn and have ambition easily come under the Captain's evil influence. David King watches helplessly as even the little good he has done is undone by the political Carpetbagger's whiskey, gimcracks, and egalitarian rhetoric.

As a result of these and other disillusionments, David prepares to return to the North. In a scene that is the obverse of the farewell in *Bricks Without Straw*, David stands before his former pupils and admits defeat. Instead of being run out by irate Klansmen, he is being forced out by the Negroes' indifference and viciousness, and by his own ignorance and *naiveté*:

> What a sight . . . when the pale Caucasian . . . asked for the prayers of these sons of Africa, and gently, . . . almost humbly received the pressure of their black . . . hands as they passed out! They had taught him a great lesson, the lesson of failure.[431]

The question Woolson raises is, why does David fail? There are several possible answers—in terms of the anti-radical position. His failure is simply the inability of New England idealism to overcome the reality of the Negro's inherent viciousness. The defeat is "inherent because David tries to treat the Negroes as equals." (This is false since he always treats them as inferiors.) A third is that only the Southron understands the Negro and, as a result, the Freedmen prefer Ole Marse to Northerners. In reality, Woolson presents the nature of David's aborted efforts as a complex of factors dividing between the Freedman and the Carpetbagger. On the one hand, there is the intractability of the Freedman as a raw material. On the other, there is David's own naïve expectations of instant success that prevent him from seeing wholly the magnitude of his task. A more subtle reason is his attitude toward the ex-African. David is ignorant of and somewhat revolted by the Freedmen as persons. Unlike his Bourbon counterpart, he neither understands the habits and folkways of the black Southerner nor can he enter into that easy relationship, supposedly common to U.S. American slavery, since he cannot endure the Negro's biophysical presence. David is, in his attitude, typical of the fastidious New Englander whose prejudice against the Negro is only barely tempered by his puritan sense of duty to the Freedman. This is the flaw that renders David incapable of exercising the kind of personal control over his wards that could have wooed them from their pleasant vices. Thus, he loses out to the Cap'n and the Bourbon: [432]

> "Our service to you, sah, all de same, ... but you had nebber quite unnerstan us, sah, nebber quite; an' you can nebber do much fo' us, sah, on 'count ob dat fack. . . . You see [our next teacher,] a color'd man [,] will unnerstan us, 'speically ef he hab libbed at de South. . . ."[433]

As an individual, David fails because of misunderstanding. As a Carpetbagger, he fails because he has not lived in the South before. As a Northerner, he fails because of the inability of Northern culture to transform the ex-slaves' alien social and moral nature. Therefore, through the failure of this well-meaning idealist, Woolson takes a hard look at those transcendental Radicals who asserted that emancipation and education were in themselves sufficient to make the ex-African slaves free men.

From the above analysis, it should be clear that while "King David" is anti-radical, it does contain within its bias some very subtle ambivalence concerning David's defeat. The author avoids the simplistic cliché of inherent failure, whether because of New England idealism, personal vices, egalitarianism, or geneticism. There are disabilities, of course, but they reside more in the Negro *as an ex-slave* than as a person, more in David as a person than as an idealistic Carpetbagger. However, ideology does eventually overcome psychological nuances. What begins as an individual failure becomes symbolic of the failure of the entire process. The source of David's lack of success lies no longer in his own nature, but in the essential flaws of Reconstruction itself. Within this symbolic action, one discovers the fullest expression of Woolson's theory of the Reconstruction.[434]

Woolson locates four flaws in the Radicals' plans. The first flaw in radical reconstitution was the belief that education and citizenship were sufficient to change two hundred years of chattelism. The second was the assumption that political power at the South could be based on material as rude and untrustworthy as David's Freedmen. It would have been better to confer such power on able, though possibly disloyal, ex-Confederates than on loyal but barbaric ex-slaves. Such an ex-Confederate is Harnett Ammerton, whom Woolson contrasts with the Freedman and the Carpetbagger. The circumstances created by the second flaw force Ammerton into a dreadful equality with his animal-like Voluntary Slaves:

> There sat the planter, his head crowned with silver hair, his finely chiseled face glowing with the warmth of his indignant words; and there passed the old slave bent and black, his low forehead and broad animal features seeming to typify scarcely more intelligence than that of the dog that followed him.[435]

Or worse, the North's misconceptions force Ammerton to admit the economic superiority of a despised Yankee teacher of Freedmen: "He endured his visitor, and he rented his field; and, with the perplexed feelings of his class, he asked himself how it was, how it could be, that a man like that—yes, like that—had money, while he himself had none."[436]

The third flaw was the belief that Northern mentors could effectively substitute for Southern masters, that the Freedmen would turn to the Carpetbagger with the same fidelity that they gave to ole Marse. The final and most important weakness was the whole course of Republican policies from Emancipation through Americanization. This is seen in one of the key statements in the work: David has returned from an argument with the Bourbon, who has placed the full burden of David's problems and Southern troubles on Emancipation. As he walks, he reasserts over and over again the moral efficacy of the Proclamation, though his inability to Americanize his Freedmen has severely tested his faith:

> "But it *is* right they should be freed, it is right, . . . and to that belief will I cling as long as I have my being. It *is* right." And then he came into Jubilee, and found three of his freedmen drunk and quarreling in the street.[437]

This juxtaposition seems to refer to that doctrine familiar in those anti-radical works that question the practicality of Emancipation, the doctrine that the destruction of slavery was a radical error growing out of the war, but the amendments were malicious blunders for which the South and the Union's honor have paid dearly.

In light of this pernicious Anti-Radicalism, the First Reconstruction is a failure in its moral conception, in its inception, and in its operations. It has failed in what was its essential task: the transformation of the slave into a Victorian. For whatever reasons, Woolson's theory goes, the Freedman has not responded to goodwill and good counsel; he has not evolved to the level of his former masters, despite the efforts of sincere, dedicated Carpetbaggers like King David. If the best of the North cannot materially affect the social, political and, most of all, moral evolution of the Freedman, then who can?

The answer is his own kind or his former masters, especially the former masters. They are the Freedman's natural leaders; they know, understand, and love him—in his place; moreover, the black Southerners reciprocate. Indeed, the Bourbons know how to do what David in all his idealism cannot do: *They know how to control the Negro.* Woolson strikes at the heart of the radical program at the South, i.e., the development of an egalitarian, multiracial coalition between the Northern émigré and the Southern Freedman and their white comrades. The scene that best symbolizes the inherent failure of such a coalition to materialize is David's departure. Here, Woolson ironically inverts a stereotypical scene.

In pro-radical sentimentalism, the departure of the teacher is framed by gathered Freedmen who have come, with tears and prayers, to wish the Yankee massa Godspeed. The function of such pathos is to underscore the personal interracial symbiosis that has sprung up between the Yankee massa and his black allies. But in Woolson's farewell scene, no weeping Negroes send David on his way; indeed, he leaves Jubilee alone—alone, that is, save for the arrival of one of his students:

> At a turn in the road dull-faced Esther was waiting for him . . . with a bunch of . . . common flowers of her small garden-bed. 'Goodbye, Esther,' said the master, touched almost to tears by the sight of the solitary little offering.
>
> 'Goodbye, mars,' . . . But Esther was not moved; she had come out into the woods from a sort of instinct, as a dog follows a little way down the road, to look after a departing carriage.

> [Then a shift back to David's hometown.]
>
> 'David King has come back home. . . . '
>
> 'Has he now? Didn't find the blacks what he expected, I guess.'[438]

It has been in the possibility of a political coalition between Esther and David that the Northern reconstitutionists had placed their hopes for the final solution to the Question and the Conflict. In light of such failure, the only course open to the North now, for Woolson, is to reset its priorities: More important than the fate of the Carpetbagger and his ally is the reconciliation between the sections.

In "King David" art makes ideology; it is Woolson's rather considerable talent as a writer, rather than the validity of her ideas about the Reconstruction (by now anti-radical redundancies), that gives her ideas a convictive energy that they would not ordinarily have. Foremost among her talents is a style possessing that fusion of imagistic restraint, precision, and subtlety reminiscent of her master, Henry James. Her art forces an assent to the truth of the particular action, while one disagrees with the broader assumptions and conclusions drawn from this single incident.

As a more general criticism of the entire collection of short stories, of which "King David" is only a part, this evaluation was foreshadowed by Henry James' commentary on *Southern Sketches*, one of the rare occasions when a major postwar figure discussed Reconstruction fiction. Henry James reacts to *Southern Sketches* on two levels. The first deals with its local color accuracy, especially in dealing with "the Negro of reality."[439] On a more significant level, James sees the *Sketches* as a Northern writer's sensitive response to the Bourbon's problems and, consequently, as a voice for their dumb anguish:

> As the fruit of a remarkable minuteness of observation and tenderness of feeling . . . of one who . . . lingered and analyzed, they have a high value, especially when regarded in light of the *voicelessness* of the conquered and reconstructed South. Miss Woolson strikes the readers as having a compassionate sense of this pathetic dumbness—having perceived that no social revolution of equal magnitude had ever reflected itself so little in literature, remained so unrecorded, so unpainted, so unsung.[440]

Among recent critics, Woolson continues to have such significance. Hubbell points out that she was that type of Northern writer in which this study is most interested: one who, though brought up in the North, is converted to the Southern point of view during the Reconstruction period. Further, he correctly notes that if "King David" had been written by a Southerner in 1875, it would not have been published. (After 1877 this rule would be modified considerably.) Quinn points out, admiringly but erroneously, that it "is to her credit . . . that while Negro rule was still being imposed upon the South with Federal bayonets, a Northern woman told through her fictional characters the truth."[441]

Put together, these critical evaluations reveal that of all anti-radical fictionists, Constance Fenimore Woolson brought to the pro-Bourbon ranks a talent and a reputation of the highest order. One can imagine that her pro-Bourbon influence on Northern audiences was considerable. Indeed, the influence of anti-radical fiction in general on the course of Reconstruction is incalculable. Whether or not the De Forest-Baker-Woolson fiction directly influenced the North's abandonment of the Southern Republicans is dubious, but that this fiction helped to change the attitude of many Northerners who had once supported that alliance is quite probable, especially since anti-radical fiction was a part of the general attack against the Carpetbagger launched by anti-radical news media, Democratic and Republican.[442]

Such media formed a massive influence on a large number of Northern readers and created an audience quite receptive to the influence of De Forest, Baker, Woolson, *et al.* Their works, in a sense, merely codified with the emotive powers of proto-realistic fiction what had already been validated by newspaper and journalistic reportage. Therefore, pro-Bourbon fiction must be considered as part of a concerted effort to discredit the Carpetbagger, rehabilitate the Bourbon and, in the process, change the North's opinion about the nature and meaning of Radicalism during the Reconstruction period, especially since the violent eruption of the Pittsburgh Commune uprising, also known as the Great Railroad Strike of 1877.

In the new vision, the Freedman of reality is no longer worthy of the disruptions resulting from the attempt to Americanize him; his Northern mentors are no longer the carriers of the North's civilizing powers; the Bourbons are no longer the enemies of the Union, but its legitimate representatives in the New South. Moreover, since the Bourbon is willing to loyally abide by the decision of 1865, it is best that *all* sociopolitical problems related to the South be left in his responsible hands, *without further intervention from the North*. De Forest's picture of the conniving Carpetbagger, Baker's image of the Afro-Saxon rascal, and Woolson's depiction of the suffering Southerner formed a montage of belief and attitude aimed at securing Northern acquiescence to this new vision. And because this montage was identified with the "factual" revelations in anti-radical media, because of the local color aesthetics that presented it, because of the authors' insistence on their objectivity, anti-radical fiction was considered not so much as the imagined creation of the romancer, or the distortions of the polemicists, but as the objective data of the realist.[443]

But it is a spurious realism: Anti-radical fiction is an even more inaccurate picture of the period than pro-radical fiction, though like the pro-Bourbon vision in general it is perhaps reliable in its details—the corruption of some Radicals, the viciousness of some Freedmen, the nobility of some Southrons. But when this literature is placed against the touchstone of Revisionist historiography, it reveals patterns of inaccuracies: The Woolsons tend to exaggerate their instances, reconstruct the historical data and, in all cases, denigrate the virtues of the enemy (this more than the Pro-Radicals). Yet such manipulation of Reconstruction history is not without its specific, political rationale. These writers show through compelling images that the verifiable atrocities unleashed at Red River, Hamburg, and Yazoo against the Radicals were both necessary and morally justified in order to redeem the South from Carpetbaggery. They, moreover, identify this redemption with the national movement toward reconciliation and "reform," thereby giving further sanctity to the Bourbon cause.

As a new vision of the First Reconstruction, as an adjunct to the anti-Carpetbagger media, as a defense of redemption, these novels and short stories are a component of those polemic forces which, in part, shaped the tragic doom of the Carpetbagger and his comrades. In Rayford Logan's work, *The Betrayal of the Negro*, one can see a dark age settling over the South and the nation *apropos* the Afro-U.S. American as citizen. That this darkness came down the Southern sky with such inexorable progress and with such little protest from the Republican establishment was in itself an ultimate demonstration of the far-reaching influence that anti-radical opinion (reflected in the fiction) would have on the new Union.

• • •

> "We will not aid you nor protect you. Though you are ignorant, from you will we demand the works of wisdom. Though you are weak, great things shall be required. . . ."
>
> Like the ancient taskmaster, the Nation said: "There shall no straw be given you, yet shall ye deliver the [quota] of bricks."[444]

Anti-radical viewpoint, then, defines the ideological thrust of the first group of fictional works; the second group is defined by the absence of a clearly articulated viewpoint or, more often, by an inclusion of a balanced one.

This is the body of short stories and novels in this survey designated as neutralist Reconstruction fiction. The neutralist position lies now clearly and now ambivalently between anti-radical and pro-radical points of view. Such centrality does not in itself imply a closer fidelity to the historical "facts" of the period. Rather, it merely indicates the manner in which the author aesthetically treats the conflict between Bourbon and Carpetbagger (though at the same time, such treatment is often quite objective when measured against Revisionist historiography).

In essence, the author's treatment meets one or more of the following criteria. First, the issues dealt with are devoid of the partisanship inherent in anti-radical and pro-radical fiction. Second, there is a deliberate balancing of the positive and the negative characteristics of the opposing factions: A vicious Carpetbagger must be balanced by a vicious Southern, a virtuous Bourbon by a radical counterpart. Finally, the neutralist writer must, as in tenuous fiction, use themes and narrative situations designed to underscore reconciliation in a style devoid of polemic rhetoric. To put it another way: A work is defined as neutralist when its themes evolve either from the absence or from the balanced presentation of the Carpetbagger-Bourbon conflict.

In light of this definition, then, an examination of six works should illustrate the fictional use of these criteria. The first is De Forest's "Parole d'Honneur" (1868),[445] a tale of the restoration period, which deals with that rather tiresome theme of sectional reconciliation, celebrated so frequently in anti-fiction. However, more interesting than the theme is the narrative texture that acts out the cliché. This texture is clearly derived from the realistic descriptions found in *A Union Officer*. As in this work, De Forest depicts the chaotic sociopolitical conditions of the period when the Confederacy lay abject under the first military occupation, numbed by the magnitude of its defeat and not yet admitted into the well-detested but much needed Union ("I do wish this miserable government would hurry up and reconstruct us—at least the mail."); when some of the great plantations were being confiscated and impoverished, aristocrats were forced to sell priceless heirlooms or, worse, were impelled by necessity to rent out rooms like common innkeepers. The narrative texture, then, derives from that moment when the South lay between Appomattox and the radical insurgence, neither in rebellion nor in the Union.[446]

Within this context and in terms of the reconciliation dynamic, De Forest describes life and love in Brownsville, a small village in the Richland district of Greenville County, South Carolina—the stamping grounds of his old Bureau days.[447] The narrative center is the *ménage à trois* first seen in this study in "Rodman the Keeper": the Bitter Belle, the Union Officer, and the Confederate Veteran. The chief figure is the Veteran, Alec M'Call; the chief action is his demoralized reactions and subsequent adjustment to the new realities. It is through him and his family that De Forest depicts the fortitude with which many Southrons faced the exigency of the restoration:

> ". . . it's horrible to be so poor. . . . to be bankrupt and beggarly and a deputy-sheriff and have no home but a boarding-house kept by one's mother! I tell you . . . that I sometimes wish I had been killed in the war. No outlook—no chance ahead—nothing but life-long bankruptcy."[448]

Despite the real agony of abandoning their old genteel ways, the members of the M'Call family make their adjustment to the new reality. Mrs. M'Call converts the family mansion into a rooming house and takes in Yankee soldiers as boarders. Her two daughters, after a period of perfunctory hostility, eventually marry two of the Blue Coat lodgers. Alex joins the military government. Because he is one of the few responsible men in the district allowed to take the "parole," he is offered a post as deputy-sheriff. He accepts in order to help his mother and sisters survive their destitution. Through the fortunes of the Veteran and Alec's family, De Forest depicts the toughness and resiliency of patricians forced by necessity to submit to Union power.

In contrast to this acquiescence, there is the intransigent enmity of the Belle, Mollie Prater. De Forest gives to her the conventional reason for this attitude: Her family had been scattered, her plantation and its wealth destroyed or freed, the cause for which so much blood and devotion had been given brought down in shattered ruins—all because of this Union power. The new reality to which Alex adapts has forced her to come to the M'Calls' as a refugee and boarder, compelled by her indigence to live partially off their charity. She who had been a highborn lady must now seek work—as a common schoolteacher.

The final member of the triangle is James Humphreys, the Union Officer, and one of the three Yankee boarders. As the Officer, he is basically without complexity, a mere illustration of the magnanimous Yankee. He is a protector of the M'Call family and becomes Alec's friend. It is he who helps him obtain his post as deputy sheriff. Thus, between the Veteran and the Officer, a Rodmanesque relationship burgeons. But his effort to achieve the conventional erotic relationship with the Belle ends in failure. Humphreys falls in love with Mollie and seeks, in his naïve gentility, to woo her from the Lost Cause. But too much desolation and suffering lie in the way. These factors, in addition to her obstinate vindictiveness, defeat Humphreys' magnanimity. Mollie responds to his kindness and concern with ostensible affection in the hopes of humiliating him as her Yankee scapegoat. The chance comes, he proposes, she turns on him with all the bitterness poisoning her life. Shocked by the suddenness of her *volte-face*, Humphreys retreats in confusion, leaving the field to his friend Alec.

De Forest avoids the easy reconciliation of *Ravenel*, "Rum Creeters," and *The Bloody Chasm*, concentrating on the reconciliation between the Confederate Veteran and the Union Officer. It is through their shared virtues, as representatives of the North and South, that Alec is converted to the new Unionism. Through this conversion is symbolized the voluntary reconciliation between the sections championed by the moderate Republicans. Thus, Humphreys, like Rodman, loses the Belle but wins the Veteran.

All the characters are brought to a moment of truth by the chief narrative event in the tale: the destruction of the Prater gang. Leroy Prater, a former

Confederate officer in a special forces group, and Mollie's beloved father, lead a band of post-Appomattox bushwhackers in bloody forays against the peace of the district. Like his daughter he refuses to surrender to Union power; instead he is still carrying on a war of massacre and fire against the Army and the new and old Unionists in the county.[449]

The destruction of this gang represents more than the elimination of pre-Klan terrorists.[450] It is a narrative act imaging in microcosm the political dimensions of the Reconstruction, especially as related to the moderate-Republican ideas about the reconstitution of the South. Both moderate and Radical Republicans eventually rejected the restoration policies of Lincoln and Johnson. Both believed in reconstitution; they differed primarily over personnel. For the Radical, this personnel was to consist of Carpetbaggers and Freedmen with the Southern Unionists (usually the poorer classes) acting as satellites. For the Conservatives, it was to be made up of Southern Whigs and their Carpetbag counterparts, with Freedmen and poor-white yeomen acting as satellites. It is this latter political concept the raid images. The narrative action divides into three parts: the makeup of the raiders as they prepare to battle the gang, the climax of their attack, and the results of the attack.

The main elements of the raiding party are white Northerners and white Southerners, represented respectively by Union Soldiers and ex-Confederate volunteers. This party is, moreover, led by the Veteran with the assistance of the Officer.[451] It is this coalition of white forces the Republican moderates saw as the essential element in their plan of reconstitution. And associated with this primary coalition in their proper roles as subordinates are the white and black lower classes who support and sustain this relationship, represented in this incident by the informants who supply the attacking raiders with important leads to the location of the gang.

At the climactic moment, the second part of this incident, Mollie reveals that the captured gang leader is her father, and she asks Alec to permit him to escape. He refuses. She then appeals to his old loyalties, arguing in effect that her father's massacres were continuations of the war against the Union, that his victims were enemies of the Confederacy, Tories whom ". . . he killed . . . for the good cause—the lost cause." When this appeal fails, Mollie tries the libidinal approach: She attempts to kiss Alec and promise him her love, gratitude, and devotion if he will allow Prater to escape. But the appeal neither to his old loyalties nor to his present affections seduces him from his *parole d'honneur*. He rejects the Belle, sacrificing her love to his new loyalties, and resolutely fulfills his duty as the Scalawag deputy sheriff of Richland district. The same *honneur* that defined Alec's life as a Cavalier now shapes his life as a Unionist. The ultimate result of the raid then is the destruction of the bushwhackers and a ratification of Alec's voluntary acceptance of the new Union: "I've sworn to be faithful in future to the United States. Word of honor! Word of a gentleman."[452]

What is discerned in the raid incident is a call for Union men and willing ex-Confederates to join together in a crusade against those irrational forces of violence and hate that threaten postwar stability and that block the meta-political reunion desired by Southern and Northern moderates. Mollie becomes those aspects of the Lost Cause psychology that prevent reunion—the nostalgic hatred, the hallowed chauvinism, the bitter sentimentality; her father exemplifies the cruel violent dimensions of the Cause. Humphreys is the Victorious Cause, not only as a military power but also as a generous triumph. Alec, by joining with this power and accepting this generosity, becomes the New Southerner who, by capturing Prater and rejecting Mollie's pleas, embraces the new Union and turns his back on the Old Cause and the Old South.

In this allegory of Reconstruction, it is precisely this political-psychological gesture that will secure the reconciliation of the sections and render the Southern acceptable to the moderate Republicans as their Southern ally. The raid on Prater's stronghold becomes for the triad, therefore, an allegoric epiphany: The Bitter Belle is rejected; the Confederate Veteran proves the authenticity of his conversion; White Southerner and White Northerner coalesce to eradicate Praterism from the southscape. This latter point is the essential theme in De Forest's tale and represents his neutralist variation on the conflict symbology. In addition, his deliberate balancing of honorable ex-Confederate and Union officers in a common cause helps to establish in a characteristic way the pervasive neutrality of the work.

The next work, Marion Harland's serialized novella, *The Wall-Flower* (1870), exemplifies the first criterion of neutralist fiction—the use of themes devoid of the fierce emotions of the more partisan works. A major theme in this group is the reconciliation cliché. As with "Parole," the interest here is more in the coalition of Carpetbagger and Bourbon than in their conflicts.

Coordinate with the cliché is the central theme of the work: the beneficent power of Carpetbaggery in its economic guise and the need for that beneficence by Bourbons broken on the wheel of impoverishment and defeat.

The Northerner is Mr. Dent, a wealthy middle-aged Yankee who embodies in his actions and attitude the contradictory virtues of financial acumen and generosity. He comes South to invest in the economic progress created in Virginia, the setting of the story, by the policies of the Reconstruction government. In this process, he joins with the Southron to form a coalition of skills through which both will exploit Southern resources for mutual benefit. The Bourbon will supply his extensive knowledge of the region; the Carpetbagger will supply his money and business knowhow. This is an additional elaboration of the Conservative Republicans' vision of the white-white coalition as an alternative to the white-black one.

The Bourbon is represented in this novella collectively by the Temple family and specifically by the eldest daughter, Bertha. She is that familiar female in this fiction, the embittered but plucky Belle whose head is turned backwards to the grandeur of 1861 and the collapse of 1865. Yet under the pressures of the new reality, it is she who leads in rejecting a dead pride.[453] Through her, Dent becomes the savior of the stricken family. Quite clearly she is the conjugal symbol in the reconciliation dynamic. She becomes Dent's bride in a flurry of literary polarities, i.e., the May-December, North-South, and Carpetbagger-Bourbon couplets. However, unlike what happens in the model reconciliation novel, the marriage does not occur as the climax of the tale, but midway in the narrative.

This gives Harland a chance to develop realistically the problems involved in such polarities, including Dent's disillusionment in discovering that Bertha still resents him as a Carpetbagger and, alas, has only married him to save the family. Eventually, through tedious but not uninteresting melodramatic events, including Dent's near death in the collapse of the Capitol in Richmond in 1870, Bertha is brought to realization of her love for her elderly Carpetbagger.

Her main function is to transform Dent's love into the shower of gold that redeems the Temples from penury and labor. Through such beneficence, a variety of admirable transformations occur: The family mansion is refurbished and once more becomes the center of brilliant social gatherings; Ellen Temple, Bertha's sister, is enabled to marry her hardworking, up-and-coming merchant; most of all, Mr. Temple is converted from agrarianism to mercantilism, becoming Dent's business partner at a high salary and thus fulfilling the demands of the coalition symbol.

In light of these remarks, it seems quite clear that *The Wall-Flower* does not fit the standard definition of the sociopolitical form. On the contrary, because the political themes are so explicitly repressed (for neutralist reasons) and because it makes liberal use of reconciliation and economic symbology, the work could be classified as semi-Reconstruction fiction. But, as in "Rodman the Keeper," the work's texture, thematic implications, and rhetorical shaping give it a strong sociopolitical thrust. This can be seen in a variety of explicit ways:

First of all, the narrative is set in Richmond, Virginia, during the Reconstruction period, and there are specific allusions to that rule. However, there is a more subtle allusion to the sociopolitical in what might be called the Temple mansion trope; that is to say, in the recurring contrast between the Southron's past grandeur and his present fall from grace.[454]

There is the poignancy of that remembered grandeur:

> Laces and jewels, that had been heirlooms for generations . . . [,] ancient silver stamped with crest-tankards, goblets, and the like—and mighty mustering of courtly "gentlemen of the old school," with white neckcloths and shaven chins, smoothly-gallant speech and Chesterfieldian bows. . . .[455]

Then the present, personal degradation:

> . . . the pretty feet and hands for which the beautiful matron was noted in the days of carriages and best French kids [i.e., kid gloves]; the feet now chilled by carpetless floors and damp pavements; the fingers roughened by labor, the dear patient eyes, strained early and late over needlework for which she was to be paid like a vulgar, illiterate sewing girl. . . . The petty anxieties . . . swarmed about the poor lady like noisy and vicious mosquitoes.[456]

All this contrast is emblematic in the condition of the once stately Temple mansion:

> The paint . . . scaling . . . in unsightly blotches as if the building had broken out with leprosy. The inner shutters

> were now a dirty yellow, and many a yawning pane bespoke . . . abject poverty. . . . The flooring was rotten and discolored. . . . And inside the lofty ceiling, defaced with dust and dampness, and massive cornices; from which pieces had fallen. . . . The furniture . . . partook of the general air of decadence. The upholstery was frayed, . . . The windows were curtainless.[457]

In terms of the Temple mansion metaphor, the Southern aristocrats find in the New Era "grimness in place of fairness, burning for beauty, ashes in heart as upon hearthstones."[458] The juxtaposition of the mansion's ancient glories with its ugly decrepitude becomes the novella's key symbol for the Southrons' loss of political supremacy under the new regime.[459]

But the clearest manifestation of the sociopolitical element occurs paradoxically, in the economic field. The explicit contrast between Dent and the Temple family stands for that recurring sociopolitical archetype in Reconstruction symbolism—the Locomotive and the Garden. Through his financial largess, Dent wins each member of the family from the older system of chattelism, agrarianism, oligarchy, and inefficiency that the *ancien regime* represented. The moderate Bourbons join the economic Carpetbaggers in a new cause: the renovation of the South through Northern men, methods, and capital. In other words, the real reconstruction begins with the acceptance of the Yankee's system of political economy. Whether in terms of Southern problems in general or the Temples' problems in particular, Mr. Dent's magic carpetbag makes all things well.

The emphasis on the economic motif also makes Harland's story clearly a neutralist work, since this is one of the themes (reconciliation is another) drained of the furious partisanship characteristic of the political issues. The assertions that the destruction of slavery freed the land for a better economic system, that the economic recovery of the South was the foremost political problem of the First Reconstruction, and that the Southrons had to adopt a work ethic if they were to aid in this recovery ("necessity made labor honorable")[460] were issues with which most Conservatives and Radicals would have had little disagreement. The economic motif then (and the reconciliation convention) makes *The Wall-Flower* a not-uninteresting example of neutralist fiction, this despite the fact that in the end the issue that eventually dominates all is whether an old man can win the love of his young wife. Perhaps this was the easiest way to achieve the neutralist stance on an aesthetic level: to raise pertinent issues about the period and then wash them away in a flood of melodramatic sentimentalism.

The neutrality in the next work, De Forest's "An Independent Ku Klux" (1872), does not, as in the previous two stories, lie in a single criterion but in a combination. First, there is the absence of a discernible point of view on the Carpetbagger-Bourbon conflict. Indeed, this conflict *per se* is absent, though technically it is automatically present in the Reconstruction symbolism associated with the Klan. The interest is instead in the social conflict between poor-white and poor-black.[461] Second, where the conflict *is* discussed, both Bourbon and Carpetbagger vices are excoriated. De Forest's mouthpiece for this view is a tertiary character, Squire Rawson, a post-Appomattox Unionist.

Finally, and more subtly, the neutrality of the work resides in the even, objective tone, generated by the work's realism. De Forest tells a straightforward tale of a low-downer named Bowen and his brief role as a Klan bully-boy. The narrative emphasis is on a realistic exploration of Bowen's character and the effect of his membership in the Klan on that character, and not on the depiction of the Kluxers as an image of the Conflict. "An Independent Ku Klux" is not so much a study of the Klan as it is a realist study of one man's participation in its terror.[462]

Bowen is more than a poor Southerner. He is that recurring figure in Southern literature, the "poor white," the Saxon counterpart to the "degraded African." In Reconstruction nonfiction, he appears as social type and cultural symbol, representing in DeForest's nonfiction one of the definitive characters of the Southern locale in its primitive state. His women are shown as barely human:

> The mother, forty-three, looking sixty, short and broadly built, haggard, wrinkled, filthy, with desperate gray eyes and unkempt gray hair. The daughter, fifteen . . . , with a white freckled face and yellow hair, . . . one garment, a ragged frock of cotton homespun, unbleached, uncolored, and foul with long wearing. Not large enough to meet in front, it was tied with twine in a loose fashion, exposing entirely one of her breasts. [In] her arms, another child, a wretched-looking baby of six weeks old, tied up in an old rag of carpet, her own illegitimate offspring. Her first words were, "How you gin'n long?" Her next, "Got anythin' for the lone wimmin?"[463]

His homes are worse than the slave's cabins:

> . . . one large room, with fireplace, two doorways, and two windows. . . . [The] windows were merely square openings, without glass or sashes, and closed by board shutters. The logs . . . were unhewn [and the mud had fallen away in spots letting the winter wind in]. The moisture which came through these hencoop sides and through the porous roof drained off though the rotten and shattered floor. No furniture . . . beyond two broken chairs, two or three cooking utensils, and a pile of filthy rags which seemed to be bedding.[464]

His neighborhoods reflect conditions not even found in the slave quarters:

> The few houses to be seen were forlorn-looking shanties, belonging to the poor white trash, with rotten steps and doors awry, and foul passages and oozy back yards. Here and there we met a creaking cart, drawn by an ox or a broken-down horse, laden with rickety pine furniture, and guided by the lank, lantern-jawed, stubby-bearded, long-haired owner. He was "toting" his goods in from some house which Sherman's "bummers" had . . . plundered. If his "woman" trudged . . . behind him, be sure she assuaged the fatigues of the journey with great quids of tobacco . . . while the ragged, frowzy children were kept busy with the vagaries of the cow.[465]

De Forest continues this image of poor white degeneration in his short story. In an almost direct parallel with his Pompey Howard descriptions, De Forest presents Bowen in loathing, local color detail as the scum of white Southern society:

> Malaria had hollowed his abdomen and gauged out his cheeks and sunk his eyes and pinched his temples . . . ; cramming him to reeking with all the monotonous tints of dumb ague; using up on him the richness of acres of decaying trees and of creeks full of oozing vegetable mud. [He was] unwholesome and ugly and dismally picturesque.[466]

Along with Bowen's physical disabilities are his moral ones. Not only is he ignorant and gullible, but he is a pig-stealer, wife-beater, and moonshiner. He is, in a word, the white savage and, for De Forest, the descendant of white savagery. His progenitors in the New World were the illiterate convicts deported to Virginia; in the Old World they were the scrofulous tramps along English highways and the *Lumpen-proletariat* within English cities; in the dim reaches of history, his Aryan ancestors were even then noted for their moral viciousness. Bowen emerges as the summation of a genetic heritage worthy of the Kallikaks and the Jukeses, mythic figures in racist genetic studies of white degeneracy. De Forest describes him as burdened with the same kind of inherent disability as he had reserved, in his anti-radical literature, for the Freedman. The white savage's only virtue is his blind obedience to the command of his betters. This then is the figure who would form the rank and file of the Bourbon terrorists in a perverse variation on the theme of social symbiosis at the South.[467]

Bowen's membership in the Klan originates in a complex of motives. As a white man, he wishes to put presumptuous ex-slaves in their place; as a paragon of civic virtue, he wishes to punish them for their vices; as a crypto-Southron, he seeks that status in the eyes of his betters that anti-radical violence afforded, e.g., "Square" Anderson and Rary Saxton, the KKK leaders, as they all "go for [the] nigger." This, of course, is Bowen's essential motive: "Folks want to put them down. An' I go for it."[468]

In order to acquire such license, Bowen undergoes an initiation that is a comic parody of the Klan ritual. Ironically, it is Squire Rawson who jokingly administers to the gullible low-downer an improvised string of gibberish, which he passes off as the sacred oath. But this comic initiation has tragic consequences. Bowen, acting under what he believes are his Klan rights, breaks into the shack of one Ham Irvine, an enterprising Negro cobbler, and tries to steal his dearest possession, a large hog. The scene in which Bowen struggles inconclusively to capture the beast is in the high tradition of frontier humor. However, when Irvine returns and tries to stop the assault on his pig, he is mercilessly shot down. At that moment comedy bursts into horror. Irvine becomes, because of accident and intent, a victim of "an outrage," to be avenged by Federal troops.

De Forest is not interested in the obvious victim, whose demise is presented without feeling; he is interested in Bowen, who emerges in this perfectly realized sketch as the true victim: victimized by his genes, his economic helplessness, his brutalizing culture of poverty and, most of all, by his betters. He emerges as the poor white savage whose unquestioning trust in his superiors is prostituted by them for ignoble ends. Bowen, not Ham, is the true victim.

As far as the larger dimensions of Reconstruction politics are concerned, the work reflects these dimensions only intermittently. Through his mouthpiece, Squire Rawson, De Forest asserts that often the White Terror offered to Bowens an excuse to rob and maltreat the ex-slave and justified under the cloak of political ideology the low-downers' natural propensity for violence against their old enemies.[469] This seems to be De Forest's main point. As in *A Union Officer*, he believes that not all crimes against the Freedman were a part of that insidious political conspiracy instigated by the Southrons in their plot to stave off reconstitution. Thus, "An Independent Ku Klux" may be seen primarily as a study of the social conditions of the pre-reconstitution period that allowed the explosion of violence against the Afro-U.S. American; it is also a study of the lower-class mentality that in part sustained that violence.

These themes are presented with a neutrality of tone that is maintained throughout: The horror of Irvine's death is balanced by the horror of Bowen's life, the political presumption of the offstage Carpetbagger by the political terror of the Bourbon. It is this objectivity that gives to this serio-comic work its inexorable movement toward the tragic in a manner faintly reminiscent of "The Blue Hotel." In this short story, De Forest returns to that realist modality missing since *Ravenel* from his Reconstruction fiction.

The next work to be considered is Mary E. Bryan's *Wild Work: The Story of the Red River Massacre* (1881), one of the major and (in some ways) one of the best Reconstruction novels that this research uncovered. It is also the key neutralist work, a rather startling fact when one considers that it was written by a faithful daughter of the Confederacy. But there are many things surprising about this, none of which is explicable by its background.

Its author, Mary Bryan, was the editor of a local magazine called *The Sunny South*, a magazine in which *Wild Work* first appeared as a serial in 1877, two years, she insists, before *A Fool's Errand*.[470] In contrast to the professional Southronism of *The Sunny South*, Bryan's novel is an excellent surprise, both in terms of its art and its thematic neutrality.[471] Bryan insists upon this neutrality: Her chief aim is to avoid "sectional prejudice" and political partisanism.[472] She seeks, instead, to lift out of the sociopolitical flux the inherent romantic and melodramatic tendencies.

Her thematic neutrality becomes a necessary adjunct to this aesthetic goal, a process achieved in several ways. Bryan balances the good Bourbon with the bad, the evil Radical against the good. She continually uses a rhetoric of reconciliation throughout her work, though she quite skillfully avoids the clichés. But her most unusual strategy is to shift the causes of the Reconstruction *agon* away from the intrinsic political nature of the Irrepressible Conflict between Bourbon and Carpetbagger. Instead, these causes reside either in the realm of purely human passions—ambition, envy, personal vindictiveness—or in the historical flux of the period. In either case, Bryan aims to see the antagonists as victims of a larger machinery of doom, whose tragic inexorability they cannot see, so intent are they on their manipulation of political forces. All these strategies combine to save her work from Charybdis (sentimental reconciliation) and Scylla (vindictive Anti-Radicalism). Of course, as a Southerner she is against the Reconstruction, and this is reflected in infrequent anti-radical distortions. But these are minor flaws in the overall neutralist design of the work, a design that, to a great degree, underlies the aesthetic success of the work.

The other contributing factor is the narrative thrust of *Wild Work*, especially the startling organic relationship of plot detail to this thrust and the way in which this detail "acts out" the work's thematic structure. There is rarely a description or an incident that does not shape that thrust and that structure. This unexpected sophistication can be seen in a variety of ways.

Bryan's choice of setting, for example, does more than just give the work's location and period; it provides a narrative context for the action that evolves directly from the historical place and the historical time. The events of Reconstruction in Louisiana (Bryan's home state) during the period 1872 to 1877 provide her with a series of readymade, melodramatic occurrences with which to construct her complications and to "act out" her ideas. This is seen in the reiterated symbol, the Garden, or more precisely, the Garden-as-Wilderness.

Louisiana was the place in Reconstruction literature where the Garden-as-Wilderness was more than a mere archetypal metaphor or trope or symbol. As the nonfictionists pointed out, it was precisely the physical existence of vast tracts of bayous, swamps, and canebrakes that gave the state its savage charm:

> It was near sunset when they entered the river-swamp. Adelle felt the difference . . . the moment that, after crossing a small bayou, she rode under the great ash-, and gum-, and cypress-trees, hung with huge, festooning vines, with a carpet of grass underneath.
>
> The shadow and stillness of death seemed to brood under those great trees and knotted vines. Not a bird sang—the rustle of a snake among the grass—the stealthy flap of an owl's wing, as the bird . . . flew away, skimming his level flight among the huge tree-trunks—these were the only sounds that broke the gloomy silence.
>
> The shrunken, muddy river glowed sluggishly between its steep banks; the poisonous night fog was beginning already to rise from it, and from the half dried-up sloughs filled with rank grass, tall blossoming weeds and croaking frogs.[473]

But this savagery of landscape had a more profound significance: It symbolized a permissiveness that presented immense potential for chaos, in which, as Bryan states, the "comparative freedom from social restraint fostered individuality and independence of character—too often to a lawless extent."[474] Bryan shows in her novel that this lawlessness afforded the fullest license for political anarchy for both her Jacobin and Royalist *personae*.

Within this archetypal landscape, the Carpetbaggers were no match for the anarchic ferocity of the Bourbon terrorists. Here, their counter-revolution was more defiantly instituted than in other states, their "protest against the 'Carpetbag dynasty' more boldly uttered." Maskless and cruelly aggressive, they launched their campaign against the Northern interloper and his allies without scruples, combining massacres, persuasion, and "maneuvres that showed a genius for statecraft" unparalleled in 19th-century U.S. American history.[475] The Radicals were, as Bryan's novel shows, overwhelmed in a surf of blood. But in the wilderness with its Social Darwinist ethic, this was as it should be: To the most ruthless belonged the victory.

Moreover, the incredible acts of violence depicted in the novel leading to that victory are no mere melodramatic posturings; the Louisiana setting validates the realism underlying her descriptions. One has only to read such Revisionist history as Buckmaster's *Freedom Bound* and much later Douglas Egerton's *The Wars of Reconstruction* to see the truth of Bryan's presentation.

On the symbolic level, then, the choice of Louisiana provides Bryan with a physiographic analogue to the Reconstruction anguish. On the literal level, it allows her to appropriate the proto-realistic element inherent in the use of the Reconstruction setting. In both cases period and location create the organic context for the narrative and hence the thematic thrust of the work.

The plot structure *per se* is another way through which Bryan creates an organic relationship between the narrative and the thematic structure. The details forming a work's plot are its complications, those specific, interrelated incidents that lead with causative inevitability to the climax and conclusion. It is with these elements that Bryan constructs the two basic lines of action that make up the plot of her novel and that help to unify the novel's variety of characters: Colonel Alver, the Bourbon antagonist; Floyd, his dark mistress; Cobb, her demon lover; Hirne, a St. Elmo (the type of Byronic hero in a famous novel of that name) as White Leaguer; Zoe, the sweet country girl who tames him; Lanier, the Southron as depraved sensualist; Witchell, the Carpetbagger protagonist; Adelle Holman, his doomed Southern wife; Omar Witchell, his genteel, doomed younger brother; Levi, the Freedman as Magua, the villainous Native American in *The Last of the Mohicans*—"He was a remarkable negro—half breed, rather, for he had Indian blood in his veins. He rode, leaped, swam, and dove like an Indian. His skin was tawny red, his nose straight, his eye keen and watchful."[476] It is within her two basic lines of action and around such characters that Bryan spells out the central idea of her novel: that the conflict between the Bourbon and the Carpetbagger originated in forces beyond their individual control.

Colonel Alver is the chief character in the Bourbon line of complications. Under other circumstances he would have been the villain of the piece, but within the neutralist dynamic such an appellation is imprecise. He is simply the antagonist to the Carpetbagger protagonist. A state leader under the old planter government and a brave though tyrannical officer during the war,[477] Colonel Alver is the natural leader of those Bourbon Democrats arrayed in sullen hostility against the Yankee.

But Alver's counter-revolution against Radicalism grows from more than the antipathies of political and sectional ideology. His pride has been outraged by the Carpetbagger's refusal to let him join the Radicals. (The Yankee recognizes correctly that Alver's profession of loyalty is hypocritical and that within radical ranks this malcontent would be a disruptive force).[478] Alver is angry because the Republicans refused to pay an exorbitant lease fee for his land. He is angry because his own hunger for power is exacerbated by the successful operation of the Carpetbagger and his scum: the benefits Witchell has brought to Cahatchie, the area he now claims as his fiefdom; the ties he has made among some of the Bourbons, the poor-whites, and the ex-slaves; and the facility with which he extracts his share from the state treasury. In a word, it is not Carpetbaggerism alone that upsets Alver; it is his pride, ambition, and envy that also underlie his hostility. More subtly, it is his desire for a share of the spoils, as well as his political ideology, that dominates his emotions and his action. Nevertheless, he sincerely conceives of himself as the chivalric redeemer.

> "I only follow out my own strong inclination when I oppose these tyrants. Justice, patriotism, as well as desire to redress my individual wrongs, make it right to use every means to root them out. Every *honorable* means—dishonorable means I will not be a party to."[479]

The egotist, the materialist, and the idealist, then, merge in Alver. Though he craves power for power's sake, "and wealth as a means to that power," he is "revolted" at using underhand means to accomplish his ends. When Floyd advocates tricking the Radicals into a trap that "will crush—kill them," Alver, in keeping with the neutralist dynamic, objects to such a bloodthirsty program. The use of "assassination, and traps, and dark plots" is not the way of honorable men. This scruple, however, does not mean he is against violence *per se*; rather, he prefers the violence of a just uprising to the violence of treachery and deceit. The uprising he envisions will be a rebellion against "tyrannical laws enforced at the point of the bayonet," against "the rule of corrupt men, who insulted and robbed us." Since "the laws, the Government [give] us no redress, [should] we not force these men to resign, even at the muzzle of the shot-gun?"[480]

But the honorable revolution and treacherous murder, noble Southron and sadistic hyena, would coalesce despite Alver's squeamishness. He too would be tied to the cowardly massacre of the Republicans, though he would not be personally involved; he too would be a part of the emotional surge toward the grotesque horrors at Yazoo, Hamburg, and the Red River.[481]

In the end, he is thrown back on the scraps of his honor at that horrific moment. He is both rationalizing and asserting a kind of truth when he pleads that his counter-revolution aimed only to free his parish "from corrupt alien rule, and to secure to the people representation by their own citizens." And this sense of honor is shown by Bryan as a reality. He helps the Carpetbaggers' widows to arrange for their property and to leave the hated South. His own sense of conscience plagues him for the rest of this life, for though he is acquitted (like many Redeemers because of the Compromise) and eventually makes a successful life in Texas, "his cheek is worn and his eyes hollow," and dark fits of gloom come upon him, growing from the memory of women's shrieks and sullied dreams of honor and renown.[482]

But behind these memories are darker ones: the recollections of passion and lust, for that which had brought Alver's plans to their dishonorable, murderous fruition was his involvement with his ironically platonic mistress, Floyd Reese.

Floyd Reese is a curious figure. On the surface, she is a precise sexist trope, the Belle-as-Bitch, presented in the archetypal form of the desirable Wanton, that libidinal image that dominated Anglo-U.S. American literature in the 19th century. Like such passionate sisters as Hester Prynne (*The Scarlet Letter*) and Charlotte Stant (*The Golden Bowl*), she incarnates that moral ambiguity inherent in the sexually attractive woman. As the female, she is the weaker sex, the Mother-Wife figure to be adored in her purity; as the Wanton, she is Lilith: sensual, fascinating, and evil. Both adultery and murder help to establish this latter characteristic in Floyd, and such a sullied past in turn surrounds her with that fascinating horror that was essential to her captivating powers, like a Bourbon version of Margaret Conrad:

> [Her dress revealed] the outlines of a most seductive shape—at once full and flexible, sumptuous and sinuous, [which] made apparent that charm of form so potent, especially in the eyes of men who are no longer very youthful.
>
> [Her] dress also [had] a negligent grace of its own; from the full sleeve falling back to show her round, white arms, to the muslin folds caught low with a rose under the large white throat. The charm of the lawless and unfettered hung about her. . . .-[483]

But beneath this surface there is another view. What motivates her actions, her rebellion against the code of purity, is more than simple immorality. With her, sexuality masks more subtle hungers. What Floyd really desires (signified by her name) is a perverse, masculine modality of will, ambition, and power:

> I was born to rule. I feel the will and the power struggling within me, and yet here I am, ruling two disgusting brats, and perhaps their commonplace father. . . . I must fly for higher game. If I could attach myself to this bold hawk [Witchell] that is preying to such good purpose on my chickenhearted states-people! Captain Witchell, if I could win your confidence, share your schemes, help you to outwit men, and rise with you to power and riches, it would be all my ambition would crave. It would fill my heart, too—[and then comes her motto] better than love can fill it. . . . Faugh! I have done with love. . . . It has been my bane: if I touch it again, it will be to make it my slave—as stepping-stone to power of some kind.[484]

Since she cannot attain this goal as a woman, she will attain it vicariously through males, using her dark eroticism and her cunning intelligence as puppet strings by which her lovers will dance to her desires. This is the complex feminist psychology undergirding the bitch-image serving as her synecdoche.

Floyd, in this quest for vicarious masculinity, first offers herself to the Carpetbagger as his confidante and his *aide-de-camp*. But Witchell's knowledge of her stained past causes him to reject her. (Through a series of Charles Dickensian complications, Witchell had saved Floyd from certain death when she had almost been lynched because of her complicity in the murder of her husband in Texas by her lover, Cobb.) He also rejects her relatively selfless offer because of his own preoccupation with the more obvious elements of power politics. In these plans, he simply sees no place for a woman's hands. This rejection is the key initial complication in the story, for Floyd, as a result, becomes that worst of all enemies, the scorned woman:

> [She looked at him,] the look full of the rage and hate of a woman who finds that she is known at her worst; who feels she has humbled herself uselessly; that her game has been seen through and despised as more contemptible even than it was, for there might have been some real honesty in that offer of devoted service to Captain Witchell. . . . He might have found such a woman a valuable ally. He would have hesitated before he turned her into an enemy. . . . But,

> preoccupied with big schemes, he lost sight of smaller policies. He had but little hypocrisy in his nature, and but little softness or flexibility. . . . He thought of this beautiful woman as a sort of human leopard. He shook her from him as such, and went on his way, thinking he had done with her forever, foreseeing not that, with more of the wolf than the leopard's nature, she would track him with her revenge.[485]

In order to effect this revenge and at the same time express her demonic will-to-power, Floyd then offers herself to the Bourbon. Alver accepts—rather is seduced into accepting her aid in his rebellion against Carpetbaggery. In a kind of perverse platonic relationship, Floyd dangles her eroticism before him but never lets him possess it, promising him fulfillment only when he redeems the parish. "He was under the influence of the wily charmer. She bewildered and attracted him, but she adroitly held him at arm's length and increased her power over him by preserving his respect for her as a woman."[486] Frustrated sexuality then becomes the key to her domination over the Southron. Indeed, sexuality is the socio-psychic basis for the counter-revolution. In this way, she becomes Alver's evil angel. When he would surrender, she goads him on with promises of sexual fulfillment and appeals to his ambition:

> 'All my hopes, [states Alver to Floyd,] are staked upon [this venture], even that of love. If I lose, I know you will despise me! If I win—but you have never . . . given me . . . one womanly token of affection—not one touch of that ripe mouth, not one throb of that white breast against mine—nothing.'
>
> 'But I will,' she whispered . . . 'Have I not promised? [When] Witchell is hurled from his seat in the Assembly, when Alver is placed upon it . . . then all the kisses of these lips, all the throbs of this heart [shall be yours].'[487]

When he counsels restraint, believing that reform "must stop short of blood," that the innocent should not suffer with the guilty, she calls for the violent purgation of Carpetbag power from the Louisiana landscape:

> They have ruined hundreds. What would even their deaths be? A small sacrifice to freedom. No great wrong can be righted without some sacrifice. . . . It is your duty to look only to the purpose. . . . Not to mind what worms you may crush.[488]

And when he would spare the captured Carpetbaggers, she orders their deaths behind his back: "It is the only way to rid our section of this pest. . . . Lop off one tentacle, and he will put out another. No lopping or crippling, but *crushing*. And if not by fair means, then by foul."[489] Indeed, the acts of terrorism culminating in the Carpetbagger deaths (and four others) are directly laid to her charge.

In a word, Floyd is the dark nemesis that, under the Bourbon aegis, rouses ex-slave against ex-master and fans into bloodshed the inherent rivalry between Conservative and Radical. She is the force of violence that Alver sought to bend to his will; instead, it controlled him and eventually brought down in ruin and bloodshed both the Carpetbagger *and* the Bourbon.

But Floyd, despite such power of enthrallment, is herself enthralled—to Cobb, her master and love-slave. He controls her with his knowledge of their previous adulterous intrigues and their joint complicity in the murder of her husband. At the same time, he is her personal agent who commits the crimes Alver refuses to countenance. She loathes Cobb but must, because of his knowledge, give to him what she refuses to give to Alver:

> "One kiss, then," and the thick, ugly mouth pressed itself on her quivering lips, on her cheeks that grew dead-white with disgust. It was gall and wormwood to the woman whose fastidious taste was her only substitute for conscience, but fear forced her to yield.[490]

In the end, Floyd is abandoned by Alver for her part in the massacre and for her corruption of his soul. In order to escape a variety of fates—her complicity in the killings, her own sense of guilt, Cobb whom she had betrayed—Floyd tries to flee by boat to Cuba:

> She stood leaning on the railing, the sunset reflection making her fair skin more dazzling, her plenteous hair more like spun red gold. The fine molding of her bust, her arms, and limbs was apparent under the soft clinging dress of gray. She knew men were looking at her with quickened pulses. She was thinking, "Once in Cuba . . . [those] meager, swarthy Spaniards will lose their senses over my white, plump beauty."[491]

But she is caught in connection with the Texas murder, and in desperation she wordlessly leaps overboard "and the dark waters closed over that fair face forever."[492]

Floyd's relationship with the Reconstruction conflicts, the Bourbon line of plot, and the thematic thrust of the work is now quite clear. She becomes not so much a separate character as Alver's alter ego, so closely do her actions help to form the Bourbon plot. As a thematic device, she is the character around whom the neutralist ideology of the work is built, for on her shoulders Bryan places the blame for the bloodiness of the conflict between the political antagonists. The cause of the sociopolitical tensions in *Wild Work* is not so much Reconstruction as it is the Bourbon's lust for Lilith and her lust for vengeance and power. The counter-revolution is no longer deliberate acts of cruelty generated by the ideology of the Mississippi Plan, but an act of blood and maneuver committed under the pressures of a demonic passion. Thus, Floyd Reese emerges as the dark fate that betrays with such tragic consequences the ambitions of the Carpetbagger and the Bourbon. Thematically and narratively, then, she emerges as the authentic villain in the novel and a dominant figure in the Bourbon line of plot.

The other line of complications in *Wild Work* centers, of course, on the Carpetbagger. His development is the model of the Reconstruction-Horatio Alger saga. He comes South, lately from New England and the Union Army and, through intelligence, shrewdness, and manipulation of radical power, parlays his carpetbag into political conquest. The complicational thrust in the narration resides in the attempt of Cap'n Witchell to become the governor of Louisiana. (By the way, this is one of the few novels that uses an actual historical figure for a character, as Witchell is based on the Radical, Marshall H. Twitchell.)

He is seen rising from a simple post to legislative and judicial eminence, culminating in his control of the Cahatchie parish, his own well-run satrapy, with its own newspaper and factory. He also speculates in tax-loss real estate deals, practices efficient nepotism, controls voter procedures, and uses appropriations from the legislature to run his personal businesses. Under his management Cahatchie becomes his county-seat and the economic center of his material reconstruction of the area. There he resides in full splendor—beneficent, grafting, utterly powerful— the Machine in the Garden. His "power with his own party and his popularity with the Negroes and 'poor whites,' together with the opportunity for controlling elections . . ." ensure his hegemony. And the very success of his operations for both Radicals and Bourbons alike—that is, those Bourbons who work directly and indirectly with him—wears off much of the "edge of aversion with which the radical ring was regarded."[493]

In the purely political area, Witchell's moves are shrewd and well-calculated. He operates independently of the two Republican factions, the Warmoth and the Kellogg groups, but keeps in good contact with both. He builds up goodwill among the party chiefs, the Freedmen, and the Scalawags. He seeks earnestly, at least initially, to conciliate the Bourbons, many of whom respect his "qualities as a leader, while he earns their goodwill in more personal ways [,]" including saving the lives of his enemies and his enemies' children. From these bases, he seeks to organize his own faction of strong "and daring spirits whom he would bind to him by ties of gratitude and interest" in order to create a more effective political organization. Consequently, "when the time came . . . , he might be strong enough to seize the supreme prize—the chief Executor's chair, now filled by the adventurer Warmoth, the shrewd, the daring, and unscrupulous." And he sincerely believes that he is using, and will use his wealth, power, and influence, to help all the members of the parish, regardless of color and sectional affiliation.[494]

This, then, is the picture of the enterprising, ambitious Carpetbagger. But as with Alver, Bryan balances this picture with another: that of the unscrupulous opportunist. Adelle Holman, an anti-radical Belle whom he once saved from drowning, asserts that he has gained power through "unjust measures and an ignorant negro vote," that he has taken over abandoned plantations and sold them to finance his nefarious operations, that he has pocketed the appropriations for "cleaning out Lake Wisteneau," a boondoggling operation in which he gets $30,000 "for clearing out of a few harmless snags!"[495] And this is Witchell's tragedy: In the beginning, states a planter-colleague, he had a chance of becoming the good ruler who, through discretion and the severest honesty, could have won the…

> head and heart of this people. You had done them many good turns; you possessed a genius for governing which they were quick to recognize; you had personal magnetism; you could

have lived down prejudice and made yourself a permanent throne in the esteem and the necessities of the people.[496]

Instead, he becomes engrossed in the drive for money and power; he will brook no interference, he will rule on his own terms.

His efforts are almost crowned with success. The 1876 campaign seems certain to place him in the governor's chair. He is powerful, and his control over his organization is complete. And though Alver is preparing a counter-offensive, nothing, it seems, will prevent the triumph. But 1876 is a bad year for ambitious Carpetbaggers. The final wars of sectional liberation are unleashed; the violence latent in the Louisiana soulscape erupts around Witchell: his brother, friends, and fellow Radicals are massacred by Alver's White Leaguers; the Republicans lose state power; the murderers are acquitted by the national Republicans as a part of the Compromise, including allowing a Democrat to become governor. Witchell's dreams of empire collapse, and he becomes the embittered but impregnable ruler of Cahatchie. Despite the Bourbon holocaust, his parish remains in his hands as one of the few Carpetbagger enclaves to survive redemption. But he is an embittered, lonely man, and his survival is a pyrrhic victory. He becomes ruthless: he has failed to win the Bourbons with kindness; his brother and friends lie unavenged; he will now rule the cowed Southrons with his personal bayonets, enforcing his basic instrument of revenge—his powers of taxation and foreclosure—to the full.[497]

But his ill-luck stalks him down. An old enemy, a tertiary character named Lanier, brutally cripples him in an ambush. When he recovers, Cahatchie has been redeemed, and he spends the remainder of his days in Europe, a U.S. American consul in bitter exile from the doom-dark South, which had swallowed up his dreams.[498] And the supreme irony is that with all his power and tactical successes, he is undone not so much by political forces as by a woman's personal enmity.

The rationale behind this "Horatio Algeriad" is given with some sympathy by Bryan. She shows Witchell using the opportunities of reconstitution to advance in typical 19th-century fashion. As usual, he had been the sole breadwinner in a household of the dead father, the invalid mother, and the dependent siblings. By the time of the war, he had through struggle brought the family to some modicum of comfort. He enlisted, and the easy democratic advancement in the Union Army allowed him to move from private to captain.

Typically, as the Union Officer, he received an appointment in the postwar South (where he had served as a soldier) and worked his way up to triumph and tragedy. His concern for his family is in part the motivation for his single-minded quest for wealth and power. For this reason he brought them South to share in his empire. The main part of the motivation, however, is the memory of the privation and struggle of his earlier years, which had so scarred him that his need for money becomes his second nature.

Thus in Bryan's hands the Yankee materialist emerges with some complexity, and this sympathetic background to his political activity is again an aspect of the work's neutrality.

On the first level, the Witchell narrative deals with the tragic Carpetbagger who came, saw, conquered, and was eventually conquered. But Bryan invests him and his narrative with other qualities. Though he is ambitious, he is noble. As indicated earlier, he performs individual acts of magnanimity toward his enemies, including saving some would-be assassins (Lanier is one of them) from his irate Freedmen. Yet even these heroic actions have ambitious qualities: "What was his motive for the generous deed he was performing? . . . Was this merely a step toward gaining popularity with that better class of citizens who were so opposed to him?"[499]

Despite such nobility, however, Witchell remains world-stained and scandalous. His "quiet cynical way" and his "bitter-sad smile," so smoothly blended into his role as the Carpetbagger, would have easily identified him to the Godeyette as being a Byronic figure. In a more orthodox novel, he would have been saved by "a little, pure-minded, country-reared girl" from his poisonous ambition.[500] It becomes clear that Bryan places his good personal qualities with those bad political ones to create a complex picture of the Carpetbagger lying between knavery and folly. Moreover, this complexity receives pathos and romance through his relationship with the Belle, Adelle Holman.

Adelle Holman's function in the Carpetbagger plot line is unusual. She is more than merely the erotic center of Witchell's political intrigue. She represents no less than the principle of erotic reconciliation applied in this case to the political Carpetbagger. The use of the principle in this way is unorthodox in the context of Reconstruction fiction. Conventionally, the Belle may marry a Union officer or an economic Carpetbagger. But she may not marry the political Carpetbagger. Indeed, any relationship with this breed would have smacked of the Taboo Conjunction (interracial sexuality between a black man and a white woman). And, in a sense, this is how Bryan depicts the relationship.

Witchell's involvement with Adelle generates several interesting complications: He saves her life and the life of her cousin, Zoe, in the first chapter. Midway through the work, he saves her brother's life during a realistically depicted yellow-fever epidemic,[501] nursing him almost singlehandedly through the sickness—to Adelle's surprise and admiration.[502] However, the high point of the relationship comes in two major incidents. In the first, Adelle attends a Bourbon soirée, the chief entertainment of which is a satiric attack on Witchell. Interestingly enough he is also there hidden partially in shadows, and Adelle sees him, outlined in rather magnificent isolation: scorned, ostracized, aloof:

> . . . with his back against the wall, his straight figure and leonine head calmly erect, as though he were not the target of the sneering looks. . . .
>
> His steely blue eyes beat back the stare of the people with cold, proud patience; his set mouth, his folded arms, his whole attitude, spoke eloquently, not of vulgar defiance or self-assertion, but of a purpose that might not be shaken, and of calm, half-sad endurance.[503]

At that moment her diminishing dislike of the alienated Carpetbagger gives way totally to pity and love. She goes up to him, and they go out together into the night. Now Bryan gives this moment a lyrical tenderness that once more reflects the neutralist stance of her work: "The next moment, the moon was tracing their shadows together on the white sandy space." In such a romantic framework, Adelle gives the ambitious Carpetbagger her heart: "If all the world should turn against you and speak evil of you, I will believe in you, honor you, be your friend." This romantic interlude is more than merely lyrical. Because of the sociopolitical context, which so obviously defines their relationship, the interlude takes on the coloration of the Taboo Conjunction, containing dramatic tensions paralleling the scene between Broderip and Margaret in *Waiting for the Verdict*. Quite properly the political reality, represented by Adelle's brother, breaks up this tender scene, reminding the reader with what dangers such a simple act is fraught: "Cursed radical dog, how dare you touch my sister; how dare you speak to her?"[504]

This unorthodox relationship reaches a melodramatic climax in the second major complication. Adelle receives a message that Witchell and his colony of Carpetbaggers and Freedmen are going to be attacked by Bourbon vigilantes. Unable to get someone to warn them, she disguises herself as a boy and goes herself.[505] Her mission is a success, but she has been recognized by one of the vigilantes, her ex-suitor, Lanier. She therefore cannot return to her family, who are themselves chief members of the anti-Carpetbagger faction. Witchell, out of recognition of her plight, out of pity, gratitude, and some affection (but no love), takes her under his protection by marrying her.[506] At this moment, the reconciliation implicit in the previous complication is fulfilled. And it seems that, despite the unconventional nature of the bridegroom, this marriage will follow the typical reconciliationist fashion.

One of the unwritten codes of the miscegenation romance is that none can marry across the color line and live. Witness *What Answer?* Such a code might also apply in this context to hetero-sectional intercourse across political lines during Reconstruction. From the moment of their marriage, Adelle is doomed, and the contributing factors to her demise are Witchell's political preoccupations[507] and her own isolation from her Southernness. In a moving, coloristic evocation of the memory of the Garden, Bryan captures the pathos and the horror of Adelle's isolation and neglect:

> . . . [the] honeysuckle shaded porch [;] . . . the scent of the pinks; the twitter of the martins in their gourd nest, hung aloft to swing and rattle in the wind; the coo of her pigeons [;] . . . the monotonous song of the kitchen darky in the backyard as he plied the churn-dasher under the mulberry-tree and pleaded,
>
> "Come, butter, come,
>
> "Here stands Miss with a free good-will;"
>
> [The taste of] ripe huckleberries in her mouth—all these sights and sounds of the sweet, lost country home.[508]

In this poignant description, Bryan transforms these local color images into symbols for all that had sustained Adelle as a Southern Belle, all that she had given up for her Carpetbagger-lover. Tormented and soothed by such memories, Adelle dies in a moving sequence, which ranks as an apotheosis of the deathbed scene in the romantic-sentimental tradition. The causes are a combination of psychological factors: ostracism, Witchell's political preoccupation, Godeyitis (a mixture of neurasthenia and self-induced consumption), and nostalgia. As a result of her death, Witchell changes from a carpetbagger to *the* Carpetbagger and enters fully into the turbulent arena of Louisiana politics.

The Alver-Witchell lines of action, then, make up the overall plot structure of *Wild Work*. It is through them that Bryan brings into clear focus the variety of characters filling out the narrative texture. This in turn contributes to the novel's organic unity. However, more important in this unifying process than our focus on character as a literary element is the thematic and narrative interrelatedness of the two lines of action. Close analysis reveals that such interrelatedness is achieved by two rather sophisticated techniques: fusion and parallelism. The first device is most clearly seen in the cluster of complications that form the climactic event for both plot lines, the White League raid on the Cahatchie Carpetbaggers.[509]

The first example of the fusion technique is the relationship of the ideological origins of the raid to its bloody fruition. Such origins lie in a strategy session convened relatively early in the Alver plot. During this meeting, Alver and Floyd postulate the principles of total insurgency against the Carpetbagger. A newspaper will be organized to inflame the passions of the Bourbons and their sympathizers.

> When the time is ripe for open opposition our newspaper shall begin the war in the most fearless fashion; shall make wit, abuse, and satire its unsparing weapons. Scatter abroad scathing truths, withering exposures. Rake up old scores and light them with fresh fires of hate.[510]

Once these passions are aroused, a White League will be formed and acts of terror will be launched against the Radicals involving the total support of an angry "Bourbonocracy."

Thus, there is seen early in the Alver plot the thematic and narrative dynamics of a raid that would profoundly affect the characters in the Witchell plot. However, the fullest manifestation of this technique is, of course, the conjunction of both plots in the events of the raid itself. The preliminaries to the raid begin with the White Leaguers' demand that Witchell surrender.

Alver offers to permit him to remain in Cahatchie as an economic Carpetbagger, but shorn of all political powers. Witchell scornfully rejects these terms.[511] Alver then promises him a war, which will be a part of the broad process of Southern redemption:

> The movement means more than a mere ebullition of personal hate. It is an extended movement—a part of the wave that is beginning to be felt throughout the South. . . . A revolutionary tide has set in. Many who have given offense will find themselves stranded high and dry; others who are innocent, will suffer . . . for being in bad company.[512]

As the election of 1876 approaches, this revolutionary confrontation between the Bourbon and the Carpetbagger shapes up (signaled narratively in the novel by the night of a Southron ball). Both sides seek to consolidate their positions by the political manipulation of violence: Witchell encourages his fellow Radicals to manufacture a bloody-shirt incident in order to stiffen up the radical ranks; Alver wants his redeemers to spread rumors of a "negro uprising" to solidify his forces. However, these plans are taken over by the Wanton. She sees these relatively mild intentions as a chance to create the real thing: "Excitement will rise to its highest, and on its tidal wave Witchell and his crew will be swept to destruction." Through her agents, virulent rumors replete with visions of rape and murder sweep the Bourbon community: "Them say the negroes are going to rise; that the night of the ball they aim to surround the ballroom and kill the men and carry off the ladies." Out of the revival of this old nightmare, the ingredients of the raid are formed: The whites begin to carry their old Confederate weaponry; families are sent from isolated plantations across the Red River; the Freedmen, alarmed at the sight of the armed clustering of their old masters, gather in sullen groups with much "restless tramping and riding up and down the river." In this volatile context, Floyd orders the first terrorist act: the killing of a Freedman leader. And according to the Wanton's plan, the Radicals blame the Leaguers, and they in turn accuse the Radicals of trying to create an atrocity to bring in the troops for the election.[513]

By now the entire area is inflamed: The bloody-shirt trick has become real, the phony Negro insurrection is becoming real, for wild with fear of impending genocidal violence and goaded to a fever-pitch of hatred and fear by the exhortations and whiskey of Floyd's double agents, the black Radicals organize to protect themselves.[514] And so clever is the impending violence orchestrated by the Dark Lady that neither faction (not even Alver) realizes that there is a more demonic force operating behind them all.

On the night of the ball, the fears of the whites become irresistible. Cobb stampedes the dance with a false report that the black rebellion has begun. Alver calls for the gathering of the Leaguers within and without the parish. The ancient cry of many a prewar night goes out, but now in its new mutation: The Negroes "incited by the Republicans had risen [;] . . . Cahatchie was in danger of being burned and its citizens massacred." And the raid is on.[515] Soon heavily armed Southrons occupy the town; they arrest all suspicious characters, surround the Carpetbagger compound, break into Freedmen homes searching for insurrectionists and weapons. And for the black Radicals, the presence of so much armed white power can only mean the fruition of the genocidal impulse. Yet Alver cannot move against the Carpetbaggers. Not only has no violence taken place against the Bourbons, but there is no real evidence that Witchell and his organization are behind even the rumored violence. The tension moves toward the critical point:

> As the [Leaguers] rode from house to house in the moonlight, their guns gleaming, their voices challenging, suddenly there came a sharp report followed by a cry. "I am shot!"
>
> . . . A bullet had pierced [a Leaguer's] arm.
>
> The first blood spilled at such a time—it is a breaking of the seals of the vials of wrath and frenzy. It is the last charm thrown into the caldron [*sic*]. At once the excitement boils over, drowning prudence and reason in the flood.[516]

Two Freedmen are captured and found guilty of firing the fatal shot. But Alver wants more than two trigger-happy black insurrectionists; he wants evidence implicating the Carpetbaggers in the "uprising." And out of fear and the coercive insistence of the Leaguers' interrogation, one of the prisoners, Saul, accuses the Carpetbaggers of instigating the uprising:

> No one reflected that the negro's answer might reasonably be false—that, confused and terrified, the weak-witted

> creature might have sought to shift the blame of his rash act upon another. [Or that he had been hired to do it with the promise he would not be punished.] The people were too wildly moved. . . . They seemed to see the climax put upon their wrongs—a hideous plot of blood and outrage unmasked. They determined to endure no more. . . . They would clear the political atmosphere by a storm of vengeance.[517]

This is the "proof" that Alver has needed; the plans formed early in his career come to fruition; now he is in command again; his control over the whites complete; all Non-Radicals must follow his lead in routing the enemy.

First, he orders the lynching of the two captured Freedmen:

> The wagon was driven underneath a gigantic oak, the ropes . . . were made fast to a large limb. . . . Up to this [moment, the freedmen] had . . . seemed to expect pardon. . . . Not till the ropes were being tied [did terror seize Saul.] His eyes roved in a wild search over the crowd, and he shifted his quid of tobacco from cheek to cheek. As the lashed team sprung forward, and the wagon rolled from under [their] feet, [the two negroes] began to tremble and shriek, and beg for a minute's time to tell "how it was."[518]

Alver then orders the imprisonment of the six Radicals (five Carpetbaggers and one Scalawag). Bryan lavishes upon their prison scene some of her most sympathetic writing:

> The prisoners met the crisis calmly. Even Howard was quiet. The old man sat with his eyes fixed on his wrinkled hands that lay on his knees; only now and then he looked up pityingly at his five young companions. Wallace and Hollin talked apart in broken sentences. Devene wrote rapidly in a pocket note-book . . . to reassure his young bride, who had shrieked and clung to him so when he was taken. Edgeville walked the narrow floor, his hands locked behind him, his thin lips compressed with scornful pain. Omar Witchell sat at a table, his face bowed on his hands.[519]

The question concerning the fate of the prisoners must now be answered. Alver wants them to resign their offices and go into immediate exile; Floyd demands their deaths as the only way to obliterate Witchell's power in the parish forever. Alver prevails, but as soon as he goes offstage Floyd plots with Cobb the death of the prisoners. He is to intercept the convoy some distance from the city and wipe out the Radicals.

To underscore the almost unendurable pathos and poignancy of the doomed prisoners, Bryan again employs a rather affecting sentimental style to frame the helplessness of the Republicans by depicting the piteous condition of their women. At this moment, Byran is clearly on the side of the Carpetbagger, though only as innocent victims among bad company:

> Through all that dreadful day their anguish had been greater than that of the prisoners. Every shout from the mob rent their hearts. The trampling of the horses in the street as parties of armed men rode by, the noise of the crowd as they carried the negroes to the gallows, struck them with fresh apprehension. [Then Bryan describes the individual women.] Omar's wife stood there with her white face, her small childish figure . . . Devene's young bride—her Southern nature less capable of control—walked the piazza wringing her hands and crying. The two sisters of Witchell were quiet. Mrs. Wallace was pale, with compressed mouth . . . Mrs. Hollin, her arms about her child, holding him to her head, with all the golden hair disheveled, bowed upon the flaxen locks of the boy.[520]

The men are allowed only to send messages to their women; Alver gives his word as a Southern gentleman that once they resign and leave the state, no harm will come to them nor their families. The men accept and ride off under escort for the Texas border. It is, of course, the last that is seen of them alive.

So far, the fusion technique is clear. The Alver plot connects with the Witchell plot at the point of the White Insurrection. Complications in both plots come to their full development at this moment. (This remains true despite the fact that Witchell himself is not present.) But then Bryan shifts her narrative and technical emphasis. She turns to a minor plot, what may be called the Hirne-Zoe line of action. These characters had already appeared earlier in the novel,[521] yet despite this preparation the shift from the Alver-Witchell conjunction seems quite damaging to the novel's unity.

However, a closer look at the Zoe-Hirne line reveals that it is not unrelated to the overall unity of the work nor to the climactic conjunction.

What Bryan has done is to make a corresponding shift in technical emphasis that helps to reassert cohesion. One discovers that the pathos related to the impending death of the Carpetbaggers is paralleled with the dread related to an impending rape of the Belle. In the first case, the Bourbons are the villains; in the latter, the Radicals.

The Radical as villain is more specifically Levi Adams, a black Republican leader and, like Yellow Jessamine, a stereotype of the treacherous mulatto. It is he who organizes the real Freedman uprising in retaliation for the murders of the three Negroes and the imprisonment of the Carpetbaggers.[522] Since he cannot attack the League-fortified town, Levi will raze the outlying plantations. Soon rumors of the impending counterraid sweep the parish.

Bryan constructs this scene with many of the trappings of the key incident in the frontier myth, the Indian raid. Her Reconstruction analogues are clear: the flight of the settlers to the fort (the Bourbons' flight to Cahatchie), the solitary woman left behind for various noble reasons (Zoe remains with a sick niece who cannot be moved), the refusal of the militia to send aid (in this case, because Zoe in the past had not shown the proper anti-Carpetbagger feeling), and, of course, the diabolical redskin chief (Levi, who is, happily enough, part-Indian).[523] And forming the frame in which the raid will take place is the Louisiana landscape.

At first glance, this landscape seems merely the pastoral moment typical of the Garden archetype; in reality it is a delusion, an idyllic moment in the anti-Indian novel that precedes the massacre; it is the wilderness anarchy out of which Magua will spring:

> Hours passed. The stillness and brightness of the summer day lay all around her. A soft breeze rippled the fields of green cotton and stirred the tops of the great swamp-forest lying back of the cultivated front lands. The white grossbeaks, flying back to the low, fish-filled bayous, were the only specks that dotted the deep blue of sky. It seemed hard to realize that any catastrophe was at hand.[524]

This local color imagery contains another related ambivalence: It *is* the Garden, the Edenic landscape of "pear and apple-trees," and "young mocking-birds," of "yellow-wasps and brown bees feasting on the red pulp of the over-ripe figs and peaches . . . ," and "vines of wild morning-glory and trumpet flowers [and] cotton . . . clustered thickly with blooms and bolls." But this Garden is also the Dionysian landscape of rank fertility, hinting of sensuous energies. And it is this latter image that emerges, for out of this landscape comes the Priapean darkness of Southern guilt. "A negro emerged from the mass of green. . . . His expression . . . was a mixture of cunning and insolence. Deceit ill-concealed the elation that lit his usually dull, pig-like eyes."[525]

This sexual symbolism is reinforced by the Freedman's intimation that a fate worse than death awaits Zoe and her niece: "Twould be mighty bad for you women and Vincent's little gal ef de men come over to you all drunk, as dey will do." And to give this libidinal threat one final turn of the screw, Levi appears suddenly in the Garden, as the Negro as Indian, a perverse amalgam of Injun Joe, Magua, and George Harris, symbolizing sexuality in its most savage mode:[526]

> his tall, straight form towered above . . . , his gun on his shoulder, a pistol and a huge bowie-knife in his rough leather belt. His saturnine face was lit with suppressed excitement; a sneer curled his mouth as he watched Zoe. His face and form, instinct with savage power, filled her with terror.[527]

Levi threatens Zoe with a doom, which means to combine psychological as well as sexual humiliation:[528]

> 'You hate us, you white-skinned women. . . . You speak to us kindly as you do to dogs, but you scringe if we chance to come close to you. It would do me good to humble you, to see you kneel to me. I'll see it, too, before sun shall set, my pretty one.'
>
> He laughed sardonically at the white horror [which his words] brought to her face. Still laughing his low, Indian-like chuckle, he strode away.[529]

Thus, the parallelism is clearly drawn: The Carpetbagger faces death at the hands of Bourbon villains; the Bourbon faces rape at the hands of radical villains. Such correspondences add to the neutralist balance of the work.[530] The parallelism is also indicated in an almost exact mirroring between the way that the Black Leaguers take over the Vincent plantation and the White Leaguers seize Cahatchie:[531]

> With strained, terror-fascinated eyes, [Zoe] watched the cloud of dust that flew into dusky ranks of negroes rapidly turning the curve in the road following the river bend. Nearer they came. The women at the cabin doors . . . watched, still as statues. Levi rode at the head. A few others were mounted, the rest were on foot; about half of them were armed with guns, the others had various weapons. Some carried fish-gigs, some axes and hoes.[532]

The attack on the Harding plantation becomes a concrete image defining in fictional terms the dreadful realities lying behind allusions to the Santo Domingo and Nat Turner revolts scattered throughout Reconstruction literature. In this way, white and black uprising now balance each other.

Levi threatens Zoe with rape and murder, in a scene whose melodramatic details are rather remarkable in themselves and in contrast to the asexuality in the domestic novels of Bryan's contemporaries:[533]

> Levi pushed past her and entered the room, partly closing the door upon her.
>
> "I see you are stubborn and proud still . . . you are in our power; . . . in half an hour this house will swarm with men—niggers, you call them—mad, drunk, furious, ripe for anything. This floor will run with blood, the roof will blaze over your head. . . . You must beg for mercy."[534]
>
> [Zoe pleads for mercy and offers him her ring.]
>
> "I don't want your jewelry. . . . Your begging is too lukewarm. Kneel to me; remember, I have your life and more, in my power. Seize my hands here in your soft palms, hug my knees with your arms, look up in my face with tears dropping from your eyes. Kneel to me, I say."
>
> [Zoe's patrician pride reasserts itself over her fears and she refuses to lower herself to an ex-slave.]
>
> "You'll see when the time comes . . . you shall feel my touch then. It shall clamp you like iron."
>
> He seized her wrist as he said the last words, his nails pressed into her flesh till the blood came.[535]

However, before Levi can make good his threats, a contingent of Leaguers (led by Hirne) appears like the United States Calvary and saves the day. The Negroes are scattered, Levi captured, and then lynched:

> I see a colored man standin' up against a tree. . . . I see it's Levi. Nobody else so tall and I see his lip turn up in dat scornin' way. I tought him 'live standing' dere till I get clost up, and, flop! A buzzard flew out from de limb by his head; an' den I see he's tied to a tree, an' his face an' bress full o' bloody holes where de shots tore, an' de buzzards done picked—[536]

No last-minute rescue comes for the Carpetbaggers, though Hirne does try to save them also. Even Witchell, hurrying to Cahatchie with Federals, arrives too late.

Bryan shifts back to the doomed Carpetbaggers following Zoe's narrow escape but without leaving the Zoe narrative. That is to say, it is Zoe who hears the description of the cold-blooded murder of the Radicals. It is her sensibilities and sympathies that frame the event with the appropriate emotions of horror and pity. This is sentimentally effective and also reestablishes the fusion technique as the dominant unity-creating device. The Zoe narrative is, narrowly speaking, outside of the specific boundaries of the Alver-Witchell conjunction, except indirectly by parallelism. But by involving Zoe in the description of the murders, Byran brings this minor plot into full relationship to the climactic moment:

> O god! All of them killed? Omar Witchell too—that gentle hearted, inoffensive soul, and young Edgeville, and Devene, who had just married one of our Southern girls, gray-haired Howard, and Wallace and Hollin, who have wives here in our midst and little children, were all these killed?[537]

Bryan adds another effect. The description of the atrocity is done in the style of the Greek tragedy: A messenger, one of the Leaguer-guards, comes from the scene of carnage and, choked by his own sense of pity and fear and by the horror that still sears his imagination, he recounts the catastrophe to Zoe. Through the combined sensibilities of these two Southerners, the cruelty of the act is poignantly articulated. The six men are escorted outside of

Cahatchie to a partially deserted spot; Cobb and his hyenas appear and the chief of the Leaguer-guards, one of Cobb's agents, turns the hapless Republicans over to their fate. Omar is the first to die:

> 'Give me a gun; I don't want to die like a dog,' he cried. The bullets rained upon him, and he fell under the horse's feet. Edgeville cried out: 'I'll die before I surrender.' He dashed ahead, and reached to the top of the hill; a bullet struck him in the head . . . Devene was killed at this same place. Wallace and Hollin and Howard were caught. . . . Howard was shot first. The old man trembled like a leaf. He got down on his knees and begged them to spare him. Wallace, too, prayed to be spared. He said: 'God is my witness, I have never done a wrong to any man in this country. . . . I have held the office only a little while. I have tried to do what is right.'
>
> They shot both of them. I counted the places where ninety buck-shot entered Howard's body. Mark Hollin stood and saw them shot. [Hollin then asks for a chance to pray and pleads with the mob not to kill his wife and children. Hirne offers a thousand dollars to spare this remaining prisoner but is refused. Hollin then says,] 'You have killed all my friends, now kill me. I will not run for my life.' Well they shot him. . . . I couldn't help feeling awful bad about the wives and children of the men, who were praying and hoping that they were safe, while they lay there dead. They deserved to be punished, I know, but it looked like a bad day's work, Miss Zoe.[538]

The ironies of the climax are many: The Freedmen were innocent of plotting an unprovoked uprising; the Carpetbagger was innocent of instigating the uprising that finally materialized or the imaginary one that caused the Bourbon revolt. And Alver's Leaguers were themselves dupes of the Dark Lady. Moreover, what had begun as games in political maneuvers ended in tragedy. Witchell had called for lawlessness, a little bloody-shirting, to ensure his election, and this had led to the death of six of his white and four of his black Radicals. Alver had called up riot to redeem the parish, and now it was awash in blood, horror, and dishonor. Even the perfidious Floyd is not untouched, relapsing for the first time into trembling femininity, horrified by the shrieks of the Republican women, fearful of Witchell's retribution. It was, indeed, a wild work.[539]

At the climax, then, all plots tie together, and that a White Leaguer and a Southern Belle, and she herself a potential victim of Radical villainy, become the sympathetic center through which one weeps for Bourbon villainy, emphasizes once again the neutralist thrust of the work. At one blow, Bryan achieves both thematic and narrative unity.

The second device used to achieve this unity is parallelism, already discussed in terms of the novel's climax. However, it was a more general application, seen in a variety of parallels: Both Alver and Witchell are ambitious; both build up political organizations to implement their ambition; both rise to triumph, suffer *peripeteia*, and are overtaken by catastrophe—all as a result of this ambition. Both have feminine counterparts who in both instances die. Both survive the tragedy sadder but wiser men. Thus, a principle of similarity within differences governs the cohesive relationship between the two plots.

The way in which Bryan uses such parallelism avoids the naïve juxtaposition of moral and sectional polarity. She could have easily created the pro-Bourbon parallel: the noble Southerner versus the knavish Northerner. She could have easily given the nefarious Floyd to Witchell and the genteel Adelle to Alver in an obvious stressing of sectional bias. Instead, it is the genteel Adelle who loves the Carpetbagger; it is the Bourbon who lusts for the Wanton. Thus, love and lust divide up in a crisscrossing of the obvious: Vices and virtues balance out. For the sake of her neutralism and more so for the sake of her art, Bryan's use of parallelism to generate unity is both complex and sophisticated.

Through fusion and parallelism, Bryan brings her multi-narrative work into clear focus, a focus in which character and incident cohere to render up the thematic structure of the work in terms of a persistent neutralist dynamic.

There have been frequent references to the neutralist nature of Bryan's thematic structure. The central idea that expresses this neutralism is Bryan's implication that the forces underlying the wild works of Reconstruction were not the political ones, but ostensibly the stubborn old Calvinist verities of human depravity—lust, greed, cruelty, and inordinate ambition. This shifting of blame from ideology to the human heart is essential to the novel's neutrality. Yet while this is true, there are other ideas in the story that qualify this neutralist concept.

There is the concomitant idea that if the first cause of the Reconstruction agony was the stubborn old verities, the necessary cause was the political condition as it impinged on the human heart:

> "The reign of the carpet-bagger"—a troublous, transition period—was rich in dramatic features. Abnormal conditions of government and society brought out unwonted lights and shades of character and gave rise to extra-ordinary incidents.[540]

Second, while this reign did generate evil, there were some good accomplishments brought forth. Witchell's rule is presented, for example, not as a picture of stagnation and corruption, but as a picture of efficiency and progress. Nevertheless, the general immorality of the period cancelled out such individual efforts, for even the most idealistic carpetbagger was contaminated by the "wide opportunities for arbitrary power and extortion that the abnormal condition of things at the South threw in the way of office-holders."[541] Despite the positive accomplishments and characters of some Radicals, Reconstruction itself had, for Bryan, "a rottenness within." It was Reconstruction that permitted Witchell to gain the kind of power that proved so abrasive to aristocratic sensibilities. It was this "rottenness within" that permitted Floyd and her gang to operate with such audacious impunity and with such atrocious results within the Louisiana soulscape. And, for Bryan, the goodness of Carpetbaggers as individuals could not overcome the great evil of their cause;[542] the evil of the Bourbons as individuals could not besmirch the rightness of their redemption. These are the secondary ideas that qualify Bryan's neutrality. But she is too sophisticated a writer to reduce her moral qualifications to a simpleminded black-and-white partisanship. Bryan may be anti-Reconstruction, but she is not blindly anti-Carpetbagger. This fairmindedness emerges as the touchstone that classifies *Wild Work* as neutralist fiction.

Perusal of the major periodicals between 1877 and 1885 reveals no critical reaction to *Wild Work*. However, our evaluation is a glowing one: Exciting, well-paced, unified, the work is the most successful of the Reconstruction short stories and novels. Melodrama, sentimentality, and proto-realistic effect rather than ideology predominate. At the same time, the very texture of the work—setting, narrative, character, language—grows organically from the sociopolitical conditions surrounding one of the worst events of Reconstruction. Around this event, "the blackest blot upon the South," Bryan has interwoven, as she puts it, the thread "of romance . . . with the warp of fact."[543] Conversely, all sociopolitical material in the work is deftly absorbed into the texture. Rhetoric and plot do not clash. In sum, *Wild Work* is clearly the result of a talented craftsman and is, therefore, a much better novel than, say, *A Fool's Errand.* Because of this fact, it would be useful to issue a reprint.

Any final evaluation of *Wild Work* must take note of its allegorical configurations. On the moralistic level, it is a parable of the dangers of overweening ambition. On the Reconstruction level it is a morality play of reconstitution and redemption. On its final pages, it seeks to become an allegory of reconciliation but does not quite succeed. Too much blood has been shed for a gratuitous handclasp across the Red River:

> It is just six years this summer of 1880 since the tragic event on which this story turns took place. . . . In this brief time the spirit of Change has moved strongly over the South. The turbulent, transition period is over; the appeals to mob law have ceased. The people have learned to assert their rights more wisely; the Government to regard them more carefully. Bitter experience has taught these lessons. Mutual sympathy and understanding open a fair prospect of union in more than name between the two sections of the Republic. In a little while our children will look back with wonder to the "dark era of carpet-bag rule." A picture of that time, even imperfect as this, may then be of interest as a curious study; and, since history repeats itself, and governments and society move in circles, such a picture may be valuable as a warning.[544]

The last two works of neutral tendency, the serial "The Valcours" and the novel *Kitty's Conquest*, are inferior in contrast to Bryan's novel, in themselves, and as Reconstruction fiction, and deserve only cursory description.

"The Valcours" by Sherwood Bonner, aka Katherine Sherwood Bonner McDowell (1881), lacks minimal complexity at all levels. Aesthetically, it is a throwback to the unsophisticated approach of the pre-realist romance: false identities, Oedipal relationships, accidental poisonings, mysterious pasts, false wills. Thematically, the social and political complexities are played down, forming only a minor part of the narrative. The major emphasis is on family conflicts within the Valcour ranks. If the Reconstruction were not so specifically present, this novella could be classified as semi-Reconstruction fiction. Those social and political elements that *are* present are articulated in terms of the simplistic reconciliation modality of Bonner's other Reconstruction novel, *Like unto Like* (1878).[545] This means that her emphasis is not on the hostility and violence of the Bourbon-Carpetbagger conflict, but on its serio-comic dimensions. In this light, those aspects of Reconstruction that do appear in the work are a precise reflection of the allegorical naiveté of Bonner's neutralist vision.

The Reconstruction plot deals with the Valcour family and its relationship to the new era in the Louisiana village of Arnville, in terms of present problems and former glories. However, unlike the M'Calls, they do not undergo the conventional suffering. Despite the destruction of slavery, they survive the war relatively well off. Nevertheless, the presence of the Carpetbagger and his power is an offense to their aristocratic sensibilities, especially the pride and pretension of General Valcour, the patriarch of the family. Bonner delineates him with the vices and virtues of his class under the new order: his unreconstructed hatred of the North, his insufferable pride, his obtuse prejudice, his manly hedonism—balanced by a love for the classics, a sense of honor and generosity, political acumen, the incarnation in him of the Cavalier vision.

The Reconstruction narrative as it relates to this family involves the hostility of the General to the new state of things in contrast to his son's adjustment to its ideas and its presence. Garry Valcour represents the young Southron under Reconstruction. Oedipally involved with his vivacious young mother and resentful of his older, dominating father, he is that familiar figure in Southern literature: the languid, indolent, young aristocrat. However, he does not remain thus. Under the influence of the neighborhood Radical, he comes to full manhood through adjustment to the new order. Pragmatically, he learns how to use free labor, how to persuade rather than flog his Negro workers. Psychologically, he learns to exploit the destruction of his father's world for the building of his own. In the contrast between Valcour *père* and *fils*, one sees the positive and negative aspect of Carpetbagger rule.

The allegorical representative of this rule is David Church, alluded to earlier as the neighborhood Radical. Courageous, generous, and intelligent, he is the editor of the pro-Carpetbagger paper, *The Arnville Avalanche*, and emerges as the typical radical hero of neutralist fiction. However, on the face of it, he is not the Carpetbagger; he is the Scalawag compleat: Before the war, he was anti-slavery; during the war, anti-secession; after the war, anti-restoration. He is, in other words, that homegrown antithesis to the Bourbon, the Southern yeoman, and belongs to the ranks of those white Dixie Unionists celebrated in pro-radical fiction and nonfiction. Nevertheless, because of his opposition to Bourbon power and because of his roots in the cultural-psychological realities of the Southscape, a major advantage and, more important, because of his subscription to Northern political idealism, Church operates in this minor plot as the Carpetbagger.

Despite his political commitment, he is no fanatic: "What difference does it make whether a man calls himself Democrat or Radical? That is not the question in making friendships."[546] And to demonstrate his tolerance, Church becomes the friend and mentor of young Valcour, despite his hostility to the Valcours as the symbol of regressive conservatism.

David Church, as the good Radical, is paired for neutrality's sake against the bad Radical, an authentic, anonymous Carpetbagger. This figure appears briefly in the Reconstruction plot, but Bonner's thumbnail sketches of his "lean and hungry look" and his demagogic appeal for Freedman support, full of "sound and fury," become signals to the reader of his hypocrisy and opportunism. In this way, Bonner again fulfills the demands of neutralist fiction. The fulfillment of these demands can also be seen in her handling of the Conflict.

The struggle between the Carpetbagger and the Bourbon appears in two forms. In the first, the Conflict is overt and specific; in the second, it is ideological and attitudinal. The scene of the first instance is a rally where the Carpetbagger gives a harangue to the Freedmen on the blessings of Radicalism. Present at the rally is General Valcour, whose Southern temper is aroused by both the Yankee's praise of Reconstruction and his egalitarian give-and-take with his auditors. It is at this moment that the patriarch joins explicit issues with Carpetbaggery, delivering a counter-speech in praise of slavery. He begins by discussing the affection between master and slave (which the Freedmen applaud) but ends by assigning "the negro his 'proper place in creation' [as a creature with neither soul nor brain,] with a plainness sufficiently unpalatable to be greeted with growls and jeers."[547]

David Church, observing the behavior of the Bourbon, takes up the cause of Freedman humanity and attacks Valcour, his speech, and his class in his newspaper by editorial and caricature, presenting the General as the embodiment of the stubborn anti-rationality of the Southern patrician. As a result, Valcour forces his son to defend the family's honor, demanding that he challenge the Scalawag editor to a duel or at least give him a flogging. Instead, the two men become friends. In this instance, the victory goes to the Carpetbagger.

In the second instance, Bonner gives the victory to the General. Here the emphasis is on the ideological and the attitudinal. Valcour assails Reconstruction as a danger to the foundation of Southern social life and reunion between the sections: "The New had once scarcely meant more than youth. . . . But now—the devil only knows what: reconstruction, topsy-turviness, and tyranny hiding its iron hand in the fair velvet of philanthropy." In contrast to the war, which was "honest and terrible" in its destruction of "the old rock of slavery," Reconstruction is a time of "Diplomacy, Cant, Carpetbaggerism, Radicalism . . . like the sneaking heathen devil. . . ." Worse, Church and his ilk have ". . . [cut] the fine invisible cords of affection that once bound together the hearts of masters and slaves."[548] In these attacks, the right seems to be on Valcour's side.

In terms of the Conflict, then, plus and minus balance out. As the Bourbon, Valcour represents anti-rationality, stubborn pride, and graciousness; as the Carpetbagger-surrogate, Church represents not only the freedom of the press and Freedman rights, but political chicanery as well. Reconstruction is both a time for youth to begin anew on the ruins of tradition and a period of exploitation and hypocrisy.

The Reconstruction elements eventually disappear, only to reappear perfunctorily at the end. Church is seen sharing his newspaper with a Democrat rival. On one side, the *Avalanche* has become an "escape-valve for the hottest Bourbon steam in the country; on the other, a sprightly Republican page. . . ." The two editors are good friends, the two sides have their views exposed, and the independents can get both sides of the story. As for the Scalawag, he is the best of friends with his Bourbon patrons.[549] Thus, there is for the first time in Reconstruction fiction a political reconciliation between the Radical and the Conservative. And those ferocious encounters that appear in the major works are now transformed into a semi-comic resolution, a benign exception to the more tragic finales in *A Fool's Errand* and *Bricks Without Straw*. As in Bonner's other novel, the reduction of the fury of the Conflict to such allegorical naiveté is the essential reason for this novel's thematic and perhaps aesthetic weakness.

The last example of neutralist fiction is Charles King's *Kitty's Conquest* (1884).[550] Its neutrality is reflected in the three typical ways: First, while it deals with the Reconstruction head-on—KK activism in Northern Alabama in 1872 and the Warmoth-Kellogg-McEnery riots in New Orleans in 1872 and 1873—the novel takes no sides. Secondly, by presenting the excesses of both the Bourbons and the Carpetbaggers, the neutralist balance is maintained. Last, the emphasis of the novel is on the activities of Union officers during the upheavals of reconstitution. But in a way already described, they are shown as immune to the partisanship of the Union's politicians. And by balancing gallant Federals with gallant ex-Rebels, the work achieves that conventional synthesis of sectional antagonisms typical of the reconciliationist romance.[551] In these three ways the plot of *Kitty's Conquest* achieves its neutral quality.

The plot is very simple: One follows the adventures of a detachment of Union soldiers on duty in the Radical South. Their first major adventure calls them into Northern Alabama to search out and destroy Klan terrorists. The KK in this case is presented as a blend of political murderers and western outlaws. In their first encounter with the soldiers, the Klan tries to rob the express train *à la* Jesse James, but are thwarted by the hero, the Union Officer. [552] As a result of this action and also because the Klan has degenerated into murderous bandits, even Southrons welcome the formerly hated Bluecoats. Thus, the United States Army emerges early in the novel as the impartial guardian of law and order against a general enemy of both Radicals and law-abiding Bourbons. And when the KK springs its captured bandits from jail, Union soldiers and Southern citizenry, including CSA veterans, successfully destroy the terrorists' stronghold.

In their second major adventure, the detachment is called to Louisiana for a protective military occupation of New Orleans during the intra-radical and radical-conservative conflicts resulting from the fraudulent election of 1872. This complex struggle, in which Kellogg Republicans battled Warmoth Republicans while Bourbon Democrats sought the overthrow of both groups, forms the major emphasis of the entire novel.

King shows us the full melodramatic outlines of this political situation. The factions are presented under siege—one group of Republicans in "the temporary State-House," another group "over a prominent bar-room in Royal Street."[553] King describes the Radicals in this situation quite objectively. The

Republicans are neither Tourgéan heroes nor Baker's villains. They are shown as merely two-dimensional reflections of the political turmoil following the 1872 election, and the suffering they endure in the State-House is more serio-comic than tragic.[554] Tired, hungry, unable to get food from the vendors because their credit is no longer acceptable, the Republicans are a sorry sight: "Scattered in groups all about the room were upwards of a hundred men, some white, some colored, stretched at length upon the chairs, others were lying asleep." This was the controlling quorum. Meantime, the Governor was blockaded in his office downstairs, while the Senate was held up in another part of the building. This "was the shape in which one Governor, at least, of the sovereign State of Louisiana was 'holding the fort' against all would-be adversaries."[555]

The most dangerous of these adversaries are the Bourbon-Democrats who, organized into paramilitary units, seek to exploit the Carpetbaggers' disarray by launching an uprising that will overthrow both factions and install the Democrat nominee McEnery. The only power protecting the Radicals from this fate is their own military group, the Negro-dominated New Orleans Metropolitan Police Force, a well-organized, well-disciplined group as fully equipped as a "battalion of infantry."[556] Against this group of ex-slaves, as the chief image of the Carpetbagger's egalitarianism, the ex-Confederate veterans have an especial hatred, and the extermination of this force is a chief goal of the uprising. Interestingly enough, the chief of the Police Force is the former Confederate-general-now-Scalawag, James L. Longstreet.

Into this tense situation comes the detachment of Federals. Once again the United States Army appears as the cosmic principle, containing within itself the full moral imperatives of Northern civilization: law and order. The Army chooses no sides, plays no favorites—at least in King's vision. The Grand Army of the Republic carries out its mandate—the maintenance of the Union's peace—in a disciplined, responsible way. And the contrast of such cosmos to the chaos of the New Orleans setting is clear. King goes behind the image of "Union bayonets," referred to so bitterly in anti-radical history and fiction, to describe the efficient dispatch with which these bayonets kept the peace. Rifle Clubsman, White Leaguer, Red Shirt, Klansman, and New Orleans' Bourbons may not have feared the "law, sheriffs, or marshals, but they would rather see the devil than the Federal uniform."[557] And more important is the fear and respect this uniform inspired in *both* sides. Thus, when the battle between

Southrons and Metros seems irresistible, the Federals roll between them and bloodshed is avoided for the moment. It is the Army then, and not the Carpetbagger or the Bourbon, that emerges as the touchstone of moral and political probity in this novel. This is a perfect neutralist ploy.

However, more interesting than this is the extension of these qualities to all military men in the story. True to his commitment, King presents Union soldiers, Bourbon paramilitary (excluding the Klan), and Negro Metros as jovial, courteous, friendly, and brave.[558] Take, for example, King's rather generous depiction of the last group. During the night of the Democrat uprising, two of the major characters are captured by this Freedman militia as Bourbon rebels. But once the truth is discovered, they are cordially treated and courteously escorted to their hotel.[559] During the siege of the Statehouse, the Metropolitans stand guard over the legislature in well-ordered ranks to prevent a Bourbon attack. King describes them with all the virtues of the Federals:

> All were very quiet, orderly, and apparently well disciplined. A colored officer in the shoulder-straps of a captain spoke in a quick, sharp tone to them; and, black and white, they sprang to their feet and respectfully drew aside. At the head of the stairs were sentries and an officer of the guard, all in police uniform, and they saluted by artillery guide with the precision of regulars.[560]

In these examples, then, one gets a clear instance of the way in which King treats all the military characters in the novel. And by concentrating on the military virtues of friend and foe, he manages to avoid any political commitment that would polarize the presentation of the Radicals, their black militia, and their Bourbon enemy.

It becomes quite clear that *Kitty's Conquest* does fulfill the basic criteria of this sub-genre; however, it does not fulfill any criteria that would make it an interesting work of art, except where it focuses on the Reconstruction. Where the work leaves the Reconstruction, the worst elements of the amateur novelist emerge and the most minimal aesthetic complexity disappears. The characters are the most obvious example of this defect: They have the typical (and by now redundant) elements of the reconciliation romance. Kitty Carrington, the heroine, is a compendium of all the clichés of the Bitter Belle: she is

> . . . the rebellious little fairy . . . with all the hatred and prejudice of ten years ago, little dreaming how matters had changed since the surrender of her beloved Lee, or imagining the quantity of oil that had been poured forth upon the troubled waters. . . .[561]

Her suitor is the Union officer Lieutenant Amory—handsome, noble, brave, tolerant, patient—who will, by the end of the story, win the heart of the little secessionist.

In the midst of these repetitive formulae are some small surprises. Southern ladies married to Bluecoats are shown suffering bitter ostracism for their betrayal of the Gray. All reconciliations are strictly personal; King makes no attempt to generalize them into the larger image of sectional reunion. The other surprise is Judge Summers, a minor character. He is Kitty's uncle, a dignified, dedicated patrician and, horror of horrors, a Scalawag. However, Summers is no mere time-server; he had believed that only through using his judicial training as a judge under the radical government in Alabama could his state return to the Union, could he bring law and stability to his community and protect it from more opportunistic types. And, interestingly enough, it is around this Bourbon-Scalawag that the glorification of the Southern aristocracy finds its clearest imagery in the climax of the first section of the novel:

> The red-gold light of the setting sun streamed in all its glory of the southern front of the quaint plantation house. The tangled shrubbery, . . . the low-hanging eaves, the moss-covered . . . porch-roof, all were tinged, gilded, gleaming . . . with the . . . glow of the . . . rays. . . . Even . . . Jake Bigg's wooly pate gained a lustre [it] never knew before. All round the evidences of approaching decay and present dilapidation, so general throughout the bright sunny South years after the war . . . there clung a tinge of gladness in answering homage to the declining king of day; but . . . the trio we left upon the steps, *they* fairly stood in halo of mellow gold. The gray-haired gentleman . . . ; the noble, womanly girl at his side . . . ; and . . . kissing her hand, waving her kerchief, her eyes dancing, her cheeks aflame, her white teeth flashing through the parted lips, her fragile form all radiance, all sweet, glowing, girlish beauty, stood Kitty Carrington; . . . [562]

That this dramatic image of the Bourbon hegemony should frame the plantation and relatives of a Radical as Southern is indeed a curious variation on the glorification of the patrician in anti-radical literature. However, the ambiguity of the Bourbon-as-Radical is not fully explored.

The novel ends with a rather magnificent picture of the detachment of Union soldiers marching off to the Indian Wars, an idealized image of the innocent power and strength of the United States Army. With flags flying, drums beating, and a great steamship waiting to receive them, Kitty, her husband, and all their fellow Bluecoats head for the renewing air of the Western frontier,[563] and the coming brutality of the military forms of Manifest Destiny.

The removal of the Army at this juncture is no mere narrative event, but a possible unintended ideological symbol. On the one hand, the departure is an image of the way in which the Federal government would leave the Southern Radicals to their fate at the hands of the Redeemers. On the other, the departure images the removal of King's apolitical Army from the scene before the real agonies of redemption began, before the Radical's serio-comic suffering would give way completely to tragedy, and before the troops would be called back in to lose their innocence and take the Carpetbagger's side against the Bourbon.

Kitty's Conquest is a good example of how a work that would ordinarily be simply an adventure-romance takes on historical complexity through its use of the Reconstruction. In this contrast, the sociopolitical events are valuable only insofar as they offer King and the other neutralist writers a readymade body of melodramatic incident with which to fill out the blood-and-thunder framework. For example, the Klan is not so much a political conspiracy as an exotic surrogate for Indians and outlaws.[564] Louisiana is not so much the symbol of radical misrule as it is an exotic locale, offering an excuse for coloristic description:

> Swiftly through a tawny waste of whirly waters a great steamer ploughs its way. From towering smoke-stacks volumes of smoke stream back along the tumbling wake and settle on the low-lying shores. Breasting the torrent, we have rushed past crowded levee, past sloop, and ship, and shallop, past steamers . . . , river monarchs, bayou traders, swamp

> prowlers. Lordly up-stream packets lead or follow; churches, domes, chimneys . . . give way to low, one-storied . . . cottages. . . . Eastward . . . the horizon but one far-reaching . . . swamp. . . . Westward, . . . the river-bank, bold barriers of forest, dense, dark, . . . shut off the view. In front lies the eddying, swirling, boiling bosom of the Mississippi,—the winding highway to the North,—sweeping in majestic curve through shores of shining green. Behind us, nestling along the grand arcs of its doubling bend, New Orleans and Algiers, close clinging to the mighty streams that at once threaten and cajole. The river is master here, yet dreams not of his power.
>
> [Proud] of its strength and grace, [the steamboat] surges ahead, rumbling in the vast caverns of its seething furnaces, panting in the depths of its powerful lungs, straining with muscles . . . , hurling aside from iron-shod beak the burdened billows of the opposing river. Black as Erebus the clouds of smoke from towering chimneys, white as snow the creaming steam-jets, deep and mellow the note of signal-bell, clear, ringing, rollicking the farewell chorus of our swarthy crew.[565]

The Southern counterpart to the Locomotive in the Garden, the north-south power of the Mississippi steamboats.

Such romantic use of Reconstruction history and locale cannot help but eliminate all partisanship—despite King's rather extensive depiction of the most important political maneuver in Carpetbagger strategy: the call for Federal bayonets. In a sense, literary form helps to create the novel's neutrality.[566]

But this is not the whole story. As in all neutralist fiction, the use of Reconstruction incident *does*, in fact, involve the ideological dimensions inherently related, by a complex of social and political associations, to the partisan interests of the average reader of the period, North and South. The controversy, emotions, and attitudes generated by events lying so close to the consciousness of reader and writer feed into the use of such incident. It is to this that King's readers must respond. The descriptions of the New Orleans riots, the Kellogg-Warmoth-McEnery battles, and the Ku Kluxers inevitably have political weight no matter how apolitically King uses such descriptions.

The use of Reconstruction incidents also has an aesthetic corollary. The fact that these events had occurred only a few years before and had been reported extensively throughout the country gives them the solidity of actual fact. This provides a gratuitous realism for an essentially romantic work.

Moreover, King's depictions have the quality of personally witnessed experiences. The kinds of realistic details he employs to describe the disposition of troops, the military train-run from Northern Alabama to New Orleans, the besieged legislators, the discipline of the Metros, and the New Orleans setting itself are textual evidence for this feeling. When the "autobiographic" is added to the historical, the bland sentimental texture of this adventure-romance is given moments of proto-realistic grittiness.

To sum up: Wherever Reconstruction incident and setting are incorporated into the novel, it makes works as vapid as King's neutralist fiction far superior in narrative and thematic power to the typical Godeyesque romance of the same period. For this reason, King's novel, like all Reconstruction fiction, becomes a valuable example of the exploitation of the Reconstruction melodrama for sensational, realistic, and unintended ideological effects.

Six works, then—"Parole d'Honneur," *The Wall-Flower*, "An Independent Ku Klux," *Wild Work*, "The Valcours," and *Kitty's Conquest*—form the neutralist canon in this descriptive analysis of Reconstruction fiction. They have in one way or the other reflected the general criteria described in the introduction of this section: the non-committal depiction of the controversial aspects of the period, the balanced presentation of Bourbon and Carpetbagger virtues and vices, and the deliberate muting of a specific political point of view. As non-polemic examples of Reconstruction fiction, these works too offer insights into the broad, complex dimensions of this period in American history. For a more polemic shaping of the First Reconstruction experience, one must now turn to pro-radical fiction.

• • •

> I'se a free man, an' ef I think a man's a gran' rascalI'se gwine to say so, whether he's black or white; an ef enny on 'em comes ter Ku Klux me I'll put a bullet t'rough dem! I will, by God! . . . I'll be damned ef ennybody shall Ku Kluck me without somebody's goin' 'long with me, when I drops outen dis world![567]

Three points form the backdrop to pro-radical fiction: First, Revisionist historiography tends to support the validity of its political position. Second, the Carpetbagger is the implicit and explicit center of this fiction. Thirdly, the Carpetbagger is central to his alliance with his white and black Southern comrades. A brief discussion of his relationship to the Freedman and Scalawag will clarify this assertion.[568]

Black and white native-born Southern Radicals are not independent nor are they merely his puppets; more correctly, they are his creations. As the viceroy of the Party of the victorious Union, the Carpetbagger brings into being the tripartite unity needed to implement the policies of the Northern Republicans through their Congressional and Executive power. As the conduit through which Northern political, military, and financial power enters the postwar South, he dominates the Southern Republican Party defining the function of the Southern Radicals, establishing their ideological frame, and serving as their operational center. Whether in the constitutional conventions of 1867 and 1868, or in the political and economic operations of the entire nine years, the Tourgées, Morgans, and Warmoths could be seen among the Radicals trailing Northern power behind them like a cloud of glory.[569] It is no exaggeration to assert that during the First Reconstruction the Carpetbagger was the central reference point in the party as the Carpetbagger dominates all implicitly or explicitly, reflected always in the character of the Freedman. This remains true despite the rise of the New Revisionism, which argues that it was black leadership that led the way in creating the First Reconstruction, a revisionism inspired belatedly by a distorted reading of DuBois' *Black Reconstruction*.

This is the third point. An analysis of Reconstruction history and literature reveals that the political symbiosis that developed between the Carpetbagger and the Freedman was the significant feature of radical rule. A reading of Morgan's memoirs suggests that the new Symbiosis evolved from a mutual helplessness and isolation in the face of the Confederate resurgence during restoration, from sociopolitical interdependence during reconstitution, and from a mutual allegorization in general: the Freedman viewing the white Northern Radical as Mistuh Linkum's man and the Northern Radical viewing the ex-slave as a militant version of Uncle Tom. Thus, necessity as well as choice underlay their mutual support. Later it would be the Black Radical who would remain faithful to the remnant Carpetbaggers during redemption, when many a Scalawag would be abandoning ship.

Therefore, it is no accident that in pro-radical fiction the Freedman and his Northern mentor are invariably featured separately or together as the narrative center. The Scalawag rarely occupies such a position, though he may often appear as a heroic tertiary character.[570] In other words, the defining attributes of pro-radical fiction become the narrative centrality of the heroic Yankee and his heroic black comrade. And in this descriptive analysis of pro-radical fiction, it is the Freedman and his struggles with his ex-master that operate as the essential symbolic reference to the larger political conflict between the Bourbon and the Carpetbagger, themselves symbols of the Irrepressible Conflict.

These three points—the closeness of pro-radical fiction to Revisionist facts, the importance of the Carpetbagger, and the symbolism of the role of black and white Southern Radicals to that importance—form the sociopolitical context for pro-radical fiction. The first work, Charles A. Deshler's rather minor sketch,[571] "Ab'm: A Glimpse of Modern Dixie" (1878), shows the Freedman representing Carpetbag power. Ab'm is clearly identifiable as such a figure. He is conversant with Shakespeare and Burns, thus justifying the Carpetbagger's faith in Negro education; he is aware of the dynamics of Reconstruction activity, thus justifying the Carpetbagger's belief in the Negro franchise. It is through Ab'm as an authentic black Radical that the Carpetbagger position is set forth.

Ab'm's first point is a familiar one: that for the Southron the most traumatic result of Reconstruction was the codification of the ex-slave's humanity into the South's political and legal structure. The refusal of the Bourbons to recognize ideologically the Negro's manhood is the root cause of the hostility between the Carpetbagger and the Bourbon, between the ex-slave and the ex-master in pro-radical literature. Ab'm, for example, scornfully describes the ridiculous extremes to which this ideology leads his old Marse. Colonel Johnson still conceives of his Negroes as grown-up children—despite the fact that they saved his life during the war and now care for him during his second childhood.

The second point is likewise familiar: that the humanization of the Afro-American, symbolized by franchise and political office, broke the symbiotic bond between slaves and masters. Black and white "friends," who grew up, hunted, and went "atter the gals" together, now battle each other politically and physically in bitter enmity. Ab'm regrets that the new order has generated such antagonism between old chums but nevertheless states, "WE WOTES."[572]

The third point is less familiar but not new: Despite the ex-slaves' sociopolitical independence, they are still dependent on white power: "We've got to 'pend on de white lawyers an' butchers an' bakers." And in case of sickness or death, Ab'm even admits that he prefers the ministrations of white Southern hands. Ab'm recognizes in this dependency that the legal, political, and economic weapons given to him by the Americanization acts offer him a way to relate himself as an equal to white power despite his dependence upon it. The white lawyers, butchers, and bakers become available to Negro needs through the countervailing power of the franchise: "but den, you see WE WOTES."[573]

The final point evolves from Ab'm's awareness of the danger of being a Freedman-as-citizen within the ruins of the old Symbiosis. While political acts have given him rights, the Southrons refuse ideologically to recognize these rights and can negate this citizenship at any moment with the extralegal powers lying to their hands. This is the existential contingency implicit in being a Negro as man within the wreck of the older but persistent definition of this non-humanity. Only in areas where the Negro does not assert himself as an equal, in the area of social equality, for example, does the Bourbon permit him physical security. However, in the area of political and economic equality, the Freedman must depend on his voting relationship with Carpetbag power to protect him from Bourbon resentment.

Implicit in Ab'm's analysis is his recognition that while white and black Southerners are tied together in a variety of socioeconomic patterns, the races are separate in the area of politics. Here there is "an antagonism of interest, which the freedmen held in restraint by massing their votes as an undivided unity."[574] So long as Ab'm's franchise would be needed, he could obtain his necessities from the reluctant, resentful Bourbon; he could use his "wotes" as a balance of power between his master's extralegal forces and his own physical safety.

It is curious that this tale should have appeared during the reconciliation period. Its emphasis on Freedman voting rights should have been outmoded by the events of 1877. In reality, while the Redeemer often advocated the disenfranchisement of the Freedman as a major objective, it was not necessarily implemented. Alcorn-type Bourbons in Mississippi and Wade Hampton-types in South Carolina more often controlled black suffrage than eliminated it. The major reason for this seemed to have been fear of Northern reaction during the period immediately following redemption. Since Negro suffrage would be under their control, at least for a while, the Southrons would use it as the

Carpetbagger had done as an undivided vote directed in this case, against anti-planter enemies within redemptionist ranks. Ex-slaves would be the base on which ex-masters would rebuild the power lost during the folly of war and restoration.[575]

The work is also a call to those readers still sympathetic to the fate of the abandoned black Radicals to keep watch over "Negro wotes" during the Hayes administration. After all, it had been those votes that had helped Republicans for the past ten years. Moreover, the power of the franchise was, for Deshler, the only dependable protection left to the Freedmen against their triumphant, resentful ex-masters. Such an emphasis—in the context of the fury of redemption and the surrender of 1877—reflected a naïve but touching faith in the power of the naked ballot to protect the humanity of such a man as Ab'm.

The next work describes the force that would render futile the power of mere "woting" to sustain the North's former wards. The then anonymous *Other Fools and Their Doings or Life Among the Freedmen*—the author turns out to have been one Harriet K. Goff—dramatizes, among other things, the irrelevance of Freedman's humanity in the midst of a hostile force committed to his dehumanization. In a ramshackle style, Goff describes a world in which even the most minimal gestures toward personal self-determination can be nullified by the quasi-military apparatus lying in Bourbon hands. It is this force—energy, rather—that walls up Freedman rights after redemption, rendering absurdly irrelevant, in Goff's eyes, the power of ballot, amendment, and law. In the novel this malevolence is unleashed by the South Carolina Redeemers during the 1876 uprising against the Carpetbagger, crushing forever that moment in Southern history (between Pike's revelations and the bloody military power of Wade Hampton's victory) when the emergence of a model, multiracial democracy seemed imminent on the American continent—at least in Goff's view. Thus, the fall of the South Carolina Carpetbaggers carried a special, tragic weight: Unlike what happened in Louisiana, they were deposed at the moment when their government was one of the best in the South.

Using the Hamburg massacre as her chief image (barely disguised in the novel as the Baconsville massacre), Goff lifts out of her clumsy rhetoric and hodgepodge of pseudo-dialects a microcosmic representation of the bloody redemption of the Palmetto State.[576] And serving as the backdrop against which this triumph progresses is the larger conflict, the Irrepressible Conflict, as an archetypal encounter repeated with monotonous insistence in each individual action in the novel.

On the surface Goff's work, like "Ab'm," describes the fortunes of the black Radicals during Reconstruction, centering on them as a symbolic reference of the larger power of the Carpetbagger. And like Deshler, she too has a contemporary message for the reconciliation moment. In contrast to his naïve hopes, Goff projects a more realistic vision of the Afro-American under reconciliation, a vision in which the new citizen exhausts himself in futile attempts to assert his political and existential manhood against the implacability of his new master, the Redeemer. It is a vision of failure—of the Radicals to keep their states, of the National Republicans to block the Bourbon resurgence, of the Union to sustain the manhood rights of those who once were its special protégés.

The Baconsville tragedy is the chief expression of these ideas. And since this tragedy is the climactic event, an analysis of the three major literary elements that make it up and that spell out Goff's vision should be helpful. These elements are character, episode, and theme.

Because Goff's novel deals with the fortunes of the black Radical, the Freedman emerges as the chief character in the novel. However, in a real sense, the work has no primary hero or villain through whom Goff articulates her pro-radical ideology and around whom she focuses her personae and episodes. Instead, she achieves a fragmentary sense of unity by grouping her personae into clusters, structured around racio-political criteria. For example, there are the doomed Freedmen—Watta, Den Pipsie, Ham Sterns, John Carr, and Moss Parker—and those Freedmen who survive—Doc, Springer, Judge Rivers, and Jesse Rome. In opposition to this grouping, there is the Bourbon cluster: General Baker, the ruthless leader of the white insurrectionists; Robert Baker, his "semi-chivalrous" cousin and second-in-command; and Gaston, the symbol of the poor white underlings. These two character clusters stand for the larger anonymous mass of black and white figures that fill out the novel's episodes. However, it is the Freedman cluster that serves as the chief unifying element. It is their deaths that dominate and shape the crude narrative variety in this tale.

The death of the Radicals contains some symbolic complexity whose importance is somewhat tangential to the main interest of this study. In most

Reconstruction literature dealing with anti-Negro atrocities, the ex-slave is shown submitting to his doom without physical defiance.[577] This is implied in the refusal of the moderate Negro leader, Jesse Roome, to go to the aid of his doomed comrades:

> [One of the black militia men asks,] "Don't ye think we ought to go down and help em! . . . but it's awful to hear them guns and stand here with my good rifle in my hands doing nothin';"
>
> [Roome responds,] "The more goes there, the worse and bigger that fuss has got to be, and the more colored people will get killed any how for the whites has got to beat. No, no, Penny you'd best keep away if you don't want to be killed."[578]

On the one hand, such submission reflects the Christological symbolism of the Negro as martyr; on the other, it reflects on his masculinity, demonstrating either his general helplessness to take care of himself or, more negatively, his poltroonery, to use De Forest's term. In this novel, there is an opposing image: The Freedmen die, but only after a stiff fight for their lives against overwhelming odds. Goff avoids the picture of a saintly or whining acquiescence; instead, there is a furious though futile gesture of defiance.

In terms of the 19th-century Cult of Masculine Prowess, Goff's image would have been a much more flattering picture of the freed slaves, especially to the Northern audience. For unintended or not, the image of Freedmen submitting to Bourbon atrocities with neither defiance nor retribution had the indirect result of reinforcing the De Forest thesis. And that the image of submission might have had this effect is hinted at in the fatigue with which some members of Northern public opinion began to greet the continuing reports of "bloody shirt" atrocities during redemption. In a sense, the Helpless Freedman was perhaps pitied for his death, but scorned for the defenselessness of his dying. Goff's use of the Doomed African archetype is, therefore, a much more powerful celebration of the Negro's humanity than the counter-image in *Uncle Tom's Cabin* and *A Fool's Errand*.

Nevertheless, despite these symbolic overtones, the Freedman characters in themselves have no individual development. They are only *papier-mâché* masks, though stained with real blood, forming an anonymous mosaic of dead and defeated faces. It is only historical knowledge of the South Carolina insurrection that charges her badly developed characterization with a sense of pity and fear, especially at the scene of their immolation. More important than their individual reality is the violence of their doom as Goff's mirror of the larger antagonism.

Character, then, is the first major element. The second is plot. Like the characters, the major complications forming the plot have no interest in themselves. Aesthetically, they proceed at an erratic pace and are often cluttered with extraneous as well as necessary incidents. However, the climax of the novel and the foreknowledge of what will happen at that moment give to this clumsily plotted work a raw kind of tension. This in turn is the key to the minimal structural unity in the work. From beginning to end, the plot fixes attention upon the Baconsville massacre—its tenuous beginnings, the pre-climactic development, the massacre itself, and then the mournful dénouement. No romantic tangents encumber this movement; no reconciliation episodes degrade the horror. From beginning to end, the narrative point of view remains directly and indirectly fixed upon the doomed Black Radicals.

The incident that leads to this destruction is in itself quite trivial: Negro militia men returning from a festive celebration of the Fourth of July Centennial of 1876 encounter Robert Baker and his son on a country road. When he seeks to force himself through them, the militia men refuse to give him the right-of-way, good-naturedly scorning his imperious commands to get out of the road. This brief episode, however, is not between a jovial group of citizen soldiers and an irate civilian; it is between black and white Southerners in the context of two hundred years of racial sociology and the political tensions of 1876. The Freedman's act is a show of masculine prowess in the context of the Bourbon's exasperation with the Freedman's legal humanity as enforced upon him by the Carpetbagger.

From this trivial incident comes the rumor of a "negro uprising." And around this ancient rallying cry, the South Carolina Redeemers launch a preemptive strike, using the encounter on the road as an excuse to do more than merely chastise some uppity Freedmen. First, the Bourbons will destroy the militia as an organized force, recognizing in them the only threat to their military supremacy in the area. Then, if these aims can be accomplished, the Hamburg Bourbons will have demonstrated in their district the model "bulldozing" operation (advocated by the Mississippi Plan) as the best way to bring down the Chamberlain Republicans despite the latter's successful reform activity, their growing acceptance by the Carolina moderates, and their access to Federal bayonets. It is clear that while the Baconsville militia is to be the immediate victim, the real target remains the offstage Carpetbaggers. The massacre will become merely a preliminary indication of the violence with which they would be deposed during the November elections. As in *Wild Work*, then, the Southrons launch a rebellion against the Carpetbagger under the cover of squelching an uprising supposedly planned by his black comrades.

It is in light of this that the plot develops. General Baker (Robert Baker's Southron cousin) and his rebels occupy Baconsville: "Armed men were still coming in, and yet more rapidly, and the sinking sun heralded a brief, southern twilight and a moonless night; while a great terror took possession of the inhabitants of the doomed village." This seizure becomes in Goff's hands a white insurrection, a rather wry, inverse fulfillment of the Bourbon's fear of the black insurrection:

> "Why, the town of Baconsville is just running over of armed white men—rifle-clubs, regular cavalry companies, and they're going to kill all the niggers, ravish the women, and burn the houses, and put all the children to death!"[579]

Baker demands that the Radicals apologize to his cousin, give up their offices, and surrender their rifles. The Republicans agree to all points except the last. Doc will only surrender his rifles to state authorities, not to an illegal body of whites. With compromise impossible, the militia and some of the political officers retreat into the Armory, besieged by their old, relentless enemies.[580] Their doom is clear: The Bourbon mounts an army of ex-Confederates and new volunteers against forty Freedmen and their twenty-five rifles.[581]

The attack is launched;[582] cannon and overwhelming rifle fire blast the defenders' strongholds; after fierce resistance, the Radicals make a run for it under the cover of night. Amidst burning buildings (fired by the white insurrectionists) and bullets, some escape but most are captured. They are taken to a place

> where fifty or sixty ruffians ('the good people of South Carolina') stood shoulder to shoulder in a circle, and backed by a crowd of hundreds. . . .

> A demoniac howl of delight arose from the drunken, bloodthirsty throng . . . and as each victim arrived, the 'high-toned gentlemen' and 'chivalrous General' and his aids [*sic*] applauded their subordinates. . . .[583]

The next day, the Freedmen are brought to the "dead ring."

> 'It is about time we began the killing,' said one of the crowd, 'We've been hunting and capturing long enough. Now who shall be killed?'
>
> 'Kill 'em all, of cose, . . .'
>
> [The Bourbon Chief then rides into the dead ring.]
>
> The poor fellows upon the ground raised their heads, and cried out each for his life, 'Oh, Gen. Baker! . . . you will save my life,' 'Gen. Baker, I surrendered right off, I did,' . . . 'I han't done nothing.' . . . and beseeching hands were uplifted, and dark faces upturned for the protection they felt sure 'a high-toned gentleman,' and 'chivalrous chieftain' would give. . . .
>
> 'Ah! Ah!' groaned the crowd, in derision of the misplaced confidence of the negroes.[584]

After lengthy discussion between those favoring a selective massacre and those favoring a total one, it is decided that only the militia leaders are to be lynched—executed, rather—since General Baker insists that they be treated according to military justices. Therefore, the South Carolina Rifle Clubs as the "natural offspring" of the "honored Confederate Cavalry" summarily court-martial the Negro leaders as representatives of the Union Army.[585] Watta is the first to die:

> As many as could lay hands upon him did so, and they carried this Second-Lieutenant of the National Guards, this county Commissioner, this graduate of a Freedman High School, this teacher of a colored school, this correspondent of the—*Times*, this influential Republican, this husband and father, this young man who bore the general reputation of being a . . . truthful man, this American citizen, and they bore him away to be sacrificed. . . .

> When he was allowed to stand . . . , he looked upon a wall of circular steel mouths, each ready to belch forth hot, blazing sulpherous [*sic*], leaden death; for every man presented the muzzle of his gun or pistol at the hapless victim.
>
> [Watta] paused and pressed his hands over his face. A tremendous volley, followed, and Alden Watta's soul leaped into the presence of that judge whom the Ku Klux Klans can [not]corrupt or intimidate; and the murderous throng hastened back to procure another victim.[586]

Ham Sterns, John Carr, and Moss Parker are also shot down; Den Pipsie is hacked to death. It is these deaths which form the climax of the novel.[587]

The work then moves downhill through an elegiac dénouement toward the conclusion:

> There arranged in a row, were the bodies of the five men; all murdered for possessing greater or less proportions of African blood, and being true to the National Government which gave them freedom—nothing more, nothing less.
>
> But for these it had been no crime to pass ordinances, protective of the public peace . . . , or to enforce them—no crime to be an intelligent leader among ones fellows—no crime to practice in the use of arms under sanction of law and the nation's flag.[588]

Character and complicational clusters then form the work's first two elements. And that which binds them together into some kind of semblance of unity, aside from the climax itself, is the work's thematic structure, the third and most important element. This structure evolves from Goff's implicit purposes in writing the novel. At first glance, her work is a passionate, retroactive defense of the Carpetbagger and his black companions; at second glance, the novel seems an 1880 attack on the Redeemers' half-exploitative, half-punitive policies toward the New Southerners. Of the two aims, it is the former that dominates the work's thematic purposes.

The offstage political Carpetbagger is the ideological center of the work, just as he is the offstage but real object of the insurrection. This ideological interest emerges in the reiterated allusions to the coming elections of 1876, which frame the narrative, and in the *raison d'être* of the massacre itself. What seems clear is that General Baker's ruthless destruction of the Freedmen leadership is meant to discredit the Freedman's faith in the protective and retributive powers of the Union and its viceroy.[589] Moreover, the immolation of the Black Radical as a proxy for the Carpetbagger becomes the local political issue around which Goff structures her conception of the Reconstruction-as-event, the struggle between the Union and the Confederacy.[590]

More interesting to this thematic analysis than the substance of these, by now, familiar polarities is the larger polemic schema in which Goff's ideological position operates as a point-by-point rebuttal of the pro-Bourbon view of the Conflict. Where the Pikes and Bakers indignantly advance Bourbon grievances as legitimate complaints, Goff scornfully dismisses them as selfish reactions to civic progress:

> Less than half the people is white to be sure, but then we own nine-tenths o' the land, and yet we must be taxed to support nigger schools, and niggers and carpet-baggers in all the offices, and new officers trumped up where there ain't enough to serve them as wants 'em—health officers in every little town, and scavengers even, under pretense of fear of yellow fever, to give salaries to dumb niggers as don't know nothing only how to rob Southern gentlemen, and all sorts of Yankee 'public improvements' as they call 'em! Why, I'm taxed this year to mend a road that runs down past me there, and nobody but niggers never travels on it. It is positively insulting and oppressive![591]

The Anti-Radicals see the Belle as struggling valiantly and tragically to maintain her gentility and culture in the midst of degrading circumstances (as found in the following image from "In the Cotton Country"):

> I do not know anything . . . for my world has been torn asunder, and I am uprooted and lost. . . . I can not adjust myself to the new order of things, I can not fit myself in new soil, the fibers are broken. . . . I will abide in mine own country. It will not be until such as I have gone . . . that the new blood can come to her. Let us alone; we will watch the old life out with her, and when her new dawning comes we shall have joined our dead, and all of us, our errors, our sins, and our sufferings will be forgotten.[592]

In contrast, Goff presents such women as intrinsically uncultivated and ignorant, with a "natural affinity" for the poor-white level to which the Trauma has degraded them. Where the Pro-Bourbons present the ex-Confederates as a noble band of brothers committed not so much to a bad cause as to a losing one, Goff shows their cause to have been evil and presents them as a new elite group within a pseudo-aristocracy, a group in which the Bakers more than the Lees predominate.[593]

The Pro-Bourbons celebrate the Cavalier's vision of Southern society as a code of idealized conduct, wholly real, operating as the moral foundation of U.S. American slavery:

> . . . and for the most part these ancient aristocrats were the kindest of Christian people—the ladies modest, frugal, home-loving, and the men wise, brave benevolent, and courtly.[594]

Goff takes a more jaundiced view of this vision. Whatever virtues the Southron may have are merely a patina over the ugliness of the slaveowner's mentality. His Cavalier courage is false: "There is a mighty sight of brag and bluster about these southern whites, though they'll dodge quick enough at sight of a United States musket with a Yankee behind it. They hav'n't forgotten their whipping yet." The aristocratic heritage celebrated by the Pro-Bourbons is more romantic than real. Goff shows that desperadoes as well as some political refugees were the ancestors of the white Carolinians. And what little nobility survived such company degenerated because of the early introduction of slavery-capitalism: "Arrogance and oppression, rapacity and murder, early became the rule and occupation of the people." Their aristocratic posturing and power is, therefore, corrupt at the core, evolving from the ignobility of that slavery defended by William Baker as the source of the Bourbon's cultural flowering:[595]

> [The Bourbon class] having utterly failed in its last great pretension in bitterness of spirit [i.e., the Civil War] still cherished its disdain for those it could not conquer, into which disdain the education of two hundred and fifty years of *irresponsible ownership of laborers* has concentrated the egotism, the selfishness and cruelty thus engendered.[596]

The ultimate meaning of the Bourbon's power, therefore, is slavery, and the ultimate meaning of slavery is Anti-Unionism in the 1850s, secessionism in the 1860s, and terrorism in the 1870s. For Goff, the anti-radical Southerner remains the Union's enemy, whose Cavalier pretensions render hypocritical what would have normally been merely savage:

> [The] feudalistic and inharmonious . . . 'aristocracy of the State'—in the year . . . 1876, and of the Republic one hundred [permitted] such brutal assault and lawless violence and outrage, as those of the worst days of feudalism. [The first families of South Carolina] committed, and defended in each other, such outrages upon the negroes and resident northern whites, as are not even admissible between civilized enemies at open war.[597]

Because of this vision, Goff can conceive of no reconciliation between the North and the resurgent Confederacy. While even a Tourgée will offer gestures of reconciliation through his commiseration with the Bourbons' suffering, Goff gloats, seeing retribution in their reduction to the level of the "cracker" families that had formerly "squatted" like caterpillars and locusts upon the skirts of their plantations," in their subjugation to poor-whites, Northern "mudsills," and ex-slaves—especially the ex-slaves.[598]

> He hates to see a nigger he has hunted in the swamps before the war, and his dogs couldn't catch, or could, practicing the use of arms with a State gun in his hands, and the Union flag over his head. He is like a mad bull, and 'the stars and stripes' is the red rag that sets him a roaring and tearing up the ground.[599]

Goff's almost fanatical denunciation spells out with the verve of an old abolitionist tract the impossibility of reunion on redeemer terms. Her harsh depiction of the Bourbon, like Albert Morgan's, is the perfect balance to the sympathetic portrayals in anti-radical literature. Within the larger polemic schema to which all partisan Reconstruction fiction thematically belongs, only her novel is the clearest Black Jacobin antithesis to the pro-Bourbon position

Her celebration of the Carpetbagger is no less partisan. With allegorical naiveté, Goff builds her novel around the thematic juxtaposition of radical virtue and reactionary villainy, the Bourbon's former hegemony over South

Carolina and the Republicans' reformism and democratic progress. Bourbonism becomes the force of Darkness, Carpetbaggery its antithetical image. In this juxtaposition, the Yankee émigré is not only the symbol of the North's political virtues, but also of the moral energy defining the North's cause.

The Carpetbagger hero operates here in his two guises. As the Black Radical, he is depicted in *Other Fools* as a vital part of the successes of the Reform Era in South Carolina. The Negro's development under Yankee tutelage is praised as the golden age of Afro-American life in the Palmetto State. There is, first of all, increasing material progress:[600]

> [The Negro lady's] iron tea-kettle shone and steamed beside a small cherry back-log upon the great hearth, which spread below the wide 'Dutch-back' chimney, while the hoe-cakes were 'keeping' between a blue-edged earthen plate, and a bright tin pan, upon a hot stone nearby, and a kettle of boiling corn, filled the room with its sweet aroma.[601]

Moreover, there is increasing political sophistication:

> It's a new thing for us to make laws and be officers . . . ; and some thinks 'cause they make the laws, that they needn't keep 'em and some is mighty ambitious, and likes to pay off old scores through the laws . . . It ain't reasonable to suppose that a man that has been a slave all his life . . . is going to rise right up and know everything at once. And the masters that has been masters over us so long . . . It's mighty hard for them to stand the nigger majorities in this State, and have the niggers that they used to have under them, just like that dog now, making laws for them, and in the offices. . . . [We] ought to think of these things on both sides, and have patience and do the best we can, and keep inside the law.[602]

In contrast to the Negro's political corruption and gullibility described in De Forest and Pike, Goff shows the Freedman leadership as becoming more discriminating about civic duty, more sympathetically aware of the Bourbon's feeling under reconstitution, and more cognizant of the need of both parties to submit to the higher power of due process.

As the White Radical, the Carpetbagger defines the pro-Union thrust of Southern Reconstruction. Denotatively, he simply stands for those pro-reconstitution Northern whites who came South after the war to take part in the political rehabilitation. Conceptually, he is both the prewar and postwar Yankee, whether as idealist, capitalist, or political, who worked with the Radicals or who had pro-Union sympathies:

> [The Bourbon] makes any man a carpet-bagger dat wa'n't baun in de South, an' some 'publicans as was. De Governor has been in de South, an' all he's got, now 'leven year; . . . an' Cummings—de head teacher o' . . . de Versity . . . — he's been in de South thirty year an' mo'; and dey calls him a carpet-bagger, too, an' all his boys; but de boys was baun here. But den dey is 'publicans an' teaches niggers, too, I wonder is dey any carpet baggers up North . . .?[603]

Of course, the Bourbons, for psycho-political reasons, take no cognizance of this complexity: "It matters not how heavy taxes they may pay, nor how long they remain in the State; if they vote the Republican ticket and maintain the principles and practice of equal justice for all men in the State, they are 'carpet-baggers.'"[604] In this wise, the Southrons' term of contempt becomes, in Goff's mutation, an insignia of honor. This is the final meaning of the appellation.

However, Goff is not so naïve as to believe that every Carpetbagger was an idealist. She recognizes that many émigrés, for example, were more interested in capitalistic opportunities than in political idealism. Many involved in politics often had little sympathy with the black power upon which their rule was built. She describes the latent prejudice existing even in former abolitionists that caused them to recoil from the reality of the Southern Negro. The black man's voice, his behavior, the very texture of his environment, offered a cultural shock that turned not a few friends of the angelic slave into an enemy of the more human ex-slave.[605]

In the Bourbon's vision of the Carpetbagger-Freedman-Scalawag alliance, contempt is the sole attitude, cynical manipulation the sole relationship. In the counter-vision, the Northerners adore all ex-slaves as the incarnation of New England political and moral virtues and work with them as father and son. "The Colored Member" treats the former, *A Fool's Errand* the latter myth. In the main Goff sees the attitude of her more typical Carpetbaggers as lying between rejection and adoration. It is one of accepting the Freedman not so much as a brother but as a man.[606] The great symbol of this idealistic thrust is, for Goff (as for most Pro-Radicals), the Yankee Schoolmarm. It is she who focuses into a sentimentally apprehensible icon the Republicans' social and political expectations of the Reconstruction moment: "If the South is saved to civilization, its chief human savior was 'the nigger school-teacher.'"[607]

But it was precisely the failure of the South to be saved "to civilization" that operates in *Other Fools* as a major idea. It is this failure that transformed the Carpetbagger from the symbol of that Northern power that had destroyed slavery to a scapegoat, when historical events caused the key Republicans to change their Dixie policy. Whatever civilization the South would develop was now to come from the triumphing redeemers. The massacres at Yazoo, Red River, and Baconsville were merely melodramatic signs of a more profound reality—the Northern elite's abandonment of their Southern allies:

> I didn't live in the No'th . . . to come back here and believe that the people there is going to stand by you in killing us off to carry the election. Maybe they're tired of protecting us, and disgusted with our blunders and our ignorance, but they won't join you . . . nor uphold nobody in killing us off that way.[608]

In Jesse Roome's plaintive declaration of faith, Goff voices the epitaph of the Radical Movement in the South. The Carpetbagger becomes a martyr, sacrificed to Bourbon heathen by the emergent indifference of the once-sustaining North's commitment to justice for all. [609] And that the South Carolina Radicals are martyred precisely at the moment when the North's older hopes in Reconstruction were being realized remains the pathetic irony in Goff's novel.

The Bourbon as Satanic villain; the Carpetbagger as Christian hero: This is the allegoric simplicity to which Goff reduces the multi-leveled complexity of the Irrepressible Conflict. Superficially, such reduction allows little subtlety; indeed, the kind of villainy that Baconsville symbolized to Goff made subtlety irrelevant. Yet there is a faint implication of complexity that can be converted by analysis into a larger, more subtle meaning for the entire work.

The battle the Northern protagonist loses at the South is not simply a political one, to repeat myself. The Carpetbagger is defeated by the broad compass of Southern mindset and mores—the Cults of Violence and Racio-sexuality, the racist ideology, the varied forms of negligence ranging from agricultural inefficiency to moral laxity. Against the Southern conception of life, the Puritan virtues of the faraway New England towns are rendered impotent, even when politically these virtues may have been succeeding. Often it was as much a psychocultural defeat as Rifle Club raids that sent many a Carpetbagger in flight from the South:

> ". . . I'm bound for dear New England, away from this land of rags and dirty, slatternly ways, lazy habits, flowing whiskey and tobacco, narrow brows and wide mouths, and people of all imaginable shades, from ebony to cream color or white. . . ."[610]

Finally, the Carpetbagger is defeated by the lawlessness of the Garden-as-Wilderness. For Goff only the tradition of extralegal violence in Southern culture could account for "the temerity of the threats and preparations for violence, and their fearful consummation, which blacken the history of the Republic's centennial year."[611] Such violence, as the defining attribute of Bourbon leadership, is the key to their victory over the law-abiding, civilized Radicals. Yet such a victory was not inevitable.

Goff, like Tourgée, believes that what gave the Bourbons their seemingly inexorable thrust for power lay not so much in their pitiless use of the Wilderness ethic as in the North's failure of nerve in 1876 and earlier in 1867 to thoroughly civilize the South. As the Scalawag, Marmor, muses:

> "And when that was over, and the No'th had us in her hand as helpless as a trapped mouse, she not only spared their lives, but gave everything back to them which they had forfeited; and now you hear them go on about the National Government and the northern people, especially [the economic carpetbaggers] in a way that is simply outrageous! You would think the South was the magnanimous *patron* of the stiff-necked and rebellious No'th. I verily believe the South would have liked the No'th better if it had put its foot upon her after she fell. Conquer your rebellious child or yield to his dictation without demur."[612]

For Goff, the death of the five Black Unionists and the eventual destruction of their ally's governments in March 1877 grow inexorably from the North's failure of nerve. It is this failure (leading to the faulty reconstitution of the South in 1867) and the inability to halt the 1876 rebellions that lead to the triumph of the Bourbon in *Other Fools and Their Doings*: "'Like the writhing beheaded serpent . . . , beheaded slave-cratic feudalism blindly ejects its spite at inevitable oncoming civilization.'"[613] This, then, is the final element in the thematic configuration of Goff's novel.

Other Fools can now be summed up in terms of this discussion and as related to our literary elements. The characters and major complications "act out" an allegory of the Carpetbagger's martyrdom at the South. Insurrection wins out over Reform, the Wilderness over Civilization, the Spirit of April 1861 over the Spirit of 1776, the Darkness over the Light. The bodies of the dead radical Freedmen stretched out in the streets of the shattered village emerge as the emblems of these defeats. For the pro-radical fictionists, more than a political party is eradicated by the Bourbons in 1876:

> The horrors of this massacre were but the commencement of a succession which blackened the history of the political campaign of the year 1876 in the State of South Carolina, and in other Southern states, and disgraced the Republic in the sight of the nations she had invited to witness the successes she had achieved under free and popular government.[614]

By the time of the book's publication, the violence launched against the Union in 1861 and its representatives in the seventies had theoretically ceased. Secession had been given up by the South, Radical Reconstruction by the North. Yet despite the presence of reconciliation as a mood and as a policy, the appearance of the pro-radical novels, of which Goff's is the most uncompromising example, is not without some design. They carry one basic message to the Northern reader: The South is no longer attacking the Union *per se* but within its borders, it is making a more insidious rebellion *against* and a far more demonic secession *from* the Union's democratic principles.[615]

Goff's presentation of the conflict motif reveals rather blatantly the intensity of her anti-Bourbon vision. Of all the pro-radical fictionists of the post-redemption period, she is the most uncompromising. No specious handclasps across the bloody chasms blur her antagonism; her indictment of redemption is as unsparing as it is partisan. For Goff, the South Carolina aristocrats are in 1880 what they were in 1861 and 1876: rebels and insurrectionists, the archetypal figures of Southern resistance to Northern enlightenment.

So far, the Black Radical has occupied the center in "Ab'm" and in *Other Fools and Their Doings*; so far, the Carpetbagger, as protagonist, has been off stage, represented only by his Negro mask. In the next novel, he appears for the first time at the center of the stage as himself. *A Year of Wreck: A True Story*: by a Victim, appeared in 1880, the same year as *Other Fools*. And like *Other Fools* and *A Fool's Errand*, *A Year of Wreck* (henceforth known as *Wreck*), it appeared anonymously. The author was in fact one George E. Benham.

There is some question if this work is a novel. In Benham's use of fictional disguises, he calls himself Harding and in the course of this section of my book, we should keep in mind we are not talking about Rebecca Harding Davis. And yet his insistence that his is a true story makes it possible, at first glance, to classify *Wreck* as either nonfiction in the form of Morgan's memoirs or fiction in the form of Tourgée's pseudo-biography. Because it foreshadows the discussion of *A Fool's Errand*, because it is a transition between Reconstruction fiction and nonfiction, and because it allows a discussion of the nonfiction as the foil to the fiction, let us initially examine *A Year of Wreck* in terms of its ambiguity of style and form.

Wreck seems to be Reconstruction nonfiction, embodying in its texture many of the qualities of the genre, especially those examples dealing with restoration. For example, the work has the kind of rhetorical stance typical of restoration nonfiction: the declamatory attacks on the recalcitrant ex-Confederates; the awed, purple evocations of the Southern landscape; the anti-Johnsonian diatribes; the Unionist outbursts. More subtly, the work makes use of the same kind of aesthetic freedom characteristic of Reconstruction nonfiction. One literary concept sums up this freedom: local color realism as the defining literary attribute.

The local color dimensions of *Wreck* can be seen, for example, in Benham's presentation of incident and character. These elements lack the conventional structuring of the 19th-century plot. Instead, as is the case within the coloristic frame of Reconstruction nonfiction, incident and character are presented without narrative strictures. Events are presented ostensibly as they occurred in real time. Personae are presented without the hero-villain polarity that defined the adventure romance (though in a very general sense, the

Carpetbagger and his planter neighbors could be considered protagonists and antagonists). Freed from such novelistic conventions, the nonfictionist could concentrate on his main aesthetic interest: regionalistic phenomena.

The incidents in *Wreck*, especially the economic scenes, reflect that interest in local color episodes found in Reid, Trowbridge, Morgan, and Andrews. The following three examples should illustrate this general local color quality. The first evokes the South-as-Garden metaphor:

> The [Harding's plantation was surrounded by] a wilderness of rose-bushes. . . . [There were also] a grand magnolia, with its thick, glossy, green leaf; . . . the laurel mundi, cape jessamine, oleander, . . . the spires, flowering shrubs, crape myrtles, pomegranate, althea . . . , the boxalder, the maple of the South; the hackberry, the counterpart of the beach tree; the sweet gum, closely resembling the oak of the West; the live oak, . . . ; the china tree, loaded with its cream-colored berries. . . . [616]

The second evokes the South-as-Wilderness metaphor within a description of the cause of malaria. While the description is medically inaccurate, it is a powerful, coloristic evocation of the "bad air" of a Mississippi riverfront area and, at the same time, an unintended metaphor of the festering ills in the reconstructing South:

> The waters in the ditches and bayous—choked up . . . soon became sour, stagnant pools, with a coating of green scum, the vapors [were] something popularly called 'malaria.' The river dropped within its banks and left the slough in front of the levee— . . . a long, narrow, slimy pond. It was overshadowed by knotted, gnarly willows, hackberries, water-oaks, and straight cotton-woods, which in turn were festooned from root to branch with enormous vine-growths. . . . When it was fed by the rains . . . , ducks had been fond of the place, but now they flew away from the sour, filthy pool, and in their stead came swarms of moccasin snakes, . . . in bunches sometimes as large as a peck basket, from their perches hissing defiance . . . or wriggling along through the green scum on the surface of the water. Occasionally an allegator [*sic*] was seen thrusting his nose through the green [scum]up against a log, . . . buffalo-fish and cat as large as a ten-year old boy, which came into the slough in the back-

> water of the Mississippi to spawn, and did not get away when the backwater ran out—now . . . gasping for the want of air in this dead-water, flopping up out of it, parting the scum and making great splashes. . . . Little lizards . . . were to be seen running up and down the sides of the trees. . . . And there was . . . insect life swarming under this density of shade. Then, there was the weed-growth rotting in the ditches; the recently turned earth exposing decayed vegetable matter—the opening up of fields with the green mold of years upon them: all filling the air with most unpleasant smells, which were passing through the lungs, and gorging the liver with bile. When the vapor began to rise at the dusk of evening, the odor was snakey.[617]

The third example is a picturesque description of the only machine permitted in the Garden, the steamboat, the depiction of which in the nonfiction is a repeated motif.

> At first the throats [of the furnaces] thus exposed looked like molten masses of fire, shining from the front of the boat, and out upon the water, but the next instant, as the fireman stirred up the furnaces, great billowing flames streamed out. . . . Then sparks and smoke rolled out from the chimneys in two great coils, the sparks veiled in the smoke looking like stars overcast by fast-flying clouds. The volume of sparks went twinkling in a long, bright band far behind the boat, hanging low over it and the water. . . .[618]

These three examples, then, illustrate the emphasis on regionalistic phenomena that, in the main, dominate the narrative incidents in *Wreck*. The same local color interest holds true for characterization. Instead of an interest in the narrative or sociopsychological evolution of character, there are only sketches exploiting the exotic differentia between Southern and Northern types for literary effect. The two following examples could have appeared in any of the nonfictional works. First, a description of a Bourbon:

> Starting out from the skirt of his hair was a pale rim of red, which gradually deepened, until centering in his enormous nose [. It] had all the color and seedy appearance of a dead-ripe strawberry. His cheeks and double chin hung down in flabby folds, and the barber's soap had brought out the blotches on his face. . . .[619]

Second, an Afro-Saxoness:

> The white blood in her veins predominated so strongly that the pink showed clearly on her cheek. Her eyes were large and coal-black and were fringed with lashes equally black, and of the most luxuriant growth, as was her long, wavy black hair, which . . . hung down her back fully two feet. Her mouth was large, and when her red, pouting lips were opened in laughter, they exposed rows of teeth of dazzling whiteness; and she had dimples in her cheeks. . . . Her . . . appearance bespoke a rich, ripe tropical growth. [She] wore a pink calico dress, so arranged that the sleeve afforded glimpses of the most finely rounded arm; and there was the small delicate hand, with tapered wrist and fingers; while from under her dress peeped a foot so diminutive it must have challenged admiration. . . . There was no super-abundance of clothing about her, so her simple pink gown wrapped her closely, bringing out her perfectly rounded form. . . . She had the expression of perfect physical health, and ripe animal growth, which made her appear so majestic.[620]

It is therefore nonfiction that, more than the fiction, best expressed the local color dynamic. Freed from the conventions of plotting and characterization in the novelistic sense, the Reconstruction nonfictionist could give full attention to regionalia. And whatever character and incident occur in this genre are presented only as having the same interest as Southern fauna, flora, and topography. Much of *Wreck* embodies this same kind of detail.

So, at the level of appearance, especially in terms of the themes (specifically the issues of restoration) and its literary stance, *A Year of Wreck* could well be classified as nonfiction. Yet despite these obvious elements, *Wreck* should be treated, in essence, as fiction masquerading as nonfiction. The slender reed upon which such an assertion is based is that Benham has chosen to speak of true experience through imagined masks, disguising the names of his characters and the setting of their adventures with imaginative identities. This approach makes *Wreck* a novel, albeit in autobiographic form. Although there was no external evidence discovered to support the belief that Benham actually participated in the events he describes, there is, nevertheless, an autobiographic "feel" about the work's texture. This "feel" gives to the novel's crude, realistic data that kind of internal consistency reminiscent of the fictionally masked "true" story, a type of docufiction. This consistency is defined as the *continual* presence of such a plethora of realistically conceived details, incidents, and characters, as to make it difficult to believe that a writer is simply "making it all up." *A Year of Wreck*, therefore, is more like *A Fool's Errand* than *Bricks Without Straw*, more like the former than *Yazoo* or *After the War*.[621]

As a foreshadowing of the Tourgée canon, as a transition work between Reconstruction fiction and nonfiction, and as an example of the organic relationship between fiction and nonfiction, *A Year of Wreck* has special significance in this study.

At the center of this novel is the saga of the Carpetbagger. Benham describes how a family of decent, apolitical, though pro-Unionist Northerners found the reconstructing South: its beauty and its terrors, its heroes and its villains. Most of all, Benham seeks to counteract the myth of immediate usurpation—that is, the legend that when the Carpetbagger first came South, he immediately found himself in possession of plantations, money, and political power, protected by the Union Army and sustained by black activism. Benham seeks to describe a more terrible reality, using the agony of the Hardings in the South as the image for the experiences of many Northern expatriates. Through such descriptions, Benham depicts with what painful knowledge the Hardings survived the sociopolitical and cultural-psychological tensions of the reconstructing South.

The saga of the Hardings takes place during the restoration and pre-reconstitution period (1866-1868). It begins with the symbolic date, January 1, 1866, that moment, lying between defeat and reoccupation, when, despite the refusal of the Radical Republican Congress to allow Johnsonian Confederate representatives to keep their seats, much of the destiny of the South's *internal affairs* still lay in Southern hands. Harding, with his family and his Northern labor force, heads for Mississippi, filled with dreams of becoming a wealthy Southern planter: "I fancied the grand sweep of an eleven-hundred-acre plantation with a roll of laborers running up in the hundreds; riding on a fine horse, with a broad Panama hat, and a ringing spur, under a Southern sky— . . . "[622] With such dreams, the Hardings arrive at their plantation ready to make the thousands of dollars glowingly prophesied by the Reids and the Andrewses.

Alas, they discover that the plantation seller has deviously exaggerated the positive conditions of the plantation and the countryside. The village is a small, sordid locality in which gambling, drunkenness, and crime fester, a place where half-wild hogs root for food in an unfenced graveyard. The manor is in ruins and the family is forced to live in an overseer's hovel. The roads are smashed and the land still smolders from the wounds of war. Despite these initial shocks, the Hardings, along with their black Southern and white Yankee laborers, begin to clear away the debris with all the vigor of new frontiersmen. However, things continue to go wrong: Their white Northern-bred overseer proves incompetent; smallpox strikes the family and the workforce; the Hardings become discouraged; the Yankee workers, unused to the Southern heat, lose their Northern efficiency and become lazy, uncooperative parasites; their young assistant dies; and the first attempt at crops ends up "in the grass."[623]

Added to these disasters are the general horrors:

> . . . chills and fever, cholera-morbus; days that were red-hot; a region so foul and filthy with its tangent pools and decaying matter . . . ; with a diet which made a man who cared anything about what he ate . . . go hungry; not a drop of milk to drink, not a pound of ice—nothing but ham, coffee, *soleratur* [sic] biscuit, hoecake, and bean soup.[624]

And all the while, beyond the tenuous perimeter of the plantation, wait the Southrons, like a foreboding presence: "We had a thorough consciousness . . . that we were living in a community where we had neither friends nor well-wishers, unless the black people were such."[625]

Thus, the year of wreck begins.

The Hardings ship off their Yankee workers and replace them with native-born Freedmen, and it seems, for a while, that things will improve. But instead the natural problems are exacerbated by the political problems. Under the Johnsonian restoration, pressures against Unionist Quislings and their Carpetbag friends increase. In the beginning, the natural antagonism was banked behind the memories of Sherman's March and the Fall of Richmond. The victorious Yankees were cheated and insulted, but they were tolerated, especially the economic Carpetbaggers like the Hardings. But as Johnson's leniency continued, the fierce passions of the anti-Unionist crusade were paradoxically awakened. The Northerners and their ways became intolerable to Southern sensibilities. Every Yankee was an enemy if he helped his men work; if he drank water out of the same gourd; if he kept "cookin' stoves, wood-saws, and India-rubber overshoes . . . [;]" if he tried to educate his Freedmen: if he, in a word, acted at all like a Northern man. And in 1867, even the most apolitical had to choose sides between the President and the Congress.[626] Those who chose incorrectly were likewise classified as Radicals and treated accordingly. The bloody-mindedness of the old anti-abolitionist crusade was revived and unleashed upon the unsuspecting Carpetbaggers through violence, death, and ostracism.

For Harding ostracism was the Bourbon's most effective method of nonviolent punishment. The planters' rigorous isolation of the Carpetbagger families was punishment having equal power with violence and death, especially for the womenfolk. In these modern times of impersonal relationships within large communal structures, such a statement might seem an exaggeration. Yet for the 19th-century frontiersperson, this statement would have been true, if one can believe Reconstruction writers. And it is easy to see why. In the frontier areas, neighborliness operated as a vital part of the technique of survival in wilderness communities, especially since one's neighbors often acted as doctors, morticians, and policemen.

The frontier community, to which much of the reconstructing South belonged, formed a fabric of interlinking individuals and families, and to have been isolated from this fabric was a form of painful exile. This many a Carpetbagger in pro-radical fiction recognized:

> "That hurts me, you know. I don't like to be looked upon with suspicion. I feel very friendly toward the people here. They seem so pleasant with each other; all the more I hate being left out in the cold. But I hope I may succeed in making them like me yet."[627]

But it is more than being left out in the cold which, for Harding, gives his ostracism a peculiar poignancy. It is the creation in the ostracized of an ill-defined feeling of deserving his punishment, as if he is somehow guilty of a moral flaw invisible to himself but clearly visible to the Bourbon neighbors. This adds a deadly psychological twist to the communal pressures on the Carpetbagger: "I began to wonder," states Harding, "if there was not something in my character to justify the Southern people in their . . . mistreatment and intolerance toward me." Thus, for all these reasons, ostracism was no easy punishment to endure.[628]

Ostracism, violence, death—the evils of the Bourbon—thus combine with drought, disease, and other natural evils to initiate the Hardings into the precariousness of their presence at the South. And with the introduction of these politically motivated evils, the year of wreck begins in earnest. The either-or demands of such contingencies, especially the pressures of the reviving rebels, force Harding to become a reconstructionist. Of course, the Carpetbagger in general went into politics for varied reasons ranging from opportunism to idealism. But those like Harding who came South during the early days of restoration had many practical reasons for becoming involved. They had too many legal tricks played on them by unscrupulous planters; they had been made victim of unfair taxation, with a corresponding lack of representation; they and their Freedmen workers had often been victims of terrorism. Worst of all, they had been unable to get legal redress from the local governments, often composed of Johnsonian ex-Confederates who considered the émigrés legitimate scapegoats for Southern troubles. And to complicate matters further, the South, because of Johnson's struggles with the Congress and because of the South's recalcitrant spirit, was still out of the Union following the expulsion of ex-Confederates in 1866.

It was this limbo condition that made the problems of Southern polity so dangerously confused. Then, when the chance to reorganize the states for admission into the Union was offered under the terms of Radical Reconstruction, the Carpetbagger was often in many communities the sole person who had the courage and the legal status to represent those Unionists who were still enfranchised. Moreover, he was often the only white man whom the newly enfranchised black U.S. Americans trusted.[629] All these factors can be combined under one term—survival—to offer a practical rationale for the entrance of many an apolitical Carpetbagger into politics. Harding, like Servosse in *A Fool's Errand*, becomes a radical judge and, like Servosse, undergoes the familiar, tragic experience of such a position.

Through the cheating, the bad crops, the uncooperative neighbors; through the ostracism, the near assassinations, the death of his radical friends, Harding and his family struggle on. By 1868 they have failed, so it seems, as economic Carpetbaggers; they have lost nearly a hundred thousand dollars instead of gaining the dreamed-of profits of one hundred eight thousand dollars. By 1875, they will also have lost political power. Through these catastrophes, the Hardings become aware with a kind of awed horror that the South is more than merely different from the North; it is rather its psychocultural antithesis in all areas. They discover that their efforts, as heroic and self-sacrificing as they were, had been doomed from the beginning in the struggle against the essential, political economic structure of Southern life, had been simply too inadequate to destroy the persistence of the Slavery Syndrome. This becomes the knowledge that frames the Hardings' defeat with tragic irony. On this note, the years of wreck seem to end.

But not quite. For following this climactic revelation, Benham adds a concluding chapter (set in 1880) that shifts Harding's political allegiance. Without warning, Harding (like Servosse) becomes an anti-Reconstructionist: "We have all grown old fast in the terrible ordeal of so-called Reconstruction, but which history will term destruction!" The abruptness of this ideological shift, in terms of the novel's tone and theme, is contradictory even by the dubious standards of unity in Reconstruction fiction. This addendum seemed to have been grafted on to a finished work as part of the reconciliation convention, since it does not "relate" to what has gone before.[630]

The sociopolitical context of this change of heart is redemption: The radical regimes have been destroyed, the political Carpetbaggers exiled, the neighborhood terrorists quieted. Harding does not see redemption, as Goff does, as a return to feudal barbarism. He sees instead real improvement. Freedman labor, which seemed so radical in 1866, is now accepted in 1880. The Negro, while curtailed politically, is allowed to own land, make use of some public accommodations, and is, in general, prospering. Of course, Harding, ex-Radical that he is, sees this general economic wellbeing for black and white Southerners as being based on the work of reconstitution, e.g., the national bankruptcy laws that eliminate so many Southern debts and the burgeoning of the embryonic enterprises founded by economic Carpetbaggery.[631]

Thus, all seems well south of the line—economically, politically, and socially. Yet the ex-Radical submerged in Harding cannot resist commenting on the flaws still persistent in the Southscape. The spirit of Reconstruction—its ideals and the manner of its defeat—still haunts the South; the old antagonism against the North remains; the terrorists, while mute, dominate

Southern communities to the extent that a non-Southernist Northerner can still get hurt.[632]

Harding, in the conclusion of his story, opts for a kind of muted reconciliation that seems more by convention than conviction. Time will eventually fuse the spirits of the two sections, just as war and Reconstruction have fused their geopolitical dimensions: ". . . and so the improvement goes on, it may be at a snail's pace, but be it remembered, given a number of years, a snail's pace means many miles."[633] And it was to be with a snail's pace that the ideals that underlay Harding's initial commitment would change the political and cultural nature of Dixie.

This, then, is the narrative aspect of the Carpetbagger saga in *A Year of Wreck*. As usual, the more important element is the thematic structure.

The problems of Reconstruction in pro-radical fiction are related to two conflicting conceptions about the ultimate nature of the South. In the sociopolitical conception, the South exists as an apprehensible construct of economic, social, and political institutions that define its ultimate nature. If the South's reality consists of such institutions, then the problems of Reconstruction reside in institutional structures, in the way in which the Garden *exists* as a sociological phenomenon. In this limited view, a change in the South's institutional nature results causally in a change in its ultimate nature. This is the Carpetbagger's perception of Reconstruction. "The South has heretofore differed from the North only in the institution of slavery." When this is removed, only the Freedman will "remain as a sign of its existence: therefore, the South is as the North would be with this element added to its population."[634]

In the cultural-psychological conception, the South "is" as an intuitional-emotional construct of psychological, cultural, and anthropological qualities, or what Harding calls "the hearts and habits of all classes of Southern people. . . ."[635] These, in essence, define the South's ultimate reality. In this conception, Southern reality is "interior" to geopolitical and socioeconomic configurations, revealed through an almost religious intuition as "a way of life" resting on a mystical complex of nostalgia, memory, and tradition (or Bourbonism), accessible only to those who have been initiated into this way of life by race, blood, and family. Within the appearance, the institutional nature, of the South—slavery, Whig and Democratic Parties, planter oligarchies—lies that defining essence that transcends such merely institutional forms. In this Faulknerian view, the South's ultimate reality is "mystical" in origin and nature.

If the ultimate nature of the South consists of factors lying simultaneously within psyche and culture, then Reconstruction by external forces is difficult, if not impossible.[636] The radical program of transforming the South by transforming the institutional nature through amendments, military pressure, and law cannot affect the Southern "anima" and therefore can have only temporary viability. This is the Bourbon's perception of Reconstruction: "It was a strange mistake. The ideas of generations do not perish in an hour. Divergent civilizations cannot be made instantly identical by uprooting a single institution."[637]

A brief examination of the conventional Southern problems, the Cult of Racio-sexuality and the Cult of Violence, will demonstrate the conflict between the sociopolitical and the psychocultural view as the thematic center of *A Year of Wreck*. Harding runs into racio-sexuality in the person of one of his Bourbon enemies, General Parker, lately of the CSA, who has had several children by his many Negro concubines. He also meets Mr. Hunt, who has three families: his white family, his Negro family in the Freedman quarters, and his "plassa quadroon wife in New Orleans, with her luxurious establishment, and her offspring educated in Europe."[638] Harding's Victorian sensibilities are shocked, but such initial outrage becomes dulled when he discovers that concubinage is normal at the South.[639]

He experiences the same kind of shock in his encounter with the Cult of Violence. But he never becomes inured to the ease with which the Mississippi Southron murderously turns on Freedman, Unionist, Yankee, and friend: (a phenomenon expressed in "Mose Evans"—"We may kill a man or so occasionally . . . but thank heaven, we do not lie . . . and steal. . . . ").[640] Violence, for Harding, becomes the key signal for the endemic lawlessness characteristic of the South-as-Wilderness and forming the chief obstacle to progress. Criminal actions in Harding's adopted village are double those in a Northern town of similar size. A man might be beaten or killed for demanding the payment of a debt, for being "different," or for some minor slight on honor. If his murderer has social status, he may be exempted from legal retribution. General Parker shoots a fellow Confederate officer in the back without warning over a few dollars. Yet his fellow citizens free him, because his status is higher than that of the murdered man.

In addition, violence becomes a form of social criticism. It is easier to kill a disliked person than to endure him. Indeed, as Tennessee Williams was later to show, violence by the lawless Southerner is often simply an expression of resentment toward non-conformists and, in this context, often represents an instinctive awareness that the unofficial individualist is the natural enemy of the Southern way of life.[641] Thus, not all Southern violence is politically or racially motivated. Rather, politics and race give the natural inclination to violence a more meaningful justification.

During the pre-reconstitution process, the average killer in Harding's village became an important figure, operating with the approval of Southron gentility, as the countervailing power to the hated reconstitutionists. Harding, like Servosse and Morgan, discovers that the moral callousness that pervaded the Southern ethos before the war remains consistent in the face of the postwar conditions. The community killers commit their ghastly crimes against the Radicals with their wonted immunity. Even those Southrons with moral qualms boast of killings as "one would talk of the killing of so many swine."[642]

As a Carpetbagger Harding would argue that the pervasiveness of the Cult of Violence (and the Cult of Racio-sexuality) was rooted in the social and political institutions of slavery, destined to pass away, with the institutional nature of slavery. As a Bourbon, General Parker would have perceived his cults of sex and blood as rooted in the very nature of things Southern, as being essential to the definition of Southern civilization.[643]

This same duality of vision carries over to the nature of the Freedman. General Parker would have looked at Freedman activity in legislature, school, and cottonfield, whether performed well or ill, and reduced it all to an essential monism: The ex-African, whether in slavery or freedom, is still a nigger. On the other hand, Harding sees the Negro socio-politically. In the beginning, for example, Harding sees the black man in the restoration phase, with the habits of sexual promiscuity and laziness still about him, ". . . with the odor of the plantation on him, just as servitude made him, with all his ways and ideas . . . , his . . . vices, and his virtues."[644] But then Harding shows that as the Carpetbagger reshapes the plantation existence, fundamental changes begin to occur in those under his tutelage, symbolized most clearly in the character of an Afro-Saxon, Jimmy Carter. The young Negro, the illegitimate son of a South Carolina legislator, would have been, in slavery, merely a house-servant. But in the new conditions, he fulfills the Southern ideals of chivalrous conduct toward his beautiful wife and develops the Northern ideals of ambition and enterprise as the overseer of the Harding plantation.[645]

The greatest split between the sociopolitical and cultural-psychological view can be seen in Harding's discussion of the need for Radical Reconstruction. In this discussion of the restoration period (chapters 28-30), Harding gives the ideological center of the novel and defines his position as pro-radical despite the "deathbed conversion" in his last chapter. Moreover, one gets the clearest discussion here of the Revisionists' view of the restoration phase.

For Harding, the realities of existence at the South during restoration were confused indeed. The Freedmen were "distrustful, suspicious [;]" the Carpetbagger "ignorant" of the Southern life; the ex-Confederates were "vicious, rebellious[:]" "We want our leaders among us, just as we always had them, and the Yankee government had better not put anything in the way."[646] The persistence of such rebellious feelings was one of the major causes of the restoration confusion. The other cause was the North's belief that it had ended the Irrepressible Conflict in April 1865 and that the Thirteenth Amendment, having eliminated the institution of slavery, had made the South, to repeat, as the North would be but with an African element.

This institutional view blinded Johnson to the political realities of the restoration phase. Acting within the transcendental haze of Lincoln's Second Inaugural ("with malice toward none, with charity for all"), Johnson disregarded the Southron's defiant rhetoric and murderous acts and attempted to implement a magnanimous policy: Pardons were freely given; self-exiled, condemned traitors returned with impunity to become leaders of state legislatures and congressional contingents; confiscated property was taken away from Union loyalists and given back to arch-secessionists.[647] Yet instead of being grateful for Johnson's concessions, the Confederates perceived them as unexpected tributes to that habit of rule supposedly inherent in a landed, slave-owning aristocracy. Thus, that magnanimity advocated and celebrated by Melville, Woolson, and De Forest as the key to reconciliation seemed to the reviving Confederacy a reassertion of the essence of the North's older relationship to the South, i.e., cowardice and servility as a kind of instinctive recognition of the South's inherent superiority.[648]

(For a reconciliationist vision of the Johnson Reconstruction policies, see the old popular front movie *Tennessee Johnson*, 1942, calling for North/South unity against Axis fascism.)

Small wonder, then, that restoration became a time of Confederate resurgency. Johnson's inept charity for Harding was doing what Johnson had hoped to prevent: the flaring-up of the South's old anti-Unionist sympathies. While state and county governments were still in their hands,[649] the Bourbon acted as if nothing basically had changed, seeing where possible to subvert the Union's power. Such blind disregard of the new conditions slowed down economic development:

> . . . the solution of the labor question of the South is in bad hands, and I predict that it will take years of patient effort to bring it out of the snarl into which this season will put it. There will be much of suffering on both sides in the meantime.[650]

In addition, the Southron's psychocultural view of restoration added fuel to the violence endemic to Southern existence, mutating into the bushwhacking of 1865 and the random violence of 1866 into the political terrorism of 1867. Believing that Johnson would not allow the Federals to punish ex-Confederate assaults on non-military personnel, the Bourbon raged like a scorching flame among the Unionist citizenry of Mississippi:[651]

> All that could be said against the Southrons now is that they would have been in better condition if they had paid less attention to the President's policy, honestly accepting the situation, and if their habits of life had been different.[652]

And so fixed were the Bourbons' eyes on their habits of life that they disregarded the radical situation that Lee's defeat had brought them. The old-time, arrogant defiance supplanted the brief humility of defeat. Reconstitution was to have been, so the Hardings hoped, the shock of realism that would open those blinded eyes.[653]

In Harding's view, the South was not altogether wrong in disregarding April 15, 1865, as the end of the Conflict. In a sense, the War against Rebellion had had two aims: first, the elimination of prejudice, "passion, hatred, and the spirit of rebellion," in the South and the creation in their stead the reign of "reason and common sense [;]"[654] and second, the abolition of slavery within the Republic's border and the giving of citizenship to the ex-slaves. In the Radicals' view, the war did not eliminate all of the sectional passion and prejudice nor bring true freedom to the slave—because it had not yet rooted out all existing forms of anti-Unionism in the South. The war had been, for the Republicans, primarily a great tactical success: The North still needed a final strategic victory over its Southern antagonists, as the day-to-day realities in the restoration South demonstrated.

This would be the function of Radical Reconstruction, envisioned by Professor Eric Foner as a Second Founding, needed to make freedom "a glowing and glorious fact"[655] and to tear down the institutional texture of Southern existence.[656] But Harding recognizes that that will not suffice:

> There are weeds to be gotten rid of elsewhere than in our fields—they are in the hearts and habits of all classes of people here. Our ditches are choked up, and hence there is no drainage to our flat plantations, and so we have stagnant pools, sickness, death, with sour, dead land, producing a puny crop. There are white ways and negro ways that must be mended, at the same time that our ditches are cleared out, before success will come to us.[657]

The above "mending metaphor" is interpreted in this wise: If the nature of the South is fundamentally changed, then true reconciliation between the sections and between the Reconstruction antagonists will become a reality creating a New South:

> But we all have to draw our nourishment from the same breast; we are all travelling the same road; our goal is a common one, and, in time, we may come to be the best of friends, though we are looking askance at each other now. The weal or woe of this Southern country is in our hands.[658]

If the cultural-psychological nature of the South—its racism—is not changed, then tragedy and agony await the Carpetbagger and his comrades in the struggle:

> Our bed will be one of roses or thorns, just as we elect. If our short-comings be the result of ignorance, we shall be pitied; if of bad intent, we shall be blamed. But, in either case, ours will be the suffering.[659]

Instead through law, constitutional conventions and constitutional innovations, legislation, and the initial support of the Union's bayonets, the Radical

Unionists proceeded to reconstitute the South's sociopolitical existence. This was to be the shock that would truly redeem the South.

But by 1876 Harding's elegiac prophecy was fulfilled. Whether the psychic and cultural bases of Southern life were, in fact, axiological noumena that could not be altered by the mere transformation of social and political details, or whether, in fact, the full weight of the North was withdrawn before renovations had been complete depends on one's ideological outlook. What is important is that an *energeia* in Southern life broke out during redemption, and the Carpetbagger's crudely wrought fabric of legal and civic innovations was torn apart, to the future detriment of the masses of black and white Southerners and to the detriment of the future peace of the Union.

These two visions of the realities of Dixie may be said to lie at the roots of the conflict between Radical and Conservative during Reconstruction. When both factions looked at the same discernible phenomena, they simply did not see the same things. Their perceptions, growing from deeply rooted preconceptions, were not subject to compromise, without deliberate, unrelenting pressures from one side or the other. In the end, it became a struggle between the possibility and the impossibility of affecting a fundamental change in the Southern way of life.

Like all dialectical polarities, both these conceptions are partially right. The South was capable of being fundamentally changed; but the superficial imposition of Northern political institutions was not enough. If the North had exerted as severe a revolutionary pressure on the Confederate states as the Southrons did their counter-revolutionary ones, it could have been that the South's essential reality, which revived so furiously during redemption, would have been irrevocably altered. But that is another story. The victory of the cultural-psychological over the sociopolitical, then, becomes another way to view the conflict between the Carpetbagger and the Bourbon.

It is clear that Benham espouses the radical cause wholeheartedly. Despite his last chapter, the novel is a retroactive celebration of the Carpetbagger's tragic glories. This celebration, however, is muted, having that peculiar, elegiac nostalgia created by the chronological juxtaposition of real and historical time that is associated with the pro-radical literature of the post-redemption period. This is the indefinable link among the works of Benham, Morgan, and Tourgée. And like all pro-radical fiction, *A Year of Wreck* sets forth what was by 1880 a heretical notion: that though Radical Reconstruction might have failed in its details and ideals, it succeeded in controlling the South long enough to purge it of its more virulent xenophobia and to force, at least, its grudging acceptance of the New Union. Moreover, this Second U.S. American Revolution did succeed in setting forth, at least for a while, the sociopolitical model of what the South would one day have to become.

The final tale in this pre-Tourgéan group is S. A. Shields' minor short story, "Harcourt V'line Mango" (1881). In this tale, Shields combines the Negro tale with a version of the Carpetbagger saga. Such a combination is rather unusual for Shields, since he first appeared in this study as a rather savage Anti-Radical in "The Man and Brother." Perhaps the answer to his change of heart lies in the fact that he is treating those idealistic Carpetbaggers, the brave New England Schoolmarms. And perhaps his positive treatment of the Freedman is due to the fact that by 1881 the Negro question was in general safely in Southern hands.

The story revolves around two centers. First, there is the encounter of two teachers with Reconstruction in Mississippi. Miss Fannie Straw and Miss Effie Joyce fulfill the best qualities of the model Freedman teacher: tough yet feminine, modest and yet quite capable of facing the antagonism and ostracism of the Bourbon community in order to open up a Negro school. The success of their school before such concerted pressures testifies to their Northern efficiency and Puritan dedication.

The leader of the opposition is their feminine counterpart, the Southern as Belle. Missus Hellum, alias Helen Harcourt. She incarnates in her bitter pride the anguish of the Lost Cause and the lost glorious days of large plantations, flowering cotton, floggings, and "fum-hangings." She had entered a convent at the beginning of the war a rich heiress; she had come home to "ruins, desolation, and misery."[660] In her bitter hatred, she is a miniature portrait of that inversion of the Southern social hierarchy that fascinated Reconstruction writers. Out of this bitterness and despair, she leads the community in ostracizing the Carpetbaggers and their protector, the Union Officer.

The Officer, after such a long absence, reappears in the character of one Lt. Bronson. He is, interestingly enough, the competent director of the community's Freedman's Bureau, which is sponsoring the Negro school. Decent, kind, honorable, he is as typical of masculine Northern virtues as the Marm is of Northern feminine ones. Naturally, this damned, niggah-loving Yankee will marry the former, niggah-owning, Union-hating Belle. The

Carpetbagger in the mask of Marm and Officer and the Bourbon in the mask of the Belle remain primarily secondary figures, and as such form the first narrative center in the work.

In the second, Shields turns to the Freedman. In his treatment of Negroes, Shields becomes a little more caustic, hinting of his earlier Negrophobic antipathies. Indeed, some of the descriptions of Freedman excess seem to have been taken from his anti-radical tale. He shows their exploitation of ruined masters, describing the way they live parasitically off the Harcourt family, refusing to work even to sustain themselves and always complaining to the Bureau for every trifle. But, unlike the interpretation in his first tale, he sees the Freedman's evils as the Frankenstein monster created by slavery. He even admits that there is an ironic justice in the turn of events. Before the war, the slave supported semi-parasitical masters; now, the master supports his semi-parasitical ex-slaves.[661]

The chief symbol of Shields' change of heart is V'line.[662] For despite the emphasis on the Carpetbagger in the initial portion of the story, it is in reality a tale of a little Black Radical. Through her destiny, Shields "acts out" the Carpetbagger's thesis that via training and education, the new U.S. Americans could be made the equal of any white man. (We emphasize here that this is an interpretation that we feel the data of the work will support.) Shields presents her first as a Topsy figure—mischievous, amoral, shrewd. Later he shows her with a hint of the Uncle Tom symbolism. For example, she is quite devoted to her Northern patrons and risks her life to save them from anti-Carpetbagger terrorists. In this minimal complexity, Shields develops the essential pro-radical theme of the tale: Can V'line's latent goodness overcome the vices of slavery?

The answer emerges not in the South but in the North. When Effie Joyce finishes her stint in Dixie, she takes V'line to New England with her as her ward (in a way reminiscent of Aunt Ophelia and Topsy in *Uncle Tom's Cabin*). In the Northern environment, V'line blossoms into a Yankee maiden and all seems well. But alas, in a melodramatic turn of events, V'line dies of consumption. It is in her deathbed scene that her full humanity is finally realized and the Radicals' faith in the possibility of rehabilitating the spirit of the new U.S. Americans justified.[663] It is this humanity that Shields defends at a time when the Bourbon's insistence on the Negro's non-humanity was ideologically triumphant throughout the redeemed South.

To sum up this chapter: The major preliminary examples of the pro-radical works are "Ab'm," *Other Fools and Their Doings*, *A Year of Wreck*, and "Harcourt V'line Mango." This handful of fiction deals, in the main, with the Black as the chief representative of the Carpetbagger. Only *A Year of Wreck* places the Carpetbagger and his conflict with the Bourbon squarely at the center of the stage. For the fullest treatment of the Carpetbagger and his conflict, one must turn to the fiction of Albion Tourgée. The preliminary works discussed in this chapter have in fragmented form what will become in Tourgée's novels and novellas a single, focused approach. His works contain the final presentation of the thematic and aesthetic configuration of pro-radical fiction detailed in this preliminary discussion. Even anti-radical and neutralist works can been seen as precursors of the Tourgée canon, the canon that forms the center of this book and the substance of Chapter V.

CHAPTER V
THE OTHER FOOL AND HIS ERRAND

"He tells the truth as nearly as a carpetbagger and a Tourgée could be expected to do. I think he tries to be fair."[664]

I was first impelled to attempt the field of romantic fiction by the weird fascination of Southern life. Thrown while . . . impressible into the very vortex of the Reconstruction Era, with the sound of the bugle yet in my ears, . . . with the shadow of slavery passing slowly over the land . . . , I walked amid the strange incongruous elements around me, as one in a dream.[665]

The year 1879 saw the publication of the then anonymous work *A Fool's Errand*. It was a bombshell that sold nearly 150,000 copies and received widespread critical attention North and South as the *Uncle Tom's Cabin* of the by-then dying radical movement.[666] Historically, it began a series of novels and short stories forming Tourgée's Reconstruction canon and containing the clearest expression of the Carpetbagger's conflict with the Bourbon. Its prominence is one reason the Tourgée canon is the model against which all Reconstruction fiction and nonfiction must be measured. His canon also sums up, both pro and con, the ideological nature of Reconstruction literature before 1879 and influences the thematic impulse of many works that follow. Tourgée's fiction, then, becomes the fullest exemplification of the presence of "The Tragic Era" in 19th-century U.S. American literature.

> Of all those authors who fictionalized the Reconstruction Era, Tourgée was the only one who lived in the South as an adult throughout the entire period, the only one who offered a first-hand account of Reconstruction in terms of the political, social and economic conflicts between Southerners and Radical Republicans. His political experiences are transcribed into writing that is personally moving and historically perceptive; his best work, unlike that of other Reconstruction authors, is a contemporaneous . . . treatment of Reconstruction. In any discussion of post-bellum popular literature, novels like *A Fool's Errand* and *Bricks Without Straw* are worth considering. . . .[667]

In addition, Tourgée's fiction has had several important functions. First, it gave his humanitarian and political theories about Reconstruction a wider audience than they would have otherwise had. On the historical level, it helped generate imitations and a renewed interest in the First Reconstruction during the declining phase, creating interest in Reconstruction as a historical rather than political event among Northerners "who had been exposed only to journalistic accounts" and who were, therefore, eager to read the "personal interpretation of a defeated carpetbagger."[668] In this same context, Tourgée sought to present a more realistic picture of Southern life during reconstitution in order to counteract the romantic-sentimental pictures of the Cotton States, which were winning over former Unionists to the Southern vision.

The third function of Tourgée's fiction (and pro-radical fiction in general) was an attempt "to persuade the indifferent Northerner of his responsibility to the Negro [by portraying] the nobility and potential greatness of the colored man who now . . . was a 'racial outcast'. . . ."[669] However, it was a task that became more and more difficult as the 1880s went toward the 1890s:

> Tourgée was fighting fictionally wars which had already been fought in the 1870s; he was presenting his vivid, persuasive interpretation of Reconstruction problems so that Northerners would realize the need of his answers for the neglected Negro. But he was addressing a minority of Northerners in magazines and newspapers which did not represent the attitude of the general public. [During President Hayes' administration, the] Northern press on the whole, wanted Negroes to remain in the South [—political commentators considered the Negro problem a Southern problem—and] by 1886 most Northerners were infernally

> tired of hearing about the Negro question. [In brief,] the Northern press was not too reluctant to sacrifice the Negro on the altar of reconciliation, peace and prosperity. (Rayford Logan is quoted here.)[670]

In the fourth place, Tourgée's radical novels acted as an apologia for the reconstructionist cause, not so much for reconstitution itself as for the men and women, black and white, émigré and native born, who tried to carry out Radical Reconstruction against Southern and, eventually, Northern opposition. His works are an impassioned defense of their courage and their cause at a time in U.S. American history when essayists and novelists were discrediting their work and denigrating their martyrdom.[671]

Finally, and perhaps most important, Tourgée (and his fictional and nonfictional comrades) recalled to the North's mind something that was fading away rapidly in the glare of the Second Industrial Revolution: that once the North had been permeated, however imperfectly and crudely, with an intense vision of the nature of the new Union. But because of the implacable violence of the redeemers and the shifting interest of its own political economic elites, especially wealthy democrats, the North had permitted the overthrow of ideals lying at the very heart of the Republic's revolutionary traditions.

Thus, within a period of reunion more rhetorical than real, within a historical context of persisting problems left over from this rhetorical resolution of the Irrepressible Conflict, the pro-radical works of Tourgée and his allies represent the Carpetbaggers' last volley before the Anti-Radicals had completely discredited them and their crusade. Because of this crusade and its validity, at least in the frame of Revisionist historiography, the Tourgée canon is a welcome relief from the reconciliation bathos that dominated and that would continue to dominate the major magazines and publishing houses in the North for years to come. It would be this reconciliation trope that would eventually move from text to other forms of media, such as the visual arts, e.g., the transformation of Pike's *Prostrate State* and Thomas C. Dixon's novels *The Clansman* and *the Leopard Spots* into a film, D. W. Griffith's *Birth of a Nation*.

These then are the historical generalizations that define, initially, the importance of the Tourgée canon.

• • •

> "That was our mistake. We tried to superimpose the civilization, the idea of the North, upon the South at a moment's warning. We presumed, that, by the suppression of rebellion, the Southern white man had become identical with the Caucasian of the North in thought and sentiment and that the slave, by emancipation, had become a saint and a Solomon at once. So, we tried to build up communities there which should be identical in thought, sentiment . . . and development, with those of the North. It was A FOOL'S ERRAND."[672]

Tourgée wrote nine fictional works during the Reconstruction period. Of these nine, three do not deal with the Reconstruction in any of the ways that have been described so far. They are *Figs and Thistles*, *Hot Plowshares*, and "John Eax." It is the other six works that form Tourgée's Reconstruction canon. Of these, two—the *Toinette* and *A Royal Gentleman* sequence—are Reconstruction fables.

Tourgée's sociopolitical fiction, therefore, consists of *A Fool's Errand* (1879), *Bricks Without Straw* (1881), "Zouri's Christmas" (1882), and "Mamelon" (1882). *A Fool's Errand* and *Bricks Without Straw* tend to emphasize the political dimensions of Reconstruction while "Zouri's Christmas" and "Mamelon" tend to emphasize its social dimensions. Because of the interest in the thematic importance of these works, it is necessary to invert the chronological order of presentation, discussing these works in the order of their ideological significance: "Zouri's Christmas" (the social problems of the Freedman), "Mamelon" (the social problems of the Bourbon), *Bricks Without Straw* (the sociopolitical problems of the idealistic Carpetbagger, the Freedmen, and the Scalawags), and the climactic work *A Fool's Errand* (the sociopolitical problems of the political Carpetbagger and his comrades).

"Zouri's Christmas" and "Mamelon" appeared (along with "John Eax") in 1882. Formally, they are novellas, miniature variations of much longer Reconstruction novels. Thematically, they are tales of reconciliation, lacking the tragic political conflicts defining pro-radical fiction. In "Zouri" and "Mamelon," respectively, Freedman and Southron, Carpetbagger and Bourbon, clasp hands across a bloodless chasm and work together toward interracial adjustment and sectional reunion.

> They give glimpses of the Reconstruction Era at the South, without the shadow that hung over the land. If the North and South are contrasted, it is but to show the fusing potency of love or the solvent power of manly friendship.[673]

Of the two novellas, "Zouri's Christmas" is the least obviously sociopolitical. It seems more a work of Negro fiction than a pro-radical tale. Yet it does exist within a specific sociopolitical context: Tourgée's 1882 conceptions about the nature and meaning of the Reconstruction-as-event. As literature, "Zouri's Christmas" has few complexities. The narrative incidents (anecdotes, rather) form a simple plot line. One sees Zouri, a twelve-year-old V'line Mango type, on a Southern plantation. Her life is delimited by her aunt and uncle in the shack, and Missus and Marse in the Big House. These scenes are fairly static; the only exciting event in the work is her near-death during a storm. As a result of this accident, Zouri's aunt and uncle, at the urging of Missus, plan a Christmas party for her. This is the climactic event of the story. Missus suggests that instead of the wild food-and-drink, debt-creating orgies that had previously passed for Christmas celebrations among the Freedmen, they cut down on such extravagance and buy presents for themselves and Zouri. She further instructs them to save some of their harvest-money to pay for Zouri's Christmas, instead of foolishly squandering it all away on gimcracks during the autumn and then going into debt during the Christmas season. Sure enough, on Christmas Day Zouri is overwhelmed with joy by the toys and clothing she receives. And, as Missus predicted, there is still enough money left over for a quiet Christmas dinner. Most of all, everything is paid for.[674]

The chief characters in this simple narration are the Bourbon stereotypes—the bluff, kindly Marse and his genteel, invalided Missus; the Freedman stereotypes—the gruff, kindly Uncle and the gruff, semi-maternal Auntie; and, of course, Zouri, the Topsy-like heroine. She is the narrative center. Tourgée avoids many of the sentimental clichés of pro-Freedman propaganda in his depiction of Zouri, describing her in rather realistic terms. Instead of being a little darkling darling, she is shown, in the beginning, much like V'line Mango: unwashed, ugly, unpleasant, neglected. Instead of being a member of a devoted loving family, she is a restoration abandonee.[675] Yet Zouri survives and, thanks to Missus and Auntie, finds happiness. At the same time, she becomes the means by which her aunt and uncle discover the joys of a Victorian Christmas celebration.

In the main the work is akin to the more tenuous forms of the Southern romance. But its kinship with the Southern romance is rather ironic. "Zouri's Christmas" can be described as a wry demonstration, from the radical point of view, that it was not necessary to locate the golden time of Negro-white relationship back in pre-Reconstruction days. On the contrary, Tourgée shows Zouri and the other Freedmen living as free laborers on a "reconstituted" plantation in symbolic contentment. In an unintended takeoff on the slavery romancers, Tourgée drenches the portraits of his Reconstruction characters with the romantic haze the Southernists had reserved for the golden age of slavery. "Zouri" emerges as an idyllic evocation of interracial harmony in the midst of Reconstruction turmoil.

At the same time, the work is a complex parable of the social progress of the Freedman in a context of implicit political conflicts. From the Freedman's rudimentary discovery that thrift equals a "responsible" Christmas celebration, two basic ideas concerning Negro social problems evolve. Tourgée describes what he considers to be the only social relationship possible between white and black in the redeemed South in the light of Northern abandonment: the Negro's submission to Bourbon paternalism in the hope of securing the help, advice, and protection of his former masters in the New South. In such a relationship, political activism on the part of the Freedman is irrelevant and its absence makes possible the development of a model, interracial society: the guidance and compassion of the White Family in the Big House, the loyalty and hard work of the Negro sharecroppers in the shacks, tilling the land not as involuntary servitors but as free laborers. The evils of the owner-chattel nexus give way to the virtues of the master-servant relationship, and because such a relationship fits the Bourbon's conceptions about the ultimate nature of Southern society it will succeed (where the Carpetbagger's conceptions had failed) in giving to the Freedman his "white man's chance," despite the contingencies of Southern redemption. This is the explicit social analysis inherent in the novella.

In the second place, "Zouri" describes the political inefficacy of the Carpetbagger's transcendental view of Negro citizenship, signaled by an allusive contrast drawn between the social virtues learned through the Christmas feast and the political rights given by the Americanization laws. The ex-slaves learn that true freedom is not that which comes by "'proclamation' and 'constitutional amendment'; but that which springs from self-denial, self-control, and self-direction."[676] Zouri and her family, therefore, emerge as the Bourbon darkies of anti-radical fiction. At this moment Tourgée's view of the political future of the Negro is hardly different from that of a Colonel Dunwoddie.

Tourgée has abandoned the doctrine of radical revolution in favor of the doctrine of gradual evolution, but this shift still reflects the radical difference between the anti- and pro-Carpetbagger position. Tourgée still believed with the mythic Carpetbagger that the Negro differed from other U.S. American citizens only because of institutional factors related to his life in slavery. These factors, in time, would be eliminated through self-development. In contrast, the Anti-Radicals maintained that the ex-slave was essentially different from real (white) U.S. Americans and no amount of social transformation would change his human distinctiveness. It is this difference in the sociopolitical and the cultural-psychological conception that distinguishes "Zouri's Christmas" ideologically from *Colonel Dunwoddie, Millionaire*, despite the novella's conservative tendencies.

In Tourgée's second work: "Mamelon" (1882), his interest in the African Question does not appear at all. He turns to the Bourbon Problem, to that "Southern Pride," which is, for Tourgée, one of the keys to the psychological and cultural tension of Reconstruction politics. This pride becomes "the substance of his tale" as "he struggles to shift his frame of reference, to place himself entirely within the context of the Southern aristocratic family."[677]

Within this new frame, Tourgée fixes his attention on two events that test the reality and relevance of Southern pride: the economic dislocations that, among other things, so paralyzed the planter's will-to-power during the First Reconstruction; and the planter's economic rehabilitation which, through non-political Carpetbaggery, revived his power, at least in the Reconstruction myth. At the same time Tourgée tentatively explored the psychocultural dimensions of the Bourbon Problem as it was affected by these economic complexities.

The narrative that "acts out" these ideas is, compared to "Zouri's Christmas," a complex one. Through the heroine, Susan Dewar, one sees the fortunes of a young Bourbon couple (Susan and her husband, Paul Dewar) in the three symbolic stages that define the Bourbon saga in Reconstruction fiction. At the first stage, the Bourbon is in his glory, surrounded by all the splendid symbols of his pride—the great estate, the noble families, the wealth, the good life:

> Two broad plantations, lying side by side upon the splashing Dan; the broad bottoms, rich with unnumbered harvests; the rolling uplands, crowned here and there with tobacco-barns, grim and unsightly, but suggestive of a wealth of golden aromatic leaf which few sections could rival. . . . Few would be wealthier than we, between the mountains, whose shadowy forms hung soft and misty in our western horizon, and the sea, whose steady breezes came to us in summer. . . . Two old families, closely connected but not of kin, would be united.[678]

Such splendor culminates in the marriage of Susan and Paul as the archetypal union of Belle and Cavalier. The presentation of this first stage gives Tourgée a chance to sketchily examine the mores and traditions of the prewar South, which had shaped the Southron's pride in self and land and blood:

> Therefore, it was that the slave-holding aristocracy of the South was so fine a race . . . physically. . . . Dissipation was cured by repose and exercise in the open air, not . . . under the whip . . . of necessity, but leisurely. . . . Excepting . . . families . . . enfeebled by inter-marriage, they were . . . the finest race . . . which has resulted from the European occupancy of America. The men were . . . harmoniously developed; not worn by useless struggle . . . nor dwarfed by . . . absorbing vices. The ladies—well, it does not become me to say much of them . . . ; but while Northern girls may be smarter . . . , we do think our Southern ones are healthier . . . than those victims of long winters, close rooms . . . and a hot-house system of education.[679]

At the second stage of the saga, one sees an obverse image. All those signs of pride and power have been destroyed by the catastrophe of 1865. In their place are failure, defeat, and humiliation. At this second stage the Dewars emerge in miniature as symbols of the effect of such a trauma upon the Bourbon's conception of himself and his culture. Through them is seen the psychological and cultural disruption attendant to the fall of a class that had once seemed so permanent, so powerful, so secure.

It is the interest in this sudden fall from grace that finds its imperfect realization in "Mamelon." And because Tourgée resists transforming artistic fascination into condemnation, "Mamelon" becomes the only pro-radical work that sympathetically explores the collapse of the Southern way of life. What is more important is that in Tourgée's explicit contrast between prewar grandeur and present disgrace, he isolates that complex of causes, signaled by the concept of "Southern pride," which generated the Bourbon's anti-rational response to the Carpetbagger's innovations. This is the sociopolitical dimension of that outraging of Southern pride reflected in Tourgée's depiction of the second stage.

Susan Dewar is the dominant figure here, used by Tourgée as his abstract of Bourbon torment. Through her he sets forth the Bourbon's bewildered helplessness before the joint disasters of military defeat and economic loss. He complicates this by-now conventional portrait of the suffering Belle with a realistic addendum: her pettiness and selfishness. Susan is definitely not that traditional Belle of the pro-Bourbon fantasies who faces the new conditions with a stiff upper lip. Instead, she whines and complains and, worse, transfers her rage and bitter resentment to Paul. She resents him because, in the beginning, he does nothing but painfully brood over the defeat, paralyzed in heart and will by the magnitude of what has been lost with the Lost Cause. When he does get a job as an insurance agent, she resents such initiative as a personal degradation of her class. When he works side-by-side in the field with his ex-slaves to keep the plantation going, she resents it as an insult and responds with hurt pride, scorn, and conjugal indifference:

> I am ashamed to confess it, but as his hands grew harder and he gathered the roughness and uncouthness that accompany manual toil I began to feel a sort of contempt, almost disgust, for him which nearly made me cease to regret our estrangement.[680]

The estrangement lasts for two years: "He could not make any allowance for my sorrow and weakness, and I had no idea what was in his heart."[681]

At the third stage of the Bourbon saga, the non-political Carpetbagger, as usual, comes to the rescue. In "Mamelon," he comes twice. As an industrial Carpetbagger (one Captain Dickson), he goes into business with the Dewars and establishes a sawmill and a handle-making factory on the plantation. For a time, the Bourbons seem to recover under the tutelage of their Northern benefactor. But this forward progress is suddenly halted when the panic of

1873 wipes out their embryonic enterprises, a panic that would be the economic basis of the Southern Radicals' abandonment by the Liberal Republican wing of the Party:[682]

> Thousands upon thousands of hearts still mourn the unseen terrible visitation which, like the blight of pestilence, swept over the land, blasting hopes, desolating homes, and crushing the strongest and proudest in its path. . . .
>
> We speak of the 'panic' or the 'crash' and it is as a belt of darkness to our minds in the brightness of the past. To the students . . . it marks a readjustment of values. To the businessman it is the beginning of a long . . . depression. To the judges and lawyers it marks one of those periodic waves of bankruptcy which are always followed by an undertow of crime and demoralization . . . oh, many a heart mourns today . . . and many another life has gone out in darkness by reason of it.[683]

Captain Dickson leaves the scene and the Dewars once more sink into the Slough of Despond. But again a non-political Carpetbagger, a Northern scientist, saves the day through a series of incredible events, including Paul's attempted suicide. In this attempt Paul has used a piece of carborundum for ammunition. From this clue the professor locates on the plantation a rich vein of this valuable industrial mineral. The discovery brings the Dewars back to power and wealth but at a qualitatively higher level than before the war, since now they arrive at this new status, not through slave exploitation but through hard work, luck, and the Carpetbagger's industrial knowhow.

Thus, Mamelon is changed, like the plantation in *Di Cary* and "The Barren Ridge," into a unit of the industrializing of U.S. America as a result of the Civil War and Reconstruction. Mamelon becomes a mining area for valuable resources, filled with turning lathes and steam sawmills. The Dewars no longer look backward to the past but forward to a New South. Their pride is now based on present survival and future accomplishments. At this final stage of triumphant resurgence, the Bourbon saga ends as a hymn to the Locomotive in the Garden.

The three stages of the Bourbon saga form the narrative content acting out Tourgée's thematic interest. However, "Mamelon" is as thematically interesting for what is missing as for what it contains. One notices immediately that political ideas are completely swallowed up in Tourgée's study of pride and economics. Yet Revisionist historians have pointed out that the South's economic thrust during Reconstruction often rested on the legislative activities of those Republicans (and their Democratic allies) friendly to factory owners and bankers and small businesses. It was their political economic encouragement that, for good and evil, attracted the Dicksons to the plantations of the Dewars. In a historical sense the rehabilitation of Mamelon is permitted by the missing political Carpetbaggers.

Second, the Conflict is missing—or so it seems. It would appear that since there is no political action, there are, correspondingly, no antagonistic encounters. Yet a mutated version of the Conflict is present, expressed in the economic clash between the Bourbon and the Carpetbagger and their mutually exclusive conceptions about the economic future of the reconstructing South. For the Bourbon this future lies in the recreation of as much of the tried- and-true methods of slave-labor capitalism as possible within the restrictions imposed by the Thirteenth Amendment. The sociopolitical activities of the Radicals are to be thwarted precisely because they interfere with the process of rechaining the ex-slave to the beloved plantation. For the Carpetbagger the South's future development lies in the full-scale introduction of Northern methods. Capital, efficiency, wages, and industrialization form the tetrarchy through which the Carpetbagger will accomplish the South's economic reconstruction, as it were, a qualitative shift from chattel slavery to wage slavery.

From these differing conceptions came the violence characteristic of the restoration, when differing economic views rather than political ones generated the bloodshed (e.g., in *Yazoo* and *A Year of Wreck*). However, unlike what usually occurs in Tourgée's fiction, the Carpetbagger resolves the conflict in his favor: the transformation of Mamelon into a symbol of Reconstruction beneficence.

The final missing thematic element is the African Question. Through the industrialization of the plantation, the troublesome African had disappeared. Perhaps Tourgée had inadvertently postulated a final solution to the African question. As factories, mills, and locomotives sprang up throughout the South, the South's chief agrarian instrument would, by some economic magic, fade away as a political economic contradiction absorbed into the new energy unleashed by a free-labor system, along with the other relics in the agrarian landscape.[684]

When both of Tourgée's novellas are added together, they give in miniature a generalized picture of some of the social problems of the reconstructing South. In this context, "Zouri's Christmas" has at its center the theme of a social reconciliation between the races through a shift from the doctrines of political revolution to those of personal evolution. "Mamelon" has as its center the theme of reconciliation between the sections through a shift from agrarianism to industrialism. In both cases the inherent conflict between Bourbon and Carpetbagger operating in these tales is muffled by Tourgée's celebration of the joys of reunion.

The third work in the Tourgée canon is *Bricks Without Straw* (1880). With this text there is a return at last to a fully developed example of the sociopolitical novel. Here the elements missing from the two novellas are clearly and precisely articulated. There is no need to engage in the kind of Procrustean manipulations, inspired by Dr. Barbara Foley's vision of "depth" as found in her *Marxist Literary Criticism* and used on the shorter fiction to render up its sociopolitical characteristics. Instead, the basic themes of pro-radical fiction—the Conflict, the Syndrome, the Question—are clearly at the surface, dominating the novel's ideological texture.

Bricks Without Straw is the only novel in this study that gives an inclusive picture of the salient characters and incidents forming the social and political context of the Reconstruction drama. These details include the standard items: the Bourbon as knight and terrorist; the Radical as Northern schoolmarm, Bourbon Scalawag, and black citizen; the redemptionist terror as the successful but cowardly tool by which the conflict between the two forces is resolved. And while the work is pro-radical in its details and in its overall thrust, its analysis of the motivation and methodology of the counter-revolution is often quite objective and sympathetic when judged by the Revisionists' interpretation of the White Terror.

In addition, the novel presents descriptive and analytical vignettes of such Reconstruction activities as the Freedman's Bureau, the registration of the new citizens, the Freedman's first election day, the operations of the Klan—all within a work that begins in slavery and ends with reconciliation. Such inclusiveness does not mean that there is a panoramic view of Reconstruction throughout the entire South; rather, there is a panoramic view of the dramatic elements of Reconstruction but localized in a small North Carolina county.

An overall view of *Bricks Without Straw* reveals two major lines of complications. In the first, there is the rise and fall of the Black Radical Nimbus Desmit, traced from his birth in slavery through the four phases of Reconstruction. What happens to him reveals in the life of one Freedman the full dimensions of the period.

The Desmit narrative climaxes with an attempted murder raid on Red Wing (Desmit's plantation) by the resentful Bourbons. The purpose of the raid is to seek out and destroy Nimbus Desmit and his intellectual advisor, one Eliab Hill, a crippled Negro minister and teacher. The Bourbons hope to destroy Red Wing as a bastion of radical power. As in all Reconstruction fiction which deals with "the raid" as melodramatic incident, Tourgée's realization of the attack from beginning to end is surprisingly well handled in its details and in its dramatic movement. First, the raiders burn the accursed church-school:

> . . . there was a gleam of light within the building, a flicker and a hiss, and then with a mighty roar the flame swept through it. . . . Here and there [the fire] surged, down the aisles and over the desks, white and clear, showing in sharp silhouette every curve and angle of building and furniture.

And in grotesque contrast, outlined against the burning building, a Klansman "stood at the detached bell-tower, and when the flames burst forth from the windows, [he] solemnly tolled the bell. . . ."[685]

The tolling bell is the signal for the full attack upon the surprised village:

> Children and women were shrieking in every direction as they fled to the . . . surrounding woods. The flame roared . . . as it licked the resin from the . . . church and leaped aloft. It shone upon the glittering needles of the surrounding pines, lighted up the ripening tobacco on the hillside, sparkled in the dewy leaves of the honeysuckle which clambered over the freedman's house and hid the starting moon with its columns of black smoke.[686]

The Klansmen discover that Nimbus and Eliab cannot be found. They then seize Nimbus' wife, Lugena, and in a scene combining erotic realism, violence, and melodramatically heightened rhetoric they brutally question her:

> 'Speak, damn you! . . .', said a third, as he struck her over the bare shoulders with a stick.
>
> 'Oh! don't! don't!' shrieked the poor woman as she writhed in an agony. 'I'll tell! I will, gentlemens—I will—I will! Oh, my God! don't! don't!' she cried as she leaped wildly about, [tearing her dress off] in her efforts to avoid the blows which fell . . . on every part of her person, now fully exposed in the bright light.
>
> Again the blows came thick and fast. She fell upon the ground and rolled in the dust to avoid them. Her round black limbs glistened in the yellow light as she writhed from side to side.[687]

Eliab, the raider's other target, interrupts this furious, psycho-sexual violence by surrendering to the Klansmen:

> 'O God, my help and my shield!' ('*Here he is, God damn him*!') Forgive them, father—! ('*I've got him!*') 'They know not-ah!'
>
> A long, shrill shriek . . . sounded above the clamor of curses, and above the roar of the blazing church. There was a fall upon the cabin floor—the grating sound of a body swiftly drawn along the surface—and one of the masked marauders rushed out dragging by the foot the preacher. . . . The withered leg was straightened. The weakened sinews were torn asunder, . . . Then there were blows and kicks and curses from the crowd, which rushed upon him. In the midst, one held aloft a blazing brand. Groans and fragments of prayer came up through the din.[688]

At that moment, the Freedmen launch a fierce counterattack, led by Lugena and Nimbus (who dramatically appears out of nowhere):

> Suddenly, Eliab saw a woman's naked figure, that seemed to rise from the ground. There was a gleam of steel, and then down through mask and flesh and bone crashed the axe . . . and the blood spurted upon Lugena's unclothed form and into the face of the prostrate Eliab.

The counterattack succeeds; the Bourbon raiders retreat in disorder ". . . and terror lent them wings as they fled. . . . Then all was still, except the roar of the burning church and the solemn soughing of the pines, as the rising west wind rustled their branches."[689]

Despite this tactical victory, the Negroes and their comrades lose the strategic battles of redemption. Therefore, after other relatively minor encounters with the Bourbon (including a massacre in Louisiana), Desmit, and later his family, flees the political resurgence of these old enemies and emigrates to the safety of Kansas. On this relatively happy note, the first narrative ends.[690]

The chief character in the second line of complications is Mollie Ainslie, the Carpetbagger as idealistic schoolmarm. Like Servosse in *A Fool's Errand* and Morgan in *Yazoo*, she is a Candide who comes to Dixie naively believing that the destruction of slavery has destroyed the culture of slavery. Her adventures in the South become a chronicle of the trials and tribulations that initiate her into the knowledge of a much crueler reality. At the same time hers is the chronicle of the suffering and triumph of the Freedman teacher in the hostile South: as it were, an authentic version of the saga of Little Miss Mouse. She undergoes ostracism, insult, and threats to her life, yet not only does she endure, she also prevails. Her acts of courage and dedication show her to be the Yankee maid "compleat" and force hostile admiration from the Southron and continuing scorn from the Belle. For example, when Nimbus defiantly leads the black Radicals in a voting-day parade to the county seat, despite the threat of Bourbon rifles, it is Mollie who gallops between the two opposing forces and persuades Nimbus to have his people vote in a less provocative fashion.

Among her grudging admirers is one Hesden Le Moyne—ex-Confederate hero: widowed, noble aristocratic. Eventually through a series of improbable complications, Mollie conquers his heart but not, at first, his will. His will belongs to his mother, a psycho-political fusion of Belle, Yankeephobe, Anti-Radical, and Jocasta. Through a mixed appeal to his Southronism and Oedipal feelings, Madame Le Moyne breaks up their romantic union, forcing Hesden to promise not to see Mollie again—so long as Madame is living. Nevertheless, Mollie has wrought some fundamental changes in Le Moyne. Through Mollie's love (and his revulsion from the Red Wing outrage), Hesden becomes a Scalawag.

In addition to converting a Bourbon to the Republican cause, Mollie also becomes a millionaire. Again via a series of improbable complications, including a secret will and the fact that Mollie and Hesden share a common 18th-century ancestry, Mollie discovers that she is the legal owner of both Red Wing and the Le Moyne plantation and, most of all, the heiress of a large fortune.

When Hesden reluctantly breaks off the romance, Mollie leaves the redeeming South and with her new wealth goes to Kansas. There she becomes a transplanted economic Carpetbagger, using her pluck and wealth to establish business enterprises and a town. Soon she is the mistress of a burgeoning economic empire. At the end of the Ainslie line of complications, all other lines converge on her Kansas plantation. To her welcoming arms come Nimbus and Le Moyne, black and white exiles from the counter-revolution: For the former, Kansas offers a new life; for the latter, a new wife. Later, Le Moyne and Mollie return to the South to continue their work, but as non-political Radicals.[691]

It is clear in this plot summary that the characters act primarily as symbolic figures in a political allegory and not so much as complex personalities. Nimbus, for example, is merely Super-Freedman, the activist representative of the Negro race.[692] Unlike the helpless pawn depicted in anti-radical fiction, Nimbus is ". . . an active outcast, . . . an ambitious, and insurgent freedman who will not complacently wait for the white man to accord him, in his daily life, rights that he legally possesses."[693] The following colloquy should illustrate Nimbus' black activist "insurgency":

> [Sheriff Gleason said,] 'Hold on, Nimbus! . . . you'd better not talk like that about a white gentlemen.'
>
> 'Whose ter hender my talkin', . . . ? Hain't I jes' de same right ter talk ez you er Marse Sykes, an' wouldn't you call me a damn rascal ef I'd done ez he did? Ain't ez free ez he is?'
>
> 'You ain't white!' hissed the sheriff.
>
> 'No, an' it seems I ain't free, nuther! . . . H'yer t'other night some damn scoundrels—I specs they wuz white, too, . . . [threatened] ter kill me an' 'Liah kase we's 'too sassy,' . . . ; an ef enny on 'em comes ter Ku Klux me I'll put a bullet t'rough dem! . . . Ef I breaks the law I'll take the consequences like a man, but I'll be damned ef ennybody shall Ku Kluck me without somebody's goin' long with me, when I drops outen dis world!'[694]

There are many reasons for Nimbus' boldness. As a former Union soldier, Nimbus has enough money and nerve to buy some seemingly worthless land from his old master, for as a former slave on a tobacco plantation he recognizes correctly that the soil is right for growing prime leaf, and sure enough, during the high Reconstruction, he becomes the wealthy lord of his own plantation, Red Wing (without the benefit of Carpetbagger tutelage, by the way). Moreover, other hardworking ambitious Freedmen flock to Red Wing, and under his sociocultural leadership and his "Yankee" initiative, they create a thriving community.

Nimbus builds the village's only church-school and contributes most to pay the salary for the imported Yankee schoolmarm. As a political leader, he leads the Freedman parade to the polling booth. Through his support the Radical Republicans in the county rise to political power. For the Carpetbagger he becomes a model of Freedman possibility under radical rule. To the Bourbon he symbolizes all the evils of that rule—black arrogance, political conspiracy, and sociopsychological rivalry. However, in the course of the allegory, one sees this vital ambitious man reduced, by the defeat of the Carpetbagger, to a furtive, frightened "boy."[695] For Tourgée it was the destruction of not so much the bodies but the spirits of such new citizens as Nimbus, which was the real tragedy of redemption.

Hesden Le Moyne is Super-Scalawag, the Arch-Bourbon converted to the Carpetbagger's cause by the love of the Yankee Maid. Such a conversion in *Bricks Without Straw* "acts out" that wistful Republican fantasy that Southrons like Hesden would flock to the Union standards (as Longstreet and Alcorn did) and join with émigrés, new citizens, and old-line Southern Unionists to reconstitute the South. In the context of this fantasy, Hesden as an allegorical figure is implicitly contrasted with the more typical Scalawag: the fearful, anti-Bourbon member of the mercantile class; the half-convinced "parole d'honneur" Unionists; the ex-Confederate opportunists; and the anti-Negro poor whites, all of whom, more often than not, made up the ranks of the Scalawag group in Tourgée's novels. In this light, Hesden is a prewar Whig as the chivalrous Southron. And although he was a reluctant secessionist, he nevertheless went with his state and was wounded in the thick of the battle. That such a man as this would turn to radicalism in the face of family and society testifies, so goes the fantasy, to the essential rightness of the new "lost cause." Again the tragedy is that the unremitting hatred of the Bourbon redeemers forces him from politics.

The defeat of this Southron-as-Radical prefigures the future tragedy of the South in the post-Reconstruction period, especially foreshadowing the cruel defeat of all the hopes of the Freedmen after reconciliation. For even as Anti-Radicals, the Bourbons of Le Moyne's breeding (once they had acquired their former power) were still willing to let the second-class citizens survive under their patronage, provided that the Negroes remained docile. Moreover, it would be to the Hesden Le Moynes of the South that Booker T. Washington was to offer his black Southerners in his desperate attempt at an intra-sectional compromise. And, ironically enough, it would be the Hesdens who, even in their reactionary guise, would offer a meager but viable alternative to the lynch spirit of the Vardamans, Tillmans, and Watsons during the Dark Age following the Separate but Equal seven-two decision of a reactionary U.S. Supreme Court:

> If we had a few men like Mr. Hesden in every county, I think it would soon be better; but if it takes as long to get each one as it has to get him, I am afraid a good many generations will live and die before that good time will come.[696]

Finally, it would be such Bourbons who would have their tragic delineation as the last of the chivalrous enlightenment at the South in the novels of William Faulkner. These are the implications symbolically discernible in Tourgée's handling of Hesden Le Moyne as Bourbon and Radical.

The Carpetbagger is, thematically speaking, the most important character in this allegorical triumvirate. But Tourgée chooses no ordinary person to play this role. He is aware in 1881 that the Carpetbaggers have acquired an unsavory reputation in the popular mind as a result of the Anti-Radical's successful polemic efforts. To give the Carpetbagger a countervailing image, Tourgée presents no mere sociopolitical figure, such as a Comfort Servosse or an Albert Morgan; he presents, instead, a fully developed literary convention. Against the Queaseys and the David Kings in anti-radical fiction, Tourgée opposes the Superwoman of the popular journals, the Yankee Virgin.

Upon Mollie Ainslie Tourgée lavishes character traits typical of this queen of the sentimental tradition. As the daughter of an abolitionist minister and the sister of a dead Union hero, she is immediately identifiable as the symbolic representative of the North. As the Northern maid who comes South to teach the Freedmen their moral and educational responsibility in the new order, she is also identifiable as the political-moral center of the novel. She is independent and strong-willed, yet modest and dependent; a superb horsewoman, full of good health and healthy spirits, yet feminine and tender; sexless yet amorous; modest yet gifted with that synecdoche of erotic power—round, plump arms:

> She raised her arm above her head. . . As she did so the loose-sleeved wrapper which had been flung about her when her own . . . clothing was removed, fell down almost to her shoulder and revealed to the . . . watcher . . . an arm of faultless outline, slender, pink-tinged, plump and soft.[697]

She is, in a word, that impossible synthesis of opposing virtues that dominated the characterization of the U.S. American girl in the proper journals and novels during the Reconstruction. Tourgée then explicitly manipulates these clichés for sociopolitical effect by making her a teacher of Freedmen. This allows him to present the pro-radical view through a character whom only a cad would dare attack.

Finally, as Tourgée's sentimental-didactic instrument, Mollie becomes in Nimbus' kingdom the White Queen whose rule brings forth in the Red Wing Freedmen their latent transcendental qualities. If Nimbus and Hesden identify the sociopolitical virtues of the cause, it is Mollie who identifies its moral ones. Again the tragedy is for Tourgée that such dedicated, idealistic persons were driven out of the South by the irrational Bourbon at a time when their efforts were needed more than ever before.[698]

The main interest of *Bricks Without Straw* is not character or plot, but theme, and like all Reconstruction literature discussed in this study *Bricks Without Straw* has the archetypal encounter between the North and the South as its central idea. But since this encounter will be fully discussed in the final section of this chapter, the interest here will be in those secondary and tertiary ideas filling out the details of the broader, thematic configuration.

For example, Tourgée, like Goff and Benham, traces the defeat of the radical governments back to the conceptual confusions about the full meaning of the North's victory over the South. Was the South "in" or "out" of the Union? Were the ex-slaves citizens or merely Freedmen? Who was the legitimate master of the conquered South? New Unionists or ex-Secessionists? "The North did not comprehend its work; the South could not comprehend its fate. The unbound slave looked to the future in dull, wondering hope."[699] Yet despite these confusions, the pro-Reconstruction North initially moved decisively. One of these was the creation of the Freedmen's Bureau. Behind a mask of ironic wryness, Tourgée makes a rather powerful, retroactive defense of the Bureau and comments poignantly on its fate since the De Forest days:

> The poor thing is dead now, and . . . the good it did has been interred with its bones. It has been buried, with curses deep and bitter. . . . its officers have been loaded with infamy. Even its wonderful results have been hidden from the sight of man, and its history blackened with shame and hate. . . . Its name became synonymous with disgrace; so that now there is hardly . . . a man can be found brave enough to confess that he . . . performed the duties of the 'Freedmen's Bureau.'[700]

In light of the critical attacks on the Bureau, some of them based on actual corruption, Tourgée's defense of this ill-fated institution is quite bold.

He also boldly defends Congressional Reconstruction, especially the reconstitution legislation creating the High Reconstruction (1867-1875) as an instrument of radical policy which, in its short span of life, paralleled the Freedmen's Bureau in importance to the radical cause. This instrument was the Registration Boards, founded for a brief span of time in 1867 and 1868 to create legally for office and franchise the new black and white citizens. In his description of the makeup of a board of registration in Nimbus' hometown, Tourgée conveys the miraculous sense of this revolutionary gesture. At the same time, he presents a humorous, unsentimental picture of the kinds of talent that went to make up the boards. The first member was Glass,

> . . . a little old white man, who had not had enough of stamina of character to have done or said anything in aid of rebellion. . . . He wrestled with the mysteries of the printed page with a sad seriousness which made one regret his inability to remember what was at the top until he had arrived at the bottom. Writing was a still more solemn business . . . but he . . . would cheerfully undertake to transcribe a list of names, which he well knew that anything less than eternity would be too short to allow him to complete.[701]

The second member of the Board was Old Pharaoh Ray, an

> old-issue free-nigger. . . . He had learned to read before the constitution of 1835 deprived the free negro [*sic*] of his vote, and had read a little since. He read about as fast and committed to memory more easily than his white associate, Glass. In writing they were about a match. . . .[702]

The final member was one Cap'n Theron Pardee, "a young man who had served in the Federal Army and afterward settled in an adjoining county. He was the chairman."[703] In these three men is symbolized the radical triumvirate. However, the figure in this group that creates the most important cluster of sub-themes is, of course, the Freedman.

The first of these sub-themes is the Black Radicals' defeat because of Northern abandonment. For Tourgée it was a political abandonment that left the Freedman's constitutional rights at the mercy of his old enemy; it was a social abandonment that turned the Freedman's chances for full sociological evolution over to those who had aimed for his devolution; most of all, it was a moral abandonment that stained the North's honor and ideals. It is, therefore, the withdrawal of Northern power, more than the ferocity of the White Terror, that defeated the Blacks:

> The colored men, [who had stayed in the woods till the election was finished] now remained in their cabins. They seemed sullen and discontented, and sometimes whispered among themselves of . . . unfair treatment; but they were not noisy . . . as they had been before . . . 'redemption!' [They] were much more respectful and complaisant to their superiors than . . . anytime since the Surrender. The old time "Marse" was now almost universally used, and few "niggers" presumed to speak to a white man . . . without removing their hats. [Only in the city were there aggressive freedmen.] On the whole, however, the result seemed . . . satisfactory, with a prospect of growing better every day. Labor was more manageable, and there were much fewer appeals to the law by lazy, impudent, and dissatisfied laborers. The master's word was rarely disputed upon the part of [proxy owners that prosperity would continue since they no longer had to worry about the] persistent clamor of their hands for payment.[704]

This picture is not only one of exploitation and cruelty; it is also a sad vision of the deadening pressures of lost hopes and failed dreams:

> It does not seem like the old Red Wing. . . . The school is small in comparison with what it used to be. Somehow the life and hope seem to have gone out of our people, and they do not look forward to the future with that confident expectation which they used to have. It reminds me very much of the dull, plodding hopelessness of the old slave time. [While there is no more Klan brutality, there are also no more rights.] With [protecting] their own property . . . and the prejudice of the white people to contend with, it does indeed seem a hopeless task for them to attempt to be anything more, or anything better than they are now. I am even surprised that they do not go backwards instead of forward under the difficulties they have to encounter.[705]

This is the tragic result of the Northern Republican Party's abandonment of its most faithful ally.

The second major sub-theme relates to solutions to the Question in the light of such total despair. Tourgée sets forth an implicit and an explicit solution. The implicit choice calls for the complete submission of the abandoned Freedman to the resurgent power of the ex-master with the hope that if the Bourbon will not forget the ten years of "black tyranny," he will at least forgive his contrite Negroes. In return for voluntary servitude (sharecropping, for example), the master will once more offer them the protection and sustenance of the old Symbiosis. In this light, the paternalistic ruthlessness of Bourbons such as the Alcorns (Mississippi), the Hamptons (South Carolina), and the Nichollsins (Louisiana) did provide an alternative, although a meager one, to the crueler designs of the negrophobic "New Man" in the redemptionist party.

For the more daring and desperate, Tourgée presents a more explicit solution: emigration, as it were, the Negroes' voluntary exile from the land of their birth. This right remained: the right to emigrate out of the southscape. It was compared to the grandiose design of the amendments, a small hope, but one that would, nevertheless, shape the future of the Negro's survival in the Union. It was this right that, after redemption, differentiated freedom from slavery.

One of the most famous Negro emigrations, popularly called the Kansas Exodus, took place during the reconciliation period between 1879 and 1880.

Tourgée gives a rather extensive picture of this toward the conclusion of *Bricks Without Straw:*[706]

> Soon [Mollie and Hesden] came upon a dusky group whose bags and bundles, variegated attire, and unmistakable speech showed that they were a party of those misguided creatures who were abandoning the delights of the South for the untried horrors of a life upon the plains of Kansas. These were all of all ages, from the infant in the arms to the decrepit patriarch, and of every shade of color, from Saxon fairness with blue eyes and brown hair to ebon blackness. . . . There was no lack of variety of incident, but a wonderful similarity of motive assigned for the exodus they had undertaken.[707]

Yet despite the optimism inherent in the black Southron's choice of emigration, the novel's vision of the Freedmen under reconciliation remains pessimistic. For all practical purposes, the essential sub-theme in *Bricks Without Straw* deals with the way the ex-slaves exhausted their idealism, their faith, and themselves in a vain attempt to remain faithful Unionists against the implacable hostility of former Secessionists and the rise of Liberal Republicanism.

Conceptual confusions, the Freedmen's Bureau, the Boards of Registration, the Freedmen—these are some of the events that cluster around Tourgée's sub-themes. And it is these clusters that are the signs of Tourgée's fundamental grasp of the realistic details of the First Reconstruction as a sociopolitical phenomenon. They are equally as interesting as the more general Bourbon-versus-Carpetbagger theme. Together, the general and the specific help to shape the novel's exciting ideological texture.

The climactic novel in this descriptive analysis of the Tourgée canon (and of this study) is *A Fool's Errand*. Like *A Year of Wreck*, it is not a typical 19th-century novel. There is neither characterization nor narration in the conventional sense. Instead, there is a montage of episodes, anecdotes, analyses, and conversations that have only a perfunctory relationship to the literary demands of the conventional novel. Characters appear and disappear without explanation; complications in one chapter often have little relationship to complications in another. A stretch of "normal" narration gives way, at recurring intervals, to static didactic interludes. The only force that holds the work together and that holds the reader's attention to the work is that it deals exclusively with the Reconstruction period.

As such the work emerges primarily as a treatise on the First Reconstruction, and the minimal literary power that it clearly has derives from obviously real Reconstruction events: assassinations, raids, floggings, attempted lynching, desperate rides to the rescue. This is due partly to the amateur level at which Tourgée wrote in 1879 and partly to the socio-historical realism of the work. Tourgée purports to present events and characters as they actually were, and the dictates of such realism demand that art remains subservient to truth. For these and other reasons, *A Fool's Errand* emerges as the most sociopolitical of all the Reconstruction fiction. It is the perfect polemic antithesis to the literary excellence of *Wild Work*, on the one hand, and anti-radical propaganda of *Colonel Dunwoddie, Millionaire*, on the other.

The narrative structure of this novel, despite is episodic quality, does have a thread of plot, dealing with the fortunes of the Servosses in the Reconstruction South and their initiation, like the Harding family, into the cultural-psychological nature of Southern institutions. This is the structure around which the major incidents are unified: the coming of the Servosses to Verdenton, North Carolina; Comfort Servosse's involvement with reconstitution politics in 1868; the KK counterattack, which creates the three most dramatic moments in the novel (the lynching of the Freedman leader, Uncle Jerry; the assassination of the Scalawag chief, John Walters; and the attempted lynching of Servosse as a Carpetbagger leader); and the coming together of the Carpetbagger's daughter (Metta Servosse) and the Bourbon's son (Mel Gurney) in the pro-radical variation of the reconciliation gambit. The novel ends with the death of Servosse—of fever, not Klan bullets—in his adopted home, mourned sincerely by his old Bourbon enemies, now that the county has been redeemed. This abstract of the plot in nowise conveys the full complexity of incident in the work, but it does give the skeleton that holds this complexity together.

The literary element that unifies the entire novel is character, especially the Fool, Comfort Servosse. First of all, Servosse, as literary persona, raises the question whether he is actually Tourgée himself hiding behind a fictional mask. Certainly, they are alike as Reconstruction personae: Both come South as Union veterans and soon become involved in restoration and reconstitution politics; both become judges and, as such, barely escape plots against their lives; finally, both become leaders in the North Carolina Republican Party. But there are no biographical similarities beyond these Reconstruction characteristics. The events of Servosse's Southern adventure may be autobiographical, but he is no mere autobiographic mask; he is more precisely the archetypal Carpetbagger.

Research has disclosed two views of Servosse as a character. In the anti-radical view, the Fool is described as pro-black, opinionated, tactless, stubborn, and definitely doomed to deserved failure against the volatile temperament of the Southron.[708] However, when one reads the work, a totally different character appears. Servosse is no "gung-ho" Radical. On the contrary, he is levelheaded and non-dogmatic toward Freedmen, Radicalism, and the Bourbons. He is quite tolerant of the beliefs of his neighbors so long as they do not seek to impose their ways on him. He will, however, be a Northern man in his operation of his plantation, in his management of his ex-slave workers, and in his opinions. He initially tries to remain out of political controversies, but he soon discovers that a "for-or-against" contingency operates in the restoration South, which will not permit such private acts of neutrality without sociopolitical consequences. At an anti-reconstitution rally, Servosse is called upon by the Southrons to give his views as the resident Yankee. He calls for loyalty from the white Southerners and a limited franchise for the black. Finally, he calls for Unionism from all Southerners, native-born and émigré.[709]

Such a conservative speech marks him as the Radical, and he is, like Harding and Morgan, reluctantly drawn into the reconstitution battles. Soon Servosse becomes by default the leader of the Union League and is later sent from his community to represent the enfranchised Southerners at the North Carolina constitutional convention of 1868. (According to Rev. W. Barber in *The Third Reconstruction*, this constitution is still operational.) From that point on the Fool becomes the complete Carpetbagger in all three aspects: the economic, the idealistic, the political. But in this evolution, Tourgée is careful to point out that the circumstances of Reconstruction politics, rather than volition, force the Fool to become the Anti-Bourbon.

Whether by will or circumstance, Servosse must put on the harness of necessity and wear it through the course of his tragedy. His family is ostracized, his workers terrorized, his life endangered. All around Servosse, like a cyclone of blood, the Bourbon murder-squads rampage with impunity. And when they are finally arrested by the radical militia, all the members, to Servosse's dismay, are acquitted or pardoned by the resurgent Bourbonist Democracy. Two years after the 1868 convention, North Carolina is in the hands of Servosse's enemies. Still, there remains a small, stubborn band of Radicals since this was before redemption (1875).

Ironically, Servosse feels a strong sense of relief. The final end of all his hopes for success relieves him of the burdensome demands of duty laid on him by the Union. Yet gazing over the ruins of the First Reconstruction, Servosse also feels elegiac and, at the same time, grudgingly envious of the power of the vicious but victorious Bourbon:

> He still believed in the cause . . . and believed in the capacity of those with whom he had worked to achieve for themselves, at some time . . . , a substantial freedom; but in that struggle he could do but little. He believed . . . that the wavering balance would hang in doubt for generations; and . . . in the meantime, that haughty . . . and instinctively dominant element which had already challenged the nation to a struggle of strength, [which had] been defeated and out of disaster had already wrested the substantial fruits of victory, would achieve still greater triumphs, and would for an indefinite period dominate . . . the national power. . . . [It] was apparent to him that a people who could perform such wonders . . . without awakening the fears . . . of those whose power they had felt, but whose prestige they had overthrown—whose glory they had already trailed in the dust until it was accounted . . . more honorable to have struck at the Nation's life [than to have defended it]—had . . . those characteristics which are necessary to secure and hold dominion.[710]

However, Servosse's humanism does not let him endure such dominion for long, and so he sends his family North and heads for Central America. Some years later he returns to his old plantation to tie up loose ends. Narratively, he has come home to die (though at the time he does not know it). He finds himself curiously welcomed by his Southern neighbors as "the last of the Carpetbaggers" in all their guises: the idealist who dreamt of an educated South, the economist who dreamt of a new agrarian-industrial South, the politician dreaming of a Republican South. In a sense the Bourbons see him as the relic of a great war, and because he is the only survivor of the enemy he is accepted by his former foes with tenderness—a tenderness that, while compassionate, indicates his helplessness and defeat:

> His old neighbors dropped in: Eyebright and Nelson; John Burleson, still clamorous and insubordinate; the irrepressible Vaughn . . . and a hundred more,—came to shake his hand, and chat of that past which was full of the shades . . . , and waken memories of those days when he was bound up with a grand idea, which had yielded . . . only a Sodom-like fruitage of ashen words.[711]

A latent strain of malaria (caught in Central America) seizes Servosse and dooms him. As he lies dying at Warrington, his eulogy is unintentionally delivered by an old Bourbon enemy, with the wonted ambivalence which characterizes the antagonists' vision of each other in Tourgée's fiction:

> He's there sick, and all alone 'cept for the niggers! He was a good fellow . . . ! I don't believe he ever had any spite. He was full of notions . . . , and was always making everybody a present of them whether they agreed with him or not. Some of 'em wa'n't so bad . . . either . . . ! [Then turning to a colored man he says,] we oughtn't to go near him at all, just to pay him for taking up with you niggers; but we ain't that kind of folks.[712]

Then Bourbons attend the Carpetbagger's last hours with much care and compassion. But the last face that Servosse is to see is a black face. This is perhaps a reminder to Servosse, even in death, of that question that had shaped, defined, and plagued his existence during his sojourn at the South.

Characterization and narration are subordinated, as indicated in the beginning, to the novel's didactic design. As with the discussion of the ideological structure of *Bricks Without Straw*, the discussion of the Conflict in *A Fool's Errand* will be saved for the third section of this chapter. Here an examination of the Reconstruction as a sociopolitical theory in the novel will be presented.

This Second Founding of the Republic appears, first of all, as resting on the ruins of the Slavocracy. While this is by now a self-evident truism, the statement does pose a problem. In this study slavery has been discussed in two aspects: as a complex of specific socioeconomic institutions and as a complex of general cultural-psychological phenomena. Of the two views it is the latter that has been emphasized as shaping the discussions of slave-labor capitalism in Reconstruction fiction. In this view the peculiar complex of psychological and cultural strategies used to defend the specific institutional forms of slavery becomes more important to the Bourbon than the actual forms themselves. These strategies (which can be called Bourbonism) become embodied in myth, memory, tradition, attitude, and concept, and give to the sociological structures of slavery their intense emotional energies, i.e., the obsessive demands for communal conformity while allowing megalomania, the repressive Protestant Evangelical ethic, the cults of blood and sexuality, the ambiguities of the Symbiosis, the anti-rational juxtaposition of nobility and barbarity, the elaborate rituals of social amenities.

At the same time (symbolically speaking), these strategies are shaped into their own intense, emotional forms by the institutional influences of slavery itself. In this way the Slavocracy becomes an ambivalent sociological reality, creating *and yet* created by cultural-psychological and socioeconomic forces in a Gordian knot of cause-and-effect. The political and economic history of slavery had been pretty much shattered by Grant, Sherman, and the Thirteenth Amendment. But its sociological reality persisted into all phases of the Reconstruction. This reality has been defined as the Slavery Syndrome, a term comparing it to "a number of symptoms occurring together and characterizing a specific disease."

Thus, when Reconstruction is described as being built on the ruins of slavery, the reference is to the Syndrome. And that the Reconstruction as a period and as a revolution rested so uneasily on this not-so-ruined structure of mindset, myth, and tradition is a recurring theme in *A Fool's Errand*. A friend of Servosse, one Dr. Garnett, succinctly sums up the nature and danger of the Slavery Syndrome to Radicals and the new Union:

> Based and builded on slavery, the ideas which were a part of the institution . . . have become ingrained and essential to the existence of the community. [This development] was even more dangerous and inimical to the nation than the institution itself. . . . [Neither] the nature, habits of thought, nor prejudice of men are changed by war or its results. The institution of slavery is abolished; but the prejudice,

> intolerance, and bitterness which it fostered and nourished, are still alive. [For Garnett, the only solutions to the problems of the Syndrome are Radical Reconstruction and time:] A new generation—perhaps many new generations—must arise before the North and the South can be one people, or the prejudices, resentments, and ideas of slavery, intensified by unsuccessful war, can be obliterated.[713]

The difficulty of obliterating the psychocultural realities of slavery was to plague the most idealistic efforts of the reconstitutionists. The Slavery Syndrome, then, is the first aspect of Tourgée's theory of Reconstruction.

The second aspect, related to the first, is the Freedman Question. Servosse experiences the ex-slave as citizen *in embryo* and in actuality. And his experiences with him, symbolized by Uncle Jerry—saint, preacher, mystic, political leader—tend to be idealized to counterpoint the degeneration described in Woodville, De Forest, Baker, and Woolson.[714] The ex-Africans that Servosse meets are either hardworking, sagacious, and brave, or are merely childish with an innate capacity for citizenship if given the magical "white man's chance." Such idealization "acts out" the Radical's solution to the Question: the transformation of the ex-slaves into white men. The Freedman differs from the white man only because of the institutional, cultural, and psychological demands of slavery. Where given a new set of demands ("the white man's chance"), the Freedman will be eventually transformed into a many-colored Caucasian, having all the civic virtues of the discredited Southern without the latter's secessionist taint.[715]

However, contrasting to this idealized, polemic image of the Negro during Reconstruction is the more realistic image of the existence after redemption. Here the bright vision of a new citizenry darkens and fades, and in its place there is painful vision of the end of Jubilee:

> Yet [Servosse] admitted . . . that if he shared [the Freedman's] poverty, inexperience, and helplessness . . . he would not think of such a thing as . . . asserting his political rights, but, on the contrary, would submit, with such patience as he could command, to whatever might impend, hoping and waiting for one of two things to occur; . . . an improvement in the . . . ruling class, or an opportunity to get away. . . . He really thought it an amazing piece of heroism that the colored man should so long have taken, not merely his own life, but the

> lives of his little ones, in his hand, and have gone to the ballot box . . . against such fearful odds of power. He thought that those who had died . . . since the time when a great nation falsely guaranteed to them safety . . . and the rights of citizenship; the thousands who fell victims to the violence of Ku-Klux and Rifle Clubs, the natural sad barbarity which inaugurated and sustained the repressive policy,—those thousands he deemed . . . an army of martyrs for those very principles which he still believed, and of which he was once so proud.[716]

It was the failure of such principles before such barbarity that changed the Freedman Question into its final form, the Negro Question.

The third aspect is Servosse's extensive analysis of the First Reconstruction itself and its failure as "the greatest political experiment of modern civilization. . . ." For Tourgée-Servosse the teleological basis for any plan of Reconstruction was clear—the prevention of the resurgence of Southern power: ". . . if the results of the war are to be secured, and the nation protected against the recurrence of such a calamity [i.e., rebellion], these States must be rebuilt from the very ground sill." Reconstruction would also create in the South a bourgeois, parliamentary, democratic-republican social order "homogeneous with that of the North, so as to render this country what it has never been heretofore—a nation."[717]

In order to accomplish these aims, the Northern victors had four possible plans of Reconstruction. The first one was the restoration program espoused by Andrew Johnson, the Northern Democrats, and the Republican right. In this plan the states were to return to the Union without change save for the abolition of slavery. Anti-Johnsonians, like Servosse, were appalled that the North "after four years of war" and an immense loss of men, money, and material, ". . . should relax its grip upon the South, with only such minor political disabilities as the disenfranchisement of a few superannuated leaders. . . ." The Sumners and the Stevenses objected to the lack of guarantees against future rebellion and the absence in the Johnson plan of the "power of reversal or modification." For the Tourgéan Carpetbagger, the restoration of the Southern states "to the position of equal, independent, and coordinate sovereignties was so incredible a proposition, that years were required for its complete comprehension." Johnson's ill-fated attempts to execute this plan "not only endangered himself, but raised hopes which he could not satisfy, and sowed the seeds of discontent with whatsoever might be done afterwards."[718]

The Bourbons, despite the suddenness of their shift "from subjection to autonomy," comprehended immediately the opportunity that Johnsonian charity offered. By September 1865, they had recreated their states in the image of the plan. It was a distorted image that, in the context of moderate Republican expectations, was rather startling. According to Revisionist historians, the Republican moderate had hoped that Johnson's lenient plan would somehow create Unionists among the ex-Confederates, if not socially then at least politically. But when the Southern states presented themselves to the Thirty-ninth Congress, it was as if the Confederacy had risen again.

The second plan was, for Servosse, equally irrelevant to the facts of 1865. In this plan the states would be restored, but those states that made the Freedman a citizen would be returned with full power; those that did not would be "shorn of such strength as they might lose by deducting from their representation . . . the ratio of representative power formally allowed to the non-voting colored race. . . ." The South, hoping for the success of the first plan, "rejected this proposition with scorn."[719]

The third plan, called "Congressional Reconstruction," was the one eventually adopted by the North. (The order is shifted here. In the novel, this is presented as the fourth plan.) This plan (discussed fully in Chapter II of this study) called for the restoration of the states as soon as they had disenfranchised their outstanding traitors, Americanized the Freedmen to allow their participation in all political processes, created new constitutions consonant with the North's theoretical vision of a bourgeois parliamentary democratic republic, and ratified the new amendments. By 1870, this was precisely what was to happen.

Paradoxically enough, this plan is also rejected by Servosse, although it would be under its aegis that he would serve as the Carpetbagger. He bitterly criticizes it as "an abortion" from the "womb of party necessity and political insincerity," designed chiefly to aid the Congressional Republicans in their attempt to overthrow President Johnson and to win the election of 1868. To accomplish these partisan ends, the plan needed the votes of the Freedmen, and this gambit—one part idealism, one part compromise, one part opportunism (what Professor Eric Foner calls "The Second Founding")—was the most dangerous aspect of the plan. It disregarded ". . . the popular feeling" against "the African population of that section," exasperating the Bourbon without guaranteeing the Negroes' safety.[720] For Servosse, this exasperation would, in turn, generate unremitting hatred between the powerful ex-Confederates and those Republicans allied with the Freedman. And by 1872, this was precisely what was to happen in North Carolina, as a first step of the redemption process (1875-1880).

The fourth plan (number three in the novel) was the only one capable of accomplishing the chief aim of Reconstruction: making the South into a homogenous part of the Union inclusive of its African and Saxon citizenry. This plan accepted "the past, and sought to guarantee the future." The states were not to be restored immediately. "Without seeking vengeance," this plan "took warning from what had been and sought to prevent a recurrence of evil," rebellion and the root of that rebellion, the doctrine of State Sovereignty. The plan

> proposed that the States which had been in the infected region should be quietly left to molder in the grave of rebellion,—the bed they had themselves prepared; that the region they once embraced should be divided up into Territories without regard to former statal lines, and so remain for a score of years under national control, but without power to mold or fashion the national legislation—until time should naturally and thoroughly have healed the breaches of the past.[721]

Behind Tourgée's fourth plan is a poignant vision of another outcome to the conflict, the "might-have-been," if the North had only instituted this kind of ruthlessness toward the defeated South. Redemptionist lawlessness would have been virtually nonexistent if only the source of that lawlessness, the Bourbon class, had been destroyed as an effective power in 1866, so Tourgée seems to imply. Such a process would have involved the destruction of the Confederate States as sociopolitical units, as indicated above. In addition, this would have meant the confiscation of all the great Southern land-holdings and their redistribution to the black and white Unionists. Politically, this would have involved the proscription of the citizenship rights of those former Southerners still possessing sociopolitical influence. Their citizenship powers would have, of course, been transferred to the new Unionist class under the tutelage of the Carpetbagger.

These economic and political penalties against the Bourbon would have theoretically stripped him of all meaningful ensigns of power, leaving him utterly dependent on the will of the victorious Union. Then to prevent internal rebellion, the full power of an implacable Federal authority would have been brought to bear. This would have meant military occupation of the South and a parallel civilian occupation under the command of the Carpetbagger. For a generation, so advocated the Jacobins, the defeated Confederacy would have been a vassal region until the reconstitution process had pervaded the South's social and political cultural fabric.

For Servosse, the beauty of this plan was that it recognized both the institutional and cultural dimensions of slavery as the defining characteristic of Southern civilization: "Slavery might be ended as a legal status by proclamation, but . . . heart and brain must have an opportunity to expand, before the freedman could be capable of automatic liberty." Here Servosse is quite aware that a broad development had to take place among the masses of Freedmen and ex-Confederates before absolute citizenship right would be meaningful, that the nation which had taken a race from bondage ". . . was morally bound to prepare" this race for freedom.[722]

However, it is "the third plan" that was accepted. And even this would not have been such an error if the North had made provision for the continuous, vigorous support and protection of the Carpetbagger and his comrades until they had been brought to their full development as self-sufficient, land-owning citizens. Instead, by 1870, the North had settled for a transcendental victory over the South under the illusion that it had achieved a far-reaching political one:

> It was all over,—the war, reconstruction, the consideration of the old questions. Now all was peace and harmony. The South must take care of itself now. The nation had done its part: it had freed the slaves, given them the ballot, opened the courts to them, and put them in the way of self-protection and self-assertion. The "root-hog-or-die" policy of the great apostle of the instantaneous transformation era became generally prevalent. The nation heaved a sigh of relief. For three-quarters of a century the South had been the "Old Man of the Sea" to the young Republic; by a simple trick of political legerdemain he was now got rid of forever. . . . The nation was safe. . . . The Republican party had accomplished a great mission. It had promised to put down rebellion, and it had done so. It had guaranteed freedom to the slave, and had redeemed its promise.[723]

That all this was true at the level of Appearance was contradicted by the reality of the Syndrome, thereby making the vision false at the level of Essence. For Servosse the essential folly of his errand was this essential falsity. In contrast to the image of triumph, Tourgée predicts a more painful development:

> The experiment must fail; and when it does fail, it will involve us all—us of the South, I mean—in ruin; but the North, and especially the Republican party of the North, will be responsible for this ruin, for its shame and its loss, for the wasted opportunity, and it may be, for consequent peril. . . . The North would not see the fact that war did not mean regeneration or perform the duty laid upon it as a conqueror. . . .
>
> . . . We Republicans of the South will go down with the reconstruction movement. Some of us will make a good fight for the doomed craft; others will neither realize nor care for its danger: but on neither will justly rest the responsibility. That will rest now and for all time with the Republican party of the North,—a party the most cowardly, vacillating, and inconsistent in its management of these questions, that has even been known in any government.[724]

The sociopolitical reality generating this bitterness, this sense of folly, was quite simply the betrayal of Radical Reconstruction itself rather than the errors intrinsic in the Congressional Plan. Tourgée sees Reconstruction as a failure insofar as it sought to root out the cause of Southern rebelliousness, State's Rights. It was also "a failure so far as it attempted to unify the nation. . . . It was a failure, too, so far as it attempted to . . secure the position and rights of the colored race."[725] Had the Congressional Plan succeeded, *A Fool's Errand* would have been a triumphant vision instead of a lament for thwarted hopes and pervasive defeats.

The delineation of the causes of this betrayal forms the most important part of the Tourgée-Servosse attack on the Reconstruction as revolution and period. The first cause was, as indicated above, the Northern Republican's failure to rebuild the South "from the groundsill."[726] Thus, there was the fact that the plans of Reconstruction were promulgated in a psychological environment still smoldering from the fires of the Battle at the Crater, the assassination of Lincoln, and the Union dead at the Andersonville Prison. This environment simply made the reconstructor and the reconstructee incapable of responding altogether rationally to the realities of the postwar situation. There was also the fact

> that the social conditions of three hundred years are not to be overthrown in a moment, and that differences which have outlasted generations, and finally ripened into war, are never healed by simple victory,—that the broken link can not be securely joined by mere juxtaposition of the fragments, but must be fused and hammered before its fibers will really unite.[727]

Finally, there was the fact of the Republican's Americanization of the African:

> After having forced a proud people to yield what they . . . [considered] a right,—the right to hold the African race in bondage,—they proceeded to outrage a feeling as deep and fervent as the . . . exclusiveness of Hindoo caste, by giving . . . the . . . dependent race—. . . who could not have lived . . . without the support . . . of the dominant one—equality of political right![728]

In addition to these general causes, Servosse describes the makeup of the tripartite alliance itself as a major cause of the Carpetbagger's defeat. The conjoining of the unclean Freedman, the undependable Scalawag, and the hated Carpetbagger was too much for many moderate Bourbons. Often deprived of the support of pro-Union planters, the Southern Radicals could not take root in the southscape as a political force on their own. They soon became, in Servosse's eyes, a party ". . . builded upon ignorance, inexperience, and poverty, and mainly composed of a race of pariahs, who are marked and distinguished by their color." Clearly such a party could not have stood unaided against "intelligence, wealth, the pride of a conquered nation, and a race-prejudice whose intensity laughs to shame the exclusive haughtiness of the Brahmin."[729]

Yet despite these odds, the Northern Republicans put upon this alliance the full weight of their policy of Reconstruction with only the infrequent protection of the Grand Army of the Republic:

> [After] erecting the rebellious territory into self-regulating and sovereign States, they abandoned these parties like cocks in a pit, to fight out the question of predominance without the possibility of national interference. They said to the colored man . . . , "Root, hog, or die!"
>
> It was cheap patriotism, cheap philanthropy, cheap success![730]

And the wonder is that against the darker terrors of the southscape and for so long the Radicals accomplished so much with this Second Founding, this Second U.S. American Revolution.

That which allowed the resurgence of the energies of Slavocratic daemon, that which caused the destruction of the New Citizen as "an emollient" in the "peaceful adjustment" of the South, that which led to the betrayal of reconstitution was, of course, the Irrepressible Conflict:[731]

> [The] Rebellion was not the mere incident of an accident: it was the culmination of a long smoldering antagonism,—a divergence of thought and sentiment which was radical and irreconcilable: it was a conflict between two divergent civilizations, and those civilizations had left their marks upon the laws of each section.[732]

But the Northern Republicans felt that a transcendental Unionism had finally bridged the chasm in 1865. And, as a result, they acted as if

> . . . the South was what the North would have been under similar circumstances, and blundered into a scheme of reconstruction from which they expected the settlement of the differences between the whites and blacks, and after that, a reconciliation and 'era of good feeling' between North and South.[733]

This was, of course, the essential error in judgment. The Conflict merely mutated within the South into forms that plague the Union even to this day, but in a startlingly new form.

Was there nothing gained, then, from nearly a decade of corruption and idealism, error and reform?

> [Reconstruction] was a great step in advance, in that it formulated a confession of error. It gave us a construction of 'we the people' in the preamble of our . . . Constitution which gave the lie to that which had formerly prevailed. It recognized the universality of manhood in governmental power, and, in one phase or another of its development, compelled the formal assent of all sections and parties.
>
> And is this all that has been gained by all these years of struggle and blood?[734]

Later in 1890, Tourgée, before he got involved in opposition to the de jure segregation struggle, gazing with horror and disgust on the new chains of terror and oppression with which many black folks were being "re-enslaved" by racism North and South, was to see the fulfillment of the worst fears he had projected in his novels. He was to give up in despair his lingering belief that the struggle had accomplished any good at all. It is this despair that is prefigured in Servosse's bitter outbursts against the failure of that struggle he had served so well.

> Short as is the story, it is full of folly and shame. Regarded with whatever charity, folly and cowardice appear as its chief elements; and it has already borne too bitter a harvest of crime to believe that the future holds enough of good springing from its gloom to make it ever tolerable to the historian.[735]

It would be the job of Revisionists to negate his subjective views.

A Fool's Errand, then, as a sociopolitical novel, fulfills all the demands of the genre in terms of Reconstruction fiction. It deals almost exclusively with the social (and psychocultural) consequences of political events. Its texture is filled out not only with examples of social and political action, but also with elaborate theories about the essence and ends of that action, as well as proposals for solving the problem growing out of such activity. Indeed, Servosse's discussions of the Reconstruction are placed throughout the work with tract-like insistence. Third, the novel is not only a critique of historical events prior to 1879, but it is also a critique of the whole policy of reconciliation in 1879.

In his description of the Bourbon reconquest of North Carolina, one can discern Tourgée's warnings to the North against a policy that was permitting the rapid resurgence of the Union's old enemies and permitting their oppression of the Union's old friends. Finally, as a vision of the Reconstruction as event and symbol in the microcosm of a small Southern town, *A Fool's Errand* emerges as the most objective analysis of sociopolitical phenomena in this study. The novel, for example, reflects Tourgée's "Growing sympathy for Southerners that was rare for a Republican who had been so passionately radical in his early political career." Indeed, as already shown, the work attacks both the Southern Bourbon and Northern Republican, especially the latter, who "betrayed the Negro, poor white, and even the impoverished Southern planter."[736]

Aesthetically the novel is an "obsolescent" specimen "of the partisan fiction of the previous decade," 1860-1870.[737] Yet the work does have balancing virtues: powerful melodramatic episodes and realistic recreations of Reconstruction events. It contains passages of such rhetorical and imagistic forcefulness that they become almost incantatory descriptions. Take, for example, the following description of the South during the restoration phase:

> If the past was sorrowful, the future was scarcely less so. If that which went before was embittered by disappointment and the memory of vain sacrifice, that which was to come was darkened with uncertainty and apprehension. The good things of the past were apples of Sodom in the hand of the present. The miser's money was as dust of the highway in value; . . . and the hoarder only had a gray piece of paper stamped with the fair pledge of a ghostly nation. . . . The home where [the Southron] had lived in luxury was almost barren of necessities: . . . [A] piece of cornbread with a glass of milk and a bit of bacon, was, perhaps the richest welcome-feast that [could be] devised for the returning hero. . . . Those whom he had been wont to see in delicate array were clad in homespun. His loved ones who had been reared in luxury were living in poverty. . . . The army of creditors was even more terrible than the army with banners, to whom he had surrendered. If the past was dark, the future was Cimmerian. Shame and defeat were behind, gloom and apprehension before.[738]

In passages such as these, the novel's thematic thrust manifests itself directly in the literary design. But this has been the aesthetic dynamic of the work in general. For whatever literary virtues the novel has come directly from the historical texture inherent in its didactic aims. The work's hard core of historicity more "than compensates for Tourgée's limitations as a novelist."[739] This core forms the socio-historical matrix of Tourgée's political experience out of which he fashions the novel's literary merits. There is no need to create heroic action or heroic personae; Tourgée merely describes his own experiences and the experiences of his old allies and comrades. There is no need to invent villains; the Klansmen are readymade characters of the darkest villainy.

In the final analysis, *A Fool's Errand*, as clumsy as it is, is a panorama of the cruelty, folly, and courageous endurance of our humanity, whether under slavery, Congressional Reconstruction, or redemption.[740] It is the outline of such a larger image in the novel that helps to further define its thematic and aesthetic force.[741]

"Zouri," "Mamelon," *Bricks Without Straw*, and *A Fool's Errand*: These then are the four works that make up Tourgée's pro-radical canon. These works are specifically united into a single ideological unit by the conflict between the Bourbon and the Carpetbagger as the symbol of the Irrepressible Conflict between the South and the North. By examining this central idea as it appears in the four works as a whole, the discussion of the Conflict as it has appeared in Reconstruction fiction, especially in pro-radical fiction, will be brought into a summarizing, if rather extensive and perhaps repetitious, focus.

• • •

> "But the government of this republic belongs to the South. It had it in large measure from the first, it would have held it still had it not been for the folly of a few when Lincoln was elected; it will assuredly come into possession of it again to hold it henceforth.[742]

The two major characters in Tourgée's fiction and in all Reconstruction fiction are, of course, the Bourbon and the Carpetbagger. It may be argued that it is, in reality, the Southron and the Freedman who dominate his narrative center. But in terms of the thematic apparatus with which this study has been structured, the Freedman is a secondary though a clearly important persona. The encounter between the Southron and the Freedman, while a dramatic clash in black and white, lacks real complexity. Their roles have been fixed by history, myth, and literary convention; they remain static figures of love and hate, compassion and cruelty, within the terrifying flux of the Reconstruction moment. The ex-slave in the fiction tends to be a complement to the emancipators and the masters. It is the more complex, more dynamic encounter between the native Bourbon and the expatriate Yankee that gives to the Reconstruction event its tragic polarity.

Inherent in this *agon* is our thematic trope, the Irrepressible Conflict. In the Tourgée canon, it appears as a clash of mutually exclusive forces at the three levels already described: the Republic against the Oligarchy, the Machine against the Garden, and the anti-rational against the rational. At this third level, the Bourbons stand as the exponents of the anti-rational as a mode of existence: ". . . the vehemence of manner and sharpness of intellect with which they defended paradoxes that affronted common sense, and assailed truths too tediously true to admit of serious debate" identify in a rather rhetorical way the Bourbon's central attribute—"They were reasoning beings without being reasonable ones."[743] And against the Bourbons are thrown, in terms of this analysis, the symbols of rationality, the Carpetbaggers.[744]

A general sampling of the journals and books of the seventies and eighties reveals quite clearly the North's fascination with the Bourbon as a literary character. He is seen in the Southern romance as the golden hero, in *Huckleberry Finn* as a satirized figure. In Henry Adams' *Democracy* (1880), he appears as the aristocratic remnant of an ancient and hallowed nobility.[745] In De Forest's fiction (*Kate Beaumont*, *The Bloody Chasm*, *Miss Ravenel's Conversion*) and nonfiction (*A Union Officer*) his virtues and vices, in his guise both as Cavalier and Belle, and as antagonist and protagonist, are analyzed.[746] However, the most comprehensive analysis is found in Tourgée's Reconstruction fiction:

> In each of the novels . . . , the figure of the "royal gentleman" has played an important role. Representing the proud Southerner as the resistant force to any progress in Reconstruction policies, Tourgée attempted to show both his salutary and pernicious effects on Southern culture. Above all, he presented him for the enlightenment of the Northern reader, who hardly comprehended such as intensity of pride.[747]

On the basis of De Forest's *A Union Officer* and Tourgée's fiction, the Bourbon as social and political figure, and as literary convention, can be defined as follows. Socially, the term encompasses both the chivalrous Southron—the wealthy, many-acred slaveowner and his poorer cousin, the semi-chivalrous Southron. Politically, the Bourbon is all those gentlemen of substance who fought against the Union and then against the program of Radical Reconstruction as members of the Democratic Party. As a literary figure, the Bourbon appears in Reconstruction fiction in two forms: as victim and as victor. These terms represent the two historical poles of the Bourbon experience in the sixties and seventies: the first signaled by the military and political defeats between 1865 and 1877. These two poles can be called in this part of our book the Trauma and the Triumph.

The Trauma—the defeat, the restoration fiasco, Congressional Reconstruction—summed up the external and internal disruptions occasioned by the North's victories. Externally, the Trauma was indicated by the destruction of the Southron's images of wealth and power. Internally, it was typified by a paralysis of will and a deep, spiritual exhaustion resulting from the debilitation of the war and the completeness of the defeat. In such exhaustion, despair was merely one component. It was these traumata that defined the Bourbon character as a victim in much of Reconstruction fiction:

> [The Southrons had ruled this nation] . . . until the right to dominate had seemed almost inherent. . . . When their will was thwarted by an aroused majority, earnestly believing themselves to be oppressed beyond endurance, they flew to arms and contested with marvelous courage . . . for the right to sever the compact which bound them to the [Republic]. Failing in this, they were at the will of the conqueror; to which they submitted sullenly, but silently, not deeming it a matter of right, not enforced by any sense of duty or obligation of honor, but simply yielding because they had been conquered, and were compelled to submit.[748]

A major symbol of this victimization is the Belle. In the treatment of this figure, some of the pain and shock of the sudden overturning of pride and class finds an objective correlative. This is especially true in such anti-radical and neutralist fiction as *Di Cary*, *The Bloody Chasm*, and "The Wallflower." In the

Belle are found the specific realities of Southern culture in its most sentimental details: her silken brocade, her dainty waist, her ethereal sexuality. To see such a figure taking in washing or, worse, cooking her own meals, was a sight guaranteed to bring tears to her sympathizers and laughter to such detractors as Goff and Morgan.

In this context Tourgée's handling of the Bourbon-as-Victim convention in "Mamelon" involves both the Belle and the Cavalier.[749] For Paul Dewar, the Cavalier, the Trauma is defined simply by a pervasive, emotional malaise occasioned not so much by the destruction of property and wealth as by the military defeat of the Cause:

> He had given himself unreservedly to the Confederate cause; . . . and he had twined his future with its fate so inseparably in all his plans . . . that he could not now bring himself to consider a future in which it had no place. . . . He seemed to have lost all interest in the future and to have forgotten that there was any past save that brief interval when the "stars and bars" floated above their unfaltering defenders. He brooded forever over their defeat, and could see no hope nor light in the future.[750]

For his wife, Susan, the Trauma is defined by the more specific humiliations of the present:

> [When I saw Paul] working in the tobacco field side by side with the niggers,—working his old war horse Bob, who seemed quite contented in his degradation . . . I was angry,—angry at Paul too. It seemed as if he were trying to humiliate me still further. . . . Paul came to supper that night all worn and weary, his hands blistered and both body and soul prostrated with fatigue and helplessness. I saw it, but I did not spare or cheer him. I poured out on his head the same reproaches I had conned over when I saw him toiling in the hot sun. I accused him of not loving me and of trying to . . . degrade me further.[751]

Here the image of a catastrophic "fall from grace" acts as the controlling symbol of the Trauma.

It is because of the image of the fall that the Trauma was so fascinating to most of the Reconstruction writers. And small wonder. This image contained inherent pathos, spectacle, melodrama; it provided the pro-radical moralists with a readymade allegory of Pride, Sin, and Retribution. What gave the planters' defeat its fascination was, of course, the sensational contrast between the Bourbon's pride and his humiliation, a contrast measured by the distance he fell as the result of his ill-fated crusade. All those glittering structures that had created the tangible contours of his psychology and culture—the gracious mansions, the broad plantations, the complex rituals of leisure and careless wealth, all overthrown, symbolically, at a blow, in a whirlwind of fire and blood and amendment. No wonder that the only parallel melodramatic enough and tragic enough to image this total devastation had to be found in the destruction of the original Bourbons some seventy years before during the French Revolution.

On a related thematic level, the victim role of the ex-Confederate articulated indirectly in easily apprehensible descriptions one of the immediate causes of the Bourbon's violence against the Carpetbagger. In the Bourbon's eyes, the Carpetbagger becomes the incarnation of all the South's traumata. And his very existence highlights the contrast between what the Bourbons had been and what they had become, highlights the contrast between their poverty and the damyankee's wealth, between their hatred of the Northerner and their need for his capital and governance.

The Reconstruction-as-trauma is defined, then, as a historical and psychological context in which the Bourbon-as-victim acts as a literary figure. The pathos, sentimentality, and perhaps tragedy of the defeated aristocrat are the immediate literary values inherent in the portrayal of the fall of such a character.

The Bourbon triumphant is, of course, the obverse of the Bourbon defeated. And in all Reconstruction fiction dealing with redemption, the former character plays a definitive role as hero and/or villain. In pro-Bourbon fiction, this role is given its literary apotheosis at that climactic moment when the aristocrat reemerges in all his splendor, sanctified by his defeats and humiliations. In pro-radical fiction, the triumph at this climactic moment is as real but decidedly less splendid. The General Parkers stand slightly outside of the "Dead-Ring," their hands dappled with the blood of their political rivals. In the Tourgée canon, the Bourbon-as-Victor appears in both versions.

In "Mamelon" and "Zouri's Christmas" the first version dominates. For example, the Dewars emerge from the Trauma as new masters of an industrialized Mamelon. In "Zouri's Christmas" this victorious image is less blatant. The only hint is in the way that the Squire runs his plantation and his Negroes during Reconstruction: "So he followed his hounds and drove his farm, cursed and beat his hands, was called 'Marse,' approached with fear, and addressed hat in hand."[752] In *Bricks Without Straw* and *A Fool's Errand*, the second image is emphasized. The Bourbon is seen sweeping through the countryside burning, beating, and hanging at will—except in those instances of defiant resistance by black folks themselves. And both state militia and Federal troops are unable to prevent his sweep to victory, only delay it.

Such power, whether in economic rehabilitation or in the more terrible triumph of the North Carolina insurrection, fascinates Tourgée and complicates his attitude toward the Bourbon as a literary figure. On the one hand, the victorious Bourbons are presented as villains—those who, for Tourgée, are still rebels "in their hearts [and] enemies of the country, striving dishonorably to subvert its laws."[753] On the other hand, they are simply the heroic enemies of the Civil War, whom a hard peace has made into terrorists. Such a figure is Servosse's arch-enemy, General Gurney. Tourgée describes him admiringly as

> . . . a tall, haughty-faced man, in whose eye there was no indecision, and whose firm-shut lips confirmed the judgment instinctively made up from eye to brow. The close-clipped beard and slightly-curling hair were . . . rich brown . . . but streaked here and there were gray. He was a man [of] formal and austere manner.[754]

And while General Gurney's antagonism toward Servosse is clear, and he works ruthlessly for Servosse's overthrow, the General nevertheless is no wolf; he wants his victory but within the Code of Chivalry. When his fellows plot to tie Servosse to a trestle and then set it on fire, it is Gurney who secretly sends the warning, which leads to their rescue.[755] Thus, as arch-Klansman and arch-Cavalier, the triumphant Bourbon is, for Tourgée, a literary figure of both horror and fascination. It is this ambiguity that, in *Bricks Without Straw* and *A Fool's Errand*, colors Tourgée's use of the Bourbon-as-Victor convention and that, at the same time, accounts for much of his objective presentation of this figure.

The use of the Bourbon in Tourgée's fiction (and in Reconstruction fiction in general) as Victim and as Victor establishes the essential literary use of this character in these works. It is in these two roles that he sums up the characteristics of Bourbonism, the inclusive characteristics of the Bourbon's psyche and culture in Tourgée's fiction in particular and in Reconstruction fiction in general.

In a non-pejorative sense, Bourbonism is merely the postwar mutation of the Cavalier attitudes previously described in Chapter I as operating in the South as cultural manifestations. Tourgée sees these attitudes primarily as the Bourbon's conservatism, his notions of chivalry, and his memories of the power that his class once wielded over the South and the old Union.

The Southron's postwar conservatism differs not a jot from the prewar form described in Chapter I. On the contrary, the defeat merely intensified it as a cultural ideology and gave it more of a religious cast. One could posit many social, economic, and cultural reasons for such persistence—the Slavery Syndrome, the Garden ethos, the lack of cultural unity between North and South, the remembrance of things past.[756] But in Reconstruction literature, these disparate reasons are subsumed under the almost obsessive need in Bourbon psychology to conserve cultural forms already proven good.[757] This lay across the revolutionary efforts of Reconstruction like a daemonic force.

The second attribute of Bourbonism, existing with and generated by conservatism, was the persistence of a chivalrous notion of wealth. This notion continued to define the Southern nobility's conception of itself and its power during Reconstruction. "Down here in the cotton country we were rich once, madam; we were richer than Northerners ever are, for we toiled not for our money, neither took thought for it, it came and we spent it, that was all."[758] In anti-radical fiction, this masterful indifference to the economic basis of Southern chivalry hid a massive structure of debt, a fact that Tourgée, Morgan, and Benham more correctly assessed.

The sociological fact accounting for such aristocratic unconcern was the Bourbon's vision of labor, not so much as an economic force but as a psychocultural symbol.

> The distinction between high and low hitherto had not been compulsory labor. [The Yankees believed that the Southron thought] manual labor was . . . menial and degrading. . . . It was not that at all,—it was the *necessity* of labor which marked the dividing line. The man who was not compelled to labor might delve unremittingly; he might, as it were, enslave his

> children, making them co-laborers with the slave without either of them losing caste by it; but if such labor was necessary for their support they were branded, with more or less rigorousness according to locality. . . .[759]

Tourgée shows that this chivalric attitude toward labor leads to those paradoxical pictures common in Reconstruction literature: helpless, poverty-stricken Bourbons in possession of fertile plantations, needing only cultivation and development to prosper:

> [Our lives were based on] having . . . burden[s] lifted from our shoulders and we were not trained in bearing them. A Northern family, reduced from almost any position in life, who yet had a good plantation, with health and youth still left to them, would not have felt themselves so utterly prostrated. We had always had so many to do *for* us, and knew so little how to do for ourselves, that we were very nearly helpless. With the science and art of oversight we were familiar. No one can direct others with so little care and so great effect as the old-time master and mistress of the plantation. But now we had no one to direct.[760]

The final attribute of Bourbonism is the Redeemer's power in his community and beyond. This power appears in the persistence of Bourbon influence as a reality, despite the Trauma, exemplified in the ease with which the Bourbons assumed command of the counter-revolution, mobilized their traditional class enemies behind their banners, and escaped punishment for heinous crimes against humanity:[761]

> It is thus that they are trained to rule. To this training . . . is due the fact, that, during all the *antebellum* period, the Southern minority dominated and controlled the government, monopolized its honors and emoluments, and dictated its policy, in spite of an overwhelming and hostile majority at the North. The Southrons are the natural rulers, leaders, and dictators of the country, as late events have conclusively proved.[762]

All told, the reality and the memory of such power testified, for Tourgée, to an energy thought forever lost at Appomattox. And in his fiction, this power of command and authority as a cultural energy stand, perhaps, as the key attribute of Bourbonism.

Conservatism, chivalry, power: These then create the nature of the Bourbon worldview in pro-radical fiction in a non-pejorative sense. However, it was the pejorative aspects, the paradoxes and dangers of this self-conception, that held the attention of the Carpetbagger and his propagandists. In the following satiric evocation of the origin of the Klan, Tourgée manages to catch the substance of the paradoxical nature of this worldview:

> The Yankee-Brother Jonathan—had long been noted as a droll. . . . The negro, too, had . . . been portrayed as an irrepressible . . . farcical fellow. But the "Southern gentleman" was a man of a different kind. . . . A sardonic dignity hedged him about with peculiar sacredness. He was . . . baronial in his instincts . . . and characteristics. He was nervous, excitable, and bloodthirsty. He hunted, fought, gambled, made much of his ancestors, hated niggers, despised Yankees, and swore and swaggered on all occasions . . . . He laughed—sometimes—not often, and then somewhat sarcastically—but he did not make himself ridiculous. He appreciated fun but did not care that it should be at his expense. . . . That was the old time idea.
>
> Yet so had the war and the lapse of half a decade changed this people that [they] banded together with solemn oaths and blood ceremonies, just to go up and down the earth in the bright moonlight and play upon the . . . fears of the . . . undeveloped people around them. They became a race of jesters, moonlight masqueraders, personators of the dead. . . . It was all in sport—a great jest, or at the worst designed . . . to induce the colored man to work. . . . It was a funny thing—the gravest . . . and [most] self-conscious people on the globe making themselves ridiculous, ghostly masqueraders by the hundred thousand! The world which had lately wept with sympathy for the misfortunes of the "Lost Cause," was convulsed with merriment at the midnight antics of its chivalric defenders.[763]

This farcical juxtaposition of the Bourbon's aristocratic self-image with the trappings of Klan activity is a rather grotesque expression of the complex nature of Bourbonism. This quality found more subtle expression in the interpenetration of pride and barbarity in Tourgée's works. Pride is the key vice and has already been presented in various sections of this study as a salient character of Bourbon culture. Here it is treated in terms of what may be called "the genealogic gambit," described in the analysis of Goff's *Other Fools and Their Doings* as the Bourbon's belief that the proper family background was necessary for social and political leadership. The gambit is clearly seen in "Mose Evans" and *Di Cary*, where an inevitable Stuart exile is shown as the founder of the family.[764] The Anti-Bourbons suggest other possibilities. Tourgée shows, for example, that sometimes a great Southern family might have ancestors as scandalous and dishonorable as a Carpetbagger. The Le Moynes discover that the founder of the family's wealth and honor was one "Black Jim" Richards, a fraudulent scoundrel who cheated his cousin (Mollie's ancestor) out of his property.[765]

In anti-Bourbon literature (and even with such an Anti-Radical as De Forest), this pride mutates into a poisonous hubris, leading to a false exaltation, as in Virginia Beaufort's rejection of her uncle's money in *The Bloody Chasm*; a false economy, signaled by a theatrical style of life based on a system of permanent debt; and a false courage, mere bluster and show often hiding malicious cruelty.[766] Out of such contradictions between the Bourbon's imperious "pride of ancient lineage" and the reality of their irrational and absurd rituals came that cultural confusion that often baffled the Carpetbagger's efforts at reform. Most of all, out of such poisonous hubris came that propensity for cruelty as culturally sanctioned behavior that thwarted even the moderate programs of Southern Reconstruction.

If the Pro-Bourbons praise the Southrons for their *noblesse oblige* toward their Negroes and their magnanimity toward their foes, the Anti-Bourbons condemn them for a strong contradictory strain of socially acceptable barbarity: "We may kill a man or so, occasionally . . . but thank heaven, we do not lie and cheat and steal . . . as is done elsewhere." It was this attitude that, during the restoration period, accounted for the ease with which genteel Belles could excuse the atrocities at Andersonville: "You call the men who sanctioned the discipline at Andersonville, wholesale murderers; now, I know some of them, and better husbands and fathers—"

Indeed, that the Southron's chivalrous gentility was composed of certain attitudes not to be mentioned again in the major Northern journals during reconciliation is the gist of the pro-radical attack on Southern culture: "That word chivalry has been brought to mean a fine generosity to your equals, and your foot on the neck of all beneath you; hospitality in the house, woman-whipping in the quarters, and starvation in the prisoners' pen."[767] Of course, as reiterated in this study, the usual act of Bourbon cruelty is directed against the "dis-placed" black Southerner and those who support his cause, an impulse originating, in Tourgée's fiction, in the

> intense and ineradicable . . . scorn of a long dominant [race] for one they have held in bondage, [A feeling which] embraces no element of individual personal dislike, but is simply utter and thorough disgust and scorn for the race,—except in what they consider its proper place,—a feeling more fatal to anything like democratic recognition of their rights as citizens than the most undying hate could be.[768]

And whatever obligation that the Bourbon felt toward the Freedman as individual was cancelled out by the Bourbon's cruelty toward the Freedman as Black Jacobin, especially as the feared black insurrectionist.[769] For Tourgée, such a fear, with its roots in the guilts and fears of the Bourbon psyche, with its imagery of fire, rape, and murder, remained as the essential hysterical vision underlying much of the Bourbon worldview:

> This formula of horrors is one so familiar to the Southern tongue that it runs off quite unconsciously whenever there is any excitement in the air about the 'sassy niggers.' It is the 'form of sound words,' which is ever forgotten. Its effect upon the Southern white man is magical. It moves him as the red rag does a mad bull. It takes away all sense and leaves only an abiding desire to kill.[770]

Yet even such barbarity has its modifying influence, at least in Tourgée's fiction. He recognizes that the Bourbon's atrocity against his political rivals was balanced by the Southerner's chivalrous inclination toward gentility and compassion:

> Scarcely one of those who had so bitterly denounced . . . the Fool, . . . perhaps not one of those who had voted to take his life by . . . barbarous violence, would have hesitated to watch over him with the tenderest care. . . . No words can overdraw the beautiful kindness and tenderness of the Southern people in this respect.[771]

Some Bourbons can even make ethical distinctions about the way that a political rival ought to be exterminated: "I was no friend o' John Walters, but I would 'a' felt better ef he'd been killed in a fa'r fight, an' not shut up like a wolf in a trap, an' killed in—in—"[772]

Thus, the Southron's ability to hold as coordinate cultural ideals the generosity of the Knight and the cruelty of the Barbarian was that quality in Bourbonism that intrigued Tourgée. And when such coordination combines with Bourbon pride, as they do in Tourgée's works, they are shown forming that facet of Southern life that fascinated and appalled the anti-Bourbon writer and which, at the same time, lent an urgency to their polemics: the need to warn the North that such a people would once more dominate the Union.

There are few major characters in the canon that adequately fulfill the Bourbonist design. The character who most nearly sums up the social, political, and literary nature of this design is Hesden Le Moyne in *Bricks Without Straw*. His very name identifies him immediately with the varied facets of the pattern. His attitude toward his ex-slaves is correct, an attitude that accepts as divinely inspired the great gulf between his race and theirs: the "thousandth part of a drop of the blood of the despised race degraded, in his mind, the unfortunate possessor."[773] However, such an attitude does not translate itself into more exotic forms of Bourbonism: racio-sexuality and anti-Negro cruelty. Instead, he has the pity and paternalistic obligation that made up the appropriate, chivalrous attitude toward the unfortunate Freedmen.

Toward their new masters he is correctly antagonistic. He remains politely aloof from their problems and dangers but does not join in with those who launch vicious diatribes and attacks against the Radicals. Finally, he is properly nostalgic for the past glories and moves grimly through the reconstitution present without hope and without purpose. Hesden is the Moderate Bourbon incarnate. He is the shining ideal in physique, class, and morality of the "way of life" with all of its foibles and glories and its nobility and culturally accepted evil, without any of its culturally disapproved vices. At this point, he defines the antithesis of the Carpetbagger in *Bricks Without Straw*. However, a more extensive glance reveals some interesting features.

Although Hesden Le Moyne owned slaves, he was never convinced of the morality of slavery. And during the war he fought not so much for slavery as for his own prideful desire for victory:

> Not that we cared so much—many of us at least—for the cause we fought for; but we dreaded the humiliation of surrender and the stigma of defeat. We felt the disgrace to our people with a keenness that no one can appreciate who has not been in like circumstances. I was opposed to the war myself, but I would rather have died than have lived to see the surrender![774]

When the surrender does come, he accepts defeat at Yankee hands as that received from a heroic foe. He endures reconstitution as the natural result of rebellion. He grows to admire the courage and endurance of the Carpetbagger and becomes a Radical.

Hesden, therefore, is symbolically the Bourbon in the first part of the novel, although a complex one. Tourgée presents him as such so that he may use the literary conventions clustering around the Southern gentleman to more emphatically dramatize Hesden's conversion to the radical cause in the authentic reconciliation between North and South.[775] By such manipulation Tourgée uses the Bourbon as a literary character for his own purposes in defending the radical cause.

But the last picture in Reconstruction literature is not of the conversion of the Bourbon, but of his apotheosis as the Anti-Radical and the Anti-Rationalist as the symbol of the Southern pole of the Irrepressible Conflict. He emerges as the complex ruler of the South, loving the slave and hating the free man, hating the Yankee and needing his capital, defeated politically and militarily and in ten years once more a power in the land. His past is glorified; his chivalric traditions are enshrined in the art of Northern and Southern writers alike. His power is reflected in the way that even Republican presidents in the 19th century acquiesced in his treatment or maltreatment of the former black Radical; his influence is mirrored in the intensifying of anti-Negro feeling in the former free states. His secessionist stance becomes changed from "treason" and "rebellion" to a kind of idealistic nationalism. The War of Rebellion changes into a heroic civil war between two equally valid moral positions; the vices presented in pro-radical works—his narrowness and volatility, his pride and cruelty, his so-called ignobility and antagonism to the Union—all disappear in pro-Bourbon fiction in the glow of the rhetoric of the Lost Cause. It is no accident that in *Democracy* a Southern gentleman emerges as the valid alternative to the evils of U.S. American democracy. This, therefore, is the antagonist who, as social, political, and literary figure, as summation of the cultural ideals of Southern society, moves through Tourgée's staging of the Reconstruction tragedy like a titan, rising as high as heroic action and skillful maneuver or sinking as low as terrorist massacre in his wars against the Carpetbagger. He becomes the victor in this momentary stage of the Irrepressible Conflict.

The Carpetbagger's image is shaped by both a historical and mythic context. Before 1870, the depiction of the Carpetbagger was quite laudatory. Trowbridge wrote glowingly of this figure in "A Carpetbagger in Pennsylvania", describing his "carpet-bag" as the "emblem of enterprise and patriotism" (p. 449). Between 1872 and 1885, anti-radical propagandists, such as Woolson, Baker, and Pike, used considerable literary and polemic skill to demolish this image:[776]

> In all history there is perhaps no instance of so . . . complete an epithet. *Sansculotes* [*sic*] is its nearest rival. 'Abolitionist,' its immediate predecessor . . . 'Carpetbagger' had . . . all the essentials of a denunciatory epithet in a superlative degree. It had a quaint and ludicrous sound, . . . It was susceptible of one significance in one locality, and another in another, without being open to any etymological objection.[777]

Socio-politically, the term always meant to Southern Anti-Radicals:

> a son of an 'abolitionist,' a creature of the conqueror, . . . a mark of their degradation. . . . They hissed the name through lips hot with hate, because his presence was hateful to that dear dead Confederacy. . . . [Finally, the Carpetbagger represented] . . . that selfish, malign, and envious North, which had sent forth the 'abolitionist' in the *antebellum* days, had crushed the fair South in her . . . struggle to establish a slave-sustained republic, and now sent . . . harpies to prey upon, to . . . jeer [the Bourbons] in their downfall and misfortune. To their minds the word expressed all that . . . hate which generations of antagonism had engendered, intensified . . . by . . . a war of passionate intensity. . . .[778]

In pro-Bourbon mythology, the Carpetbagger is depicted as lacking the heroic dimensions of the Bourbon, even in the latter's barbaric modes. The

Carpetbagger's virtues as idealist, economic renovator, and political inventor are rendered nonexistent or, at best, subordinate to Bourbon virtues. At worst, the Carpetbagger's good qualities disappear within a haze of charges that he is a hypocrite, exploiter, and corrupter. At best, his evils are shown to lack the heroic proportions of satanic villainy. Rather, his malice toward the Bourbon is meanspirited; his vices—venality, cowardice, opportunism—are demeaning by their very pettiness.

The Carpetbagger also in this mythology lacks the heroic past cocooning his Southern counterpart. His only antecedent in the prewar period is the mythic Yankee Pedlar and Southern Yankee Merchant (e.g. the Coldfield family in *Absalom Absalom*). This caricature of Northern business-mindedness generated not so much hate or admiration as contempt, even among Northern writers. Whether travelling through the Cotton Kingdom selling nostrums or quietly holing up in offices in Southern cities (where he often carefully controlled the Southron's indifferent luxury through credit and speculation and dry goods), the Northerner in the South remained always the Yankee Pedlar. Then there was the darker myth of the prewar Yankee ironically created by a Northern abolitionist. This is the figure of Simon Legree, the Northerner as apostate who, more Southern than the Southron, became the symbol of the vices of slavery. Into this figure are gathered the various negative traits of the Southern-based Northerner during the antebellum period. It is to ending the Conflict that this figure must be sacrificed.

During the First Reconstruction, this older image underwent few changes. The "instinct for money as of a rat-terrier for vermin"[779] merely found a larger field to play in among the enslaved Bourbons; the cruelty toward the Negro was simply disguised by a hypocritical espousal of his cause for selfish benefit. In all the varied aspects of the Reconstruction experience, the Carpetbagger in anti-radical myth emerges as the corrupt but absolute master of the defeated Confederacy. After 1877 even once-sympathetic Republican journals would join in this abuse, presenting the Carpetbag as the emblem of a disruptive, political helplessness and an anachronistic radicalism—as, for example, in the "Studies in the South". Later in the so-called non-partisan history and fiction to follow 1885, the "Yankee" and his bag would become fixed in the popular imagination as symbols of corruption.

Between 1879 and 1885, our small group of writers appeared as apologists for the discredited Carpetbagger and sought to recover the nobility that had once aureoled his name during the high Reconstruction in the same way that pro-Southrons had rehabilitated the Cavalier. However, the Pro-Radicals' efforts, unlike those of their rivals, met with failure in stemming the growing influence of the myth of the villainous Carpetbaggers. Yet their literature does successfully identify in the Carpetbagger's fall from grace, in the defeat of his idealism and courage, the characteristics of a tragic hero. Their literature also tells the truth of Reconstruction from the Revisionist point of view. These are the chief purposes of Tourgée's key novels insofar as they are sagas of the Carpetbagger as the heroes of the Conflict.

To begin with, Tourgée gives a juster picture of the Northern emigration into the South than the one found in anti-radical myth. In his fiction and in his nonfictional work, *The Invisible Empire*, the Yankees are described as coming with their families instead of as lone wolves. Those that do come alone become attached to native Southerners. All intend to make the South their home, not their dominion. Rather than being freelance opportunists without any skills save in Republican demagoguery, many are members of honorable professions, ranging from medicine to agriculture. Some are Union veterans who have come South because of an economic and socio-aesthetic interest in the other country generated by their wartime tour of duty. One such veteran described the reasons for the immigration thusly:

> Many of them were poor, hoping to make fortunes; others were rich, and thought to increase their store fourfold . . . from the great productive wealth of the rich soil. Born amid the rigors of the North, they were enamored by the glorious sunny sky and the most genial climate on the face of the earth. . . . The greater number of them were cast out of the army, with restless minds and impulses readily quickened by the same [republican] influences [that they held during the war].[780]

In the second place, the Carpetbagger as the Reconstruction hero in Tourgée's fiction is quite human and strangely fallible in contrast to the images of dominance in the opposing myth. His helpless innocence rather than his cunning, his fearfulness rather than his malice, and the folly of his naiveté rather than the absoluteness of his control are the substance of *Bricks Without Straw* and *A Fool's Errand*. Such fallibility can be clearly seen in the way that the hatred of the white community discomforts the Tourgéan hero: "You

Servosse can not understand why they should feel so, because you were never submitted to the same influences. You have a right to be angry, but your surprise is incredible to them, and pitiable to me."[781] Later as the hatred of the Carpetbagger manifested itself in social isolation and violence, surprise and anger would change into dread and a despairing helplessness, which eventually mutates into a desperate resistance.

In the main, however, it is through the depiction of the Carpetbagger in his three guises—the idealistic, the economic, and the political—that Tourgée presents the counter myths. Through such depictions, one obtains the most complete picture of the positive attributes of the Yankee Radical in Reconstruction literature.

Let us review to make clear the vital importance of white leadership among the Black Republicans. The idealistic Carpetbagger usually appears in Reconstruction fiction in the form of Bureau workers ("V'line Mango"), teachers ("King David"), and those economic and politically minded Northerners who sought to teach the ex-slave the holiness of wage-labor and the vote. In a real sense the term "idealistic Carpetbagger" could embrace examples of all types since the term is a cumbersome designation for a stance rather than a specific sociological label. Nevertheless it is used in this discussion to distinguish them from the political-economic types.

In anti-radical myth he appears in the form of a hypocrite, especially in his espousal of an idealistic relation to the Freedman. Publicly the Radical Idealist pretends to prefer Negroes to Caucasians; privately he is contemptuous and disgusted with his black ally. Moreover, his insistence on Freedman citizenship rights leads to black insurrection and the necessity of white terrorism. Even when the David Kings seek to do good, their ignorance brings forth chaos.

If the idealistic Carpetbagger is a woman, more sordid details emerge in the myth. The Bourbons see her as a woman with whom "high bred Christian dames and dainty maidens would not deign to associate." She and her sisters stand "on the plane of the courtesan—they [are] *seen* but not *known*." The Schoolmarms' teaching relationship with her Nimbuses and Eliabs is by necessity licentious.[782] While Tourgée does not dwell upon the sordid details of such vile imaginings, he does use a brief episode in *A Fool's Errand* to reveal the intensity of this feeling against the idealistic Carpetbagger. A Bourbon newspaper article describes some teachers of Freedmen as participating in an interracial orgy, organized at Servosse's home as a part of a Thanksgiving celebration: They "ate and drank and sung 'John Brown' . . . and similar melodies. It is said that one of the 'N.T.'s became so full of the spirit . . . that she kissed one of the colored boys who waited at the table."[783] It is, in Tourgée's view, against piety and selflessness that the Anti-Radicals hurled their most savage insults: "Christian tongues befouled with calumny! Christian lips blistered with falsehood! Christian hearts overflowing with hate!" As the result of this type of calumny as well as the general hostility of the Southron community, the Belle snubbed the Schoolmarm, while the Cavalier approached her with "a shamed-faced curiosity." In more sociopathic communities, she became the target for terrorist raids.[784]

The intrusion of Northern women into the Southern soulscape was both courageous and naïve. Their race and sex were red flags to the anti-rational propensities of the Southron. They stumbled into a thicket of taboos and restrictions, which was the natural outgrowth of the Cult of Racio-sexuality and the Bourbon's obsessive fear of the Taboo Conjunction. The wonder is that their work did manage to succeed in the face of such opposition. Hesden Le Moyne sums up, in a realistic way, the feeling of the average Southron community toward such idealists: "We find it hard to believe that anyone who will come down here and teach niggers is of very much account at home. . . ."[785]

Tourgée seeks to redeem the Teacher-Radicals from such calumny. In his fiction all idealistic characteristics come together in the person of the Yankee Schoolmarm. Perhaps she and her profession could stand as the basic symbol of this group of Carpetbaggers, since in her Tourgée sees the fullest flowering of the ideals inherent in the Northern Radicals' side of the Conflict. Mollie Ainslie in *Bricks Without Straw* is the most fully developed representative of the idealistic Carpetbagger described above.

Tourgée allows only some of the ambivalence which he uses on the other Reconstruction types to appear in his treatment of the Yankee Maid-as-Carpetbagger. In this context, such a picture is to counteract the more negative image in "Miss Mouse" and "King David." Tourgée emphasizes her allegoric simplicity, defining her motivation and her vision of her task more in terms of Puritan morality than psychological fact. He hails these New England nuns as the "white souled angels of peace."[786] In his novels they exist primarily as the didactic center of Tourgée's romantic apprehension of the idealist's "meta-historical" impact on the events of Reconstruction history:

> Perhaps there has been no grander thing in our history than the eager generosity with which the Christian men and women of the North gave and wrought to bring the boon of knowledge to the recently-enslaved, [and to the Southron.] The civilization of the North in the very hour of victory threw aside the cartridge-box, and appealed at once to the contribution box to heal the ravages of war. . . . [There were] thousands of schools organized in the country of a vanquished foe, almost before the smoke of battle had cleared away, free to the poorest of her citizens . . . and taught by kindly-hearted daughters of a quick-forgiving enemy. . . . Even to this day, two score of schools and colleges remain, the glorious momentoes.[787]

It is in this laudatory frame of reference that the Mollies seem to appear. Unlike the difficulties encountered by David King in teaching, hers give way without effort.[788] Whether courageous with "Mouth clear-cut and firm" or frightened with lips "drawn and quivering with deep emotions," she is, as indicated earlier, that Godeyesque paradox, the Maiden-Matriarch.[789]

Woolson's complex portrayal of the idealistic Carpetbagger in "King David" is perhaps more artistically compelling than Tourgée's often rhetorical images. Yet he too—beneath the surface of his didactic exuberance—manages to render up a relatively intricate picture of the Schoolmarm, oscillating rather deliberately between allegoric simplicity and psychological complexity. For example, he is aware of the reality of the psycho-social hardship she had to endure in the context of the ambivalent relationship she had with the black-and-white South. To begin with, Mollie does not come South only for the standard missionary reasons. She also comes because the South's genial climate will be therapeutic for an inherent predisposition toward tuberculosis.[790] Moreover, while she works mightily to transform her students from brutes into men, she, like David King, has difficulty entering into that close affectionate relationship that, in the other myth, the Belle had with her slaves. She is reduced to a strained, semi-paternal, semi-idealistic, but rarely personal relationship with her charges:

> She had never once thought of making companions . . . of those whom she labored [*sic*]. They had been so entirely foreign to her early life. [She never had] . . . any inclination

> to that intimacy which would have been sure to arise if her pupils had been of the same race as herself.[791]

(Of course, this was to change somewhat after the Red Wing attack.)

Mollie personally prefers her more familiar relationship with the white community—even though it imposes upon her a rigorous system of ostracism. The effect of such ostracism (as already pointed out) upon women raised in the culture of the New England village would have been rather grim, even on the most morally committed. For Mollie Ainslie, even the grudging, cold relationship with the hostile Madam Le Moyne is a welcome relief from total isolation. Such hunger for acceptance is in clear contrast to the myth of the Carpetbagger's arrogant, moral aloofness.

The most startling aspect of Tourgée's analysis of the idealists is found not so much in his comments on the psychological complexity of her motives toward her relation with the Freedman as in his comments on the mixed nature of radical idealism itself. It becomes clear that Tourgée is critically aware of the idealistic Carpetbaggers' misconceptions and philosophic errors about the nature of Reconstruction politics. He attacks their naïve faith in the transcendental reality of political rhetoric and attributes such blindness to the innocence he praises elsewhere. For example, Mollie's hope for Reconstruction relies solely on the Northern Republicans' campaign oratory:

> To her undiscriminating mind the mere fact that this honor and power were pledged to the protection and elevation of the Negro had been an all-sufficient guarantee of the accomplishment of that pledge. In fact to her mind, it had taken on the reality and certainty of a fact already accomplished.[792]

For Tourgée, such faith on the part of the idealistic Carpetbagger in the Union's promises is as touching and as futile as the Freedman's faith in the transcendental efficacy of the ballot.

Throughout *A Fool's Errand* and *Bricks Without Straw*, Tourgée is impatient with all idealism not tested against the complex reality of Southern culture. If it is the idealism of the truly committed, he sees it as merely naïve:

> As the war went on, and I saw the bulwarks of slavery crumbling away, until finally the light of freedom shone upon

> the slave, I rejoiced at the wonderful power of God, who wrought out the ends of his glory through the instrumentality of human passion and human greed. . . . Who could have believed that the blood, the tears, . . . and woes of God's stricken . . . people . . . were so soon to become the forces which could destroy the oppressor, root and branch![793]

If it is the arrogant idealism of the merely ideologically committed, he sees it as pernicious. Tourgée saves some of his most angry writing for those idealogues who, from the safety of the North, dispensed oracular advice to the struggling Radicals and who remained complacently ignorant of the realities of Southern culture:

> If the colored people and the Union men of the South expect to receive the . . . moral support of the country, they must show themselves . . . able to take care of themselves. The government has done all it can be expected to do. . . . It has given the colored man the ballot, . . . and now he must show himself worthy. . . . The same is true of the poor white and of the Union man. Instead of whining over the wrongs they suffer at the hands of the rebels, they should assert themselves, and put down such lawless violence. . . . The doctrine of government by majorities is based upon the idea that the majority will be sufficiently bold and self-asserting to . . . maintain its rights. . . . If people are killed by the Ku-Klux, why do they not kill the Ku-Klux?[794]

Tourgée (through Servosse) answers such political transcendentalism with bitter anger:

> It is all well for you, sitting safely and cosily in your easy-chair under the shadow of the dome of the Capitol, to talk about asserting ourselves, . . . and retaliating upon our persecutors. Either you have not apprehended our condition, or you are inclined to 'mock at our calamity.'[795]

This type of idealist, the political transcendentalist, became, for Tourgée, a more pernicious enemy to the Southern Radicals than the Bourbon. Because the transcendentalists believed in a kind of politico-verbal magic in which allegorical and rhetorical utterances somehow partook of the substance of reality, and because they espoused a symbolic politics through which melodramatic legislative acts *in and of themselves* transformed social and cultural realities, they could neither see nor comprehend the difficult and dangerous actualities that pressed in around the embattled Carpetbaggers. Had not Emancipation been proclaimed? Had not the Amendments been promulgated? Then how could there be Klan terrorism, save at the sufferance of the Southern Radicals themselves? Such lofty attitudes led the political transcendentalists to misunderstand the Southern Republican's predicament and led them to attack the Carpetbagger for failing to instantaneously transform the South into a utopia. These attitudes, for Tourgée, were more damaging to radical morale than the atrocities. For the transcendentalists, the Conflict was over by 1870; in the South it was beginning at another level.

Many of these attitudes grow from an ambiguous, idealistic vision that the transcendentalists (the "Wise Men") had of the Reconstruction-as-event. On the one hand, this vision mixed metaphysical verities and unacknowledged (but normal) human weaknesses or what today we would call burnout:

> We have assumed that slavery was dead, because we had a Proclamation of Emancipation, a Constitutional Amendment, and 'laws' . . . . The Antislavery Society met, and congratulated itself on the accomplishment of its mission, on having no more . . . victim to succor. And thereupon, in the odor of the self-laudation, it dissolved its own existence. . . . It was an end that smacks of the millennium; but, unfortunately it was farcical in the extreme. I don't blame Garrison and Phillips and yourself. . . . It was natural that you should at least wish to try on your laurels while alive.[796]

On the other hand, these verities were often entangled with more immoral characteristics, such as political manipulation and opportunism:

> The Wise Men of that day looked upon the supporters of reconstruction at the South as mere instruments in their hands,—to be worked as puppets, but to be blamed as men, for the results of their acts. They had not yet arrived at that refinement of cruelty which also made them scapegoats for the results of others' ignorance and folly. That was to come afterward.[797]

It was with such idealists and with such an ambivalent vision that the Reconstruction was launched in a blaze of Emersonian rhetoric. And that the

Northern transcendentalists could not or would not sustain their rhetoric with unstinting political support is, for Tourgée, the tragedy of the Carpetbagger at the South: "I don't wonder, though, that men who had been in the 'racket' of the anti-slavery reform should be tired. I fully realize that a life-time of struggle takes away a man's relish for a fight."[798] Tourgée lays bare here the essential psychological weakness of the idealistic dynamic in the Radical Republican Movement: the inability of the human psyche to sustain over a long period of time either a zealous intensity toward abstract moral concepts or a zealous commitment to even the most deserving victim of oppression, unless grounded in a deeply held social humanist understanding of the political economic nature of class society.

By the time he had written his two key Reconstruction works, Tourgée had become rather impatient with transcendental sentiments as the sole basis for truly ending the Conflict.[799] Yet he always remained aware that it was this idealism that gave to the Reconstruction cause, as tragic as it was, its moral dynamism. As Gross correctly, though negatively, reminds us:

> The Northerners' mission of salvation was an unequivocal failure, but Tourgée realized too that their folly was not entirely ludicrous. These men were men of faith: and so, despite the futility of their attempt to reconstruct the South, they became the superior individuals of the nation.[800]

The final vision of the idealistic Carpetbaggers in Tourgée's fiction is the fact that, for a while, they stood heroic watch on the picket line of freedom in the reconstructing South.

The Carpetbagger's second guise, that of the capitalistic entrepreneur, seems to be a less melodramatic image. But in anti-radical myth, the economic Carpetbaggers are seen rather sensationally as Robber Barons, moving like locusts through Dixie seizing plantations, factories, and railroads right and left through legal confiscation and heartless exploitation of Bourbon poverty. Their establishment of mines and manufactories is viewed as the demonic eroding of the beauties of the southscape, their investments in Southern businesses become an octopus-like control over the Southron's economic life. At the same time, their capitalistic acumen contributes nothing to the life of the South, since their maneuvers are designed solely for self-aggrandizement. They bring to a land used to the genteel luxury of Bourbon wealth the swinishness of Yankee materialism and profligacy.[801] In neutralist fiction, however, the economic Carpetbagger is accorded honor and status as the carrier of the redeeming "magic carpetbag."

In Tourgée's fiction (and in pro-radical fiction in general), the depiction of the entrepreneurial type picks up from the neutralist vision. From the Carpetbagger's view, the Northern entrepreneur is simply the economic agent of the great crusade. In handling him from the Southern point of view, Tourgée presents the dollar-driven Radicals from a dual perspective. Some Southrons see the economic Carpetbagger as in anti-radical myth. And despite the South's need for the North's economic powers, such planters seek to destroy their emissaries: "The fools who had removed to these States from motives of ease or profit, engaging in [economic activity,] ought not complain" if they are maltreated by their neighbors. The generation of "antagonism which war had fused into hate" has made "kindliness, favor, or even fair play" difficult to come by.[802] This view, of course, represents the pro-radical position that the economic Carpetbagger, like his idealistic counterpart, was invariably the put-upon victim of shrewd, dishonest ex-Confederates who manipulated his naiveté, the law, and their social power to exploit him for his Yankee gold, at least during restoration.

Then there are those Bourbons who are politically anti-Radical Reconstruction, but who, nevertheless, see the need for "Northern energy, and Northern men" to carry the South down the "high road of prosperity" in the new Union.[803] In the beginning Servosse is such a Northern type. He takes over the old Warrington plantation and, with the energy and capital of the mythic Northern man, transforms it into an economically successful North Carolina farm. However, as soon as he begins to dabble in such non-economic activities as Negro education and pro-Unionist meetings, he falls from grace.

A purer version of the acceptable economic Carpetbagger is Captain Dickson, who in "Mamelon" is clearly symbolic of the influence of Northern economics, reflecting such influences on the Yankee personality. Susan Dewar observes in his face that "restlessness of manner" and "look of eager watchfulness" which, for her, are signs of the Northerners' economic struggle:

> With the world from boyhood . . . —an appearance of being ever on the alert. . . . Usually this was absent from the face of the Southern man of the better classes because such struggle . . . comes only when he has arrived at maturity. . . . With the [Northerner] of almost any grade it begins early and is unceasing.[804]

It is this restless energy in the Northerner's personality that, for Tourgée, is the major reason for the influx of economic Carpetbaggers into the South during restoration—and afterwards:

> After a little, groups of Northern men settled, to engage in commerce, or to till the soil. The cotton and tobacco which remained of the slender crops of the years of war brought fabulous prices.[805]

Simultaneously, Dickson serves as the general symbol for the total infusion of Northern economic ideas and economic methods into the ex-Confederacy, standing for that powerful, residual force that survived the failures of the First Reconstruction's idealistic and political dimensions:

> Of course the old economies of the plantation and the negro-quarters will have to give way. The labor of that section must be organized, or rather taught to manage itself, to become automatic in its operations. The former master is not prepared to do this. . . . In this reorganization, I think men who have been acquainted with free labor will be able to give valuable aid, and accomplish good results. . . . Should the present controversy be concluded, and new States erected in the recently rebellious sections, without a large increase of the Northern element . . . I am confident that . . . the future peace of the country [will be] insecure.[806]

In this context the economic Carpetbaggers act as political and industrial symbols of the drive and the power of the Machine. It is this power—admired, feared, and needed—that the Bourbon is praising in the economic Carpetbagger. And from this standpoint, he is a creature desired by both sides. Moreover, it would be the Carpetbagger's free labor economic force that would persist with varying intensity beyond reconciliation as the Henry Grady-Booker T. Washington version of the New South. It would be this force that would gradually untangle the knotty sociological structure of the South and reshape it into a more democratic image.

The most important guise in which the Carpetbagger appears in Tourgée's fiction remains the political one. This is by now the most familiar and the most important manifestation of Northern power in this study. Indeed, the term

"Carpetbagger" has traditionally referred only to those Northern men who came South specifically to take part in the governmental reconstruction. As villain, hero, or both, the political Carpetbagger defines the sociopolitical definition of Reconstruction fiction as central to the sociopolitical revolution, which this fiction chronicles as symbolic of the Conflict. His presence or absence in the fiction becomes a touchstone to the tenuousness or explicitness of a work's Reconstruction characteristics. In this final discussion of the Bourbon and Carpetbagger as symbolic-mythic figures in the Conflict, he is the key character.

In anti-radical myth the political Carpetbaggers find themselves political masters immediately and miraculously after the Surrender through their adroit capacity for political opportunism. Then for twelve cruel years they control the defeated Bourbons with a tyrannical efficiency and relentless malice:

> I can't supplant them; . . . They have too firm a hold here, and they have had it so long now that it seems a thing of course for them to be our masters, to absorb all our offices, to make money out of us, and to whistle up the bayonets if we dare expostulate.[807]

In this image of absolute political power, the Carpetbagger becomes for the Bourbons their "representative, tax-receiver, magistrate, and everything else."[808] He becomes, in other words, the master of masters.

In the second image, they are the new masters of ex-slaves. The Freedmen's insistence on social rights, their insolent behavior, their use of the ballot—all stem from the Carpetbagger's malevolent control. Whether in public meetings or offstage caucus rooms, the Carpetbagger remains the boss of the new citizens' hopes and actions and the demonic instigator of black political activity—the white power behind the black power.

Through Servosse, Tourgée seeks to counteract the various images in anti-radical myth. The first image relates to the Émigré's unadulterated political opportunism. Tourgée (like other pro-radical fictionists) shows that this so-called opportunism resulted directly from the fiasco occasioned by the Johnson plan of restoration. With the overthrow of the Johnson plan, Southern governments were left in disarray. It was the function of the Carpetbaggers to bring order to this chaos while at the same time satisfying, in some instances, personal ambitions, re: Twitchell.

Another reason for the Carpetbagger's political activity was the need for economic self-preservation. The absence of legal redress during restoration, as indicated by Morgan and Harding, in the area of contract violation and fraudulent sale and lease procedures forced the purely economic Carpetbaggers into politics in order to protect their investments:

> . . . the sad conviction was forcing itself upon me that there were not courts open for our class; that a new-comer had no rights which any one respected; that we were simply regarded as so many fat geese tied in the market, and every passing Southerner was at liberty to pluck a feather from us.[809]

The second myth that Tourgée attacks related specifically to his main concern: the concept of Carpetbagger power within and beyond the South. In this myth, the Carpetbagger's power *within* the South is absolute, resting firmly on his control over Freedmen and Scalawags and on his immediate and continuing access to Federal power, a power that can be brought to bear any time that the Bourbon threatens his role. The destruction of the North Carolina Radical Republican Party testifies, for Tourgée, to the falsity of this myth. At the same time, his novels articulate his own myth: that of the helplessness of the *émigré* Radical. This mythic apparatus is, of course, clearly seen in his chief political symbol of the radical pole of the Conflict, Comfort Servosse.

As previously noted, there are several examples of the political Carpetbagger in Reconstruction fiction. They range from subsidiary characters such as Hiddikel Queasey in *Colonel Dunwoddie* and Jack Hunt in "The Colored Member" to such major figures as Witchell and Servosse. It is Servosse, however, who is the original pattern of the political Carpetbaggers. Yet while he is a progressive, he is not the Radical of the pro-Bourbon myth. This is clearly seen in his sociopolitical relationship with the black and white Southerner.

Initially, Servosse's political relation with the Freedmen is nonexistent, since his main interest in them is economic and educational. But as reconstitution proves imminent, the relationship becomes somewhat more political. He gives them some minimal information about their civic rights and advises the more active to join the Union League in order to become educated in Republican ideals and the important responsibility of the ballot. And, as stated earlier, on the question of the vote—that touchstone of Southern Republican principles, he is no Political Radical. Finally, the act that precipitates his political career—being chosen as a convention delegate—results not from ideology but from a courageous sense of duty.[810] Thus in more ways than one, Servosse is not the archetypal Radical of the Bourbon nightmare.

Yet his presence as Northerner among the Freedmen automatically renders his relationship with them both political and radical:

> These people feel that you, by the very fact of Northern birth, and service in the Federal army, represent a power which has deprived them of property, liberty, and a right to control their own, and that now, in sheer wantonness of insult, you are encouraging the colored people to do those two things which are more sacred than any other to the Southern mind; to wit, to *buy and hold land* and to *ride their own horses*.[811]

Over his head, for black and white Southerner alike, emanate the symbolic energies of Northern polity: republicanism, abolitionism, the victorious ending of the Sectional Conflict. Eventually, through the social needs of his Negro workers, through the hostile pressures of the Southrons, Servosse's symbolic power is transformed into political reality: He is chosen by Negro votes as the delegate to the constitutional convention and then to the legislature. As he is isolated more and more from the white community, he becomes not only the Freedmen's political leader but a kind of tribal chief as well. His danger is their despair; his safety, their joy:

> From almost every house . . . [the Servosse family] saw white faces peering at them with troubled and apprehensive looks, while the cabin of every colored man gave them looks and words of cheerful greeting; and, long before they reached Warrington, it became evident that the negroes [*sic*] were hastening from all directions to meet Servosse.[812]

It is at this moment that Servosse's role as the beneficent political Carpetbagger among his faithful Freedman comrades achieves the symbolic dimensions of the pro-radical myth. But nowhere in the work is Servosse shown, like Witchell, actively or ambitiously seeking such power for the political purposes of the Radical Party.

His political relation with the Bourbons is likewise conservative. While he recognizes them as his political rivals and opposes their political vision of the Conflict, the Union, and the Question, he is not as aggressively hostile to the Bourbon vision as Tourgée was supposed to have been.[813] He is quite moderate in his analysis of the Bourbon's governmental problems and history and is only reluctantly drawn into their civic affairs. Servosse attends the Bourbon rally, for example, and only because of his neighbor's insistence does he make his speech on limited black enfranchisement.[814] Further, Servosse lacks the mythic Radical's faith in the Congressional Plan of Reconstruction, representing those who went along with the Plan because it was the only one available. Nevertheless, the results of his relatively mild progressive ideas are ostracism and threats against his life since, in the Bourbon worldview, all progressive ideas are radical.[815] Despite Servosse's efforts to walk cautiously between Northern views of government and Southern mores, he finds himself in absolute conflict with his Southron neighbors.

Interestingly enough, it is a sociopolitical rivalry without personal animosity. It is precisely because Servosse and his Bourbon antagonists like each other as persons that the terrorism, the ostracism, and the tension of their ideological conflict become so poignantly ambivalent:

> While his neighbors did not seem to have towards him any especial distrust in their personal intercourse, and generally met him with affability, he gradually became aware that a current of wonderful strength was setting against him. He became an object of remark at public assemblies; the newspaper at Verdenton had every now and then made alighting allusions to him. . . . [816]

But all through this vindictiveness, Servosse's attitude of sympathetic interest in Bourbon behavior remains constant, showing an understanding of the anti-rationality that generates his political violence. As a political Carpetbagger Servosse's radicalism, such as it is, contains little that is violently anti-Bourbon.

There is a strong metaphysical radicalism in Servosse's vision of Reconstruction that does shape his actions. Though he prophesies that as government officers he and his friends will eventually break their hearts and bodies on the shards of the Union's promise, nevertheless he will hazard the die for the sake of his political vision.[817] With almost existential stoicism, Servosse submits to the Harness of Necessity associated with the Reconstruction tragedy in the hope that some of his political and humanist ideals will, through his efforts, survive the Union's betrayal. These ideals must be distinguished from the more naïve hopes with which Servosse begins his Southern experience.

Before his long-day's journey into night, Servosse has certain naïve presuppositions about the nature of the South, the chief of which is, of course, the delusion about the institutional nature of slavery:

> Oh, . . . there must be great changes, of course! Slavery has been broken up, and things must turn into new grooves; but I think the country will settle up rapidly now that slavery is out of the way. Manufactures will spring up, immigration will pour in, and it will be just the pleasantest part of the country. I believe one-fifth of our soldiers—and that the very best of them too—will find homes in the South in less than two years, ...[818]

With slavery "out of the way," utopia is at hand: The South, for Servosse as the specifically idealistic Carpetbagger, will become a center of learning and culture for all its citizens; for Servosse the economist, a region of a new industrialism and Northern agrarianism; for Servosse the politician, the model of multiracial democracy in the New World. However, Servosse discovers, like Harding in *A Year of Wreck*, the reality of the Slavery Syndrome. Against this reality Servosse's naïve hopes are shattered but not his deeper faith.

This deeper faith, Servosse's political-humanistic ideals, ideals representing the progressive side of the Conflict, is based upon those 18th-century rationalistic-romantic notions about the nature of humanity undergirding the American experiment, from the Arctic to the Antarctic, especially those notions that cluster around the philosophic assumption of human equality. In terms of such notions, Servosse's humanism is composed of the traditional tenets celebrated in the history and letters of the American Republics: the belief in "the equality and inherency of right," either as principle or prejudice, regardless of ". . . race, color, or previous condition . . . "; the belief that the vote is not a privilege but a political necessity; the opposition to any trick—philosophical, constitutional, or violent—that denies legal rights to any citizen; the rejection of slavery as an unnatural condition and a supreme evil.[819] Furthermore, Servosse accepts the doctrine of political egalitarianism as the essential truth to the specific U.S. American experience, seeing it as the doctrine inclusive of all other tenets and diametrically opposed to any form of exclusionism: "He felt that ignorance, poverty and an ebon skin, were each of them terrible afflictions, and acknowledged that they might all . . . be classed as public evils . . . ;" but that they should not limit "political power or inherent right."[820]

This tougher idealistic stance, too, collides against the cultural reality of slavery, symbolized by the Bourbon victory. Servosse sees his 18th-century vision of the human condition, aka the Enlightenment, defeated by the much older feudalistic vision. He is aware that the Bourbon's redemption of North Carolina renders his humanism irrelevant in terms of pragmatic action. Nevertheless, he does not indulge in any bitter repudiation of the inherent morality of his stance. He stoically accepts the fact that it is the tragedy of the U.S. American experience that at that historical moment the younger political vision faltered and gave way before the power of the older. It is at this moment of choice that Servosse becomes, on a symbolic level at least, the political Carpetbagger in full, in the context of the Irrepressible Conflict.

But it is only symbolic, for even on the narrative level political realities as image and event are missing. The political operations forming the texture of the Reconstruction experience do not appear in Tourgée's fiction in a detailed way as they do in *Yazoo*. Despite the obviously important political activity that has been described in this discussion, *A Fool's Errand* is not a political novel. More specifically, one rarely sees Servosse engaged in governmental or party operations. One merely hears that he participated in the Constitutional Convention, that his resolution against the slavery-based penal code was passed, that he was eventually elected state senator. But these occurrences are not experienced as events. One reads of his political philosophy in letters, tracts, and recorded conversations, but it is not perceived at the legislative level. Indeed, none of the basic civic actions involved in reconstitution as a local color event—the stump speeches, the registration, the voting—appear in a detailed way in the novel. This does not mean that there is no political activity at all. Certainly, Servosse becomes the leader of the Union League, and the narrative of *A Fool's Errand* clearly derives from political action.

But such activity lacks the details lavished on his social conflicts with the Southern community. Tourgée wants to show the effects of Reconstruction politics on a small Southern town, on Servosse, as victim of offstage legislative acts. Servosse and his narrative actions are the clearest exponent in Reconstruction literature of the aesthetics of sociopolitical fiction. Such fiction does not describe political operations, but the results of such operations on social and cultural structures. In a sense, the offstage political reality is only important insofar as it defines and structures the reality of Servosse's power and weakness and his reality as sectional symbol and tragic protagonist.

In light of this, Servosse emerges as an allegorical representative of the deeper sociopolitical conflict between the North and the South; it is as such a political symbol rather than a political character that he has his importance in Tourgée's vision of Reconstruction:

> He was not one of them. he represented another civilization, another development, of which they were naturally suspicious, and especially so on account of the peculiar restrictions which slavery had put around them, and which had acted as an embargo on immigration for so many years before the war.[821]

It is not only as a political symbol that Servosse has his fullest reality. It should be clear by now that Servosse is the most complete expression in Reconstruction fiction of the general and essential attributes of all three types of Carpetbaggers, fusing into a single character idealistic, economic, and political manifestations. In the cycle of Servosse's rise and fall can be discerned the life and death of the archetypal Carpetbagger. And the teleology that underlies this fusion and that, in Tourgée's myth, defines the meaning of this cycle is not some heroic apotheosis, but Servosse's defeat at the hands of the Bourbon. At this moment, Servosse becomes a more interesting type of symbol: the Carpetbagger as modern hero in a conflict much longer than this manifestation on the U.S. American soil.

The defeat of humanist idealism in a world made absurd and chaotic by a malevolent physical, social, or metaphysical power forms the essential fate of the tragic hero in modern literature. This hero struggles to gain an Elysian moment, only to be crushed in the last chapter by some relentless doom beyond his will. *The Old Man and the Sea* is an immediate instance. Likewise,

Servosse discovers that while privately held idealism may not fail in itself, its articulation in public acts of heroism and honor must inevitably end in failure when challenged by a ruthless, countervailing power. Beneath the feudalistic, somnolent beauty of the Southern soulscape, Servosse finds such an implacable power. And, aroused paradoxically by the very humanist principles he thought would protect his cause, this force swallows up the most honorable intention and the most heroic person in an abyss of fire and blood. At such furious moments, it is not the idealistic and the dedicated who survive; rather, it is the powerful and the ruthless who not only survive but prevail—at least in the arena of public action.

This is the rather hyperbolic image that Tourgée conveys in this description of the fate of his *alter ego* during the White Terror: "The Fool feels himself a bewildered child, lost in a kind of frightening, surrealistic maze of Southern life; all exits seem to be only *culs de sac*."[822] Through the course of the narrative, it is Servosse's fate to sink through an abyss of increasing hostility, violence, and dread so that he might, in this interpretation, become initiated into a world of sociopolitical conflict bordering on the Absurd.

Faced with this condition (and the fact of Union powerlessness or indifference), Servosse finds himself, following redemption, in a moral position somewhat similar to that of characters in many contemporary novels, especially those dealing with the so-called "existential ethic." More specifically, Camus' *The Fall*, Sartre's *The Respectful Prostitute*, and Anouilh's *Antigone* come to mind. According to this school of thought, existential ethics presuppose that one is absolutely free to act in terms of one's personal moral vision. Yet how can one be truly free to act when he has painful, mutually exclusive choices to make between his moral vision and his own annihilation? This is precisely the kind of dilemma that Servosse, as a social humanist, faces after redemption: "… he was, in a sense, at liberty to act as he chose; but the consequences of his action [to himself and] others were so terrible that he must have been either more or less than man to have invited them."[823] Servosse can choose to continue to lead an idealistic though futile resistance against the triumphant Southrons. But if he does, he and his dwindling radical comrades will be massacred.

The only power capable of protecting the Carpetbagger is, of course, the North. But when the Northern Republicans finally abandon the Carpetbagger, the basis for any heroic action disappears, rendering all public heroism impossible if not absurd: "Until he felt that he was betrayed . . . and condemned by [the Union] . . . which had thrust this burden on him, he never thought of surrender. . . . When the power of the Nation was withdrawn, the struggle was at an end."[824]

The final result is that Servosse opts for a meager compromise between foolhardiness and cowardice, allowing a protective alienation to spring up between himself and his cause. He simply avoids translating his social humanism into public action and resigns from participating in the Conflict. He will no longer urge his black allies to make "any further stand for what were termed their rights. . . ."[825] While not surrendering his egalitarian concepts, Servosse no longer acts them out as visible realities, falling back on a cynical form of moral relativism:

> So, without abandoning his principles, as he called them,—for . . . what are termed 'principles' are only ingrained habits of thought, and hereditary systems of belief,—he submitted quietly to having them rendered inoperative by the suppression of the . . . majority, or, rather, by excluding from the estimate those who were opposed to the white majority.[826]

Eventually, Servosse achieves a kind of bitter, stoic solace that fits the contingency of the Bourbon triumph:

> . . . he found himself enjoying a personal peace . . . which was very grateful, after what had gone before. Where he had been hated . . . , he was now tolerated with an 'if,' or commended with a 'but.' . . . They excused his views because of his Northern birth and education, and he excused their acts because of their Southern nativity and training; they disregarded his political convictions because a method had been discovered to prevent their crystallizing into results, and he refrained from urging them because to do so was a useless travail.[827]

Thus, once Servosse cuts the links between a heroic display of his moral concerns (duty, revolt, commitment) and his personal survival, he is allowed to enjoy...

> what was pleasant in his surroundings. . . . So there was peace at Warrington. Servosse blessed the sunshine and the shade,

thought less of the welfare of his fellows and more of his own comfort, and rejoiced that the struggle . . . was at an end.[828]

As a result of this initiation into the abyss of things as they exist, Servosse, like other modern heroes, learns the limits of idealism within the frame of a class-structured society: "He saw that he had expected too much, that he had been simple enough to believe that the leopard might change his spots, while yet the Ethiopian retained his dusky skin."[829] At this moment, Servosse ceases to be a symbol of Carpetbaggery in its various positive facets and emerges more comprehensively as a symbol of the Reconstruction tragedy in the cycle of its rise and fall.

It should be quite clear from this discussion, especially from the analysis of Servosse as a modern hero, that Tourgée, in his depiction of the various Carpetbagger mutations, has countered anti-radical mythology with one of his own. If the Bakers build their myth on the basis of vilification, Tourgée's is based on edification—but in a manner that is rather subtle for such a minor talent. It would have been quite easy for him to have presented the Carpetbagger as a purely heroic figure, melodramatically overcoming all odds—only to be defeated in the end by a joint alliance of Republican Copperheads and ex-rebels. Instead, Tourgée structures this defeat around a less melodramatic image: a myth of victimization. To reiterate: Servosse the archetypal Carpetbagger is a tragic victim of a duty imposed upon him against his better judgment. Moreover, by foregoing heroic melodrama, Tourgée is able to deal more effectively with the problem of Carpetbagger evil. In a sense Tourgée admits that the Anti-Radicals were right: There were crimes, but in Tourgée's hands the nature and meaning of these crimes undergo an interesting transformation. In place of the corrupting manipulation described by De Forest and Woolson and Baker, there is a courageous helplessness. If there are vices, they are the vices of folly, weakness, and human error, not opportunism, greed, and hypocrisy. Tourgée seeks to appropriate for his own purposes the fact that the Carpetbaggers were wrong—but wrong in their ignorance and idealistic innocence before the reality of Southron evil. Their defeat reveals they were in error—but an error on the side of the angels. This is the mythic apprehension of Reconstruction with which Tourgée comes to terms with the defeat of his cause.

If a Baker loads the Carpetbagger down with infamy, a Tourgée loads him down with crosses. Whether as Satan or Christ, the reality of the

Carpetbagger's complex nature is still missing; anti-radical and pro-radical exaggeration both distort the fullness of a figure at once guilty of political exploitation and symbolic of political idealism. To substitute one myth for another is still to remain on a mythological, not historical, level. The truest picture of such a complete reality still remains Morgan's novelistic memoirs and Bryan's historically based melodrama. However, if one recognizes and accepts Tourgée's mythic apparatus as part of his polemic design, his version of the Irrepressible Conflict, one can discover that, as a realistic picture of the Carpetbagger's *positive* nature, Tourgée's descriptions are more inclusive and, as far as Revisionist history goes, more factual than those of anti-radical detractors.

The Bourbon and the Carpetbagger: These then are the two major figures in the Reconstruction *agon*. Together, they articulate the essential symbology that defines the nature of Reconstruction fiction and nonfiction: the violent struggle between the North and the South for the possession of the Union. It is as sociocultural characters in an allegory of intersectional rivalry that these two figures live and have their being both as masks and realities.

• • •

> Twenty-two years ago a great nation was broken in twain in an hour. There was no splintering of the parts, no strain, no lesion. The cleavage was sharp and smooth. The day before there was no sign of severance. The day after there was no trace of the union that had been. The one Republic became two without a ripple in the daily life or relations of the people. Governors, judges—all officers, state and federal—continued to perform the same duties under the new as under the old organization. . . . Before the sword was drawn the separation was as complete as if the ocean rolled between.[830]

The irrepressibility of the conflict between Bourbon and the Carpetbagger originates in the political economic infrastructure of their geographic sections and then expands outward through opposing ideological-cultural presuppositions about the ex-African into their political vision of the First Reconstruction itself. The essential factor defining their conflict as a national reality is the archetypal and historical fact of the North-South rivalry for economic-political possession of the Union. On an archetypal level, the issue is the battle between the Machine and the Garden as economic forces; on the historical level, it is between North and South as sociopolitical forces. In Chapter I and II, these conflicts were presented in their historical guise; here they are seen again in terms of an extended fictional analysis.

The Tourgéan hero comes into the Garden as the exponent of the Locomotive, dreaming of mining on Barren-Ridge, textile mills on the Farley Moors, and a handle-making factory at Mamelon.[831] Even when circumstances do force him into politics, the Carpetbagger's aggressive attempt to reconstruct the social, political, and ideological structure of the South demonstrates those cultural imperatives that Leo Marx defined as the nature of the Machine and what that other Marx would have called industrial capitalist development. At this level, the Carpetbagger's chief image is, as repeated earlier, that of a Locomotive bearing down relentlessly on the calm, natural order of the Bourbon's landscape:

> Horace Dunwoddie stood for an instant, watch in hand, listening to the noise of the incoming train, and conscious that the new era in his life was coming upon him as speedily and surely, and that it was a something which was much more apt to crush him under its revolving wheels, rushing upon him . . . with a force simply incalculable. He knew that he did not comprehend all that was coming, but this he did know, that he could come to understand it better than his father.[832]

In opposition to such fatal power is the Bourbon, incarnating in his feudalistic economic vision of the world the virtues and vices of the Garden. In terms of this vision, he sees the Locomotive as an energy aiming for the destruction of his existence. Therefore, he battles the Carpetbagger both as a political *and economic* opponent. During the restoration, the Anti-Radicals exploit and harass the Carpetbagger because of his financial power and economic innovations, mocking his use of cultivators, plows, and hay-cutters; denouncing the coming of his factories and railroads as pollutions of their ancestral homes; attacking him for those innovations in labor relations affecting the traditional slave-master Symbiosis.[833] At all points the Bourbon recognizes the enmity of the Locomotive as a sociopolitical power threatening with destructive inevitabilities the calm, hierarchical order of his Garden.

On the historical level their antagonism is a symbolic action for the more important conflict between the North and South as distinct, geopolitical worlds. This is the sense of the thematic design of all Reconstruction literature, but especially of pro-radical fiction. While pro-Bourbon and neutralist fiction seeks to gloss over the differences between the sections for reconciliationist reasons, the Pro-Radicals, and Tourgée in particular, emphasize the two-nation hypothesis to defend the Carpetbagger's struggle as an "inter-national" one:

> The North and the South had been two households in one house—two nations under one name. The intellectual, moral, and social life of each had been utterly distinct and separate from that of the other. They no more understood or appreciated each other's feelings or development, than John Chinaman comprehends the civilization of John Bull. It is true they spoke the same language, used the same governmental forms, and, most unfortunately, thought they comprehended each other's ideas. . . . The Northern man despised his Southern fellow-citizen in bulk, as a good-natured braggadocio, mindful of his own ease, fond of power and display, and with no animating principles which could in any matter interfere with his interest. The Southern man despised his Northern compeer as cold-blooded, selfish, hypocritical, cowardly, and envious.[834]

For the pro-radical writer, the South remains that other country in hostile antipathy to the North. It deserves none of that reconciliationist charity that permitted redemption and prevented a thorough reconstitution of the ex-Confederacy. There can be no authentic reconciliation in this view until one of the nations dominates the other.

In Tourgée's fiction this archetypal and historical rivalry culminates within the South itself as a symbolic-political struggle between two "antagonistic civilizations . . . for mastery" over the South, a struggle in which allegorical forces—knowledge "and ignorance, slavery and freedom, Northmen and Southron, Caucasian and African" join as "opposing forces and contrasted elements."[835] The goal in such a battle is the codification of the Union's victory in total continental mastery: "Now that the bars of slavery are down, I suppose you Yankees will New Englandize the continent."[836]

More generally, this struggle takes on additional importance as an analogical paradigm of the specific *postwar* problems that plagued the twenty-year transition (1865-1885) from ancient to modern America. The tension between the Carpetbagger's republican principles and the Bourbon's aristocratic ones, the racial warfare, the battle for political power, the desire for land, the factional infighting, the growth of *city-based* commerce at the South—all mirrored obliquely such larger issues as the rise of urbanization, the emergence and stabilization of the plutocracy, the growing dominance of industrial capitalism, the resulting hostility between agrarian and industrial interests, and political variation on this theme—the battle between oligarchy and populism on the local and national levels. The struggle between ex-slave and ex-master may be said to foreshadow the specific worker-capitalist polarity into which the difficulties and agitations of the transition would eventually crystallize in social-conscious fiction.

Within this general context of prewar rivalry and postwar agitation, the specific nature and meaning of the conflict between the Bourbon and the Carpetbagger in the Tourgée canon will be examined as these figures relate to the Reconstruction. In this frame (to repeat myself), this conflict had three major aspects, our familiar triad—the psychocultural, the ideological, and the political, with the political being the most important. This familiar triad has its clearest articulation in Tourgée's fiction, summed up in the violence of the White Terror, the most melodramatic symbol of the intensity generating the irrepressibility of their hostility.[837]

The term cultural-psychological has been bandied about frequently, along with other hyphenated, sociological neologisms in this work. It is a jargon word borrowed from social psychology to describe the close interrelation between cultural expectations and the mindset of people in a society and the artifacts, rituals, mores, institutions, and customs that form their culture. Cultural demands create psychological strategies; cultural pressures generate mental patterns. The cultural-psychological means, further, that while some emotions do have their origins in the individual psyche, most are created by sociocultural expectations. For example, the Bourbon's abhorrence of the Taboo Conjunction is an emotional reality, but engendered and sustained by Southern mores. In pro-radical fiction the specific manifestation of the cultural-psychological, aka psychocultural, is the effect of slavery on both North and South. Slave-labor capitalism was the political economic underpinning of Bourbon culture before and during Reconstruction.[838] What is not so familiar is the assumption in this study that slavery paradoxically can also be considered as a force that helped to form the cultural dimensions of Northern society insofar as it related to the Carpetbagger as a psychocultural symbol. In this interpretation the Carpetbagger's conception of the North is also formed by slavery in all its complexity but formed in a *reverse* manner by the ethics of the anti-slavery movement. It is the belief here that abolitionism became, for a while, a specific sociological as well as ideological entity that exemplified in the North this psychocultural fusion.

In this hypothesis, the decades preceding Secession beginning with the Missouri Compromise of 1820 saw the intensifying influence of anti-slavery agitation in many Northern communities. Church and political meetings, newspapers and popular fiction, intellectual salon and family gatherings became sounding boards for the abolitionist crusade. The general configuration of the Northern *ethos*, represented mainly by the residue of New England philosophy and religion, aided in giving the abolitionist ideology first sociopolitical and then sociocultural currency. So it was that during these intense decades when the expansionist drive of the two sections was already clashing in the near-western territories, when Southern chauvinism was creating in the North a kind of Unionist nationalism, the anti-slavery issue became fused with both the religious ethics of a new revivalism and the politics of a new Unionism as cultural forms. Abolitionism evolved into a touchstone, in many Northern communities, of a person's emotional commitment to Christian *and* patriotic idealism. Consequently, Northerners within such communities could not help but be influenced psychologically by the intense sociopolitical anti-slavery fervor raging around them, particularly as abolitionism came to be more and more identified with Northern society.[839]

Among such Northerners, Yankeelandia became more defined by its distinctiveness *from* the slaveholding society. In Tourgée's fiction the North's salient attributes as a cultural entity—its democratic polity, its work ethic, its commercial impetus, its emphasis on education and self-development, its theoretical egalitarianism, its family and religious life, its growing cities and farms were all considered artifacts of a world whose social reality resulted from the *absence* of the peculiar institution.[840] If slavery defined the essential cultural nature of the South, the lack of it, for the anti-slavery Yankee, becomes the defining attribute of the North. Therefore, slavery and its complementary antithesis, abolitionism, define the psychocultural antagonism between the two sections.

When the Carpetbagger and the Bourbon meet in the South, fresh from the moral and physical trauma of the war, they merely stake out in the ruins of the Confederacy their ideological and political positions as extensions of this older antagonism. What emerges in Reconstruction fiction is a social collision in which Southern culture defeats Northern psychology.

Because the Carpetbagger's psychological perceptions of the South are rooted in Northern abolitionism, he is at an epistemological disadvantage so long as s/he depended on the National Republican Party. Empirical observations of freed Negroes taking power and an empirical awareness of emancipation as a constitutional fact force him to conclude that the slave society, as the opposite of the anti-slavery one, no longer exists. The Abolitionist-Radical victory *has* New Englandized the South; the task of the Carpetbagger is simply to instruct the new black and white Bostonians in governing their transformed society. This is the psychocultural distortion that repeats itself in Reconstruction fiction, for since the Carpetbagger's modes of feeling and reasoning about the postwar South had been conditioned by the anti-slavery movement as a cultural imperative and as a victorious crusade led by the Republican Party and its Black Vanguard, he was unable to fight effectively against the Bourbons' counter-revolution, once he was abandoned by the liberal wing of that Party. The force of the slaveowners' resurgence so surprised the Tourgéan hero that, in the end, it was not only the absence of Federal troops that made him helpless. The persistence of slavery as an emotional, psychic reality (the Slavery Syndrome in all its forms) rendered the Carpetbagger's *own sociocultural, Northern conceptions* so utterly alien to the unexpected ferocity of the counter-revolution that they became hindrances to his survival, paralyzing him with false expectations and irrelevant actions, leaving him desperate, bewildered, and vulnerable. He was used to due process and around him there was lynch-law; he had been taught respect for governmental officers and around him they were being assassinated; he had known the solidarity of law-abiding neighbors as a moral force against criminal action, and around him his neighbors *were* the criminals. Before such powerful tides rolling against him from the dark springs of Southern existence, the Carpetbagger's own sectional misconceptions made him unable to either fly or fight:

> That you should be unable to measure the strength of prejudice in the Southern mind is not strange. You should remember that the war has rather intensified than diminished the pride, the arrogance, and the sectional rancor and malevolence of the Southern people
>
> . . . . All that made the Southern slaveholder and rebel what he was, still characterizes him since the surrender. The dogma of State-sovereignty has been prevented from receiving practical development, but as a theory it is as vital and as sacred as ever. The *fact* of slavery is destroyed: the *right to enslave* is yet as devoutly held as ever. The right of a white man to certain political privileges is admitted: the right of a colored man to such, it will require generations to establish.[841]

But it is the persistence of this kind of reality that marks Comfort Servosse as the alien, the representative of the hated abolitionist culture, and that therefore makes him in Bourbon's eyes a legitimate target for persecution.

The Carpetbagger in Tourgée's fiction transcends his cultural misconceptions *via* the agony of his persecution and discovers those two essential facts of Reconstruction as a symbol of the Conflict between South and North. To reiterate: First, slavery as a psychological-ideological force had not disappeared with the abolitionist victories of 1865 and 1868:

> We ought to have seen and known that only the shell was gone. Slavery as a formal state of society was at an end: as a force, a power, a moral element, it was just as active as before. Its conscious evils were obliterated; its unconscious ones existed in the dwarfed and twisted natures which had been subjected for generations to its influence,—master and slave alike. As a form of society [it is abolished by law; as a psychocultural reality, it is as] indestructible as the souls on which it has left its mark.[842]

Second, abolitionism as a cultural antithesis no longer existed in the North as a universal imperative. Paradoxically, the victories of 1865 and 1868 had destroyed anti-slavery idealism both as a viable, moral commitment and, in terms of this hypothesis, as a psychic imperative among the Northern crusaders. From 1870 on whatever defined the North's ultimate nature as a society in the eyes of the Greeleys and Higginsons would no longer be related to the problem of slavery and freedom, but to economic expansionism. The Wormley House Compromise merely codified this fundamental shift in the North's social and emotional priorities. Thus in the cultural and psychological conflict between Carpetbagger and Bourbon, slavery was to prove to be more organic to Southern life than abolitionism was to Northern life. It would be the slave-master's vision, not the slavery-destroyer's, that would reassert itself both above and below the line.

Slavery was destroyed; its Syndrome was not: Out of this overly repeated fact grows the second aspect of the Reconstruction conflict—the ideological antagonism. The doctrines, opinions, and ways of thinking that characterize the antagonists' ideological commitments cover a variety of issues ranging from the aesthetic to the political. However, in the Reconstruction fiction, the crux of their opposition is the mutually exclusive ideas about the nature of the Negro as a sociopolitical entity developed during the intense decade by the Fitzhughs and the Garrisons to defend or oppose slavery.

Bourbon ideology rests on the same basic assumption as the pro-slavery position:

> The slave is now free, but he is not white. We have no ill will towards the colored man as such and in his place; but he is not our equal, cannot be made our equal, and we will not be ruled by him as a co-ordinate with the white race in power. . . .[843]

This is, of course, the doctrine of racial subordination, constantly discussed in this study:

> The bulk of the Southern people . . . regard the abolition of slavery only as a temporary triumph of fanaticism over divine truth. They do not believe the Negro intended or designed for any other sphere in life. They may think the relation was abused by bad [corrupt and incompetent] masters and [speculators] and all that, and consequently God permitted its overthrow; but they have no idea that he will permit the permanent establishment of any system which does not retain the African in a subordinate and servile relation.[844]

This doctrine of subordination has both a humane and brutal side. At its best, the Southron merely seeks to fix in the Reconstruction flux the fabled (and in some instances verifiable) affection between black and white: "'Ah! Momsie,' [says the heroine of "The Barren Ridge" to her Aunt Segis] bending her soft white cheek to touch the dusky fingers . . . . In riches or in poverty, you and I must be always to each other just what we have ever been."[845] Here the doctrine is couched in terms of the humanitarian impulse intrinsic in Southern paternalism.[846] At its worst, racial subordination assumes the absolute non-humanity of Aunt Segis: She is still the "living creature" of prewar Southernist anthropology, a kind of animal with human "passions, appetites, and motives."[847] Any gestures that give Aunt Segis recognition as a human being mean, for the Bourbon, to be in favor of

> abolitionism, negro-equality, miscegenation, rape, murder, arson, and anarchy, with all the untold horrors which Southerners believed would follow the uprising or liberation of a race of untaught savages, lustful as apes, bloodthirsty as cannibals, and artful as satyrs.[848]

In this context, racial subordination defines the black and white Radicals as monstrosities to be destroyed at any cost:

> For generations the South had regarded . . . the assertion of [the Negro's] manhood and autonomy, as the *ultime thule* of possible evil. San Domingo and hell were twin horrors . . . with the odds . . . in favor of San Domingo. To prevent negro domination anything was justifiable. It was a choice of evils, where on one side was placed an evil which they had been taught to believe . . . infinitely . . . outweighed . . . all other evils in enormity. [Anything,] they cried aloud to the world, was better, is better, must be better, than negro rule, than African domination.[849]

The idea that save for the pressures of the Yankees the ex-slave assents in his subordination (discussed elsewhere as voluntary servitude) is another important concept in the Bourbon's ideological conflict with the Carpetbagger. The Freedmen, in this view, also longs to be to the ex-master just what he had ever been. But confused and misled by the Carpetbagger's gifts of liberty and citizenship, many black Southerners go against the old way—to their sorrow. For Hesden Le Moyne (in his Bourbon phase), liberty and citizenship make the ex-slaves poor dogs without masters, "the blameless instrument by which a bigoted and revengeful North seeks to degrade and humiliate a foe overwhelmed by the accident of numbers. . . ."[850] If the Bourbon can overthrow Reconstruction, racial subordination will automatically return to the South.

Of equal importance to the Bourbon is his conception of the rationale that shaped the Carpetbagger's activities. For Tourgée, the Bourbon's ideological misapprehension of Yankee motives exacerbated the natural tensions created between Northerner and Southerner by the Americanization of the Freedmen. The Southron views the general range of Radical Reconstruction activity, and Americanization in particular, not as legislative acts growing from the Northerners' ideological commitment to certain legal and constitutional propositions, but as manifestations of a complex of malevolent motives, e.g., malice, vengefulness, and hypocrisy, originating in the texture of Northern life. Making a Hesden Le Moyne socio-politically coordinated with "a race despised beyond the power of language to express . . . —mere ethnological ciphers . . ." is simply an act of malice, "given in mere wantonness of power, and for the sole purpose of revenge." The sin of such an act is the vengeful humbling of the dignity of princes "who had but lately dominated the nation, and had . . . given four years of . . . blood and toil for the right . . ." to enslave Aunt Segis. [851]

Coeval with this malice and vengefulness is that endemic vice of the abolitionist tyranny: hypocrisy. The Carpetbagger espouses Freedman rights and racial equality in order to control the black plebeians and to degrade and disgrace white patricians. If the North had been sincere, so went Bourbon reasoning, it would have Americanized its own Negroes before the war. Americanization is a cheap gesture, since it only affects the South. The Yankees need not fear the results of Negro citizenship on *their* political and social institutions since so few Negroes live above the line. For the Bourbons, therefore, the imposition of black power on their country was the fullest expression of the North's hypocrisy and vengefulness.[852]

Convinced then that immorality rather than politics lay behind the Carpetbagger's assaults on racial subordination, the Bourbons in Tourgée's fiction feel ideologically justified in using any means necessary to destroy the radical menace. For if the Carpetbagger is not so much a political rival as he is a demon, then no crime is too horrible that will exorcise him and his influence from the Southern Garden. This is the basis of the violence to which the Bourbon's ideological commitment would lead him in his opposition to the Carpetbagger's point of view.

The Carpetbagger's ideological position *vis-à-vis* the ex-slave is less complex. In the first place, the "Negroes are free now, and must have a fair chance to make themselves something." While they may be socially inferior at this stage of their development, there is no scientific proof that they are anthropologically inferior. Therefore, "they have a right to equality before the law." This was one of the solemn promises of the Northern Radical's crusade against the Rebels. In the second place, with political equality, especially with the ballot, the Negro will become a vital element in Southern politics, and the possession of the franchise will ensure his good treatment from Southrons anxious to woo his vote in order "to retain permanent control of [their] States." Moreover, once the political issue is settled along radical lines, the "negroes will go to work, and things will gradually adjust themselves."[853] Out of this general statement of hopes and principles evolve the three major tenets of Carpetbagger ideology: abolitionism, Unionism, and egalitarianism, undergirding the Irrepressible Conflict.

Just as the basis of the Bourbon's ideological position evolves from the Intense Decade, so does the Carpetbagger's. The Garrison-Douglass faction of the movement demanded the destruction of slavery in all its symbols, the chief of which was the political and legal non-existence of the slave. Very well then, so the Radicals reasoned in 1868, the purpose of reconstitution would be to give the ex-slave the fullest political and legal rights possible in a 19th-century Republic. Only when the Negro was safely visible in legislature and polling-booth with his rights guaranteed by the once-hated Constitution would slavery be officially dead within the Union. Of course, such idealism had its practical side.

The Union had been preserved from Secession by men, North and South, who had remained steadfast to the Republican-Unionist cause throughout the war. Several hundred thousand of these Unionists were Negro soldiers who had fought in almost every major battle since 1863. Now they and their civilian brothers were needed to ensure that rebellion never again threatened the peace of the nation. The chief insurance was the Americanization amendments, which had created some four million new political Unionists in the South, even though many could not vote. They would be the basis upon which loyal Republican states would be raised, states whose climatic, cultural, and racial distinctiveness would never again evolve into the kind of geopolitical antagonism that had plagued the old Union.

Abolitionism and Unionism may also be subsumed under the key proposition in radical doctrine, egalitarianism. It is this doctrine that sets the Yankee in diametrical opposition to the concept of racial subordination. In Tourgée's fiction the Carpetbaggers in all their faces assume the basic humanity of their black comrades. From this assumption proceed the various legislative acts that implement the doctrine of egalitarianism during Reconstruction.

Tourgée, however, admits that Bourbon ideologies are partially correct "in believing that the North cared little or nothing for the Negro as a man." Indeed, Tourgée describes in *Hot Plowshares* a corresponding anti-egalitarian strain in the Northern Republic that emerged after the Missouri Compromise, one with a strong anti-Negro cast. The North's specific response was, in many instances, to follow the South's lead, to assent legally to Negro subordination in state and national legislation from Massachusetts to Illinois: "Many of the subtlest exertions of [American] intellect were those which traced and defined the line of demarcation [between black and white] until there was built up between the races, considered as men, a wall of separation as high as heaven and as deep as hell."[854] In this wise, not a small part of the prewar social and political development of the North (outside abolitionist communities) also involved the suppression of African-Saxon marriage in some states, Supreme Court and Congressional decisions, legal conundrums over white Negroes, the political helplessness of many a Northern Freedman, aspects of the Constitution itself—all testified to the anti-egalitarian reaction generated by the pressures of the African enigma above the line. And now in the postwar period, this very same North joins with the Radical Republicans, one of its smaller political factions, to insist that this creature become the Bourbon's political equal. Furthermore, Tourgée in implementing the egalitarian principle in the South *was* entangled with some sense of maliciousness, though only at an ironic level:

> [The Southrons have no complaints if Negro equality is now the order of the day.] They would have the Negroes as slaves, kept the country in constant turmoil for the sake of them, brought on war because we would not catch their runaways . . . ; and now they cannot complain if the very weapon by which they held power is turned against them, and is made the means of righting the wrongs which they have themselves created.[855]

But Tourgée insists they were wrong to believe political egalitarianism and manhood suffrage grew "from any thought of malice . . . [or] revenge." Rather, this principle was a real and dominant psychocultural one, despite the betrayal of this principle in 1877. [856] The agitation of the fifties, the war in the first half of the sixties, and the Radical Movement in the second half combined to reawaken egalitarianism as the key to Northern sociopolitical idealism and as the meaning of the Civil War and Reconstruction. For Tourgée, social and cultural conceptions remain the essential rationale for radical activity. The political equality of the Negro is the uncompromisable reality emerging from the very center of the Northerner's vision of society and politics. It is over this vision that the ideology of the two antagonists clashed.

In the Reconstruction upheaval described in the fiction, one sees the last flareup in the 19th century of the doctrines, opinions, and ways of thinking that had formed the ideological substance of the abolitionist and pro-slavery positions. By 1877, the pro-slavery position had, through its postwar mutation, become victorious, though it would take another twenty-one years, so resistant was the egalitarian principle, before it would become judicially codified into national terms. In 1898 the U.S. Supreme Court would once more assent to the ideology of racial subordination, though this time behind a legal paradox that would permit equality, but in separate and eventually inferior social and political forms. Once more the pressures of the African enigma would generate among the majority of the Northern bourgeoisie the anti-egalitarian response. These were to be the long-range meanings of the Bourbon's ideological victory over the Carpetbagger.

Thirdly, the movement from the ideological to the sociopolitical conflict follows rather naturally, since the former usually leads to the latter. The history of Reconstruction is the struggle between opposing ideologies at the legislative levels. Moreover, the political antagonism between Bourbon and Carpetbagger relates to and, at the same time, evolves at the level of appearance from their psychocultural misconceptions of each other and the Reconstruction experiences. Finally, the sociopolitical struggle is the key theme in Reconstruction literature, forming the most important rationale for the violence of the Irrepressible Conflict at the South.

In Tourgée's key works the sociopolitical battle begins where ideology leaves off. The Bourbon had called for racial subordination; the Carpetbagger for political equality. By 1870 the Freedman's political rights, especially his voting rights, were a reality. The Bourbon was now forced by the North's military and moral surveillance to deal with the fact that the key to the states was the enfranchised Freedmen, that where they outnumbered enfranchised whites they were the power of the state.

To obtain this power the Bourbon had to compete with a rival who had suffered and worked to bring about this reality. He had to enter into equal combat with the Yankee, who in Bourbon ideology represented demonically ". . . a distinct people—sometimes generous and brave, but normally envious, . . . treacherous, and malignant," and the natural enemies of the Southern way of life.[857] Worst of all, he had to play his old games by new democratic rules, rules that were the familiar tradition of his rival. The former slavocrat had to go among his former slaves at churches, stump-rallies, and crossroads, and compete with the Yankee in respectfully soliciting Negro votes. This shattering of nearly a hundred years of tradition and custom accompanied the politicization of the ex-slave and forms the context for the first aspect of the sociopolitical struggle, the battle for Negro votes.

For Tourgée, both sides have advantages in this competition. The Southron comes as the father-figure of the plantation ethos, the manifestation of ambivalent elements that formed Southern paternalism: "Why, your blatant freedom-shriekers have no idea of the close and patriarchal relation subsisting between a master and his slaves."[858] As ole Marse, the Southron, seeks to transform a hundred years of guidance, affection, and personal loyalty between master and slave into social and political power, the Carpetbagger also appears before the Freedman as a father-figure, mainly because of his white skin, his intelligence, and his Northern ways. But he is also a white Unionist among black ones, and this gives an element of equality and fraternity to this new patriarchal relation. The Carpetbagger's paternalism is a manifestation of the mystique of Jubilee and Mistuh Linkum, the tangible evidence within the Garden itself of the alert, watchful concern of the faraway Emancipators.

In the first round of their political competition, the Bourbon loses. The Carpetbagger and his children-brothers take over the symbols and offices, from clerk ordinary to governor, once reserved solely for the Bourbon and his race. Where the Bourbons do win, they are an embattled, embittered minority. The Freedman's steadfast loyalty to various radical factions and Carpetbagger-instituted coalitions is the sociopolitical fact of life at the South. On the basis of this loyalty, the Carpetbagger-as-patriarch proceeds to reconstitute the legal and judicial foundations of Bourbon culture: "property qualifications for voters, officers, and jurors" are eliminated; direct "election of all officers . . . " is instituted; the "whipping-post, the stocks, the branding-iron" "are abolished and capital felonies are reduced from *seventeen* to one, or at most two." The tax structure is reformed so that a "uniform and *ad valorem* taxation" is levied on all property. Finally, an "effective system of public schools" is established for all citizens.[859] These were some of the social effects of the Carpetbagger's political victory in one state.

Such legislation stood in Bourbon eyes as the signs of a heinous Jacobinism, [860] indicating all around him the abandonment of the old ways. The cause of this abandonment and the most galling symbol of its reality remained, in the Bourbon's eyes, the emerging loyalty and affection of Aunt Segis for her new patriarchs. This, among other inconceivable transformations in his world, forced the Bourbon to conclude that his slaves were being duped, magically abused, by what he knew was the corrupting power of a Mephistopheles whose oratory and legislation of egalitarianism and uplift mask sociopolitical manipulation, hypocrisy, and hatred of the Negro: "Now, look at your Radicals, your Abolitionists. It is the abstract idea of freedom they care for, not the black man. On the contrary, there is a personal antipathy to the Negro in the North, which does not exist with us."[861] Therefore (so goes this melodramatic view of Reconstruction politics), since the Carpetbagger's spell is too strong for normal party rivalry, the Bourbon decides to neutralize or gain the Freedman vote through terror. The struggle for the black ballot, then, at both the civic and terroristic level, is the first aspect to the sociopolitical conflict between Bourbon and Carpetbagger.

The prize in this struggle, the second aspect of this conflict, is control of the Southern state houses. The Bourbon has lost the Union, his chance to rule a confederacy of independent states and his state governments. But if he could regain control over the Southern capitols through controlling or constraining the Negro franchise, he can at least return near the center of Federal power, the halls of Congress. Therefore, home rule and federal representation become the interrelated goals of Bourbon sociopolitical strategy. And the power that could make this strategy work was the persistence of the doctrine of State's Rights among many Northerners.

The Congressional Radicals' commitment to this doctrine shaped their plan of Reconstruction. Initially, they wanted the CSA destroyed, but then restored as soon as possible under Unionist control. They believed that Unionists would either dominate state powers permanently through the black franchise or fend off indefinitely Bourbon resurgence by making sure that the Freedman would be connected by principle and profit to the radical cause. Furthermore, the immediate reorganization of the states was necessary to help the Northern Republicans win in 1868. For Tourgée, such cynical use of the doctrine of State's Rights was the time bomb that destroyed the Radical Movement:

> So it must have been well understood by the wise men who devised this short-sighted plan of electing a President . . . that they were giving the power of the re-organized . . . republics, into the hands of a race unskilled in public affairs, poor to a degree hardly to be matched in the civilized world, and so ignorant that [many] could not read their own ballots, joined with such Adullamites among the native whites as might be willing to face . . . proscription . . . , together with the few [Northerners] either knaves or fools, or partaking of the nature of both,—who might elect to become permanent citizens, and join in the movement.[862]

Under such conditions the "power of the re-organized republics" had been guaranteed by the North. It was available to whomever could grasp and hold it. Servosse recognizes that, even in states with pro-radical majorities, controlling this power would be difficult, since the Radicals were not organized enough nor protected enough for a long contest with the Bourbons. For the Tourgéan hero, therefore, the North's continuing allegiance to the doctrine, despite the lessons of Secession and the Civil War, remains the Union-wide problem that neither war nor Reconstruction was able to solve. North and South only disagreed over the political makeup of the states; both agreed that the states were the key to the Federal arrangement. In this context, Tourgée describes State's Rights as

> . . . that Juggernaut of American politics by which so many hecatombs have been crushed and mangled. This demon required a million lives before he would permit slavery to be abolished: perhaps as many more would induce him to let the fettered souls be unbound and made free.[863]

This juggernaut presides over the crucial sociopolitical incident in the Reconstruction *agon*—the violent struggle for the Southern state houses.

In this battle the two forces are theoretically equally matched. Despite the disadvantages created for him by reconstitution, the Bourbon in Servosse's eyes still has sociocultural power. Despite war losses, many Southrons had more wealth than their ex-slaves, since many still owned their plantations. They had "the intellect, organizing capacity, the determined will," and "the pride, and hate of a people who [*sic*] it had taken four years to conquer in open fight. . . ." Furthermore, the Southern patricians had in their ranks powerful men who fought in and led the secessionist crusade. Some were heroic leaders; many were "the most reckless and unworthy" of the rebels. Both groups were united by their hatred of the Carpetbagger as a political rival, as the representative of the Yankees, and as the advocate of Negro equality.[864]

The essential factor here is the Bourbon's traditional sociopolitical prominence in the South: "Every family . . . has its clientelage, its followers, who rally to its lead as quickly . . . as the old Scottish clansmen, summoned by the burning cross." The reconstitutionists supposed that by simply depriving this class "of actual political position, they would be shorn of political influence." For Servosse this "was a fatal mistake. . . . The king of every village was dethroned. . . . Henceforward, each and every one of their satellites was bound to eternal hostility" against the Radicals. [865] The leadership of the Bourbon and his family over the hierarchical structure of the Southern community accounts in Tourgée's fiction for the boldness with which the counter-revolution is launched against the Carpetbagger and his comrades.

The tactical aims of the counter-revolution are simple. Under a variety of terrorist strategies known generically as Klan violence or the White Terror, the Bourbons will first isolate the masses of Freedmen from their white and black leaders through persuasion, assassination, and torture; the leaderless masses will then be either prevented from voting altogether or will be forced to vote for Bourbon candidates. In this manner the Anti-Radicals hope to regain the state houses, a strategy described by Servosse in rhetoric that is ironically sympathetic. At the same time his description presents in summary a general history of anti-radical crusade as a sociopolitical and sociopsychological phenomenon:

> [Such] was the indomitable spirit of this people, that they scorned to yield or submit to what they deemed oppression. . . . It was a defiance openly and fairly given; and to the redemption of this challenge was plighted the honor of a people even more scrupulous of their collective than their individual rights, exasperated by defeat, and aroused by . . . unpardonable wrong and oppression.[866]

When the Reconstruction acts approached, the

> Fool saw them resisting bravely every step leading to the adoption of this plan, . . . denouncing with rage, and finally submitting almost with tears. No conquered foe ever passed under the yoke which they conceived to mean . . . infamy to them, with more unwilling step, or with more deeply muttered curses. He saw men and women afflicted with the keenest sense of . . . humiliation because of . . . enforced submission to . . . a people they had always deemed their inferiors,—the . . . 'groveling and greedy Yankee,'—.[867]

In the face of Union power without and within their country, the Bourbons

> could not fight . . . ; but by infinite patience, matchless organization, unremitting and universal zeal . . . they could turn against that enemy the weapon [i.e., universal suffrage] by which he had sought to secure their degradation [*sic*]. . . . It was a daring conception for the conquered people.[868]

To accomplish this, all Southerners of the patrician class had to be accessory, and

> be worthy of implicit mutual trust. Having eyes, they must see not; and having ears, they must hear not. . . . The whole South must be . . . welded into one . . . mass, having . . . one relentless will. It was a magnificent conception, and, in a sense, deserved success![869]

Furthermore, Servosse sees this entire sociopolitical strategy as one that had to be made "in the face of . . . an enemy . . . of overwhelming strength." It had to be disguised until the Bourbons had defeated the Reconstruction forces and presented the Northern foe with an accomplished fact. Servosse concludes on a note of admiration: Such a revolution would require skill, patience, and courage. "Should it succeed, it would be the most brilliant revolution ever accomplished."[870]

Within this sociopolitical strategy and its potential success, there is a moral corruption that will make the Bourbon victory dangerous to the future spiritual health of the Union. It will be the handiwork of traitors and terrorists.[871] And this is Servosse's major point in his apprehension of the Bourbon counter-revolution: that despite the heroic genius that redemption might manifest, it would be an immoral force, generated by the darker emotions of the ex-Confederates' psyche, aiming at destruction and a more subtle form of re-enslavement. This was the reality that no amount of heroism or brilliance could disguise.

Against this power, the Carpetbagger has, *theoretically*, his own countervailing political measures. On the one hand, he has tangible assets such as economic, political, and military resources. Economically the Carpetbagger is the viaduct through which locomotives, manufactories, and scientific agriculture can come into the Garden. Politically he has the voting power and united loyalty of white and black Unionists who more than outnumber the disenfranchised, cowed Southrons. If the Bourbon, therefore, seeks a purely sociopolitical struggle, the Carpetbagger is more than his match.

If the Bourbon turns to terrorist warfare, the Carpetbagger has military resources at his fingertips. There were the state militia, composed of Scalawags and Freedmen. Armed, trained, and paid by radical government, they were the *Garde Republican* of the Carpetbagger cause. Supporting the militia was an armed citizenry that had a vested interest in the survival of the Radical Reconstruction, ready to defend it against an enemy who had once enslaved the black Unionist and repressed the white. Many Carpetbaggers were former soldiers, familiar with military tactics and discipline. In the event of a white uprising, they would stand ready to take the lead in organizing the radical communities in support of the state militias. Finally, there was the presence, actual or implied, of the Grand Army of the Republic, the national guardians of the Union's peace North and South. In the event of a Southern counter-revolution and the failure, for some reason, of state authority to defend itself, the Army would be as near as the telegraph.

Adjunct to the Carpetbagger's tangible power was an important intangible resource: the moral support of the Northern supporters of the bourgeois democratic republic. While abolitionism as a psychocultural force had passed into history, the moral idealism it had generated still remained as a continuing memory. The Radical Movement is seen as the direct heir to the ethical commitment of the Intense Decade. While reconciliationists may preach the joys of reunion with ex-Rebels, the memories of the Union dead from Shiloh to Andersonville remind the North of the price paid for suppressing their rebellion. The great Northern heart (so continues the Carpetbagger's vision) will know that its true friends at the South are not the supporters of the defunct Confederacy, but the grateful ex-slaves, the white Southern loyalists, and the sons and daughters of the North's own loins.[872]

Economic, political, and military power within the South; moral support from the North: these then are the Carpetbagger's resources. Now, what is his strategy? Basically, it complements in reverse Bourbon tactics. The Southron aims to seize the state houses by using terror. The Carpetbagger seeks to keep power by protecting his white and black followers from that terror and, where defenses break down, to retaliate with the full power of the state.

Unfortunately, Carpetbagger power proved to be ineffective in practice: Federal military support was insufficient; Northern elite opinion shifted; the franchise was nullified; and the Carpetbagger's prior military experience was rendered irrelevant against the discipline, numbers, and the community support of the white terrorists. Most of all, the Carpetbaggers failed to make effective use of their black power—the Negro-dominated state militias. The reasons for this were several. Many ex-slaves were often reluctant and afraid to fight back against white attack because of the conditioning of slavery. Where they were willing to give battle, they were often restrained by pro-Negro Carpetbaggers who feared an even bloodier counter-response from the Southron community. This same reluctance affected the Carpetbagger's deployment of his militias. Often the state troops were not as well-trained as their ex-Confederate counterparts.[873] And where ill-trained troops did fight back, they were decimated by overwhelming odds, as at Baconsville. Where they were well-trained, timid leaders refused to call them out (e.g., Governor Ames of Mississippi) because of fear of massive retaliation and, more interestingly, because of the fear of Northern conservative resentment against the use of Freedman violence *under any circumstances*.[874]

And so the sociopolitical conflict between postwar forms of abolitionism and slavery, Unionism and Secessionism, was joined. The Bourbons had lost the first round, but would win the second. In that round political terrorism rather than inter-party maneuvers and intra-party factionalism decided the outcome. But whether bullets or ballots were involved, political mastery over the South remained the essential goal. The sociopolitical, therefore, remains the definitive aspect of the general conflict between the Bourbon and the Carpetbagger.

The Reconstruction antagonists sum up in their character and action the opposing psychocultural, ideological, and social and political forces forming the thematic structure of pro-radical fiction in particular, and shaping the texture of the Conflict that, in general, this fiction articulates. But their conflict is also "acted out" in a more deadly historical and metaphoric reality—in what may be called the wars of redemption. It is the acts of ruthless violence with which the Bourbons bring down the power of their rivals that stand in Reconstruction literature as the symbol for the complex of antagonisms defining their opposition.

Not all Reconstruction fiction treats the Bourbon as the instigator of this violence. In "King David," Freedmen create drunken disturbances that cause the Bourbons to arm themselves. In *Colonel Dunwoddie*, Radicals attack the black Bourbon, Parker Anderson, burning his church and administering to him the flogging, which eventually leads to his death. And in the same work, Yellow Jessamine, the Freedman leader, and his henchmen murder a Belle and her daughter. In general, however, Reconstruction fiction dealing with redemptionist violence—*Wild Work*, *Kitty's Conquest*, *Other Fools and Their Doings*, *A Year of Wreck*, *A Fool's Errand*, and *Bricks Without Straw*—features the Bourbon as prime actor, for good or evil. And that the Southron more often than the Yankee was the instigator of terrorism is attested by history.

Reconstruction historians support the above assertion with qualifications indicating Revisionist and Dunningite points of view. Dunningites insist that massacres of Carpetbaggers and their comrades were quite rare and that the severity and frequency of Bourbon violence were exaggerated by pro-radical sensationalists. And, besides, the White Insurrection was the only response possible to the "mobocratic" hegemony of Carpetbagger rule, especially since the Freedman franchise, the key to state power, was the Radicals' private monopoly. In contrast, the Revisionist historians show that the Carpetbagger's crimes, real or imagined, were not so depraved or excessive in terms of the general historical conditions of the period as to justify the horror with which they were driven from office. Railroad speculation, ignorant legislators, and bribery were not, in this view, commensurate with the Bourbon response, represented by the Hamburg, Chisholm, and Red River massacres.

Whether justified or not, violence as it originates among the Bourbons is the emphasis in most Reconstruction works. The burning schoolhouse, the Dead-Ring, and the lynching become the definitive incident in Reconstruction history. They become symbols of the distinctive mindset and cultural values that differentiate the two antagonists; become the visible sign of their ideological incompatibility; become, finally, the image of the breakdown in the normal political dialectic between their two parties. It is violence, then, that emerges in Reconstruction fiction as the key metaphor of the complex of antagonism that defines the encounter between Carpetbagger and Bourbon.

While Tourgée's presentation of Bourbon ruthlessness is quite comprehensive, it is not the best source for examples of specific attacks on the Carpetbagger. The specific victims in Tourgée's fiction are usually the Carpetbagger's more vulnerable comrades: the Freedmen (Eliab Hill, Nimbus, Uncle Jerry) and the Scalawags (John Walters). This does not mean that there is no anti-Carpetbagger violence at all. Rather, where it does take place, it is muted, narratively speaking.

For instance, one usually "hears" that a Carpetbagger sheriff has been assassinated or a political leader has been flogged, but always in the next county. Or if on-stage violence does occur, it is in the form of an attempt that is always thwarted at the last minute. On one occasion terrorists try to ambush Servosse, but he manages to escape. At another time Bourbon assassins plan to waylay Servosse and a fellow Carpetbagger in order to burn them alive on a railroad trestle. In this instance Metta Servosse warns them in time. Because of these literary strategies, Tourgée's narrative depiction of anti-Carpetbagger atrocities is muted and lacks intensity.

Perhaps this is an unintentional, symbolic awareness of the self-imposed restraints in Bourbon tactics *à propos* the Northern Radicals. Historically speaking, the indiscriminate attacks against all men of Northern birth and Unionist sentiment, which had characterized the restorationist movement, ceased during the redemption wars:

> "It's not been from any kindly feeling [that Yankees have not

> been attacked]; but there has been a notion that if . . . Northern men of . . . prominence . . . were interfered with, it might stir up a hornet's nest that would make us trouble. This very fact is all that has saved more than one man whom I could name."[875]

The Terror became more selective, used against those like Servosse, Morgan, and Witchell, who insisted on actively identifying themselves with radical politics, especially black political power. In a sense the Northerner is only a victim by association, when in a thrust against the Radicals he is standing in the Bourbons' way. Where he disassociates himself from the Republican alliance, he is relatively safe.

This historical reality might account for the absence in the Tourgée canon of the vivid description of anti-Carpetbagger violence, which is found in *Yazoo* and *Wild Work*. Yet if the Carpetbagger *per se* is not depicted in his scapegoat guise, the symbols of his principles are. The descriptions of the hanging of Uncle Jerry, the stabbing of John Walters, and the raiding of Red Wing are quite powerful examples of "bloody shirt" atrocities, in which the immolation of the Carpetbagger is "acted out" in ritual disguise.

The second aspect of Tourgée's presentation of violence is its aesthetic dimension, specifically the way in which the scenes of blood and fire are depicted in his works. At the literary level, such descriptions in Reconstruction fiction offer the writer a chance for some powerful, often naturalistic writing, as in *Other Fools*, *Wild Work*, *A Fool's Errand*, and *Bricks Without Straw*. In Tourgée's novels this aesthetic dimension is expressed in three ways that relate implicitly to his larger polemic design. They are direct narration, indirect narration, and what may be called rhetorical impressionism. The only example of the first method is the attack on Red Wing in *Bricks Without Straw*. The second method is exemplified in *A Fool's Errand* in the deaths of Uncle Jerry and John Walters. In each case, there is a narrative indirectness that screens the reader from the actual horror of the deed. For example, one sees how Uncle Jerry is captured:

> Each masked sentry sat his horse as if horse and rider were only some magic statuary with which the bleak night cheated the affrighted eye. Then a whistle sounded on the road toward Verdenton. The masked horsemen turned their

> horses' heads in that direction, and slowly and silently moved away. Gathering in twos, they fell into ranks with the regularity and ease of practiced soldiery, and, as they filed on toward Verdenton, showed a cavalcade of several hundred strong; and upon one of the foremost horses rode one with a strange figure lashed securely to him.[876]

Later, Jerry's body is seen hanging in the square, but what is not seen is the act itself, as with the lynching of the two Freedmen in *Wild Work*.

In the case of John Walters' murder, by far the most vivid scene in *A Fool's Errand*, the indirection is less noticeable, created by the fact that the scene is recounted by a Freedman informer, who in turn is reporting verbatim an overheard conversation:

> 'Dar was ten on us, an' he seed de game we was up to in a second; but he didn't even wince.' 'Law sakes! . . . but dat was monstrous cool.' 'Cool? I should tink in was, as cool es hell. . . .' Jack Bradshaw [then] whipped a slipnoose over his neck, an' pulled him back. . . . '
>
> 'He jest give one groan when he seed all was over. It was de fust an' last. Der wsn't no use tryin' ter hold de boys back no longer. Jim Brad, he drew de cord till it fairly cut inter de flesh. Den dey turned him half over all on us holdin' hims arms an' legs, an' Jack Cannon stuck a knife inter his throat. He bled like a hog; but we caught de blood in a bucket, an' arterwards let it down out o' de winder in a bag to de fellers outside. . . . We stowed him away in the wood-box, an', arter it comes on good an' dark de boys are goin' to take him ober, an' shove him away under dat damned nigger school-house o' his; and' den you see we'll claim de niggers done it, an' perhaps hev some on 'em up, an' try 'em for it.'[877]

Despite the fact that this description is twice removed from reality, it is still a good example of the kind of naturalistic writing that flickers from time to time in Reconstruction rhetoric. It is an understated, almost clinical description, created mainly by the dialect, of the cruelty and helplessness that accompany Walters' murder. But again, as vivid and realistic as it is, it is still indirect narration and hence lacks the kind of bloody immediacy that pervades Goff's intense depiction of the Dead-Ring in *Other Fools*.

Tourgée is at his best with the third method, rhetorical impressionism.

This simply means that one gets an impressionistic mosaic of redemptionist violence in a rhetorical rather than narrative mode. In this process Tourgée moves from individual instances to a montage of the general scale of the Terror. Usually these impressions are scattered through his novels. Sometimes they occur in an intensely concentrated passage. The White Terror was:

> a strange history of peaceful years;—bloody as the reign of Mary, barbarous as the chronicles of the Comanche!
>
> Of the slain there were enough to furnish forth a battle-field, and all from those three classes, the negro, the scalawag, and the carpet-bagger,—all killed with deliberation, . . . roused from slumber at the murky midnight, [and] . . . upon the riverbrink, on the lonely woods-road, . . . shot, stabbed, hanged, drowned, mutilated beyond description, tortured beyond conception.
>
> And almost always an unknown hand. Only the terrible, mysterious fact of death was certain. Accusation by secret denunciation; sentence without hearing; execution without . . . appeal. In the deaths alone, terrible beyond utterance; but in the manner of death—the secret doom from which fate springs—more terrible still: in the treachery which made the neighbor a disguised assassin, most horrible of all the feuds and hates which history portrays.
>
> And then the wounded,—those who escaped the harder fate,—the whipped, the mangled, the bleeding, the torn! Men despoiled of manhood! Women gravid with dead children! Bleeding backs! Broken limbs! [And the dead as numerous as at Gettysburg.] Dwellings and schools and churches burned! The poor, the weak, the despised, maltreated and persecuted—by whom?
>
> [Thus, a reign of terror descended on the Carpetbagger and his comrades, originating always from] the same intangible presence, the same invisible power. Well did it name itself 'The Invisible Empire.'[878]

In this impressionistic vision, Tourgée evokes in the polemic design of his rhetoric the archetypal outlines of the Wilderness ethos. In Reconstruction literature, this ethos is still latent in the semi-barbaric state that characterizes the postwar South and reflects the deeper anti-rationalism attendant to the Slavery Syndrome:

> All over the county, the process of "redemption" was being carried on. The very air was full of horrors. Men with bleeding backs, women with scarred and mutilated forms, came to Mollie to seek advice and consolation. Night after night, devoted men, who did not dare to sleep in their own homes, kept watch around her, in order that her slumbers might be undisturbed. It seemed as if all law had been forgotten, and only a secret Klan had power in the land. . . . Her heart bled for the people she had served, and whom she saw bowed down under the burden of a terrible haunting fear.[879]

And to reveal the danger of this ethos to both the South and the new Union is precisely the polemic aim behind Tourgée's use of his three literary methods. Through these devices Tourgée seeks to symbolize from all points of view—the direct, the indirect, the impressionistic—the pervasiveness of violence as a cultural imperative for Southern behavior, an imperative that had rendered the Carpetbagger helpless without outside help during the redemption wars and that would continue to dominate the reconciling South, paralyzing all progressive impulses with its demonic energy.

It is the nature, cause, effect, and symbology of this energy that Tourgée seeks to uncover in his analysis of Klan violence. While the presentation of redemption in the Tourgée canon is not as aesthetically satisfying as in the other fiction, his analysis of its meaning is the most comprehensive and therefore applies to all fiction dealing with the White Insurrection.

When one speaks of the "nature" of Klan violence, the first aspect of Tourgée's discussion, the term is used on two levels. On a narrative or rhetorical level, the reference is to those surface realities that made up the texture of the violence treated as a whole. There are, first, those incidents of terror that appear in Tourgée's presentation both as specific acts of cruelty for sociopolitical aims and, more interestingly, as sacred acts within a ritual. Second, the reference is related to a ghostly ludicrousness surrounding this ritual. At this narrative-rhetorical level, the nature of the Terror is a fusion of laughter and violence in which Hallowe'en masks and gobbledygook rituals join with murder and mutilation for psychological and sociopolitical purposes. At this level Tourgée discusses the makeup of the Terror via the descriptive rather than analytical mode. On the thematic (or ideological) level, the "nature" of the Klan violence refers to a structure of specific elements. It is the isolation of these defining elements that is the aim of Tourgée's analysis.

To begin with, "Ku Klux Klan" is used in Tourgée's analysis as a generic and symbolic term for all anti-radical terrorism. Historically speaking the Klan was a separate organization from the other like-minded groups that developed during the wars of redemption. While the Klan was a secret underground organization, the redemption groups tended to be almost arrogantly "out in the open" as paramilitary groups with only minimal camouflage as social clubs. Alver and his Leaguers, for example, are known by all when they seize Cahatchie. And in contrast to the Hallowe'en paraphernalia with which the Klan disguised its attacks, the Leagues and Rifle-Clubs of the redemption period launched their raids on Yazoo and Baconsville without need for cumbersome masquerades. The Klan may have been ludicrous with its hoods and sheets, but not Wade Hampton's private, well-armed troops with their rifles and red shirts. In the second place, the Klan *qua* Klan reached the height of its power (in most Southern states) before redemption. By 1871 this power brought it under Union scrutiny, and through congressional investigations, Northern opinion, anti-Klan legislation, and military action, the Kluxers were curbed—all before redemption, the key moment of Reconstruction violence in this study. This is the chief distinction.[880]

Nevertheless, the Klan emerges in Tourgée's fiction as the symbol for all Bourbon terrorism, before and *during* the wars of redemption. While the Klan was outlawed as an organization, it was never extirpated from the reconstructing South as its spiritual energy and its model for anti-radical activity. For Tourgée in 1879, according to this hypothesis, whether Bourbon violence is expressed through League or Club—before, during, or after the chronological moment—its ultimate nature derives for the same sentiment that had energized the Ku Klux Klan during reconstitution:

> Yet it was a magnificent sentiment that underlay it all, an unfaltering determination, an invincible defiance to all that had the seeming of compulsion or tyranny. One can not but regard with pride . . . the indomitable men, who, being conquered in war, yet resisted every effort of the conqueror to change their . . . customs, or even the personnel of their ruling class; and this, too, not only with unyielding stubbornness, but with success. . . . How they laughed to scorn the Reconstruction Acts . . . ! How boldly they declared the conflict to be irrepressible, and that white and black could

> not and should not live together as coordinate ruling elements! How lightly they told the tales of blood,—of the Masked Night-Riders, of the Invisible Empire of Rifle Clubs and Saber Clubs (all organized for peaceful purposes), of warnings and whippings and slaughters! Ah, it is wonderful![881]

Thus the Klan in Tourgée's analysis of the nature of Reconstruction violence subsumes under its meaning all organized forms of Bourbon terrorism against the Carpetbagger. It becomes the prototype for all counter-Radical Reconstruction activity, defining its *genus* and symbolizing, especially in the necromantic impulse, the entire redemption movement as an archetypal force:

> Unseen and unknown! In one State ten thousand, in another twenty thousand, in another forty thousand, in all an army greater than the Rebellion, from the moldering remains of which it sprung, could ever put into the field. An invisible Empire, with a trained and disciplined army of masked midnight marauders, making war upon 'the weakling powers' which the Wise Men had set up in the lately rebellious territory![882]

The first element forming the nature of the White Terror is the Klan's personnel.[883] In Tourgée's fiction the Klan's ranks are made up, allegorically speaking, of the South's most noble sons and her most despicable. Southern gentility may accuse "a base, lawless element" in their community for being responsible for Reconstruction violence, but they are themselves the lawless element and the leaders of it:

> They were good horses, though. . . . Oh, it was a respectable crowd! . . . I don't know when I have seen so many good horses together since the Yankee cavalry left here after the surrender. They were well-drilled too. Plenty of old soldiers in the crowd. . . .[884]

Within this general lawlessness Tourgée describes two groups, separated by a thin, almost irrelevant, line of moral scrupulousness: those for whom bloodshed was merely a tool to be used disinterestedly and selectively for patriotic reasons and those for whom it satisfied sadistic drives. These groups can be labelled, metaphorically, the lions and the wolves. Infrequently, the lion's scruples acted as a restraint on the inherent tendency toward excess among the Klan's rank-and-file:

> Men are just like dogs, anyhow. Just let them get a taste of blood, and they are as savage as wolves. As soon as Jerry was killed, it seemed as if the whole Klan was wild for blood. Only a few opposed it,—just enough, and of the right sort.[885]

There is a tendency for Tourgée to see this division along class lines, allocating the lion's role to the patrician class. It is General Gurney, a high-toned Klansman, who warns Servosse's daughter of the attempt to burn her father alive. But such acts of restraint by aristocrat (or villain) are the exception to the rule. The Klansman of scruples differs only quantitatively from his more bloodthirsty followers. An Alver will kill only two Freedmen; he will not countenance the death of six Carpetbaggers. If the moral restraints of the "right sort" prevent a bloodbath after the death of Uncle Jerry, it is not an ethical principle that will prevent a future massacre should one be necessary for the anti-radical crusade.

In the main the excesses of the wolves grow directly from the controlling hands of the lion. It is not the semi-chivalrous Southrons and poor-whites, but the chiefs of the Southern communities, the future governors and judges of the redeemed states, who control the Klan:

> They don't look like Ku-Klux, do they? . . . I don't believe there are a dozen white men on this platform whom I don't know to be such. . . . They are most of them church-members, and all of them respectable. You ought to see them with their gowns and masks on! They look savage enough then. . . . There's right smart of men here who to my knowledge deserve a hanging.[886]

Therefore, in Tourgée's fiction, the Klan is made up of nobility and cruelty, Bourbon and Poor-White, a fusion signaling the total complicity of the Bourbon-controlled Southern community in the horrors committed during redemption and indicating, further, that all classes of anti-radical citizens— lion, wolf and even lamb—were members of the Klan and thereby helping to generate its brutal audacity.

The second and most important constituent of the Bourbons' violence is the audacity with which they brought down the Carpetbagger governments throughout the South. Tourgée sees this as the unique characteristic of the Terror: Verdenton, Yazoo, Baconsville, and Cahatchie are captured by masked and unmasked armies, the radical leaders hunted down and publicly executed; rank-and-file Republicans are seized from among their friends and ostensible neighbors and tortured and assassinated with impunity. This audacity, which may be described as the melodramatic shape of Bourbon violence, appalls Tourgée and identifies for him an essential element of Reconstruction violence. However, it is not so much this factor in itself that is important.

What is important is that such audacity symbolizes in Tourgée's analysis the social power of the Bourbon leadership in Southern society. This, of course, grows directly from the discussion of the first element. The Klan, for example, seized a town like Verdenton without fear of alarm precisely because it is a community-supported organization and can depend on anti-radical citizenry, which is the majority of Southerners, to protect its movement. Anti-radical terrorists can murder a John Walters or an Uncle Jerry with impunity precisely because the non-Klan Bourbons assent to such actions through their support and protection:

> Everything was as still as the grave—no . . . stir about town. It was evident that a great many of the citizens experienced this movement, and were prepared to co-operate with it by manifesting no curiosity, or otherwise endangering its success. . . . Here the town was in the hands of two or three hundred armed and disciplined men, . . . and having friends and co-workers in almost every house, I knew that resistance was useless.[887]

The Bourbons need have no fear of reprisals, legal or otherwise, after such raids—at least on the non-Federal level. As a community-supported organization, the Klan was immune to judicial punishment, not only because of its disguises, but moreso because "so large . . . a proportion of those competent to serve as jurors [on the local level] were quite likely to be *participis criminis*."[888]

Thus the impunity and audacity of the Klan raids as the expression of communal will gradually render the Carpetbagger's position more and more absurd. A bitter persecution descends upon him from invisible foes, increasingly unopposed, save for infrequent rescue by Army and militia. His neighbors, instead of rallying around him with that cooperation Tourgée identifies as the meaning of civilization and social cohesion, assent to his immolation.[889] The codes and rituals of chivalric gentility, defining the meaning of the Bourbon social order, melt away, revealing to the Carpetbagger the permissibility of the mutilation and death:

> Many openly approved the course of the mob; others faintly condemned; and no one took any steps to prevent the consummation of the outrage threatened. No one seems to think that the Fool was entitled to any support or sympathy. That he should sell land to colored men, and assist them to purchase stock, was considered by nearly the entire community as an offense deserving the worst punishment.[890]

Again, the Syndrome accounts for such communal acquiescence, even among those whose morality might have been outraged by Klan atrocities:

> The terrible suppressive power which slavery had exercised over liberty of thought and speech had grown into a habit of mind. Men who for generations had been unable to express their thoughts above a whisper, as to one of the institutions by which they were surrounded, became cautious to the verge of timidity.[891]

Because of this tradition of suppression and mandatory conformity on the question of slavery, Bourbon violence derived its community sanctions from both admiration *and fear*:

> You will find out that this old pro-slavery, aristocratic element don't allow people to differ from them peaceably and quietly. If I were you, I'd be mighty careful who I talked to. You don't know anything about what trouble you may get into any day.[892]

Thus if the community assents to evil out of fear or desire, then the individual toward whom it is directed reaches the ultimate limit of that alienation that defines the absurd condition:

> Some of the most atrocious outrages which even the annals of this modern barbarity can furnish were perpetrated in this

> very county; and yet no word of censure has ever come from the 'people of Verdenton and vicinity.' No meeting of sympathy, . . . no utterance of horror, is heard from ' . . . Verdenton and vicinity,' . . . when men are whipped, women beaten almost to a jelly (white women too), children made imbecile by fright. . . . The scourged and mangled victims had no claim upon your sympathy; but its masked . . . assassins who perpetrated these fearful, bloody deeds—ah— . . . .Whoever speaks of their crimes above a whisper must be 'noticed and condemned.'[893]

Suddenly, it must have become clear to many a Radical faced with the Terror as an act and as a *communal imperative* just how vulnerable they were within the depths of the Garden-Wilderness. Once more Tourgée arrives at the informing thesis that shapes his presentation and analysis of Reconstruction violence. Because the Federal government did not intervene to restore minimal law and order, the Carpetbagger and his cause were lost—since he could expect no help from the normal instruments of law and order in Southern society itself. For whether the Bourbons rode with the Klan or merely protected the operations out of admiration or fear, the commitment to Southern ideology and the interlock of social and political aims was the same. Psycho-culturally speaking, the Southern-dominated community was the Klan, giving in Tourgée's analysis their audacious ruthlessness, their image of invincibility and invisibility:

> They are thoroughly united, and are instinctive, natural rulers. They are not troubled with scruples, nor do they waste their energies upon . . . immaterial issues. . . . The North is disunited: a part will adhere to the South for the sake of power; and, just as before the civil war, the South will again dominate and control the nation.[894]

Yet Tourgée indicates two major weaknesses that a determined North could have used in support of the Radicals to destroy, if not contain, the racist ruthlessness of the White Insurrection. First, there was the danger of loss of confidence. Because of the vast number of men of all classes and types involved in the Terror, there was the statistical probability that one day the oaths that bound them in secrecy would be broken:

> Surrounded year after year by this terrible organization, whose secret blows has fallen upon every side, . . . there had grown up in the minds of these men a conviction that there would . . . come a day when confidence would be lost between the perpetrators of these crimes, and they would turn upon each other, and confess their evil deeds.[895]

One of the forces that realized this fear was the Klan's second weakness: the psychological and moral reality of what might be imprecisely called human decency. Tourgée points out that there were Klansmen who participated in anti-radical atrocities and later suffered a kind of moral revulsion, generated by their sense of decency, which caused them to turn informer. This reality appears in Kirkwood's confession to and disclosure of Klan activities in Verdenton:

> When we got in there, they rode down by the trees nigh the Court-house. I had been feeling mighty bad all the way; and when they halted, and began to make preparations, I rode out toward the Court-House, so as not to see anything more. But I turned around . . . and I saw the face of Uncle Jerry as he hung there on the limb. I've been seeing it ever since, gentlemen.[896]

However, it is the elements of strength rather than of weakness that Tourgée is mainly interested in. In his novels he locates the strength and intensity of Reconstruction violence in three elements: the pervasiveness and persistence of the Klan as a meta-historical reality in all phases of Reconstruction, the kind of men who directed and participated in the Klan, and the audacity of their raids as a symbol of the dynamics of the main aspects of Southern communities. These are the elements that define the nature of anti-radical atrocities at that level below the surface reality of fire and blood. When these two levels—what have been called the narrative and the thematic—combine as they do in Tourgée's major novels, they show the White Terror at once implacable and inexorable.

As to causative factors, Tourgée locates the roots of Reconstruction violence in a familiar complex of rationales and motives: the political, psychological, and cultural aspects of Reconstruction-as-society. This complex incorporates and yet goes beyond those reasons directly attributable to the Irrepressible Conflict. In describing such causation, Tourgée presents both the

Bourbon and Carpetbagger viewpoints.

Of least importance for the Anti-Radicals is, ostensibly, the communal rationale, although the structure and texture of Carpetbagger rule was, for the Bourbon, cause enough for counter-revolutionary atrocities:

> We were rebels in arms: we surrendered, and by the terms of surrender were promised immunity so long as we obeyed the laws. This meant that we should govern ourselves as of old. Instead . . . they put military officers over us; they imposed disabilities on our best . . . ; they liberated our slaves, and gave them power over us. [Then to add insult to injury,] the outcasts of Northern life were sent [South to] induce the former slave to act against his former master. . . .[897]

As a result of this seduction, the Yankees "were give [*sic*] place and power by the votes of slaves and renegades[,]" and proved to be corrupt and incompetent. Yet the Tourgéan Bourbon, curiously enough, dismisses the importance of politics *per se* as part of the rationale of the White Terror: "We did not do these acts of violence from political motives, but only because the parties had made themselves obnoxious."[898]

The other causes, to reiterate, have their roots in the psychic and cultural dimensions of the Southron's "worldview," especially as shaped by the Lost Cause and the plantation *ethos*.

The psychological wounds created by the Lost Cause fed directly into the postwar period like suppurating lesions. There were the memories of the wartime traumas—the painful deprivations and the physical devastation of the last two years of the war, symbolized by the thoroughness and magnitude of the Union victory. To these realities were added the collapse of the myth of the Southron's military invincibility and the sudden destruction of his golden illusions about the permanence of slavery. All these traumas grew out of Appomattox and left a festering wound across the souls of the Bourbons: "Pride the most overweening, and a prejudice of caste the most intense and ineradicable, stimulated by the chagrin of defeat and inflamed by the sense of injustice and oppression—both these lay at the bottom of [redemption]."[899] In this context, Klan terrorism can be envisioned, from a Freudian point of view, as a cauterization of that wound. The ferocity that swept the South with two great bursts of bloodshed (1868-1870; 1874-1876) acts out a wish-fulfillment in which defeat and Reconstruction are undone and the Lost Cause is won.

Interrelated with these psychological motivations are those cultural factors originating long before Appomattox. There is, of course, the violence endemic to slavery (described earlier as the Cult of Violence), which passes unchanged into the Reconstruction. And there is the plantation *ethos* as the sociocultural adjunct to slavery defining the importance of land in the Bourbon's world view. The ownership of broad plantations (like Sutpen's 100 in Faulkner's *Absalom, Absalom*) was the criterion of power in the Southern hierarchy and was, aside from mere skin coloring, the difference between white ex-master and black ex-slave. The redemption of the land as property, as a state-national framework, and as the chief symbol to the Southron of his existence, becomes another key motive of Reconstruction violence:

> [It was necessary to redeem] the land to which they were attached with such unalterable devotion, from the oppression of foes whom they regarded with hereditary contempt and hate. . . . All else could be forgiven and forgotten; all other sins might be condoned. . . . [The desire to liberate the land] gave tone and color to . . . this people, and made that appear . . . insignificant which would otherwise have been counted horrible and atrocious.[900]

The psychological turmoil stimulated by defeat and the cultural attitudes formed by nearly sixty years of indoctrination combine to give to the Bourbon his diabolistic apprehension of the Carpetbagger as a destructive force. In terms of this apprehension, states Tourgée in a sympathetic mood, KK violence ". . . must be counted but as the desperate effort of a proud, brave, and determined people to secure and hold what *they deemed to be their rights*."[901] Psychological and cultural factors once more become the chief non-political motives for that terrifying outpouring of anger and revenge called, in this study, the White Terror:

> The time he had dreaded had come! The smouldering [sic] passion of the South had burst forth at last: For years—ever since the war—prejudice and passion, the sense of insult and oppression had been growing thicker and blacker all over the South. Thunders had rolled over the land. Lightnings had

fringed its edges.[902]

In contrast to such an elaborate rationale, the Carpetbagger sees the primary motive for Reconstruction violence in less complicated, more basic terms. The political, despite the Bourbon's disclaimer, remains the essential cause. In the Carpetbagger's vision of War and Reconstruction, the purpose of the Union's victory was to end the North-South struggle militarily, while the purpose of Reconstruction was to end it civically. Since the Bourbons lost the military round, they turned to the wars of redemption in order to nullify this sociopolitical process. The common motive behind the Klan and its sympathizers was the "subversion of liberty" in order to prevent the exercise of the Radicals' political rights. Klan depredations against these rights became merely a continuation within the former Confederacy itself of the "spirit and essence of the Civil War."[903] All other reasons are mere textural details around this fact. Therefore, within a complex of motives and rationales, the interlocking of apparent causes which, for the Carpetbagger, drove the Bourbon to violence remain the familiar triad—the effect of laws on social conditions, the psychocultural, and the ideological: "It was these things that so blinded the eyes of a whole people that they called this bloody masquerading, this midnight warfare upon the weak, this era of unutterable horror, 'redeeming the South!'"[904]

But Tourgée does not stop here. Bourbon villainy and Carpetbagger folly are the factors *within* the South leading to the midnight warfare. For him, the ultimate source of this violence lies north of the line, in the Northern Republicans' almost brutal complacency toward the difficulties attendant to reconstitution after 1869:

> The nation had looked on with smiling face, and declared the sunshine undimmed. It had taken no note of exasperation and prejudice. It had unconsciously trampled underfoot the passionate pride of a conquered people. It had scorned . . . a sentiment more deeply inwrought than that of caste in the Hindoo breast.[905]

Then after Reconstruction began to falter before The Terror, Northern reaction to Klan violence went, for Tourgée, through stages:

> This new Reign of Terror had come so stilly and quietly upon the world, that none realized its fearfulness and extent. At first it had been a thing of careless laughter to the . . . unsuspecting North, then a matter of contemptuous ridicule, and finally a question of incredulous horror.[906]

Tourgée depicts the first stage in language whose hyperbolic thrust reflects his continuing resentment of Northern complacency and, at the same time, gives the description an incantational quality:

> The old claim of the South, that the colored man could be . . . induced to labor only by the lash or its equivalent, had many believers still, even among the most earnest opponents of slavery, and [many] of these even laughed good-naturedly at the grotesque pictures in illustrated journals of shadowy beings in horrible masks and terrified negroes cowering in the darkness with eyes distended, hair rising in kinky tufts upon their heads, and teeth showing white from ear to ear, evidently clattering like castanets. It was wonderfully funny . . . and it made uproarious mirth in the aristocratic homes of the South. From the banks of the Rio Grande to the waters of the Potomac, the lordly Southron laughed over his glass, laughed on the train, laughed in the street, and laughed under his black cowl of weirdly decorated muslin—not so much at the victims . . . , as at the silly North which was shaking its sides at the mask he wore. It was an era of fun. Everybody laughed. The street gamins imitated the *Kluck*, which gave name to the Klan. It was one of the funniest things the world had ever known.[907]

Later such humor and "contemptuous ridicule" change to incredulous horror: "But, when the cries became so clamorous that they could no longer be ignored, the Wise Men appointed a committee who should investigate the matter, and hear all that could be said both *pro* and *con*."[908]

During the last stage the North's reactions to the reports of murders and beatings were either indifference or the more interesting feeling that the Radicals somehow deserved their fate. This last point is exemplified in *Wild Work* by the Northern Republicans' response to the Cahatchie massacre. First, there is the outrage and a call for an investigation. But then the Republicans delay, feeling that the Bourbon charges against the men might be true—as, states Bryan, such charges had been in the past. To avoid any embarrassment on that score, the Republicans let a jury of Southerners try (and acquit) Alver and his Leaguers. In the end, the Northerners eventually adopt the Bourbon view that the Cahatchie Six must have been guilty of much woe to deserve such pain.[909] Thus, the Northern Liberal Republicans join with their former enemies to condemn their only friends in the South.

This is an important point and deserves reiteration. As Northern moderate opinion moves from outrage against the Bourbon to exasperation with the Radicals, it becomes difficult for the beleaguered Carpetbaggers to receive aid from the Federal government. Where it does intervene, such intervention tends to be ineffective in the long run. A sense of growing public disaffection in significant numbers with the Radical Movement begins to hamper even this limited aid. In the final analysis, the Northern Liberal-Conservative coalition, described in Gore Vidal's modern anti-radical novel, *1876*, lets the Klan win its insurrection, if only to end the eternal agitation south of the line. In Tourgée's analysis the Union defeats the Old South militarily but betrays the New South politically. That the intensity and fervor of the Abolitionist-Unionist coalition should come to this is the painful reality that goads Tourgée on in his continual attacks on "the North" as a Bourbon ally.

> Servosse was ashamed of the halting, shuffling indecision of his own people, and how they had pandered to a sickly sentimentalism, relinquishing therefore the substance of power, betraying and abandoning their allies, and heaping upon them the contempt and shame of the failure which resulted thereby, . . . [Servosse looked with almost pride on those Bourbons] . . . who had thus thwarted and overthrown their conquerors [because they were] born rulers of men, whose empire was not likely to fail from any lack of vigor. He looked forward to see them regaining the proud supremacy of *antebellum* days,—not . . . with satisfaction . . . , but . . . with admiring pride in the capabilities of the [Southern] branch of the American stock.[910]

The question of Northern support of Carpetbagger power is, of course, a complex one. During the high Reconstruction the Carpetbaggers were not so completely powerless against Bourbon counter-revolution as they were later to become. The Carpetbagger was the symbol of that Northern power that had marched through Georgia three years earlier. The memory of the

"Shermanization of the South" laid an oppressive weight over concerted anti-Carpetbagger terrorism:

> And still, out of the two openings in the dark pines upon the other side of the stream, poured the two blue-clad, steel-crowned columns! Still the staff officer shouted the glad tidings, "Lee-surrendered-unconditionally!" Still waved aloft the dispatch! Still the fierce flame raged, and from the column which had gone into the forest beyond came back the solemn chant, which sounded at that moment like the fateful voice of an avenging angel:
>
> "John Brown's body lies a-mouldering in the grave, His soul is marching on!"
>
> One who looked upon the scene thinks of it always when he reads of the last great day—the boundless flame—the fervent heat—the shouts—the thousands like the sands of the sea—all are not to be forgotten until the likeness merges into the dream reality![911]

In the second place the Northern Republicans, Radical and Liberal, gave active, untiring support to their Southern representatives during this period. The idea of the military reoccupation of the South showed revolutionary commitment to making sure that the Confederates understood that they had been defeated. The overthrow of the Johnson plan must be seen as the most radical act of a series of radical acts, using black and white troops to make clear to Southern states that the days of their Black Codes and Klan terror were over and that change was coming. And so we must conclude that through these efforts Federal troops were present throughout the redistricted South as protectors of the reconstitutionists. As a result, the Klan violence of 1868 proved ineffective against the Republican North's determination to put, at least, political power in the hands of its Southern party. The Bourbon's realization of such unstinting support, his memories of Appomattox, the sight of the Bluecoats patrolling his capitals prevented him, initially, from attacking this the chief representative of Union power.

But during the wars of redemption, this support began to disappear. In the myth Grant sends troops hither and yon at the Carpetbagger's whims to quell Bourbon insurrections large and small. In reality Grant's intervention in

Mississippi, North Carolina, South Carolina, and Louisiana became, after the 1872 elections, the exception rather than the rule. Key Northern Republicans began to get weary of the continual cries from embattled Radicals for more troops to protect this small town and to avenge that bloody outrage. Tourgée shows that as military and moral support began to ebb, the Carpetbaggers found themselves more and more powerless and their position at the South more untenable: ". . . and if their master was inherently or accidentally too weak to protect them, or disinclined to compel obedience and respect from the recently vanquished enemy, it was only the fault of their employer, whose service was purely voluntary."[912]

For Tourgée, this abandonment was more than merely the disappearance of the ensigns of power south of the line. It was, instead, an insidious moral and spiritual abandonment or, more precisely, a gradual, startling mutation of "the North" from a supporter of the Carpetbagger to a supporter of his enemy—so that whether he looks within or beyond the South, he saw the face of Bourbon power:

> Perhaps there is no other instance in history in which the conquering power has discredited its own agents . . . , espoused the prejudices of the conquered foes, and poured . . . contempt upon the only class in the South who defended its acts, supported its policy, . . . or desired its preservation and continuance.[913]

In a bitter summation of the meaning of "the North's" betrayal of the Émigré, Tourgée climaxes his attack on the myth of the North's unconditional support of its servant. To give his point more irony, he allows John Burleson, a Klansman, to serve as spokesman:

> Horrible?—it's hellish, Mel . . . ! That's what it is! If I were the Yankees, and had the power of government, I wouldn't see these things go on one hour. By Gad! I'm ashamed of them as Americans! . . .
>
> I told our fellows on the start, they would burn their fingers; for I could not forget that the men they were whipping and hanging were the friends of those same Yankees, that *such* men would suffer them to be abused at that rate. . . . For a time I looked every day for an earthquake, and, when it didn't

> come, I felt an unutterable contempt for the whole Yankee nation; and damn me if I don't feel it yet! I really pity . . . Servosse! He feels ashamed . . . , and knows that even the white [Southern] Republicans . . . despise the whining . . . sycophancy which makes their Northern allies abandon helpless friends to powerful enemies. . . . [If] we Southerners had come out ahead, and had such friends as these niggers and Union men . . . scattered through the North, we would have gone through *hell-fire* before we would have deserted them in this way![914]

The lack of Northern support combines with Klan terrorism to render the Carpetbagger's protective resources "a cumbrous rope of sand[:]"[915]

> Ah! these villains have a terrible sight of crime and agony to answer for. I hear they are raiding all about the country, whipping and mutilating without restraint. . . . Is our government so weak that it can not protect its citizens at home?[916]

For Tourgée the answer is yes, as the Carpetbagger's helplessness makes him an unwitting accomplice in his own destruction, as Northern disunity permits the state capitols to return one by one to Bourbon hands, as one of the Carpetbagger's most important defenses—the support of Northern public opinion—shifts, at the level of appearance, to the side of his enemy:[917]

> I can't understan' it, Colonel. They say our side whipped; that the Union won, an' the Confederacy lost: an' yit here they be a-puttin' it on to me like all possessed day after day, an' abusin' my wife an' children too bad for white folks to hear about, jes cos I was a Union man. There must be some mistake, Colonel, about the matter. Either 'twas the t'other folks that surrendered at Appomattox, or else you an' I was on t'other side, an' hev jes been a-dreamin' that we was Yank an' Union all this time![918]

This betrayal of Northern Yanks and Southern Unionists was in sharp contrast to the united front generated by the Bourbons. Among them there were two groupings: slavocrats before 1800 and those who emerged afterwards, but all mostly united.

In Servosse's eyes Northern perfidy and complacency became the chief cause of Reconstruction violence that subsumes all others, rendering the White Terror at once the most dramatic and the most horrifying dimension of the Reconstruction experience. This defines the moderate North as the enemy against whom the Carpetbagger was struggling all the while.

Thus far, the nature and cause of Reconstruction violence have been seen as derived directly from Southern sociology and indirectly from Northern political strategies during Reconstruction. The *results* of this violence, as a reflection of both its nature and its rationale, also relate directly to Southern society and Northern politics.

First of all, there is in Tourgée's presentation a sense of the Terror's corruption of the Southern community. The Klan remains a befouling of the boasted honor and pride of the Southern patricians. More specifically, Tourgée refers to the way that the Klan degraded its youthful members.[919] This meant that those who had come of age after the rancor of the Intense Decade and the war and who, therefore, offered to the Southern community a generation unburdened by the virus of the Conflict were now to carry that virus into a coming future. Thus, this corruption, aided by legal segregation, generally creates a permanent state of anarchy as a result of the magnitude and intensity of anti-radical atrocities. Terror becomes acceptable as a "meta-legal" device by which a minority (or a majority) can enforce its will on much of Southern life, tolerated by Northern moderates. It must give to the Bourbon of whatever moral restraint, young or old, a sense of the satanic power of violence as the ultimate arbiter of the South's social and political development. Hence, the White Terror was to corrupt and disrupt social restraint, political and due process, and moral behavior in the Southern Garden for generations to come, a fact more dramatically symbolized in the periodic recurrence of the lynch-syndrome years after Reconstruction had ended.

The effect of the wars of redemption on the North's political commitment to the Carpetbagger's cause is another aspect of the violence symbolism. In Tourgée's analysis, this effect is rather complex. It has already been shown how the North responded either inadequately or not at all to the Terror and that this, in turn, helped to stimulate the violence. Here the effort is to pinpoint more specifically the effect on the North as a political ally of the Carpetbagger and as a chief representative of the new Union. To do this, it is necessary to go beyond the scope of Tourgée's analysis to pose the following hypothesis: For whatever reasons—Constitutionalism, Democratic objection, Liberal

Republican indifference—the Federal government permits the use of violence below the line as a form of legitimate political behavior. Such permission may have eventually corrupted the Northern use of legal power during the violence occasioned by the labor struggles of the seventies and eighties—or even much later, the political violence of the Second Reconstruction.

However, it is not these corrupting effects on the North and South, nor the quality of Northern response to the Terror, that are central to Tourgée's analysis. His main concern is with the basic intrasectional result of Reconstruction violence—the violent overthrow of the Carpetbagger and his vision of the Union. This, for Tourgée, is the chief aim and result of the Terror, all with the complicity of Northern moderates—liberal and conservative:

> To Mollie Ainslie the departure was a sad farewell to a life which she had entered upon so full of abounding hope and charity, so full of love for God and man, that she could not believe that all her bright hopes had withered and only ashes remained. The way was dark. The path was hedged up. The South was 'redeemed.'[920]

More specifically, Bourbon violence results in a twofold victory. In the North, Republican leaders feel themselves forced to negotiate a political Appomattox with the Bourbon's *de facto* and *de jure* power. In the South, the Northern Republicans' allies are deposed or contained, exiled, or killed. Bourbons who led the violence, like Alver and his Leaguers, escape punishment under the new rule of "beauty of peace and reconciliation" being "heralded throughout the land":[921]

> Fortunately, the Legislatures of the several states were in session, and most of them passed . . . an act of amnesty and pardon for all who had committed acts of violence in disguise, or at the instigation of any secret organization. . . . [They] pardoned not only the perpetrators of these outrages, but, in a reckless determination to forgive, they even pardoned the victims! [But those governors who tried to suppress the KK during the Terror were gotten rid of.] There are some things which can not be forgiven, even in an era of 'reconciliation!'
>
> So the Ku-Klux was buried, and such is the influence of peace

> and good-will, when united with . . . pardon, that in a twelvemonth it was forgotten, and he who chanced to refer to so old . . . a joke was greeted with the laughter-provoking cry of the 'bloody shirt.'[922]

Extralegal violence, then, ceases throughout the old Confederacy, though it would be revived from time to time to "restrain or punish some daring leader . . . ,"[923] like Chisholm in Mississippi or, more frequently, be revived to execute ex-Freedmen suspected of general and specific crimes against public safety. Thus did the Bourbon victory finally bring his vision of law and order to the reconstructed states:

> The revolution had been inaugurated, and its feasibility demonstrated. . . . The rule of the majorities had been overthrown, the power of the Government boldly defied, and its penalties for crime successfully evaded, . . . the enfranchisement of the colored man [was] rendered a farce, and the obnoxious Amendments and Reconstruction legislation . . . nullified. . . . [The] triumph of the ancient South was incredibly grand; in the then present there was little lacking to give it completeness; in the future—well, that could take care of itself.[924]

The effect of the Bourbon's use of violence is total: on the North and South in general, on Republicans and Democrats, on the course of the nation itself in regard to the Question and the Conflict. By 1885, the mainstream Union had accepted, for all practical purposes, the Bourbon's conception of the failure of so-called Negro freedom and the diabolism of the white traitor who had championed that freedom.[925] For decades to follow, the Southron's rationale would become the morally acceptable view of that reign of blood and fire that marked his resumption of sectional and national power. This was the all-pervasive effect of the Bourbon's skillful use of bloodshed during redemption, and as Servosse himself would agree, "It was a magnificent conception, and, in a sense, deserved success!"[926]

Such a victory in such a manner makes Reconstruction violence more than a simple historical reality. In this analysis, the meaning of this violence is greater than the sum of its nature, cause, and effect. It may be seen instead as an historical phenomenon but whose very virulence gave it a symbolic dimension.

On the first symbolic level, the defeat of the Carpetbagger through midnight warfare stands as a successful attack on the United States by the so-called vanquished South to avenge the humiliations of 1865 and 1868:[927] "It was not the individual negro, scalawag, or carpet-bagger, against whom the blow was directed, but the power—the Government—the idea which they represented."[928] And that was Lincoln's dream of a new birth of freedom.

On a second level, however, one finds a more melodramatic symbology inhering in the ruthlessness of the violence, a ruthlessness finding its clearest articulation in the necromantic imagery with which this ruthlessness was disguised:

> Here and there throughout the South, by a sort of sporadic instinct, bands of ghostly horsemen, in quaint and horrible guise, appeared, and admonished the lazy and trifling of the African race and threatened the vicious. They claimed to . . . be the ghosts of departed Confederates who had come straight from . . . hell to regulate affairs about their former homes.[929]

It was also a ruthlessness masked by ghostly ludicrousness:

> The most vaunted race of warriors seized the cap and bell and stole also the plaudits showered upon the fool. Grave statesmen, reverend divines, legislators, judges, lawyers, generals . . . all who could muster a good horse . . . joined the jolly cavalcade and rollicked through the moonlight night, merely to make fun for their conquerors by playing on the fear of the sable allies of the Northmen. . . . So the North laughed, the South chuckled, and the world wondered.[930]

It is no accident that the Bourbons use such necromantic symbology. Their metaphoric exhumation of the Confederate dead becomes a mirror of the three Souths forming the Wilderness image: the Gothic South of ghosts and phantoms, incubi and succubi, imaged in Reconstruction literature by descriptions of pineries at midnight, solitary "deadenings," and magnolia-drenched cemeteries, a sense of the *Thanatos* of Freudian mythology, the triumph of death over life. Secondly, there is the sadistic South of Simon Legree and Andersonville prison, an eruption from the Southrons' collective unconscious of an ancient atavism, to use the Jungian trope. The description in *A Fool's Errand* of the grotesque but deadly procession of hooded horsemen moving toward Verdenton with their victim lashed to the lead horse hints of an esoteric violence, reflecting rites of blood sacrifice once practiced by the Bourbon's Druid ancestors. The Klan murders become sacrifices to the final symbol, the nostalgic South—the South, according to William Faulkner, the voice of that South, whose eyes were forever to be fixed over its marvelous moment in 1863 at Gettysburg when secessionist generals Stuart, Lee, and Pickett held the destiny of Union and Confederacy in their valorous hands. To this nostalgia the Carpetbagger is immolated.

All aspects of Reconstruction violence are structured around this symbolism: the psychic obliteration of the Spring 1865 and the recreation in its place of a corrupted past—slavery as a John C. Calhoun utopia, if not as a legal reality, then almost religiously as a socio-psychic reality to be sustained by a ghostly confederacy in which the dignity of the Lees is overwhelmed by the barbarity of the Legrees. In this light Tourgée's analysis of Reconstruction violence is an objective critique but also a visionary apprehension of daemonic occurrences. But this symbolism was to become obscured, save among the Carpetbagger and his dwindling friends, by the dream of reconciliation over a new bloody chasm.

In terms of this symbolical exegesis, the problems that reconciliation masks will remain as a source of future violence—if not between the North and South as geopolitical areas, then between civilization and the Wilderness as antagonistic moral polarities. No real solution to this potential for bloodshed will emerge until "the North learns to consider facts, and not to sentimentalize" or until

> the South shall have worked out the problem of race-conflict in her own borders, by the expiration or explosion of a system of unauthorized and illegal serfdom. The lords of the soil are the lords of the labor still, and will so remain until the laborers have grown, through the lapse of generations, either intelligent or desperate.[931]

Violence as a mode of sociopolitical behavior, condoned by Southern culture and tolerated by the indifference of Northern elites, will be the ultimate legacy of the Reconstruction terror. Because of this legacy, the South's ultimate progress will be delayed and its internal social, economic, and political problems exacerbated. Thus from the Bourbon side the Klan triumph is a pyrrhic victory. From the opposing side the Carpetbagger can claim some important moral victories. His sociopolitical programs, as inefficient as they sometimes became, were better in the long run for the ultimate reconstruction of the South than Bourbon violence. Further, it was only through this violence, and not through normal political competition, that he was hounded from office. And while the political Carpetbagger was banished from the Southscape, the hopes he nurtured still remained. Remnants of his educational system, though surrounded by a quiescent foe and only receiving limited Northern and Bourbon support, still survived. In this context of moral and pyrrhic victories, the Carpetbagger, too, achieves a kind of triumph, like a flaming chalice of the future, an eternal flame of freedom in the heart of an immense darkness of failure and defeat, the true ending of the Irrepressible Conflict.

Violence, then, is the clearest expression of the Irrepressible Conflict between the Locomotive and the Garden, giving thematic form to Tourgée's presentation of the Terror and shaping into an ideological whole his analysis of the four elements: its nature, cause, effect, and symbolism. The narrative and rhetorical use of episodes of blood and fire in Reconstruction fiction in general, but in pro-radical fiction in particular, gives to these works an emotional force lacking in the fiction that forgoes this treatment. Thus, anti-radical atrocities have aesthetic as well as thematic value for Reconstruction literature. Thematic importance remains in the forefront; the Bourbon-Carpetbagger antagonism defines the violence, as it defines the importance of Reconstruction fiction in general, even when most victims were black and white Southerners, as depicted in Howard Fast's *Freedom Road*.

The violent conflict between the Bourbon and the Carpetbagger in pro-radical fiction demonstrates that, despite the political and military superiority won at Appomattox and Washington, despite the reconciliation fraternalism preached by the moderates, the North in 1885 still did not culturally dominate the rival country within the borders of the new Union. A sociopolitical chasm still divided the Union along sectional lines. The oligarchic-democratic polarity, which had defined the "international" conflict in political terms and which had created social problems within the reconstructing South itself, still persisted. The South, so goes the pro-radical vision in Tourgée's novels, would be a danger to the Union so long as the psychocultural, ideological, and sociopolitical ideals remained in opposition to Northern civilization. This, then, is the logical structure symbolically "acted out" in the broad range of literary elements describing the issues shaping the Bourbon-Carpetbagger conflict, in which the sociopolitical remains the clearest expression (and hence the operational image) for the struggle between Radical and Anti-Radical, between good and evil. It is the way that this issue is defined by the complex of myths, metaphors, and historical realities of the Irrepressible Conflict that renders the Carpetbagger and Bourbon absolutely incompatible: "We are so different, have been reared under such different influences, and have such different thoughts, that it does not seem as if we should ever get nearer to them."[932]

Perhaps the ultimate source of the conflict lies, in turn, in the way that dialectical materialism shaped that contradictory substance called human nature. The passions of the heart, the commitment of the will, the perceptions and thoughts of the mind—shaped on the Bourbon side by slavery and on the Carpetbagger's side by abolitionism—are the forces that both made and sustained the Conflict:

> It's human nature, and there's no more use of asking questions of human nature than of an owl. 'What' and 'Why' are things that don't concern human nature. It don't care no more for reason than a mule does for persuasion. Human nature is a sullen, obstinate, unreasonable brute; but it always has its own way with on [*sic*] us. . . .[933]

Was this then the enemy against whom the Carpetbagger and the Bourbon were battling all the while?

No! For, within the Reconstruction *agon*, the sociopolitical conflict remains the stubborn simplicity emerging as the force within forces preventing the opposing powers—black and white, Carpetbagger and Bourbon, Machine and Garden, North and South—from peacefully coexisting. For Tourgée and the other pro-radical writers, the Conflict would never end, so long as the "two nations" differed at this ultimate level and, more importantly, so long as they differed fundamentally over the legal definition, political reality, and racial inclusiveness of "human nature": "Ended? . . . It is just begun!"[934]

> The North and the South are . . . convenient names for the distinct . . . irreconcilable ideas,—the civilization. . . . At the North there is . . . more of intellectual arrogance; and we . . . speak of the one as civilization, and of the other as . . .

> barbarism. These two must always be in conflict until the one prevails. . . .To uproot the one, and plant the other in its stead, is not the work of a moment or a day.[935]

In Reconstruction history itself, the struggle is concluded when the two nations are, ostensibly, reunited by the triumph of the Bourbon. In a like manner, most Reconstruction fiction ends with this reunion motif. The general exception to this is pro-radical writing. The literature is not concerned with handclasps across the blood-filled chasm. It so obsessively reiterates the themes of irrepressible antagonisms and irreconcilable differences that they almost become a significant attribute of the genre. Nevertheless, so strong perhaps was the reading public's demand for an aesthetic of reconciliation during the post-redemption period that even some anti-Southron writers managed to bring it in, even if in a low-key manner. Such is the case with Tourgée.[936]

Some literary historians go so far as to call Tourgée an out-and-out reconciliationist. This is only partially true. For example, his fiction is not as aggressively reunionist in tone as *Di Cary* and *The Bloody Chasm*. In these works reconciliation takes place only when the Northern hero submits to Southern indoctrination in order to marry the Belle. When this marriage does occur, it is a symbol of civic harmony. In Tourgée's novels, this symbolism is mute. There is no change of Northerner into Southerner; if anything, it is just the reverse. There has been too much midnight marauding, too much new blood in the chasm, for there to be any facile conjoining of opposing communal ideals (as in "The Valcours," for example). There is then no political reunion in his novels. For Tourgée, tyranny and freedom remain mutually exclusive. Servosse is merely silent about the civic evils of redemption, not reconciled to them. What reunion there is in Tourgée's fiction takes place on either a personal or socioeconomic level.

In the two major novels, there is a brace of intersectional marriage typical of the reconciliationist aesthetic. A Bourbon (Hesden) becomes a Scalawag to win the hand of an idealistic Carpetbagger (Mollie); the daughter of a Radical (Metta Servosse) marries a repentant ex-Klansman, the only son of a redeemer (Mel Gurney). In terms of Tourgée's treatment of the textural details framing these marriages, they do not seem to be synecdoches for North-South harmony but instead remain strictly personal unions.

In the novellas this motif is more pronounced. In "Zouri's Christmas," the Freedmen learn the meaning of real liberty not from some Northern outsider but from the kindly ministrations of their Missie, thus demonstrating the reestablishment of the older patriarchal relation. In "Mamelon," the Machine and the Garden become one, as the North's economic power is shown redeeming the Garden from the blight of slavery and war:

> The ceaseless rumble of the unwearied waterwheel came up from the river bank a mile away, while the glare of the furnace fire upon the opposite hill-side lighted up the cedars of Beaumont. . . . [The] neighboring plantation showed the lack of prosperity. The hedge-rows were upgrown and the ditches clogged. The old South was dying around us. The new South was springing into life about us—the spirit of the North and the manhood of the South its matchless elements.[937]

Thus in these four examples one can see that while there is no triumphant reconciliation between opposing forces in Tourgée's works, there is at least an armistice, enforced by the defeat of the radical cause. Historically, reunion occurs when the two sections achieve certain mutually inclusive victories. The North obtains the presidency; the South wins the state capitols. Further, the redeemers of 1877 are not the same as the arrogant ex-Confederates of 1867; the Hayes Republicans are of a different temper from Stevens and Butler. The North had been able to use Reconstruction to maintain for some fifteen years its wartime hegemony over the Union; the South would be able to use Reconstruction as the satanic image around which it would unify its discordant political elements in a common stance against this hegemony—at least for a while. Later, these tragic victories would find their ultimately sad symbolism in the North's acceptance of the Bourbon's handling of the Question as the method least likely to disrupt the new domestic tranquility.

Thus, historically and literarily, the major phases of the Conflict end when the battle between the two sections reaches an armistice at Wormley House. For the Carpetbagger who had placed his life, honor, and the safety of his family and compatriots on the picket lines, there was little consolation. Among these new irreconcilables, there was, perhaps, only a despairing bitterness, a painful sense of national dishonor, as the spirit of reunion became the dominant mood of the new Union. This is the final vision that pervades pro-radical fiction, despite the reconciliationist aesthetic that qualifies—but only in a halfhearted way—its treatment of the Irrepressible Conflict.

• • •

> Tourgée occupies a unique position among the writers of Reconstruction literature. He was the only Northerner who wrote extensively about the period; the only writer who had lived in the South during the Reconstruction era; and, of greater importance, he was the only author who was an active politician in the carpetbagger regime. His best work has a personal and authoritative spirit that humanizes Reconstruction and forces the reader to share the suffering of all men—Southern as well as Northern—in this tragic era.[938]

Let us now summarize and conclude this study. Tourgée's novels of the First Reconstruction period sum up both the aesthetic and the thematic dimensions related to the use of the Reconstruction-as-ideology in all forms of the fiction. His sociopolitical canon—*A Fool's Errand*, *Bricks Without Straw*, "Mamelon," and "Zouri's Christmas"—makes up the model through which the isolation of the defining attributes and illustrative examples of this fiction has taken place. Such attributes help to differentiate Reconstruction fiction from Southern and Negro fiction. They help to group the novels and short stories into semi-Reconstruction, fable, and sociopolitical modes: for example, *Toinette*, *The Bloody Chasm*, and "Mose Evans" as fable, semi-Reconstruction novel, and sociopolitical fiction, respectively.

Examining the Tourgée canon as sociopolitical, pro-radical fiction is the culmination of this study. On the one hand, his works contain the characteristics that relate anti-radical, neutral, and pro-radical works together as sub-genres. On the other, *A Fool's Errand* and *Bricks Without Straw* are the chief works that demonstrate the contrast between pro-radical fiction and its neutralist and pro-Bourbon counterpart. Both as literature and polemics, his works contain the comprehensive picture of the Carpetbagger's position as a political and moral philosophy. The allegorical strategy typical of pro-radical fiction (and all of the fiction, for that matter) finds its clearest articulation in the didactic and melodramatic richness of his narrative. For example, as in "Ab'm" and "Harcourt V'line Mango," there is the Freedman in his ennobling light. As in *Other Fools*, the Freedman's and Scalawag's unswerving loyalty to the Union's cause is presented as a spiritual resource squandered by the North in the blind quest for reunion with ex-Rebels and Redeemers. Finally, in the sympathetic portrayal of the Carpetbaggers and their cause in all the mutations, Tourgée's works complete the picture given in *A Year of Wreck* of the White Northerner as idealist, economic innovator, political hero, and tragic victim.

In addition to the presentation of the Radical as personae, there are the analyses of sociopolitical ideology in Tourgée's fiction that sum up the thematic interest of the pro-radical allegory. Tourgée alone presents critical analyses of radical ideology and tactics as a primary concern. In his short stories and novels, the sociopolitical *motives* are given their most complete exposition. Of his works, Tourgée's novels and novellas are the best examples of using allegory for such exposition. Freedman, Scalawag, and Carpetbagger become embodiments of moral abstractions, e.g., courageous endurance, steadfast loyalty, and moral idealism. They are characters in a Reconstruction morality play whose theme is the failure of U.S. American transcendentalism. It is through this strategy that Tourgée's works emerge as the chief representatives of the pro-radical position in Reconstruction fiction.

The difference between Tourgée and neutralist fictionists is primarily a matter of tone. In terms of what can be vaguely called a "sociopolitical" aesthetic, Tourgée's works contain that polemic bias and rhetorical excess necessary to the emotional impact of Reconstruction fiction. It is precisely this impact that is muted in neutralist fiction by the subordination of political and social forces to novelistic conventions and reconciliationist demands. Tourgée's polemic fervor invites a more powerful reaction when contrasted with the neutralist decorum of, for example, "The Valcours" and *Kitty's Conquest*.

The contrast of Tourgée's key fiction to anti-radical works is more complex, since they share the same rhetorical aesthetic. Not only are those works different because they espouse opposite positions, but also because in terms of literary and thematic details *Bricks Without Straw* is more objective than "King David," despite Tourgée's biases. Such objectivity can be seen first in the treatment of the Freedman. In "Sambo: A Man and Brother" and "The Call Meeting," the Freedman is at best a Voluntary Slave, at worst a beast. In the canon both Cousin Berry and Eliab Hill are presented, illustrating Freedman vices and virtues respectively. Of course, there is idealization of the ex-slave. Tourgée sees his vices as merely the result of slavery, rather than as acts of immorality. Nevertheless, Tourgée's vision of the Freedman's desire for freedom and his attempt to better himself economically and socially is more balanced than in Woodville's limited vision.

In the treatment of the South and the Southron, Tourgée again demonstrates an awareness of complexity that eludes Baker and Woolson. He recognizes the South's mixing of good and evil: The courage, courtliness, and humanness of the Bourbon, which Servosse grows to respect and admire, are shown combined with the cruelty and terror that mutilated his dreams and hopes. Such interpenetration of good and evil allows a more realistic depiction of the Southern patrician under Reconstruction as Klansman *and* courtier.

The Carpetbagger, too, is given a relatively complex analysis. Tourgée presents Servosse, Mollie, and Dickson as human figures, guilty at worst of the folly of naïve idealism. Further, much of his work is a denunciation of Congressional Reconstruction and a bitter recognition of the weaknesses in the radical cause. Yet here Tourgée's objective treatment is not flawless. There are no depictions of the specific criminal acts that the unscrupulous Carpetbagger did commit. He is shown sinning, all right, but it is the sin of omission and not commission. Still Tourgée's characters remain more humanly complicated than those sleazy cartoon figures found in *Colonel Dunwoddie, Millionaire* and "The Colored Member."

It is, therefore, the wholeness of Tourgée's vision, in spite of his mythic distortions, that makes his four works thematically superior to those of the Anti-Radicals. Indeed, compared to the pro-Bourbon position in Southronist and Reconstruction fiction, his novels and short stories have a refreshing realism. Susan Dewar's unreasoning bitterness about her poverty is much more compelling than Mrs. Dunwoddie's saintly endurance. His vision of slavery and Reconstruction contrasts strongly with the reconciliationist bathos that was submerging the post-reconstitution period with a "torrent of romantic fiction . . . perennial in our day." His description of the ex-slave's appreciation of freedom and yet the difficulties preventing the immediate realization of that freedom comes as a welcome relief to those racist caricatures in Woodville and Baker in which the Freedmen are shown as devotees of slavery, "the miserable victim of emancipation, whom only the kindness of his former master gives any place in society."[939] Thus, as literature, the canon may lack the psychological subtlety of Woolson and the narrative skills of a Bryan, but as sociopolitical fiction these works are compelling examples of the use of the First Reconstruction as event and as experience within a literary framework.

In the third place, Tourgée's key works also conclude the treatment of Reconstruction literature in general, represented here by their relationship to the nonfiction. It is against his novels and short works that the nonfiction acts as the foil. One of the chief values of the travel books and sketches used in Chapter II is that they offer from another genre illumination into the themes of Tourgée's works and that they augment through information and imagery the textural detail surrounding these themes. For example, the descriptive details with black life and manners in *A Fool's Errand*, "Zouri's Christmas," and *Bricks Without Straw* parallel the treatment of Afro-U.S. American sociology in *A Union Officer*, *Afoot and Alone*, and *Yazoo.*

A specific example of this crossover is the use of the "Civil War prison" trope found in a few pro-radical travel books. The following extensive passage is a remarkable parallel to Sidney Andrews' description of the Salisbury camp in North Carolina in *The South since the War*, but the time is now some years later:[940]

> It was a beautiful enclosure. . . . Across it ran a stream, with green banks sloping either way. A single great elm drooped over its bubbling waters. . . . In front, and a little to the right, lay a sleepy Southern town half hidden in the embowering trees. Across the little ravine within the cemetery . . . were the graves, marked, in some cases, by . . . white monuments of polished marble, on which was but the single word, 'unknown.' A few bore the names of those who slept below. But on one side there were five long mounds, stretching away, side by side, as wide as the graves were long, and as long as four score graves. Smoothly rounded from end to end, without a break or a sign, they seemed a fit emblem of silence. . . . Cannon battered and grim, the worn-out dogs of war, gaped with silent jaws up at the silent sky. No name was carved on base or capital, nor on the marble shield upon the shaft [above the long mounds.] Only, 'Sacred to the memory of the unknown hero who died—'
>
> . . . There had been a military prison of the Confederacy just over the hill yonder, where the corn now grew so rank and thick. Twelve thousand men died there and were thrown into

> those long trenches where are now heaped-up mounds that look like giants' graves—not buried one by one . . . but one upon another heaped and piled, until the yawning pit would hold no more. No name was kept, no grave was marked, but in each trench was heaped one undistinguishable mass of dead humanity!
>
> As she wandered back to the town [here referring to Mollie Ainslie], she gleaned from what she had seen a lesson of charity [for the Southrons].
>
> 'It was thus, . . . that they treated brave foemen of their own race . . . who died, not on the battle-field, but of lingering disease in crowded prison pens, in the midst of pleasant homes. . . . None cared enough to give to each a grave. . . . And if they did this to their . . . foeman and kinsmen, . . . why should we wonder that they manifest equal barbarity toward the living freedman—their recent slave, now suddenly exalted. It is the lesson and fruitage of slavery.'[941]

In this context the connection of Tourgée's fiction to nonfictional literature can be seen from a thematic point of view as an articulation of the pro-radical position of Sidney Andrews, Albert T. Morgan, Whitelaw Reid, and John Trowbridge and as a vigorous response to that intensifying anti-radical abuse, originating with James Pike, which was to find its apotheosis in the anonymous "Studies in the South."[942]

Therefore, as pro-radical fiction in particular and Reconstruction literature in general, "Zouri's Christmas," "Mamelon," *Bricks Without Straw*, and *A Fool's Errand* bring into a clear focus that thematic thrust denoting the presence of Reconstruction-as-event in U.S. American literature and demonstrate what is meant by a Reconstruction aesthetic. In terms of his literary output, Tourgée's sociopolitical fiction crystallizes into a clearly apprehensible whole the social and political themes clustering organically around the Conflict and the Question. It is this crystallization that binds the canon to his fables (*Toinette* and *A Royal Gentleman*), his non-Reconstruction historical novel (*Hot Plowshares*), his Negro fiction (*Pactolus Prime*), his Southronist novella ("John Eax"), his apolitical novel (*Figs and Thistles*), and his nonfiction (*An Appeal to Caesar*) and articles in his magazine (*The Continent*). Through all these works, appearing between 1874 and 1890, he covers the chronology of the two great interrelated issues of the U.S. American republic narratively and analytically, from 1848 to 1890. And in this Reconstruction fiction especially, he analyzes, describes, and allegorizes the Freedman-Southron Symbiosis and the Bourbon-Carpetbagger Conflict with obsessive concern, seeking to extract from the flux of their agony principles, insights, and warnings that would be helpful to the evolution of the New Union. Therefore, it is to his works that this treatment of Reconstruction literature has been tending; it is in terms of his vision, codified in these works, that this First Reconstruction has important significance to an understanding of the social, political-economic, and moral dynamics of that period.

• • •

> Popular fiction and the other popular arts have considerable sociological interest in that they illustrate the attitudes and expectations shared by the larger mass audiences. Since they take the form largely of wish-fulfillments, they show what kind of wishes are current in a particular society at a particular period.[943]

What, then, is the literary and historical significance of Tourgée's fiction specifically and Reconstruction literature in general for the students of U.S. American culture? Although these works belong to a minor school, they are, nevertheless, directly related to the 1865-1880 transitional period in U.S. American literature. They use many of the literary devices and aesthetic modes that came to define later literature; they are definitely a part of the proto-realistic development in general and the local color movement in particular. And the references to sexuality and the use of the pungent language of patricians, poor-whites, and poor-blacks make Reconstruction literature a part of greater frankness in U.S. American literature.

The evolution toward U.S. American realism found many avenues of expression. Journalistic essays, political melodrama, and historical romance as well as regionalist writing became caught up in this burgeoning movement. Reconstruction literature, then, demonstrates how when a new literary movement appears, its presence is not signaled by some sudden eruption but is quietly heralded by a broad diversity of instruments, often quite humble and subterranean in relationship to the dominant, older tradition. It is only in retrospect that these phenomena can be seen as a part of an overall thrust of tendencies that shape the character of the new tradition. Realism was such a movement; Reconstruction writing was such a humble instrument.

These works also have socio-historical value. They give to the reader in concrete images contemporaneous accounts of this paradoxical, revolutionary period, a period marking the consummation of a kind of metaphysics of innocence that had, since the first Revolution, shielded the nation from an awareness that here, too, in the Western Garden were evil, violence, and corruption. The myths and accurate depictions, the truth and hallucinations, the valid insights and the biases form a vision of one of those sociopolitical events in the U.S. American experience when, for an instant, idealistic and practical politics merge and threaten to become manifest as an historical reality. It is this vision encompassing the mundane and the momentous that is realized in these half-forgotten works and that, along with Dunningite and Revisionist historiography, helps the student of U.S. American social and literary history to better understand this controversial era, a period that during the 20th century was echoed in a Second Reconstruction (the Civil Rights Movement and the Indiana Peace and Freedom Party/Black Panther Party Rainbow Coalition) and that even now is being echoed in the 21st century in calls for a Third Reconstruction, e.g., Rev. William Barber's *The Third Reconstruction* and Peniel E. Joseph's *The Third Reconstruction*.

Whatever other value Reconstruction literature in general and Tourgée's fiction in particular may possess for the modern reader lies in the unscholarly hinterlands of radical idealism. If there is a universal thrust in a literature of such categorical appeal and of such aesthetic limitations, it is related dialectically to the tension between human's fate and human's hope. In the end, it would be the idealistic hopes of Servosse and Morgan that would survive into the latter half of the 20th century and the first half of the 21st, as sustaining forces, limited and discredited as they were to be in U.S. American historiography—for a while, while the fatal doctrines of Alver and Pike would reach their apotheosis in the death camps of Eastern Europe and the hamlets of South Vietnam.

In the victories of that Second Reconstruction, which extended to North and South alike, it is the Fool's vision that dominated a continuing Irrepressible Conflict between our hopes for a social humanist society and our fate to rise above and temporarily fall beneath recurring spirals of oppressive tyrannies based on class, race, property, and party—until such a society is achieved through, perhaps, multiracial unitarian universalism or its secular equivalent, and with that victory, the end of the Conflict. And so whether he looked north or south, east or west, Tourgée saw the face of Bourbonism.

But until then…:

> Ended? . . . It is just begun! I do not mean the physical tug of war between definitely defined sections. That is a mere incident of a great underlying struggle,—a conflict which is ever going on between two antagonistic ideas. It was like a stream with here and there an angry rapid, before the war; then, for a time, it was like a foaming cascade; and since then it has been the sullen, dark, but deep and quiet whirlpool, which lies below the fall, full of driftwood and shadows, and angry mutterings, and unseen currents, and hidden forces, whose farther course no one can foretell, only that it must go on.[944]
>
> Or more optimistically:
>
> Tis the Final Conflict
> Let each stand in their place
> The multiracial Working Class
> Shall be the human race;
> Tis the Final Conflict
> Let all stand in their place
> The International Working Class
> Shall be the human race

APPENDIX:
UNITARIANS AND UNIVERSALISTS IN THE RECONSTRUCTION PERIOD 1865-1885

UU Reparations You Never Heard About
Wesley V. Hromatko, D.Min.

For former slaves there was aid and some measure of Government reparations from the establishment of the Freedmen's [sic] Bureau and the private and institutional reparations of the Unitarians and Universalists as well as other doners [sic]. The memory of the substantial aid Unitarians and Universalists provided freed slaves following the Civil War even though there were great sacrifices during the war has been largely forgotten.[945]

The Freedmen's Bureau built hospitals and schools and provided food and medical care for former slaves; its biggest success was in education and establishing historically black schools and colleges. Now forgotten and unknown to most people, it really was an effort of restorative justice and reparations. It did not, however, succeed in giving the land of the slave holders to the freed slaves because of President Andrew Johnson's veto.[946] Unitarian and Universalist Volunteers went south to work in the Freedmen's [sic] schools[947] after the war in the time of the first Klan, who were still fighting for the lost cause and its structural racism. It was dangerous to be a teacher in the South, because they were trying to build a new and better educational structure in the South. Even with all the war losses and expense of the Sanitary

Commission, Unitarians and Universalists went south and the AUA contributed as an organization to help those who had been freed.[948]

While it is clear that Universalists as a whole supported every law that would give the freed equality with other citizens, it is much harder than the case of the Unitarians to put a monetary value on their efforts. Funds were collected as well as volunteers, but how much was collected through churches and conventions is hard to know and there is room for more research.[949]

Those who went south to work with the Bureau for former slaves discovered that the education of the white population was often just as bad as for the freed slaves, and they wanted to improve or establish schools for everyone. Universalist Rev. W. N. Van de Mark, former Chaplain of the 92nd U.S. Colored Infantry, became the head administrator of the Freedman's Bureau for Louisiana and was the Superintendent of the New Orleans Negro Schools with 14,000 pupils.[950] Also, Universalists strongly supported the amendments to the Constitution and Civil Rights Act and citizenship. Following the war they volunteered to help with the Freedmen's [sic] Bureaus. W. N. Van de Mark, a Chaplain of the 92nd Colored Infantry, became agent of the Freedman's Bureau of Education in Louisiana. For a time he was superintendent of all the Negro schools in New Orleans with 14,000 students. For the Unitarians Rev. Mayo, for example, worked to improve schools in Cincinnati.[951] As we had for the Union soldiers, we sent boxes of books to schools. The 1868 aid for former slaves from the American Unitarian Association, as an institution, was administered by AME, African Methodist Episcopal, churches just as our Service Committee in our time has worked through local existing organizations. By one measure the value of the aid in today's dollars "...would be the same proportion of output as measured by GDP as $10,730,070.53 is today."[952] The majority of the aid was for what are now traditionally black colleges such as Wilberforce, and Hampton. Professors from Antioch, including President George Hosmer[953] came to teach at Wilberforce.

Years later, Gene Reeves, who was once Meadville President, told me a story about his experience with Wilberforce. As a new Ph.D. he was having a hard time finding a teaching post. Having failed at other colleges, he decided to try to apply to Wilberforce. In the interview he was asked if he was a Unitarian. His heart sank, because the university was A.M.E. He said yes because he was one of us. He was then warmly welcomed by the interviewer, who said that they remembered Unitarians had given them books and professors to start Wilberforce. We had cast our bread upon the waters and it didn't come back soggy.

The Tuskegee Institute on July 4, 1881, and for the first eight years, was given 6,000 dollars a year—or, by the same measure of conversion, $11,274,799.83—by individual Unitarians and churches, but it was not a project of the A.U.A. as the 1868 effort was.[954] The amount from Unitarians then went up to $10,000 a year or to $15,772,550.91 in today's dollars. [955] When the contributions stopped is not known to me. The amounts seem astronomical. If you find errors on my part, let me know. We seem to have been far wealthier than we are today.

To these past efforts must be added those closer to our time. There was the important social settlement movement. In Chicago there was Abraham Lincoln Center, open to all; the Universalist Unity House in Minneapolis,where Henry Fonda worked. He continued to donate for years. Others could be named, like Chicago's Ryder House, which became the Darrow Center in 1960. The Universalist Service Committee aided in desegregation in the Civil Rights years. We cannot forget all the money raised for the now free-standing Chicago Children's Choir, which started in 1956. I have no idea of how much money was raised and spent on these efforts to bring people together. To the total would have to be added the costs of money actually spent in 1968 and the recent 5.3-million-dollar commitment. We have already given reparations; we have only forgotten.

BIBLIOGRAPHY

1. *List of Works Cited*

Reconstruction Nonfiction

Andrews, Sidney. *The South Since the War*. Boston, 1866.

De Forest, John W. *A Union Officer in the Reconstruction.* Edited by James H. Croushore and David M. Potter. New Haven, 1948.

King, Edward. *The Great South: A Record of Journeys*. Hartford, 1875.

Morgan, Albert T. *Yazoo; or On the Picket Line of Freedom in the South.* Washington, D.C., 1884.

Pike, James S. *The Prostrate State: South Carolina under Negro Government.* New York, 1874.

Powers, Stephen. *Afoot and Alone: A Walk from Sea to Sea by the Southern Route*. Hartford, 1872.

Reid, Whitelaw. *After the War: A Southern Tour*. London, 1866.

Somers, Robert. *The Southern States since the War: 1870-1871*. New York, 1871.

"Studies in the South." Parts 1-11. *Atlantic Monthly* XLIX-LI (January-February, May, July-December, 1882; January, 1883), 76 ff., 179 ff., 673ff., 99 ff., 194 ff., 349 ff., 476 ff., 623 ff., 750 ff., 87 ff.

Trowbridge, John T. *A Picture of the Desolated States: and the Works of Restoration.* Hartford, 1868.

Reconstruction Fiction

[Baker, William M.] *Colonel Dunwoddie, Millionaire: A Story of To-Day.* New York, 1878.

[________.] "Little Miss Mouse and Her Marvelous Scholar." *Harper's*, LVII (October, 1878), 770-79.

Baker, William M. "Mose Evans." *Atlantic Monthly*, XXXIII (January-June, 1874), 44 ff., 205 ff., 324 ff., 464 ff., 597 ff., 714 ff.

_________. "Two Couples: A White and Yellow." *Scribner's* XVIII (July, 1879), 375-81.

[Benham, George F.] *A Year of Wreck: A True Story*. New York, 1880.

Bonner, Sherwood. "The Valcours." *Lippincott's* XXVIII (September-December, 1881), 243 ff., 345 ff., 444 ff., 555 ff.

Bryan, Mary E. *Wild Work: The Story of the Red River Tragedy*. New York, 1881.

Davis, Rebecca Harding. "Two Women." *Galaxy*, IX (June 1870), 799-815.

_________. *Waiting for the Verdict*. New York, 1868.

De Forest, John W. *The Bloody Chasm*. New York, 1881.

_________. "The Colored Member." *Galaxy*, XIV (March, 1872), 293-302.

_________. "An Independent Ku-Klux." *Galaxy*, XIII (April, 1872), 480-88.

_________. "Parole d'Honneur." *Harper's*, XXXVI (August, 1868), 372 ff., 483 ff.

_________. *Miss Ravenel's Conversion from Secession to Loyalty*. New York, 1939.

_________. "Rum Creeters Is Women." *Harper's* XXXIV (March, 1867), 484-91.

Deshler, Charles D. "Ab'm: A Glimpse of Modern Dixie." *Harper's*, LVII (September, 1878), 489-95.

Dickinson, Anna E. *What Answer?* Boston, 1868.

Eggleston, George Carey. "My Friend Phil." *Galaxy*, XXI (December, 1875), 737-42.

Flagg, William J. "A Good Investment." *Harper's*, XLIV-XLV (February-September, 1872), 45 ff., 221 ff., 364 ff., 541 ff., 717 ff., 894 ff., 95 ff., and 231 ff.

[Goff, Harriet N. K.] *Other Fools and Their Doing or Life Among the Freedmen*. New York, 1880.

Harland, Marion. The Wall-Flower. *Godey's*, XXXXI (July, 1870), 29 ff., 125 ff.

Harris, Joel C. "Free Joe and the Rest of the World." *Scribner's*, XXIX (November, 1884), 117-23.

King, Charles. *Kitty's Conquest*. Philadelphia, 1892.

Melville, Herman. "Supplement." *Battle-Pieces and Aspects of the War*. Edited by Sidney Kaplan. Gainesville, Fla., 1960.

Palmer, Fanny Purdy. "A Woman." *Galaxy*, II (November, 1866).

Peters, M. Sheffey. "The Barren Ridge of Ridgeway." *Godey's* CV (November, 1882), 411-42.

Pool, Maria Louisa. "Pharaoh's Horses." *Galaxy*, I (July, 1866), 395-407.

Shields, S. A. "Harcourt V'line Mango." *Lippincott's*, XXVIII (July, 1881), 84-89.

_________. "Sambo: A Man and a Brother." *Lippincott's*, XXII (August, 1878), 242-46.

Sikes, W. W. "Absalom Mather." *Harper's*, XXXIII (September, 1866), 463-70.

Spencer, Edward. "Low-Down." *Appleton's*, VIII (August, 1872), 157-60.

Thornton, M. Jacqueline. *Di Cary*. New York, 1879.

Tourgée, Albion W. *Bricks Without Straw*. New York, 1880.

_________. *A Fool's Errand . . . and The Invisible Empire*. New York, 1880.

_________. *A Fool's Errand*. New York, 1879.

_________. *Hot Plowshares*. New York, 1883.

_________. *John Eax and Mamelon or the South without the Shadow*. New York, 1882.

_________. *A Royal Gentleman and Zouri's Christmas*. New York, 1881.

Woolson, Constance Fenimore. *Rodman the Keeper: Southern Sketches*. New York, 1886.

Woodville, Jennie. "The Call Meeting." *Lippincott's*, XXVII (January, 1881), 52-61.

_________. "Dogwood Bitters." *Lippincott's*, XXV (May, 1880), 612-19.

Background to Reconstruction Literature

Secondary Sources

Allen, James S. *Reconstruction: The Battle for Democracy*. New York, 1937.

Beatty, Richmond C.; Bradley, Sculley; Long, H. Hudson. *The American Tradition in Literature*. Rev. ed. 2 vols. New York, 1961.

Becker, George J. "Albion W. Tourgée: Pioneer in Social Criticism." *American Literature*, XIX (November, 1947), 59-72.

Blair, Walter; Hornberger, Theodore; Steward, Randall. *The Literature of the United States*. Rev. ed. 2 vols. Chicago, 1953.

Brogan, D. W. *The American Character*. New York, 1944.

Buckmaster, Henrietta. *Freedom Bound*. New York, 1965.

Carter, Hodding. *The Angry Scar: The Story of Reconstruction*. New York, 1959.

Chase, Richard. *The American Novel and Its Tradition*. London, 1957.

Cohen, Hennig. "Review of the Machine in the Garden . . . [by] Leo Marx." *Saturday Review*, XLVIII (January, 1965), 32.

Morrison, Samuel E.; and Commager, Henry Steele. *The Growth of the American Republic*. 2 vols. New York, 194.

Dibble, Roy F. *Albion W. Tourgée*. New York, 1921.

DuBois, W. E. B. *Black Reconstruction in America*. New York, 1964.

Dunning, William A. *Reconstruction, Political and Economic: 1865-1877*. New York, 1962. (Reprint.)

Fiedler, Leslie. *Love and Death in the American Novel*. New York, 1960.

Franklin, John Hope. *Reconstruction after the Civil War*. Chicago, 1961.

Fulbright, William. "The Uses of Flexibility." *Saturday Review*, XLVIII (May, 1965), 20.

Gianakos, Perry E. "The Spanish-American War and the Double Paradox of the Negro America." *Phylon*, XXVI (Spring, 1965), 34-39.

Gross, Theodore L. *Albion W. Tourgée*. New York, 1963.

Hansen, Harry. "Old Vision of a New South." *Saturday Review*, XLVIII (April, 1965), 42-43.

Henry, Robert Selph. *The Story of Reconstruction*. New York, 1951.

Hesseltine, William B., ed. "Introduction." *The Tragic Conflict: The Civil War and Reconstruction*. New York, 1962, 11-33.

Hubbell, Jay B. *The South in American Literature: 1607-1900*. Durham, N.C., 1954.

James, Henry. "Miss Woolson." *Partial Portraits*. New York, 1899. Pp. 117-92.

Jones, C. H. "Sectional Literature." *Appleton's*. New Series, IX (July, 1880), 563-70.

King, Henry. "A Year of the Exodus in Kansas." *Scribner's Monthly*, XX (June, 1880), 211-18.

Lee (Smith), Rebecca Washington. *The Civil War and Its Aftermath in American Fiction, 1861-1899*. Chicago, 1937.

Logan, Rayford. *The Betrayal of the Negro from Rutherford B. Hayes to Woodrow Wilson*. Enlarged edition. New York, 1965.

Marx, Leo. *The Machine in the Garden: Technology and the Pastoral Ideal in America*. New York, 1964.

Moers, Ellen. "The 'Truth' of Mark Twain." *The New York Review of Books*, V (January, 1966), 10-15.

Nevins, Allan. *The Emergence of Modern America: 1865-1878*. New York, 1935.

"The Other South." *Time*, LXXXV (May, 1965), 48-49.

Quinn, Arthur H. *American Fiction: An Historical and Critical Survey*. New York, 1936.

Runnion, James B. "The Negro Exodus." *The Atlantic Monthly*, XLIV (1879), 222-30.

Simkins, F. B. *A History of the South*. New York, 1953.

"Some Political Novels," *The Atlantic Monthly*, 47 (January, 1881), 119-22.

Spears, Morris E. *The Political Novel: Its Development in England and in America*. New York, 1924.

Stampp, Kenneth. *The Era of Reconstruction: 1865-1877*. New York, 1965.

Steiner, George. "Review of The Machine in the Garden . . . by Leo Marx." *The Reporter*, XXI (December, 1964), 36.

Taylor, William R. *Cavalier and Yankee*. New York, 1961.

Trowbridge, John T. "A Carpet-bagger in Pennsylvania." *Atlantic Monthly*, XXIII (April, 1869), 449-61.

Van Doren, Carl. *The American Novel: 1789-1939*. New York, 1940.

Wilson, Edmund. *Patriotic Gore: Studies in the Literature of the American Civil War*. New York, 1962.

Woodward, C. Vann. *Reunion and Reaction: The Compromise of 1877 and the End of Reconstruction*. Boston, 1951.

2. *List of Works Consulted*

Selected Bibliography—Reconstruction Nonfiction

Cable, George W. "The Freedman's Case in Equity." *Century Magazine*, XXIX (January, 1885), 409-18.

Crayon, Porte. "On Negro Schools." *Harper's*, XLIX (September, 1874), 457-68.

Dennett, John Richard. *The South as It Is: 1865-1866*. Edited by Henry M. Christman. New York, 1965.

Fitzhugh, George. "The Freedman and His Future." *Lippincott's*, IV (October, 1869), 436-39.

G. H. [Fitzhugh, George.] "The Freedman and His Future." *Lippincott's*, V (February, 1870), 191-97.

[Editorial.] *Godey's Lady Book and Magazine*, CVI (June, 1883), 573.

Handy, Mrs. M. F. "On the Tobacco Plantation." *Scribner's* IV (May, 1872; January, 1873), 651 ff., 273 ff.

Hopkins, Isabella T. "In the M. E. African." *Scribner's*, XX (July, 1880), 422-29.

How I Found It North and South. New York, 1880.

Lester, J. C.; and Wilson, D. L. "The Ku Klux Klan." *Century Magazine*, XXVIII (July, 1884), 398-410.

"Moral Significance of the Republican Triumph." *Atlantic Monthly*, XXIII (January, 1869), 124-28.

Pollard, Edward A. "The Negro in the South." *Lippincott's*, V (April, 1870), 383-96.

_________. "The Romance of the Negro." *Galaxy*, XII (October, 1871), 470-78.

_________. "The Virginia Tourist." *Lippincott's*, V (May-June, 1870), 387 ff., 599 ff.

R. P. S. "Revolution at the South." *Lippincott's*, V, (June, 1870), 620 27.

Pyle, Howard. "Chincoteague." *Scribner's* XIII (April, 1877), 737-45.

Rhodes, Albert. "The Louisiana Creoles." *Galaxy*, XVI (August, 1873), 252-60.

Seabrook, E. B. "The Poor Whites of the South." *Galaxy*, IV (October,

1867), 680-90.

"Sketches in Color." *Putnam's*, IV-V (December, 1869; January-March, 1870), 741 ff., 31 ff., 205. Ff.

Stearns, Charles. *The Black Man of the South, and the Rebels*. New York, 1872.

"Symposium: 'The Future of the Negro.'" *North U.S. American Review*, CXXXIX (July, 1884), 78-99.

Webster, Albert Jr. "A Jaunt in the South." *Appleton's*, XI (August-October, 1878), 262 ff., 297 ff., 322 ff.

Webster, Albert F. "Southern Home Politics." *Atlantic Monthly*, XXVI (October, 1875), 464-67.

Woolson, Constance Fenimore "The Ancient City." *Harper's*, L (December, 1874), 1-25.

Southern and Negro Fiction

Baker, William. "Curious Couples." *Lippincott's*, XIX (June, 1877), 751-60.

Bonner, Sherwood. "In Aunt Neely's Cabin." *Lippincott's*, XXI (February, 1878), 245-50.

Davis, Rebecca Harding. "The Colonel's Venture." *Lippincott's*, XXIII (February, 1879), 186-97.

__________. "A Night in the Mountain." *Appleton's*, new series, III (December, 1877), 505-10.

__________. "The Rose of Carolina." *Scribner's*, VIII (October, 1874), 723-26.

__________. "The Yares of Black Mountains." *Lippincott's*, XVI (July, 1875), 35-47.

Epes, Sergeant. "Strategy at the Fireside." *Atlantic Monthly*, XVI (August, 1865), 151-67.

Kellogg, Sarah Winter. "Little Lizay." *Lippincott's*, XX (October, 1877), 442-55.

"My Village in the South." *Lippincott's*, XXIII (March, 1879), 343 ff., 492 ff., 590 ff., 714 ff.

Tourgée, Albion W. *Figs and Thistles*. New York, 1879.

__________. *Pactolus Prime*. New York, 1890.

Woolson, Constance Fenimore. "Up in the Blue Ridge." *Appleton's*, new series, V (August, 1878), 104-25.

Woodville, Jennie. "The 'Death-Rain'" *Lippincott's*, XXIV (May, 1880), 612-19.

_________. "Uncle Pompey's Christmas." *Lippincott's*, XXI (January, 1878), 90-96.

Background to Reconstruction Literature Secondary Sources

Beard, Charles; and Beard, Mary H. *The Rise of American Civilization*. New York, 1936.

Bettersworth, John K.; and Burger, Nash. *South of Appomattox*. New York, 1959.

Canby, Henry Seidel; Johnson, Thomas H.; Spiller, Robert E.; and Thorp, Willard. *Literary History of the United States and Supplement*. 4 vols. New York, 1948.

Cowie, Alexander. *The Rise of the American Novel*. New York, 1948.

Danziger, Marlies K.; and Johnson, W. Stacy. *An Introduction to Literary Criticism*. Boston, 1961.

Dickinson, A. T. Jr. *US Historical Fiction*. New York, 1958.

Franklin, John Hope. *From Slavery to Freedom: A History of American Negroes*. 2d ed. New York, 1956.

H. A. B. "Fiction and Social Science." *Scribner's*, XXIX (November, 1884), 153-55.

Hacker, Louis M.; and Zahler, Helène S. eds. *The Shaping of the American Tradition*. New York, 1947.

Hicks, Granville. *The Great Tradition: An Interpretation of American Literature since the Civil War*. New York, 1933.

Howard, Leon. *Literature and the American Tradition*. Garden City, N.Y., 1960.

Leisy, Ernest E. *The American Historical Novel*. Norman, Okla., 1950.

Morse, James H. "The Native Element in American Fiction since the War." *Scribner's*, XXVI (July, 1883), 362-75.

Olsen, Otto. *Carpetbagger's Crusade: The Life of Albion Winegar Tourgée*.

Baltimore, 1965.
Quilibet, Philip. "Darwinism in Literature." *Galaxy*, XV (May, 1873), 695.
Rozwenck, Edwin C., ed. *Reconstruction in the South*. Boston, 1952.
Schlesinger, Arthur M. *Political and Social Growth of the United States: 1852-1933*. New York, 1934.
Starr, Harris E. "John W. De Forest." *Dictionary of American Biography*. V, 199.
Tourgée, Albion W. "Aaron's Rod in Politics." *The North American Review*, CXXXII (February, 1881), 10-162.
_________. "The Liberal Movement in North Carolina." *The Continent*, II (July, 1882), 57.
Van Cleve, Thomas C. "James Pike." *Dictionary of American Biography*. XIV, 595-96.
Wann, Louis, ed. *The Rise of Realism: American Literature from 1860 to 1900*. Rev. ed. New York, 1949.

RECENT WORKS CONSULTED AS OF 2023

Barber, William, *The Third Reconstruction*: a call for the kind of multiracial unity reflected in the two preceding periods of Reconstruction, but with an emphasis on coalitions rather than a unitary organization.

Challenge-Desafio, "Black Reconstruction": an essay based on a misreading of Du Bois' *Black Reconstruction*, using the concepts from the Afro-centric neo-racist doctrine of decentering whiteness, rejects the leadership role of the Carpetbagger and white Radicals in general in the First Reconstruction.

Faulkner, William, *Absalom Absalom* (a novel): deals with the negative effects of negrophobic racism on a powerful Slavocratic family as seen in the symbology of an Afro-Saxon, Charles Bon, the son of the lead white character, one Thomas Sutpen.

Foley, Barbara. *Marxist Literary Criticism Today*: mainly used to justify my theme and variation approach to Reconstruction literature, especially the idea of going deep into the text to recover its political ideological elements.

Foner, Eric. *Reconstruction: America's Unfinished Revolution, 1863-1877*: best of the post-John Hope Franklin Revisionists, and *The Second Founding*, a brilliant explication of the impact of the Americanization amendments on U.S. Constitutional history, especially their contradictory role in buttressing Lincoln's call for a new birth of freedom.

Peniel, Joseph, *The Third Reconstruction*, another work in the decentering whiteness movement as related to the First and Second Reconstruction seen in his call for a Third Reconstruction to be based on the Black Lives Matter movement as a mono-racial reality.

Vidal, Gore, *1876 (A Novel)*: "The political backdrop to the story is the 1876 presidential election, a close contest between Tilden and the Republican Rutherford B. Hayes. Tilden won the popular vote, but there was a dispute over the results in Louisiana, Oregon, South Carolina, and Florida. In Florida, the Republican leaders of the State and the Electoral Commission initially reported a victory for Tilden, before deciding that in fact Hayes had won. Vidal builds up to this historic crisis through the activities of a mixed cast of historical and fictional characters. Vidal also describes sympathetically the support for Redemptionist movement as a reform movement among Northern liberals and conservatives in the upper class, thereby revealing his anti-radical bias."

AUTHORS INDEX

A note on the Index for this edition of the book: I have chosen to use a selective Authors Index divided into nonfiction books and fiction texts. The second edition will make use of traditional indexing. I thank you for your patience.

Nonfiction

Pike, James S. *The Prostrate State.* Bourbons under reconstitution, page 38; South Carolina under Radical Reconstruction, page 40; calls for redemption, page 40-41

Powers, Stephen. *Afoot and Alone.* South as wilderness, page 6; suffering of the Freedmen, page 48-49.

Reid, Whitelaw. *After the War: A Southern Tour* South as wilderness, page 5; Taboo Conjunction, page 21; racio-sexuality and incest, page 21; Afro-Saxons, pages 22, 47; Freedman power, page 35; physical ruins of the war, page 35; need for reconstitution, page 37; rise of the Scalawags, page 42; distinctions within the Freedmen as a class, page 44; wealthy Freedman, page 45; multiracial nature of the Freedmen, page 47-48; the genocidal impulse, page 49; Freedmen poverty, page 49; Freedmen ignorance, page 50; the Slavery Syndrome, page 51; the Freedmen's need for land, page 51; creating a legal Freedmen family, page 52; Freedman school, page 53; sharecropping, page 54; Freedman and the wage system, page 56; free-labor system, page 57; restraining genocidal violence, page 62; genocidal violence, page 63; natural symbolism indicating Bourbon decadence, page 73.

Somers, Robert. *The Southern States since the War: 1870-1871* the South as the Garden, page 7; Bourbon virtues, page 16.

Trowbridge, John T. *A Picture of the Desolated States: and the Works of Restoration* Afro-Saxons as slaves, page 22.

Fiction

Baker, William M. "Little Miss Mouse and Her Marvelous Scholar," 132-135, 314 "Mose Evans," 64, 130-132, 133-135, 250, 306, 381 "Two Couples: A White and Yellow," 154-156 *Colonel Dunwoddie, Millionaire*, 3, 11-12, 85, 93, 132, 137-152, 153-156, 232, 265, 282, 323, 333, 352, 384

Benham, George F. *A Year of Wreck*, 164, 240-256, 258, 269, 281, 326, 352, 383

Bonner, Sherwood *The Valcours*, 11-12, 211-215, 221, 380, 383

Bryan, Mary E. *Wild Work: The Story of the Red River Massacre*, 184-211, 221, 229, 282, 352, 354, 355, 368

Davis, Rebecca Harding "Two Women," 86-87 *Waiting for the Verdict*, 14,46, 94, 97-110, 115, 197

END NOTES

[1] The geographical area covered will be only those Southern states that existed immediately before the Missouri Compromise (1820-21): Virginia, Tennessee, North Carolina, South Carolina, Georgia, Alabama, Louisiana, Mississippi, and the Florida territory. Kentucky, Maryland, and West Virginia are not included because they did not undergo the Reconstruction experience; Arkansas, Missouri, and Texas are excluded because they are more Southwestern than "deep" Southern.

[2] So spoke Stephen Vincent Benet: Samuel E. Morison and Henry Steel Commager, *The Growth of the American Republic* (New York, 1942), I, 736.

[3] So spoke James M. Mason, *Ibid.*, p. 652.

[4] Edmund Wilson, *Patriotic Gore: Studies in the Literature of the American Civil War* (New York), 1962, p. xv.

[5] Hodding Carter, *The Angry Scar: The Story of Reconstruction* (New York, 1959), p. 399.

[6] William B. Hesseltine, ed., "Introduction," *The Tragic Conflict: The Civil War and Reconstruction* (New York, 1962), p. 13.

[7] Hennig Cohen, "Review of *The Machine in the Garden* . . . by Leo Marx," *Saturday Review*, XLVIII (January 16, 1965), 32.

[8] In Marx' work, it is a general rather than a sectional conflict.

[9] Leo Marx, *The Machine in the Garden: Technology and the Pastoral Ideal in America* (New York, 1964), p. 26.

[10] *Ibid.*, p. 343. This is a subsidiary theme in Tourgée's non-Reconstruction work *Hot Plowshares*.

[11] [William Baker], *Colonel Dunwoddie, Millionaire: A Story of To-Day* (New York, 1878), p. 101.

[12] Marx, pp. 216-19.

[13] Albion Tourgée, "Mamelon," *John Eax and Mamelon*, or *The South Without Shadow* (New York: Fords, Howard, and Hulberts, 1882), p. 233. Hereafter cited as "Mamelon," unless a specific reference to "John Eax" is required.

[14] Marx, pp. 191, 192, 214.

[15] William R. Taylor, *Cavalier and Yankee* (New York, 1961), p. 259.

[16] Marx, pp. 23, 15.

[17] M. Jacqueline Thornton, *Di Cary* (New York, 1879), p. 50. However, the antebellum South did permit one machine in the Garden, the steamboat, but as an organic part of the pastoral texture of the South because of its dependence on the Southern rivers.

[18] Henry Nash Smith, *Virgin Land: The American West as Symbol and Myth* (Cambridge, Mass., 1950), p. 123.

[19] Marx, pp. 28, 143.

[20] Whitelaw Reid, *After the War: A Southern Tour* (London, 1866), pp. 492-93.

[21] De Forest's *Kate Beaumont* (1872) is an example of an objective treatment of these virtues.

[22] Edward King, *The Great South* (Hartford, 1875), p. 85. For more of the same see pp. 86-87.

[23] Stephen Powers, *Afoot and Alone: A Walk from Sea to Sea by the Southern Route* (Hartford, Conn., 1872), p. 98.

[24] Robert Somers, *The Southern States Since the War: 1870-71* (New York, 1871), p. 268.

[25] George Steiner, "Review of *The Machine and the Garden . . .* by Leo Marx," *The Reporter*, XXXI (December 31, 1964), 36.

[26] It might be argued that this analysis has viewed the North as one vast roundhouse and the South as a machineless, farming community. Such an obvious exaggeration was useful only in exploring the polarity involved in the antithesis, agrarianism versus industrialism. Moreover, it was a method helpful in presenting the archetypal conflict intrinsic in this antithesis, a conflict that symbolizes the cultural and historical struggle between the North and the South. Finally, that the Garden image would persist as a peculiar Southern appropriation is seen in the Southern Fugitive Movement. See Steiner, p. 36.

[27] The basis of this discussion is Taylor's *Cavalier and Yankee*.

[28] Since the emphasis in this research is on the reconstructing South, there is no need to give a detailed analysis of the North, except where such an analysis will help to define the clash with the South. By describing the Cavalier society, we indicate not only what the North was not, but what it preferred not to be.

[29] William Fulbright, "The Uses of Flexibility," *Saturday Review*, XLVIII (May 8, 1965), 20.

[30] Taylor, p. 133.

[31] Cf., "The Other South," *Time*, LXXXV (May 7, 1965), 49. Here we get a glimpse of the factual insufficiency of the South's cultural myths. But in this discussion, we see the Cavalier society as the fusion of its realities and its mythology. And while the mores and traditions forming the culture of this society are often surrealistic phenomena, they are often more important than the concrete sociocultural facts. The myths of the Cavalier become collective names for the mores and traditions identifying the Southerners' society. That this society was also involved in realities that contradicted its pretensions does not diminish the sociocultural vitality of its myths.

[32] See Wilson, p. 439; also Morison, I, 546.

[33] In a sense, Scott became the poet laureate to the Southron's nostalgic temperament at a time when his society was feeling more and more besieged. See Morison, I., 546. Even the term "Southron" is derived from Scott's novels of the Scottish border.

[34] Taylor, p. 183.

[35] *Colonel Dunwoddie, Millionaire*, pp. 121, 109-10.

[36] Sherwood Bonner, "The Valcours," *Lippincott's*, XXVIII (September–December, 1881), 251-52.

[37] Albion Tourgée, *Bricks without Straw* (New York, 1880), p. 442.

[38] Tourgée, *John Eax*, pp. 71-73.

[39] Taylor, p. 164.

[40] Cf. Carter, p. 399.

[41] Rebecca Harding Davis, *Waiting for the Verdict* (New York, 1868), p. 248.

[42] *The Other South*, p. 49.

[43] See Taylor, 317.

[44] *Ibid.*, p. 97.

[45] Somers, p. 112.

[46] Wilson, pp. 615-16.

[47] Marx, pp. 330-31.

[48] Cf. Morison, I, 544; Wilson, p. 390.

[49] See Morison, I, 632.

[50] Wilson, p. 293.

[51] Morison, I. 538.

[52] Carter, p. 297.
[53] In most cases in U.S. American literature, the "black" mistress is usually a fair-skinned slave.
[54] See Taylor, p. 169.
[55] Carter, p. 399.
[56] Reid, in the notes, p. 282.
[57] John W. De Forest, *A Union Officer in the Reconstruction*, ed. James H. Croushore and David M. Potter (New Haven, 1948), pp. 73, 4, 132.
[58] Reid, p. 282.
[59] Wilson, p. 290.
[60] Reid, p. 243.
[61] John T. Trowbridge, *A Picture of the Desolated States; and the Work of Restoration* (Hartford, Conn., 1868), p. 183.
[62] See Leslie Fiedler, *Love and Death in the American Novel* (New York, 1960), p. 381.
[63] Fiedler's term. For his full discussion, see Ibid., pp. 381-82.
[64] Wilson, p. 292.
[65] See Taylor, p. 18.
[66] Cf. *Ibid.*, p. 324.
[67] Carter, pp. 29-30.
[68] Margaret Leech, *Reveille in Washington: 1860-1865*, Time Reading Program edition (New York, 1962), p. 2.
[69] See Wilson, p. 423.
[70] Leech, pp. 26, 515, 37.
[71] Morison, I., 648.
[72] Because much of the literature of Reconstruction emphasizes the sectional conflict, this introduction has been built around an analysis of the kind of struggles that are explicitly or implicitly present in these works. However, some of the authors—De Forest, King, Woolson—emphasize the resolution of the conflict through reconciliation and remind us that, after all, the two sections had much actual unity. This is historically true. It was this sense of community that enabled the rebellion to come to an end without a long, drawn-out war of attrition and that enabled the agreement of '77 to be reached.

There were the cohesion of national political parties (*Ibid.*, p. 551), the interdependence of economic interest, the shared Protestant theology, the similarity of Anglo-Saxon traditions and political values, the participation in the same aesthetic traditions, and the surprisingly widespread feeling of Unionism in some areas of the South (Taylor, pp. 335, 16, 17). The myths celebrate total separation; the reality shows more unity than each side could have seen in 1860 or in 1865. But as with all myths, there is a core of truth in the vision of the two antithetical societies (Hesseltine, p. 17).
[73] Henrietta Buckmaster, *Freedom Bound* (New York, 1965), p. 3.
[74] John Hope Franklin, *Reconstruction after the Civil War* (Chicago, 1961), p. viii.
[75] D. W. Brogan, *The American Character* (New York, 1944), p. 113. This position finds its clearest expression in William A. Dunning's *Reconstruction, Political and Economic: 1865-1877*, Harper Torch book reprint (New York, 1962).
[76] See Kenneth M. Stampp, *The Era of Reconstruction, 1865-1877* (New York, 1965), pp. 3-7.
[77] Cf. Harry Hansen, "Old Vision of a New South," *Saturday Review*, XLVIII (April 10, 1965), 42. Also see Stampp, pp. 18-20.
[78] See Hansen, p. 42.
[79] See Franklin, p. 231.
[80] Cf. Stampp, p. 11.
[81] Here is a table presenting the works in terms of their historical chronology and

political allegiances:
1865: *The South since the War* (pro-radical)
1865-1866: *After the War* (pro-radical)
1865-1868: *The Desolated States* (pro-radical)
1866-1868: *A Union Officer* (anti-radical)
1868: *Afoot and Alone* (neutral)
1870-1871: *The Southern States* (anti-radical)
1872-1873: *The Great South* (anti-radical)
1873: *The Prostrate State* (anti-radical)
1865-1875: *Yazoo* (pro-radical)
1882: "Studies in the South" (anti-radical)

82 Cf. Franklin, p. vii.

83 Cf. Stampp, pp. 44-47, 51, 64.

84 Albion Tourgée, *A Fool's Errand and the Invisible Empire* (New York, 1880), p. 393. Henceforth cited as *A Fool's Errand* (1880).

85 See Franklin, p. 229.

86 Cf. James S. Allen, *Reconstruction: The Battle for Democracy* (New York, 1937), p. 106.

87 Stevens had died in 1868 before he saw the fruits of his labors harvested.

88 The most comprehensive account of the election, the issues, and the resulting compromise is Vann Woodward's *Reunion and Reaction* (1951).

89 The etymology of these names may be of some interest. "Scalawag" derives from "Scalaway," a term denoting a filthy sheep, cow, or hog. "Freedman" was a euphemism that sought to remove racial labelling from the former Negro slave, to describe his new status between citizenship and slavery, and to differentiate the term from "free man," the epithet usually applied to the white U.S. American citizen. The word "Bourbon" was applied by the *New York Herald* to the anti-radical planter class to identify them with the doomed French dynasty, which "had never learned anything or forgotten anything" (Carter, *The Angry Scar*, p. 346). And, of course, "Carpetbagger" referred to the legend that all the Northern émigrés came into the South with nothing but large cloth-covered valises called carpetbags. Tourgée gives a more elaborate analysis of this term, an analysis to be presented later.

90 Dunning, p. 86.

91 Sidney Andrews, *The South since the War* (Boston, 1866), p. 1.

92 See Allan Nevins, *The Emergence of Modern America: 1865-1878* (New York, 1935), p. 6.

93 See Morison, II, 13.

94 De Forest, *A Union Officer*, p. 66.

95 *Ibid.*, p. 66.

96 *Ibid.*, p. 561.

97 Reid, pp. 425-26.

98 Cf. Carter, pp. 23-24, 236.

99 Reid, p. 68.

100 *A Union Officer*, p. 198.

101 Franklin, p. 43.

102 *A Union Officer*, pp. 28-29.

103 Albert Morgan, *Yazoo: or on the Picket Line of Freedom in the South* (Washington, D.C., 1884), p. 274.

104 Reid, p. 297.

105 Morgan, pp. 328-29.

106 King, *The Great South*, p. 431.

107 James S. Pike, *The Prostrate States: South Carolina under Negro Government* (New

York, 1874), pp. 13-14.

108 Cf. *A Union Solider*, p. 195.

109 King, pp. 673-74.

110 Morgan, pp. 210-11.

111 Pike, p. 12.

112 *Ibid.*, pp. 56-57.

113 *Ibid.*, p. 60.

114 "Studies in the South," parts 5 and 6, *The Atlantic Monthly*, L (July-August, 1882), 109, 204-5, 201.

115 *Ibid.*, part 3, XL (May, 1882), 677.

116 *A Union Officer*, p. 203.

117 *Ibid.*, p. 172.

118 Reid, p. 266.

119 Morison, II, 49.

120 *A Union Officer*, p. 55.

121 King, p. 789.

122 Reid, p. 55.

123 King, p. 429.

124 Cf. Morgan, p. 45.

125 Reid, pp. 183-84.

126 *A Union Officer*, p. 121.

127 Morgan, p. 51.

128 Albion Tourgée, *Hot Plowshares* (New York, 1883), p. 464-65.

129 The best treatment of this theme is Twain's *Pudd'nhead Wilson* (1894). In a sense, Twain's work can be seen as a parable on the failure of Reconstruction. Despite all the training and advantages the Afro-Saxon villain has had from infancy, he still retains, genetically, the vices of a slave. One might even argue that Twain's attitude here may reflect anti-racial leanings and that while he might have favored the emancipation of a Jim, he did not favor his reconstruction at the expense of the cultural values of the white South. (Cf. Ellen Moers, "The 'Truth' of Mark Twain," *The New York Review of Books*, V (January 20, 1966), 14.)

130 Reid, p. 245.

131 *Ibid.*, 243.

132 *Ibid.*, p. 81.

133 Powers, pp. 100-1.

134 *Ibid.*, p. 100.

135 King, p. 598.

136 Reid, p. 456.

137 *Ibid.*, p. 293.

138 King, pp. 790-91.

139 Reid, pp. 369-71.

140 Morgan, p. 358.

141 King, p. 781.

142 It is interesting to note the literary handling of these defects of Negro life. The nonfiction writers are cushioned against the shock of unadulterated *négritude* by the romantic circumstances that surrounded the Freedmen. These circumstances are based on the fact that, despite the U.S. Americanizing process even before the war, the ex-slave still carried the exoticness of the African. He was still freighted with those picturesque and comic characteristics acquired through nearly fifty years of mythologizing. This freight forms special psychocultural associations in the Northern mind and, therefore, originates the nonfiction writers' apprehension of the ex-slave as a local color object. Even Pike's horror of black tyrants contains both moral outrage and the colorist's fascination with a sectional peculiarity. The result

in Reconstruction literature is a discernible aesthetic tension between the realities of the Freedmen's existence and the blurring exoticism of his "African" past; between the writers' desires to see the Freedman Victorianized and their fascination with the literary values surrounding his pre-Victorian state.

[143] Reid, p. 107.

[144] King, p. 341.

[145] Reid, p. 59.

[146] *Ibid.*, p. 126.

[147] *A Union Officer*, pp. 56-57.

[148] Morgan, p. 274.

[149] Reid, pp. 256-57.

[150] *A Union Officer*, p. 117.

[151] King, p. 554.

[152] *Ibid.*, pp. 52, 54.

[153] Reid, pp. 501-2.

[154] *Ibid.*, 525-29.

[155] *Ibid.*, pp. 496-97.

[156] Morgan, p. 425.

[157] Pike, p. 15.

[158] Morgan, p. 435.

[159] King, p. 291.

[160] *Ibid.*, p. 297.

[161] It is not necessary to point out in detail that the Symbiosis has been implicit in our discussion of the Freedman. See also the preliminary discussion in Chapter I.

[162] King, p. 290.

[163] Cf. *A Union Officer*, p. 101; Morgan pp. 60-61, 448.

[164] *A Union Soldier*, pp. 73-74.

[165] *Ibid.*, p. 110. Reid also believed that some reports of atrocities were exaggerated. Commenting on "bloody shirt" outrages in the Delta, Reid asserted that even "in Mississippi murder is not practiced with as much safety as the other fine arts. . . ." Reid, p. 418.

[166] Cf. *Ibid.*

[167] King, p. 779.

[168] *Ibid.*, pp. 778-79.

[169] Reid, pp. 418.

[170] *Ibid.*, p. 420.

[171] Morgan, p. 121.

[172] Reid, pp. 52, 352.

[173] Morgan, pp. 31-32.

[174] Reid, pp. 386-87.

[175] Morgan, p. 111.

[176] In *Wild Work*, *Other Fools*, and *Yazoo*, this is the rationale for the overthrow and massacre of the Radicals.

[177] Morgan, p. 274.

[178] Reid, p. 51.

[179] Cf. Morgan, pp. 318-19. "The shifting color line," states Morgan in an aside, "proved a great blessing, I'm certain, to several of the most hightoned and honorable ladies and gentlemen in Yazoo" (p. 318). That some of the anti-radical Bourbons were of Negro descent is an irony not lost on Morgan's sardonic sense of humor.

[180] *Ibid.*, p. 322.

[181] *Ibid.*, pp. 433 ff.

[182] *Ibid.*, pp. 434-35.

[183] *Ibid.*, pp. 85-89.

[184] The Revolution accomplished other things in this area. It allowed those planters of conscience and love to legitimize their offsprings and to provide for their legal inheritance, acts forbidden under the old constitution. *Ibid.*, p. 344.

[185] Morgan's allusion to the Freedwoman's "dissolute mistresses" is rather unorthodox for his period.

[186] *Ibid.*, p. 321.

[187] *Ibid.*, p. 274.

[188] *Ibid.*, p. 321.

[189] *Ibid.*, pp. 361-63.

[190] *Ibid.*, p. 358.

[191] *Ibid.*, p. 446.

[192] *Ibid.*, p. 511.

[193] *Ibid.*, pp. 349, 511.

[194] *Ibid.*, pp. 455-56.

[195] Eldridge Cleaver's discussion of the Black Sex-Machine is a more recent "black power" treatment of this myth in *Soul on Ice*.

[196] Morgan, p. 510.

[197] *Ibid.*, p. 322.

[198] Reid, pp. 140-41. While the immediate idea is the military destruction that slavery brought on the South, the richness of the texture suggests a vast range of corruption and destructiveness wrought by the peculiar institution: the Cult of Violence and Racio-sexuality, the inordinate pride and stubbornness of the protectors of the Southern way of life. And the juxtaposition of sturdy oaks and the ever-present moss suggests the ambiguity of the Bourbons, whose virtues as Cavalier were so entangled with their racism as slave masters.

[199] Carter, p. 165.

[200] Morgan, pp. 317-18.

[201] Franklin, p. 198.

[202] See Carter, p. 313.

[203] Hesseltine, p. 321.

[204] Robert S. Henry, *The Story of Reconstruction* (New York, 1951), pp. 587-88.

[205] Cf. Stampp, p 188.

[206] Cf. Franklin, p. 219.

[207] Buckmaster, p. 176.

[208] Richard Chase, *The American Novel and Its Tradition* (London, 1957), p. viii.

[209] *A Fool's Errand*, p. 324.

[210] R. G. Beatty, et al., *The American Tradition in Literature* (rev. ed.; New York, 1961), II, 5-7.

[211] Walter Blair, et al., *The Literature of the United States* (rev. ed.; Chicago, 1953), p. 102.

[212] Beatty, et al., p. 13.

[213] Carl Van Doren, *The American Novel: 1789-1939* (New York, 1940), p. 225.

[214] *Godey's Lady Book and Magazine*, CVI (June, 1883), 573.

[215] Cf. Van Doren, p. 204.

[216] Edward Spencer, "Low-Down," *Appleton's*, VIII (August, 1872), 157, 159.

[217] Mrs. W. H. Palmer, "A Woman," *Galaxy*, II (November 1, 1866), 413.

[218] Jay B. Hubbell, *The South in American Literature: 1607-1900* (Durham, N.C., 1954), p. 733.

[219] Cf. Taylor, *Cavalier and Yankee*, pp. 302, 304.

[220] See Rebecca Washington Lee (Smith), "The Civil War and Its Aftermath in American Fiction, 1861-1899 (unpublished dissertation, Chicago, 1937), p. 42.

[221] Theodore L. Gross, *Albion W. Tourgée* (New York, 1963), p. 8.

[222] *Galaxy*, IX (June, 1870), 804-5.
[223] *Ibid.*, pp. 807, 809.
[224] *Ibid.*, p. 813.
[225] William J. Flagg, "A Good Investment," *Harper's*, XLIV-XLV (February-September, 1872), 722.
[226] *Ibid.*, p. 367.
[227] *Ibid.*
[228] *Ibid.*, p. 901.
[229] Thornton, *Di Cary*, p. 226.
[230] *Ibid.*, p. 145.
[231] *Ibid.*, p. 29.
[232] John W. De Forest, *The Bloody Chasm* (New York, 1881), p. 23.
[233] *Ibid.*, p. 298.
[234] The contrast between her ineffectual ex-Confederate father and her own success hints also of the feminist revolution of the period.
[235] This parallels the discovery of a corundum deposit in Tourgée's "Mamelon."
[236] John W. De Forest, *Miss Ravenel's Conversion from Secession to Loyalty* (New York, 1932), p. 225.
[237] *Ibid.*, p. 237.
[238] *Ibid.*, p. 242.
[239] *Ibid.*
[240] *Ibid.*, p. 219.
[241] *Ibid.*, p. 220.
[242] *Ibid.*, p. 225.
[243] *Ibid.*, p. 219.
[244] One might argue here that Ravenel is more of a paternalist than a true Radical.
[245] De Forest's vision of the Freedman is quite generous in *Miss Ravenel's Conversion* and in *A Union Officer*. In "A Colored Member" (to be discussed later), he opens up a box of racist insults and virulently attacks the Negro as a racial type. Such attacks are surprising in contrast to his charity in these earlier works. But by 1874 much of the charity for the Freedman, especially with the reports of black misrule emanating from the anti-Reconstruction press, had evaporated. In a sense, so long as the Freedman was still a ward of the North (Ravenel and the Bureau) and not yet a complete citizen, he was more acceptable. The Negro's sudden elevation to citizenship and political equality could have been unacceptable to De Forest. This is reflected in Ravenel's insistence that the ex-slave must be civilized before he can become a free man.
[246] Cf. *Miss Ravenel's Conversion*, pp. 157-60.
[247] The siege of Ravenel's plantation by guerillas foreshadows the KK raids throughout Reconstruction fiction. And all such raids are literary descendants of those Indian attacks in Cooper, Simms, *et al.*
[248] *Miss Ravenel's Conversion*, p. 448.
[249] It appeared in book form a year later.
[250] Davis, *Waiting for the Verdict*, pp. 11-12, 27.
[251] *Ibid.*, p. 5.
[252] *Ibid.*, p. 230.
[253] *Ibid.*, p. 95.
[254] *Ibid.*, p. 259.
[255] *Ibid.*, pp. 233, 250.
[256] *Ibid.*, p. 250.

[257] And there is also the tiresome "magic carpetbag" but now slightly inverted: It is the Yankee Cinderella who ends up the mistress of the prince's land, paralleling the legal tricks in *Bricks without Straw*.

[258] *Waiting for the Verdict*, pp. 163-64.

[259] *Ibid.*, p. 58.

[260] *Ibid.*, p. 172.

[261] *Ibid.*, p. 229.

[262] *Ibid.*, p. 164.

[263] *Ibid.*, p. 113.

[264] *Ibid.*, p. 12.

[265] *Ibid.*, pp. 262-63.

[266] *Ibid.*, p. 295.

[267] *Ibid.*, p. 272.

[268] *Ibid.*, p. 164.

[269] *Ibid.*, p. 163.

[270] It is interesting to note here that Ross' phobia against her bastard blood parallels Broderip's disgust with his Negro blood. Their final acceptance of their total natures gives us in multiple images the full impact of the *mana* of "blood" in 19th-century U.S. American literature.

[271] *Ibid.*, p. 300.

[272] For example, she discovers a dead Union soldier in the woods and calmly orders Garrick to bury him.

[273] *Ibid.*, pp. 326, 226, 209.

[274] *Ibid.*, p. 309.

[275] Cf. *Ibid.*, pp. 123-24.

[276] Davis in "Two Women" and "A Night in the Mountain" is quite detailed in her evocation of a masculine atmosphere, replete with whiskey, cigars, sexuality, profanity, etc.

[277] *Waiting for the Verdict*, p. 326.

[278] *Ibid.*, pp. 113, 326.

[279] *Ibid.*, p. 312.

[280] *Ibid.*, p. 315.

[281] *Ibid.*, p. 303-13.

[282] *Ibid.*, pp. 43, 324.

[283] *Ibid.*, pp. 359, 361 ff., 33.

[284] *Ibid.*, p. 354.

[285] Rebecca Harding Davis' only Reconstruction novel is a landmark, one of the few aesthetically satisfying examples of the genre. When its subject matter, themes, language, and characterization are placed against the Victorian aesthetic (from which her work is not entirely free), it has the shock of a fresh discovery. Professor Arthur Quinn supports this assertion in his study of U.S. American fiction. He correctly characterizes Davis as an unappreciated realist whose frankness is quite modern, especially in discussing the race question. Quinn further notes that her sensitivity to and sympathy with the complexity of the Question made her see it more fully than Tourgée. (Arthur H. Quinn, *American Fiction: An Historical and Critical Survey* [New York, 1936], p. 186.) In this context, she can be seen as a feminine counterpart to the hardheaded, compassionate Dr. Ravenel. In *Waiting for the Verdict*, she unknowingly isolated Northern racism as the force that would eventually undo the Reconstruction she supported. Quinn's final judgement is, like that of this study, pro-Davis. Her novel is one of the best examples of the transition. Rebecca Harding Davis, along with De Forest, stands as the "most uncompromising of the realists who

prepared the way for what was to come" (*Ibid.*, pp. 185, 204).

286 As usual, she dies from such presumption, though narratively speaking her death is due to a delayed shock caused by a mob attack on the Ercildoune home in which her firstborn son is killed.

287 She is probably related to that elite "old issue" Freedman group that dominated the Philadelphia Negro community in the fifties and sixties. Cf. Anna E. Dickinson, *What Answer?* (Boston, 1868), p. 300.

288 *Ibid.*, pp. 173, 199, 197.

289 *Ibid.*, pp. 75, 153.

290 *Ibid.*, p. 35.

291 *Ibid.*, pp. 195, 190.

292 The description of the assault has a curious stylistic tension. The language, couched in the rhetorical mode, is a celebration of a heroic, magnificent decimation. Yet beneath the grandiloquent imagery, one catches the oblique reflection of that vision in Bierce, Crane, and De Forest: the horror of wave after wave of charging soldiers being cut to pieces by rifle and cannonfire. It is clear that Dickinson has based this scene on factual accounts, accounts that can still be seen beneath the romantic-rhetorical surface. See *Ibid.*, pp. 299-301.

293 *Ibid.*, p. 247.

294 *Ibid.*, p. 259; see also *Ibid.*, pp. 247 ff.

295 *Ibid.*, pp. 247, 159 ff.

296 *Ibid.*, p. 297.

297 Dickinson's handling of this scene contains a brief complexity. Robert Ercildoune represents the intense faith of the Northern Freedmen in the significance of 1776. During the war their commitment to the Union is more poignant than that of the slave. The slave fights to free himself, his family, and to get revenge. The Yankee Freedman is one "who is free already and so has nothing to gain in that way,—without the promise of gaining anything . . . for himself [—] all . . . because he has faith that the great republic will ultimately be redeemed. . . ." *Ibid.*, p. 219.

298 *Ibid.*, p. 298.

299 See (Smith) p. 18.

300 Tourgée deals with the Afro-Saxon for the last time in *Hot Plowshares* (1885) and *Pactolus Prime* (1890).

301 For the "Toinette" ending, see Otto Olson's *Carpetbagger Crusade: The Life of Albion Winegar Tourgée* (Baltimore, 1965), p. 215.

302 Gross points out that Tourgée was strongly opposed to interracial sexuality. As a state senator, he introduced an amendment "making sexual intercourse between the races a misdemeanor." Gross argues that this was to prevent the continuation of racial eroticism as a form of suppression of the Negro. Gross, *Albion W. Tourgée*, p. 44.

303 Albion Tourgée, *A Royal Gentleman and Zouri's Christmas* (New York, 1881), pp. 327-28.

304 *Ibid.*, p. 367.

305 *Ibid.*, p. 312.

306 See *Ibid.*, p. 464.

307 *Ibid.*, pp. iii-iv.

308 Roy F. Dibble, *Albion W. Tourgée* (New York, 1921), p. 48.

309 See also Gross, p. 44.

310 Joel C. Harris, "Free Joe and the Rest of the World," *Scribner's*, XXIX (November, 1884), 120.

311 Cf. Morris Speare, *The Political Novel: Its Development in England and in America*

(New York, 1924), pp. 26, 16, ix.

[312] *Ibid.*, p. 17. To use Speare's terms.

[313] *A Union Officer*, p. v.

[314] Speare, p. 29.

[315] *A Royal Gentleman*, p. v.

[316] A modified version of a statement by Henry James in "Miss Woolson," *Partial Portraits* (New York, 1899), pp. 179-80.

[317] A modified version of Gross' more general statement. *Albion W. Tourgée*, p. 8. When the anti-radical position passes totally into Southern hands, it undergoes no startling mutations. On the contrary, ex-Confederate writers remain faithful to the models of villainous or stupid Radicals given to them by the Northern writers. It is the pro-Bourbon Northern writers whose sympathy had been "extended toward the displaced Southern gentry" in the fiction and the nonfiction, who originate the stereotypes and prepare the way for the anti-radical vision in the authentic Southern writers.

[318] Herman Melville, "The Freedman," "Supplement," *Battle-Pieces and Aspects of the War*, ed. Sidney Kaplan (Gainesville, Fla., 1960), p. 268.

[319] See *Ibid.*, pp. 233 ff.

[320] *Ibid.*, p. 234.

[321] *Ibid.*, pp. 234, 236.

[322] Although the locale is not explicitly identified as South Carolina, one can locate it here for two reasons. First, this is De Forest's favorite locale for his Southern works (*Miss Ravenel* would be the exception). Second, the political activities he describes, especially the orgy at the Governor's mansion, parallel those attributed to Governor Moses' reign.

[323] John W. De Forest, "The Colored Member," *Galaxy*, XIV (March, 1872), 294-95; 296-97.

[324] *Ibid.*, p. 297.

[325] *Ibid.*, p. 299.

[326] *Ibid.*, p. 301.

[327] See *Ibid.*, p. 299.

[328] *Ibid.*, p. 300.

[329] *Ibid.*, pp. 293-94.

[330] *Ibid.*, pp. 293, 295, 294.

[331] Though there are hints of De Forest's racism in *A Union Soldier*, they are so muted as to be inoffensive. Another point: De Forest's tale precedes *The Prostrate State* by one year. In a sense, it is a fictional preview of the racist tone in Pike's essays, and thus it is also a plea for a change in Northern attitude toward Reconstruction in the light of such corruption.

[332] If *What Answer?* was written for the Pro-Radicals during the 1868 presidential election, it is quite possible that De Forest's short tale was written for the Conservative Republican revolt during the 1872 elections.

[333] William Baker, "Mose Evans," *The Atlantic Monthly*, XXXIII (January–June, 1874), 51 ff.

[334] *Ibid.*, p. 213.

[335] *Ibid.*, pp. 45, 46, 726.

[336] *Ibid.*, p. 206.

[337] *Ibid.*, p. 474.

[338] *Ibid.*, p. 334.

[339] *Ibid.*, p. 467.

[340] Again, as with De Forest's story, this is a surmise based on Baker's interest in South

Carolina and on the fact that a reference is made to the Dunwoddies, a South Carolina family, which will appear later.

341 *Ibid.*, p. 775.

342 *Ibid.*, p. 776.

343 *Ibid.*, p. 779.

344 *Ibid.*, pp. 778-79.

345 S. A. Shields, "Sambo: A Man and Brother," *Lippincott's* XXII (August, 1878), 242, 743.

346 In further support of an implicit environmentalism in S's sketches is his admission that the murders result as much for the Freedwoman's conditioned reflex to obey absolutely a white command as from her lack for maternal instinct. *Ibid.*, pp. 245, 242.

347 His work could also be a part of a grand design, imputed to Conservative Republicans, to forge a coalition with Southern neo-Whigs at any cost in order to retain Republican influence in the South.

348 The continuity of this vision in our literature throughout Reconstruction and beyond to the film *The Birth of a Nation* is quite significant when one considers the influence of the film on the development of the Klan in the twenties. Moreover, it is the memories of Klan power during the twenties that feed into the Klan activity during the Second Reconstruction. In a sense, one sees a literary vision articulated continually in sociopolitical action. One also sees the long-range effects of Reconstruction literature.

349 *Colonel Dunwoddie, Millionaire*, p. 111.

350 *Ibid.*, p. 26.

351 *Ibid.*, pp. 59, 111.

352 *Ibid.*, p. 20.

353 *Ibid.*, p. 114.

354 *Ibid.*, pp. 41, 59-60.

355 *Ibid.*, p. 88.

356 *Ibid.*, p. 144.

357 *Ibid.*, p. 145.

358 *Ibid.*, p. 181.

359 *Ibid.*

360 *Ibid.*, p. 182.

361 *Ibid.*, p. 114.

362 *Ibid.*, 179.

363 *Ibid.*, pp. 86, 79.

364 Cf. *Ibid.*, p. 120.

365 *Ibid.*, p. 84.

366 *Ibid.*, pp. 95, 131, 62, 26.

367 *Ibid.*, p. 100.

368 *Ibid.*, pp. 43-45, 64.

369 *Ibid.*, p. 130.

370 *Ibid.*, pp. 43 ff.

371 This is perhaps the first lynch scene on such charges in U.S. American fiction.

372 *Ibid.*, p. 143. It is important in Baker's symbolism that such anarchic sentiments be voiced by a Yankee. First, Middleton expresses the sentiments of the Southrons without their having to bear the onus of the statement. Second, his statement becomes a contradiction in general to the Northerner's vaunted commitment to law and due process. His sentiments imply that when the chips are down, the Northerner

too has a kinship with so-called barbaric vigilantes. Finally, for those Northern readers who feel that lynching for any reason is wrong, Middleton's views reveal his moral degeneracy.

373 *Ibid.*, p. 86.

374 *Ibid.*, p. 96.

375 *Ibid.*, p. 94.

376 *Ibid.*, p. 137.

377 *Ibid.*, p. 136.

378 *Ibid.*, p. 137.

379 *Ibid.*, pp. 137-38.

380 It is curious that Baker will still permit the Freedman to vote. This is related to the idea that disenfranchisement was not always a Bourbon goal in his counter-revolution.

381 Baker's view of a Haitian-style hatred between black and non-black Negroes is obviously a literary form of the anti-radical strategy of pitting Freedman against Freedman.

382 While Baker's Victorian reticence does not permit the term to appear in the work, and while he concentrates only on the murder, it becomes increasingly clear by his veiled references, by the motivelessness of the crime, and by the references to mulatto lechery that rape is a component of the actual murder.

383 *Ibid.*, p. 139. The mulatto as villain appears for the first time in Reconstruction fiction in this novel. (He will appear again in *Wild Work.*) In post-1885 Reconstruction fiction, he appears most prominently in *The Clansman* (1903). And if, as we believe, sexual assault is a part of the villainy, then Baker's work also introduces the Negro rapist to the reading public for, perhaps, the first time in U.S. American literature. When this reference is added to those in Reconstruction nonfiction, one has the possibility that rape as the standard image of the Taboo Conjunction in Southern fiction originated in Reconstruction literature. Baker's use of these characters—the mulatto villain and the Negro rapist—prefigures in a clear way some key attributes of future Southern fiction.

384 *Ibid.*, p. 141. While Parker knows "instinctively" that Afro-Saxons are the guilty party, he has no definite proof that Jessamine specifically committed the crime. However, Jessamine's guilt is revealed later.

385 *Ibid.*

386 *Ibid.*, p. 140.

387 *Ibid.*, p. 154.

388 *Ibid.*, p. 115.

389 *Ibid.*, p. 90.

390 All these feelings are not completely susceptible to rational analysis since they are tied in with the socio-psychic bases of 19th-century Southern culture and the various archetypal and psychological symbols this culture appropriated to express its deepest fears and longings.

391 Baker's insistence on a universal Southern prejudice against the mulatto is a gross distortion, masking the actual complexity of the Bourbon's attitude toward the mulatto. To begin with, the Afro-Saxon was clearly a desirable and valuable commodity during slavery, as Harriet Beecher Stowe pointed out. Then there was the fact that some planters acknowledged their Negro children with pride and love precisely because of their white blood and their physical proximity to the Saxon ideal (or, in the case of Cable's aristocrats, the Gallic ideal). And, of course, there were those who did loathe their left-handed children precisely because the above characteristics were the physical evidence of the debasement of white pride in an act of guilt, shame, and desire.

392 Baker disturbs the consistency of his obsessive phobia by an unintended (that is,

unintended in terms of our hypothesis) reconciliation of the races. It is the mulatto, Leonidas Dunwoddie (an ex-slave in the house of the Colonel, perhaps even a relative), who warns of the attack on Parker, who cleans Parker's wounds, who prays for him as he dies, and elegizes his importance to the total Freedman community. Yet even in this scene, he is presented as a shallow, trivial creature. Cf. *Ibid.*, pp. 152 ff.

393 Cf. *Ibid.*, pp. 867-87.

394 *Ibid.*, p. 100.

395 *Ibid.*, p. 125.

396 *Ibid.*, p. 135.

397 In this light, Baker's novel represents the first articulation of the racio-political symbology that would dominate the Southern Reconstruction novel after 1880. And the fact that such a novel was published by such a well-known Northern firm as Harper and Brothers reflects how the political atmosphere stimulated by the Compromise would open up to Yankee homes the Southern polemics. Another point: The initial anonymity of the work perhaps demonstrates Baker's feelings (as a Southern writer in need—typically—of Northern markets) that while the new atmosphere permitted a reconciliationist Anti-Radicalism, it would not tolerate his more rabid views of the Conflict and the Question. Thus, through anonymity, he protected his foothold in Northern journals.

398 It is precisely because of the chauvinist, racist distortions in Baker's fiction that we have been reluctant to use Southern writers in large numbers. The Southerners' biases are all too obvious; it is only when these same biases are found in Northern writers (or pro-radical sentiments in Southern writers) that we discover an interesting sociopolitical tension. Our rule of thumb governing the inclusion of ex-Confederates is that they be published either in major, popular Northern journals or by major, well-known Northern publishing houses.

399 His treatment of the white couple is so perfunctory that it deserves no comment in our study, particularly since this couple had nothing to do with Reconstruction.

400 William M. Baker, "Two Couples: A White and Yellow," *Scribner's Monthly*, XVIII (July, 1879), 337.

401 *Ibid.*

402 *Ibid.*, pp. 379-80.

403 Cf., *Ibid.*, p. 380.

404 *Ibid.*, p. 318. James H. Morse, in "The Native Element in American Fiction Since the War," describes Baker as one of the better Reconstruction fictionists, particularly in his presentation of "the social and transitional" aspects of the period. *Scribner's Monthly*, XXVI (July, 1883), 381.

405 Jennie Woodville has appeared in our study before as an Anti-Radical and a writer of Negro tales.

406 Jennie Woodville, "Dogwood Bitters," *Lippincott's*, XXV (May, 1880), 612. Though the Carpetbaggers do not appear in either of Woodville's works, their presence is, nevertheless, clearly defined by the action of the aggressive Freedman, by a social atmosphere that makes his displacement possible, and by their influences as the "low and vicious class of politicians who now came down to deceive and defraud," the Freedmen. *Ibid.*

407 *Ibid.*, p. 615.

408 *Ibid.*, p. 616.

409 *Ibid.*, pp. 619, 615.

410 This same device is used in *Di Cary*. An ex-slave woman journeys to the North during restoration to partake of the fabled freedom there. But she is so maltreated that she eventually returns to the old plantation and dies. Hers and Milly's experience then stand for the hypocrisy of the Yankee's concern about the Negro.

[411] In keeping with her anti-radical leanings, Woodville presents all the Northerners in the story as malicious and hypocritical. A sub-narrative deals with the battle between the Southern Belle and the Yankee Woman for the hand of an ex-Confederate officer. The Belle wins when Aunt Milly reveals the dishonest behavior of the Yankee and further identifies her as the one who most mistreated her in the North.

[412] Jennie Woodville, "The Call Meeting," *Lippincott's*, XXVII (January, 1881), 59 ff.

[413] *Ibid.*, p. 53.

[414] Does the frequent appearance of Woodville's tales in *Lippincott's* reflect the post-Reconstruction views of the editors or of just the author? There are rarely any opposing positions present after 1874. It seems clear that, as Rayford Logan points out, the anti-radical fiction and articles in journals like *Lippincott's* may have helped to ratify emotionally in Northern audiences their acceptance of the redemptionist movement. And it is also possible they prepared the way for the victory of that movement.

[415] This work appeared in 1886 and is technically out of the purview of this study by one year. However, all the Reconstruction stories were published in magazines prior to 1884, e.g., "Old Gardiston" in *Harper's* (1875), "Rodman the Keeper" in *The Atlantic* (1877), and "King David" in *Scribner's* (1877). The stories received favorable reviews in the 1880s. An anonymous reviewer in *Scribner's* saw the anthology as typical of the literature of reconciliation by a Southernized Yankee. Another reviewer in *Appleton's* correctly pointed out that her main purpose was to describe the South as a local color phenomenon in order to help in the interpreting of "The North and South to each other." ("Review," *Appleton's*, VIII, new series (May, 1880), 479.) Further, he saw her depiction of the "pathos, pitifulness, [and] the splendor" of the South as a link to the colorful sketches of Harte and Cable. (*Ibid.*)

[416] Woolson's interest in the South seems to have gone through two literary phases: neutral, colorist nonfiction depicting Southern physiography and mores in North Carolina, South Carolina, and Florida in the late sixties and early seventies; and then her less neutral fiction of the late seventies and early eighties. *Southern Sketches* climaxes this last phase, in this survey, and it often has passages that are clearly grafts from the descriptive style of the first period.

[417] Probably the Florence, North Carolina, prison referred to by Andrews and Tourgée.

[418] Constance Fenimore Woolson, "Rodman the Keeper," *Rodman the Keeper: Southern Sketches* (New York, 1886), p. 28.

[419] Cf. *Ibid.*, pp. 23-24, 27.

[420] *Ibid.*, p. 24.

[421] *Ibid.*, p. 41.

[422] In tenuous fiction, the Reconstruction only forms a rather generalized context and the emphasis is on other themes; in modified sociopolitical Reconstruction fiction, the period is specifically present and the emphasis is on its personal and social aspects. In the clearly sociopolitical form, the emphasis is on these elements, but as they are affected by the specific political conflicts.

[423] Woolson, "Old Gardiston," p. 134.

[424] *Ibid.*, p. 116. Here we have the Dunningite vision in its most concise form. And like all the Anti-Radicals, Woolson completely blanks out the restoration phase. She accepts the lie that the South went directly from military defeat to radical control.

[425] This convention is clearly seen in *Kitty's Conquest*.

[426] Woolson, "In the Cotton Kingdom," pp. 195-96.

[427] Like "Rodman the Keeper," this sketch could be classified as tenuous fiction. But it is too clearly shaped within the Reconstruction event; it too obviously depends on the politics of that event to charge its episodes with pathos and sympathy. In addition, while the Carpetbagger is absent as a character, he is present as the force that gives

the anonymous Belle her postwar sorrow.

[428] Woolson, "King David," p. 255.

[429] *Ibid.*, p. 256.

[430] *Ibid.*, pp. 256, 264, 257.

[431] *Ibid.*, p. 274.

[432] Hubbell, p. 737; Quinn, p. 335.

[433] "King David," p. 274.

[434] When we speak of discovering her ideology, we mean both "uncovering" as well as "finding out." Woolson avoids direct commentary; it is, rather, in her superb artistic shaping of the story that we must "discover" her theory. In a word, her handling of the tale is the ideology.

[435] *Ibid.*, p. 784.

[436] *Ibid.*, p. 261.

[437] *Ibid.*, p. 263.

[438] *Ibid.*, p. 275.

[439] James, pp. 180, 179.

[440] *Ibid.*, pp. 179-80.

[441] Hubbell, p. 736; Quinn, p. 335.

[442] E.g., the Boston *Evening Transcript*, the Cincinnati *Enquirer*, the Washington *Star*. Indeed, some of the strongest attacks appeared in the Republican press under the bylines of such former Pro-Radicals as Whitelaw Reid and Carl Schurz. In addition to the newspaper accounts, there were reports of such widely read correspondents as Edward King and James B. Pike.

[443] Another point is this: The research for this study reveals no major pro-Carpetbagger nonfiction between 1872-1877 either in book form or in the journals. Indeed, the major pro-radical nonfiction appears before 1872 and after 1878. Thus, anti-radical fiction and nonfiction dominated the media during redemption and their versions of the truth become *the truth* for many Northern readers.

[444] Albion W. Tourgée, *Bricks without Straw* (New York, 1879), p. 400.

[445] De Forest is represented in all classifications of Reconstruction fiction save the Pro-Radical: the fable (*Miss Ravenel's Conversion*), tenuous fiction (*The Bloody Chasm)*, anti-radical fiction ("The Colored Member"), and two examples of neutralist fiction. Then when these are added to *Kate Beaumont*, "Rum Creeters is Women," and *A Union Officer*, we can see that De Forest's Southern output was considerable.

[446] John W. De Forest, "Parole d'Honneur," *Harper's*, XXXVII (August and July, 1868), 485, 373 ff.

[447] *Ibid.*, p. 273.

[448] *Ibid.*, p. 377.

[449] The work has several allusions to atrocities committed during the period against native Unionists and postwar converts. For example, seven persons, including two women and three children, are reported to have been burned to death. *Ibid.*, p. 485. And this occurs before the so-called provocation of the Union Leagues. Among the bushwhackers referred to in the tale are Champ Ferguson, Joly, Largent, and Texas Brown alluded to in *A Union Officer*. These incidents and allusions reveal how profitably De Forest worked the vein discovered during his stint as a military Carpetbagger in Greenville. These references are a further link between this tale and the first section of *A Union Officer*.

[450] The raid on the Praterites parallels the attack on the KK stronghold in *Kitty's Conquest*.

[451] The interesting realistic details that De Forest uses in describing the raid suggest to me that it is based on a personal experience.

[452] *Ibid.*, pp. 489, 375.

[453] Marion Harland, *The Wall-Flower*; *Godey's*, LXXXI (July-September, 1870), 31-32.
[454] *Ibid.*, p. 29.
[455] *Ibid.*
[456] *Ibid.*
[457] *Ibid.*, pp. 29-30.
[458] *Ibid.*, p. 29.
[459] Of course, Virginia is a special case. It was the one state on which the iron glove of radical power rested most mildly, mainly because the Bourbons, where they could, entered into that model coalition espoused by moderate Republicans.
[460] *Ibid.*, p. 31.
[461] The irony in this conflict is that because of their "inherent vices" both lower-class white and lower-class blacks share, in De Forest's eyes, the only real moral and social equality in the reconstructing South. Cf. John W. De Forest, "An Independent Ku-Klux," *Galaxy*, XIII (April, 1872), 400.
[462] Since this is the emphasis, the story has little partisan commentary and only the briefest allusion to the larger political ramifications of violence. Indeed, De Forest's only comment *as an author* on the KK is to label its massacres and floggings a "silly and savage reign of terror." (However, the work does seem to be in general a tragi-comic condemnation of the excesses committed in the South Carolina highlands.) In a real sense, "An Independent Ku-Klux" is the companion-piece to "The Colored Member." They both appeared the same year, and together they reflect in a thematic way the technique of balancing Carpetbagger vices with Bourbon ones. If corruption was the essential sin of the Radicals, KK terrorism was the sin of the Anti-Radicals. Pompey Howard and Bowen are the Frankenstein monsters created on each side, respectively, by these sins. Considering these works as a related pair, De Forest's neutrality could be seen in the balancing of the evils of Bourbons and Carpetbaggers.
[463] De Forest, *A Union Officer*, p. 50. We see again how De Forest's work as a Bureau officer feeds directly into another work of fiction.
[464] *Ibid.*, p. 51.
[465] Reid, *After the War*, pp. 138-39.
[466] "An Independent Ku-Klux," pp. 481-82.
[467] *Ibid.*, p. 485.
[468] Cf. *Ibid.*, pp. 486, 480.
[469] *Ibid.*, p. 483.
[470] Bryan suggests that her work might have influenced Tourgée's publication. In fact, she maintains that the chapter "A Race Against Time" in *A Fool's Errand* parallels the chapter in which her heroine gallops off to save her Carpetbagger hero. Mary E. Bryan, *Wild Work* (New York, 1881), p. vii.
[471] The work has the following bibliographic history: published in 1877 in serialized form, revised in 1879, and in 1881 republished in book form by the Northern house, D. Appleton and Co. The book version was published obviously to take advantage of the interest in Reconstruction fiction stimulated during the 1880s by Tourgée's novels.
[472] *Ibid.*, p. v.
[473] *Ibid.*, pp. 60-61.
[474] *Ibid.*, p. v.
[475] *Ibid.*
[476] *Ibid.*, p. 239.
[477] Bryan's description of the aristocrat reflects her neutralist position. She allows him to be described as a "tyrant by nature. The position he had as head of a regiment in the late war pampered his love of ruling men and over-riding them" (*Ibid.*, p. 135).
[478] *Ibid.*, p. 136.

[479] *Ibid.*, p. 155.
[480] *Ibid.*, pp. 157, 155, 205.
[481] Cf. *Ibid.*, p. 241.
[482] *Ibid.*, pp. 324, 325, 409.
[483] *Ibid.*, pp. 15, 17, 144.
[484] *Ibid.*, pp. 24-25.
[485] *Ibid.*, pp. 38-39.
[486] *Ibid.*, p. 157.
[487] *Ibid.*, p. 208.
[488] *Ibid.*, pp. 206-7.
[489] *Ibid.*, p. 155.
[490] *Ibid.*, p. 220.
[491] *Ibid.*, p. 404.
[492] *Ibid.*, p. 405.
[493] *Ibid.*, pp. 51, 132.
[494] *Ibid.*, pp. 37, 51-52, 83, 136-37.
[495] *Ibid.*, p. 14.
[496] *Ibid.*, p. 212.
[497] *Ibid.*, pp. 359, 380, 406.
[498] *Ibid.*, p. 409.
[499] *Ibid.*, p. 67.
[500] *Ibid.*, p. 92.
[501] Here are three examples of Bryant's proto-realistic evocation of the yellow fever epidemic, examples that further reveal her genius as a minor talent. First, the burial of Tom Wallace. "Most the Negroes did do was to dig a grave in one corner of de yard, and knock up cypress coffin, and slide it onto de gallery. His young wife and her father—him wid de fever on him, too-had to do the rest—to git de body in the coffin somehow, and den roll and push de coffin till dey roll it into de grave, and cover it theirselves" (*Ibid.*, p. 72). Second, the death of Major Copley: ". . . de fus' ting he done, when the lirum tuck him, was to jump up outer de bed and stave in the whisky-bar'l. Den he paddled and splosh about in de licker over de floor, and holler bout he's in de lake o' fire and brimstone. . . . Died a cussin', and a hollerin' out de debil had 'im" (*Ibid.*, p. 62). Third, the sentimental blurring of realistic details typical of the local color style: The swamp fever was terrible, "chilling and burning its victims by turns and tingling them a saffron deep as that of the helianthus, whose bloomy mass burned like a flame beside the bayous; . . ." (*Ibid.*, p. 45).
[502] *Ibid.*, pp. 63-64.
[503] *Ibid.*, p. 87.
[504] *Ibid.*, pp. 91, 92, 93.
[505] Bryan's description parallels Tourgée's, a fact she attributes to accident. However, she does indicate that in point of time, her description precedes Tourgée's depiction. For the interested student, an examination of these two incidents does reveal startling similarities.
[506] *Ibid.*, pp. 103 ff.
[507] *Ibid.*, pp. 158-59.
[508] *Ibid.*, p. 162.
[509] The incident begins with Chapter XX and ends in Chapter XXXI. See *Ibid.*, pp. 209 ff.
[510] *Ibid.*, p. 152.
[511] *Ibid.*, p. 212.

[512] *Ibid.*, p. 211.

[513] *Ibid.*, pp. 234, 236, 238.

[514] *Ibid.*, p. 241.

[515] *Ibid.*, p. 245. During all this Witchell is away on pre-election business, not dreaming of the suddenness with which the Bourbons would launch their preemptive strike.

[516] *Ibid.*, p. 246.

[517] *Ibid.*, p. 247.

[518] *Ibid.*, p. 248. Bryan suggests here that these victims were perhaps pawns in a larger game, instigated no doubt by Floyd Reese.

[519] *Ibid.*, p. 249.

[520] *Ibid.*, p. 255. Devene also effects the unorthodox reconciliation. But the law remains. He, like Adelle, dies.

[521] Hirne is a White Leaguer-St. Elmo type. We first meet him on the way to a Federal penal island for flogging a Freedman teacher. Zoe is the virginal Belle, the little country girl, who will transform the world-stained Hirne. She was also Adelle's best friend.

[522] *Ibid.*, p. 262.

[523] Cf. *Ibid.*, pp. 252-64.

[524] *Ibid.*, p. 264.

[525] *Ibid.*, p. 266.

[526] *Ibid.*, p. 269. Actually, by making Levi an "Indian" mulatto, Bryan avoids a direct treatment of the Black Rapist image, especially since Indian assault was a more conventional pattern of rape on the 19th-century U.S. American frontier. As in *Colonel Dunwoddie*, it was, perhaps, too psychologically untenable to articulate in fictional form this nightmare figure in his true colors. By making Afro-Saxon and Afro-Indian characters the Rapist figure, Bryan and Baker were able to hold in their imagination *as separate personalities* the black Southerner as being both the kindly Uncle Remus and the savage Uncle Nat (Turner). One would suppose that surrounded by the Darkness of Blackness, it was unthinkable for Bryan and Baker to articulate in consciously designed images a picture of the Dark Rapist as a "black" man.

[527] *Ibid.*, p. 269.

[528] Levi's kinship to Magua and Injun Joe is quite clear in these scenes.

[529] *Ibid.*, p. 271.

[530] Again, this neutralism is emphasized by placing the ultimate cause of the Freedmen's behavior not on the ideological nature of black radicalism, but on exterior forces, i.e., the terrorism unleashed upon the Negroes by Floyd's machinations. *Ibid.*, p. 270.

[531] It also parallels the way the Klan seized Verdenton in *A Fool's Errand*, the Red Shirts seized Beaconsville in *Other Fools*, and the Rifle Clubs Yazoo in Morgan's memoirs.

[532] *Ibid.*, p. 274.

[533] This scene illustrates again the readymade dramatic incident that Reconstruction offered the minor talents of the period.

[534] Notice that Levi does not speak with a dialect.

[535] *Ibid.*, pp. 274-76.

[536] *Ibid.*, p. 302.

[537] *Ibid.*, p. 309.

[538] *Ibid.*, pp. 311 ff. In a footnote, Bryan states, "The circumstances of the pursuit and killing of these six office-holders are given almost word for word as they were told me by one of the men who accompanied the prisoners as a guard. The man who offered a thousand dollars for every life the mob would spare was a Southerner." *Ibid.*, p. 315.

[539] Adaptation of statement by Bryan, *Ibid.*, p. 321.

[540] *Ibid.*, p. v.
[541] *Ibid.*, pp. 130-32, 142.
[542] In this case, it is Floyd who is allowed to pronounce this "truth." *Ibid.*, pp. 153, 360, 151.
[543] *Ibid.*, p. vi.
[544] *Ibid.*, pp. 409-10.
[545] Bonner was an English woman who, after the Civil War, came South to live. Like Somer, our English nonfictionist, she had no special political commitment to either side of the North-South conflict. Her bias is that of the interested outsider, anxious to understand both sides of that impassioned conflict.
[546] Sherwood Bonner, "The Valcours," *Lippincott's*, XXVIII (September-December, 1881), 353.
[547] *Ibid.*, p. 247.
[548] *Ibid.*, pp. 246, 247.
[549] *Ibid.*, p. 570.
[550] We are using the 1892 reissue.
[551] Cf. Lee (Smith), p. 34. Charles King was a member of the United States Army during this period. Thus, many of the incidents recounted in his novel have the quality of directly observed experience. However, since research reveals nothing about his background, this comment is merely a surmise.
[552] Charles King, *Kitty's Conquest* (Philadelphia, 1892), pp. 23-25.
[553] *Ibid.*, p. 144.
[554] The historical background to this situation is rather confusing. The essence of the struggle seemed to have been as follows: If the Warmoth legislature could maintain its quorum control of the State House, it could prevent Kellogg, the reputed elected governor, from taking complete control. By remaining in session and not losing their quorum, the Warmoth Radicals could ensure through this parliamentary technicality at least a tenuous hold on the Louisiana throne. For a fuller elaboration of the complicated politico-legal maneuvers that led to this situation and that finally resolved it, see Buckmaster, pp. 149-51; and W. E. B. DuBois, *Black Reconstruction in America* (New York, 1935), pp. 480-82.
[555] *Ibid.*, pp. 144, 145.
[556] *Ibid.*, p. 136.
[557] *Ibid.*, p. 42. A modified use of the quotation.
[558] In a sense, this celebration of the inherent virtue of the military could be considered a variation on the reconciliationist doctrine of the Civil War Veteran. In this doctrine all who fought in the War have become sanctified; both Reb and Yank partake of some expiation of evil through the ritual of the Red Badge of Courage. Any soldier who fought well and did his duty, whether as Secessionist or Unionist, achieves a transcendental merit.
[559] *Ibid.*, p. 156.
[560] *Ibid.*, pp. 142-43. Of course, the major reason for this sharp performance is the fact that the Metros were trained by a West Point graduate, General James Longstreet, lately of the CSA.
[561] *Ibid.*, p. 19.
[562] *Ibid.*, pp. 112-13.
[563] *Ibid.*, pp. 291-93.
[564] See *Ibid.*, p. 21.
[565] *Ibid.*, pp. 295-96.
[566] However, as we have pointed out earlier, this neutrality can be a relative thing. For if King could be described as having a bias, it would be in the direction of the Radicals' rank and file: the soldier, the ordinary legislator, the city policeman, the

conscientious Scalawag, the loyal Freedman. But this tenuous lapse in the work's neutrality is balanced by King's romantic shaping of the Southron's milieu and his women.

567 *Bricks Without Straw*, p. 272.

568 Cf. our discussion of the Scalawag, David Church, as a Carpetbagger symbol in *The Valcours*.

569 Cf. Franklin, pp. 92 ff.

570 The Scalawag rarely appears as a central character in pro- or anti-radical works. (Even Le Moyne Hesden appears merely as an active tertiary character to the Freedman-Carpetbagger nexus.) The reason for this is obscure. It could not be that Yankee and Negro Radicals were more exotic than a Southerner-turned-Radical. Certainly, the political shift of an Alcorn or a Longstreet would have had a like exoticness. Perhaps the answer lies in the fact that historic-romantic interest lay with the black and émigré Radicals in terms of audience reaction, the political concepts related to Union and abolition, and the writer's interest in "aliens" at the South.

571 Two points need to be emphasized here. First, eight works are featured in this discussion and all were written after the reconstitution phase. The main reason for this could be that pro-radical nonfiction carried the brunt of the battle during the period itself; that Northern readers were not interested in works defending heroes discredited by many of the major Northern newspapers and by such persuasive Anti-Radicals as De Forest, Woolson, Pike, and King; that the sympathetic interest of many Northern readers lay with the victims of "mis-rule" and not with the rulers; and that only after it was over could the Carpetbagger side of the issue be presented without the fear of negative reactions from pro-Southern Northerners. Perhaps also, after it was over, the participants themselves had time to write about their commitment.

Second, because of the importance of the Tourgée canon to this group of works and to this study, we are modifying the chronological presentation that has so far structured our descriptive analysis. The Tourgée canon, especially his two major Reconstruction works, *Bricks Without Straw* and *A Fool's Errand*, will be featured last in a separate chapter as the climactic works of this study.

572 Charles P. Deshler, "Ab'm: A Glimpse of Modern Dixie," *Harper's*, LVII (September, 1878), 493.

573 *Ibid.*

574 *Ibid.*

575 Cf. F. B. Simkins, *A History of the South* (New York, 1953), p. 348. Between 1877 and 1890, control of the Negro franchise became a key instrument in intraparty politics at the South between the Bourbons and the non-aristocratic classes (called the New Men). It was only when these New Men emerged that disenfranchisement became the major political strategy vis-à-vis the Negro. Anti-Bourbon factions united behind such anti-Southron, anti-Negro demagogues as Tillman and Vardaman to eliminate this black power base. (*Ibid.*, p. 351.) And following the intraparty disruptions attendant upon the populist moment when Negro votes went to New Men like Tom Watson, Bourbons also turned against the black franchise. Never again, vowed aristocrat and commoner, would the Negro be allowed to interfere in the politics of white men. (Cf. *Ibid.*, pp. 352-58.) But in 1878, such widescale legal disenfranchisement was twelve years in the future.

576 Goff's novel gives in a fuller, fictional way the same picture of redemption described in such contemporary articles as "The Political Condition of South Carolina" and "The Results in South Carolina." Again we see how political reality feeds into Reconstruction fiction.

577 Exceptions would be Levi's attempted counterstrike against Zoe in *Wild Work* and Nimbus' successful defense of Red Wing in *Bricks Without Straw*.

578 [Harriet K. Goff], *Other Fools and Their Doings* (New York, 1880), p. 142.

[579] *Ibid.*, pp. 114-15, 137.

[580] In terms of the psychoanalytic aspect of this study, the rifles become an expression of the phallic archetype. If there is a complex racio-sexual anima permeating Black-White conflict in Reconstruction literature—as we have suggested—then the antagonism toward the Freedman's possession of weaponry mirrored the sexual-masculine rivalry between White and Black Adam. The Rifle Clubs' destruction of the militia's potency in *Other Fools* is a psychocultural act, involving political, racial, and sexual motives. The final step, then, is to see the battle at the Armory not only as a military operation but as an act of castration as well. This is the deeper meaning that can be read into the insurrectionists' cry that the weapons can only be surrendered to them.

[581] *Ibid.*, pp. 159, 161.

[582] *Ibid.*, p. 160.

[583] *Ibid.*, pp. 170-71.

[584] *Ibid.*, pp. 180-81.

[585] *Ibid.*, p. 182.

[586] *Ibid.*, p. 190.

[587] The horror of these climactic incidents overshadows the lack of art in the work, demonstrating again that even the least talented of our Reconstruction writers can depict the violence of the era with a certain crude, compelling power.

[588] *Ibid.*, p. 215.

[589] Of course, as in all pro-radical works of the reconciliation period, chronology is an important aspect of their power. The "prophecy" in *Other Fools* has retroactive application in the chronological juxtaposition of fictional and real time. The reader's awareness through the *Nation* and *Harper's Weekly* of how the prophecy was fulfilled makes him/her a part of the story. The narrative time, July 1876, is complemented by the reader's real time, 1880. What was supposed to have happened has, in fact, already happened. It is the tension between the fictional prophecy and the historical fulfillment that, I would suppose, gave to these works a special poignancy, especially in the minds of those readers with some pro-radical sympathies.

[590] Structurally speaking, the clearest presentation of Goff's vision of the Reconstruction event is in Chapter IX. Aesthetically, the chapter is a break in the somewhat suspenseful momentum of the narrative action. Thematically, it is the bridge between the horrors of the event and the ideological discussions about it.

[591] *Ibid.*, p. 9.

[592] Woolson, "In the Cotton Country," p. 196.

[593] *Ibid.*, pp. 27, 151-52, 156.

[594] Thornton, *Di Cary*, p. 169.

[595] *Ibid.*, pp. 34, 87.

[596] *Ibid.*, p. 150.

[597] *Ibid.*, pp. 88, 150.

[598] *Ibid.*, p. 150.

[599] *Ibid.*, p. 33.

[600] Cf. *Ibid.*, p. 221.

[601] *Ibid.*, pp. 129-30.

[602] Jesse Roome on the Reconstruction. *Ibid.*, p. 138.

[603] *Ibid.*, p. 16.

[604] *Ibid.*, p. 44.

[605] *Ibid.*, pp. 44, 36.

[606] *Ibid.*, p. 37.

[607] *Ibid.*, p. 154.

608 *Ibid.*, p. 25.

609 *Ibid.*, p. 88.

610 *Ibid.*, p. 35.

611 *Ibid.*, p. 88.

612 *Ibid.*, p. 43.

613 *Ibid.*, p. 155.

614 *Ibid.*, p. 233.

615 The novel was reputedly well-received by the remnant anti-Bourbon press. (Cf. *Ibid.*, pp. 235-36.) Reid's old paper, *The Cincinnati Gazette*, and the paleo-abolitionist *Boston Watchman* gave the work glowing blurbs, while the *InterOcean Chicago* goes the author one better in anti-Southronism, calling for the extermination of the Bourbons from "the face of the earth." The anti-radical press dismissed the work as more lies on the South. The *Louisville Courier* states, "'Another fool is now in the field with his slavering idiocy. . . . The book is a series of gross exaggerations, vindictive calumnies, and insipid lies. . . ."
The work was endorsed by S. W. Dorsey, Secretary of the National Republican Committee. The political reason for such an endorsement is obvious. The work came out in 1880, evidently before the presidential elections, and as such would have made a handy anti-Democratic polemic. Since it was obvious to many in the national Republican leadership by 1880 that reconciliation with the Bourbon *qua* Whig would not reinstate Republicanism in the South, this novel, and others like it, can be seen as the removing of the kid gloves. At the same time, *Other Fools* is a part of the polemic strategy that aimed to get some final mileage out of the bloody-shirt device during a presidential election.

616 George E. Benham, *A Year of Wreck* (New York, 1880), pp. 46-47.

617 *Ibid.*, p. 259.

618 *Ibid.*, p. 240.

619 *Ibid.*, p. 27.

620 *Ibid.*, p. 172. Local color technique permits a little Victorian erotic-realism to appear in this example. The female form becomes, ambivalently, both a sexual object as well as a coloristic object.

621 Mrs. Smith, in her dissertation, points out that *Wreck*, like *Other Fools*, *Bristling with Thorns*, and *Bricks Without Straw*, is one of the novels spawned by *A Fool's Errand.* Interior evidence clearly supports the contention that *Wreck* does derive from Tourgée's masterpiece.

622 *Ibid.*, p. 17.

623 *Ibid.*, pp. 69, 205.

624 *Ibid.*, p. 268.

625 *Ibid.*, p. 205.

626 *Ibid.*, p. 137. But this is just the point: These innocent acts become political symbols of defiance in the Bourbon's anti-rational vision of Reconstruction. Small wonder that in minds trained during the forties and fifties to view any non-Southern action by the hated Northerner as anti-Southern, these simple gestures became symbols of subversion against what remained of the Southern way of life during restoration.

627 Bryan, p. 133.

628 Benham, p. 415. Such ostracism is described in "Miss Mouse," "King David," "Harcourt V'line Mango," *A Fool's Errand*, and *Bricks Without Straw*.

629 See *Ibid.*, p. 190.

630 *Ibid.*, p. 471. Both Harding and Servosse turn against Congressional Reconstruction in their "old age." On the one hand, this shift represents an authentic disillusionment with the failure of the North to institute a vigorous policy of reconstitution; on the

other hand, it could be the reconciliation gambit, designed, in this case, for the disenchanted Republicans in 1880. This seems especially true, in the case of *Wreck*, since the preceding chapters were an impassioned defense of the necessity of Congressional Reconstruction.

631 *Ibid.*, p. 472.

632 *Ibid.*

633 *Ibid.*

634 Tourgée, *A Fool's Errand*, p. 129.

635 Harding, p. 434.

636 One might surmise that if the change originates among the Bourbons, the guardians of the mystique, the change might take root. But even then, we would suspect that such changes would not really be substantial, as witness the shift from slavery to the Black Codes in 1866.

637 Tourgée, *A Fool's Errand*, p. 129.

638 *Ibid.*, p. 370.

639 *Ibid.*, p. 35.

640 "Mose Evans," p. 325.

641 *Ibid.*, pp. 391, 36-37, 285.

642 *Ibid.*, pp. 285, 286, 462.

643 Carrying this perception still further, we would describe this informing essence negatively as basically the South's persisting Wilderness dynamic.

644 *Ibid.*, p. 168.

645 Harding attacks the Baker view of the essential corruption of the mulatto. It is precisely the existence of white blood in Carter and his wife that, for Harding, is their most attractive point. Indeed, it is Carter's blood that helps to change him from slave to prosperous Freedman through the influence of the radical program.

646 *Ibid.*, pp. 169, 141.

647 Cf. *Ibid.*

648 Cf. *Ibid.*

649 *Ibid.*, pp. 133, 415.

650 *Ibid.*, p. 132.

651 *Ibid.*, p. 324.

652 *Ibid.*, p. 403.

653 Cf. *Ibid.*, p. 141.

654 See *Ibid.*, p 137.

655 *Ibid.*, p. 134.

656 Cf. *Ibid.*, p. 145.

657 *Ibid.*, p. 368. This statement is almost an exact parallel to a similar "mending metaphor" in *A Fool's Errand.*

658 *Ibid.*, p. 145.

659 *Ibid.*, p. 169. Harding also includes the Bourbon in this elegiac prediction.

660 S. A. Shields, "Harcourt V'line Mango," *Lippincott's* XXVIII (July, 1881), 86.

661 Cf. *Ibid.*, p. 87.

662 The title of the short story is a corruption of "Harcourt's Eveline Mango."

663 *Ibid.*, p. 89.

664 Thus spoke a Mrs. Cornelia Spencer. Hubbell, *The South in American Literature*, p. 34.

665 Tourgée, *John Eax*, pp. v-vi.

666 George J. Becker, "Albion W. Tourgée: Pioneer in Social Criticism," *American Literature*, XIX (November, 1947), 66.

667 Gross, p. 146.

668 *Ibid.*, pp. 53, 83.

669 *Ibid.*, p. 53.

670 *Ibid.*, p. 142. In his later life, Tourgée would despair of any solution—educational, Christian, or governmental—to this question, a question that, in his fiction, he thought capable of being solved by a Federal system of education in the South. Cf. *Ibid.*, p. 143.

671 Cf. *Ibid.*, pp. 7-8.

672 Tourgée, *A Fool's Errand*, (1880), p. 309.

673 *John Eax*, p. ix. Thus spoke Tourgée in the preface to the work.

674 See "Zouri's Christmas," pp. 525-29.

675 Cf. *Ibid.*, pp. 310-311, 314.

676 *Ibid.*, p. 529. One might add here that this was the strategy of many Negro leaders during reconciliation in the kind of "back-to-Massa" movement.

677 Gross, p. 103.

678 "Mamelon," pp. 168-69.

679 *Ibid.*, p. 197.

680 *Ibid.*, p. 203.

681 *Ibid.*, p. 202.

682 *Ibid.*, p. 237.

683 *Ibid.*, pp. 235-36. In this brief description of the effects of the Panic, Tourgée foreshadows the kind of social criticism that would be leveled more pointedly at the developing industrial oligarchy by later writers. This description also hints at the national dislocations occasioned by the Republicans' economic policies (or lack of them) during the Reconstruction period. Finally, the descriptive passage is no mere rhetorical outburst. Tourgée himself established a similar handle-making outfit in North Carolina. And since he too lost his factory during the Panic, this outburst can be seen as a real lament. Cf. Dibble, p. 106.

684 This same kind of disappearance occurs in *Di Cary* and "Barren Ridge."

685 Tourgée, *Bricks Without Straw*, p. 279.

686 *Ibid.*, p. 281. The similarity between the Klan raid and Indian attack is quite evident here.

687 *Ibid.*, p. 282.

688 *Ibid.*, p. 289. This entire scene perhaps foreshadows (as do all such scenes in Reconstruction fiction) the lynching scenes in William Faulkner, Erskine Caldwell, and Richard Wright.

689 *Ibid.*, pp. 289, 290. This furious co-mingling of the symbolism of blood ritual, eroticism, and violence is quite powerful. Once more one has an example of the way in which Reconstruction fiction manifests those underground sentiments usually forbidden to reader and writer in the Godeyesque aesthetic.

690 *Ibid.*, p. 487.

691 In the final chapters, Tourgée's didactic predilections take over. He permits Hesden and a Northern Republican friend to have a dialogue. First, there is a rather explicit discussion of the sociopolitical differences between North and South. Second, there is a elaboration of Hesden's proposal for a federally financed system of public education throughout the entire South as the only solution to the sociopolitical problems in the ex-Confederacy.

692 Tourgée is not so simpleminded as to present all the Freedmen in such a light. Nimbus has an alter ego, his cousin, Berry. He is the anarchistic Freedman: good-hearted and good-humored, yet lazy and ignorant, driven hither and thither by his animal spirits. For him freedom means irresponsibility, not the fulfillment of moral imperatives; the suffrage means free barbecues, not civic action.

693 Gross, p. 87.

694 Tourgée, *Bricks Without Straw*, p. 272.

695 Cf. *Ibid.*, p. 480.

696 *Ibid.*, p. 447.

697 *Ibid.*, p. 236.

698 Tourgée's juxtaposition of Mollie and Nimbus has both an explicit purpose and an implicit, unintended effect that slightly contradicts that purpose. Tourgée explicitly seeks to attack the calumnies levelled against the white women who taught among the lowly Freedmen. He boldly "answers" those critics who had accused the schoolmarm and the ex-slave of sexual as well as sociopolitical unity by using the Yankee Virgin as his chief character. He places her with all her shining virtues squarely in the middle of Red Wing, and by depicting her dedication to the Freedmen and their respect for her, he virtually dares the anti-radical reader to cast the first aspersion.

Yet there is an opposing though unintended effect that, at the same time, Tourgée unconsciously exploits. The juxtaposition of the Eve and Black Adam in Reconstruction fiction—whether in a student–teacher relation (as in "Pharoah's Horses"), the Taboo Conjunction (*Waiting for the Verdict*), or the preliminaries to a rape (as in *Wild Work*)—carries psycho-sexual energies that heighten the "meta-literary" interest of these works. Such an assertion, for the purposes of this study, must be allowed to lie beyond the threshold of a precise, evidential analysis. However, this inference is drawn from a detailed study of the descriptive and rhetorical textures that shape these scenes. Within this general frame of reference, one can assert that in *A Fool's Errand* and *Bricks Without Straw*, Tourgée presents his encounters between the Black Adam and the Northern Eve within a highly charged, surrogate-erotic matrix, curiously vibrant with the implicit echoes of the Taboo Conjunction. In *A Fool's Errand*, it occurs when he juxtaposes the Virgin with the Uncle in an idyllic setting clearly evocative of the fecund energies of the Priapean Garden. In *Bricks Without Straw* it occurs between Mollie and her student, the older Eliab Hill (as the Virgin and the Cripple, respectively). Here, the scene is depicted in straightforward emotional terms. Eliab tearfully confesses his feelings of intellectual inadequacy to Mollie, chiding himself for his mental slowness and begging her to spend more time on the "younguns." She moves forward to comfort him and he exclaims, "Don't come nigh me, Miss Mollie" (*Ibid.*, pp. 172-75). The intimacy of the moment causes one to feel that if Eliab had been White Adam, Tourgée might have allowed those feelings of inadequacy to evolve into, at least, platonic love.

In other words, these are scenes in which confessional and sentimental rhetoric blunts but does not suppress a latent erotic content. Fortunately, Tourgée covers his tracks by making Black Adam, in both cases, physically incomplete.

All this is said to indicate that though Tourgée answers his critics on the conscious level, he seems to be aware that it would not have been so monstrous for there to have been some normal male-female eroticism operating in the relationship between the Yankee Maiden and the African. (See Tourgée, *A Fool's Errand*, the 1879 version, pp. 195 ff. and Tourgée, *Bricks Without Straw*, p. 173.)

699 *Ibid.*, p. 35.

700 *Ibid.*, p. 107.

701 *Ibid.*, p. 43.

702 *Ibid.*

703 *Ibid.*

704 *Ibid.*, p. 409.

705 *Ibid.*, p. 445.

706 The Kansas Migration was one of the most astounding events of the reconciliation

period as related to the Negro Question. It received detailed coverage in the major Northern newspapers and in *The Atlantic*, *Harper's* and *Scribner's*. It was such a large movement that there were calls for congressional investigations. The main reason for the migration was political oppression and an increase in genocidal violence, despite the fact that the political cause of the violence—radical rule—had been eliminated: "The negroes have suffered the more because they have not resisted and defended themselves." [James B. Runnion, "The Negro Exodus," *The Atlantic Monthly*, XLIV (August, 1879), 227.] More than any other reason, to flee the slaughter pens of Mississippi and Louisiana was the consistent rationale for those who participated in the Exodus. (*Ibid.*) For more details, see also Henry King, "A Year of the Exodus in Kansas," *Scribner's* XX (June 1880), 211-18. The King article has scenes in it that closely parallel those in *Bricks*.

[707] *Ibid.*, p. 488. The inclusion of these scenes serves two purposes: Thematically, they are a demonstration to the 1881 audience of the contemporary results of the great abandonment and show the persistence of Reconstruction problems despite the Compromise; in literary terms, they demonstrate how Tourgée could bring his art to bear on topical questions and at the same time use such questions to increase the verisimilitude of his works.

[708] C. H. Jones, "Sectional Fiction," *Appleton's*, new series, IX (July, 1880), 565.

[709] Tourgée, *A Fool's Errand*, pp. 58-69.

[710] *Ibid.*, p. 325.

[711] *Ibid.*, p. 370.

[712] *Ibid.*, p. 377.

[713] *Ibid.*, pp. 96-97.

[714] *Ibid.*, pp. 91-94.

[715] *Ibid.*, p. 154.

[716] *Ibid.*, p. 322.

[717] *Ibid.*, pp. 148, 22, 154.

[718] *Ibid.*, pp. 120, 162-63.

[719] *Ibid.*, p. 121.

[720] *Ibid.*, pp. 122-23. Servosse, unlike the other Pro-Radicals, does not defend the Congressional Plan. In many ways, he is quite a conservative Radical when compared to Harding and Morgan. But, on the other hand, he condemns the plan because it was not radical enough.

[721] *Ibid.*, pp. 121-22.

[722] *Ibid.*, p. 122.

[723] *Ibid.*, p. 158.

[724] *Ibid.*, p. 159.

[725] *Ibid.*, p. 357.

[726] *Ibid.*, p. 22.

[727] *Ibid.*, p. 20.

[728] *Ibid.*, p. 126.

[729] *Ibid.*, pp. 154-55.

[730] *Ibid.*, p. 126.

[731] Cf. *Ibid.*, p. 154.

[732] *Ibid.*, p. 156.

[733] A remark made by Tourgée in 1886 in an interview. Gross, p. 53.

[734] Tourgée, *A Fool's Errand*, p. 358.

[735] *Ibid.*, p. 118.

[736] Gross, pp. 82-83. This objectivity is aesthetically sustained through the novel by

the fact that, as author, Tourgée remains (with effort) pretty much outside the narrative. Comfort Servosse is such an excellent spokesman for his views that Tourgée can keep a literary distance between himself and the novel. This, in turn, contributes to the thematic objectivity in the work.

737 Lee (Smith), p. 28.

738 Tourgée, *A Fool's Errand*, p. 119.

739 Gross, p. 57.

740 Cf. *Ibid.*, p. 81.

741 In 1881 the novel was dramatized on the New York stage. Lee (Smith), p. 28.

742 Baker, *Colonel Dunwoddie, Millionaire*, p. 114.

743 "The Moral Significance of the Republican Triumph," *The Atlantic Monthly*, XXIII (January, 1869), 125.

744 It is an interesting facet of Reconstruction history that the French Revolution is the constant analogy. But in light of the trauma that the Revolution of 1789 inflicted on the psyche of western man, it is quite understandable. Using the Bourbon metaphor as a guide, one can see additional political images from the French Revolution. The Bourbons are, of course, those Southerners, primarily the Southron planter class and their allies, who wish to remodel the defeated Confederacy as closely as possible on the basis of the old society. They will not repudiate the war without a struggle; they accept emancipation but demand racial subordination with as little human, legal, or civil rights as possible. They are implacably hostile to the Union and especially the Union's representatives in the South. The Girondins could be those Southern moderates who accept the terms of the Surrender, including Emancipation, and even envision some limited rights for the Freedman. The Danton Jacobins could refer to those poor white and poor black Unionists who desire a complete overhaul of Southern society so as to give the poor more power. They would tend to be pro-Union and anti-Freedman. The Robespierre Jacobins would be the Stevens-type Radicals, demanding total annihilation of the power of the Southron and the complete transformation of the South for the benefit of Freedmen, Scalawags, and Carpetbaggers.

745 While the work is by no means related formally to Reconstruction fiction, it does have in it some of the secondary themes of the anti-radical novel: There is the paean to George Washington, as the archetype of Southern aristocracy, which also appears in "Mose Evans." There is the coalition of Southron and Northron, as reconciliation symbol, in the friendship between Carrington and Gore. This coalition reminds us of the North-South alliance attempted in 1874 and 1877 and of the metaphor in "Parole d'Honneur." In this coalition symbol, one sees the articulation in *Democracy* of the hope that Southern and Northern aristocrats would join forces against the rabble everywhere. In the novel this common enemy is Senator Ratcliffe, a "Scalawag" from Illinois who symbolizes venal corruption and unscrupulous demagoguery. See Speare, pp. 291-93.

746 De Forest in 1868 comments rather wryly and accurately on this interest in the Bourbon as a literary figure; because the "chivalrous Southron" had been "too positively and authoritatively a political power," he could not get "fair treatment in literature. People had not described him; they had felt driven to declaim him. . . . Northern pens have not done justice to his virtues nor southern pens to his vices." Gross, p. 38.

747 *Ibid.*, p. 103.

748 Tourgée, *A Fool's Errand*, p. 306. Notice how similar this last sentence is to the Faulkner style.

749 See *Ibid.*, pp. 39-40; Tourgée, *Bricks Without Straw*, p. 101. Tourgée's treatment of the Bourbon-as-Victim is, aesthetically, unsatisfying. He deals with the Bourbon Trauma abstractly and never quite gives the kind of emotional rhetoric capable of expressing the despair of the Bourbon as he had done for the defeated Radicals,

though there are moments of close approximation as, for example, in Susan Dewar's humiliation and petty bitterness. And certainly "Mamelon" does attempt an emotional examination of the psycho-social effects of the Trauma within a Bourbon family. But his examination remains abstract and superficial when compared to the portrayal of the Freedman's anguish, for example. The reason for this lies in the fact that, despite his intellectual sympathy with the plight of his old enemies, his emotional sympathies rested always with their victims. Thus, for the most emotionally compelling portrayal of the Bourbon-as-Victim, one must ultimately turn to pro-Bourbon and neutralist fiction.

750 Tourgée, "Mamelon," pp. 190-91.

751 *Ibid.*, pp. 201-2.

752 Tourgée, "Zouri's Christmas," p. 322.

753 Tourgée, *Bricks Without Straw*, p. 382.

754 Tourgée, *A Fool's Errand*, p. 349.

755 *Ibid.*, pp. 354, 351.

756 Cf. Thornton, *Di Cary*, p. 226; Tourgée, *A Fool's Errand*, p. 155.

757 Davis, *Waiting for the Verdict*, p. 240.

758 Woolson, "In the Cotton Country," p. 185.

759 Tourgée, "Mamelon," p. 199.

760 *Ibid.*, p. 198.

761 Cf. Goff, *Other Fools*, p. 17.

762 Tourgée, *A Fool's Errand*, p. 261.

763 Tourgée, *Bricks Without Straw*, pp. 251-52.

764 It is interesting to note that one of the best attacks on Southern pride in family is found in the pro-Bourbon work, *Di Cary*: "The old Southern States have played out [their ancestry]. They're all pickin' around now, as poor as rats, and that kind of talk don't git um a red cent, does it. . . ? Lord love you, sir, I've seen a dozen on um sittin' on a store bench, talkin' about their grandfathers with their elbows and toes out, tellin' who was the greatest, Jack Randolph or Gin'ral Jackson, when there wa'n't a furrow run in their cropland, their nags' bones were comin' out through the skin. I tell you . . . the South wants Northern emigrants, or it'll git to be wilderness. Jack Randolph nor Gin'ral Jackson ain't coming back to work the land." Thornton, p. 30. However, one must point out that this is said by a rather opportunistic Yankee entrepreneur.

765 Tourgée, *Bricks Without Straw*, pp. 434 ff.

766 De Forest *The Bloody Chasm*, pp. 49-50, 76; Goff, p. 25. Goff points out rather hyperbolically that even when making social calls in antebellum times, the Southrons went armed for possible violence with horse-pistols, nine-shooters, hidden derringers and double-barreled shotguns. *Ibid.*, p. 85.

767 Baker, "Mose Evans," p. 325, Davis, *Waiting for the Verdict*, p. 329. Says a character about the Southron family in *Verdict*: "The Randolphs are indolent, selfish, chivalric to their equals, cruel to those beneath them. It is the legitimate outgrowth of the Southern creed. Weak, dull, with a slaveholder's conscience—" *Ibid.*, p. 245. This is the kind of language that was banished during reconciliation for such former pro-radical journals as *Harper's* and *The Atlantic Monthly*.

768 Tourgée, *A Fool's Errand*, p. 155.

769 An ex-master in *Waiting for the Verdict* drives his faithful Freedmen during the planting and harvest season and then gives them only enough wages to pay their rent to him, but not enough for food. When several die of starvation, his response is that ". . . when Congress made his niggers free, it meant it. . . . Their dead bodies was nothing out of his pocket now. Then agin, the old uns and babies ain't counted in the payment of rations." (Davis, *Waiting for the Verdict*, p. 334.)

[770] Tourgée, *Bricks Without Straw*, p. 153.
[771] Tourgée, *A Fool's Errand*, p. 377.
[772] *Ibid.*, p. 219.
[773] Tourgée, *Bricks Without Straw*, p. 310.
[774] *Ibid.*, p. 300.
[775] The Southron-as idealistic Radical appears in *Wild Work*, *Kitty's Conquest*, and *A Year of Wreck*. But in Reconstruction fiction, his fullest development is in the character of Hesden Le Moyne.
[776] According to Tourgée, the term "Carpetbagger" originated in one of the Northwestern states "during the early days of 'wildcat money'. . . . It described the member of a financial organization which secured its issues by the mortgage of land, which mortgage the State had power to enforce as upon forfeiture, on behalf of the creditors, whenever the notes of the organization (they called it a bank) 'should go to protest.'" To avoid this contingency, the organization instituted "walking agents." "As the law had neglected to provide that the banks organized under it should have a permanent place of business, the 'banks' were in reality simply agents, who carried the bills (for circulation) about the country in carpetbags, and were hence denominated 'Carpetbaggers.'" Tourgée states that an unnamed Copperhead from Wisconsin (who once was a "Carpet-bagger" of the old school) first used the term as an insult toward the Northern émigrés. (Tourgée, *A Fool's Errand*, p. 166).
[777] *Ibid.*, pp. 166-67.
[778] *Ibid.*, pp. 166-68.
[779] Baker, "Mose Evans," p. 50.
[780] Tourgée, *A Fool's Errand*, pp. 494-95, from "The Invisible Empire" portion of the novel.
[781] *Ibid.*, p. 99.
[782] Tourgée, *Bricks Without Straw*, pp. 133, 164, 134.
[783] Tourgée, *A Fool's Errand*, p. 48.
[784] Tourgée, *Bricks Without Straw*, pp. 134, 164-65. Gross, in his somewhat Dunningite study of Tourgée's novels, makes the following statement, which demonstrates how even in the 20th century the reputation of the idealistic Carpetbaggers still lies under a shadow among the non-Revisionists: "Southern hostility toward Northern teachers was understandable, for the Southerner felt that these teachers were supported and manipulated by Radical Republican reconstructionists like Tourgée; and in most cases they were." Gross, p. 62.
[785] Tourgée, *Bricks Without Straw*, p. 71.
[786] *Ibid.*, p. 133.
[787] *Ibid.*, pp. 132-33.
[788] *Ibid.*, pp. 125-26, 127, 149.
[789] Cf. *Ibid.*, p. 125.
[790] See *Ibid.*, p. 217.
[791] *Ibid.*, p. 218.
[792] *Ibid.*, p 219.
[793] Tourgée, *A Fool's Errand*, p. 192.
[794] *Ibid.*, p. 232. Tourgée describes the tone of this letter from an idealistic ideologist as petulant and whining, as if the glory of establishing Reconstruction "had already soured upon his stomach. . . ." *Ibid.*, p. 230.
[795] *Ibid.*, p. 234.
[796] *Ibid.*, p. 359.
[797] *Ibid.*, p. 236.
[798] *Ibid.*, p. 360.

[799] See *Ibid.*, pp. 152, 356.

[800] Gross, p. 61.

[801] The best symbol of this particular aspect of the myth is Middleton in *Colonel Dunwoddie*. In a scene with Emmiline Anderson, Middleton describes how capitalistic speculation can increase the Dunwoddie millions. As she listens, Emmiline becomes increasingly disgusted: ". . . there was, under his eager description, a certain unpleasant sound, as of the swinish crunching of acorns, which was offensive. When she herself was alluded to . . . in that connection, there was an instinctive recoil from being classed with the swine which fared so sumptuously, or the acorns upon which they fed." (Baker, *Colonel Dunwoddie, Millionaire*, p. 65.) Baker further describes Middleton as the economic Carpetbagger, as a show pig and as a tulip that has been made beautiful by manure. (*Ibid.*, p. 46.)

[802] *A Fool's Errand* (1880), p. 164.

[803] Tourgée, *A Fool's Errand*, p. 33.

[804] Tourgée, "Mamelon," p. 206.

[805] Tourgée, *A Fool's Errand*, p. 120.

[806] *Ibid.*, p. 164.

[807] Bryan, p. 149.

[808] *Ibid.*, p. 151.

[809] Harding, p. 95.

[810] Tourgée, *A Fool's Errand*, pp. 144, 147.

[811] *Ibid.*, p. 99.

[812] *Ibid.*, p. 294.

[813] See Gross, pp. 21-23.

[814] Tourgée, *A Fool's Errand*, pp. 147 ff.

[815] *Ibid.*, p. 59.

[816] *Ibid.*, p. 85.

[817] *Ibid.*, p. 360.

[818] *Ibid.*, p. 20.

[819] *Ibid.*, p. 321.

[820] *Ibid.*, p. 322.

[821] *Ibid.*, pp. 85-86.

[822] Gross, p. 72

[823] Tourgée, *A Fool's Errand*, p. 323.

[824] *Ibid.*, p. 325. Some historical discussion is necessary here. The North Carolina Republicans were defeated as a ruling power in 1870. As a powerful minority party, they continued to operate until the Compromise of 1877. The Compromise not only ended Reconstruction governments in the Deep South, it also paralyzed the Southern Republican Party as an opposition force to the Southern Democrats. As long as there was even a tenuous policy of federal intervention and concern, there was a possible hope of a resurgence. Once this policy was discarded by the Compromise, all hope for another chance, according to this theory, vanished. This is the full meaning of the statement "The struggle was at an end."

[825] *Ibid.*, p. 322.

[826] *Ibid.*, p. 223

[827] *Ibid.*, pp. 323-24.

[828] *Ibid.*, p. 324.

[829] *Ibid.*, p. 323.

[830] Tourgée, *Hot Plowshares*, p. 4.

[831] Cf. Peters, p. 414; and Thornton, p. 146.

[832] Baker, *Colonel Dunwoddie, Millionaire*, p. 44.

[833] Harding, p. 136; cf. Thornton, p. 50.
[834] Tourgée, *A Fool's Errand*, pp. 126-27.
[835] Tourgée, *A Royal Gentlemen*, p. v.
[836] Baker, "Mose Evans," p. 454.
[837] As stated before the ideological and political antagonisms characterizing the hostile juxtaposition of the key figures are merely specific forms of their more general psychocultural postures as representatives of their respective sections. This is particularly true since, psycho-analytically speaking, such postures precede political and ideological concerns. (We prefer "psychocultural" to "cultural" because we view the Bourbon-Carpetbagger conflict as involving both personal and emotional drives growing from societal imperatives.)
[838] The best scholarly work presenting this point-of-view is Professor Genovese's *The Political Economy of Slavery*. Also, for a fuller discussion, see Chapter I.
[839] For many Southrons, *all* of Northern culture became equated with abolitionism. Cf. Tourgée, *A Fool's Errand*, p. 167.
[840] Tourgée, *Bricks Without Straw*, p 461.
[841] Tourgée, *A Fool's Errand*, p. 99.
[842] *Ibid.*, p. 360. This is one of the better definitions of the Slavery Syndrome as a psychocultural trope in Reconstruction fiction.
[843] *Ibid.*, p. 127-28.
[844] *Ibid.*, p. 76.
[845] Peters, p. 440.
[846] Also cf. Tourgée, *A Fool's Errand*, pp. 127-28.
[847] Cf. Tourgée, *Bricks Without Straw*, pp. 176-77.
[848] Tourgée, *A Fool's Errand*, p. 167.
[849] Tourgée, *Bricks Without Straw*, p. 309.
[850] *Ibid.*, p. 310.
[851] Tourgée, *A Fool's Errand*, pp. 307, 309.
[852] *Ibid.*, pp. 128, 307.
[853] *Ibid.*, pp. 127-28.
[854] This is a major theme in Tourgée's pseudo-Reconstruction novel, *Hot Plowshares*. Tourgée, *Bricks Without Straw*, p. 177.
[855] Tourgée, *A Fool's Errand*, p. 128.
[856] *Ibid.*, p. 129.
[857] Tourgée, *Bricks Without Straw*, p. 419.
[858] Davis, *Waiting for the Verdict*, p. 238.
[859] Tourgée, *A Fool's Errand*, p. 147.
[860] Cf. Ibid.
[861] Davis, Waiting for the Verdict, p. 238.
[862] Tourgée, A Fool's Errand, p. 215.
[863] *Ibid.*, p. 367.
[864] *Ibid.*, pp. 125, 161.
[865] The burning cross allusion is an apt comparison, by the way. *Ibid.*, p. 130.
[866] *Ibid.*, p. 308.
[867] *Ibid.*
[868] *Ibid.*, p. 309.
[869] *Ibid.*
[870] *Ibid.*, p. 310.
[871] *Ibid.*, p. 161.
[872] This rather hyperbolic, rhetorically heightened interpretation of what was the

general Carpetbagger view of Northern support during the high Reconstruction is based on statements, hints, and implications scattered throughout pro-radical literature.

[873] *Ibid.*, pp. 234-35.

[874] See DuBois, p. 482.

[875] Tourgée, *A Fool's Errand*, pp. 285-86.

[876] *Ibid.*, pp. 225-26. The way Bourbon forces seize radical strongholds is a recurring *motif* of some of these works.

[877] *Ibid.*, pp. 217-19.

[878] *Ibid.*, p. 246. The sources of the scenes of Reconstruction violence in Tourgée's works are dual: Tourgée's own personal experience as a Republican judge in North Carolina and the reports of the Congressional Committee that investigated Klan terrorism in the South in 1871. Indeed, some editions of *A Fool's Errand* carry a "key" to the novel entitled *The Invisible Empire.* This work is both a compendium and summary of some of the testimony made before the Committee.

[879] Tourgée, *Bricks Without Straw*, p. 280.

[880] Redemption is both a technique and a chronological phase of Reconstruction history. Historically it begins in 1872 as a South-wide movement. As a technique it had already rescued two states before 1872: North Carolina and Georgia. And while Tourgée's description of the Terror specifically refers to the North Carolina campaign of 1869 and 1870, it is quite applicable to the redemption campaigns that follow in 1872. This is especially true since his major novels were written after 1877 and absorb within their texture a retrospective vision of redemption primarily as the historical moment in which the Redeemers operated. Hence, while the term does refer to a technique, it is also used in this study primarily as a reference to the chronological moment in which this technique operated to fullest advantage.

[881] Tourgée, *A Fool's Errand*, p. 247.

[882] *Ibid.*, p. 246. This statement that the Klan in its totality was larger than the Confederate Army need not necessarily be an hyperbole. First, there was a stimulus-response situation during Reconstruction that differed psychologically from the situation that began the Civil War. The stimulus for the attack on Fort Sumter was, in the South, "Look what might happen if the Republicans won the election." The stimulus for redemption was "Look what has happened since they won the war." Thus for the former case the issues were only emotionally apprehended possibilities. In the latter, however, they were emotionally apprehended actualities.
Secondly, the issues that initiated the Civil War touched only a relatively small segment of the Southern classes. In contrast, the issues of Reconstruction touched, with one aspect or another, the Negrophobe Unionists, the Whig-moderates disgusted with high taxes and corruption, the ex-Scalawags whose factions lost out in the division of spoils, as well as ex-Confederates. Add to these those persons who participated in Klan activity but could not, because of age, sex, or infirmity, participate in the war, and one might have an army "greater than the Rebellion."

[883] One must indicate here that the comments making up Tourgée's analysis are scattered throughout his two major novels. Thus, when one speaks of his "analysis," one is in reality referring to the thematic shaping of data culled from these scatterings.

[884] *Ibid.*, p. 227. This conjunction of nobility and baseness is, of course, not new in Reconstruction fiction. It appears also in *Wild Work*, "An Independent Ku Klux," and *Other Fools*.

[885] *Ibid.*, p. 331.

[886] *Ibid.*, p. 292.

[887] *Ibid.*, p. 228.

[888] *Ibid.*, p. 229.

[889] Cf. _Ibid_., p. 87.
[890] _Ibid_., pp. 87-88.
[891] _Ibid_., p. 136.
[892] _Ibid_., p. 137.
[893] _Ibid_., pp. 243-44.
[894] _Ibid_., p. 362. Here Servosse is more bitter than absolutely correct in his prophecy. Still, the South has managed to manipulate its power in the Congress to great advantage and behind the scenes has exerted a great deal of influence out of proportion to its size over the social and political evolution of the post-Reconstruction Union. That the Republican presidential campaigns of 1968 and 2000 were based on a Southern strategy reflects some truth in Servosse's prophecy.
[895] _Ibid_., p. 298.
[896] _Ibid_., p. 301.
[897] _Ibid_., p. 248.
[898] _Ibid_., p. 247.
[899] _Ibid_., p. 308.
[900] _Ibid_., p. 309.
[901] _Ibid_., p. 248.
[902] _Ibid_., p. 307.
[903] See _Ibid_., p. 137.
[904] Tourgée, *Bricks Without Straw*, p. 308.
[905] _Ibid_., p. 307. It is not necessary to point out that Tourgée is rather unfair to the 1868 Radicals. Very few people could have seen how quickly the Bourbons were to recover their power. With military defeat, constitutional amendments guaranteeing the rights of the new citizenry, and pro-radical forces in nearly all of the state capitols, who could have foreseen the pro-Bourbon resurgence of the seventies? Tourgée's pronouncements about the North prove again the old rule that hindsight makes the best prophecy.
[906] Tourgée, *A Fool's Errand*, p. 245.
[907] Tourgée, *Bricks Without Straw*, p. 250.
[908] Tourgée, *A Fool's Errand*, p. 245.
[909] Bryan, p. 323.
[910] Tourgée, *A Fool's Errand*, pp. 325-26.
[911] Tourgée, *Bricks Without Straw*, p. 99.
[912] Tourgée, *A Fool's Errand*, p. 164.
[913] _Ibid_., p. 169.
[914] _Ibid_., pp. 281-82.
[915] _Ibid_., p. 161.
[916] _Ibid_., p. 184.
[917] See _Ibid_.
[918] _Ibid_., p. 165. Tourgée, of course, overemphasizes the Federal government's dereliction of duty in his analysis to stress the inadequacy of national aid during redemption. There was some significant intervention during the early days of Reconstruction, especially in his own state of North Carolina, where whole counties were put under military control. Moreover, influential Pro-Radicals, like Philip Sheridan of Civil War fame, advocated strenuous Federal supervision of the South, including a military reoccupation where necessary. And during the insurrections of 1876, such supervision was partially put into action in Louisiana, Florida, and South Carolina.

But Tourgée would have argued that in 1876 it was only the desperation of the Republican Party North and South that motivated Grant to send aid to the

beleaguered Carpetbaggers, and not concern for their fate *per se*. Such aid did come in time to barely save the national administration for Republican hands, but it was too late to save the remaining Southern states for Carpetbagger hands. (Cf. DuBois, p. 482.)
We might add here that Tourgée tends to equate "North" and "Union" with the Republicans as the Civil War-Abolitionist Party. By 1874, the Union and the North were no longer the exclusive property of this Civil War Party. Therefore, it was in no position to intervene at will. However, in terms of the specific violence in North Carolina in 1869 and 1870, his criticism of Federal neglect is more accurate and hence more just.

[919] Cf. Tourgée, *A Fool's Errand*, p. 302.

[920] Tourgée, *Bricks Without Straw*, p. 399.

[921] Tourgée, *A Fool's Errand*, p. 304.

[922] *Ibid*., pp. 304-5.

[923] *Ibid*., p. 252.

[924] *Ibid*., p. 252.

[925] The fullest study of this is Rayford Logan's *The Betrayal of the Negro* (1965).

[926] Tourgée, *A Fool's Errand*, p. 309.

[927] See Wilson, p. 543.

[928] Tourgée, *A Fool's Errand*, p. 249.

[929] *Ibid*., p. 170.

[930] Tourgée, *Bricks Without Straw*, p. 252.

[931] Tourgée, *A Fool's Errand*, p. 362.

[932] *Ibid*., p. 90.

[933] *Ibid*., p. 80.

[934] *Ibid*., p. 359.

[935] *Ibid*., p. 360.

[936] Among the Reconstruction novels, the ones in which this aesthetic is completely missing are *Waiting for the Verdict*, *What Answer?*, *Other Fools and Their Doings*, and *Colonel Dunwoddie, Millionaire*. *Yazoo* is the chief example of this fact from the nonfiction list.

[937] Tourgée, "John Eax," *John Eax and Mamelon*, pp. 143-144.

[938] Gross, p. 7.

[939] Becker, p. 70.

[940] Andrews, pp. 102 ff. Cf. also Woolson's description, pp. 10-13.

[941] Tourgée, *Bricks Without Straw*, pp. 403-5.

[942] It is quite clear that all pro-radical fiction that appeared after 1877 is specifically designed to counteract the rising tide of pro-Bourbon abuse.

[943] Perry E. Gianakos, "The Spanish-American War and the Double Paradox of the Negro American," *Phylon*, XXVI (Spring, 1965), 36.

[944] Tourgée, *A Fool's Errand*, p. 359.

Appendix End Notes

[945] George Willis Cooke. Unitarianism in America (Boston: AUA, 1902), 176. See also Russell E. Miller, *The Larger Hope: The First Century of the Universalist Church in America 1770–1870* (Boston, MA: The Unitarian Universalist Association, 1979),

630f.

[946] U.S. Bureau of Refugees, Freedmen, and Abandoned Lands. *https://www.britannica.com/topic/Freedmens-Bureau*, September 29, 2020.

[947] Russell E. Miller. *The Larger Hope: The First Century of the Universalist Church in America 1770–1970* (Boston, MA: The Unitarian Universalist Association, 1979), 637.

[948] Cooke, 197.

[949] Miller, 637.

[950] Miller, 637.

[951] Cooke, 410-411.

[952] *Measuring Worth. www.measuringworth.com/dollarvaluetoday/relativevalue.php?year_source=1868&amount=4000&year_result=2020.*

[953] Hosmer, George Washington. "An address delivered before the Erie County Common School Education Society at Buffalo, N.Y.," 3 February 1840. *Courtesy of Library of Congress. https://iowaculture.gov/history/education/educator-resources/primary-source-sets/reform-movements-america/george-hosmer.*

[954] Cooke, 338-339.

[955] *Measuring Worth. www.measuringworth.com/dollarvaluetoday/relativevalue.php?year_source=1889&amount=10000&year_result=2020.*

POSTSCRIPT:
A BRIEF INTRODUCTION TO LITERARY TERMS USED IN THIS BOOK

Texture: The name we give to all the literary characteristics of a work of fictionality or to works of nonfiction classified as literature. The literary characteristics in this study are based upon the Nine Elements of Literature:

1. form, the inner and outer structure; in terms of outer structure, whether the work is a poem, a play, or a novel;
2. conflict, the creation and resolution of antagonistic/non-antagonistic contradictions between an x and a y; e.g., nihilism versus humanism;
3. plot, the arrangement of episodes and complications within a narrative;
4. character, the personae who inhabit the narrative and their personality traits; primary, secondary (protagonist/antagonist) tertiary, and peripheral;
5. language or diction, the use of figurative and nonfigurative words, phrases, clauses, etc.; also the use of prosody and poetic meter; specifically, the imaginative use of diction to trigger neuro-psychological responses in the reader;
6. setting, the location of the work; geographical and environmental factors;
7. tone, the emotional content as based on the tonal axis: comic/tragic—happy/sad;
8. point of view, the angle of vision through which the author involves

the reader in perceiving the work of literature, signaled by the use of personal pronouns;

9. and that ambiguous element irony—look up the definition in an *American Heritage Dictionary*; e.g., tragic irony, ironic foreshadowing.

Thematic structure. AKA theme. The central and controlling idea or ideas or concepts in a work of literature as acted it out in the texture. There are four basic types of concepts in a work of literature:

- the paraphrastic meaning of the work (a paraphrase or summary of the salient concepts);
- the personal imperative of the work represented by a character or persona within the work;
- the categorical imperative, denoting the category to which the persona belongs [borrowed from Immanuel Kant but with a different meaning]; and
- the universal imperative, which could apply to all categories of human experience at the universal level.

An imperative is a valid and compelling idea or concept. The universal imperative in the form of an interpretational hypothesis defines the center of the thematic structure and can exist whether the writer intended it or not, provided that the texture of the work supports the hypothesis. The image of the thematic structure can be compared to that of a cesium molecule.

For more detailed explanation, check out this link:

https://www.sparknotes.com/writinghelp/glossary-of-literary-terms/

www.ingramcontent.com/pod-product-compliance
Lightning Source LLC
LaVergne TN
LVHW052216200926
848481LV00001B/124
9798889254300